C0-BKK-221

American Jewish Year Book

American Jewish Year Book 1988

VOLUME 88

Prepared by THE AMERICAN JEWISH COMMITTEE

Editor
DAVID SINGER

Associate Editor
RUTH R. SELDIN

THE AMERICAN JEWISH COMMITTEE
NEW YORK
THE JEWISH PUBLICATION SOCIETY
PHILADELPHIA

ISBN 0-8276-0313-4

Library of Congress Catalogue Number: 99-4040

PRINTED IN THE UNITED STATES OF AMERICA
BY THE HADDON CRAFTSMEN, INC., SCRANTON, PA.

Preface

Two articles on the Jews of South Africa are featured in the present volume. The first, by Gideon Shimoni, examines the paradoxes and pressures in the situation of South African Jewry—a privileged minority in a society based on racial discrimination. Shimoni traces changes in Jewish attitudes to the apartheid system over the years, describes responses to the present crisis, and discusses prospects for the future. In the second article, Sergio DellaPergola and Allie A. Dubb present a comprehensive analysis of the social and demographic characteristics of the South African Jewish community—similar in many ways to other Western Jewish communities, yet distinctive.

The regular articles on Jewish life in the United States are written this year by new contributors: Earl Raab on "Intergroup Relations" and Kenneth Jacobson on "The United States, Israel, and the Middle East." "Jewish Communal Affairs," prepared by Lawrence Grossman, is a new feature that will, it is hoped, appear regularly from now on. The section on U.S. Jewish population, which presents 1987 estimates, is again provided by a team of researchers associated with the North American Jewish Data Bank: Barry A. Kosmin, Paul Ritterband, and Jeffrey Scheckner. Accompanying the estimates is an essay describing the methods used to count Jews in the United States.

The reports on Jewish communities abroad are augmented this year by articles on Australia, Italy, and Austria, the last an account of the election of Kurt Waldheim and its effect on the country's small Jewish community. Updated population estimates, as of 1986, are presented for Jewish communities around the world.

Carefully compiled directories of national Jewish organizations, periodicals, and federations and welfare funds, as well as religious calendars and obituary notices, round out the 1988 AMERICAN JEWISH YEAR BOOK.

We note with sorrow the death in June 1987 of Arnold Mandel, distinguished French writer on Jewish affairs, novelist, and critic, who contributed the article on France to this publication for over a quarter of a century, beginning in the 1961 volume.

We are very grateful to Michele Anish and Diane Hodges for their proofreading efforts and to Diane Hodges for compiling the index. We also acknowledge the aid of Cyma M. Horowitz, director of the Blaustein Library, Lotte Zajac, and all our other co-workers in Information and Research Services.

THE EDITORS

Contributors

HENRIETTE BOAS: journalist, Amsterdam, Holland.

SUSAN BURES: editor, *Australian Jewish Times,* Sydney, Australia.

SERGIO DELLAPERGOLA: director, Division of Jewish Demography and Statistics, Institute of Contemporary Jewry, Hebrew University of Jerusalem, Israel.

SIMONETTA DELLA SETA: Jerusalem correspondent, *Il Giornale,* Italy.

ALLIE A. DUBB: former director, African Studies Institute, University of Witwatersrand, South Africa.

ZVI GITELMAN: professor, political science, University of Michigan.

LAWRENCE GROSSMAN: director of publications, American Jewish Committee, New York.

NELLY HANSSON: researcher in political science and sociology, Paris, France.

KENNETH JACOBSON: director, Middle Eastern Affairs, Anti-Defamation League of B'nai B'rith, New York.

LIONEL E. KOCHAN: honorary fellow, Oxford Center for Post-Graduate Hebrew Studies, England.

MIRIAM KOCHAN: writer, translator, Oxford, England.

BARRY A. KOSMIN: director, North American Jewish Data Bank, Graduate School, City University of New York.

RALPH MANDEL: journalist, translator, Jerusalem, Israel.

JOANNA NITTENBERG: publisher and chief editor, *Illustrierte Neue Welt,* Vienna, Austria.

EARL RAAB: executive director emeritus, San Francisco Jewish Community Relations Council, California.

PAUL RITTERBAND: professor, sociology and Jewish studies, City College and the Graduate School, City University of New York.

FRIEDO SACHSER: editor, *Allgemeine Jüdische Wochenzeitung,* Bonn, West Germany.

JEFFREY SCHECKNER: administrator, North American Jewish Data Bank, Graduate School, City University of New York.

U.O. SCHMELZ: professor emeritus, Jewish demography, Institute of Contemporary Jewry, Hebrew University of Jerusalem, Israel.

GIDEON SHIMONI: Shlomo Argov Chair in Israel-Diaspora Relations, Institute of Contemporary Jewry, Hebrew University of Jerusalem, Israel.

HAROLD M. WALLER: associate professor, political science, McGill University, Canada.

Contents

DIRECTORIES, LISTS, AND OBITUARIES

Special Articles

South African Jews and the Apartheid Crisis

by GIDEON SHIMONI

THE WIDESPREAD ERUPTIONS of unrest in South Africa in the 1980s have focused attention on various aspects of that society, including its small but influential Jewish community. That community occupies a special place within South Africa itself and also on the worldwide contemporary Jewish scene. In the South African context, Jews have been very important in the economic and cultural development of the country; at the same time, they have been prominent in manifestations of resistance to the apartheid system by which the whites have dominated the society as a whole. In the Jewish context, the situation of South African Jews is highly unusual: a Jewish community that shares in the castelike status of the privileged in a society based upon a system of legalized racial discrimination.

The Distinctiveness of South African Jewry

In 1987 the estimated 115,000 Jews of South Africa constituted no more than one-half of 1 percent of the country's composite population, consisting of 19.7 million blacks, 4.9 million whites, 3.0 million coloreds (people of mixed race), and 900,000 Asians (mainly Indians). Jews belonged inherently to the dominant white minority, forming 2.3 percent of the total. As for the history of the community: it began as an incidental offshoot of British Jewry in the nineteenth century, was consolidated by a broad wave of immigration from Eastern Europe between 1880 and 1930, and was finally augmented by a small influx (numbering some 6,000) of Central European Jews fleeing from Hitler's tyranny in the 1930s.[1]

Note: The author gratefully acknowledges the access granted him by the South African Jewish Board of Deputies to its extensive library and archives and the research assistance in South Africa of Jonathan Penkin.

[1]According to the South African census of 1980 there were 117,963 Jews. The population figures cited here are estimates for mid-1986. They exclude the independent Transkei, Bophuthatswana, and Venda. See Sergio DellaPergola and Allie A. Dubb, "South African Jewry: A Sociodemographic Profile," in this volume. On the origins of the Jewish community, see Louis Herrman, *The History of the Jews in South Africa* (London, 1935); Israel Abrahams, *Birth of a Community* (Cape Town, 1955); Gustav Saron and Louis Hotz, eds., *The Jews in South Africa: A History* (London and Cape Town, 1955). A perceptive study of South African Jewry in the comparative context of some other New World communities is Daniel J. Elazar and

In many important respects, the Jews of South Africa were no different from those of other New World Jewish communities. South Africa offered Jewish immigrants postemancipation freedom in all essentials, as well as great economic prosperity. It also took its toll in the erosion of Jewish identity resulting from acculturation to the surrounding society. Yet a number of factors converged to confer a distinctive character upon South African Jewry.

One was the relatively homogeneous composition of the community. Although the founding generation, numbering some 4,000 by 1880, came mainly from Britain, the formative East European wave, which brought some 40,000 immigrants from 1880 to 1910 and a further 30,000 until 1948, was predominantly from Lithuania. The synthesis of Anglo-Jewish institutional forms with "Litvak," non-Hassidic religious orthodoxy and deep Zionist sentiment that characterized South African Jewry may be attributed largely to this factor. This has been aptly described as the "pouring of Litvak spirit into Anglo-Jewish bottles."[2] This synthesis endowed South African Jewry with a Jewish Board of Deputies modeled on the Anglo-Jewish prototype, on which were represented most synagogue congregations and communal organizations. Hence, too, the blend of the Orthodox "*misnaged*" tradition of the Litvaks with London's United Synagogue form of synagogue ritual, which led to a kind of "conservative traditionalism" and a normative mode of religiosity that has been described as "non-observant Orthodox."[3] In contrast to the situation in Britain and the United States, the Zionist orientation that most Litvak immigrants brought with them to South Africa did not come into conflict with an established mold of Reform Judaism, with its attendant antagonism to Jewish nationalism. Indeed, Reform Judaism was only introduced into South Africa in 1933, and its founder, Rabbi Moses C. Weiler, endowed it with a moderate mode of Reform and a marked Zionist sentiment. Consequently, Zionism met with only slight resistance in South Africa, and in fact the Zionist Federation that was founded in 1898 became the first Jewish institution to achieve a countrywide organizational framework. What is more, from the outset

---

Peter Medding, *Jewish Communities in Frontier Societies* (New York, 1983). The most recent work on South African Jewry is Marcus Arkin, ed., *South African Jewry: A Contemporary Survey* (Cape Town, 1984), which also contains an extensive annotated bibliography by Reuben Musiker. An illuminating contribution to the economic history of the community is Mendel Kaplan, *Jewish Roots in the South African Economy* (Cape Town, 1986).

[2]The expression is that of the doyen of South African Jewish historiography, Gustav Saron. See Gustav Saron, "The Making of South African Jewry: An Essay in Historical Interpretation," in *South African Jewry 1965*, ed. Leon Feldberg (Johannesburg, 1965), 9–48.

[3]See Jocelyn Hellig, "South African Judaism: An Expression of Conservative Traditionalism," *Judaism* 35, no. 2 (Spring 1986):233–42; also Jocelyn Hellig's chapter "Religious Expression" in Arkin, *South African Jewry,* 95–116.

South African Zionism was deeply involved in local community life. It remained the preeminent ideological orientation of South African Jewry, providing an anchor for Jewish ethnicity no less important than the synagogue was for Jewish religiosity.

At least as important a factor in shaping the distinctive character of South African Jewry was the societal environment into which the immigrants entered. It was one in which an ascriptive attribute—race—was the primary determinant of people's lives. In sociological terms, South Africa was, as it remained, a pluralistic society characterized by the existence of several sociocultural segments with parallel institutional structures within the same overarching political and economic system.[4] The traditional norms which determined this segmentation long before the term "apartheid" entered the country's political lexicon were buttressed and enforced by the apartheid laws of the state. They remained potent even as the apartheid system, having become largely dysfunctional, was in the process of disintegrating.

It is of interest to note how this mode of what may be described as a "mandatory" pluralism differed from the "laissez-faire" pluralism of American society. In the latter, the sociocultural segments maintained institutions supplementary to all-embracing ones common to the society as a whole. Moreover, the professed attitude of the state to these supplementary institutions was neutral, so that their maintenance was a wholly voluntary matter. By contrast, in the mandatory pluralism of South Africa, the state actively compelled strict separation of the segments and the maintenance of parallel, rather than merely supplementary, sets of institutions for each of them. Indeed, South Africa's pluralism could be said to be multiply segmented. Its primary segmentation was into racially defined, castelike groups, one of which—the whites—was in all respects dominant, but all of which possessed parallel, if unequal, sets of institutions. Its secondary segmentation divided even the dominant group into Afrikaners and English-speakers (in a ratio of about three to two) by compelling further institutional duplication in certain spheres, particularly language and education.

Jewish immigrants to South Africa belonged from the outset to the privileged white segment and normally lived their lives within its confines. Exempt by virtue of skin color from the discrimination suffered by all nonwhites, they enjoyed full civic rights in the parliamentary democracy of the whites. Outside of the economic sphere in which, in common with all whites, they related to the other segments of society as masters to servants

---

[4]For a fuller discussion see Gideon Shimoni, *Jews and Zionism: The South African Experience (1910–1967)* (Cape Town, 1980), 1–4. Cf. Elazar and Medding, *Jewish Communities in Frontier Societies,* 211–13.

or as employers to employees, they would never normally participate in any social or cultural institutions whatsoever with nonwhites.

Since the privileged white segment was itself culturally dualistic and of inchoate national identity, the circumstances were highly conducive to the preservation of a separate Jewish group identity. The Jews certainly became acculturated to the white part of society, but it was overwhelmingly the English segment which served as their reference group. However, the most formative factor in the country's history proved to be not the English but the Afrikaners, descendants of the seventeenth-century Dutch settlers, who were marked by an organic national consciousness, Calvinist religiosity, and a sharp sense of grievance against British imperialism. Consequently, the pull of acculturation, with its attendant erosion of distinctive Jewish identity, was considerably weaker than in England itself, where English culture was indigenous and unchallenged. Nor was it as strong as in the United States, where a new all-embracing American identity exerted a powerful attraction. There was, in fact, no unhyphenated South Africanism—no agreed-upon, all-inclusive identity equivalent to that provided by the concept of being "British" or "American." Hence, considerably more leeway remained for Jews to retain their distinctive identity, not only in the religious sense but also as far as the national element—expressed through Zionism—was concerned.

Jewish Political Orientations Prior to Enforced Apartheid

From the beginnings of a significant Jewish presence in South Africa—and this can be dated to the last quarter of the nineteenth century—the pattern of their political involvement reflected their acculturation mainly to the English-speaking segment of society. Most of the Anglo-Jews involved in politics at the municipal and parliamentary levels, both before and immediately after the creation of the Union of South Africa in 1910, were attached to the pro-British imperial parties.[5] At that time, when people spoke of the "race question" they usually meant the conflict between Boer (Afrikaner) and Briton. Within that context, by the 1920s Jews tended to identify mainly with the centrist South African party led by the former Boer generals Louis Botha and Jan Christiaan Smuts. This party followed a policy of conciliation between the Afrikaners and the English and looked toward the molding of a united, bilingual (white) South Africanism. Ever since the British government's Balfour Declaration of November 1917, favoring the development of a Jewish national home in Palestine, in the making of which Jan Christiaan Smuts played a role as a member of the

[5]For the period prior to the creation of the Union of South Africa, see Saron and Hotz, *Jews in South Africa,* 179–212; also Shimoni, *Jews and Zionism,* 61–73.

imperial war cabinet, Jews had held him in high regard. This sentiment, in turn, reinforced their support for his conciliatory, centrist political position. In a major realignment of political forces that took place in the early 1930s, the Afrikaner nationalist leader J. B. M. Hertzog combined forces with Smuts to form the United party. One segment of the nationalists, however, did not agree with this fusion and, under Daniel F. Malan, split off in 1934 to form what was called the "Gesuiwerde" (purified) National party. As minister of the interior in 1930, Malan had introduced the Quota Act, which greatly restricted further Jewish immigration to South Africa. Moreover, his new party succumbed to anti-Semitic influences largely emanating from Nazi Germany. From 1933 until well after the Second World War, pro-Nazi, anti-Semitic groups proliferated in South Africa. The "Jewish problem" became a political issue, and widespread agitation against a loophole in the Quota Act culminated in the Aliens Act of 1937, which halted the entry of Jews fleeing from Hitler's Germany. By 1938 the Afrikaner nationalist opposition headed by Dr. Malan was campaigning on a platform that demanded total prohibition of Jewish immigration and even the imposition of a quota system directed against Jews in commerce and the professions. In these circumstances, all Jewish candidates for political election and the entire Jewish public were clearly associated with Jan Smuts's wing of the United party (with the exception of a lesser number who supported the small Labor party). Furthermore, the Jewish Board of Deputies, intensely engaged in the defense of the Jewish community against anti-Semitic defamation, even departed somewhat from its traditional policy of noninvolvement in politics and lent discreet support to a liberal group centered on the personality of Smuts's political lieutenant, Jan Hofmeyr.[6]

When Hertzog and Smuts split in 1939 over the question of whether South Africa should enter the war on Britain's side against Germany, it was a foregone conclusion that Jews would lend their support overwhelmingly to the Smuts wing of the party, which conducted South Africa through the war period in alliance with Britain. Under Smuts as premier a Jew reached cabinet rank, for the first and only time to this day—Henry Gluckman, who became minister of health in 1945. In light of the Afrikaner National party's attitude toward Jews, they contemplated its victory over Smuts's party in the elections of May 1948 with great trepidation.

---

[6]See Shimoni, *Jews and Zionism,* 152–55. The term "liberal" is used here and throughout this study in its customary South African sense. In Hofmeyr's time this connoted opposition to Nazi influences, the upholding of civil liberties, and the desire to uplift the underprivileged sections of the population and alleviate discrimination and the indignities that were their lot. After 1948, liberals generally meant those who were actively concerned to abolish racial discrimination and to extend equal civic rights to nonwhites within the existing parliamentary system. See Janet Robertson, *Liberalism in South Africa 1948–1963* (Oxford, 1971).

Throughout the period until 1948, very few Jews showed political concern that transcended the interests of the white group. Indeed, when there was an incidental convergence of Jewish and Indian concerns over proposed immigration legislation which, although primarily aimed at stopping Indians from coming to South Africa, would also have hampered the free flow of Jewish immigration, Jewish representatives were at pains to dissociate their case from that of the Indians.[7] This detachment from the fate of the Indians, who in some respects suffered from disabilities similar to those that applied to Jews in the Russian Pale of Settlement under czarist rule, characterized the Jewish community's political orientation within South African society at that juncture. Preoccupied as they were with their own interests and advancement in a white societal environment not free from anti-Semitism, they showed little concern for the underprivileged racial groups, not even for the Indians whose fate occasionally touched theirs.

At the same time, however—and this too was characteristic—Jews predominated among those few whites who were dissenters and took up the cause of the underprivileged masses. This was especially marked in the struggle for the rights of Indians led by Mohandas K. Gandhi from 1906 until 1914, in which he developed his doctrine of *satyagraha,* later to be employed with empire-shaking effect in India itself. The closest of Gandhi's white associates were in fact Jews, notably Henry Polak, who had come from England, and Hermann Kallenbach, who was Lithuanian-born but had qualified as an architect in Germany. Differences of opinion over the question whether Jews had a moral imperative to support the cause of the Indians or whether Jewish interests rather dictated that they not deviate from the behavior of other whites already encapsulated the controversy, which remained substantially the same thereafter. Polak, for example, explained that he had been drawn into the Indian *satyagraha* struggle "as a Jew who has tried to remember that Judaism is a matter not only of belief but also of action." He said that after coming to South Africa and learning about the Indian problem there, he had realized that "this was the Jewish problem all over again," for there was not a single argument advanced against Indians which had not already been urged against Jews in one or another European country. He was ashamed at the failure of Jews in South Africa to champion the Indians' immigration rights, while defending their own. Drawing a parallel with discrimination against the Jews in czarist Russia, he complained that "either in ignorance or by design, Jews have lent themselves to, or at least not openly dissociated themselves from, racial

[7]This convergence of Indian and Jewish immigration problems occurred in 1902, 1911–13, and 1924. See Shimoni, *Jews and Zionism,* 76–80, 90.

persecution." The only consolation he found as a Jew was "that those non-Indians who have taken a leading part in the effort to expose and do away with this persecution are most of them members of our faith."[8]

As for the Litvak immigrant generation in South Africa, they were generally too preoccupied with their economic integration into the country to be concerned with the problems of the social system as a whole. Gauged by the adaptiveness of Jews from Eastern Europe to the codes of behavior underlying the castelike separation of the races and the norms, legal and customary, of white domination, it is doubtful whether their own experiences of discrimination and persecution in the Russian Pale of Settlement had as ennobling an effect upon them as is sometimes imagined. Indeed, most Jewish immigrants quickly became accustomed to regarding blacks as inferiors fit solely to be servants and unskilled laborers.[9] Yet even among these immigrants there were some early manifestations of revulsion over the indignities and exploitation to which blacks were subjected. In 1917 a Yiddish-speaking group was formed within the South African International Socialist League, the forerunner of the South African Communist party, which rejected all distinctions based on color and recognized only class differences. Moreover, an early Zionist-socialist group, Poalei Zion, formed in 1918, evinced deep sympathy for the oppressed black masses. Still another organized Jewish group which nurtured a leftist-oriented opposition to the South African societal system was the Yiddisher Arbeter Club. It existed from 1928 to 1948, and its membership overlapped somewhat with the similarly aligned Afrikaner Geserd that functioned in the 1930s.[10] In the late 1930s and 1940s the Zionist Socialist party, which formed an integral part of the South African Zionist Federation, also evinced concern for the cause of the black population and participated to a degree in some left-wing alignments.[11]

---

[8]See the London *Jewish Chronicle,* Sept. 5, 1913. On Gandhi's Jewish associates, see Mohandas Karamchand Gandhi, *Satyagraha in South Africa,* trans. V. G. Desai (Stanford Academic Reprints, 1954); also Gideon Shimoni, *Gandhi, Satyagraha and the Jews* (Leonard Davis Institute of International Relations of the Hebrew University, Jerusalem, 1977).

[9]See Leibl Feldman, *Yidden in Johannesburg* (Yiddish) (Johannesburg, 1956), 241–46; also Michael Pesah Grossman, "A Study of the Trends and Tendencies of Hebrew and Yiddish Writing in South Africa Since Their Beginnings in the Early Nineties of the Last Century to 1930" (unpublished D.Phil. diss., University of the Witwatersrand, 1973), 347–49.

[10]See Feldman, *Yidden in Johannesburg,* and also his *Yidden in Dorem Afrika* (Yiddish) (Wilno, 1937), 102–16; also Taffy Adler, "Lithuania's Diaspora: The Johannesburg Jewish Workers' Club 1928–1948," *Journal of Southern African Studies* 6, no. 1 (1979):70–92; Evangalos Mantzaris, "From the History of Bundist Activity in South Africa," *Bulletin of the Bund Archives of the Jewish Labour Movement,* no. 3/31 (Winter 1981–82):1–3.

[11]See Shimoni, *Jews and Zionism,* 188–92.

Political Involvement of Jews Under Apartheid

The ascent of the Afrikaner nationalists to power in 1948 was a critical turning point in the history of South Africa and also for the Jewish community. It inaugurated a new era of anxieties and moral dilemmas. The innovative aspect of Malan's new government lay not in the invention of the system of white domination and racial segregation—this long preceded Malan's ascent to power—but rather in its ideological rationalization and in the institution of far-reaching social engineering to fortify it against the winds of change in Africa. The term "apartheid" entered political usage in the mid-1940s. Although at its crudest level it signified the preservation of *baasskap,* meaning white domination in all aspects of South African society, it underwent a steady process of ideological refinement. Hendrik Verwoerd made the major contribution to the process, starting in 1950 when he first became minister of native affairs ("native" then being the term used for blacks), through his ascent to the premiership in 1958, and until an assassin took his life in 1966. At its most refined level, apartheid purported to be a regulated system of race relations that would guarantee white self-preservation while at the same time providing parallel "separate development" for all the racial groups comprising South African society.

As a program of action, apartheid meant reinforcement of white domination of the political and economic life of the country. It also meant systematization of social and residential separation between the various racial groups on the basis of racial classification of the population. At the same time, it purported to provide frameworks, institutional and territorial, for the proposed separate development of each racial group. Accordingly, measures were taken throughout the 1950s to remove residual irregularities in the political system, such as the long-standing right enjoyed by enfranchised coloreds in the Cape to vote for Parliament on a common voters' roll with whites. Similarly, segregation became more stringently enforced in public places and services, such as railways, buses, and parks. Controls over black migration to the towns were significantly tightened, and harsh measures were taken against those who broke the rules. Job reservation (disqualifying nonwhites from certain jobs) was systematized, and separate industrial conciliation machinery was instituted.

In the field of black education, control was transferred to the government, which sought to withhold from blacks such education as might fit them for positions in society which they were in any case not allowed to hold. Similarly, blacks were now denied access to those English-language universities which had previously admitted them along with whites and were directed to separate colleges that were created for the various racial groups, under strict governmental supervision. At the same time, long-term planning was instituted for the consolidation of territories historically associated with the various black tribes into projected "homelands." All urban blacks were ultimately to hold citizenship and political rights in the respective homelands of their particular ethnic groups, rather than in the white state of South Africa. This aspect of the policy was called "grand" apartheid, in contrast to the "petty" apartheid of segregated services, pass laws, and the like.

The enormous disruption and suffering resulting from the apartheid system aroused bitter opposition. Ranged against it were an array of black, colored, and Indian political movements, supported by a number of white liberals and radicals, some struggling to reform, others to overthrow, the societal system. Under the leadership of the African National Congress, whose founding dated back to 1912, nonviolent opposition swelled to unprecedented proportions. The 1952 Defiance Campaign openly violated apartheid laws, with the protesters allowing themselves to be arrested. A second wave of protest led to a "Congress of the People" in 1955, and a third wave to the famous Sharpeville demonstration of March 1960, in which the police opened fire on the crowd, killing 69 people and wounding 180.

To this unrest the government reacted with an escalating series of repressive measures. Thousands of protesters of all racial groups were arrested, and hundreds were put on trial and charged with plotting the violent overthrow of the state. It was at this point that the African National Congress and its offshoot, the Pan-Africanist Congress, went underground and launched a campaign of violence.

Apart from the effect of these dramatic events upon the lives of Jews simply as white citizens of South Africa, they had significant consequences for South African Jewry as a community. The reason was the extraordinary prominence of Jewish individuals in the white opposition to the regime of apartheid. Throughout this period Jewish names kept appearing in every facet of the struggle: among reformist liberals; in the radical Communist opposition; in the courts, whether as defendants or as counsel for the defense; in the lists of persons banned (i.e., placed in political quarantine); and among those who fled the country to evade arrest. The prominence of Jews was particularly marked in the course of the great Treason Trial, involving 156 people of all races, which received wide media attention throughout the second half of the 1950s. Twenty-three of those who were put on trial were white, and more than half of them were Jews. Leading the defense was advocate Israel Maisels, who was also a prominent Jewish communal figure. After dragging on for five years, the trial ended in March 1961; the prosecution finally conceded defeat and all the accused were released.

As the battered opposition forces retreated into undergound activities, resorting to the use of violence, the government reacted with emergency legislation of an even more drastic nature, notably the notorious "90-day clause" enacted in 1963, which permitted 90 days' detention without either the need for a warrant or recourse to the courts. In this phase of the conflict the prominent involvement of individual Jews was even more in evidence. Most dramatic were the circumstances of the "Rivonia Arrests" of July 1963, in which leaders of the African National Congress underground were captured. Of the 17 people arrested, 5 were white, all of them Jews. The dramatic effect of this arrest was exceeded only by its sequel: in August, while awaiting trial in a Johannesburg prison cell, four of the prisoners made a spectacular escape. Two were Jews, Arthur Goldreich and Harold Wolpe; the latter settled in London, the former in Israel.

Reacting to this prominence of Jews in the opposition, the Afrikaans press bristled with editorial observations and letters to the editor charging or insinuating that Jews were unsympathetic to the Afrikaners' legitimate political aspirations and that all too many Jews were responsible for liberal trouble-mongering and Communist subversion. Nor were the critics satisfied by declarations of the Jewish Board of Deputies reiterating that the Jewish community had neither collective political allegiance nor responsibility for the political actions of individual Jewish citizens.[12]

It must be borne in mind that the involvement of Jews in the opposition to the apartheid system, notwithstanding its public salience, actually reflected the attitudes of only a very small segment of the total Jewish population. With compelling inherent socioeconomic factors reinforcing their position within the white racial group, for the most part Jews conformed to the norms of English-speaking whites. Empirical studies published in the 1970s indicated that the political preferences of Jews tended to be much the same as those of English-speaking non-Jews of the same socioeconomic status. Factors such as level of education and family income appeared to be more important determinants of political preference than the quality of their Jewishness. On the other hand, some pertinent sociological research on Jewish youth conducted earlier, in 1959, led to the conclusion that "Jews are more favourably disposed towards Natives [blacks], Coloureds and Indians than are the members of any other White group. Jews were found to be consistently more tolerant than other groups in their attitudes to non-Whites."[13]

---

[12]Ibid., 228–30.

[13]Henry Lever, "The Jewish Voter in South Africa," *Ethnic and Racial Studies* 2 (Oct. 1979). See also H. Lever and O. J. M. Wagner, "Ethnic Preferences of Jewish Youth in Johannesburg," *Jewish Journal of Sociology* 9 (June 1967):34–37; and Henry Lever, *Ethnic Attitudes of Johannesburg Youth* (Johannesburg, 1968). Since these works, there has been no published research of note on Jewish political behavior. Nor has there been research on the sociology of the community since the publication of Allie Dubb's *Jewish South Africans: A Sociological View of the Johannesburg Jewish Community* (Rhodes University, Grahamstown,

One rough indicator of Jewish political behavior may be found by examining the allegiance of Jewish candidates for election. It appears that throughout the two decades following the 1948 elections the majority of candidates for Parliament, and almost all of those who gained election, belonged to the centrist United party, which followed the political tradition of Jan Smuts. In 1948, for instance, all five of the Jews elected to Parliament belonged to the United party. It should be noted that at that time there already was a further option provided by the small Liberal party, which advocated abolition of apartheid and a discrimination-free, multiracial democracy, whereas the United party, while opposed to apartheid laws, still upheld white political supremacy in all essentials. Jews were certainly prominent in the Liberal party, but gauged by the record in a number of specific constituencies known to have a high proportion of Jewish voters, most Jews still preferred the United party.[14]

The Liberal party did not survive long in the political climate of South Africa under Verwoerd and his successor, John Vorster. Multiracial political parties having been forbidden by law, it disbanded in 1968. However, a rather more equivocal liberal option had emerged in 1959 out of the ranks of the United party itself. This was the Progressive party, which, by stages, absorbed other fragments of the disintegrating United party to become finally the Progressive Federal party in 1977. While advocating the abolition of apartheid, in its initial stages the Progressive party spoke of a universal educational qualification for the franchise in a federally ordered, multiracial democracy. The Progressives immediately attracted a considerable segment of Jewish supporters. Two of the five United party members of Parliament who were Jews opted to become Progressives. One of these, Helen Suzman, was reelected in 1961 and remained the sole Progressive member of Parliament for the next three sessions. That the centrist United party still had Jewish support was shown by the fact that five, two, and three Jewish United party members took their seats in Parliament in 1961, 1966, and 1970, respectively. In the 1974 elections Helen Suzman was still the only successful Jewish Progressive party candidate, and there were three successful Jewish United party candidates. However, the United party disintegrated during the ensuing parliamentary session; thereafter, barring a few Jewish National party candidates who repeatedly failed to get elected, all Jewish candidates stood for the Progressives. By 1980 the Progressive Federal party was clearly the one with the greatest Jewish affiliation, and in the 1981 elections all four Jews elected were Progressives.

1977). An illuminating theoretical analysis taking inductive account of the South African case is Peter Y. Medding, "Towards a General Theory of Jewish Political Interests and Behaviour," *Jewish Journal of Sociology* 19, no. 2 (Dec. 1977):115–41.

[14]See Shimoni, *Jews and Zionism,* 303, 304.

Jewish Political Responses to Apartheid in Transition

By the mid-1960s the radical onslaught on the apartheid regime had virtually been suppressed, allowing the system a further lease on life. Although it was again convulsed by the Soweto outburst in 1976, another apparent respite followed, lasting until the great resurgence of resistance that began to envelop the country in 1985. Under B. J. Vorster's premiership, from 1966 to 1978, implementation of "grand" apartheid continued apace. Forced resettlement of population in the homelands, mostly under appalling conditions, encompassed as many as 3.5 million people. Three of the homelands accepted the offer of "independence," while the others remained only self-governing. In other respects, however, this was a period of transition in the apartheid policy. Signs of dissonance began to appear as increasing numbers of urbanized Afrikaners became upwardly mobile in business, manufacturing, and professional occupations.[15] Pragmatic tendencies began to erode ideological dogmatism, and Afrikaner businessmen, no less than their English counterparts, began to balk at the dysfunctional aspects of apartheid in the economic sphere. These were primarily the failure to satisfy industry's hunger for more permanent and skilled black workers and the limited consumer capacity of blacks.

Against this background, a division emerged between two main ideological factions which came to be loosely labeled as *verkramptes* (narrow-minded) and *verligtes* (enlightened). In general terms, adherents of the former were characterized by rigid insistence upon Afrikaner national exclusivism and domination of the South African polity and by uncompromising resistance to modification of the apartheid system in accommodation to criticism from outside the country. *Verligtes* tended to relinquish a measure of Afrikaner exclusivism for the sake of more white unity and to adopt an open-minded attitude to modifications of apartheid which, while not substantially altering long-term goals of "separate development," would soften the hard image of apartheid. Examples of such modifications that aroused the ire of *verkramptes* were mixed sports, admission of black diplomats to the country, mixed audiences in theaters, and the general amelioration of "petty apartheid" measures that offended the dignity of nonwhites more than was necessary for implementation of basic policy.

In the late 1960s this division of opinion led to a split in the ranks of the National party, the *verkramptes* forming the Herstigte (reconstituted) National party, which became the core of the Afrikaner backlash against the *verligte* thrust of Prime Minister Vorster and even more so of his successor, P. W. Botha, who took over in September 1978. In due course an additional

---

[15]On these changes in the Afrikaner sector see Heribert Adam and Hermann Giliomee, *The Rise and Crisis of Afrikaner Power* (Cape Town, 1979), 104–27, 217–21.

wave of right-wing reaction led to the foundation of the Conservative party (in 1982), which succeeded in becoming the main opposition party in the all-white chamber of Parliament when it gained more seats than the Progressive Federal party in the 1987 elections.

Having already undergone considerable refinement in Verwoerd's time, the rhetoric of apartheid was further transformed by *verligte* ideological ferment. Racist suppositions were disavowed, blacks were no longer spoken of pejoratively, and less emphasis was placed on the specters of miscegenation and social mixing of the races. By the mid-1970s, *verligtes* tended to exchange faith in separate development as a total ideological solution for more pragmatic considerations of economic reality and ethnic survival. They inclined not only toward removal of petty apartheid discrimination and such racist legislation as the Immorality Act (which made interracial sex a punishable offense), but even toward relinquishing job reservation for whites.

Under P. W. Botha, who served as prime minister from 1978 until 1984 and then, under the new constitution, became state president with executive powers, these tendencies gathered momentum and culminated in a series of reforms. However, with the introduction of emergency regulations to cope with the widespread black unrest that erupted in 1985, the momentum of reform flagged. The centerpiece of these reforms was the new constitution instituted in 1984. It replaced the Westminster-model system with a new tricameral parliament, with one chamber each for the whites, the coloreds, and the Indians. This ostensible step toward political power sharing was greatly flawed, however, not alone by the calculated preeminence of the white chamber but, even more importantly, by the total exclusion of the black (African) majority of South Africa's population. The channel for black political expression was relegated to the various "homelands," four of which had by then accepted independence, while the remaining six were self-governing. As for South Africa's vast population of urban blacks, little more was held out to them than local urban councils with authority limited to what the current lexicon of reformed apartheid referred to as their "own affairs."

At the same time, other specific reforms modifying the apartheid structure erected by earlier Afrikaner governments were introduced, which, in the context of Afrikaner political traditions, certainly represented far-reaching change. Thus, the South African government permitted the creation of legal black trade unions, modified job reservation practices and the pass system, and even took the odious article 16 of the Immorality Act and the Mixed Marriages Act off the statute books. The cumulative effect of these reforms signified the virtual dismantling of most of the petty apartheid dogmatically erected in the first two decades of National party rule. Yet, in practice, it could not be said that apartheid had ceased to exist, since the hard core of apartheid legislation, namely classification of the population according to race and residential segregation, still remained intact—although less rigidly enforced than in the past.

Be that as it may, the ideological rhetoric of government policy was certainly transformed. This rhetoric, and the delicate balance between change and continuity which it veiled, may be illustrated from the National party's electoral campaign of May 1987. The party declared that it would continue the policy of reforms, but only by its own lights and not in surrender to sanctions and threats. It upheld "individual freedom without race discrimination" but predicated this on preserving "the group character" of South African society. Moreover, the National party affirmed that "separate residential areas and voters' rolls for the various groups" still remained official policy. It promised political "power sharing," but qualifed this as "own decision making on own affairs and joint decision making on matters of common concern, without the domination of any group by another." The party contrasted this formula for power sharing with the policy of the Progressives, which, it declared, "amounts to a handing over of power."[16]

The Progressive Federal party, for its part, in 1987 advocated "an open society, free from statutory apartheid," to be shaped by a national convention comprising the acknowledged leaders of all sections of the population. This implied the inclusion of African National Congress leader Nelson Mandela, who would have to be released from prison. The party would negotiate a new federal constitution which would not exclude the blacks, as the government's constitutional changes had done, and would not divide the population on the basis of racially classified "own affairs."

On the other side of the political spectrum, the Conservative party, born of the right-wing reaction of Afrikaners to Botha's reformist policy, rejected "power sharing" out of hand, advocated partition, and demanded "the restoration of separate development in practice, especially with regard to white residential areas and public amenities." It called for the retention of all apartheid laws, including those that forbade miscegenation and mixed marriages. The Conservatives, furthermore, affirmed what they called "Christian white civilization," although at the same time claiming to "respect freedom of conscience and worship for others."

Although Jews were aware, for the most part, of the still inherent moral defects of reformed apartheid, the fact that it combined renunciation of racist premises with an appeal for the right of the whites to ensure their own survival and welfare against black majority rule struck a responsive chord

---

[16]The quotations in this and the following paragraphs are from pamphlets and brochures issued by the parties during the election campaign of May 1987.

among more and more of them, along with other English speakers. This tendency was perhaps best illustrated in the views of Israel Pinshaw, who was appointed to the State President's Council in 1984. Pinshaw was as identifying a Jew as any in the Jewish community but also an active member of the National party. It is a telling testimony to the transformation of National party political discourse that Pinshaw could depict his role in its ranks as that of a Jew inspired by Jewish values, which were solicitous of human rights irrespective of color or creed, but at the same time insistent upon ethnic-cultural particularism (one may read for this, "own affairs") as a legitimate structural basis for society. Pinshaw claimed that, as a Jew, he urged the National party leadership to move faster and more convincingly toward reforms. In the Jewish press he was reported as stating:[17]

> I sincerely believe that the philosophy of the National party has completely changed over the years. . . . As a Jew I find bigotry and discrimination repulsive and I believe that through the efforts of the National party accommodation can be achieved amongst our various race groups . . . and as a Jew I will endeavour to see that the decisions to which I am a party will be so designed that they are equitable, just and fair.

Already in the parliamentary elections of 1977 there were indications that the National party was gaining credence in the eyes of Jews. Against a background of some opinion polls that indicated almost a doubling of English-speaking supporters since 1974, the party sponsored the candidacy of a Jew, Abe Hoppenstein, in a Johannesburg constituency (Bezuidenhout) known to have a considerable Jewish population. Hoppenstein, a lawyer by profession, was a National party member of some 20 years' standing and at the same time an identifying Jew associated, *inter alia,* with the Revisionist party of Zionism. In 1974 he was appointed South Africa's trade commissioner in Israel and shortly after that became political counselor in South Africa's Washington embassy. Fresh from that post, he entered the electoral lists to challenge an Afrikaner candidate of the Progressive Federal party, Japie Basson, who had undergone a leftward odyssey in politics after expulsion from the National party. Hoppenstein declared: "Voting for the National party is the best way to provide for our survival in the face of pressure from abroad. We are the only party that can and will bring about effective, meaningful change."[18] In the end, although Basson was elected, he gained a mere 50 votes more than Hoppenstein, and it was evident that

[17]*Jewish Herald,* Nov. 27, 1984. Also the author's interview with I. Pinshaw, Sept. 1986. The State President's Council functioned as an advisory body under terms of the reformed constitution. It had 60 members, 41 of whom were white, 13 colored, and 6 Indian. Pinshaw was its only Jewish member until 1987, when he was joined by another Jewish appointee, S. Spilken.

[18]The source is newspaper clippings in South African Jewish Board of Deputies Archives (hereafter BD, and in accordance with its classification system), 311.12 and 303.12.

a considerable number of Jewish votes had been cast for the latter. Although his defeat meant that there was still no Jew on the National party benches in Parliament—whereas five Jewish candidates for the Progressives took their seats in the Parliament of 1977—Hoppenstein's close miss was a sign of the times.

To be sure, it was also indicative of the political orientations of Jews that Hoppenstein's candidacy stirred quite a controversy within the Jewish community, with members of the South African Union of Jewish Students (SAUJS) declaring that support of National party policies was a travesty of Jewish ethics and deprecating what they termed Hoppenstein's "contorted rationalizations" in justifying his actions.[19]

The increase in the number of Jews tending to vote for the National party was evident in subsequent contests. One was a municipal election in the affluent and largely Jewish ward of Houghton, Johannesburg, an electoral district that had for many years been represented in Parliament by the Progressives' most famous personality, Helen Suzman. In March 1984 the National party ventured to challenge the Progressives, putting up Israel Pinshaw as a candidate. Although the Progressives won the election decisively, with 1,310 votes, Pinshaw managed to gain 573. It is reasonable to assume that most of these votes were cast by Jews.[20]

In the municipal by-election in the Bellevue-Judith's Paarl ward of Johannesburg in February 1986, in a contest between two Jewish candidates—the Progressives' Tony Leon and the National party's Sam Bloomberg—the Progressives just scraped through with a margin of 39 votes. Since it was reliably estimated that some 35 percent of the eligible voters were Jews, there can be little doubt that many of them voted for the National party candidate. During the contest emotions ran high in the Jewish community: on the one hand, National party posters were defaced; on the other, ultra-Orthodox Jewish residents in the area, mostly elderly persons, were conspicuous in support of the National party's candidate.[21]

Notwithstanding these indications of growing Jewish support for the National party, the main political orientation of Jews was still toward the Progressive Federal party. This may be adduced, in part, from the prominence of Jews in that party's active membership and among its candidates for election. It should be recalled that on the eve of the May 1987 elections all four Jewish members of the white chamber of Parliament were Progressives. At the provincial and municipal levels the prominence of Jews in the

[19]See *S.A. Jewish Times,* Oct. 26, Nov. 9, Nov. 23, 1977. Hoppenstein returned to the South African Foreign Service. In 1979 he was appointed consul general in Washington, and in 1980 he took charge of the South African consulate in New York.

[20]The source is newspaper clippings in BD, 199; 311.12; 100.4A; and 313.12.

[21]Ibid.

Progressive Federal party was even more marked. For example, in the March 1977 municipal elections, Jews accounted for 19 of the 38 Progressive candidates.[22] In 1986, 16 of the Progressives' representatives on the Johannesburg City Council, as well as the mayor himself, were Jews.[23]

At the parliamentary level, the name of Helen Suzman had been the very symbol of opposition to the apartheid system for more than a quarter of a century. She was the South African-born daughter of a Jewish immigrant from Lithuania who prospered in his new country. After a spell in academe teaching economics, she entered Parliament in 1952 as a United party member for the affluent Houghton district in Johannesburg, which had always had a significant Jewish voting population. In 1958 Suzman participated in the first of a series of splits from the United party that ultimately led to the formation of the Progressive Federal party in 1977. For 13 years, from 1961 to 1974, Suzman was the sole Progressive representative in Parliament. Singlehandedly, relentlessly, and with superb analytic prowess, she assailed the apartheid system from the floor of Parliament, where she also had to endure an occasional anti-Semitic taunt.

Suzman, being Jewish, willy-nilly symbolized the relatively liberal stance of South African Jews for people both in and out of South Africa. However, it is perhaps her fellow Progressive Harry Schwarz who came closer to epitomizing the normative orientation of politically aware South African Jews. For whereas Suzman had never taken particular interest in Jewish communal life, Schwarz had been actively involved and, indeed, could be regarded as one of the community's foremost leaders. Born in Cologne, Germany, in 1924, Schwarz came to South Africa in 1934. During the Second World War he served as an officer in the South African Air Force. Afterward he practiced law and engaged in business and merchant banking. After entering Parliament in 1974 as a representative of the United party, Schwarz broke away to found the Reform party, which joined the Progressives, and went on to form the Progressive Federal party in 1977. Within the South African political spectrum, Schwarz was generally identified with the conservative wing of the Progressive Federal party, at least on matters

[22]At that stage the name was Progressive Reform party. The United party had not yet disbanded, and 9 out of 31 of its candidates in the municipal elections were Jews. BD, 401.6. See especially the *Jewish Herald,* Feb. 8, 1977.

[23]There was a remarkable prominence of Jews in municipal politics, reflected particularly in the number of Jewish mayors. In the 31 years between 1956 and 1987, 12 Jews were elected mayor of Johannesburg; in the 19 years between 1968 and 1987, 8 were elected. (Mayors served a one-year period in office.) In Cape Town, of the 57 aldermen and councillors who held office in the city council from 1976 to 1987, 19 were Jews, and 4 of them had served as mayor in that 11-year period. In mid-1987, 12 of the 34 incumbent councillors were Jews. BD, 100.5A. See also Nathan Mendelow, "Johannesburg's Eighteen Jewish Mayors," *Jewish Affairs,* July 1966, 18–31.

of law and order and the need for military conscription. Much as Suzman was consistently returned to Parliament by the Houghton electorate, so Schwarz was repeatedly successful in the Yeoville constituency of Johannesburg, which also had a considerable Jewish population.

Beginning in the mid-seventies, Schwarz played an increasingly important role on the Jewish Board of Deputies, serving as chairman of its committee on international relations and often acting as spokesman for the board to Jewish agencies abroad. He argued that violent change could ultimately lead to a nondemocratic regime that was not compatible either with Jewish ethics or with the legitimate interests of the Jewish community. He emphasized that Jews needed not only a democratic society for all, but also "the right to follow [their] own religion and love for Israel freely." Typical of his many expressions on this matter was the following:[24]

> To be against apartheid is one thing, but what do we want in its place? What will the post-apartheid regime be like? Will it be a free world type democracy in which human rights are respected and minorities protected? Will it be a regime under which South African Jews will, like other citizens, have religious freedom and under which our communal institutions can be maintained and our love for Zion expressed?

The developing trends in Jewish political orientation were rather more clearly confirmed in the June 1987 general election to the white chamber of Parliament. It was still the Progressive Federal party that fielded the majority of Jewish candidates for election—five out of seven—and that gained most of the votes of Jews in districts known to have large Jewish concentrations.[25] Only three Jews gained election—Harry Schwarz and Helen Suzman for the Progressive Federal party and Sam Bloomberg for the National party, the latter thereby becoming the first Jew ever to be elected to Parliament as a representative of the National party.[26] As mentioned earlier, Bloomberg had been narrowly defeated when he contested a Johannesburg municipal by-election as a National party candidate in 1986. He now succeeded in the Johannesburg constituency of Bezuidenhout, whose considerable body of Jewish voters, although not predominant,

---

[24]Quoted in the *Zionist Record and S.A. Jewish Chronicle,* Dec. 27, 1985, 11; Feb. 6, 1987, 5.

[25]Four electoral districts had major concentrations of Jewish voters: Houghton, Yeoville, and Bezuidenhout in Johannesburg, and Sea Point in Cape Town (represented by Colin Eglin, the leader of the Progressive Federal party). Only in Bezuidenhout was the Progressive candidate defeated. The Jewish candidates were listed in the *Jewish Times,* May 1, 1987, and the full election results were given in the *Cape Times,* May 8, 1987.

[26]Another Jew, Theo Aronson, had preceded Bloomberg as a member of Parliament for the National party. However, he was not an elected member. Having suffered defeat when he stood for election in 1981 as a National party candidate, he was appointed to Parliament according to the terms of the new constitution of 1982. BD, 100.4A.

certainly contributed to the 60-percent majority gained by him. His fellow party candidate in the Cape, Esme Chait, was defeated in her constituency, but entered Parliament as a member nominated, under the terms of the constitution, by the National party. The total number of Jewish members of the white chamber thus remained at four, the same as at the close of the previous parliamentary session, but the fact that this number was now equally divided between the government party and the progressive opposition was surely indicative of the trends we have noted.

Yet another noteworthy trend was evident in the 1987 elections, affecting a part of the Jewish vote. Following the example of F. van Zyl Slabbert, who, about a year earlier, had resigned both from Parliament and from the chair of the Progressive Federal party to form the Institute for a Democratic Alternative for South Africa, some of the most fervent opponents of the government's policies chose to demonstrate their conviction that the white chamber of Parliament was irrelevant to the real issues facing the country by boycotting the election altogether.

Involvement of Jews in Social Action

The suppression of the radical opposition to the apartheid regime in the 1960s left most of the Jews involved in one or another branch of that opposition either in exile or in prison or under severe banning orders that placed them in political quarantine. Jewish individuals did not, however, fall away from what might be called the liberal-reformist opposition functioning within the bounds of South African laws. To be sure, even this form of opposition was subjected to harassment under the 1986 Emergency Regulations, resulting in new arrests and banning orders. At the English-speaking universities, Jewish students were prominent as opponents of the apartheid system within the leadership of the various Students' Representative Councils and the National Union of South African Students (NUSAS). Some of these were at the same time actively involved in Zionist groups off and on the campus. Others, having been awakened to social awareness in the Zionist youth movements, severed their particularistic Jewish bonds and threw themselves wholly into the struggle for a transformed South African society.

Individual Jews were prominent across the entire spectrum of organizations and political groups engaged in the struggle against the government's policies and emergency powers, and on behalf of their victims. In recent years a broad array of new organizations and groups arose, often acting as thorns in the side of the government. The names of Jews were ubiquitous in the leadership of many of these, ranging from Lawyers for Human Rights, headed by Jules Browde, to the End Conscription Campaign, which demanded changes in the law regarding compulsory military service for whites so that individuals could choose either not to serve in the black townships or do alternative national service.

One outstanding example of activity aimed at alleviating the iniquities of the system was the Legal Resources Center established in 1979 with private funds. It provided desperately needed legal services for thousands of victims of the day-to-day operation of the apartheid system. It also trained paralegal personnel in the elementary legal skills needed to help blacks cope with the maze of apartheid laws which governed their lives. The director and moving spirit of this entire legal aid enterprise was Arthur Chaskalson, who left a brilliant practice as senior counsel at the Johannesburg bar in order to dedicate himself to it.[27] Other Jews involved in the founding and progress of the center were Sydney Kentridge, widely regarded as the preeminent lawyer practicing in South Africa, and Basil Wunsh, who was also active in some Jewish organizations. By 1986 the center's staff had grown to some 20 lawyers, 2 paralegal assistants, 8 fellows, and more than 20 administrators. Illustrative of the center's far-reaching achievements were judgements in the cases of two ordinary working blacks, one of which established the right of certain migrant workers to qualify for permanent urban residence, and the other, that of certain black urban dwellers to have their families live with them.

The work of Arthur Chaskalson demonstrated a form of activity which, far more than direct political involvement, characterized the endeavors of Jewish individuals in numbers quite disproportionate to the size of the Jewish population. It was the activity of people born into the privileged status of whites but whose moral conscience drove them to dedicate themselves, within the parameters of what remained legal and possible, to the alleviation of the day-to-day indignities and deprivations inflicted by the apartheid system. At the same time, their efforts formed part of the broader struggle for the reform and ultimate abolition of that system.

Another example of a Jew involved in this manner was educator Franz Auerbach. The author of an academic study of prejudice in history textbooks and syllabi of white high schools, he served from 1981 to 1983 as president of the South African Institute of Race Relations, one of the great pillars of liberal values in South African society. In addition, Auerbach organized the teachers' program of the Funda Center, which provided black teachers with supplementary training.[28] Born in Germany, Auerbach fled with his family from the Nazis in 1937, when he was 14 years old. Concurrently with his tireless activities in the broader societal arena, he was active

[27]BD, biographical files containing, *inter alia,* Rex Gibson's profile in *Optima* 34, no. 1 (Mar. 1986):32–35.

[28]BD, biographical files.

on the Jewish Board of Deputies and other Jewish communal bodies, notably the South African Yad Vashem Foundation.

Auerbach drew parallels between the Nazi regime in Germany and apartheid. He argued that there was a key parallel in "the organization of a society in which the most important attribute of human beings is their race, as assigned by the state." In defense of similar comparisons made by Archbishop Tutu, Auerbach said that forced removal of black people to "homelands" where there was little food and work was an inhuman practice, even if in the South African case there was no intention of killing them. "The persistence of legally enforced race discrimination," Auerbach said, "makes a comparison between apartheid and Nazism a perfectly valid analogy. . . . In fact I have always held that the experience of the Holocaust obliged me to oppose racial discrimination, especially where it is enforced by law."[29]

In the business sphere the role of Jews was inherently more ambiguous. Whether big business was a factor either in buttressing apartheid or undermining it was a moot point among academic analysts as well as political activists.[30] Be that as it may, in recent years Jews had been in the forefront of those businessmen who, out of enlightened economic self-interest as well as social concern, advocated the dismantling of apartheid restrictions. At the same time, of course, they vigorously called upon foreign corporations not to disinvest and boycott South Africa but rather to remain "constructively engaged" and add their weight to the strategy aimed at attaining change via the economy. In this regard, two particularly important Jewish businessmen were Raymond Ackerman, head of a flourishing chain of supermarkets, and Tony Bloom, head of the mammoth Premier Milling Group. In 1985 they took the lead in drawing up a manifesto signed by 92 of the country's top businessmen, calling for an end to apartheid and for government negotiations with black leaders, not excluding those in detention. Much to the chagrin of the government Bloom also formed a delegation of business leaders who met with African National Congress representatives in Lusaka.

Mendel Kaplan, a prominent businessman who was at the same time South African Jewry's single most important Jewish communal leader, authored a book on the historical role of the Jews in the South African economy, in which he averred that the solution of South African society's

[29]See F. E. Auerbach's article in the *Rand Daily Mail,* Feb. 24, 1971, and his letter to the editor, *Rand Daily Mail,* Jan. 15, 1985, in defense of Archibishop Tutu's comparisons between apartheid and Nazi Germany.

[30]See, e.g., F. A. Johnstone, "White Prosperity and White Supremacy in South Africa Today," *African Affairs* 69, no. 274 (1970):124–40, and Merle Lipton, *Capitalism and Apartheid: South Africa 1910–1986* (London, 1985).

problems "will be dependent on the acceptance of every South African by his fellow South African with equality, irrespective of race or religion." Kaplan concluded his study with the statement that "if Jewish businessmen, in particular, fail to give leadership in the movement to abolish all discriminatory practices, they will be betraying their heritage in the country which gave the Jewish people their freedom and opportunities."[31]

Measured against the record of the Jewish community in the past, the most innovative development was the emergence in late 1985 of groups of Jews dedicated to collective Jewish expression of opposition to the apartheid system. In Cape Town one such group initially called itself Jews Against Apartheid, but, with a view to adopting a more positive, less provocative posture, soon changed it to Jews for Justice. Among its founders were Jewish individuals associated with various groups active in resistance to government policies, such as NUSAS and area committees of the United Democratic Front, a broad alignment comprising some 60 groups. At the outset, it also included members of the Habonim-Dror Zionist youth movement. At about the same time, a group of similar composition was founded in Johannesburg under the name Jews for Social Justice. The combined enrolled membership of these groups was only a few hundred, but their public meetings attracted up to a thousand participants.

What made these groups distinctively different in the South African Jewish experience was their attempted synthesis of two foci of identification—bold public protest against the apartheid system, on the one hand, and self-affirming Jewish identification, of which Zionism formed an intrinsic part, on the other. To be sure, the attempt to organize a collective Jewish voice in opposition to apartheid was not entirely without precedent. In the 1950s a minuscule and short-lived group called the Jewish Democratic Association had been formed by Michael Szur. It was a residual manifestation of the leftist Yiddish groups that were referred to earlier in this study. Much as the Jews for Justice groups were now doing, that association invoked the memory of recent Jewish suffering in Europe and argued that if Jews "complained justifiably that the people of the world did not rally to our defense," then "as a community we cannot hide ourselves behind the false slogan of neutrality and keep silent when other peoples are in distress." Unlike the contemporary Jews for Justice, however, the Jewish Democratic Association had upheld the diminutive legacy of leftist anti-Zionism. It had accused Zionism, among other charges, of propagating the false view that

[31]Mendel Kaplan, *Jewish Roots in the South African Economy* (Cape Town, 1986), 28, 389. Kaplan was a Jewish leader of international importance; he was treasurer of the World Jewish Congress, chairman of the board of trustees of the Keren Hayesod, and in June 1987 was elected chairman of the board of governors of the Jewish Agency for Israel.

Jews were really no more than temporary sojourners in the Diaspora, thereby lulling them into passive acquiescence in apartheid.[32]

In a newsletter appealing to Jews to join its ranks, Jews for Social Justice declared that it was intended to fill the need for a "united Jewish response" to the South African situation:[33]

> Our history of persecution imposes a special duty on us to protest any form of discrimination against any people. Judaism is a religion of faith expressed in action; therefore its teachings about human dignity and social justice make it unacceptable for us to be guilty of the complicity of silence in an oppressive society. . . . A vast proportion of the Jewish population does desire a just society and wishes to stake its claim to a future in a democratic South Africa. It is therefore essential for a united Jewish voice to be heard in the struggle for justice. . . . South African Jews are already choosing between leaving South Africa or adapting to changes. If Jews are sincere about staying in South Africa, but are fearful of the changes which must come, it is their responsibility to play a part in these changes and thus participate in the formulation of a new South Africa.

An example of the protests made by Jews for Justice on particular issues was that against the government's legislation of June 1986, which gave the minister of law and order unlimited power to declare an "unrest area" without possibility of challenge by any court. "Our historical experience of persecution and oppression impels us to protest in the strongest terms against this Bill," declared Jews for Social Justice. Another example was its protest against the further curtailment of individual freedom enforced by Section 50A of the Internal Security Act, which allowed the police to increase the period of detention without trial to 180 days. In Johannesburg, members of Jews for Social Justice joined a public demonstration against this legislation in June 1986, alongside the Black Sash (a veteran women's social-action group), the Johannesburg Democratic Action Committee (JODAC), and the End Conscription Campaign.[34] In April 1987 Cape Town's group held a "freedom seder" during Passover, addressed by Archbishop Desmond Tutu—his first to a public meeting under Jewish auspices. Despite a bomb threat, a thousand people came to hear him say, *inter alia,* that although Jews had been in the forefront of the anti-apartheid struggle from the outset, South Africa's blacks currently felt a sense of disappointment with the Jewish community because of Israel's close ties with the white regime.

In March 1987 Johannesburg's Jews for Social Justice participated in the founding of the Five Freedoms Forum, a broad grouping of about 25 white organizations opposed to apartheid, including the Progressive Federal

---

[32] *Jewish Opinion: A Newsletter,* July 1954. This newsletter of the Jewish Democratic Association appeared monthly from Apr. 1954 until June 1962.

[33] *Newsletter of Jews for Social Justice,* Nov. 17, 1985, in BD, 303.12.

[34] Jews for Justice leaflet calling a protest meeting for June 8, 1986, in BD, ibid.

party, the Black Sash, JODAC, and NUSAS. This forum was oriented toward the white elections set for May 6, 1987. Similarly, Cape Town's Jews for Justice, while declaring that "the major source of change in South Africa is to be found in the extra-Parliamentary struggle," formulated an appeal "for those who wished to oppose apartheid by voting in the 1987 election" to support only those candidates who "oppose a social system based on statutory racial classification; oppose a legal system in which detention without trial forms an integral part; support a political system in which all South Africans will enjoy the same rights irrespective of colour and in which all will be able to be represented by persons of their own choice."[35]

Some of the anti-apartheid forces with which the Jewish groups aligned themselves fell victim to bannings under the Emergency Regulations imposed in June 1986. Indeed, of the 22 political, religious, and communal groups with which Cape Town's Jews for Justice was associated at the outset of its involvement in assisting the destitute black inhabitants of the Crossroads squatter camp, all but Jews for Justice itself and the women's Black Sash were afterward muzzled. This may well indicate the authorities' perception that the Jewish group was not really dangerous.[36] Also, given the antagonistic attitude toward Jews evinced by some of the Muslim groups associated with the United Democratic Front and the fact that many members of Jews for Justice concurrently had other, more compelling political affiliations, this expression of Jewish social action bore the marks of an ephemeral phenomenon much like its kindred predecessors in the history of the community.

The Policy of the Jewish Board of Deputies

Turning from an analysis of the political orientations of Jewish individuals and groups to the Jewish community as an organized entity, it is the South African Jewish Board of Deputies that must now engage our attention. The board was recognized, by convention, as the representative organ of South African Jewry. Ironically, a retrospective survey of the official statements issued by the board since 1948 reveals an inverse relation between the harshness of the apartheid system and the daring of the board in criticizing it. When crudely racist apartheid was at its zenith in the late 1950s and early 1960s, the board's stance was at its most timid. However,

---

[35]*Jews for Justice Newsletter,* no. 2, Apr. 1987, 3.

[36]Those associated with Jews for Justice who experienced detention were concurrently active in other protest groups. For example, Lisa Seftel of Johannesburg, who was an organizing secretary of JODAC, an affiliate of the United Democratic Front, and Raymond Suttner, a university law lecturer who was an executive member of the United Democratic Front in the Transvaal.

as the ideology of apartheid became more refined and less overtly racist, and as its practice began to crack and reach a stage of near disintegration, the board's statements became progressively bolder and clearer in condemnation of apartheid.

From the inception of the Board of Deputies in 1912, its purposes were perceived in narrowly particularistic terms: to "watch and take action in all matters affecting the Jews in the southern portion of the continent of Africa."[37] Its honorary officers, generation after generation, never considered their terms of reference to include a collective Jewish response or contribution to the shaping of South African society as a whole. The board's record is best understood as a characteristic minority-group phenomenon of self-preservation. This dictated a policy of noninvolvement in politics: "that Jews participate in South African public life as citizens of South Africa and have no collective attitude to the political issues which citizens are called upon to decide."[38]

The explicit justification most often proffered for not formulating a collective viewpoint was that it simply did not exist; that there was "as much diversity of political viewpoint in the Jewish community as in the general population." The implicit justification, more rarely enunciated, was that even if it were possible to formulate a single viewpoint, this would be ill-advised from the point of view of the community's self-interest.

Until 1948 the context in which the board navigated this policy was the intrawhite conflict between the centrist United party, associated with the name of Jan Smuts, and the Afrikaner nationalists, who evinced pro-German and anti-Semitic tendencies after 1933. In that context, as has already been mentioned, the board did align itself, at least discreetly, in the late 1930s with the liberal forces associated with Smuts's lieutenant, Jan Hofmeyr. However, this was hardly inconsistent with the fundamental policy of political noninvolvement, since it was motivated by the wish to resist the anti-Semitic forces in the Afrikaner nationalist camp, and only by association did it implicate the board in the broader political arena.[39]

After 1948, in the wake of the National party's electoral victory—which was repeated at every election from that time on—and its enforcement of apartheid, the context widened to include issues that transcended intrawhite politics. The crucial question became whether one condoned or opposed a societal system based on legally enforced racial discrimination. Poignant moral dilemmas concerning basic human dignity and rights descended

---

[37]A Jewish Board of Deputies was founded in Johannesburg in 1903 and in Cape Town in 1904. The two bodies united to form the South African Jewish Board of Deputies in 1912. See Saron and Hotz, *Jews in South Africa,* 226–69.

[38]*South African Jewish Board of Deputies Report, April 1958 to August 1960,* 9.

[39]For a full discussion of this, see Shimoni, *Jews and Zionism,* 152–55.

insistently upon the leadership of the Jewish community. The question whether, as the acknowledged representative body of the community, the Board of Deputies at least ought to say something about those fundamental moral issues which transcended formal party politics was hotly debated at every congress of the board. Some argued that it was impossible to separate moral from party political issues and that the board had no business, in the first place, making statements on any controversial public issue not directly affecting Jewish rights. Others asserted that the agreed principle of noninvolvement in politics did not preclude some statement against racial prejudice and in affirmation of fundamental human rights.

The upshot was the periodic passing of resolutions giving expression to a Jewish ethos sufficiently generalized to be politically innocuous. An example is the one passed in 1955, stating that "the welfare of all sections of the population depends on the maintenance of democratic institutions and the enjoyment of freedom and justice by all," and that "the elimination of inter-group conflict and the abatement of racial prejudice are vital for the national good." At the same time, the board repeatedly declared that "every individual Jew has the right to his own political views and actions" (adding cautiously, "of course within the framework of the law"), and urged every Jewish citizen "to make his individual contribution in accordance with the teachings and precepts of Judaism."[40]

In this way, at a time when apartheid was at its worst, the board trod a precarious path between noninvolvement in the political thicket, on the one hand, and the muffled impulses of Jewish moral conscience, on the other. There can be no doubt that most of the board's executive members throughout the 1950s would have wished to speak out against apartheid but were severely constrained by their concern for the safety of the Jewish community. What intimidated them was not so much the presence of anti-Semitism but rather the very fact that the Afrikaner nationalists had consciously abandoned anti-Semitism ever since coming to power in 1948. A process of Afrikaner-Jewish rapprochement was in progress, facilitated largely by genuine Afrikaner sympathy for the new State of Israel, and the purpose uppermost in the minds of the Jewish communal leadership was to cultivate that rapprochement. In these circumstances they were anxious not to do anything that might undermine it.

The transformation of apartheid's ideological rhetoric, which was discussed earlier, had the effect of extending the boundaries of public moral criticism permitted by the white consensus. By the 1970s it became possible for the Board of Deputies to vent views that would have been regarded as

---

[40]The seminal resolution adopted at the board's 20th congress in 1955 was reiterated at later congresses. See, e.g., *South African Jewish Board of Deputies Report, September 1962 to June 1965,* 9.

disloyal, if not treacherous, only ten years earlier. Accordingly, the board continued to uphold its traditional policy of noninvolvement in politics but formulated statements which, while clearly liberal in connotation, were sufficiently equivocal to be compatible with the rhetoric of *verligte* Afrikaners. Thus a resolution was passed at the board's congress in 1967 and reiterated in 1970 calling for "the promotion of understanding, goodwill and co-operation between the various races, peoples and groups in South Africa and toward the achievement of a peaceful and secure future for all inhabitants of the country, based on the principles of justice and dignity of the individual."[41]

Incrementally more outspoken, yet venturing only ever so slightly beyond the norm of *verligte* rhetoric, resolutions of the board's congresses throughout the 1970s called for the elimination of "unjust discriminations so that all, regardless of race, creed or colour, be permitted and encouraged to achieve the full potential of their capabilities and live in dignity and harmony.[42] A somewhat less equivocal augur of the real change yet to come in the 1980s was the speech delivered by David Mann, president of the Board of Deputies, at a banquet for Prime Minister Vorster on his return from a visit to Israel in 1976. He said:[43]

> I believe that there is a wide consensus today that attitudes and practices, the heritage of the past, bearing upon the relations between our various racial groups are no longer acceptable. I believe that there is a new sense of urgency abroad in our land, a realization that we must move away as quickly and effectively as is practicable from discrimination based on race or colour, and that we must accord to every man and woman respect and human dignity and the opportunity to develop to their fullest potential. Our task is to translate into concrete patterns of living, and of relationships between man and man and group and group, the great injunction of the Bible, "Justice, justice shalt thou pursue, that thou may live and inherit the land which the Lord thy God gave thee."

In later years, as new waves of black resistance pounded against the apartheid system with unprecedented force, and as President P. W. Botha's government itself began to dismantle old-style apartheid and institute reforms calculated to preserve white supremacy in alternative ways, the Jewish Board of Deputies abandoned its noninvolvement policy, in practice if not in theory. In 1981 there were periodic statements by the board condemning evictions of blacks and pass-law arrests; in 1982, condemnation of detention without trial; in 1983, objection to a university quota system for blacks and to the treatment of squatters at the Crossroads camp near Cape

---

[41]*Report to South African Jewry, 1967–1970* (S.A. Jewish Board of Deputies, 1970), 8.

[42]See resolution adopted at the Jewish Board of Deputies' 29th biennial congress, May 29–31, 1976, cited in *Report to South African Jewry, 1976–1978* (S.A. Jewish Board of Deputies, 1978), 10.

[43]*Jewish Affairs,* May 1976, 12.

Town; and in 1982, representations to Parliament calling for the repeal of the racial provisions of the Mixed Marriages and Immorality Acts.[44]

The culmination of this new direction of policy was the unanimous passing of a resolution at the 33rd national congress of the board in 1985, which, for the first time, explicitly rejected apartheid: "Congress records its support and commitment to justice, equal opportunity and the removal of all provisions in the laws of South Africa which discriminate on grounds of colour and race, and rejects apartheid." This was reiterated and elaborated upon at the board's April 1987 congress in a series of unequivocal resolutions, including the following:[45]

> Congress resolves that there is an urgent need for enhanced and accelerated dialogue, negotiation and meaningful reform in South Africa, and records its dismay at the lack of meaningful progress in this direction, whilst acknowledging the steps already taken by the Government to repeal certain laws and abolish certain discriminatory practices. Congress also expresses the hope that a climate for peace and calm will speedily be re-established including the lifting of the state of emergency, and that the rule of law will be re-established. . . . Congress endorses the efforts of the National Executive Council in seeking to maintain channels of open communication with all sections of the South African population. . . . Congress recognizes that apartheid is the principal cause of political violence in South Africa and that continued oppression under that policy exacerbates the climate of political unrest and believes that apartheid and racial prejudice are in complete contradiction to the teachings of Judaism.

The Jewish Board of Deputies also continued to concern itself with its original and primary function of monitoring anti-Semitic manifestations and taking action against them where necessary. Although such manifestations ceased to be a serious problem by the mid-1950s, they never entirely disappeared. In this respect South Africa cannot be said to differ from other Western countries. However, something of the thematic admixture endemic to the South African variety of chronic anti-Semitism may be demonstrated by the following extract from a vitriolic news sheet published by the veteran anti-Semite S. E. D. Brown. Responding to the board's resolutions calling for the abolition of apartheid laws, he wrote that these "posturing moralists" had "virtually declared open war on the White nation in South Africa!"[46]

> Yet it is they themselves who are the one race—racists par excellence who know just how to discriminate and do so in no uncertain terms, against everyone and

---

[44]See *Report to South African Jewry, 1980–1983* (S.A. Jewish Board of Deputies, 1983), 17, 18; *Report to South African Jewry, 1983–1985* (S.A. Jewish Board of Deputies, 1985), 11.

[45]See the resolutions adopted at the 34th national congress, Apr. 1987, in *Jewish Affairs,* Apr. 1987, 28–29.

[46]*South African Observer,* Feb. 1986. The article is entitled "The Total Zionist Onslaught on South Africa."

everything that is non-Jewish. They long ago decided that they were the "chosen people" of all the peoples on earth, and the world's most enduring ethno-centrism began. Their endless and bitter campaigns against "racism" imposed with the fervour of the inquisition of the Middle Ages, are serving no other purpose than to break down the racial and national dynamism of all the peoples of the West, while at the same time building up their own fanatical racism. . . . Moreover, they openly identified themselves with world Zionism's "total onslaught" on South Africa . . . in complete phase with the "total onslaughts" of world Communism and the forces of international finance. Furthermore, the S.A. Jewish Board of Deputies and their coracialists made themselves guilty of wilfully stabbing an old friend in the back—South Africa—after all that South Africa had done, and is still doing for Israel and World Jewry.

There was also something of a resurgence of anti-Semitism emanating from a right-wing, reactionary group founded in 1981 under the name the Afrikaner Weerstandbeweging (resistance organization). This was a racist, neo-Nazi organization that harked back to the various "Greyshirt" movements that mushroomed in the 1930s as purveyors of Nazi and anti-Semitic views. Its leader, Eugene Terre-Blanche, stated openly that South African Jews would be deprived of political rights under an Afrikaner Christian people's government controlled by his organization. He said that "the Jews must decide between two things in this country—political rights or economic freedom. They cannot have both. They cannot have political rights. It is Israel, not South Africa, which they recognise as their fatherland."[47] President Botha condemned the views and activities of the Weerstandbeweging on a number of occasions. In late 1982 it was reported that the police had uncovered arms caches belonging to the group and that a number of arrests had been made.

Although overt anti-Semitism was not expressed in the more respectable sections of the right-wing Afrikaner opposition to the government party, their political character and policies also did not augur well for the Jewish community. The Herstigte Nasionale party (reconstituted national party), founded as far back as 1969, was committed to what it called "Christian Afrikaner Nationalism," a formulation evoking those ideological trends in pre-1948 Afrikaner nationalism that were hostile to Jews. The party's newspaper, *Die Afrikaner,* frequently carried articles emanating from so-called revisionist historians who denied the truth of the Holocaust.

The main political group to the right of the present National party was the Conservative party. Formed in 1982, it had already gained more seats than the Progressives in the 1987 elections to the white chamber of Parliament, thereby displacing them as the official opposition. Although disavowing anti-Semitism, this party too emphasized the strictly Christian basis of

---

[47]Cited in "Anti-Semitism in South Africa," a report by the S.A. Jewish Board of Deputies, issued in Jan. 1986.

the state in ways that had disconcerting associations for Jews. Jewish concern was compounded by the formation of a new cultural organization called Die Afrikaner Volkswag (the Afrikaner people's sentinel) in May 1984. As well as harking back to the Ossewa Brandwag (ox-wagon sentinel), which agitated against participation in the Second World War and against Jews, it presaged a popular drawing together of all right-wing Afrikaners in an extraparliamentary framework conducive to the spread of Terre-Blanche's influence.

The Rabbinate's Response to Apartheid

A balanced evaluation of the record of the rabbinate on the question of apartheid in South Africa requires awareness of some basic differences between its position and that of the Christian clergy. Unlike the major Christian churches, whether Anglican, Dutch Reformed, or Roman Catholic, Judaism had no adherents outside of the white population of South Africa. Consequently, the rabbinate was never answerable to, or responsible for, a black membership suffering directly from the apartheid system; it never had to formulate theological or practical principles either justifying or denouncing discrimination among its members.

On the other hand, the rabbinate had to contend with the minority-group status of Jews within the white racial group. The non-Jewish majority did not differentiate between the statements and actions of rabbis and the position of the Jewish community. This greatly constrained those rabbis who were, over the years, genuinely perturbed by the acute moral issues peculiar to South African society but, at the same time, had a primary sense of responsibility for the safety and welfare of the Jewish community. This situation was most marked in the peak years of racist apartheid—the 1950s and early 1960s—when the leadership of the Jewish community felt intimidated by the assertive Afrikaner devotees of that apartheid ideology. The rabbis, hardly less than the lay leadership, instinctively sensed that outspoken condemnation of apartheid, and even more so public action against it, would have endangered the Jewish community.

Account must also be taken of the inherent proclivity of the Orthodox rabbinate—who served over 80 percent of synagogue-affiliated Jews—for a societal order that fostered ethnic-religious particularism. In recent years, as apartheid ideology began to shake off its racist trammels and to project an ostensibly purified rhetoric of ethnic-cultural survival as the basis for government policies, this was bound to strike a chord of ambivalence, if not actual understanding, in the Orthodox rabbinate.

Since the conventions of South African society always recognized the prerogative of the clergy to speak out on moral issues, rabbis potentially enjoyed considerably more scope in this respect than did lay bodies like the

Jewish Board of Deputies. However, the record shows that most rabbis, particularly the East European-born and the more traditionalist ones, gave but scant attention to the issue of apartheid over the years, some even speaking out in support of government policy in South Africa.[48] This does not mean, however, that they were oblivious to the glaring evils of the system. Their behavior is explicable, rather, as a function of their essentially insular outlook; their tendency to compartmentalize Jewish concerns and to dissociate them from responsibility for the society as a whole. By their lights, apartheid and its attendant evils were the doing of the non-Jewish majority of white society. Collective Jewish involvement—and the actions of rabbis inevitably would be interpreted as such—was imprudent. It would only invite hostility to the Jews and divisiveness among themselves.

In the first decade of apartheid rule, rare were the occasions when a rabbi adopted a stand of unequivocal opposition to the apartheid system, and when it did happen, the response within the Jewish community was anything but enthusiastic. A case in point is that of Andre Ungar, a young Progressive (Reform) rabbi, newly arrived from England, whose outraged protestations against apartheid led to the withdrawal of his permit of residence in 1956. Neither his own congregants, nor the Jewish Board of Deputies, nor even his rabbinical colleagues, rallied to support him.[49] Yet it is also true that the head of the Orthodox Federation of Synagogues in that period, Rabbi Louis I. Rabinowitz, chafed at the bit of communal restraints and became increasingly irrepressible in the last years of his tenure before settling in Israel in 1960. His sermons became progressively more outspoken against apartheid, and in one Yom Kippur sermon in 1959 he gave vent to his anguish and frustration in a frank outburst:[50]

> . . . What do we do to loosen the bonds of wickedness, to undo the bonds of oppression? . . . There are some Jews in the community who do attempt to do something . . . and when, as a result, they fall foul of the powers that be, the defence put up by the Jewish community is to prove that these are Jews only by name, that they do not belong to any synagogue. . . . Have Jewish ethics ever descended to a more shameful nadir? . . . I have practically abandoned all hope of effecting any change in this matter. The power of fear and of the possibility of our security being affected is too strong. . . . Do not think that I am proud of my record in this matter, that I do not squirm inwardly at the thought that on many occasions I have been infected with that same fear and that same cowardice

---

[48]An example of a traditionalist rabbi who urged Jews to support government policies is a certain Rabbi Pfeuffer, who is reported to have said that helping black people to power in South Africa would be like giving guns to a kindergarten. See BD, "Press Items of Jewish Interest," no. 23, Dec. 11, 1986, citing the *Star,* Dec. 4, 1986. For the record of the period until the late 1960s, see Shimoni, *Jews and Zionism,* 277–86.

[49]Shimoni, *Jews and Zionism,* 277–86.

[50]The mimeographed text of Rabbi Rabinowitz's Yom Kippur Sermon, Oct. 1959, is in BD, biographical files.

> and have failed to rise to the level which my calling demands of me. But when from time to time a blatant, glaring case of injustice occurs, and it is one in which there is a hope that my intervention may possibly have a salutary effect, then no power in the world can prevent me giving expression to what I conscientiously believe to be the authentic voice of prophetic Judaism. . . .

Another important religious leader was Rabbi Moses C. Weiler, chief rabbi of the United Progressive Jewish Congregation until he settled in Israel in 1959. Like Rabbi Rabinowitz, he occasionally joined Christian clerics in protests against particularly outrageous manifestations of apartheid. Weiler upheld the view that the appropriate collective expression for Jewish ethical concerns lay in the practical field of welfare and education for the underprivileged black population. Hence he encouraged the sisterhood of the Progressive congregation to set up such projects as an elementary school with attached health facilities in a poverty-stricken black township near Johannesburg. His successor, Rabbi Arthur Saul Super, continued his policy until he too settled in Israel in 1976. He frequently preached to his congregants against the evils of apartheid and joined Christian leaders in protests against specific iniquities of the system.

Not a few other rabbis, both Orthodox and Reform, who were quite outspoken against apartheid, left South Africa to take up pulpits elsewhere, at least in part out of the conviction that it was unconscionable to participate in such a system. They included the South African-born Orthodox rabbi Abner Weiss, a protégé of Louis Rabinowitz, who left his pulpit in Durban for the United States. Another was the Progressive rabbi Richard Lampert, also South African-born, who left Johannesburg for a pulpit in Australia. Rabbi David Rosen, born in England, is a notable example of another category of those who raised their voices against apartheid, namely, rabbis who spent only a temporary period of service in South Africa.

Over the last two decades, the majority of the Orthodox rabbinate followed the lead of Bernard Casper, chief rabbi of the United Hebrew Congregations of Johannesburg and the Federation of Synagogues. From the outset of his incumbency in 1963, he perceived his task to be limited to nurturing the religious life of the Jewish community; it did not, by his lights, extend to the reformation of the societal order as a whole. To be sure, Rabbi Casper, too, sporadically expressed, in the name of Judaism, revulsion against racism and various particular injustices manifest in South African society. On occasion, he even joined Christian clerics in peaceful demonstrations of protest against extraordinarily acute travesties of justice. However, he was at all times judiciously cautious. When, in 1986, in the wake of the campaign to end compulsory military conscription, Rabbi Casper was called upon to answer the question whether the *halakhah* permitted conscientious objection to military service, since it might involve serving in the black townships, he ruled that it did not.

Taking leave of the community on the eve of his *aliyah* to Israel in March 1987, after 25 years in South Africa, he cautioned the Jewish community to adopt a low profile:[51] "In South Africa we are a small identifiable foreign body and we fool ourselves if we think otherwise, and we as a Jewish community should be careful not to act in such a way as to convey the impression that we can influence the course of events." At the same time Rabbi Casper outspokenly opposed international sanctions against South Africa, saying "I have appealed to my colleagues overseas to adopt a stand against sanctions. . . . Sanctions can only mean hunger and frustration and riots and chaos. I think that is a moral stance that all of us should be emboldened to pursue." To the youth of the community, grappling with the incompatibility between "Jewish values" and the realities of South African society, Rabbi Casper held out a Zionist message: "Go home to the land which belongs to our people, where your views will be welcomed in the society we believe in."

In recent years a few Orthodox and traditional rabbis cast caution aside and ventured to condemn the structural essence of the apartheid system, not just particularities of injustice, going beyond the boundaries of the conventional white consensus. One such rabbi was South African-born Ben Isaacson. A former protégé of Orthodox Chief Rabbi Louis Rabinowitz, Isaacson was a maverick whose checkered career included *aliyah* to Israel in the mid-1960s, return to South Africa in 1974 to serve as a Progressive (Reform) rabbi, and, after disagreements in that framework, formation in 1982 of Har-El, an independent traditional congregation (resembling American Conservative congregations) in the prosperous Houghton suburb of Johannesburg. Throughout these mutations, however, Isaacson was a consistently outspoken critic of the apartheid system.

Isaacson tongue-lashed the Jewish communal leadership and castigated Jews at large for tacitly enjoying the evil fruits of the apartheid system. He also accused Jewish leaders of distorting Bishop Tutu's statements and wilfully spreading the false notion that anti-Semitism was rampant among blacks. To Jewish youths entering military service, Isaacson did not shrink from advising that they respectfully request the authorities to refrain from using them to suppress blacks in the townships. An example of the tenor of his sermons as reported in the general press was this comment:[52]

> The Jewish establishment, taking its cue from the ruling political party, has slowly begun to jump onto the bandwagon of reform and now at least makes the right sounds—albeit spluttering and gurgling sounds. . . . As Jews we should have

---

[51]Reported in the *Zionist Record and S.A. Jewish Chronicle,* Mar. 6, 1987, 3.

[52]*Sunday Star,* Sept. 15, 1985, 3. The heading of the report of Rabbi Isaacson's sermon is "Jews Should Know Better: Rebel Rabbi Slams Establishment for Not Speaking Out Against Apartheid Exploitation."

> known better. We should have instinctively recoiled from perpetrating on others the injustices that we, more than any other people, have suffered.

Rabbi Isaacson's tempestuous style of protest was not only frowned upon by most other rabbis and Jewish communal leaders but also increasingly alienated his own congregants. Finally, in mid-1987, after a fiery lecture tour in the United States, which he made with a black clergyman from Soweto, in the course of which Isaacson was reported to have disparaged his own congregants together with South African Jews in general, the lay leaders of Har-El served him notice and disbanded the congregation.

In Cape Town, another South African-born rabbi, Selwyn Franklin, of the large Orthodox congregation of Sea Point, took a leading role in Jews for Justice. In doing so he initially exceeded the limits of propriety as understood by his congregation's board of directors. At Jews for Justice's first public meeting, he sat on the speakers' platform but refrained from speaking in deference to his board's reservations. With other members of Jews for Justice, Rabbi Franklin assisted the victims of intercommunal fighting in the Crossroads squatter camp near Cape Town and joined multiracial church and Muslim leaders in a series of interfaith services dedicated to peace and justice in South Africa. While on a visit to Israel in mid-1986, Rabbi Franklin also outspokenly criticized the conduct of Israel's relations with South Africa. At that time, notwithstanding moves toward sanctions against South Africa taken by Western countries, Israel sent a treasury delegation to South Africa to renew a trade and investment cooperation agreement. Franklin challenged the claim that such links were in the best interests of the South African Jewish community, suggesting that in the long run, it was bad policy to antagonize the blacks.

Another leading figure was American-trained Rabbi Norman M. Bernhard, who had served the important Oxford Synagogue-Center in Johannesburg for over 20 years. In 1980 his congregation launched a social-action program aimed at improving the quality of life of blacks employed in its area of Johannesburg. In late 1985 Rabbi Bernhard lent his support to the founding of Jews for Social Justice in Johannesburg. However, his cautiously measured statements criticizing the injustices of the apartheid system, and his intimate involvement in the Zionist Federation and the Jewish Board of Deputies, contrasted greatly with the style of the impetuous Rabbi Isaacson. Indeed, Bernhard took issue with the latter's excoriation of the Jewish public and commended Jews for their record as employers and as opponents of apartheid.[53]

Distinctive to Rabbi Bernhard's stance was his repeated insistence on an

---

[53]Deon Delport, "Rabbi Raps Rabbi: You've Got It Wrong—Most Jews Are Eroding Apartheid," *Tribune*, Sept. 9, 1986, 12; in BD, biographical files.

optimistic prognosis for the future of South Africa. His inspiration for this derived from the Lubavitcher Rebbe, Menachem Schneerson, whom Bernhard revered as one endowed with *ruah hakodesh,* the gift of divinely revealed insight and foresight. To his coterie of followers in South Africa, the rebbe had repeatedly expressed optimism that South Africa would ultimately provide a bright and prosperous future for all its peoples and urged Jews not to leave. Echoing the rebbe, Bernhard pointed approvingly to the reforms implemented by the South African government and averred that there still was a great reservoir of residual goodwill between all the races in the country.[54]

The Progressive (Reform) rabbis, whose congregants accounted for some 18 percent of synagogue-affiliated Jews in the community, followed a somewhat more uniform approach than the Orthodox. In sermons and through projects, such as those of their sisterhood organizations, they emphasized the application of Jewish precepts to the problems of society at large and encouraged contributions to welfare work and education in black townships. Following his arrival from Israel in South Africa in 1985, Rabbi Ady Assabi, who was trained at London's Leo Baeck College, took the lead in Johannesburg. Starting close to home, he issued a pamphlet stipulating minimum requirements regarding wages and other working conditions for domestic employees. He also identified with the Jews for Social Justice group.

In sum, it may be said that the rabbis in South Africa differed in their approaches to the country's race crisis no less than the Jewish public in general.

The Impact of Israel's Relations with South Africa

The State of Israel was established in the same month and year as that in which the Afrikaner National party under Daniel Malan ascended to power in what was then the Union of South Africa. Initially, Israel's was the more eager of the two governments to establish relations. To be sure, just two days before his election defeat, Prime Minister Smuts, long an ardent sympathizer with Zionism, had been among the first to recognize Israel *de facto.* However, Malan delayed *de jure* recognition for another full year. It should be remembered that at that juncture South Africa still looked rather more to the vast Arab world for the advancement of her interests than to the weak State of Israel, and that it maintained diplomatic relations with Egypt until as late as 1961. Not until 1972 did South Africa

---

[54]See the report on Rabbi Bernhard's views in the *Herald Times,* Oct. 10, 1986, 5.

take up reciprocal diplomatic representation in Israel. Israel, in contrast, not only wished to expand its limited diplomatic relations but was also drawn to the warm Zionist Jewish community in southern Africa, at a time when Zionist fund raising was still of weighty significance for Israel's infant economy. Consequently, Israel was willing unilaterally to open a diplomatic mission in July 1949.

It was only toward the end of her first decade of independence, when Israel launched an imaginative policy of diplomatic relations, technical assistance, and trade with the new African states, that the tables were turned. Indeed, the South African government soon felt itself to be the injured party as Israel aligned itself progressively with black Africa's attacks on apartheid in the international forum. This development reached a peak in September 1963, when Israel downgraded its level of diplomatic representation by recalling its minister plenipotentiary and leaving only a chargé d'affaires.

Very few Diaspora communities were as affected as that of South Africa by oscillations in the relationship between Israel and their own country. The grave dilemmas precipitated for South African Jewry have been analyzed in detail elsewhere.[55] In the present context, only a brief overview is required. Between 1961 and 1967, as Israel sided increasingly with the black states against South Africa's white regime, South African Jewry was much discomfited. Somewhat ironically, it was a former South African, Michael Comay, who was Israel's permanent representative at the United Nations in this critical period. In the press, aspersions were cast on the loyalty of Jews to South Africa, and some government ministers exerted subtle pressure on the Jewish community to influence Israel. These were resisted, by and large, by the Jewish leaders.

The deterioration of relations with Israel was compounded by the prominence of Jewish names in the radical opposition to apartheid in the same period. The acutely uncomfortable atmosphere in which Jews found themselves in relation to the surrounding white majority was reflected in a critical article by the editor of an important Afrikaans paper, in which he posed the question: "Where does the Jew stand in the white struggle for survival?"[56] Although on visits to Israel, South African Zionist leaders discussed the situation with Israeli government ministers, and certainly

---

[55]See Shimoni, *Jews and Zionism,* especially 235–304. For a survey of the same subject with emphasis upon the attitude of black Americans to the relations between Israel and South Africa, see the chapter "Israel, South Africa and Black America," in Robert G. Weisbord and Richard Kazarian, Jr., *Israel in the Black American Perspective* (Connecticut, 1985), 93–119.

[56]Dirk Richard, "Where Does the Jew Stand in the White Struggle for Survival?" (Afrikaans), *Dagbreek en Sondagnuus,* Sept. 26, 1965.

expected their situation to be taken into account, they were uncomplainingly cognizant of Israel's sovereign considerations.[57] Israel's policymakers, for their part, certainly took cognizance of South African Jewry's delicate position; however, their solicitude did not extend so far as to override the convergence of considerations, moral as well as politically self-serving, that motivated the cultivation of relations with many African states and Israel's correlative alignment with them against the white regime of South Africa.[58]

At issue was not the stance of Israel in principle but rather the question whether, out of consideration for the Jewish community, finer discretion could not be shown by keeping within the parameters of anti-apartheid actions set by the major Western powers. What particularly irked the South African government was Israel's tendency to go to excess in offensively toeing the line of the black states of Africa at the United Nations, even when the Western powers abstained. In December 1961 the South African government gave vent to its resentment by disallowing the transfer of funds raised by South African Jewry for the Jewish Agency in Jerusalem. This stricture, which remained in force until mid-1967, precipitated for the Zionist movement in South Africa the most trying test of its traditional hold over the Jewish community.[59]

The Six Day War of 1967 proved to be the turning point in relations between Israel and South Africa. A wave of public sympathy for Israel swept over white South Africans as the noose tightened around the neck of the Jewish state. This was followed by wonderment and admiration as news came through of Israel's dramatic preemptive strike and decisive victory in the six days of fighting that ensued. At that point Jewish community leaders made an urgent appeal to the South African government to lift the ban on transfers of funds to Israel. It was granted, presaging a return to normalcy in the relations between the two countries. Indeed, the South African government was also responsive to some emergency military needs of Israel during the war.[60]

---

[57]On one occasion only did South African leaders adopt a self-serving stance and present their objections demandingly. This was in anticipation that Israel would stop El Al flights to Johannesburg at the end of 1963. The upshot was that Israel refrained from doing so. See Shimoni, *Jews and Zionism,* 346.

[58]See ibid., 320–26, and Michael Brecher, *The Foreign Policy System of Israel* (London, 1972), 234ff.

[59]It is noteworthy that although there was a decline in contributions to Zionist funds (the Israel United Appeal), because Jews knew they could not be transferred to their destination, very few Jews reacted to these events by dissociating themselves from Zionism and its fund-raising functions. See Shimoni, *Jews and Zionism,* 350.

[60]Details of this will be known only when archival records become accessible. However, the military materiel involved was probably related to the Mirage planes used both by Israel and South Africa at the time, spare parts for which were being withheld by France. Some conjectures in this regard are made in James Adams, *The Unnatural Alliance* (London, 1984), 32.

To be sure, the Six Day War did not immediately undermine the position of Israel in Africa. Apart from a breach with one country, Guinea, Israel's bilateral diplomatic relations with African states even expanded, reaching 32 missions by 1972, as did her various technical-assistance programs and trade ventures. However, in the long term, the war proved to be the beginning of a process of alienation from Israel.[61] Between March 1972 and May 1973 seven African states broke off relations with Israel. South Africa, on the other hand, at last took up its option to reciprocate Israel's diplomatic representation there by opening a consulate general in Israel in 1972. On the eve of the Yom Kippur War in October 1973, two more African states broke relations with Israel. Finally, the Yom Kippur War precipitated a landslide of diplomatic ruptures with Israel, with nine more African states severing relations before the fighting was over, and another ten soon after. By 1974 Israel was left with diplomatic relations with only four African states: Mauritius, Lesotho, Malawi, and Swaziland, four small countries which also maintained relations with South Africa.

Full analysis of the factors that drove Israel toward normalization, and then proliferation, of relations with South Africa, in the course of which trade burgeoned in military-related spheres, must await the time when researchers will have access to archival sources. It does seem obvious, however, that the desertion of Israel by so many African states was a key factor in driving Israel into the arms of South Africa. The latter, prudently setting aside its pique at Israel's earlier behavior, recognized its primary geopolitical interest in associating with the Jewish state and was forthcoming in matters of important strategic need to Israel. An example was the South African government's willingness to permit the use of its ports and fueling facilities by the Israeli Navy, something which no other state in Africa was prepared to grant, not even those that continued to trade with Israel after halting diplomatic relations. With the Suez Canal blocked, this was extremely helpful to Israel.

The facts of Israel's conventional trade with South Africa have always been available. Compared to that of many Western states it was always

---

[61]For the factors involved in Israel's diplomatic displacement in Africa, see Susan A. Gitelson, *Israel's African Setback in Perspective* (Jerusalem, 1974); R. Kochan et al., "Black African Voting Behavior in the U.N. on the Middle East Conflict 1967-1973," in *Israel and the Third World,* ed. M. Curtis and S. A. Gitelson (New Brunswick, N.J., 1976), 289–317. A highly critical analysis of Israel-South Africa relations, arguing that they are in every respect detrimental to Israel, is Naomi Chazan, "The Fallacies of Pragmatism: Israeli Foreign Policy Towards South Africa," *African Affairs* (Apr. 1983):169–99. On the factors influencing more recent attitudes of black states, see Arye Oded, *Africa and Israel: African Attitudes Towards Resumption of Diplomatic Relations,* Leonard Davis Institute for International Relations Policy Studies, 18 (Dec. 1986).

small, reaching, by 1985, $174,654,000 in imports from South Africa and $63,896,000 in exports. This accounted for less than 1 percent of the total foreign trade of both countries.[62] Trade related to military materiel, however, was kept secret. Although it was well known that already in the 1970s Israel had sold a number of patrol boats and surface-to-surface Gabriel missiles to the South African Navy, the existence of ramified trade of a military nature was consistently denied by both countries, rumors to the contrary notwithstanding.

Whatever the motives and circumstances may have been, it is evident that Israel's post-Yom Kippur War Labor government, under Prime Minister Yitzhak Rabin and Minister of Defense Shimon Peres, embarked on a course of pragmatic self-interest in regard to South Africa, while continuing to condemn the racial discrimination practiced under apartheid. In 1974 and 1975 Israel and South Africa raised their diplomatic representation to ambassadorial level, and in April 1976 Prime Minister John Vorster visited Israel and signed a series of trade and technical cooperation agreements. On this basis Israel's ambassador, Itzhak Unna, pursued a policy that encouraged bilateral relations on all levels of mutual interest, while at the same time frankly disapproving of apartheid—at times more demonstratively than any other ambassador to South Africa.[63] The relationship was much enhanced under the Likud government headed by Prime Minister Menachem Begin and during Ambassador Eliahu Lankin's tenure in South Africa from 1981 to 1985.

While the full facts of Israel's arms-related trade with South Africa remained elusive, it is evident that Israel was motivated primarily by the needs of an economy based inordinately on military industries, which, in

[62]These figures are from *Statistics of Foreign Trade* 18 (Hebrew), Central Bureau of Statistics, Jerusalem, 1986. Figures given in the International Monetary Fund's *Direction of Trade Statistics,* published in Washington, do not differ substantially. The diamond trade is not included since it is conducted through the international commodity market, but it is known that Israel cut about half of all gem diamonds sold through De Beers's central selling agency. See Marcus Arkin, "Israel and South Africa: The Economic Connection," in the supplement to *Barclays Business Brief* (Johannesburg, May 1979). The small scale of Israel's conventional trade with South Africa was evident from comparison with that of some other countries. *International Trade Statistics Yearbook* 1 (U.N. Publishing Division, New York, 1986) gives the following figures for South African trade in 1984 (in millions): with Israel—imports $83, exports $129; with U.S.A.—imports $2,375, exports $1,458; with U.K.—imports $1,660, exports $742; with West Germany—imports $2,339, exports $676.

[63]Unna frequently declared that similarities between the geopolitical position of Israel and South Africa did not efface fundamental differences in the internal social purposes and policies of the two countries. An example of his frank criticism of apartheid was his refusal to attend a performance of the play *Golda* in a Pretoria theater on the grounds that it was not open to all races. See BD, "Press Items of Jewish Interest," no. 12, May 22, 1978; no. 13, June 7, 1978.

turn, was an inescapable function of Israel's struggle against a hostile Arab world.[64] Likewise, there can be little doubt that, at least as perceived by the South African government, its relationship with Israel was regarded as specially beneficial and cordial, particularly in periods when the Likud party held the offices of prime minister or foreign minister. Yet, outwardly, relations were kept in low profile.

Within Israel's Labor party and also among Foreign Office professionals, a measure of dissatisfaction long existed under the surface. As Western pressures against South Africa intensified after 1985, some elements agitated more insistently for a serious reassessment of Israel's relations with South Africa. The impetus which at last precipitated such a reassessment was a forthcoming U.S. State Department report on other nations' arms trade with South Africa, which carried with it a threat to cut U. S. military assistance to countries engaged in that trade. The very act of reassessment and the ensuing decisions ostensibly to phase out what had never been acknowledged to exist served to confirm that covert military-related trade on a formidable scale had been going on between the two countries. Informed estimates reported in the Israeli press ran as high as half a billion dollars worth of such trade per annum. In due course, the unclassified part of the State Department report issued to Congress confirmed that Israel, together with six Western European countries, had indeed provided considerable military assistance to South Africa.

The Israeli government's timely announcement of a reassessment, on March 18, 1987, a month before the release of the American report, helped to avert the anticipated harm to American relations with Israel. The Israeli announcement reiterated its condemnation of the policy of apartheid and went on to state that it had been decided "to continue to curtail Israel's relations with South Africa" and "to refrain from new undertakings between Israel and South Africa in the realm of defense." In September 1987 Israel's inner cabinet approved a series of sanctions conforming with those adopted by the European Common Market countries. These covered a range of industrial, commercial, scientific, and cultural activities.[65]

---

[64]An informed analysis of the connection between Israel's external relations and its arms sales (acknowledged to have approached the $1-billion mark annually in the early 1980s) is Aaron S. Klieman, *Israel's Global Reach: Arms Sales as Diplomacy* (Washington, 1985). On Israel's relations with South Africa, see especially pp. 151–54. In addition to military-related cooperation, it is possible that there was also cooperation in nuclear development between Israel and South Africa. Far-reaching conjectures are made on this in James Adams, *The Unnatural Alliance* (London, 1984). However, no firm evidence has ever come to light confirming such conjectures. See Gerald M. Steinberg, "The Mythology of Israel-South African Nuclear Cooperation," *Middle East Review* 19, no. 3 (Spring 1987): 31–38.

[65]Israel Ministry of Foreign Affairs Information Division, briefings, Mar. 27, 1987; Sept. 16, 1987.

Judged by the moderate response of the South African government, and in the studied absence of any indications as to the duration of existing contracts in the realm of defense, it could reasonably be inferred that some mollifying understanding on essentials had been reached between the two governments. At the same time, as was attested by the resistance which the new guard at Israel's Foreign Ministry had to overcome (notably from Minister of Industry and Trade Ariel Sharon of the Likud party), a perceptible change of course in relations with South Africa had certainly been inaugurated, one which carried within it the seeds of a possible serious breach in the future.

The process of reassessment in early 1987 temporarily thrust the question of Israel-South Africa relations to the forefront of Israeli public attention.[66] Apart from some demands voiced at small demonstrations sporadically conducted by a minuscule group of anti-apartheid activists, some of whose members were former South African Jews (notably Arthur Goldreich, who dramatically escaped from the hands of the South African security police in 1963), there was no popular call for extreme measures. Regret at the extent of Israel's involvement in arms trading with South Africa was manifest in most newspaper articles, compounded by concern for Israel's long-term relations with the blacks of southern Africa. Yet, on balance, there was acceptance of the fact that, given Israel's economic exigencies and existing arms-trade commitments, anything more than their gradual phasing out would be excessively damaging to Israel's economy. Although apartheid as such was universally condemned by political spokesmen and the press in Israel, the Israeli public was suspicious of international sanctions and all too aware of the close alignment between the most extreme proponents of sanctions, like the African National Congress, and Israel's enemies in the Middle East. Indeed, politically conservative Israelis associated with the Likud party and groups farther to the right evinced considerable sympathy with the dilemma of South African whites and were receptive to the ostensibly survivalist rationale of President Botha's white government, insofar as it disavowed racism and promised reforms.

Anguish over Israel's relations with South Africa was far more intense within the South African Jewish community than in Israel. The leadership of the organized community, whether of the Board of Deputies, the Zionist Federation, or the rabbinate, certainly favored good relations between the

---

[66]Throughout March 1987 most of Israel's dailies carried reports and comments on Israel-South Africa relations. See especially the views of Eliahu Lankin, Israel's ambassador to Pretoria from 1981 to 1985, in the *Jerusalem Post,* Oct. 10, 1986, and Apr. 8, 1987, and the contrary views of Prof. Shlomo Avineri in the *Jerusalem Post,* Aug. 2, 1985, and in *Maariv,* Feb. 13, 1987. The parliamentary debate is in *Knesset Debates,* no. 21, session 309, Mar. 19, 1987, 2250–64.

two countries and had welcomed the comfortable atmosphere that displaced the tensions of the 1960s and prevailed until 1987. Indeed, the Zionist Federation as well as individual Jewish entrepreneurs had been instrumental in the development of trade between their country and Israel. Yet, the scale of the arms nexus between Israel and South Africa surprised even the leadership of South African Jewry. As late as September 1986, at the biennial conference of the South African Zionist Federation in Johannesburg, queries were raised, in a spirit of protest, by the large youth and student delegation concerning rumors and random bits of information about ongoing visits of Israeli military personnel and the use of Israeli weapon systems in the South African Army, which often aided the police in suppressing black unrest. The unanimous response of leaders of both the Zionist movement and the Jewish Board of Deputies was that these reports were highly exaggerated and malicious, and they cautioned the young people not to grant them credence.[67]

The moral conundrum generated by Israel's arms-related trade with South Africa was most intense among the leaders of the Zionist youth movements, especially the largest of these, Habonim-Dror. (The others were Bnei Akiva, Betar, and Maginim.) *Aliyah* to Israel was the educational goal of these movements, yet they were hard put to understand Israel's policy. It seemed to run counter to their conviction that Zionism rested on values correlative with those underlying the struggle of the blacks for liberation and a just society in South Africa. This was a source of dissonance in the Jewish community, since its distinctively Zionist character had long rested upon the extraordinary importance of these Zionist youth movements. Unlike the North American scene, there had never been other than Zionist youth movements in South Africa, with their combined membership of some 6,000 encompassing about 35 percent of the eligible age group in the community in 1987. Since the entire leadership of the youth movements was made up of university students, there was a considerable overlap with the membership of the South African Union of Jewish Students (SAUJS) on the various campuses. They found themselves torn between their identification with Israel and their wish to support the cause of their fellow black students who, however, were stridently anti-Israel.

The embarrassment caused by Israel's relations with South Africa might well have inflicted serious damage on the identification of Jewish students with Israel, were it not for the grotesque, malicious slanders propagated by Muslim students on the various campuses. To the accompaniment of cries of "Death to Zionist imperialism," their propaganda fliers flooded the

---

[67]The author personally witnessed the discussion at the S.A. Zionist Conference in Sept. 1986.

campuses at "Al-Quds Day" demonstrations with such inflammatory statements as: "These crimes by Begin and gang make Hitler look like an amateur. The illegitimate State of Israel was formed with the blood and lives of innocent men, women and children and has ever since continued its bloody legacy."[68]

These crass excesses tended to galvanize Jewish students, whose total number at South African universities was estimated at over 5,000. The atmosphere contrasted sharply with the relative tranquility of the 1960s and 1970s, when Zionism and the Middle East question attracted no particular interest at South African universities. By 1987, SAUJS was more active than ever before and conducted a spirited campaign in defense of Zionism. Indeed, the provocative calls of the Muslim students for exorcising "Zionists" from the struggle against apartheid tended to vindicate the Zionist contention that Jews could be fully at home only in their own sovereign state.[69]

The publications of SAUJS reflect the poignant ideological dilemma of politically aware segments of South African Jewry. Some of the debates call to mind, if on a smaller scale, the classic ideological conflicts characterizing the Jewish experience in European countries from the beginning of the period of Jewish emancipation until recent times.

On the one hand, views are aired castigating the Jews for prospering from the fruits of the apartheid system, and the organized Jewish community for "abdicating moral responsibilities in favour of ingratiating oneself with the government of the day." According to one student critic, "a twisted morality is produced when Jewish youth are taught to concern themselves with moral issues thousands of miles away from their own reality [in support of Jewish refuseniks in Russia or of issues in Israel] and remain silent on the moral issues of their immediate environment." He goes on to argue that leaving South Africa with "the skills and wealth acquired under apartheid," whether to "Kibbutz Tuval, Dallas, Texas or Adelaide" is abdication of

---

[68]From a flier issued by the Muslim Students Association at Natal University on May 22, 1987, entitled "Liberate Palestine . . . the Stolen Land." Other typical examples of anti-Semitic motifs spawned by the Muslim Students Association are: "The link between apartheid and Zionism may be expressed in close economic and military ties but is, however, organically rooted in ideology"; "Zionism sees and recognizes itself in the death throes of the apartheid regime"; "The brutality with which this regime handles the Palestinians makes all the alleged tortures of the Nazis seem insignificant." These citations are from leaflets issued at the University of the Witwatersrand, May 22, 1987.

[69]A typical statement of the Muslim Students Association is: "The oppressed in South Africa can never be liberated if we collaborate with Zionism and imperialism in any of its guises." From a newsletter issued at the University of the Witwatersrand Medical School: *Our Message,* May 22, 1987.

responsibility. "The real moral challenge," he avers, "is to fight to end apartheid and build a new South Africa."[70]

On the other hand, the distinctively South African ideological matrix of Zionism is reflected in the following account of one Jewish student leader's intellectual odyssey until settling in Israel.[71]

> I had always thought that I was a South African and my contribution should be there: to work toward the abolition of the apartheid system and all the iniquities arising out of it. My degree in social anthropology and African culture was, I felt, further testimony to my commitment to the African struggle. . . . My decision to get involved in the South African Union of Jewish Students, and later in the formation of "Jews against Apartheid" was based on the premise that the South African reality had to be taken cognizance of from a Jewish perspective. . . . A large part of the last five years has been spent attempting to reconcile my Jewishness with my South African identity. The turning point came, ironically enough, as a result of my participation in a seminar on the Holocaust at Yad Vashem in July 1985. . . . "Thou shalt not be a perpetrator; thou shalt not be a victim; and thou shalt never, ever be a bystander." The awful clarity hit me then; by returning to South Africa, I would be guilty of violating all three, whether or not I wanted to. . . . In the ultimate analysis, the bitter truth for me was that the South African diaspora had been unable to accommodate both my Jewish and African identities and, however difficult, I had to confront reality and be brutally honest with myself and finally make a choice. . . .

The circumstances of Israel's announced reassessment of policy toward South Africa alleviated but little the dilemma of the Jewish community. The real core of the problem—arms-related contracts—remained, and the South African government's response had been accordingly moderate. President P. W. Botha set the tone during an election rally in March 1987, when he said that he sympathized with Israel's position, as it had been "bullied" by the United States and intimidated by the prospect of losing billions of dollars in American aid.[72]

The announcement of the Israeli cabinet's sanctions decision in September 1987 evoked predictable disappointment and resentment from the South African government and press, but not out of proportion to their reaction to other countries that had preceded Israel in adopting similar sanctions. For their part, both the Jewish Board of Deputies and the Zionist Federation had decisively declared themselves opposed to the application of

---

[70]Tony Karon, "South African Jewry: An Alternative to Complicity," *Strike,* May 1985, 4–7.

[71]Barbara Meltz, "From African Culture to Jewish Identity," *Hame'orer* 5 (Journal of the Movement for Zionist Fulfillment in Israel) (Winter 1986):35.

[72]One newspaper, the *Star,* provided the following vivid metaphor: "Israel has been handed a knife and told to stab a friend—or be stabbed instead." See BD, "Press Items of Jewish Interest," no. 6, Mar. 26, 1987; no. 17, Sept. 18, 1987. These are the sources for all the citations which follow, unless otherwise stated.

sanctions of any sort against South Africa. Moreover, between the announcement of reassessment in March 1987 and the adoption of specific measures in September, they made persistent representations to the government of Israel urging it not to embark upon a course of sanctions. The Israeli Foreign Ministry was flooded with letters from Jewish citizens of South Africa making similar appeals.

Statements issued by the Jewish Board of Deputies together with the Zionist Federation recognized that Israel, like any other sovereign state, "takes its own decisions to protect its own national interests," but added that "in this regard it is noted that Israel has been subjected to significant pressures from the United States." They declared their opposition to sanctions "on the ground that it undermines the ability to create conditions in which steps can be taken toward the achievement of an apartheid-free and just society in which all peoples can attain their legitimate aspirations." At the same time, these statements averred that the "deep-rooted religious and cultural affiliations" felt by Jews with Israel would endure. The *Zionist Record* reported the president of the Zionist Federation, Julius Weinstein, as saying: "We abhor apartheid—it is un-Jewish, inhuman and we do not accept it as Jews, but we will not participate in any threats or blackmail or sanctions that the western world or any other countries wish to impose against this country." He added: "It has to be explained to the Israelis in no uncertain terms that sanctions which they wish to impose against South Africa will in fact harm the very people that we want to help—and that they want to help."[73]

A major factor in the considerations determining the Zionist Federation's policy was the encouragement of *aliyah.* One of the attributes of South African Zionism's preeminent strength was the emphasis it had always placed on personal *aliyah,* its record in this area being distinctly superior to that of Zionist organizations in the United States. It was estimated that in 1987, some 14,000 former South Africans were living in Israel, constituting what might be described as a daughter community about 12 percent the size of the mother community in South Africa.[74]

In the atmosphere of uncertainty that prevailed after 1985, causing Jews—not unlike other middle-class whites—to contemplate emigration, there was an unprecedented intensification of efforts to encourage the choice of Israel rather than other Diaspora destinations, such as Australia, Canada, the United States, and Britain. It was of some significance both to

[73]*Zionist Record and S.A. Jewish Chronicle,* Mar. 27, 1987.

[74]For brief surveys of the history and status of Zionism in South African Jewry, see Arkin, *South African Jewry,* 79–94, and Gideon Shimoni, "Zionism in South Africa: An Historical Perspective," *Forum* 17 (Spring 1980):71–91.

South African Jewry and the State of Israel that the South African government had not hindered activity along these lines. Indeed, the trade agreements periodically renewed between the governments of Israel and South Africa had always included the latter's granting of "approved enterprise" status to certain categories of investment in Israel, among them residential housing. These were limited, however, to agreements renewable every two years and had not been in excess of some 40 million rands (approximately $19 million) per annum. Moreover, the proceeds from the sale of such investments had to be repatriated to South Africa. Emigrants from South Africa were permitted to take only 100,000 rands (approximately $34,000) of capital out of the country.

The range and scale of activities now developed to promote *aliyah* were unparalleled anywhere in the Western Diaspora since the establishment of Israel. They included subsidized pilot tours of Israel; group settlement projects in new towns in Israel, such as Kohav Yair; provision of subsidized, furnished apartments as an alternative to absorption centers; creation of loan funds for small businesses; a series of short visits by emissaries who were former South Africans successfully settled in various walks of life in Israel; and an organized letter-writing campaign from former South Africans settled in Israel to friends and relations urging them to "make the right move—to Israel," and "if you want to leave home, come home." In addition, South African Zionists succeeded in setting up a coordinating committee of the Israeli government's Absorption Ministry, the World Zionist Organization, and their own Israel office. One outcome of this committee's recommendations was an exemption for South African settlers from limitations on the size of apartments purchasable with subsidized government housing loans.

Despite the troubled situation in South Africa, the record of emigration was very far from presaging the disappearance of South African Jewry. It was estimated that between 1970 and 1980 about 12,000 Jews settled abroad permanently, one-third of them (4,000) in Israel. After the most recent wave of unrest in South Africa, the number of immigrants to Israel rose rather moderately from 246 in 1985 to 565 in 1986 and 737 in 1987. Moreover, it was estimated that at least 6,000 Israelis were living in South Africa in 1986.[75] (In the Jewish community rumors had long exaggerated the number to as many as 20,000.) This inflow of Israelis and, even more so, the fact that considerably more of those who emigrated from South Africa chose to settle in other Diaspora lands—mainly Australia, Canada, Britain, and the United States—was a cause of distress and soul-searching among the leaders of a community long considered among the most Zionist in the world.

---

[75]For these estimates, see Sergio DellaPergola and Allie A. Dubb, "South African Jewry: A Sociodemographic Profile," in this volume.

Attitudes of Black Political Leaders Toward the Jews

Almost no research, historical or sociological, has been conducted into public attitudes toward the Jews outside of the white group. Indeed, the only serious study ever to address itself to this area of inquiry was a 1971 survey of attitudes of matriculation pupils resident in the black township of Soweto, near Johannesburg. Its author was Melville L. Edelstein, at the time chief welfare officer there. His findings showed that the sense of "social distance" experienced in relation to Jews was greater than toward English-speakers in general and was exceeded only by that felt toward Afrikaners.[76] The explanation for this did not fall within the scope of Edelstein's research, but, noting that his respondents had only the barest actual contact with Jews, and that there appeared to be some correlation between antipathy to Jews and membership in white-oriented churches, he suggested that the explanation possibly lay in New Testament teaching and the cultural transmission of anti-Jewish stereotypes. Edelstein himself, no less than the Jewish community's leadership, was surprised by these findings. Ironically, Edelstein, who had devoted himself to welfare work in Soweto, tragically lost his life in the 1976 Soweto riots.

Similar indications of negative stereotyping of Jews by blacks and coloreds can be culled from incidental references in other works of research. An example is a study of social groups and racial attitudes in a small South African town called Port Nolloth. Although there were very few Jews in the town, it was found that insofar as colored people distinguished between Jews and other whites, Jews were considered more tolerant; however, there was also "a stereotype of them as being avaricious and cunning."[77]

A valuable new source of information was provided by two young scholars, Alan Fischer and Tzipporah Hoffman, who conducted extensive interviews with leading personalities across a broad spectrum of political and ethnic groups in South Africa.[78] The candid answers elicited by the interviewers' probing questions cast new light on the prevailing attitudes toward Jews of major political activists outside of the white group. In the main, they reflect considerable hostility. This mostly assumes the form of so-called "anti-Zionism," but the anti-Jewish undertones are recognizable.

One current of thought distorts the character of Zionism in order to

[76]Melville L. Edelstein, *What Do Young Africans Think?* (Institute of Race Relations, Johannesburg, 1972); also, "The Urban African Image of the Jew," *Jewish Affairs,* Feb. 1972, 6–8.

[77]Martin E. West, *Divided Community* (Cape Town, 1971), 79.

[78]The interviews were to be published in late 1988 by Southern Book Publishers (Johannesburg), under the title *The Jews of South Africa: What Future?* Unless otherwise indicated, the quotations that follow are from these interviews. I am deeply indebted to the authors of this innovative work for making available to me their tapes and transcripts.

delegitimize it. This is accomplished by attributing to it (and by extension to the State of Israel) an innate "Chosen People" ethos of arrant exclusivity and discrimination against outsiders. This putative ethos is then facilely equated with apartheid, so that Israel is criticized for collaborating with the white regime of South Africa, not so much out of self-interest as out of an alleged inherent empathy. Although ostensibly directed against the State of Israel, this hostility attaches itself to the local Jewish community, whose intimate affinity with Israel is all too evident. While the interviews contain some expression of appreciation for those individual Jews who had been active in the opposition to apartheid over the years, a clear distinction is drawn between them and Jews as a community.

Another indication that criticism of the Jews ran deeper than the question of Israel's relations with South Africa was the perceived role of Jews in the South African economy. For example, Saths Cooper, a leader of the Azanian People's Organization (AZAPO, a "black consciousness" movement open only to black membership), told his interviewers that the Shylock stereotype was prevalent among blacks and that it was common for the term "Jew" to be used synonymously with "exploiter," whether the reference was to white or black. He said, furthermore, that "the Jewish community, rightly or wrongly, has been seen to be based in capitalism and capitalism has meant propping up apartheid. Oppenheimer [the diamond magnate, actually a convert to Christianity] has been responsible for the greatest single exploitation in this country."

A key black figure was Desmond Tutu, archbishop of the Anglican Church in South Africa, who was recognized throughout the world as a symbol of the struggle against apartheid. Archbishop Tutu repeatedly condemned Israel's ties, military and other, with South Africa, and called upon the Jews of South Africa to oppose the apartheid system with vigor. Tutu also considered Zionism to have "very many parallels with racism," since it "excludes people on ethnic or other grounds over which they have no control." He told his interviewers, rather obscurely, that "in Israel you exclude people and treat those that are excluded as lesser humans." To recognize that Archbishop Tutu, in common with most black leaders, had imbibed the anti-Zionist stereotype was not, however, to say that he was anti-Semitic. Nor had Tutu ever denied Israel's right to exist, as had some of the more extreme detractors of the Jewish state among the black leadership. Indeed, he said that he considered it unrealistic of the Arab world to pretend that Israel did not exist, and that while sympathizing with the PLO, he did not accept its methods. Some of Archbishop Tutu's comments aroused resentment in Jewish quarters and even insidious rumors that he had made blatantly anti-Semitic remarks, but these rumors were given short shrift by the South African Jewish Board of Deputies itself.

Typical of Tutu's acerbic rhetoric is the parallel he repeatedly drew between apartheid and the Holocaust perpetrated by the Nazis. He said, for example, that the South African government deliberately resettled children where there was no food, thereby condemning them to starvation, adding, "You might even say that the gas chambers made for a neater death." Some Jews took exception, arguing that the evils of apartheid had never extended to systematic annihilation of the blacks and pointing out that no rabbi in Nazi Germany had been allowed the freedom to criticize the regime which Archbishop Tutu enjoyed. His response was to describe this "as a kind of Jewish arrogance." "Jews seem to think that they have cornered the market on suffering," he complained to his interviewers.[79]

Another important figure in the bitter opposition to apartheid was the Reverend Allan Boesak—a colored according to apartheid race classification—who was president of the World Alliance of Reformed Churches and a patron of the United Democratic Front. Reverend Boesak was less vocal than Archbishop Tutu in criticism of Jews and more sensitive in his rhetoric. He told his interviewers that he rejected as "shameful prejudice" the notion that God did not hear the prayers of the Jews. Yet he too averred: "Zionism is an ideology that does not accept the values of the Jewish heritage as I understand it."

More typical than these reasonably qualified criticisms of Israel in the broad spectrum of views recorded by Fischer and Hoffman were those of Dan Habedi, a leader of AZAPO. Although in regard to the local Jewish community Habedi declared, "We do not split hairs and say the Jewish people are more to blame than other people," he brusquely denied the legitimacy of the State of Israel, stating: "That land as far as I am concerned belongs to the Palestinians." Moreover, he equated Zionism with Afrikaner Calvinism: "They believe that they are the Chosen People, like those who colonized this land believe they are the Chosen People; that they were sent here to teach black people their right ways."

Gatsha Buthelezi, president of Inkatha (the National Cultural Liberation Movement) and chief minister of the KwaZulu semiautonomous territory, was an exception to the general rule of hostility toward Israel. Although undoubtedly an important figure in the South African political constellation, Buthelezi was something of an outcast from the mainstream of the black liberation movement. His commitment to an ethnic Zulu constituency was considered dangerously divisive. He refused to toe the African National

[79]On the controversy over Archbishop Tutu's allegedly anti-Semitic statements and the denials issued by the Board of Deputies, see BD, "Press Items of Jewish Interest," no. 3, Feb. 13, 1987; Feb. 26, 1987; also the *Herald Times,* Feb. 20, 1987. Tutu's comparisons with the Holocaust were reported in the *Jerusalem Post,* Mar. 11, 1987. He made much the same remarks in interviews with ABC television on Oct. 16, 1984, and Israel Radio on July 23, 1987.

Congress line on a range of matters, including advocacy of sanctions by outside countries. Moreover, defying the prevalent black taboo on Israel, Buthelezi accepted an invitation to visit there in 1985. In a revealing comment to his interviewers, Fischer and Hoffman, he explained: "I accepted the visit to Israel because I need friends too. The ANC have got Arafat and Cuba." Buthelezi refrained from aiming selective criticism at Israel compared to other countries in the world. However, he was critical of the South African Jewish community for failing "to stand up and be counted." He told his interviewers that Jews "criticize, through their liberal press, the policies of the government" but secretly pray for the retention of Afrikaner power because they feel more secure with it.

The worst manifestations of hostility toward Jews, equaled only by the anti-Semitism of the Afrikaner right-wingers, emanated from political groups in the Muslim community. (This community numbered some 353,000, of whom 176,000 were members of the colored community situated mainly in the Cape, and another 166,000 were part of the Indian population found mainly in Natal and the Transvaal.) A case in point was the political group Call of Islam, formed in 1983 and active in the framework of the United Democratic Front. Interviewed by Fischer and Hoffman, one of its founders, Farid Essak, expressed hatred for the Jews, drawing freely upon anti-Jewish stereotypes found in the Koran. Essak also espoused use of anti-Zionism as an instrument in the struggle against apartheid in South Africa. Ironically, it was with Call of Islam that the Jews for Justice group, to which we referred earlier, cooperated in coming to the aid of the black population at Crossroads near Cape Town. Yet Essak had no kind words for the members of Jews for Justice, seeing in them not "liberated Jews" but really Zionists in disguise, insidiously infiltrating the freedom movement in South Africa.

Similar deep-seated hostility was expressed by Sheikh Nazeem Mohammed, president of the Muslim Judicial Council in South Africa, who argued that the white press and universities, no less than the country's finances, were wholly controlled by Jews. To his interviewers the sheikh explained candidly that it was inherent to the doctrine of Zionists that they gain control of the media and the educational and financial institutions of the country: they "must have control of the brain structure of the community."

An example of crude anti-Semitism emanating from Muslim sources was a leaflet distributed anonymously in 1985. It listed the names of major business companies, some owned by Jews and others mistakenly attributed to Jewish ownership. "If you have any policies or accounts with these companies," it exhorted blacks, "please cancel them and take out with other companies. These companies are Zionist organizations and send 80 percent of their profits to Israel . . . who buy arms to murder our Arab brothers. . . . By exploiting our black workers these companies are keeping alive the illegal regime of Israel as well as South Africa."[80]

Ironically, it was the modification of the apartheid system, one aspect of which was the reentry of growing numbers of blacks, coloreds, and Indians into the English-speaking universities, that led to hostile confrontations between Jewish and Muslim students on campuses in Johannesburg and Cape Town. One such clash took place at the University of the Witwatersrand in June 1982, when Israel invaded Lebanon. The most recent clash, involving scuffles and fisticuffs, was in May 1987 at Cape Town University, after the Muslim Students Society held a meeting under the banner "Death to the Zionist Imperialists." Moulana Ebrahim Mousa, regional coordinator of the Muslim Youth Movement, declared: "We will not tolerate Zionism's attempts to infiltrate the liberation movements in South Africa," and "if Arafat is a terrorist, then so are Mandela and Tambo."[81]

Although the Muslim groups constituted only a small part of the forces of resistance to the apartheid regime, their influence was considerable within the United Democratic Front (UDF). Moreover, as revealed by Fischer and Hoffman's series of interviews, criticism of the Jews bore much the same marks across the entire spectrum of black groups struggling against the apartheid regime.

In the final analysis, it was probably the banned African National Congress (ANC) that would determine the future of South African Jewry, no less than that of the country as a whole. In early 1986 leaders of NUSAS, defying progovernment white public opinion, met with ANC leaders outside of South Africa, in Harare, Zimbabwe, to ascertain their views on a variety of subjects. One of the questions raised concerned Zionism and the PLO. The students reported back that "the ANC distinguishes between the religious manifestation, with which it has no problems, and the political manifestations of Zionism, which they argue, has denied the fundamental rights of the Palestinian people to independence." They said the ANC supported the PLO out of recognition of "the right of oppressed people to struggle," and condemned Israel for acting, especially in the military sphere, "as a third party for the imperialist powers in supporting the South African government and other repressive states." At the same time, the

[80]Leaflet entitled "Urgent Appeal!! Boycott," in the author's possession.

[81]See BD, "Press Items of Jewish Interest," no. 10, May 27, 1987, and also the exchange of letters from readers in the *Cape Times,* May 23, 1987. Characteristic of the delegitimization of Zionism is one letter calling upon Jews to acknowledge "the distinction between true Judaism and racist Zionism imperialism. We call on all South African Jews . . . to declare Zionism a heresy, as Christians declare apartheid heretical and as Muslims are continuously denouncing Malayism, Indianism and corrupt Saudi Arab states as heresies."

ANC claimed that it was "opposed to anti-Semitism and any form of racism and was not antagonistic to the Jewish community in South Africa," which, it noted, "had offered up many white democrats who actively opposed apartheid."[82]

Amplification of this attitude may be drawn from an interview with Neo Mnumzama, an ANC spokesperson stationed at the United Nations.[83] Recognizing the "different political colours" of South African Jews, he said that the ANC regarded "in a positive light" those Jews who belonged to the broad struggle against apartheid and, above all, "those active in the ANC itself." (The most prominent of these was Joe Slovo, a Communist of long standing and one of the ANC's foremost leaders.) However, it disapproved of those members of the community who had Zionist affiliations. Claiming that there was a distinction between anti-Semitism and anti-Zionism, Mnumzama averred that "the people of South Africa . . . see parallels of apartheid in Zionism"; that "a major obstacle to Jewish participation in the struggle against apartheid has by and large been Zionism"; and that "Zionism as an ally of apartheid is certainly an accomplice in the perpetuation of the crimes that Pretoria commits against the South African people." Asked to define Zionism as perceived by the ANC, Mnumzama answered that Zionism was "an exclusive organization to which only Jews can belong," "a segregationist movement" on religious and ethnic lines that carried a strong reminder "of the reality of apartheid under which we have to live." He said that Israel, like South Africa, was based on the uprooting and dispossession of the indigenous majority population, and that the exclusion of blacks from the South African national experience as constituted by apartheid was paralleled by the exclusion of anyone who was not in the first place Jewish from "entry into the total experience of Zionist-Israel." Hence "you cannot struggle against apartheid and still adhere to Zionist positions."

Mnumzama also criticized Jews for wilfully refraining from translation of their "dominant role in the South African economy" into political power against apartheid. Moreover, he scoffed somewhat at recent statements of the Jewish Board of Deputies calling for the abolition of apartheid. He said that the situation was too far gone for mere statements of condemnation; "people must translate verbal denunciations into active struggle." Asked what was in store for South Africa's Jews after the attainment of the ANC's objectives, and whether Jews would one day be punished, Mnumzama considered that while a free South Africa would "not tolerate a Zionist

[82]*NUSAS Talks to the ANC,* report on meeting between the National Union of South African Students and the African National Congress, held from Sunday, 31 March to Tuesday, 2 April, 1986, in Harare, Zimbabwe, 28.

[83]One of the series of interviews recorded by Fischer and Hoffman.

presence in our country," Jews, like all people, would "have a choice to either abandon segregation as practice and join with the rest . . . in building a free, united, non-racial and democratic South Africa or, to exercise their freedom to leave the country and go to those climates which would be more conducive to Zionism."

In light of both the black perceptions of Israel surveyed here and the closely related record of Israel-South Africa relations discussed earlier, it was hardly surprising that neither Israel itself nor the organized Jewish community of South Africa had meaningful communication with black leaders. The conspicuous exception was Gatsha Buthelezi, himself in an ambiguous situation within the politics of black liberation. Beginning in 1980, the Jewish Board of Deputies' executives in the various provinces of South Africa initiated some "outreach" forums and invited various black leaders to address them.[84] These included, for example, Nathan Motlana, a prominent civic leader in Soweto, persons in the trade union and labor relations field, and Archbishop Desmond Tutu, who addressed a committee meeting of the board in June 1986. Given the gravity of the situation in South Africa and the issues at stake, these activities appeared rather perfunctory and futile. Indeed, the Jewish Board of Deputies' invitations to some black bodies met with blunt refusals, and Harry Schwarz candidly commented that addresses by those who have agreed "have been masochistic experiences for the audiences and have probably achieved very little."[85]

As for the State of Israel, the only ray of light penetrating the dark cloud of relations emanated from the Histadrut labor confederation. Its Afro-Asian Institute in Tel Aviv and its Na'amat women's organization sustained some ties with various black civic organizations and trade unions.[86] By late 1987, a series of groups, numbering in all about 80 black men and women, had attended three- to four-week courses in organizational and leadership training at the institute, which exposed them to Israel's rich experience in these fields. In fact, one of the Israeli government's decisions regarding South Africa, announced in September 1987, was that steps would be taken to create a fund for the expansion of such training programs. Within the Labor party and the Histadrut and in the Foreign Ministry, the advocates of a serious change of course in relations with South Africa were hopeful

---

[84]On these contacts with blacks see *Report to South African Jewry, 1985–1987* (S.A. Jewish Board of Deputies), 11, 64; *Report to South African Jewry, 1980–1983* (S.A. Jewish Board of Deputies, 1983), 17. For Buthelezi's comments in Israel, see the *Jerusalem Post,* Aug. 16, 1985, 5.

[85]Arkin, *South African Jewry,* 142.

[86]The Los Angeles-based Center for Foreign Policy Options, whose research director was Steven Spiegel, was involved in the genesis of this activity. Its field director in Israel was Shimshon Zelniker, a lecturer on African politics at Labor's Beit Berl College. See the article by Tom Tugend in the *Jerusalem Post,* Apr. 18, 1986, 8.

that this modest channel of contact with blacks might one day open wider prospects.

Conclusion

South Africa was a society in transition, the ultimate outcome of which could not be predicted. Whether as dictated by the unilateral reforming policies of the National party government, or as generated by the agitation of revolutionary forces at work in the black population, a transformation was taking place. Relative to changes of political attitudes within the white segment of the population, especially among Afrikaners, over the previous quarter of a century, attitude change in the small Jewish component of that population had only been slight. After all, the political orientation of South Africa's Jews had always placed them, normatively speaking, somewhat to the left of center in the conventional white political spectrum. Concurrently, there had always been an extraordinary prominence of Jewish individuals in the nonconventional political groups seeking to transform the society as a whole on the minimum basis of one-man one-vote. Both of these phenomena had long characterized the Jewish experience in South Africa.

What did change for Jews was less their own political orientation than the gradual political moderation of the dominant Afrikaner group, on the one hand, and the dramatic political awakening and radicalization of the black majority, on the other. By 1987, the National party was situated at the center of the white political spectrum. On its right it was assailed by the reactionary backlash of Afrikaner parties, ranging from the Conservative party through to the neo-Nazi Afrikaner Weerstandbeweging. On its left were the Progressives and some of its own people who chose to become independents in the 1987 elections. Beyond the white parliamentary spectrum was a complex array of radical forces, political and trade unionist, overt and covert. To the extent that these frameworks were still open to whites, or at least to alignment with like-minded white groups, Jewish individuals were disproportionately prominent—almost as much as in the first decade and a half of apartheid rule.

The gap between the National party and the Progressives had narrowed. Notwithstanding the fundamental difference between the Progressives' advocacy of genuine multilateral negotiations for a new polity and the government party's essentially unilateral reordering of the existing polity, the two approaches were far closer to each other in 1987 than they had been 25 years earlier. Both catered, if with different intensity, to the whites' fear of revolutionary chaos and an ensuing nondemocratic regime; both opposed international sanctions, arguing that they were misguided and counterproductive as a strategy for effecting change in South Africa.

Already in the early 1960s it was quipped that most Jews spoke like

Progressives, voted for the United party, and hoped that the National party would stay in power. By the mid-1980s it could be said that most Jews both spoke as Progressives and felt most at ease with their consciences voting for the Progressives, but still relied on the National party to keep control of the situation. Moreover, increasing numbers of Jews were no longer constrained by a sense of moral unease from actually voting for the National party.

Something of a paradox was evident. On the one hand, much of the Jewish communal leadership was gripped by a sense of crisis. Many young Jews were leaving the country and many more, old and young, were talking of leaving, but probably never would. There was also a disheartening sense of failure at the fact that so many of those who left chose destinations other than Israel. South African Jewry had never been rich in intellectual resources rooted in Judaism itself, and now there was a brain drain of scholars, rabbis, and teachers. Yet, on the other hand, the Jewish leadership was ideologically more at ease than before because the boundaries of liberal opinion permitted by the white consensus had broadened. The Jewish Board of Deputies was now able to say what it had always felt at heart but was constrained from saying, and Jews were able to articulate a collective Jewish voice through groups such as Jews for Justice, without embarrassing the Board of Deputies. Even the South African Union of Jewish Students no longer felt at odds with the board.

The nature of Israel's relations with South Africa, however, aroused some dissonance among Jews. Whereas it embarrassed those who identified strongly with the forces of opposition to the apartheid system, whether in its pristine or reformed shape, the relationship was gratifying for the communal leadership and probably for the average Jew. In this regard the announcement during 1987 of Israel's reassessment of policy and sanctions measures, moderate as they might have been, appeared like a cloud on the horizon, threatening to discomfort them in a manner reminiscent of their experience in the 1960s. Much depended on how far Israel would go against the white regime of South Africa in the future. The Jewish communal leadership, for its part, had made its opposition to sanctions crystal clear.

It was difficult to escape the impression that South African Jewry found itself in a highly deterministic situation, with very little room for maneuver. Jews were inextricably embedded in the white segment of South African society and shared with all whites in the anxieties of the present crisis. Yet an additional dimension peculiar to the Jewish situation compounded their anxiety, as they viewed the growing right-wing Afrikaner reaction and its attendant anti-Semitism with mingled repugnance and fear. Nor did they contemplate with pleasure the prospects on the left. As well as sharing with all whites the fear of socioeconomic upheaval, revolutionary violence, and chaos, they contemplated with growing trepidation the hostility toward

Israel prevalent in black political groups and its attendant anti-Semitic undertones.

Jews could have no more than the most peripheral influence on the determination of South Africa's future. In a sense characteristic of the Jewish minority experience in many past climes and times, South African Jewry was held in a vise. Actions of Israel calculated to gratify black political leaders were likely to raise the level of hostility toward Jews in the ranks of the reactionary white political groups and could even awaken old animosities in the government party itself. At the same time, so-called anti-Zionism and hostility to Israel were already so prevalent among black leaders that it was difficult to imagine how they could be eradicated by any but the most improbably extreme actions of Israel against the South African government. This fostered a despairing frame of mind in the community concerning the chance that a future black regime would tolerate the Jews' natural bonds with Israel. One consequence was the inclination of many Jews to throw in their lot with the present South African government's policies. Another was the example set by Jews for Justice groups and progressive political figures like Harry Schwarz, who worked for the transformation of South African society but who, as Jews, would settle for nothing less than full and free expression of Jewish identity.

South African Jewry: A Sociodemographic Profile

by SERGIO DELLAPERGOLA AND ALLIE A. DUBB

Background

PERHAPS THE MOST SALIENT FEATURE of South African society today is that racial classification determines the basic constitutional rights of each citizen—work opportunities, place of residence, participation in the political sphere, use of public amenities, and so on. Within this legalized castelike hierarchy, whites occupy the most privileged position, coloreds (people of mixed race) and Asians (largely Indians) an intermediate status, and blacks the lowest. According to the 1980 census, the total population of South Africa was 25,016,525, with 17,022,248 blacks, 4,551,068 whites, 2,624,007 coloreds, and 819,202 Asians (see table 1). By mid-1986, the total population was estimated at some 28.4 million.[1]

While Jews have been in South Africa since the first British occupation in 1795,[2] major Jewish settlement dates from the 1880s. From the outset, Jews were part of the dominant white group and, more specifically, of its English-speaking segment. The latter fact is partly explained by the tendency of Jews to gravitate to the main towns and cities, which were predominantly English in character. Also important was the fact that the Afrikaners (the descendants of the original Dutch settlers), like the Jews themselves, were a relatively closed group, maintaining strict social, cultural, linguistic, and religious boundaries. British culture in South Africa, in contrast, was the idiom of the rich and powerful; it was cosmopolitan and not bound up

---

Note: The research reported in this article was carried out at the Division of Jewish Demography and Statistics, the Institute of Contemporary Jewry, the Hebrew University of Jerusalem. Prof. Uziel O. Schmelz read the manuscript and offered valuable comments. Arin Poller and Benny Anderman ably assisted in the preparation of this study.

[1]The 1980 total excludes the black homelands of Transkei, Bophuthatswana, and Venda, which were already independent, while the latest midyear estimate also excludes Ciskei. The UN, which still regards these territories as an integral part of South Africa, estimates the 1986 population at just over 32,000,000.

[2]Histories of the Jewish community include Louis Herrman, *A History of the Jews in South Africa* (Johannesburg and Cape Town, 1935); Gustav Saron and Louis Hotz, eds., *The Jews in South Africa: A History* (Cape Town, 1955); Gideon Shimoni, *Jews and Zionism: The South African Experience 1910–1967* (Cape Town, 1980). See also Gideon Shimoni, "South African Jews and the Apartheid Crisis," in this volume.

with membership in a rigidly exclusive social group. To this open and accessible culture, with its more amorphous social identity, were attracted those immigrants—including Jews—who could not or would not become part of the Afrikaner people. Jews who went to live in the smaller towns and villages spoke Afrikaans and often established close and warm relations with their Afrikaner neighbors, but they remained strangers and outsiders.

The difference between Afrikaans- and English-speaking whites and the position of Jews in the ethnic stratification of South Africa is at least partially reflected in the religious distribution of the population (table 1). A breakdown of religious denomination by home language among whites in 1980 shows that three-quarters of all Afrikaans-speakers belonged to one of the three Dutch Reformed churches and a further 9 percent subscribed to the Apostolic faith. English-speaking whites, in contrast, showed allegiance to a wide spectrum of religious denominations, including 6.8 percent who were Jews. In turn, white, mostly English-speaking individuals constituted 97.4 percent of all those who identified themselves as Jews, the remainder being black (1.9 percent), colored (0.5 percent), and Asian (0.2 percent).

The South African Jewish community is relatively homogeneous in respect to its origins, religious patterns, and commitment to the Zionist cause and Israel. The community is relatively small in size and geographically concentrated in the two major metropolitan centers, Johannesburg and Cape Town. For these and other reasons the South African Jewish community has long been regarded in the Jewish world as a model of effective and disciplined organization. Virtually all Jewish religious and secular activities take place within the framework of national coordinating bodies. The most important of these are the South African Zionist Federation, the South African Jewish Board of Deputies, the South African Board of Jewish Education, and the Federation of Synagogues of South Africa (which includes the Beth Din).[3] Virtually all fund raising is done on a national level through the Israel United Appeal and the United Communal Fund.

From a global point of view, the South African Jewish community ranks eighth in size, seventh in the Diaspora. However, it has contributed beyond its size not only to the financial needs of Israel but, more significantly, to Western *aliyah* (immigration to Israel). In some ways it resembles various Jewish populations in the West, but in others—especially those related to the particular type of pluralism characterizing South Africa—it differs markedly. This article will focus on the major social and demographic characteristics of the Jewish community, viewing them mainly within the context of the white population, which the Jewish community most closely

[3]Until recently Johannesburg and Cape Town had separate *batei din*.

resembles and of which it is, most immediately, a part. At the same time, some characteristics will also be compared with the South African population as a whole so as to obtain a broader perspective.

Sources

From the point of view of sociodemographic information, South African Jewry is among the best documented Jewish communities in the Diaspora. There are a variety of sources in which the main components of Jewish population structure are described and by means of which selected aspects of population change over the last 100 years can be traced. The data available since the beginning of the twentieth century are especially rich.

The principal sources are the periodic official population censuses. Beginning in 1904, and again in 1911, 1918, 1921, 1926, 1936, 1946, 1951, 1960, 1970, and 1980, censuses have provided information on the various religious denominations, including Jews.[4] This information includes not only the total size of each group and its geographic distribution, but also selected demographic and socioeconomic characteristics. The proportion of the total (white) population which does not report a religion in South Africa's censuses is usually low, which enhances reliability of the results.

The data published by the South African Department of Statistics on the Jewish population have usually included a moderate amount of detail. However, the South African Jewish Board of Deputies was able to arrange for special detailed processing of the 1970 and 1980 data files on the white

---

[4]The main published sources of data from South African censuses include: *Results of a Census of the Colony of the Cape of Good Hope, 1904* (Capetown, 1905); *Census of the Colony of Natal, 1904* (Pietermaritzburg, 1905); *Census of the Orange River Colony, 1906* (Bloemfontein, n.d.); *Results of a Census of the Transvaal Colony and Swaziland, 1904* (London, 1906); South Africa Bureau of Census and Statistics, *Census of the Union of South Africa: Annexures to General Report, 1911,* part 6 (Pretoria, 1912); South Africa, *Census of the European or White Races of the Union of South Africa 1918* (Capetown, 1920); South Africa Bureau of Statistics, *Third Census of the Population of the Union of South Africa, Enumerated 3rd May, 1921,* part 7 (Pretoria, 1923); South Africa Bureau of Statistics, *Fourth Census of the Population of the Union of South Africa, Enumerated 4th May, 1926,* part 8 (Pretoria, 1929); South Africa Bureau of Statistics, *Sixth Census of the Population of the Union of South Africa, Enumerated 5th May, 1936,* vol. 6 (Pretoria, 1941); South Africa Bureau of Statistics, *Seventh Census of the Population of the Union of South Africa, 7th May, 1946,* vol. 4 (Pretoria, 1954); South Africa Bureau of Statistics, *Population Census, 8th May, 1951,* vol. 3 (Pretoria, 1954); South Africa Bureau of Statistics, *Population Census, 6th September, 1960,* vol. 2 (Pretoria, 1966–1967); vol. 3 (Pretoria, 1966); Sample Tabulations by Census Tracts (Pretoria, n.d.); South Africa Department of Statistics, *Population Census, 6th May, 1970,* Report no. 02–05–03 (Pretoria, 1975); Tabulations by Area and Religion, Metropolitan Areas (Pretoria, n.d.); South Africa Central Statistical Services, *Population Census 80, Religion by Statistical Region and District,* Report no. 02–80–06 (Pretoria, 1985); *Social Characteristics,* Report no. 02–80–12 (Pretoria, 1985).

Jewish population to be provided to the Institute of Contemporary Jewry of the Hebrew University of Jerusalem. In 1970 the Department of Statistics prepared a comprehensive set of tabulations based on a 10-percent sample of South African Jewry; in 1980 it provided a computer tape of individual records of Jews living in the six major centers of Jewish settlement: Cape Town and Port Elizabeth in the Cape province; Durban in Natal; and Pretoria, Johannesburg, and Germiston in the Transvaal.[5] Further processing of these data was performed by the authors of this article.

In addition to the censuses, official data are also available on the number and characteristics of Jewish international migrants for the period from the beginning of this century up to the 1950s.[6]

Community-sponsored surveys of the Jewish population of the major cities have provided a wealth of information covering both essential demographic and socioeconomic variables and several aspects of Jewish identity, attitudes, behaviors, and community activities. Surveys of Johannesburg Jews were undertaken in 1935 by Henry Sonnabend,[7] and in 1968 by Allie A. Dubb.[8] The major research effort was the 1974 South African Jewish Population Study, sponsored by the South African Jewish Board of Deputies in cooperation with the Hebrew University of Jerusalem, and directed by Dubb.[9] The 1974 study used a sample of 2,074 Jewish households in

---

[5]The more detailed data available for 1980 refer to the six statistical regions which included the largest numbers of Jews. Statistical regions are divided into districts. In each of the regions for which we have data, most of the Jewish population is concentrated in the district named after the largest regional city. The Cape Town region also includes the Wynberg, Simonstown, Goodwood, and Bellville districts; Port Elizabeth includes Uitenhage and Kirkwood; Durban includes Pinetown and Inanda; Pretoria includes Wonderboom; Johannesburg includes Randburg; Germiston includes Alberton, Boksburg, Kempton Park, and Benoni. For the sake of simplicity, in this paper only the names of the chief regional centers will be mentioned. The data, however, relate to the entire respective regions. It should also be noted that an area bearing a particular name frequently has different boundaries in the census than it does when defined according to other criteria (e.g., magisterial district, municipal area, suburb from point of view of municipality, etc.). Furthermore, the census enumeration areas have themselves been altered from census to census. The result is that comparison of areas bearing the same name (e.g., the major metropolitan centers) over a period of years is subject to some error.

[6]See Stuart Buxbaum, "A Profile of Jewish Immigration to South Africa Between 1924–1948 and Its Impact upon the Local Community," in U. O. Schmelz, P. Glikson, and S. DellaPergola, eds., *Papers in Jewish Demography 1981* (Jerusalem, 1983), 145–62.

[7]Henry E. Sonnabend, "Statistical Survey of Johannesburg Jewish Population" (Johannesburg, 1935), mimeo; Henry E. Sonnabend, "Notes on a Demographic Survey of a Johannesburg Group," *South African Journal of Science* 33 (Mar. 1937):1055–60.

[8]Allie A. Dubb, *Jewish South Africans: A Sociological View of the Johannesburg Community,* Rhodes University, Institute of Social and Economic Research, Occasional Paper no. 21 (Grahamstown, 1977).

[9]Allie A. Dubb, Sergio DellaPergola, Dorit Tal, Beryl Unterhalter, and Stuart Buxbaum, *South African Jewish Population Study* (Jerusalem, Hebrew University, 1977–1978). Several advance reports were issued summarizing the main findings of the 1974 study. In this paper

Johannesburg, Cape Town, Durban, Pretoria, Port Elizabeth, and Bloemfontein, randomly selected from current Jewish community lists. The sample, therefore, did not adequately cover the more marginal members of the Jewish population, nor very recent arrivals who were as yet unknown to the organized community. These biases must be taken into account in interpreting the findings.

Records concerning Jewish marriages and Jewish burials have been routinely accumulated for many years by Jewish communities in South Africa. While these vital statistics have not been studied systematically, some of this information relating to Johannesburg Jewry in the late 1960s and early 1970s was analyzed.[10] Some data on synagogue marriages have also been published by South Africa's Department of Census and Statistics.[11] An investigation of Jewish births, using records of maternity wards, was carried out in Johannesburg in 1972.[12]

Jewish education in South Africa has been coordinated over the years by two central boards of education which publish periodic reports. In 1982 a systematic census of Jewish schools was taken, as part of the First Census of Jewish Schools in the Diaspora, by the Project for Jewish Educational Statistics at the Hebrew University's Institute of Contemporary Jewry.[13] Information was collected about the basic characteristics of institutions, pupils, and teachers.

Other, more specific, pieces of social-science research are also available.[14] All these sources are helpful in obtaining an overview of the changing characteristics of the Jewish population and the Jewish community in South Africa over the last several decades.

---

these are referred to as SAJPS Advance Reports. See, in particular, SAJPS Advance Report no. 1, *Methodology of the Study.* It should be noted that Bloemfontein, the main center in the Orange Free State province, was included in the 1974 survey but not in the detailed 1980 census processing. The entire Germiston statistical region was covered in the 1980 census tabulations, while in 1974 only parts of the Germiston statistical district were included, and those as part of the Johannesburg survey area.

[10]SAJPS Advance Report no. 5, *Mortality,* and no. 13, *Marriage and Mixed Marriage.*

[11]See Stuart Buxbaum, "Synagogue Marriages in South Africa: An Analysis of Official Statistics," in U. O. Schmelz, P. Glikson, and S. DellaPergola, eds., *Papers in Jewish Demography 1973* (Jerusalem, 1977), 171–94.

[12]SAJPS Advance Report no. 7, *First Data on Fertility.*

[13]Nitza Genuth, Sergio DellaPergola, and Allie A. Dubb, *First Census of Jewish Schools, 1981/2–1982/3—International Report,* Project for Jewish Educational Statistics, Report no. 3 (Jerusalem, 1985).

[14]See U. O. Schmelz, ed., *Demography and Statistics of Diaspora Jewry, 1920–1970—Bibliography,* I (Jerusalem, 1976), 254–62; Paul Glikson, "Selected Bibliography, 1969-1971," in U. O. Schmelz, P. Glikson, and S. J. Gould, eds., *Studies in Jewish Demography—Survey for 1969–1971* (Jerusalem-London, 1975), 242–43; Paul Glikson, "Selected Bibliography, 1972–1980," in U. O. Schmelz, P. Glikson, and S. J. Gould, eds., *Studies in Jewish Demography—Survey for 1972–1980* (New York, 1983), 139–44.

EVOLUTION OF THE JEWISH POPULATION

Growth of the Jewish Population

By 1880 there were about 4,000 Jews, mostly from England and Germany, in the four territories that were to become the Union of South Africa in 1910 (the Cape of Good Hope, Natal, the Orange Free State, and the Transvaal). During the two decades that followed, the discovery of gold and diamonds in South Africa and deteriorating conditions in Eastern Europe drew thousands of Jewish immigrants from Lithuania, Russia, Poland, and Latvia. By the turn of the century, in 1904, the Jewish population had increased ninefold to over 38,000, and constituted 3.4 percent of the total white population of the territories (see tables 2 and 3). Seven years later, the first census after the formation of the Union indicated that the number of Jews had grown by almost a quarter, to 47,000, constituting 3.7 percent of all whites.

As East European immigration moved into high gear, the Jewish population of the Union increased significantly faster than the total white population, until by 1936 it stood at over 90,000, comprising 4.5 percent of all whites. However, with the enactment of the Quota Act in 1930 and the Aliens Act in 1937, this immigration was reduced to a trickle. The last relatively large influx, which occurred between 1933 and 1939, was of refugees from Nazi Germany, which had not been one of the "quota" countries.

The cessation of large-scale Jewish immigration since 1939, a low rate of natural increase, and, during the last ten years or so, a rise in emigration, have led to a decline in the rate of growth of the South African Jewish community, both absolutely and relative to the total white population. Between 1970 and 1980 the number of Jews actually decreased by some 200 persons, to 117,963. By 1986 it is estimated that there was a further reduction—due mainly to a new wave of emigration—to around 115,000, constituting 2.3 percent of all whites.

The breakdown of the South African population in 1980 by religion (see table 1) shows that Jews constituted the smallest major religious group in the total population and that only Islam, Buddhism, Confucianism, and Hinduism had fewer white adherents. Compared with specific Christian denominations in a more detailed census tabulation, however, the number of Jews ranks with medium-sized white churches, such as the Presbyterians, and well above the Baptists, individual Pentecostals, and the various ethnic churches.

Another interesting fact is that a small proportion—less than 0.1 percent in each case—of coloreds, Asians, and blacks declared themselves to be Jews. In 1980 this represented a total of 3,125 individuals (2,320 black, 533 colored, and 272 Asians) in addition to 117,963 white Jews. While it is possible that colored and Asian Jews were either "reclassified" white Jews[15] or their offspring, they had in fact increased by more than 150 percent since 1970 and seventeenfold since 1960.[16] The characteristics of colored, Asian, and black Jews in South Africa will not be discussed in further detail here, but the subject is worthy of research.

International Migrations

IMMIGRATION

Historically, immigration constituted the main determinant of growth of South African Jewry. During the last two decades of the nineteenth century, a large number of Jews, mainly from the West, joined the diamond and gold rushes in Kimberley and on the Witwatersrand. However, the largest and most important stream of immigration, which also began in about the 1880s and continued until the 1930s, was that of Lithuanian and other East European Jews. The early 1930s saw the arrival of Jews—a large proportion being from Germany—seeking refuge from increasing Nazi pressure and persecution. This immigration continued until the outbreak of World War II. The relative magnitude of each wave of immigration can be estimated with a fair degree of accuracy. Gustav Saron gives the following figures: "I estimate that in the thirty-year period from 1880 to 1910, some 40,000 Jewish immigrants entered the country. Thereafter, for various reasons, the numbers decreased, with the exception of the years 1924 to 1930. In all, in the half-century 1910 to 1960, I estimate that perhaps 30,000 Jewish immigrants entered the country. The bulk of these were East European Jews."[17]

Year-by-year official statistics relating to the number of Jewish immigrants show a peak in 1928 (2,293 admitted persons) and 1929 (2,788

---

[15]In terms of the Population Registration Act, 1950, all permanent residents were classified according to "population group," i.e., black, white, etc. Reclassification in any direction could be requested by the person him/herself, or by the authorities acting on their own initiative or on the reports of neighbors or others.

[16]There were rumors during the 1970s of an Israeli rabbi, who has since left the country, selling conversions to blacks. The probability, however, is that almost all the black Jews in 1970 and 1980 belonged to a sect founded by the self-styled "Rabbi" Mshizana in Soweto, Johannesburg. The sect was never accepted by either the Orthodox or Reform communities as authentically Jewish. First encountered by anthropologist Martin West (now professor and head of the Department of Anthropology, University of Cape Town) in the 1960s, the sect was later reported in the press from time to time. The "rabbi" was detained during the recent disturbances.

[17]Gustav Saron, "The Making of South African Jewry," in Leon Feldberg, ed., *South African Jewry, 1965* (Johannesburg, 1965), 13.

persons), and an all-time record in 1936 (3,330 persons).[18] In earlier and later years the volume of Jewish immigration was much smaller. From the available statistics we can also evaluate past fluctuations in the percentage of Jews as a proportion of total immigrants to South Africa. The general trend was a decrease—from a peak of 35 percent in 1929 to 7 percent on the eve of World War II. During the 1960s and 1970s the level of Jewish immigration was below 1 percent of the total.

Action by the South African government in the form of restrictive legislation had profound effects on the volume and nature of Jewish immigration. In May 1930 the Immigration Quota Act came into force. This established a limited quota of immigrants of any race from all those countries specified in the act. Among the regulated countries were those of Eastern Europe, from which most Jews had come. Although it was officially denied that the act was aimed at curbing Jewish immigration in particular, it had exactly that effect. The reasons given for the restrictions emphasized that immigrants from the quota countries were culturally too different to be satisfactorily assimilated into a South Africa wishing to maintain its homogeneity, its basic ethnic composition, and its type of civilization.[19] In 1937 further restrictive legislation, the Aliens Act, was enacted.

During the late 1920s and early 1930s, almost 90 percent of Jewish immigration originated from countries affected by the 1930 Quota Act (see table 4). More than 50 percent of all immigrants came from Lithuania and nearly 20 percent from Poland. Jews constituted 80 percent of all immigrants from quota countries between 1924 and 1932. This pattern changed completely when the Nazis came to power in Germany. Between 1933 and 1939, the proportion of Jewish immigration coming from quota countries was reduced to 30 percent (of which half was from Lithuania), while 70 percent came from nonquota countries, which included Germany (59 percent of the total), other countries under German rule, and the British Commonwealth. The Jewish share of the total immigration from quota countries was reduced to 30 percent.[20]

In the years 1941–1945 Jewish immigration to South Africa ceased almost entirely. With the end of World War II, immigration resumed. During the early postwar period it was over 500 persons per year, with about half coming from the United Kingdom. Survey data collected in 1974 suggest that between the mid-1950s and the early 1970s the net inflow of Jewish immigrants probably declined to a yearly average of 200–300. Of these, about 25 percent came from Rhodesia/Zimbabwe, about 20 percent from Israel, 15 percent from the United Kingdom, and the rest from other

[18]See Buxbaum, "A Profile of Jewish Immigration," 146.
[19]Ibid., 145.
[20]SAJPS Advance Report no. 4, *Country of Birth and Period of Immigration.*

European countries, the Middle East, North Africa, North America, and Australia.

The demographic profile of Jewish immigrants changed during the different periods of immigration. During the 1920s a disproportionate number of young, single Jewish males arrived in South Africa (see table 4). Later, the sex ratio of immigrants was more balanced. Some married women and minors were brought to South Africa by husbands and fathers who had preceded them by a few years. Concentration of interwar immigrants in particular years and age groups had an impact on the demographic composition of the Jewish population in subsequent years (see below).

Fragmentary data on occupation before immigration of Jews from Eastern Europe during the 1920s indicate a predominance of salesmen and industrial workers.[21] By contrast, the occupational composition of Israelis migrating to South Africa between 1975 and 1984 was more than one-half professionals, about one-fifth production workers, and a smaller proportion of other occupations.[22]

EMIGRATION

As already noted, a positive international migration balance was for many years the most important factor in Jewish population increase. Nevertheless, while emigration from South Africa has generally been much lower than immigration, it has usually represented a sensitive indicator of changes both within the Jewish community and within South African society at large.

During the period 1924–1945, the ratio between the number of emigrants from South Africa per 100 immigrants was only 4 percent among Jews, as against 59 percent among non-Jewish whites.[23] This reflects differences in the frequency of return migration, different motivations of Jews and non-Jews for immigration and emigration, and the different options for actually moving back and forth that were available to members of each group during the interwar period.

The only country for which detailed data on Jewish migration from South Africa exist is Israel. Between 1924 and 1948, 954 Jews emigrated from South Africa; of these, 265 (28 percent) went to Palestine (see table 5). With the establishment of the State of Israel, the flow of South African *olim* increased significantly, though the pace varied over time. Yearly numbers

---

[21]Buxbaum, "A Profile of Jewish Immigration," 156–57.

[22]Israel Central Bureau of Statistics, *Migration of Israelis Abroad: A Survey of Official Data from Selected Countries,* Supplement to the Monthly Bulletin of Statistics, no. 6 (Jerusalem, 1986), 69.

[23]See Buxbaum, "A Profile of Jewish Immigration," 158.

of migrants tended to increase throughout the 1950s and 1960s, particularly after the Six Day War. However, of much greater significance were the repercussions of political unrest in South Africa during the late 1970s, which led to an *aliyah* of more than 1,000 *olim* in each of the two years 1977 and 1978. After a temporary slowdown during the early 1980s, emigration to Israel began to increase in 1985. The total pool of Jews of South African origin living in Israel was estimated at about 14,000 at the end of 1987, including Israeli-born children of South African parents.[24] This amounts to about 12 percent of the size of the Jewish population in South Africa in 1980.

In 1974 Jewish heads of households surveyed in the six major centers reported a total of 28,000 children of all ages living at separate addresses. Of these, over 5,000 (19 percent) did not live in South Africa. Of all children whose place of residence abroad was indicated, 33 percent lived in Israel, 32 percent in the United Kingdom, 13 percent in the United States, 7 percent in Canada, 3 percent in Australia, and 12 percent in various other countries. On the other hand, when asked about their intention to stay in South Africa, 78 percent of heads of households stated that they would remain (52 percent definitely and 26 percent probably), 8 percent were not sure, 13 percent contemplated leaving, and 1 percent indicated that they would definitely leave. Of those who specified a possible country of destination, 80 percent indicated Israel, 9 percent the United Kingdom, 7 percent the United States, 2 percent Canada, and 2 percent another country.[25] While these attitudes may have changed, and actual behavior may not have been consistent with them—under the impact of more recent events—Israel did stand quite high among possible destinations for those who were considering emigration or whose kin had already emigrated.

Natural Increase and Affiliative Changes

BIRTHS AND DEATHS

In general, the size of a religious-ethnic minority group can be affected by three types of factors: the balance of internal demographic changes—births vs. deaths; the balance of international migrations—immigration vs. emigration; and the balance of identificational changes—accessions vs. secessions.

---

[24]Our estimate based on Israel Central Bureau of Statistics, *Demographic Characteristics of the Population, National Data from the Complete Enumeration, 1983 Census of Population and Housing,* Publication no. 7 (Jerusalem, 1985), and evaluation of changes between 1983 and 1987. The estimate is based on figures on the South African-born and an appropriate inflation factor to account for persons who immigrated from South Africa but were not born there.

[25]SAJPS Advance Report no. 2, *Emigration.*

With the decline of Jewish immigration during the 1930s, natural increase emerged as the principal factor in the growth of the Jewish population. Birth and death rates are not available, but rough orders of magnitude can be obtained by looking at the number of young Jewish children at various dates and subtracting the known amount of growth due to migration from the total Jewish population growth. It would appear that the rates of natural increase were generally modest and tended to decline—from 6–7 per 1,000 Jews during the 1930s to 3–4 per 1,000 during the 1960s.

Retrospective and recent fertility rates are available from the 1974 South African Jewish Population Study, from a 1972 special investigation of Jewish fertility in Johannesburg, and, indirectly, from the age structure of the Jewish population in successive censuses.[26] While some substantive findings are discussed below, it should be noted here that South African Jews exhibited a relatively high level of fertility during the 1940s and 1950s—as compared to most other Diaspora communities—and showed a tendency to decline in the 1960s and especially toward the end of the 1970s.

Given the apparent high levels of natality after World War II, the explanation for the modest rate of natural increase must come from relatively high death rates. The older age composition of the Jewish population appears to have resulted in crude death rates somewhat above those of total whites. Relatively high death rates should not, however, be confused with the intrinsically low levels of mortality among South African Jews. The results of a study of Jewish mortality in Johannesburg in the late 1960s and early 1970s point to a life expectancy at birth of 71.9 years for men and 73.4 for women, as against 64.1 and 71.1, respectively, for total South African whites.[27] A similar advantage in the life expectancy of Jews probably prevailed in earlier decades too.

CHANGES IN IDENTIFICATION

Due to a lack of systematic data on changes in affiliation and identification among South African Jews, it has been assumed that the balance of conversions and other identification changes is nil. An inquiry conducted in 1966 found that Christian missionary activity among Jews was minimal, due to a notable lack of success in the past. Moreover, interviews with ministers of several Christian denominations suggested that very few Jews converted on their own initiative or because of outmarriage.[28]

Regarding assimilation without religious conversion, it should again be noted that although the Jews belong to the white group, this is a legal definition and not a social or cultural one. The Afrikaners maintain strict

---

[26]SAJPS Advance Report no. 7, *First Data on Fertility.*

[27]SAJPS Advance Report no. 5, *Mortality.*

[28]The inquiry was undertaken by Allie A. Dubb for the national weekly *Zionist Record.*

social and cultural boundaries which cannot easily be crossed, while English speakers do not form a coherent or cohesive social group. Thus, the country lacks clear-cut, generally accepted definitions of what constitutes a "true South African," and this has reduced the pressure on Jews to conform. Moreover, certain advantages (see below) in being Jewish might well play a significant role in minimizing the tendency of individuals simply to drift away from the Jewish community and from self-identification as Jews.

In spite of conversion to Judaism related to marriage (see below), there is no evidence showing that the accretion of converts has been a major factor in Jewish population change in South Africa.

The Jewish Population Equation, 1970–1980

Probably the most intriguing finding about the Jewish population from the 1980 South African census was the final count of the number of Jews. Since the 1970 census, in which 118,200 Jews were enumerated, the emigration of several thousand might have led to the expectation of Jewish population decline, this in spite of the moderate natural increase that still prevailed around 1970. The figure of 117,963 Jews for 1980 contradicted this expectation, pointing instead to surprising stability of Jewish population size during a decade of intense change.

Although every census, even the most sophisticated, carries some problems of quality, there is no way of ascertaining the extent to which the 1970 and 1980 totals may be explained by differences in the general quality of responses or in the coverage of the Jewish population in particular. Only on one specific point is there a known difference: the percentage of the total white population whose religious affiliation was unknown or who did not admit to any affiliation increased from 2 percent in 1960 and 2.7 percent in 1970 to 4.5 percent in 1980. However, the extent of nonresponse to the question on religion—although increasing—was low compared to that found in other Western countries. Were we to assume that a proportional share of Jews was included among those with unreported religion or none, the total would increase to 121,500 in 1970 and 123,500 in 1980. The size of the Jewish population would thus have grown over the intercensal period, making the actual demographic changes even more at variance with popular perceptions.

In order to reconcile the 1970 and 1980 figures on Jewish population, we must rely on partial and sometimes circumstantial evidence. In spite of their limitations, the available data do suggest the main direction and determinants of population change during the intercensal period.

An attempt should first be made to estimate the expected course of Jewish population growth between 1970 and 1980, assuming no international migrations and no identificational changes. These estimates are based on the age structure of the Jewish population in 1970 and on the levels of mortality and fertility that have been ascertained or inferred from the 1970 and 1980 censuses and other sources. It should be noted that while age composition around 1970 was quite favorable to population growth, structural transformations during the 1970s were bringing about rapid changes in the prospects for growth. Thus, the proportion of those aged over 65 was rapidly increasing, and the number of women of procreative age was beginning to decline—the end of natural increase was approaching.

Applying the available five-year age-specific death and birth rates to the 1970 Jewish age structure, we obtain projected totals of 121,200 for 1975 and 122,400 for 1980, as against 118,200 in 1970. This amounts to an expected excess of 4,200 Jewish births over the number of Jewish deaths. Some moderate increase in life expectancy that might have occurred during the 1970s, which was not taken into account here, has probably led to some overestimate of the expected number of Jewish deaths and an underestimate of the expected growth of the Jewish population (assuming the absence of external migrations).

Considering the actual decline of about 200 in Jewish population size between 1970 and 1980, the total of 4,400 Jews "missing" from the 1980 census can only be explained by a negative balance of international migration. It must again be emphasized that there are no systematic and definitive data on Jewish immigration and emigration. Nevertheless, the few reliable items of information that are available, plus a set of reasonable hypotheses, provide the basis for an interpretation of the migration process.

Let us first consider immigration to South Africa during the 1970–1980 period. This factor has generally been given little attention, aside from periodic rumors about a growing community of Israelis—said to include as many as 20,000 people. In reality, the 1980 census reported a total of 2,261 persons born in Israel and (partially overlapping) 1,927 Israeli citizens. However, to obtain a fuller estimate of the number of Israelis we must also include those who were neither born in Israel nor were citizens of the country, but who had been resident there. Recent Israeli and South African migration statistics show a ratio of former Israeli residents to Israeli-born of about 1.6 to 1.[29] If we apply this ratio to the South African census figure of Israeli-born, we obtain a 1980 estimate of 3,618 persons, including a few non-Jews.

The notion of a large Israeli community in South Africa in 1980 must, therefore, be dismissed, although the above estimates of the number of

[29]Over the period 1975–1979, 1,171 immigrants whose last country of permanent residence was Israel came to South Africa; the number of Israeli-born immigrants was 742. In 1980–1984, the figures were 2,443 and 1,507, respectively. See Israel Central Bureau of Statistics, *Migration of Israelis Abroad,* 68–69.

Israelis should be considered as minimal (see below). They do not include people who might have been defined as Israelis but who either did not report an Israeli origin in the census or escaped the enumeration altogether. Among these were: (a) tourists and other temporary residents who were not obliged to report in the census; (b) persons who were not born in Israel and, being entitled to multiple citizenship, may not have appeared as Israeli citizens; (c) former South African immigrants to Israel who were recorded as both South African-born and South African citizens; (d) any other Israelis who concealed their birthplace or citizenship; (e) those located in the independent black homelands, which are excluded from the census but which in popular perception are still seen as part of South Africa.

A useful clue in the 1980 census on the volume of immigration to South Africa is the number of children born outside of the country since 1970 and thus immigrating to South Africa between 1970 and 1980. There were 837 such children in the six major metropolitan areas for which we have detailed data. Of these, 167 were born in African countries (mostly Zimbabwe), 109 in the United Kingdom, 48 in other European countries, 427 in Israel, and 86 in other countries (mostly the United States and Canada). There was no unusual pattern of concentration in any of the six major centers, other than some underrepresentation in the Cape province. Proportionate weighting of the total figure for the six selected centers (837) gives an estimate for the whole country of 914 foreign-born children aged 0–9.

How many Jewish adults entered South Africa together with these children? We may speculate that the migrants included a disproportionate share of unattached adults; at the same time, some portion of the migrants consisted of entire families. We shall assume, as the central value of a range of hypotheses, that the proportion of the 0–9 age group among the migrants was slightly below that of all South African Jewry in 1980: 12 percent vs. 13.7 percent. Based on this assumption it is estimated that a total of about 7,600 individuals immigrated to South Africa between 1970 and 1980 and remained there in 1980. If the real proportion of children out of all migrants was higher, the total estimate of immigrants would decrease; if it were lower, the estimate would increase. It should be noted that some of these migrant children were probably born abroad to South African parents who emigrated and later returned to South Africa.[30] Any children that were born

[30]As noted above, about one-half of all immigrant children in 1970–1980 were Israeli-born. Children probably constituted a higher proportion of Jewish immigrants from Israel than from other countries. If we relate the 1980 census figures on Israeli-born children to the figures on immigration mentioned in footnote 29, a percentage of 20–25 percent of children is obtained, which seems not unlikely. We assume that the overwhelming majority of the Israeli-born immigrant children were born to Israeli parents and not to former South African *olim.*

in South Africa and that emigrated and returned during the 1970–1980 period are not included at this stage in the calculation. If they were, they would entail an additional number of accompanying adult return migrants.

Before suggesting a fuller estimate of return migration to South Africa, it would be well to consider the matter of emigration. Regarding the latter, the only hard facts are provided by the Israel Central Bureau of Statistics. Over the 1970–1979 period, 7,893 South African residents came to Israel as "new" or "potential" immigrants[31] (see table 5). At the same time, many more Jews emigrated to other countries. Partial evidence from Australian censuses suggests an estimated net inflow of up to 1,400 South African Jews between 1971 and 1981.[32] The United States, Canada, and the United Kingdom were other destinations reported by emigrants, but no precise figures are available. Some emigrants might even have moved from one destination to another after a period of a few years. Again the only clue upon which an estimate of further migratory mobility can be based comes from Israel: the proportion of immigrants from the period 1970–1979 who were still in the country in 1983 could be determined from the 1983 Israeli census. It was found that Israel had retained 47.5 percent of these *olim,* and that 52.5 percent, or over 4,100 out of the almost 7,900 individuals, no longer lived in Israel.[33] Some had presumably gone back to South Africa, while others had moved to a third country.

We must now reconcile our estimates of immigration and emigration in order to complete the picture of Jewish population movements between 1970 and 1980. The total number of new immigrants and return migrants to South Africa could range between the 7,600 estimated on the basis of the foreign-born children and accompanying adults in the 1980 census and the 11,700 arrived at by adding all 4,100 former *olim* of the period 1970–1979 who were "missing" in Israel. Lacking further information, we shall choose a middle estimate of about 2,000 returning *olim,* with the rest, presumably,

---

[31]A "new immigrant" is a person entering to take up permanent residence in Israel under the Law of Return or the Law of Entrance. A "potential immigrant" is a foreign subject who is entitled to an immigrant visa according to the Law of Return and intends to stay in Israel for a period exceeding three months. Potential immigrants are not Israeli citizens nor permanent residents but may apply to obtain either or both statuses. The data also include tourists who changed their status to new or potential immigrant. In recent years, over 90 percent of South African *aliyah* has been composed of potential immigrants. It should be noted that because of different classification criteria in the two countries, persons registered as immigrants in Israel may not have been recorded as emigrants in South Africa.

[32]See William D. Rubinstein, *The Demography of the Australian Jewish Community 1981,* Australian Institute of Jewish Affairs, Research Report no. 1 (Melbourne, 1986).

[33]Israel Central Bureau of Statistics, unpublished data. The number and percentage of the 1970–1979 South African *olim* staying in Israel in 1980 was probably higher, which results in some overestimate in the assumed number of return migrants. See also footnote 34.

having gone to other destinations.[34] This would produce a total of 9,600 Jewish immigrants and returning emigrants entering South Africa between 1970 and 1980. In order to attain the previously estimated South African Jewish migration deficit of 4,400 for the same period, an estimated 14,000 Jews would have had to have left South Africa during the intercensal period.

With regard to the destinations of these 14,000 Jewish emigrants, we know that 7,900 initially went to Israel and that 6,100, therefore, went to other countries. In the following years, the latter were joined by former South African *olim* who left Israel and chose not to return to South Africa. If our assumptions are correct, Israel represented the destination of first choice for more than half of those Jews who left South Africa between 1970 and 1980, but retained only roughly one-third of the estimated 12,000 South African Jews (14,000 emigrants minus 2,000 returnees) who had settled abroad permanently.

The basic results of this attempt to reconstruct Jewish population changes between 1970 and 1980 are summarized in table 6. It should be emphasized that only the central values from a much wider range of possibilities are presented. Thus, the Jewish population experienced a moderate annual rate of natural increase: 3.5 per 1,000 vs. 11.4 per 1,000 for total whites. The Jewish birthrate was lower and the Jewish death rate higher than that of total whites, mainly because of the different age structures of the two groups. Immigration rates were similar among Jews and total whites, but Jewish emigration rates were higher. The balance of international migrations was negative for the Jewish population and positive among total whites, despite a deficit in the net migration flows of whites in 1977 and 1978.[35] The average annual net migration rates for the 1970–1980 period were estimated at -3.7 per 1,000 Jews and 4.8 per 1,000 total whites. Overall, the Jewish population declined by a yearly rate of -0.2 per 1,000, as against a yearly increase rate of 18.7 per 1,000 among total whites.[36]

---

[34]The main assumption, here, is the total of 2,000 returning immigrants to South Africa. For the sake of simplicity, we assume that all came from Israel. We might also assume that fewer former *olim* returned directly to South Africa, while more went from Israel to other countries, and the balance returned from these countries to South Africa. The assumed fixed constraint of 2,000 return migrants seems to fit better with other data and estimates discussed in this paper. While the extremely tentative nature of these estimates is emphasized, it should be noted that some of the biases introduced by our various assumptions tend to mutually compensate.

[35]The main countries of origin of white immigrants were the United Kingdom and "other African countries" (mainly Zimbabwe). The main countries of destination of white emigrants were the United Kingdom and "other countries in Europe." See *South Africa 1980–81, Official Yearbook of the Republic of South Africa* (Johannesburg, 1982).

[36]There was an unexplained discrepancy in published data on total whites between the total amount of population growth between the 1970 and 1980 censuses and the sum of change components: births, deaths, immigration, and emigration. See South Africa Central Statistical Services, *Births: Whites, Coloured and Asians, 1983,* Report no. 07–01–11 (Pretoria, 1985).

Changes Since 1980

After a decline at the beginning of the decade, beginning in 1985 emigration again started to grow substantially. Using figures from South African Jewish community records for 1983 to March 1987 and Israeli immigration statistics for the same period, it is possible to arrive at an assessment of Jewish emigration since 1980. According to these sources, of a total of 3,500 Jewish emigrants,[37] about 50 percent went to Israel. Applying this proportion to the known number of *olim* for the whole period between 1980 and 1987—about 3,000 (see table 5)—we obtain a total of about 6,000 Jewish emigrants. Although not all other destinations can be ascertained, it is known from Australian census returns that between 1981 and 1986, 1,500 to 2,000 immigrated to that country.[38]

While it is difficult to determine the level of total Jewish immigration to South Africa since 1980, official South African sources suggest that from Israel there has been a net influx of about 2,500[39] (this would raise the total number of Israelis from an estimated 3,600 in 1980 to over 6,000 in 1987). Nevertheless, although Jewish immigration and return migration to South Africa have continued as in the past, it is assumed that there has been an ongoing negative migration balance since 1980. Furthermore, by 1985 the increasingly aging Jewish population (see below) had already produced a negative balance of births and deaths. The cumulative effect of these two processes has resulted in a further decline in Jewish population size—estimated conservatively at 115,000 at the end of 1986 (see table 1).

SOCIODEMOGRAPHIC CHARACTERISTICS AND TRENDS

The South-Africanization of South African Jewry

BIRTHPLACE

The major transformation of South African Jewry over the years has been its gradual change from an immigrant to a predominantly local-born group.

---

[37]Information kindly supplied by Sally Frankental, Kaplan Center, University of Cape Town. The figure is based on the number of Jewish households known to have left and a multiplier of 2.5 persons per household.

[38]Based on the increase in the number of South African-born Jews according to the censuses of Australia, from 1,938 in 1981 to 3,425 in 1986. Information kindly supplied by Walter M. Lippmann, Jewish Social Service Council of Victoria.

[39]See Israel Central Bureau of Statistics, *Migration of Israelis Abroad,* and unpublished data.

This process of South Africanization of the Jewish population has had significant consequences for most other sociodemographic characteristics and trends. Around 1930, a majority of Jews were foreign-born as compared with about 15 percent of total whites. Subsequently, the diminished impact of immigration brought about a steady increase in the proportion of local-born individuals. The process can be followed by looking at the birthplaces of different age groups among South African Jews in 1980 (see table 7). The South African-born represented 46 percent of the group aged 65 and over, 74 percent of the 45–64 age group, 85 percent of the 30–44 group, and 94 percent of the children below age 15.

According to the 1980 census, 79 percent of Jews were born in South Africa, in comparison with 87 percent of all whites (table 8). The proportion of South African-born Jews in 1980 might have been somewhat larger had it not been for a significant increase of Jews born in Zimbabwe and "rest of Western Europe" as compared with 1970; natives of those countries had grown from 1.0 percent and 0.2 percent, respectively, in 1970, to 1.7 percent and 1.1 percent of the Jewish population in 1980. Furthermore, since emigrants were drawn disproportionately from the younger age groups, increased emigration also reduced the percentage of those born in South Africa. It is also probable that the proportion of local-born Jews was greater outside the main metropolitan areas, since new immigrants tended to concentrate in the larger cities.

The different timing of immigration from various countries is reflected in the age structure of different origin groups within the Jewish population (see table 9). In 1980 the oldest group was the East European, with a median age of 69.4, followed by immigrants born in other West European countries, including Germany (65.1) and the United Kingdom (59.8). On the other hand, immigrants born in other African countries (including Zimbabwe) and Israel were younger, with a median age, respectively, of 30.4 and 28.5. South African-born Jews had a median age of 29.8, as compared with 61.0 for the foreign-born.

CITIZENSHIP

Despite the relatively high proportion of the foreign-born in the Jewish population, 93 percent of Jews were South African citizens in 1980, as compared with 91 percent of all whites (see table 10). This reflects both the tendency of Jews to become naturalized and their relatively low level of immigration since World War II. On the other hand, the influx of Jews from Zimbabwe, Israel, and Western Europe, and probably the emigration of South African nationals as well, led to a 2-percent decline in the proportion of Jewish South African citizens since 1970.

LANGUAGE

One further index of the steady South Africanization of the Jewish community is the decrease in the use of Yiddish and "other European languages" as the primary language at home. Table 11 shows that whereas in 1936 nearly 18,000 Jews (19 percent) spoke Yiddish, this number declined to such an extent that after 1960 it was no longer listed separately in the census returns. In a survey of Jews in six major cities in 1974, 2 percent spoke Yiddish or Hebrew as a primary language and a further 7 percent used one of these languages together with English.[40] By 1980, 94.5 percent spoke English or Afrikaans at home, 1.1 percent spoke a Western European language, and 4.3 percent spoke Yiddish, Hebrew, or some other non-European language. This was similar to the proportion of total whites who spoke a foreign language at home.

Table 11 also provides interesting evidence of the direction of Jewish acculturation in South Africa. Whereas 36 percent of whites spoke English at home and a further 5 percent were bilingual (Afrikaans and English), 92 percent of Jews were English-speaking and 1.5 percent were bilingual. Only 1 percent said that their home language was Afrikaans. Within the white group, Jews constituted only 0.04 percent of Afrikaans-speakers and 6.8 percent of the English-speaking section (see table 1). This reflects the exclusivism of the Afrikaner group, as well as a clear preference on the part of Jews for the more open and cosmopolitan culture of English-speaking South Africans.

Geographical Distribution

COUNTRYWIDE PATTERNS

The earliest Jewish settlement in South Africa was in the Cape Colony, and it was in its capital city, Cape Town, that the first Jewish congregation was formally established in the mid-1840s. With the discovery of gold on the Witwatersrand, many Cape Jews, as well as a large proportion of immigrants, moved northward. In the 1904 census (table 12), out of a total 38,000 Jews, 51 percent were in the Cape Colony, 41 percent were in the Transvaal Republic, and 4 percent each were in Natal and the Orange Free State. After the formation of the Union, the Jewish population of the Cape continued to decline until stabilizing at just over one-quarter of the total, while the proportion of Jews in the Transvaal had increased to about two-thirds by 1970. In the Orange Free State, after some years of modest

---

[40] SAJPS Advance Report no. 6, *Educational Attainment and Languages.*

growth, the proportion and number of Jews dropped steadily during the post-World War II period. Natal has remained with between 5–6 percent of all Jews over at least two decades.

The distribution of Jews in the four provinces paralleled the movement from rural areas and smaller towns into larger towns and cities, and from the larger towns into the major metropolitan areas. Jews had always been one of the most highly urbanized white groups—91 percent in 1911 and 99 percent in 1980 lived in urban areas as compared with 52 percent and 88 percent of total whites for the same years—but had, nevertheless, been scattered throughout the country in communities ranging between a few score and some tens of thousands. This process is reflected in table 13; whereas in 1918, 40 percent of Jews had lived outside of the major urban areas, this proportion had decreased steadily so that by 1980 it was only 7 percent (if the towns on the East and West Rand are included). On the other hand, Jewish settlement in Port Elizabeth and East London increased up until 1960, and in Pretoria up until 1970. Thereafter, with the exception of Durban, these communities also began to decline. By 1980, 57 percent of the total Jewish population of South Africa, or 67,820 out of 117,963 individuals, lived in Johannesburg,[41] with a further 23 percent (26,977) in Cape Town.

INTERNAL MIGRATION AND URBANIZATION

The patterns of internal migration have not been unidirectional. The two main stages of past geographical mobility within South Africa have been, first, diffusion into a large number of localities, and, more recently, concentration in the largest metropolitan areas. An examination of places of birth of South African-born residents of the major metropolitan areas in 1974 and in 1980 suggests that most of those born in Johannesburg and Cape Town had remained in those cities, and that they constituted the large majority (two-thirds and three-quarters, respectively, in 1974)[42] of the local Jewish population. In the smaller cities, however, locally born Jews made up 47–57 percent of the population. Of the remainder, 18–33 percent had migrated from the two largest cities, the rest being from the smaller towns and villages. Whereas the migratory balance was ultimately positive for

[41]In the case of the Jewish population, redefinition of census areas affected, primarily, the boundaries of Johannesburg and Germiston and the towns constituting the East Rand between 1960–1970 and 1970–1980. In table 13, the composition of the East Rand is held constant, while Johannesburg and Germiston have been combined. In other tables, the three areas are as defined in the 1980 census, with the East Rand being included as part of "Rest of Country."

[42]SAJPS Advance Report no. 9, *Geographical Distribution and Mobility.*

Johannesburg and Cape Town, it was zero for Durban and negative for the remaining cities.

Reasons for migrating to Johannesburg and Cape Town were not only the lure of the big city, but, in many cases, opportunities for study and work. On the other hand, migration from the two largest cities included many professionals and entrepreneurs who felt that the smaller centers offered better economic opportunities. The numerical stability of the Pretoria and Port Elizabeth communities was maintained primarily by the steady influx from the nearby smaller towns. It is partly because of the virtual disappearance of this source of replenishment that these communities, too, began to decline in recent years. Another possible factor is that with the increased emigration abroad during the 1970s and 1980s of many professionals and others in the higher occupational categories, fewer big-city Jews found it necessary to seek a niche in the smaller centers. The exception to the general trend was Durban: while 15 percent of its Jewish population came from smaller towns, 33 percent were from Johannesburg and Cape Town, and a further 7 percent from the other metropolitan areas. This reflects the general economic expansion of the city during the post-World War II years, and its attractiveness for entrepreneurs, professionals, and others.

One consequence of internal migrations has been the collapse and even the disappearance of organized Jewish community life in scores of small towns and villages throughout South Africa. In most of these places, synagogues and other property have been sold, and all that remains are cemeteries. In many areas there are no longer any Jews at all, while in others only one or two Jewish families are to be found.

Since the mid-1970s and early 1980s, the Jewish population decline of the smaller metropolitan areas has led to serious impoverishment of community life. A case in point is Port Elizabeth. Some 20 years ago the community numbered just under 3,000 persons, maintaining a full set of communal officials, institutions, and amenities—two Orthodox and a Reform synagogue; a Jewish day-school system from preschool to matriculation, a resident *shohet* and a kosher butcher, and so forth. By 1987 the secondary division of the day school had absorbed a large number of non-Jewish pupils (constituting over 40 percent of the total enrollment) in order to maintain itself; there was no longer a *shohet, mohel,* or Orthodox rabbi in town; and the large synagogue was relatively empty on the High Holy Days when, previously, extra sitting space had been needed.

RESIDENTIAL DISTRIBUTION IN JOHANNESBURG

Jewish settlement within the metropolitan areas in South Africa follows a pattern common throughout the Jewish world—Jews tend for the most part to concentrate in certain areas. As their socioeconomic position improves, they move into more desirable locations, but the pattern of concentration is constantly repeated. In South Africa residential separation of the various population groups—black, white, colored, Indian, and Chinese—is enforced by law;[43] Jews, as whites, therefore reside in white residential areas.

Although Jews in Johannesburg did not create a ghetto as they did, for example, in Chicago, they tended to cluster within a continuous area. Thus the earliest locus of Jewish residence was concentrated mainly in a band running east and west from downtown (Central, South-Eastern, and South-Western suburbs in table 14). As the community became more affluent, and many of these suburbs became industrialized and run down, Jews started to move northward, toward the northern parts of the central area, the eastern and northern suburbs. These areas remained roughly contiguous, but represented a fairly wide spectrum of socioeconomic levels. By 1960, 80 percent of Johannesburg Jews were concentrated in these areas, constituting in them over a quarter of the total white population. In the period 1960–1980 some Jews began to move out of the central and northern suburbs, mostly eastward to the newly developed suburbs in the east and northeast. To some extent this movement was a response to the establishment of major facilities, such as day schools, in what was at the time a developing residential area most convenient to existing concentrations of Jewish population. As a consequence of movement outward from the city center, synagogues and other facilities built in the areas of early settlement were closed down (though there are some exceptions), and the major Jewish institutions in Johannesburg today are to be found in a broad band running from northeast to west through the northern suburbs. In some of these suburbs Jews constitute the majority of the total white population.[44]

In the other major cities Jews have also tended to concentrate heavily in certain areas, but unlike the situation in Johannesburg, these areas have been scattered, resulting in several geographical foci of Jewish life.

Demographic Characteristics

In discussing the demographic characteristics of the Jewish population, comparisons will be made with other whites rather than with the population as a whole. The justification for this approach is that demographically South

---

[43]The Group Areas Act, 1966. Although the act is still in force, it has become government policy to allow areas to become "mixed" if the residents agree. One such area is a central Johannesburg high-rise residential suburb, Hillbrow.

[44]See also SAJPS Advance Report no. 9, *Geographical Distribution and Mobility;* T. Hart and J. G. Browell, *A Multi-Variate Spatial Analysis of the Socio-Economic Structure of Johannesburg, 1970,* University of the Witwatersrand, Urban and Regional Research Unit (Johannesburg, 1976).

African whites resemble other Western populations, while blacks and, to some extent coloreds and Asians, have characteristics more typical of the less-developed countries. Thus, whereas 88 percent of whites, 90 percent of Asians, and 75 percent of coloreds, respectively, lived in urban areas in 1980, this was true of only 38 percent of blacks. The nonwhite groups all had appreciably higher birth and death rates than did whites, resulting in markedly different age distributions. Thus, 28 percent of whites were aged 0–14, 64 percent aged 15–64, and 8 percent aged 65 and over; the proportions of Asians—who differed least from whites—were 37 percent, 61 percent, and 2 percent for the same age groups; among coloreds, children aged 0–14 constituted 39 percent of the population, 58 percent were aged 15–64, and 3 percent were 65 and older; and among blacks the percentages were 40 percent, 57 percent, and 3 percent, respectively.

SEX RATIOS

The sex composition of the Jewish population at the beginning of the twentieth century reflected the recency of its migrant origins (see table 15). High ratios of males per 100 females point to selective immigration of young male adults. Higher sex ratios, as compared to total whites, prevailed among the Jews until about 1960. Subsequently, the decline of foreign-born Jews and the aging of the Jewish population, together with the normally greater longevity of women, brought about a growing numerical predominance of women in the community.[45]

An examination of sex ratios of total whites in 1980, by age, reveals that besides the usual excess of males among young children, sex ratios at ages 30–64 were rather high—an effect of a long period of migratory inflow. On the other hand, sex ratios for Jews of the same ages were rather low, which could be a consequence of stronger emigration or assimilation of Jewish males. The higher sex ratio of Jews at ages 65 and over was an echo of selective immigration in the past, but also reflected comparatively greater chances of survival among elderly Jewish males than among total whites in the same age group. This finding is confirmed by investigations of mortality patterns and estimates of average life expectancy for Jews and total whites of each sex (see above).

The composition of the Jewish population by sex varied in different communities, with a few exceptions to the moderate predominance of women that existed nationally and in the largest cities (see table 18). In 1980 males were more numerous in Pretoria—probably because young men were attracted by government employment opportunities in the nation's capital

[45]SAJPS Advance Report no. 3, *Demographic Characteristics.*

(see below); in Germiston—because of the comparatively higher proportion of children, and thus, of males, among the Jewish population; and in the very small communities and isolated Jewish households scattered all over the country.

AGE COMPOSITION

The age composition of the Jewish population was greatly affected by immigration until the late 1930s. Thereafter, it was more decisively shaped by changing birth and death rates, although the continuing effects of immigration and emigration remained evident. A significant feature was the "age bulge" formed by the comparatively large number of Jews born during the pre-World War I period, which moved conspicuously through the age structure over time (see table 16). From the 1920s on, South African Jewry witnessed a continuous growth in the proportion of those aged 60 and over—from less than 5 percent in 1926, to 13.1 percent in 1960, and 22.5 percent in 1980. Some of these changes reflected the age composition of Jewish immigration to South Africa. On the other hand, the proportion of children below age 10 declined from 18.2 percent in 1926 to 14.6 percent in 1936, and, following the postwar fertility increase (see below), from 17.3 percent in 1960 to 13.7 percent in 1980—reflecting further reduction in the birthrate and, possibly, the emigration of children. The median age of the Jewish population increased from 25.8 in 1926 to 34.9 in 1980, as compared to 22.8 and 28.1, respectively, among total whites.

In 1980 there were proportionally fewer Jews than total whites in each age group below age 50 and more Jews in each age group above age 50 (table 17). The net effect of recent migration exchanges on the age composition of the Jewish population can be judged by comparing detailed data from the 1970 and 1980 censuses. The strongest decline appeared among the 25–29 age group in 1980 (aged 15–19 in 1970), and more generally among the 20–34-year-olds (aged 10–24 in 1970). On the other hand, the group aged 35–44 in 1980 was, on balance, the most stable between the two censuses. It may thus be inferred that the age composition of Jewish emigrants was younger than that of Jewish immigrants. This is confirmed by the age distribution of South African Jewish immigrants to Israel, which included proportionally far more children and young adults below age 30 than did South African Jewry in both 1970 and 1980. Recent migration movements, therefore, have further accelerated the aging process set in motion by the lowering of fertility since the 1960s.

The consequences of the aging process were quite remarkable at the older end of the Jewish age structure. In absolute numbers, between 1970 and 1980 the 65+ age group increased by over 6,400 persons, or 47 percent of its size in 1970. The 65–69 age group grew by 1,300, or 23 percent; the 70–74 group grew by 1,900, or 46 percent; and the 75+ group grew by 3,200, or 85 percent. Some of these changes reflect the ascent of the already mentioned "age bulge" into the elderly age range. The prospects for further aging are now somewhat less extreme than they were in previous years, because of the relatively "flat" age composition of the age groups from 40–44 to 60–64. But further emigration of younger adults, together with the reduced propensity for emigration among the elderly, may further speed up the aging trend.

Some differences were evident in the age structures of the various local communities (table 18). In 1980 the most youthful group was in suburban Germiston, bordering on Johannesburg, a reflection of the tendency of younger households to move into the newer developing areas. Pretoria appeared to have the highest proportion of adults below age 30. The highest proportion of elderly (aged 65 and over) was found in Port Elizabeth, while Durban and Cape Town, too, had fairly high percentages. Johannesburg differed the least from the country total, which it determined in large part. Finally, the aggregate of smaller communities was probably losing youth and generally stagnating, as shown by the high proportion at ages 45–64.

MARITAL STATUS

About 60 percent of South African Jews aged 15 and over were currently married in 1980 (table 19). Close to 29 percent of males and 20 percent of females were never-married; 3 percent and 17 percent, respectively, were widowed; and smaller percentages were divorced or living together.

The tendency to postpone marriage that has been exhibited in recent years in all Western countries also occurs among South African Jews. Between 1970 and 1980, the proportion already married at ages 25–34 declined from 77 percent to 71 percent among Jewish males, and from 91 percent to 85 percent among Jewish females (table 20). (Marriage postponement did not significantly affect the total whites, among whom in 1980, 83 percent of males and 90 percent of females aged 25–34 were already married.) Between 1970 and 1980, relatively more Jews than non-Jewish whites married after ages 25–34, but not enough to compensate for the much diminished frequency of marriage among younger Jewish adults—males up to 35 and females up to 25. The proportion of ever-married Jews at ages 45–54 continued to be high—above 95 percent and similar to total whites—but this was mainly a reflection of the higher marriage propensities of the past. Based on the continuation for an indefinite period of the rhythm of family formation observed in the different age groups between 1970 and 1980, over 95 percent of total white males and over 92 percent of total white females could be expected to marry at some time. Among Jews, the percentage ever marrying would be substantially smaller than in the past—88 percent of males and 82 percent of females.

Compared to other Western countries, the recent slowdown in family formation among South African Jews was moderate. In North America, the expected rates of eventual marriage—based on a continuation of the trends of the 1970s and early 1980s—would be lower.[46]

The male-female differential in expected marriage (if the conditions that prevailed during the 1970s were to continue indefinitely) reflected a temporary asymmetry or "squeeze" in the structure of the marriageable Jewish population by sex and age. Considering that men usually marry somewhat younger women, both the 1970 and 1980 census data suggested a more favorable position of Jewish males from the point of view of potential spouse supply. In 1970 there was a countrywide ratio of 185 never-married Jewish women aged 20–34 per 100 Jewish men aged 25–39. In 1980 the same ratio was somewhat more balanced, but, countrywide, there still were 153 never-married females aged 20–34 per 100 males aged 25–39.

The unbalanced sex composition of the marriageable Jewish population reflects past fluctuations in fertility levels and consequent sharp changes in the size of age cohorts, from the smaller ones born during the 1940s to the larger ones born during the 1950s and 1960s. Further reasons could be a higher level of emigration of Jewish males from South Africa, and, possibly, stronger assimilatory processes—with a consequent withdrawal from the Jewish group—among males. Another factor affecting sex ratios at the local level was the different pace of internal migration among young adults of each sex. In Johannesburg, in 1970, the ratio of never-married Jewish women aged 20–34 to five-year-older single Jewish men was 244 to 100—more than twice as many. In 1980 the same ratio was still very high—172 to 100. In several of the smallest communities the imbalance was even greater, though in some cases young Jewish single males were in excess. In turn, these age-sex-marital status imbalances, aside from their direct effect on frequency of marriage and the age-assortment of couples, may powerfully affect other Jewish population trends, enhancing the rate of outmarriage and of outmigration of individuals who cannot find a Jewish marriage partner locally.

The proportion of unmarried young adults living together increased by a factor of four to five over the period 1970–1980. However, the actual percentages reported as living together in 1980 were quite small—overall 1.4 percent of Jewish males and 1.2 percent of Jewish females aged 15 and

[46]See Sergio DellaPergola and U. O. Schmelz, "Demographic Transformations of American Jewry: Marriage and Mixed Marriage in the 1980s," in *Studies in Contemporary Jewry* (New York-Oxford, 1988).

over. The highest frequencies of Jewish persons living together appeared among men 25–29 years old (3.8 percent) and women 20–24 years old (3.4 percent). These rates were only slightly higher than among total whites. We lack information concerning further instances of cohabitation included in the larger "never-married" category.

An increase in the proportion of divorced persons is another aspect of changing family behavior. Thus, 3 percent of Jewish men and 5 percent of Jewish women per 100 ever-married in the 35–44 age group were divorced in 1970. The corresponding figures in 1980 were 5 percent and 8 percent, respectively. Among total whites the increase in divorced persons per 100 ever-married aged 35–44 was somewhat less, from 3 percent among males and 4 percent among females in 1970 to 4 percent and 6 percent, respectively, in 1980. Proportionately more Jews than total whites were currently divorced. This increase contrasts with the high value placed on family cohesion within the Jewish community in the past. It also suggests that there were fewer remarriages than in the past—especially of women—in cases of family disruption. According to 1974 survey data, over one-half of Jewish divorcees were granted a civil divorce only, and less than half were divorced by a Jewish rabbinical court (with or without a civil divorce).[47]

MIXED MARRIAGE

Only fragmentary data exist on the frequency of mixed marriage among South African Jews. According to the 1974 survey, in the major Jewish communities only 1.3 percent of married Jews of all ages had a currently non-Jewish spouse—2.3 percent of Jewish husbands and 0.3 percent of Jewish wives; another 1.1 percent were married to a spouse who had been converted to Judaism. Translated into household terms, this 1.3 percent of outmarried Jews corresponded to an overall figure of 2.6 percent of existing mixed couples, ranging from 5.1 percent in Durban and 4.9 percent in Bloemfontein, to 3.5 percent in Cape Town, 1.9 percent in Johannesburg, and 1.6 percent in Pretoria.[48] While these in all likelihood are underestimates, some sense of the ongoing trend can be obtained by comparing these same data across two generations. The percentages of the outmarried among adult children of heads of households—again, regardless of age—were higher: 7 percent had a currently non-Jewish spouse and another 3 percent had a converted Jewish spouse.

---

[47]SAJPS Advance Report no. 13, *Marriage and Mixed Marriage.*

[48]The proportion of mixed marriages is always greater for couples than for individuals, because a homogamous Jewish marriage appears only once in the count of couples but twice in that of the component individuals. See SAJPS Advance Report no. 13, *Marriage and Mixed Marriage.*

Some further, admittedly outdated, indication of the extent of mixed marriage comes from a survey of synagogue marriages in Johannesburg over the period 1966–1970.[49] At that time 85 percent of marriages were Orthodox and the remainder were Reform. Of grooms marrying in an Orthodox synagogue, 1 percent were converts, while the figure for brides was 2 percent. Among Reform marriages, however, 7 percent of grooms and 27 percent of brides were converts, with another 5 percent of each sex not reporting religion at birth. Considering that Johannesburg was at the low end of the South African continuum in terms of outmarriage frequencies, and that civil marriages or marriages with a non-Jewish religious ceremony were not reported in these data, it was tentatively suggested that the percentage of Jewish grooms or brides marrying a non-Jewish spouse who did not convert to Judaism might range between 8 percent and 14 percent in the 1970s and between 15 percent and 24 percent in the 1980s.[50] While these figures are little more than conjectural, it seems quite certain that in the particular context of South African society, the diffusion of mixed marriage was slower and at lower levels than among Jewish communities in most other Western countries.

That this may indeed have been the case is reinforced by some further comparative data on attitudes toward intermarriage that may underlie differences in actual outmarriage rates. In 1974 only 5 percent of Jewish heads of household in South Africa were indifferent to, or held a positive attitude toward, possible intermarriage of their children.[51] The corresponding percentage in one Jewish community in the United States, Boston—roughly twice the size of South African Jewry—was 37 percent in 1975 and 39 percent in 1985.[52] The actual percentages of Boston Jewish residents who outmarried in their first marriage were 20 percent in 1971–1975 and 29 percent in 1981–1985.[53] Assuming the existence of some relationship between social attitudes and behavior, the corresponding percentages for South African Jews must be considerably lower.

FERTILITY

The evolution of South African Jewish fertility levels over the past 50 years can be reconstructed along broad lines on the basis of several sources of data. According to a survey conducted in Johannesburg in 1935, Jewish

---

[49]Ibid.

[50]Ibid.

[51]Ibid.

[52]Sherry Israel, *Boston's Jewish Community: The 1985 CJP Demographic Survey* (Boston, 1987).

[53]Ibid.

women aged 45 or over had borne an average of 3.9 children, compared with an average of 4.6 for urban whites and 6.4 among rural whites.[54] The average number of children per Jewish woman was 4.0 in the least affluent Johannesburg suburbs and declined to 3.2 in the most affluent areas. It could be expected that the increasing socioeconomic status of Johannesburg Jews would result in a further decline of Jewish family size. Taking into account the younger women as well, married Jewish women had 2.6 births on average, as compared to 3.6 in the white population. These figures, while showing lower Jewish fertility than among total whites, also indicated that in South Africa fertility levels were higher than in the United States or England at the same time.[55]

Detailed birth histories collected in 1974, in the framework of the sample survey in the six major Jewish centers, offered the basis for a retrospective evaluation of Total Fertility Rates (TFR)[56] between the early 1940s and the mid-1970s (see table 21). Around 1940 the Jewish TFR was 2.1—the level that ensures generational replacement and population stability in the long term, under conditions of low mortality and the absence of external migrations—as against 3.1 among total whites. From the experience of Jewish populations in several other Western countries, we know the TFR had declined to below replacement level during the 1930s. In the United States, for example, the Jewish TFR was estimated at 1.3 around 1935, and 1.5 around 1940, as against 2.1 and 2.3, respectively, among total whites.[57] In South Africa, too, the Jewish birthrate appeared to be quite low during the 1930s, at a time of economic depression and under the impact of Jewish immigration from low-fertility European countries. Jewish fertility had probably started to rise by the beginning of World War II. This trend continued until the mid-1950s, when the TFR reached a level of 3.1 among Jewish women vs. 3.4 among total white women. The late 1950s and 1960s witnessed a moderate reduction in Jewish fertility levels, which preceded a similar trend among total whites by several years.

It should be noted that during the 1940s the fertility levels of Jewish women—though lower than average—increased much more rapidly than among total whites, and that subsequently the TFRs of Jews in South Africa

---

[54]Sonnabend, *Statistical Survey of Johannesburg.*

[55]See Patrick Festy, *La fécondité des pays occidentaux de 1870 à 1970,* Institut National d'Etudes Démographiques, Travaux et Documents, Cahier no. 85 (Paris, 1979); Sergio DellaPergola, "Patterns of American Jewish Fertility," *Demography* 17, no. 3 (1980): 261-73; Barry A. Kosmin, "Nuptiality and Fertility Patterns of British Jewry 1850-1980: An Immigrant Transition?" in D.A. Coleman, ed., *Demography of Immigrants and Minority Groups in the United Kingdom* (London, 1982), 245-61.

[56]The TFR expresses the number of children that would be born under the assumption of continuation of the age-specific fertility levels observed for a certain period.

[57]DellaPergola, "Patterns of American Jewish Fertility."

were closer to those of the total (white) population than had been the case in the United States, Canada, or France.[58]

For the more recent period, only the cruder fertility measure represented by the Child-Women Ratio (CWR)[59] is available. Around 1970, for which year both TFR and CWR are available, the ratios between Jews and total whites obtained from either measurement technique were quite consistent. This allows for cautiously inferring more recent trends in fertility levels. Moderate declines occurred during the early 1970s for both Jews and total whites. During the late 1970s the fertility decline was much sharper—close to 20 percent less than in the preceding five-year period. The TFR for Jews possibly reached a level of about 2.4 in 1970–1974 and 1.9 in 1975–1979, as against roughly 2.9 and 2.3, respectively, among total whites.[60] The TFR for Jews in the United States and Canada at the same dates was estimated at 1.5–1.6, as against 1.7–1.9 among total whites.[61] In South Africa, fertility started declining later, and current levels at the end of the 1970s were higher than in most other Western countries. Thus, Jewish fertility patterns, although also low, were quite exceptional in the framework of the contemporary Diaspora.

Data from the 1974 survey on the number of children born to Jewish women, according to socioeconomic characteristics of husbands, provide further details.[62] Among older women, aged 55 and over in 1974, a reverse relationship prevailed between the occupational status of husbands and family size. This was consistent with the conventional relationship between educational levels and fertility and probably reflected the preference for smaller families and more effective family planning of the more educated and upwardly mobile Jewish households. Among the intermediate 35–54 age group in 1974, the relationship between socioeconomic status and family size had shifted to a U shape. This probably indicated a positive impact of higher income on fertility after the general spreading of moderately high educational levels among the Jewish population. Among younger women up to 35, whose families were still incomplete, the socioeconomic status-fertility relationship tended again to be negative, pointing to a later start and slower pace of family growth among the more educated and upwardly mobile.

The major explanation for South African Jewish fertility patterns at the

---

[58]Sergio DellaPergola, "Contemporary Jewish Fertility: An Overview," in U.O. Schmelz, P. Glikson, and S. DellaPergola, eds., *Papers in Jewish Demography 1981* (Jerusalem, 1983), 215-38.

[59]Ratio between the number of children aged 0–4 and the number of women aged 20–39.

[60]See South Africa Central Statistical Services, *Births: Whites, Coloureds and Asians, 1983.*

[61]U. O. Schmelz and Sergio DellaPergola, *Basic Trends in U.S. Jewish Demography,* Jewish Sociology Papers, American Jewish Committee (New York, 1988).

[62]SAJPS Advance Report no. 7, *First Data on Fertility.*

community level, then, seems to be tied to the substantial improvement in socioeconomic standards since the end of World War II and continuing through the late 1970s. Relatively high income, adequate housing, and, in particular, easily available domestic help probably facilitated the formation of comparatively larger families. In a broader societal perspective, this clearly reflected the preferential status of whites, including Jews, in the unequal socioeconomic context of multiracial South African society. Nevertheless, the postponement of marriage among younger Jewish adults, which has already been noted, more efficient fertility control, and the general political and socioeconomic situation in recent years combine to make it highly probable that a further decline of Jewish fertility levels must already have begun by 1980.

FAMILY SIZE

In 1974 the average number of persons in Jewish households in the six major centers was 3.35, of whom 3.30 were Jews.[63] The survey did not cover Jewish persons in institutions; servants and other permanent household personnel were also not counted as household members. Household structure by relationship to the head was typically nuclear, with 30.1 percent being heads of households (including persons living alone), 23.6 percent spouses, 42.6 percent children, 3.3 percent other relatives, and 0.4 percent nonrelatives. Since 1974, the decline of fertility, an increase in the percentage of the elderly, postponement of marriage, and international migrations can be expected to have resulted in a steady decline in Jewish household size.

Socioeconomic Characteristics

EDUCATIONAL LEVEL

Even during the early years of settlement, Jewish immigrants, while struggling to make a living, realized the value of education in optimizing the opportunities offered in their new country, which itself was young and full of potential. This was consistent, of course, with traditional attitudes toward study—albeit primarily in the religious sphere—which characterized Lithuanian and other Eastern European Jewry. Thus one hears again and again of immigrant parents stinting themselves in order to educate their children, including, if at all possible, giving at least one of them, particularly a son, university training. During these early days it was not only parents

[63]SAJPS Advance Report no. 3, *Demographic Characteristics.*

who made sacrifices but also often other relatives. Even siblings frequently helped to educate a promising brother or sister. As Jews prospered, however, it became possible for more families to provide all or most children with whatever education and training they were capable of receiving.

Over several decades, census and other data have shown that South African Jews have been better educated than total whites and, more specifically, than the urban whites whom they most closely resemble.[64] In more recent years, especially since 1960, the overall educational levels of both urban whites and the Jewish population have steadily improved. Among Jews, the older immigrant generation, whose level of general education was relatively low, was gradually being replaced by the better-educated local-born, and by more recent immigrants from Western countries. At the same time, both Jews and total whites lost a proportionately large number of the better-educated through heavy emigration during the second half of the 1970s.

The improvement in educational standards was more marked among whites as a whole than among Jews, so that by 1980 the educational gap between them had narrowed somewhat—although it remained substantial (see table 22). Thus, while 4 percent of both Jews and total whites aged 20 and over had not gone beyond primary education, 70 percent of Jews and 49 percent of total whites had at least completed secondary school (grade 12)[65] or attained a nondegree diploma.[66] Of these, 14 percent of Jews and 6 percent of total whites had a bachelor's degree or the equivalent, and another 1.4 percent and 0.8 percent, respectively, held a master's degree or a doctorate.

It should be noted that levels of education of the main racial and ethnic groups reflect the effects of conventional and legal discrimination against people of color in South Africa. Thus, in 1980 more than half of coloreds and blacks and 39 percent of Asians aged 20 and over had no more than primary schooling. At the upper levels, 15 percent of Asians, 7 percent of coloreds, and 4 percent of blacks had matriculated or obtained a nondegree diploma; of these, 2 percent of Asians and less than 1 percent of coloreds and blacks had obtained university degrees. Although the educational levels of these groups have been steadily improving, both the quantity and quality of their education is still far inferior to that of whites.

---

[64]SAJPS Advance Report no. 6, *Educational Attainment and Languages.*

[65]Each province in South Africa uses its own terminology to designate grades and its own cutoff points between primary and secondary school. In this paper, Sub (standard) A, Sub B, and Standard 1 through Standard 5 represent grades 1 through 7 and are defined as primary education. Secondary education is from Standard 6 through Standard 10 (or Matriculation), i.e., grades 8 through 12.

[66]"Nondegree diplomas" did not, in all cases, require matriculation level. The category includes a proportion of persons, therefore, who did not complete secondary school.

Variation in educational level of the Jewish population aged 15 and over in 1980, by sex, age, and major metropolitan area is shown in table 23. The major difference, by sex, was the higher proportion of Jewish males with completed university education: 20 percent, compared with 10 percent of women.

Educational differences between age groups clearly reflect the continuous improvement of the overall level over time. The oldest group, those aged 65 and over, included fairly high percentages of persons with a low level of education: 12 percent below grade 8, and, overall, 55 percent below grade 12. These proportions decreased, while the percentage of university graduates increased, from 7 percent among the 65+ age group to 14 percent among the 45–64 age group and to 20 percent among the 30–44 age group. The youngest group (15–29) included a high proportion who had not completed their education and, therefore, a lower proportion with degrees. A similar growth pattern appeared across age groups with regard to the proportion holding nondegree diplomas—from 7 percent at ages 65 and over to 23 percent at ages 30–44.

Only minor differences existed in the educational level of Jews in the different metropolitan areas. The proportion with a completed university education ranged between a maximum of 17 percent in Pretoria and a minimum of 13 percent in Durban, while the proportion of those without matriculation was 28 percent in Pretoria and 36 percent in Durban.

OCCUPATIONAL CHARACTERISTICS

In common with other Western Jewish communities, South African Jews are better educated than other whites and are overrepresented in professional and managerial occupations. This, together with their income and residential distribution, suggests a disproportionately middle- and upper-middle-class population.

Upward economic mobility of Jews in South Africa has been rapid. To a much greater extent than in the United States and Britain, which already had highly developed economies, South Africa was a land of opportunity for immigrants. Hard work, initiative, and a measure of good luck were sufficient to establish an individual independently in business in a country with a large and unsophisticated rural population. The discovery of gold and diamonds, the consequent need for goods and services, and the easy spending habits of the miners also provided economic openings. If the urban experience and skills of Jews were an asset to their advancement in the United States, they were an even greater asset in South Africa at the end of the nineteenth century. The South African situation also favored Jewish economic progress in another way: whereas in the United States and Britain

Jewish immigrants without skills or training were absorbed as laborers, this was not the case in South Africa. There, most unskilled labor was performed by blacks, so that the immigrants were virtually forced into entrepreneurial activities. Thus, in South Africa it was often the immigrants themselves who moved up the socioeconomic ladder.

Considerable changes in the structure of the Jewish labor force were involved in this process of integration and mobility within South African society.[67] Table 24 compares the occupational characteristics of Jews before World War II with those of more recent years. The number and percentage of Jewish professionals and administrators dramatically increased at the expense of salesmen and production workers—although even in the 1930s the latter constituted a relatively small part of the Jewish labor force.

Although in recent years many of the laws governing the strict division of labor between the races have been amended or repealed, the castelike arrangements of the South African labor force were still evident in the 1980 figures. A comparison of the occupational distribution of the major racial and ethnic groups exhibits, as in the case of education, a wide cleavage between whites on the one side and coloreds, Asians, and blacks on the other. Regarding participation in the total work force, whites had a higher proportion of economically active persons than all other groups—which is mostly explained by the lower proportion of children among whites (table 25). Within only the male work force, however, proportionately three times more coloreds and blacks than whites were agricultural workers; half the coloreds and blacks and 40 percent of Asians were production workers. Women in service and production numbered 9 percent among whites as against 58 percent among coloreds, 46 percent among Asians, and 53 percent among blacks. For the latter three groups these categories involved mainly menial work, including, especially among black women, domestic service. Higher-status blue- and white-collar occupations were consistently and significantly less frequent among coloreds and blacks. Among the highly urbanized Asians, however, the proportion of professionals was about half that of whites; the proportion of male clerical and sales workers was greater than that for whites and the same was true of female Asian sales workers.

Looking at Jews in the context of the white population, we find that the overall differences between Jews and total whites remained relatively stable. Even the comparatively urbanized and high-status white Anglicans (Episcopalians) had intermediate characteristics between Jews and other whites (see table 25). Jews retained their concentration and overrepresentation in professional, administrative, and sales occupations, while relatively few of

[67]SAJPS Advance Report no. 10, *Occupational Characteristics.*

them were engaged in the lower white- and blue-collar occupations. Among Jews, as among all whites, between 1970 and 1980 there was an increase in the proportion of professionals and administrative personnel and a decrease in sales and production workers, as well as among the few Jews in agriculture.

Changes in the overall white occupational structure were probably due to real occupational mobility as well as to a significant positive migration balance among professionals in particular. Upward changes in the Jewish occupational structure reflected the retirement of elderly and less educated workers and their replacement by younger and better-educated ones. Moreover, a unique combination of immigration and emigration possibly resulted in a bias toward an occupationally better-established population. The significant emigration of younger adults, still at the beginning of their working careers, and their replacement by somewhat older immigrants, is also reflected in the higher proportion—and absolute size—of the work force in 1980 as compared to 1970, despite an overall decrease in Jewish population size.

Table 26 analyzes the changes in the occupational distribution of Jews over the periods 1960–1970 and 1970–1980. The net balances mainly reflect the outflow from the labor force of elderly persons in production and sales and the inflow of younger people in professional, technical, and service occupations. Between 1970 and 1980 the professionalization of the Jewish labor force was the leading theme of change, especially for males. Occupational changes among women involved their entering a broader range of occupations—sometimes as substitutes for upwardly mobile men—but here, too, professionalization prevailed.

Jews were not only concentrated in certain characteristic occupational groups but also in specific occupations. Thus, among professionals, 30 percent of Jews in 1980, as compared with 18 percent of whites, were in medical and allied fields (see table 27). There were similar large and disproportionate concentrations of Jews in public accounting, the legal profession, and, to a lesser degree, in the arts. On the other hand, only about a third as many Jews as other whites were engineers, architects, and physical scientists. It is difficult to gauge the proportion of Jews employed in university teaching and research, as the various fields are included in several professional categories.

The major sex-related differences in the Jewish occupational structure in 1980 were in administrative, managerial, and clerical occupations (see table 28). About one in four (24 percent) economically active Jewish males in 1980 was an administrator or manager, as against only 6 percent of females. On the other hand, 7 percent of males and 45 percent of females were clerical workers. Professional and technical work constituted the largest major occupational group for Jewish males (31 percent) and the second largest for females (28 percent). Men were also relatively more numerous in sales and production.

The occupational profiles of different age groups reflected the significant socioeconomic structural changes within the Jewish population over the past decades. Passing from older to younger age groups, the proportion employed in professional and technical occupations generally increased. The same occurred with administrative and service occupations, the latter also including managerial posts. On the other hand, consistent declines related to age appeared in the once dominant sales sector (from 33 percent of employed Jews aged 65 to 14 percent at ages 15–29), in the small blue-collar production sector, and among the few Jews in agriculture. The comparatively large proportion of Jews in clerical occupations and the low share of administrators among the 15–29 age group reflected for many a stage of entrance into the labor force that would be followed by movement to higher occupational categories.

Some minor variations in the occupational distributions of the six major Jewish communities may be observed in table 28. The single most salient difference was that in Pretoria, the administrative capital of South Africa, 13 percent of Jews were in service occupations, compared with 4 percent for all Jews nationally. As might be expected, few Jews in the metropolitan areas were engaged in agriculture, while farmers constituted a small but visible (6 percent) share of the Jewish labor force in smaller towns and rural areas. These small communities also featured comparatively high proportions of Jews in sales, services, and production, and relatively low proportions in professional, administrative, and clerical occupations. The highest percentage of professional and technical workers was in Cape Town (32 percent); Durban had the highest share of administrators and managers (21 percent); Johannesburg the highest clerical concentration (23 percent); and Port Elizabeth the highest proportion of sales workers (31 percent).

WORK STATUS

A relatively large percentage of the Jewish labor force was made up by employers, including the self-employed. According to the 1980 census, 25 percent of all economically active Jews and 34 percent of Jewish males were employers. The comparable figures for whites were 11 percent for both sexes and 14 percent for males. Looking first at the relationship between occupation and work status (table 29), the two extremes were agriculture, where over 80 percent of Jews were independent farmers, and clerical occupations, in which over 97 percent were employees. In each of the other occupational branches, the proportion of Jewish employers ranged between 35 percent (sales) and 24 percent (services).

Variation in work status by sex and age was significant and reflected the occupational differences already noted. Being an employer was over three times more frequent among males than among females (see table 30). A more interesting feature, however, was the constant decline in the proportion of employers from the older to the younger age groups. Along with life-cycle effects, this reflected a turn from small, family-owned businesses in trade and manufacturing to employee status in large business corporations, professional firms, and public administration. These changes, which directly stem from the much increased educational level of the younger generation, carry significant implications for the position of Jews in the general socioeconomic fabric of South Africa. These same factors probably also account for the 3-percent decrease in the proportion of Jewish employers between 1970 and 1980.

While the proportion of Jewish employers was quite similar in the different metropolitan areas, it was lowest in Johannesburg. In part this may be due to the fact that most public companies are based in Johannesburg, and while Jews may be employed in high-status positions there, they are nevertheless employees in those firms. Secondly, it may be that occupational opportunities in Johannesburg attract many young Jews, who are at the start of their careers, from the smaller centers. Interestingly, Port Elizabeth had a significantly higher proportion of employers than the other larger centers. This is consistent with the large number of Jews who classified themselves as sales workers. These people were probably owners of small shops and reflected an earlier developmental stage in the economic structure of South African Jews. A similar situation, in all likelihood, prevailed in the smaller centers.

INDUSTRY AND TYPE OF EMPLOYER

Turning now to the various economic branches, table 31 shows that Jews were heavily overrepresented in trade (33 percent), finance (20 percent), services (23 percent), and manufacturing (19 percent). Somewhat paradoxically, given their large involvement in trade, only 22 percent of Jews defined themselves as sales workers (see table 29), despite the fact that about 40 percent of the Jewish labor force was employed in sales occupations and/or in the trade sector. The probability is that owners of, or workers in, medium-sized businesses may have preferred to describe themselves as managers and administrators. What is of particular importance, however, is that Jewish participation in manufacturing (according to more detailed data not presented here) is, more often, as owners—17 percent against 4 percent for all whites—or administrators, rather than as production workers. This gives Jews a pivotal position in the manufacturing industry. The role of Jews as large employers of black labor in industry and trade, especially in the Johannesburg and Witwatersrand areas, could also have important and possibly negative implications for black attitudes during the present period of economic and political upheaval.

About 86 percent of economically active Jews were employed in private business enterprises, including public shareholder corporations, as against 11 percent overall employed by the government and other public authorities, and 3 percent employed by nonprofit organizations (see table 31). With only a few exceptions, private employment, including corporations, was predominant in each industrial branch. Thus, the proportion in the private sector ranged from over 99 percent of Jews in finance and trade to over 95 percent in manufacturing, construction, and agriculture, over 80 percent in transport, and 42 percent in services. In the latter branch, central government and provincial and local authorities constituted the main employers (44 percent), with nonprofit organizations employing 13 percent (see bottom line of table 31). Public-authority corporations were significant employers only in the small transport branch.

From the point of view of type of employer, it appears that the central government and the provincial and local authorities and nonprofit organizations were almost exclusively concentrated in the services branch, while public utilities—mainly gas, water, and electricity suppliers—appeared as employers in transport and manufacturing. With regard to the private business sector, 38 percent of economically active Jews were employed in trade, followed by finance (23 percent), and manufacturing (21 percent) (see upper part of table 31).

The basic characteristics of the Jewish labor force, by type of employer, did not vary substantially by sex, age, or place of residence (see table 32). Jewish women worked more often than men for provincial administrations and nonprofit organizations, but still almost 80 percent of those employed worked in the private sector. A steady increase in the propensity to work for government and other public authorities appeared among younger adults, reaching 20 percent among the 15–29 age group. This was mainly the result of the concentration in Pretoria of a group of highly trained young professionals and administrators attracted by employment opportunities with the central government. But even in Pretoria the overwhelming majority of young adults was employed in private business enterprises.

In comparison with the United States and other Western communities, the proportion of South African Jews with a university education or in professional occupations was not particularly high in 1980. There probably remains substantial room for further socioeconomic mobility in the same direction as has been experienced over the last decades. There is, however, one area in which some alteration in the previous pattern of occupational mobility might be expected. Given the increasing tendency in South Africa toward large corporations, many Jewish family businesses have become public companies with boards of directors, salaried executives, and, frequently, large minority shareholders. Thus, whereas previously a son could expect favorable employment in his father's store or factory, with the possibility of eventually taking over, these expectations have now been modified by the more complex and competitive administrative structure of the large public corporations. It is possible that in future years the upward occupational mobility of Jews—which has already slowed in relation to the general population—may show a leveling-off trend, although this will not be precisely reflected in occupational and work-status categories as used in the census.[68]

INCOME

Income levels reflect the differences in socioeconomic stratification of Jews and total whites. According to the 1980 census, 68 percent of Jews and total whites aged 15 and over reported some income (table 33). Of these, Jews reported a median annual per capita income of 8,323 South African rands (worth US $6,658 in 1980), vs. 6,139 rands ($4,911) among total whites—36 percent more. Among total whites the rural population had a slightly higher average income than urban residents, which points to the relatively prosperous economic situation of white farmers in South Africa. Among Jews, professionals and administrators had higher incomes than workers in other occupations; at peak career ages (45–64), the median income of Jewish professionals was 35 percent higher than that of total Jews with some income.

ASPECTS OF JEWISH COMMUNITY LIFE

Jewish Identification

While an analysis of demographic characteristics and trends is basic to an understanding of past growth and future prospects of any population, these demographic features are themselves closely bound up with a wide range of values, attitudes, and behavior. These last-mentioned factors are

[68]Mervin Cohen and Allie A. Dubb, "Some Socio-Economic Aspects of the South African Jewish Population According to the Official Census of 1970," in U. O. Schmelz, P. Glikson, and S. DellaPergola, eds., *Papers in Jewish Demography, 1973* (Jerusalem, 1977), 149–70.

especially relevant in any discussion of the patterns of continuity and cohesion of a religious-ethnic community. Brief reference has already been made to some aspects of formal community organization among South African Jews, as well as to the issues of assimilation and mixed marriage. In this section we will discuss some of the ways in which Jews identify themselves as such and as part of a Jewish community.

The 1974 survey, which included several questions on religious observance, showed that over 80 percent of Jewish households lit Sabbath candles, participated in some kind of Passover seder and/or fasted on Yom Kippur.[69] Between one-half and two-thirds observed at least some of the dietary laws, had a festive meal on Friday nights, and/or, where relevant, celebrated bar/bat mitzvah. Moreover, in over one-third of the households one or more members attended synagogue on the Sabbath, which in the majority of cases referred specifically to the Friday-night service. Only 9 percent described themselves as "fully observant."

These findings match those of an in-depth study of Jewish identification conducted on a sample of Johannesburg Jews in 1968.[70] Both studies suggest, therefore, that select public and family-oriented rituals are most commonly observed, whereas private rituals, such as regular prayer or *tefillin* are performed only by very observant Jews. Similarly, those public and private rituals which require greater effort or commitment—full Sabbath observance, meticulous adherence to dietary laws, rules regarding "family purity," and the like—are also neglected by most Jews. The 1968 study also indicated that the combination of rituals observed by any individual or within a household tended to be arbitrary and idiosyncratic. Furthermore, apart from the completely nonreligious and nonobservant, on the one hand, and the fully observant, on the other, there was no strong relationship between the degree of religious belief and actual observance. The conclusion from the 1968 study was that religious observance, including attendance at Friday-evening and festival synagogue services, was primarily a means of identifying as Jews, rather than an expression of religiosity.

The most significant aspect of Jewish identification among Johannesburg Jews, according to the 1968 study, was in the area of social relations. Thus, three-quarters of the respondents were members (paying and nonpaying) of a synagogue,[71] although less than one-quarter attended services at least once a week. Clearly synagogue affiliation was an important means of formally identifying with the community. Informal social relations were also

---

[69]SAJPS Advance Report no. 11, *Religion and Religious Observance.*

[70]Dubb, *Jewish South Africans.* Based on a sample of 283 Jews.

[71]In the 1974 survey, for six major metropolitan areas almost 90 percent were paying or nonpaying members. See SAJPS Advance Report no. 12, *Jewish Community Activities.*

important: 83 percent of the respondents had only Jews among their closest friends, while 87 percent had only or mostly Jewish acquaintances. In addition, 45 percent said that all their business associates were Jewish, and another 13 percent indicated that most were Jewish. An important conclusion that emerged from the study was that, in Johannesburg at least, it was perceived as being advantageous, both socially and economically, to be Jewish and that this perception was supported by reality.[72]

Jewish Education

As in other Jewish communities in the West, the main source of Jewish education in South Africa was, for a long time, the afternoon *heder* or some other part-time arrangement. Of all Jews over the age of 15 in 1974, some 70 percent had received a Jewish education in part-time classes, with only 10 percent having attended day schools (table 34). Thus, although over 80 percent had received some Jewish education, the level attained was, on the whole, fairly low, with no more than 17 percent having continued for a while after bar/bat-mitzvah—mostly on a part-time basis—and only 9 percent having taken Jewish studies/Hebrew as a matriculation subject.[73] Until the establishment of a teachers' seminary in 1945, the only facilities for postsecondary or advanced studies were in the university Hebrew departments, and these attracted few Jews. The first yeshivah was started in Johannesburg in the 1960s.

Although day schools for Jewish pupils had been established in the earlier period, the first serious attempt by the community to set up a regular school that would provide not only a Jewish milieu but also Jewish studies as an obligatory and integral part of the curriculum was made in Johannesburg in the mid-1940s, with the opening of the King David School. Over the years the day-school movement expanded, and by 1981-82 there were 24 primary and secondary schools in six centers (table 35). In contrast, the *heder* system had declined in the cities and remained important mainly in the small and dwindling outlying communities.

The First Census of Jewish Schools in the Diaspora, conducted between 1981 and 1983, provides a picture of the current state of Jewish education in South Africa.[74] In 1981-82 a total of 146 schools with 14,300 pupils were

[72]Dubb, *Jewish South Africans,* 92ff.

[73]SAJPS Advance Report no. 12, *Jewish Community Activities.*

[74]Sponsored by the Joint Program for Jewish Education of the State of Israel's Ministry for Education and Culture, the Jewish Agency for Israel, and the World Zionist Organization. See Genuth, DellaPergola, and Dubb, *First Census of Jewish Schools 1981/2–1982/3,* and unpublished data.

affiliated with two boards of education—the larger in Johannesburg and the smaller in Cape Town. This represents a total enrollment of about 55 out of every 100 Jewish children between the ages 3–17. Of these, only 8 out of 100—a total of 2,224 pupils—were enrolled in supplementary schools (*hadarim*). Of the remainder, 3,765 attended Jewish nursery schools and 8,311 Jewish day schools. Although overall enrollments in the two main cities and in the rest of the country were similar, the distribution differed; the *hadarim* had the highest proportion (one-third) of postnursery enrollment in the smaller centers. In Johannesburg one-fifth of primary- and secondary-school pupils attended afternoon schools, while in Cape Town the proportion in these schools was only 6 percent. It is also noteworthy that, unlike the situation in the United States and several other countries, there appears to be little fall-off between lower and higher grades (1st to 6th and 7th to 12th, respectively) in day schools, so that enrollment at the two levels is quite similar.

An important feature of the Jewish educational system in South Africa, as compared with that in many other Diaspora communities, is the strength of Jewish nursery schools. Indeed, the Jewish community has played an important role in the development of the nursery-school movement in South Africa and, in many places, provides the best available facilities. These facilities are, in most cases, open to non-Jews as well; in 1982 these pupils constituted 20 percent of the total enrollment in Jewish nursery schools. Of all Jewish children of nursery-school age (3–5 years), about 80 percent attended these schools.

While there have always been non-Jewish pupils in Jewish nursery schools, less than 1 percent of day-school pupils were not Jewish in 1981/82. Since then, however, the numbers and proportions have increased considerably. In the smaller centers, the declining number of Jews has made it essential to open the day schools to non-Jews in order to ensure their continued viability. In one of these centers—Port Elizabeth—over 40 percent of pupils in 1987 were not Jewish.

By 1987, due at least partly to emigration and to the falling birthrate, enrollment of Jewish children in Jewish nursery and day schools had fallen by 24 percent and 16 percent, respectively.[75]

In the 1981-82 school census, some 991 teaching posts were reported. Of these, 160 were for Jewish studies in day schools and a further 101 posts were in *hadarim*. Overall, over two-thirds of Jewish-studies teachers in day schools and three-quarters of the teachers in *hadarim* were women, who

[75]Allie A. Dubb, "Emigration, Population Change and Jewish Education in South Africa in the Eighties," in U.O. Schmelz and S. DellaPergola, eds., *Papers in Jewish Demography 1985* (Jerusalem, forthcoming).

also comprised 81 percent of general-studies teachers. Two-thirds of Jewish-studies teachers in day schools had some postsecondary Jewish education and 15 percent were ordained rabbis.

All the day schools in South Africa were Orthodox, as were over 90 percent of the nursery schools. The remaining 6 percent of nursery schools, as well as 12 percent of *hadarim,* were affiliated with the Reform movement. It should be pointed out that the actual orientation of most of the day schools in South Africa is locally defined as "national traditional"; there are also one modern Orthodox school (in the American sense) and two small *haredi* (ultra-Orthodox) schools. The average number of hours of schooling, in particular of Jewish studies, was lower than in most other countries of the Diaspora: out of an average 26 hours a week of schooling in the three lowest grades on the primary level, 6 hours per week were devoted to Jewish studies. The weekly number of hours increased in the three highest grades of secondary school to a total of 32 hours, with 9 hours of Jewish studies.

SUMMARY AND CONCLUSION

The sociodemographic profile of South African Jewry is similar in its broad outlines to that of the Jewish populations in other Western countries. Most Jews had arrived in South Africa from Eastern Europe as part of the mass migrations which began in the last decades of the nineteenth century. Now, a century later, the community is overwhelmingly native-born, highly acculturated to the host society, largely middle- to upper-middle class, relatively better educated than the rest of the population, and concentrated in the professions and other white-collar occupations.

Compared with the total white population, of which they are a part, Jews are an aging population, with a significantly lower (and declining) birthrate, a high life expectancy, and, because of the age structure, a considerable death rate; they also marry later and have a greater proportion who remain unmarried. Jews are an essentially urban population, gravitating toward the major metropolitan areas, where, in general, they have tended to form distinct residential concentrations.

There are, however, certain characteristics of the South African Jewish community that distinguish it from most others in the Western Diaspora. Thus, an increase in age at marriage, a tendency not to marry at all, a decline in family size, and an increasingly unfavorable balance of births and deaths have all appeared later and developed at a slower pace among South African Jewry. It is the only Western Diaspora community in which fertility was still probably above replacement level as recently as 10–15 years ago.

Moreover, South African Jews are not as educated or as highly professionalized as, for example, Jews in the United States.

It is on the community level, however, that the uniqueness of the Jewish population in South Africa is most clearly evident. South African Jewry has a highly centralized structure, with a number of national institutions responsible for funding, planning, and organizing facilities and activities in the fields of education, religious life, welfare, and Zionism. In terms of Jewish identity, the particular kind of pluralism of South African society has minimized both the need for, and the possibility of, large-scale assimilation, while at the same time lending legitimacy to the preservation of a distinctive Jewish ethnic identity. Consistent with this, Jews themselves exhibit a high level of commitment to the local community, Israel, and the Jewish people as a whole. This is expressed primarily in a well-developed Jewish educational network, wide-scale synagogue affiliation, and strong support for Zionism.

The issue of Jewish continuity is an important one throughout the Diaspora. Whereas, however, in Europe and North America the focus is, primarily, on an excess of deaths over births and increasing losses through outmarriage and assimilation, the problem in South Africa is different and more immediate. Since the mid-1970s the country has been in a state of tension and turmoil as a result of black uprisings, riots, and strikes. As the situation has become increasingly serious—and with every sign that blacks are determined to continue the struggle at whatever cost—growing numbers of whites have been leaving the country. With regard to Jews, it is estimated that about 14,000 left South Africa between 1970–1979 (mostly as from 1976), and had it not been for a relatively large number of returnees, as well as relatively large-scale immigration from Zimbabwe, the United Kingdom, Western Europe, and Israel, the Jewish community would have been severely depleted. As it is, these migratory movements significantly affected the demographic and social structure of the Jewish population during the 1970s. In addition, there are indications that the quality of community life suffered through these sociodemographic transformations.

After a period of reduced activity, blacks once again stepped up antigovernment action in the mid-1980s, and this led to another peak in white—and Jewish—emigration, as well as reduced immigration. It is probable that the Jewish rate of emigration will continue to be higher than that of whites in general, for two reasons. In the first place, Jews are relatively better educated and are concentrated in those occupations that are more easily transferable. Secondly, increasing numbers of Jews may begin to feel that the future will be worse for them than for other whites as a consequence of black anti-Semitism and anti-Zionism.

The sociodemographic future of South African Jewry is, then, difficult to predict. While the present balance of internal demographic and identificational factors points to the beginning of a moderate decline in Jewish population size, the crucial factor of external migrations escapes simple projections based on assumed continuation of "present trends." The number and composition of South African Jews will depend, above all, on political developments in the country and on the ways in which Jews respond to them.

APPENDIX

TABLE 1. POPULATION OF SOUTH AFRICA, BY RELIGION, ETHNIC GROUP, AND WHITE LINGUISTIC GROUPS, 1980

Religious Denomination	Total	Whites, According to Home Language				Coloreds	Asians	Blacks
		Total[a]	Afri-kaans	English	Bilingual			
Total no.[b]	25,016	4,551	2,465	1,610	233	2,624	819	17,022
Row %	100.0	18.2	9.9	6.4	0.9	10.5	3.3	68.0
Column %	100.0	100.0	100.0	100.0	100.0	100.0	100.0	100.0
Dutch Reformed churches	15.9	45.8	78.8	2.5	36.3	26.1	0.5	7.1
Anglican churches	6.6	10.1	0.5	26.4	7.5	13.8	1.0	4.8
Methodist	8.9	9.3	1.3	21.0	19.0	5.7	0.5	9.7
Presbyterian, Congregational	4.1	3.4	0.4	8.2	4.7	7.4	0.4	3.9
Lutheran	3.6	1.0	0.2	0.7	0.6	3.9	0.1	4.4
Roman Catholic	9.6	8.5	0.6	15.4	6.3	10.2	2.5	10.2
Apostolic	3.1	6.1	9.3	1.8	8.0	9.8	0.5	1.3
African Independent churches	20.8	—	—	—	—	3.1	—	30.1
Other Christian	5.5	8.5	6.0	10.2	11.5	8.5	6.9	4.2
Jewish/Hebrew	0.5	2.6	0.0	6.8	0.8	0.0	0.0	0.0
Islam	1.4	0.0	0.0	0.1	0.0	6.7	20.2	0.1
Buddhism, Confucianism, Hinduism	2.2	0.0	0.0	0.1	0.0	0.1	64.2	0.1
Other or no religion	2.4	1.2	0.5	2.1	1.6	0.8	0.7	3.1
Object to state	2.7	0.8	0.3	1.5	1.0	0.5	0.5	3.7
Unspecified	12.7	2.7	2.1	3.2	2.7	3.4	2.0	17.3

Source: South Africa Central Statistical Services, *Population Census 80, Social Characteristics,* Report no. 02-80-12 (Pretoria, 1985).

[a]Including linguistic groups other than Afrikaans and English.

[b]Thousands.

TABLE 2. THE JEWISH POPULATION OF SOUTH AFRICA, 1880–1986

Year	Total Population	Total Whites	Total Jews	Whites as % of Total Population	Jews as % of: Total Population	Jews as % of: Total Whites
1880[a]	n.a.	474,309	4,000	n.a.	n.a.	0.8
1904[b]	5,174,827	1,116,806	38,101	21.6	0.7	3.4
1911	5,972,757	1,276,242	46,919	21.4	0.8	3.7
1918[c]	n.a.	1,421,781	58,741	n.a.	n.a.	4.1
1921	6,927,403	1,519,488	62,103	21.9	0.9	4.1
1926[c]	n.a.	1,676,660	71,816	n.a.	n.a.	4.3
1936	9,587,863	2,003,857	90,645	20.9	0.9	4.5
1946	11,415,925	2,372,690	104,156	20.8	0.9	4.4
1951	12,671,452	2,641,689	108,497	20.8	0.9	4.1
1960	15,994,000	3,077,699	114,762	19.2	0.7	3.7
1970	21,447,982	3,773,282	118,200	17.6	0.6	3.1
1980[d]	25,016,525	4,551,068	117,963	18.2	0.5	2.6
1986[e]	28,400,000	4,900,000	115,000	17.3	0.4	2.3

Sources: Unless otherwise noted, all figures in this and subsequent tables are based on official census results published by South Africa Central Statistical Services (formerly Department of Statistics). The figures for Total Population include blacks, Asians, and coloreds (people of mixed race) as well as whites. Because of difficulties in enumerating blacks, in particular, total population figures are underestimates, especially in earlier censuses.

[a]Estimate of total whites for 1880 is the midpoint between 328,000—an unreferenced figure for 1875 quoted by Gustav Saron and Louis Hotz in *The Jews of South Africa* (Johannesburg, 1955), 85, and 620,619—the 1890–91 total for the two Crown Colonies (Cape and Natal) and the two Boer Republics (Transvaal and Orange Free State) published in the *Official Year Book* of 1910–1922. Estimate of Jews in 1880 from Saron and Hotz, 89. No estimate of the total population is available.

[b]Official census of the two Crown Colonies and two Boer Republics after the Anglo-Boer War. First census after Union was in 1911.

[c]The 1918 and 1926 censuses were of whites only.

[d]Between 1976 and 1979, three former black homelands (reservations)—Transkei, Bophuthatswana, and Venda—were granted independence by the government of South Africa and were therefore excluded from the 1980 census. After 1980 a further homeland, Ciskei, was granted independence, and its population has been excluded from all population estimates since 1982 as well as from the 1985 census. The exclusion of these former homelands has not affected the white, colored, or Asian populations significantly, except to increase their proportions within the reduced borders of the republic.

[e]Total and white population figures from South Africa Central Statistical Services, "Mid-Year Estimates: 1970–1986." The UN, which does not recognize the independence of the former homelands, has estimated the total South African population at 32,392,000. Jewish population estimate from U.O. Schmelz and Sergio DellaPergola, "World Jewish Population, 1986," AJYB, vol. 88, 1988.

Note: "n.a." indicates data not available.

TABLE 3. GROWTH OF JEWISH AND TOTAL WHITE POPULATIONS, 1880–1980

	Intercensal Change			
	Jews			Total Whites
Period	No.	Total %	Annual %	Annual %
1880–1904	34,101	852.5	9.8	3.6
1904–1911	8,818	23.1	3.0	1.9
1911–1918	11,822	25.2	3.3	1.6
1918–1921	3,362	5.7	1.9	2.2
1921–1926	9,713	15.6	2.9	2.0
1926–1936	18,829	26.2	2.4	1.8
1936–1946	13,511	14.9	1.4	1.7
1946–1951	4,341	4.2	0.8	2.2
1951–1960	6,265	5.8	0.6	1.7
1960–1970	3,438	3.0	0.3	2.1
1970–1980	−237	−0.2	−0.02	1.9

TABLE 4. JEWISH IMMIGRANTS TO SOUTH AFRICA, BY COUNTRY OF BIRTH, SEX, AND AGE, 1924–1948

	1924–1932	1933–1939	1940–1948
Total no.	13,880	9,070	1,895
% of total white immigrants	27.9	22.8	3.3
Country of Birth			
Total %	100.0	100.0	100.0
Quota countries[a]	88.5	30.4	18.4
Lithuania	55.5	15.2	5.6
Latvia	10.8	4.6	2.5
Poland	16.3	8.5	6.7
Russia[b]	5.9	2.1	3.6
Nonquota countries[a]	11.5	69.6	81.6
United Kingdom[c]	5.4	5.3	49.7
Germany	0.6	58.8	10.8
Other	5.5	1.3	20.9
Sex			
% Males	58.9	49.8	45.1
Age at Immigration			
Total %	100.0	100.0	100.0
0–14	20.0	17.6	15.9
15–29	47.1	34.6	23.6
30–44	23.8	25.5	31.8
45–64	7.8	16.3	20.7
65+	1.3	6.0	8.0
Median age	24.4	29.4	34.5

Sources: SAJPS Advance Report no. 4, *Country of Birth and Period of Immigration;* Stuart Buxbaum, "A Profile of Jewish Immigration to South Africa Between 1924–1948 and Its Impact Upon the Local Community," in U. O. Schmelz, P. Glikson, and S. DellaPergola, eds., *Papers in Jewish Demography 1981* (Jerusalem, 1983), 145–62.

[a]See explanation in the text.

[b]Including other quota countries.

[c]Including other British Empire.

TABLE 5. JEWISH EMIGRANTS FROM SOUTH AFRICA TO PALESTINE/ISRAEL, 1919–1987

	Born in South Africa		Resident in South Africa		
Year	Total (A)	Yearly Average (B)	Total (C)	Yearly Average (D)	Ratio (A)/(C) %
1919–1923	0	0			
1924–1931[a]	61	8			
1932–1938[a]	125	18			
1939–1945	49	7			
1946–5/14/1948	30	12			
5/15/1948–1949	406	271			
1950–1954	386	77	447	89	86
1955–1959	520	104	661	132	79
1960–1964	1,131	226	1,252	250	90
1965–1969	1,467	293	1,719	344	85
1970–1974	2,747	549	3,064	613	90
1975–1976	869	435	1,000	500	87
1977–1979	3,283	1,094	3,829	1,276	86
1980–1982	788	263	837	279	94
1983–1984	574	287	605	303	95
1985–1986	758	379	811	406	93
1987	707	707	737	737	96

Sources: Moshe Sicron, *Immigration to Israel (1948–1953), Statistical Supplement,* Israel Central Bureau of Statistics, Special Series no. 60, and Falk Project for Economic Research in Israel (Jerusalem, 1957); Israel Central Bureau of Statistics, *Statistical Abstract of Israel* (Jerusalem, annual publication).

[a]Figures for 1924–1934 relate to South African citizens.

TABLE 6. ESTIMATED POPULATION CHANGES AMONG JEWS AND TOTAL WHITES, 1970–1980

Components of Change	Jews[a] No.	Jews[a] Yearly Rate per 1,000	Total Whites[b] Yearly Rate per 1,000
Population in 1970	118,200		3,773,300
Internal change, 1970–1980			
Total	+4,200	+3.5	+11.4
Births	18,700	15.8	19.7
Deaths	14,500	12.3	8.3
External migrations, 1970–1980			
Total	−4,400	−3.7	+4.8
Immigrants	9,600[c]	8.1	7.8
Emigrants	14,000	11.8	3.0
Total change, 1970–1980	−200	−0.2	+18.7
Population in 1980	118,000		4,551,100

[a]Rough estimates, medium hypothesis. See text for explanations.
[b]Rates for total whites do not add and are reported here as they appear in the original official publication. See South Africa Central Statistical Services, *Births: Whites, Coloureds and Asians, 1983,* Report no. 07-01-11 (Pretoria, 1985).
[c]Including return migrants.

TABLE 7. JEWISH AND TOTAL WHITE POPULATIONS, BY COUNTRY OF BIRTH, 1926–1980 (PERCENT)

Year	Total	Born in South Africa	Foreign Born
Jews			
1926	100.0	45.0	55.0
1970	100.0	76.7	23.3
1980[a]	100.0	79.1	20.9
1980, by age:			
0–14	100.0	93.9	6.1
15–29	100.0	90.7	9.3
30–44	100.0	85.4	14.6
45–64	100.0	73.8	26.2
65+	100.0	45.6	54.4
Total whites			
1926	100.0	85.0	15.0
1970	100.0	89.0	11.0
1980	100.0	87.0	13.0

[a]Authors' processing of census file for the six major metropolitan areas of Jewish residence: Cape Town, Port Elizabeth, Durban, Pretoria, Johannesburg, and Germiston. In 1980, 91.5 percent of all Jews lived in these areas.

TABLE 8. JEWISH POPULATION, BY BIRTHPLACE, 1970 AND 1980

Birthplace	Jews 1970 No.	Jews 1970 %	Jews 1980[a] No.	Jews 1980[a] %	Whites 1980 %
Total	118,120	100.0	108,007	100.0	100.0
South Africa	89,950	76.2	85,725	79.4	87.3
Zimbabwe	1,220	1.0	1,830	1.7	1.1
Other Africa	1,120	1.0	949	0.9	2.6
United Kingdom and Eire	5,110	4.3	4,402	4.1	4.7
Germany (W and E), Austria	3,030	2.6	2,358	2.2	0.8
Rest Western Europe[b]	290	0.2	1,250	1.1	2.4
Lithuania			3,592	3.3	0.1
Latvia and Estonia			227	0.2	0.0
USSR	13,250	11.2	2,622	2.4	0.1
Poland			1,719	1.6	0.1
Rest Eastern Europe			473	0.4	0.2
Israel[c]	2,590	2.2	1,830	1.7	0.0
Other Asia			288	0.3	0.2
Americas	580	0.5	514	0.5	0.2
Australasia	130	0.1	123	0.1	0.2
Unknown	850	0.7	105	0.1	0.0

[a]Six major metropolitan areas, authors' processing.
[b]Includes other unspecified European countries.
[c]In the full 1980 census returns, 2,261 persons stated that they were born in Israel. This figure includes non-Jewish persons.

TABLE 9. JEWISH POPULATION, BY COUNTRY OF BIRTH AND AGE, 1980[a]

Age	Born in South Africa	Foreign Born						
		Total	Other Africa	United Kingdom	Other Western Europe	Eastern Europe	Israel	Other
Total no.	85,843	22,524	3,021	4,402	3,212	9,020	1,830	1,030
Total %	100.0	100.0	100.0	100.0	100.0	100.0	100.0	100.0
0–9	16.3	3.7	5.5	2.5	0.8	0.2	23.3	8.3
10–19	17.3	5.5	17.2	6.1	0.7	0.5	15.6	9.0
20–29	16.7	6.8	26.5	5.8	1.8	0.8	13.0	10.3
30–39	14.8	9.6	20.3	12.4	6.4	2.7	21.3	15.3
40–49	10.6	7.1	10.9	12.1	8.2	2.7	7.8	8.7
50–59	9.6	15.5	7.8	11.3	16.5	21.6	7.8	13.3
60–69	9.3	19.2	7.6	18.8	30.8	22.8	3.8	15.5
70+	5.4	32.6	4.2	31.1	34.8	48.7	7.4	19.5
Median age	29.8	61.0	30.4	59.8	65.1	69.4	28.5	48.2

[a]Six major metropolitan areas, authors' processing.

TABLE 10. JEWISH POPULATION, BY CITIZENSHIP, 1970 AND 1980

Citizenship	Jews 1970 No.	Jews 1970 %	Jews 1980[a] No.	Jews 1980[a] %	Whites 1980 %
Total	118,120	100.0	108,007	100.0	100.0
South Africa	112,100	94.9	100,488	93.0	91.3
Zimbabwe	690	0.6	978	0.9	0.5
Other Africa			132	0.1	0.9
United Kingdom and Eire	2,520	2.2	2,630	2.4	3.9
Germany (W and E), Austria	260	0.2	206	0.2	0.6
Rest Western Europe[b]			859	0.8	2.2
Eastern Europe	440	0.4	299	0.3	0.1
Israel[c]			1,699	1.6	0.1
Other Asia	1,810	1.5	76	0.1	0.1
Americas			465	0.4	0.2
Australasia			96	0.1	0.1
Unknown	300	0.2	79	0.1	0.0

[a]Six major metropolitan areas, authors' processing.
[b]Includes other unspecified European countries.
[c]In the full 1980 census returns, 1,927 persons stated that they were Israeli citizens. This figure includes non-Jewish persons.

TABLE 11. JEWISH AND TOTAL WHITE POPULATIONS, BY HOME LANGUAGE, 1936–1980 (PERCENT)

Year	Total %	English	Afrikaans	Afrikaans and English	Yiddish or Hebrew[a]	English and Yiddish or Hebrew[a]	Other
Jews							
1936	100.0	76.0	2.0	1.0	19.0	n.a.	2.0
1974	100.0	88.4	0.0	1.9	1.8	6.9	1.0
1980	100.0	92.3	0.8	1.5	b	b	5.4[c]
Total whites							
1980	100.0	35.4	54.2	5.1	b	b	5.3[d]

[a]In the census of 1936 there were 17,686 people whose home language was Yiddish, in 1946 there were 14,045, and in 1951 there were 9,970. In subsequent censuses, Yiddish was no longer treated as a separate category. Yiddish and Hebrew were combined in the 1974 survey.
[b]Neither Yiddish nor Hebrew were tabulated.
[c]Thereof 1.1 percent described as "Western European Languages" and 4.3 percent as "Other Languages." Both Yiddish and Hebrew were presumably included in the second category.
[d]Thereof 3.3 percent described as "Western European" and 2.0 percent as "Other."
Note: "n.a." indicates data not available.

TABLE 12. JEWISH POPULATION, BY PROVINCE, 1904–1980

Province	Jews						Whites	Jews as % of Whites	
	1904	1911	1936	1960	1970	1980	1980	1904	1980
Total no.	38,101	46,919	90,645	114,762	118,200	117,963	4,551,068[a]		
Total %	100.0	100.0	100.0	100.0	100.0	100.0	100.0	3.4	2.6
Cape	51.2	35.7	31.1	28.0	27.1	27.5	28.0	3.4	2.6
Natal	3.9	3.1	4.1	5.4	5.7	5.5	12.4	1.5	1.2
Transvaal	40.7	55.2	59.5	63.8	65.3	65.9	52.4	5.2	3.3
Orange Free State	4.2	6.0	5.3	2.8	1.9	1.1	7.2	1.1	0.4

[a]27,329 whites, or 0.6 percent of the total, were living in the black homelands (reservations) in 1980. Thus percentages of whites in each province have been calculated from the base 4,523,739.

TABLE 13. JEWISH POPULATION, BY METROPOLITAN AREA, 1918–1980[a]

Metropolitan Area	Jews 1918	Jews 1926	Jews 1946	Jews 1960	Jews 1970	Jews 1980	Whites 1980	Jews as % of Whites 1980
Total no.	58,741	71,816	104,156	114,762	118,200	117,963	4,551,068	2.6
Total %	100.0	100.0	100.0	100.0	100.0	100.0	100.0	
Johannesburg[b]	34.2	36.0	48.4	51.6	53.7	57.5	17.2	12.1[c]
Thereof: Germiston	n.a.	n.a.	n.a.	1.2	5.1	2.9	5.5	1.4
Cape Town	15.5	16.3	18.8	19.8	21.7	22.9	10.3	5.7
Durban	2.8	3.4	4.0	4.7	5.1	5.0	7.0	1.8
Pretoria	2.9	3.3	3.3	3.1	3.2	2.9	9.2	0.8
Port Elizabeth	2.0	2.1	2.4	2.6	2.4	2.1	4.1	1.3
Bloemfontein	1.6	1.9	1.2	1.0	1.0	0.6	2.1	0.7
East Rand[d]	n.a.	n.a.	n.a.	3.3	2.5	2.0	6.2	1.1
West Rand[d]	n.a.	n.a.	n.a.	1.7	1.9	1.1	4.7	0.6
East London	0.7	0.9	0.9	0.9	0.7	0.5	1.5	0.9
Rest of country	40.3	36.1	21.0	11.3	7.8	5.4	37.7	0.3

[a]Boundaries of metropolitan areas in 1980 have been adjusted, as far as possible, for consistency with those for 1960 and 1970. For this reason there are minor discrepancies between this and other tabulations referring to metropolitan areas. The term "metropolitan areas" in Department of Statistics and other published reports refers to several large urban-industrial complexes, each of which comprises one central city plus one or more contiguous smaller cities and/or towns. In some publications, reference is made to the "PWV area," which combines Johannesburg with Pretoria, the East and West Rand, Germiston, Vereeniging, and van der Bijl Park.

[b]Including Germiston. The increase in the number of Germiston Jews between 1960–1970 is probably due to the inclusion of some of Johannesburg's eastern suburbs in the Germiston census district. The subsequent decrease between 1970–1980 may be partly due to further redefinition of districts as well as to a real decline in the Jewish community of Germiston proper. For these reasons Johannesburg and Germiston have been regarded as a single metropolitan area for the purposes of this table. It should also be noted that the towns of Sandton and Randburg are also regarded as part of the Johannesburg metropolitan area and are treated as such in the census tabulations.

[c]Johannesburg only: Jews and total whites in Germiston census district are excluded.

[d]East Rand and West Rand include all the smaller towns and cities on the Witwatersrand goldfields outside of the Johannesburg/Germiston conurbation. For the years 1918 to 1946 they are included in the category "Rest of Country."

Note: "n.a." indicates data not available.

TABLE 14. JEWISH POPULATION IN JOHANNESBURG, BY AREA OF RESIDENCE, 1960–1980

Residential Area[a]	1960 No.	1960 %	1960 % of Total Whites	1980 No.	1980 %	1980 % of Total Whites
Total	55,613	100.0	14.0	63,204	100.0	12.9
Southern	841	1.5	1.3	430	0.7	0.5
South-Eastern	4,329	7.8	7.1	1,390	2.2	3.1
South-Western	380	0.7	0.6	346	0.5	0.6
Central[b]	15,551	28.0	25.8	11,679	18.5	17.8
Eastern	16,761	30.1	40.3	25,802	40.8	39.0
Western	5,359	9.6	24.2	6,064	9.6	13.8
Northern	12,392	22.3	25.3	8,446	13.4	23.9
North Eastern[c]	—	—		7,899	12.5	20.0
North Western[d]	—	—		590	0.9	1.3
Far Northern[c]	—	—		558	0.9	2.9

[a]"Residential areas" comprise groups of suburbs. Germiston (see table 13) and "Unknown" have been excluded.

[b]Downtown Johannesburg makes up part of the Central area.

[c]Sandton, a separate municipality, makes up most of the North Eastern and Far Northern suburbs.

[d]Randburg, a separate municipality, makes up most of the North Western suburbs.

TABLE 15. SEX RATIOS (MALES PER 100 FEMALES) AMONG JEWISH AND TOTAL WHITE POPULATIONS, 1904–1980

Year	Jews	Total Whites
1904	211	132
1918	125	105
1926	112	105
1936	114	103
1946	106	101
1951	103	101
1960	99	99
1970	98	99
1980	95	99
1980, by age:		
0–14	107	103
15–29	106	104
30–44	93	105
45–64	85	97
65+	83	69

TABLE 16. JEWISH POPULATION, BY AGE, 1926–1980

Age	1926	1936	1960	1970	1980
Total no.	71,816	90,645	114,762	118,120	117,963
Total %	100.0	100.0	100.0	100.0	100.0
0–9	18.2	14.6	17.3	15.6	13.7[a]
10–19	21.2	16.9	17.3	17.0	14.8[a]
20–29	18.2	21.0	10.4	14.4	14.4
30–39	15.2	17.6	12.6	10.4	13.6
40–49	13.3	12.9	14.6	11.8	9.9
50–59	8.4	9.7	14.7	12.7	11.1
60+	4.9	7.3	13.1	18.1	22.5
Median age	25.8	28.8	34.0	32.8	34.9

[a]Published census data on Jewish population by age do not provide a detailed breakdown within the age group 0–19. The distribution given here is based on the Jewish population of the six major metropolitan areas with a combined Jewish population of 108,007. The same percentage of Jews aged 0–19 (28.5) resulted for the six major centers and for the total of South Africa.

TABLE 17. JEWISH AND TOTAL WHITE POPULATIONS, BY AGE AND SEX, 1980

	Jews				Total Whites			
	1970	1980[a]			1970	1980		
Age	Total	Total	Male	Female	Total	Total	Male	Female
Total no.	118,120	117,963	57,478	60,485	3,727[b]	4,551[b]	2,268[b]	2,283[b]
Total %	100.0	100.0	48.7	51.3	100.0	100.0	49.8	50.2
0–4	7.8	6.4	3.3	3.1	10.7	8.6	4.4	4.2
5–9	7.8	7.3	3.9	3.4	10.3	9.5	4.8	4.7
10–14	8.1	7.3	3.7	3.6	10.0	9.4	4.8	4.6
15–19	8.9	7.5	3.8	3.7	9.0	8.9	4.5	4.4
20–24	7.9	7.4	3.9	3.5	8.8	8.6	4.4	4.2
25–29	6.5	7.0	3.5	3.5	8.1	8.1	4.1	4.0
30–34	5.4	7.3	3.6	3.7	6.9	8.1	4.1	4.0
35–39	4.9	6.4	3.1	3.3	5.9	7.3	3.8	3.5
40–44	5.8	5.3	2.5	2.8	5.6	6.0	3.1	2.9
45–49	6.0	4.6	2.2	2.4	5.3	5.0	2.5	2.5
50–54	5.8	5.3	2.4	2.9	4.7	4.6	2.3	2.3
55–59	6.9	5.7	2.6	3.1	4.4	4.2	2.0	2.2
60–64	6.5	5.4	2.5	2.9	3.8	3.6	1.7	1.9
65–69	5.0	6.1	2.9	3.2	2.5	3.2	1.4	1.8
70–74	3.6	5.2	2.5	2.7	1.7	2.4	1.0	1.4
75–79	} 3.1	3.2	1.4	1.8	1.2	1.3	0.5	0.8
80+		2.6	1.0	1.6	1.1	1.2	0.4	0.8
Median age	32.8	34.9	33.1	36.7	26.1	28.1	27.4	28.8

[a]Distributions for the 0–19 and 65+ age groups reflect their respective actual sizes in the total South African Jewish population, and their internal breakdown by 5-year age groups among the Jewish population of the six major metropolitan areas.

TABLE 18. JEWISH POPULATION, BY METROPOLITAN AREA, SEX, AND AGE, 1980[a]

	Johan-nesburg	Germis-ton	Cape Town	Durban	Pretoria	Port Elizabeth	Rest of Country
Total no.	64,367	4,812	26,975	5,930	3,487	2,436	9,956
Total %	100.0	100.0	100.0	100.0	100.0	100.0	100.0
Sex							
Male	47.7	51.3	48.0	48.9	54.3	49.7	54.0
Female	52.3	48.7	52.0	51.1	45.7	50.3	46.0
Age							
0–14	21.3	27.0	19.3	19.5	20.6	21.7	20.6
15–29	22.6	22.3	22.6	17.4	24.4	15.6	18.6
30–44	18.7	24.5	18.6	19.4	19.4	19.4	18.1
45–64	20.6	17.4	20.7	23.8	20.8	23.1	25.8
65+	16.8	8.8	18.8	19.9	14.8	20.2	16.9
Median age	34.1	30.4	35.6	39.8	34.1	39.6	36.6

[a]Six major metropolitan areas, authors' processing. The "Rest of Country" category was obtained by subtracting the totals for the six major metropolitan areas from those for the total of South Africa.

TABLE 19. JEWISH POPULATION AGED 15 AND OVER, BY SEX, MARITAL STATUS, AND AGE, 1980[a] (PERCENT)

Age	Total	Never Married	Married	Living Together	Divorced	Widowed
			Males			
Total	100.0	28.9	63.6	1.4	2.9	3.2
15–29	100.0	78.3	19.2	1.7	0.8	0.0
30–44	100.0	10.3	83.3	1.9	4.1	0.3
45–64	100.0	5.6	87.6	1.1	4.0	1.7
65+	100.0	6.6	76.1	0.8	3.2	13.3
			Females			
Total	100.0	20.5	57.0	1.2	4.5	16.8
15–29	100.0	61.8	34.2	2.0	1.8	0.2
30–44	100.0	7.3	82.5	1.6	7.0	1.6
45–64	100.0	4.4	75.4	0.7	5.7	13.7
65+	100.0	6.3	34.4	0.4	3.7	55.1

[a]Six major metropolitan areas, authors' processing.

TABLE 20. PERCENTAGE EVER-MARRIED AMONG JEWISH AND TOTAL WHITE POPULATIONS, BY SEX AND AGE, 1970–1980

	% Ever-Married				Changes, 1970 to 1980		
	Jews		Total Whites			Increase in % Married	
Age	1970	1980[a]	1970	1980	Age	Jews	Whites
				Males			
15–24	6.0	5.3	14.8	15.0	5–14 to 15–24	5.3	15.0
25–34	77.2	70.9	82.8	83.2	15–24 to 25–34	64.9	68.4
35–44	93.0	93.5	94.0	93.7	25–34 to 35–44	16.3	10.9
45–54	92.8	94.5	95.1	95.4	35–44 to 45–54	1.5	1.4
					Period PEM[b]	88.0	95.7
				Females			
15–24	25.9	18.4	34.0	32.2	5–14 to 15–24	18.4	32.2
25–34	90.5	84.6	91.9	90.3	15–24 to 25–34	58.7	56.3
35–44	95.3	94.4	95.8	95.5	25–34 to 35–44	3.9	3.6
45–54	94.5	95.9	94.0	96.1	35–44 to 45–54	0.6	0.3
					Period PEM[b]	81.6	92.4

[a]Six major metropolitan areas, authors' processing.

[b]Percent of a hypothetical cohort that would ever-marry, assuming the age-specific increases in ever-married during observed period remain constant.

TABLE 21. SELECTED MEASURES OF FERTILITY AMONG JEWISH AND TOTAL WHITE POPULATIONS, 1940–1980

Approximate Date	Jews Fertility (A)	Jews % Change (B)	Total Whites Fertility (C)	Total Whites % Change (D)	Ratio (A)/(C) %
a. Total Fertility Rates[a]					
1940	2.1		3.1		68
1945	2.7	+29	3.2	+3	84
1950	3.0	+11	3.4	+6	88
1955	3.1	+3	3.4	=	91
1960	3.0	−3	3.5	+3	86
1965	2.7	−10	3.5	=	77
1970	2.7	=	3.2	−9	84
b. Child-Woman Ratios[b]					
1970	0.589		0.726		81
1975	0.547	−7	0.660	−9	83
1980	0.445	−19	0.551	−17	81

Sources: Sergio DellaPergola, "Contemporary Jewish Fertility: An Overview," in U. O. Schmelz, P. Glikson, and S. DellaPergola, eds., *Papers in Jewish Demography 1981* (Jerusalem, 1983), 215–38; Allie A. Dubb, *Patterns of Fertility and Family Formation Among South African Jewish Women* (Jerusalem, 1979), unpublished paper.

[a]Children that would be born on the average according to age-specific fertility levels prevailing during five-year period around indicated dates. For Jews, five-year periods should be read as follows: 1937–41, 1942–46, 1947–51, etc.

[b]Ratio of children aged 0–4 to women aged 20–39 at date indicated. Based on retrospective estimates from 1980 population census. Jewish population: six major metropolitan areas, authors' processing.

TABLE 22. JEWS AND TOTAL WHITES, COLOREDS, ASIANS, AND BLACKS, AGED 20 AND OVER, BY EDUCATIONAL LEVEL, 1980[a] (PERCENT)

Standard of Education[b]	Jews	Whites	Coloreds	Asians	Blacks
Total					
Total	100.0	100.0	100.0	100.0	100.0
No education	2.9	1.8	12.6	12.6	23.0
Up to std. 5	1.1	2.4	41.0	26.5	40.9
Std. 6–9	26.0	47.1	39.7	45.6	32.0
Std. 10	38.5	27.9	3.2	9.8	2.6
Nondegree diploma	15.8	13.7	3.2	3.7	1.4
Bachelor's degree	14.3	6.3	0.3	1.7	0.1
Master's and doctorates	1.4	0.8	0.0	0.1	0.0
Males					
Total	100.0	100.0	100.0	100.0	100.0
No education	1.5	2.3	12.0	5.6	24.9
Up to std. 5	1.0	2.0	37.5	20.8	41.3
Std. 6–9	21.7	43.2	42.4	53.3	29.7
Std. 10	36.7	29.4	4.7	12.9	2.9
Nondegree diploma	16.5	14.1	2.9	4.5	1.0
Bachelor's degree	19.5	8.4	0.5	2.7	0.2
Master's and doctorates	2.3	1.4	0.0	0.2	0.0
Females					
Total	100.0	100.0	100.0	100.0	100.0
No education	3.4	2.1	13.2	19.5	20.5
Up to std. 5	1.2	2.7	44.1	32.1	40.4
Std. 6–9	29.9	51.0	37.1	38.1	35.1
Std. 10	40.1	26.4	2.0	6.7	2.0
Nondegree diploma	15.0	13.3	3.5	2.9	1.9
Bachelor's degree	9.8	4.3	0.1	0.7	0.1
Master's and doctorates	0.6	0.2	0.0	0.0	0.0

[a]The category "Unknown" was excluded from computations.
[b]See text footnotes 65 and 66 for an explanation of terms relating to grade divisions and diplomas.

TABLE 23. JEWISH POPULATION AGED 15 AND OVER, BY EDUCATIONAL LEVEL, SEX, AGE, AND MAJOR METROPOLITAN AREA, 1980[a] (PERCENT)

	Total	Up to Std. 5	Std. 6–9	Std. 10	Nondegree Diploma	Bachelor's Degree	Master's and Doctorates
Total	100.0	3.8	29.1	38.5	14.4	13.0	1.3
Sex							
Males	100.0	3.1	25.7	36.8	16.9	17.5	2.0
Females	100.0	4.4	32.3	40.0	13.9	8.9	0.6
Age							
15–29	100.0	1.2	27.0	43.8	13.2	14.2	0.6
30–44	100.0	1.3	18.9	36.3	23.2	18.1	2.2
45–64	100.0	2.2	30.1	40.5	13.6	12.1	1.5
65+	100.0	12.1	42.7	31.2	6.8	6.6	0.8
Metropolitan area							
Johannesburg	100.0	4.2	29.2	38.1	14.2	13.0	1.3
Germiston	100.0	3.0	28.9	37.5	17.0	12.7	0.9
Cape Town	100.0	3.3	28.6	39.3	14.5	13.0	1.1
Durban	100.0	2.7	33.2	37.3	13.9	11.6	1.3
Pretoria	100.0	2.7	25.3	41.1	13.9	14.6	2.4
Port Elizabeth	100.0	2.3	30.0	38.7	13.5	14.0	1.5

[a]Six major metropolitan areas, authors' processing.

TABLE 24. ECONOMICALLY ACTIVE JEWS, BY OCCUPATION, 1936–1980

Occupation	1936	1960	1970	1980
% Economically active	45.4	40.8	42.6	43.6
Total no.	41,170	45,887	49,750	51,422
Total %[a]	100.0	100.0	100.0	100.0
Professional and technical	9.7	20.0	22.1	29.1
Administrative	2.0	19.7	16.3	17.5
Clerical	15.5	20.6	22.7	20.3
Sales	48.0	29.1	28.6	23.0
Services	5.3	1.8	3.9	4.4
Production	17.6	7.5	5.4	4.9
Agriculture	1.9	1.3	1.0	0.8

[a]Percentages were computed after excluding the "Not classified/unknown" category.

TABLE 25. ECONOMICALLY ACTIVE JEWS, ANGLICANS, AND TOTAL WHITES, COLOREDS, ASIANS, AND BLACKS, BY OCCUPATION, 1970–1980

Occupation	Jews		Anglicans		Total Whites		Coloreds	Asians	Blacks
	1970	1980	1970	1980	1970	1980	1980	1980	1980
Total									
% Economically active	42.6	43.6	43.7	44.4	40.0	41.9	35.4	31.2	32.9
Total economically active	100.0	100.0	100.0	100.0	100.0	100.0	100.0	100.0	100.0
Professional and technical	22.7	28.7	20.3	25.3	15.4	19.8	5.7	8.9	3.4
Administrative	17.5	17.2	8.6	11.9	5.3	7.3	0.3	2.1	0.1
Clerical	20.7	20.0	28.6	25.5	26.7	27.0	7.6	21.1	3.7
Sales	26.8	22.7	12.2	12.3	10.3	9.8	3.8	14.7	3.0
Service	4.0	4.3	5.4	5.9	6.8	7.9	16.5	6.6	19.8
Production	5.3	4.8	18.7	14.6	26.1	21.9	41.1	39.7	38.4
Agriculture	1.0	0.8	3.4	3.0	6.4	4.8	17.1	2.2	20.1
Not classified/unknown	2.0	1.5	2.7	1.5	3.0	1.6	7.9	4.7	11.5
Males									
% Economically active	59.7	58.0	59.7	58.6	56.4	56.3	44.4	46.7	43.9
Total economically active	100.0	100.0	100.0	100.0	100.0	100.0	100.0	100.0	100.0

Professional and technical	24.0	29.8	20.8	26.4	14.4	18.9	3.8	7.8	2.2
Administrative	23.1	23.5	12.2	17.0	7.1	10.0	0.5	2.7	0.1
Clerical	8.2	7.0	14.9	10.3	15.1	13.0	6.8	20.4	4.3
Sales	30.5	25.8	12.5	12.8	9.4	9.5	3.1	15.7	2.3
Service	4.2	4.5	5.5	6.2	7.3	8.8	6.6	6.4	9.2
Production	7.0	6.8	26.8	21.6	35.5	31.4	51.2	40.1	51.2
Agriculture	1.4	1.2	4.9	4.3	8.7	6.9	22.2	2.7	22.0
Not classified/unknown	1.6	1.4	2.5	1.5	2.5	1.6	5.8	4.2	8.7
Females									
% Economically active	26.0	29.9	28.7	31.0	23.7	27.7	26.8	16.0	21.2
Total economically active	100.0	100.0	100.0	100.0	100.0	100.0	100.0	100.0	100.0
Professional and technical	19.8	26.7	19.2	23.4	17.9	21.7	8.7	12.0	5.9
Administrative	4.8	5.6	1.6	2.9	1.1	1.9	0.1	0.5	0.0
Clerical	48.7	43.9	55.5	52.7	54.1	55.2	8.9	23.3	2.5
Sales	18.5	16.8	11.7	11.4	12.6	10.3	4.9	11.5	4.6
Service	3.6	3.9	5.2	5.3	5.7	6.0	32.6	7.1	43.1
Production	1.5	1.2	2.9	2.1	3.8	2.7	24.9	38.7	10.5
Agriculture	0.2	0.1	0.7	0.8	0.9	0.7	8.7	0.8	15.9
Not classified/unknown	2.9	1.8	3.1	1.5	3.9	1.5	11.2	6.1	17.5

TABLE 26. CHANGES IN OCCUPATIONS OF JEWS, 1960–1970 AND 1970–1980

Occupation	Difference 1960–70 Total	Difference 1960–70 Males	Difference 1960–70 Females	Difference 1970–80 Total	Difference 1970–80 Males	Difference 1970–80 Females
			Absolute Nos.			
Total	3,438	1,165	2,273	−237	−886	649
Not economically active	−163	983	−1,146	−1,275	596	−1,871
Total economically active	3,601	182	3,419	1,038	−1,482	2,520
Professional and technical	2,264	1,063	1,201	3,335	1,584	1,751
Administrative	−232	−120	−112	37	−228	265
Clerical	1,003	−445	1,448	−169	−524	355
Sales	140	−661	801	−1,860	−2,026	166
Service	1,182	962	220	186	47	139
Production	−779	−541	−238	−174	−150	−24
Agriculture	−92	−98	6	−102	−94	−8
Not classified/unknown	115	22	93	−215	−91	−124
			Percentage Change[a]			
Total	3.0	2.0	3.9	−0.2	−1.5	1.1
Not economically active	−0.2	4.4	−2.5	−1.9	2.5	−4.2
Total economically active	7.7	0.5	28.2	2.1	−4.3	16.2
Professional and technical	24.7	14.6	64.1	29.2	19.0	57.0
Administrative	−2.6	−1.5	−13.0	0.4	−2.8	35.4
Clerical	10.6	−13.4	23.7	−1.6	−18.3	4.7
Sales	1.0	−5.9	38.6	−13.8	−19.0	5.8
Service	141.1	194.7	64.0	9.2	3.2	24.6
Production	−22.6	−18.2	−50.2	−6.5	−6.2	−10.2
Agriculture	−15.1	−16.7	27.3	−19.7	−19.2	−28.6
Not classified/unknown	12.8	4.1	26.1	−21.3	−16.3	−27.6

[a]Percentage change for each cell = $\frac{\text{Total change between the two dates}}{\text{Total number at the earlier date}} \times 100$

TABLE 27. JEWISH AND TOTAL WHITE PROFESSIONALS, 1980, DETAILED BREAKDOWN

Professions	Jews	Total Whites
Professionals as % of total economically active	28.7	19.8
Total no.	13,750	378,570
Total %	100.0	100.0
Physical scientists and related technicians	0.9	2.4
Architects, quantity surveyors, engineers, and related technicians	10.7	29.4
Aircraft and ships' officers	0.3	1.1
Life scientists and related technicians	1.4	2.5
Medical, dental, veterinary, pharmaceutical, and related workers	30.1	17.6
Statisticians, mathematicians, systems analysts, and related technicians	2.1	2.5
Economists	0.4	0.4
Public accountants	15.3	7.5
Lawyers, judges, and other legal occupations	9.2	2.5
Teachers and other educational workers	16.8	22.8
Workers in religion	0.8	2.3
Professional, technical, and related workers not elsewhere classified	4.3	3.4
Authors, journalists, and related workers	2.2	1.8
Sculptors, painters, photographers, and related creative artists	3.2	2.4
Composers and performing artists	1.8	1.0
Sportsmen	0.5	0.4

TABLE 28. ECONOMICALLY ACTIVE JEWS AGED 15 AND OVER, BY OCCUPATION, SEX, AGE, AND MAJOR METROPOLITAN AREA, 1980[a] (PERCENT)

	Total	Professional/ Technical	Administrative	Clerical	Sales	Service	Production	Agriculture
Total	100.0	29.8	17.6	21.0	22.4	4.0	4.9	0.3
Sex								
Males	100.0	31.0	24.4	7.5	25.6	4.1	7.0	0.4
Females	100.0	27.6	5.5	45.1	16.7	3.8	1.2	0.1
Age								
15–29	100.0	33.9	7.6	29.2	14.4	8.5	6.2	0.2
30–44	100.0	33.5	20.6	17.2	21.9	2.4	4.2	0.2
45–64	100.0	25.9	21.9	19.9	25.4	2.3	4.3	0.3
65+	100.0	21.2	19.1	17.5	32.6	3.4	5.7	0.5
Metropolitan area								
Johannesburg	100.0	29.2	17.1	23.4	21.7	3.5	5.0	0.1
Germiston	100.0	27.9	19.5	19.9	23.6	3.5	4.8	0.8
Cape Town	100.0	32.0	18.1	17.1	23.3	4.0	5.1	0.4
Durban	100.0	29.6	21.3	17.3	21.6	5.3	4.5	0.4
Pretoria	100.0	28.5	15.5	15.2	23.6	12.7	4.0	0.5
Port Elizabeth	100.0	30.0	17.7	14.0	30.8	3.1	3.8	0.6
Rest of country	100.0	22.3	15.8	12.9	29.4	8.1	5.2	6.3

[a]Six major metropolitan areas, authors' processing. Percentage distributions were computed after excluding the "Not classified/unknown" category. The "Rest of country" category was obtained by subtracting the totals for the six major metropolitan areas from those for the whole of South Africa.

TABLE 29. ECONOMICALLY ACTIVE JEWS AGED 15 AND OVER, BY OCCUPATION AND WORK STATUS, 1980[a]

Occupation	Work Status			
	Total	Employer	Employee	Unemployed
		Column %		
Total no.	46,127	11,769	34,272	86
Total %	100.0	100.0	100.0	(100.0)
Professional and technical	29.8	37.2	27.3	(29.1)
Administrative	17.6	19.8	16.9	(5.8)
Clerical	21.0	1.9	27.5	(41.9)
Sales	22.4	30.9	19.5	(12.8)
Services	4.0	3.8	4.1	(5.8)
Production	4.9	5.6	4.7	(4.7)
Agriculture	0.3	0.9	0.1	(0.0)
		Row %		
Total %	100.0	25.3	74.1	0.6
Professional and technical	100.0	31.8	68.0	0.2
Administrative	100.0	28.7	71.3	0.1
Clerical	100.0	2.3	97.4	0.4
Sales	100.0	35.2	64.7	0.1
Services	100.0	24.3	75.4	0.3
Production	100.0	29.1	70.7	0.2
Agriculture	100.0	81.1	18.9	0.0

[a]Six major metropolitan areas, authors' processing.

TABLE 30. ECONOMICALLY ACTIVE JEWS AGED 15 AND OVER, BY WORK STATUS, SEX, AGE, AND MAJOR METROPOLITAN AREA, 1980[a]

	% Economically Active	Economically Active			
		Total	Employer	Employee	Unemployed
Total	55.9	100.0	25.3	74.1	0.6
Sex					
Males	74.2	100.0	33.6	65.9	0.5
Females	37.6	100.0	10.5	88.6	0.9
Age					
15–29	48.7	100.0	8.8	90.2	1.0
30–44	73.6	100.0	27.1	72.3	0.6
45–64	65.4	100.0	32.1	67.3	0.6
65+	29.7	100.0	37.2	62.5	0.3
Metropolitan area					
Johannesburg	57.0	100.0	22.5	77.0	0.5
Germiston	62.2	100.0	29.9	69.8	0.3
Cape Town	49.2	100.0	29.1	70.0	0.9
Durban	51.0	100.0	28.5	70.4	1.1
Pretoria	60.5	100.0	28.7	70.9	0.4
Port Elizabeth	55.7	100.0	41.0	58.7	0.3

[a]Six major metropolitan areas, authors' processing.

TABLE 31. ECONOMICALLY ACTIVE JEWS AGED 15 AND OVER, BY INDUSTRY AND TYPE OF EMPLOYER, 1980[a]

		Type of Employer				
Industry	Total	Central Govt.	Provincial/ Local Authority	Public Authority Corporation	Private Business Enterpr.[b]	Nonprofit Organization
			Column %			
Total no.	45,130	2,038	2,731	355	38,596	1,410
Total %	100.0	100.0	100.0	100.0	100.0	100.0
Agriculture	0.5	0.1	0.2	0.0	0.6	0.0
Manufacturing[c]	18.7	1.8	1.8	29.3	21.3	2.3
Construction	2.6	0.4	1.5	0.8	2.9	0.1
Trade	33.0	2.0	0.4	0.8	38.4	0.3
Transport	2.3	0.5	0.5	47.3	2.1	0.1
Finance	20.1	0.4	0.1	2.0	23.5	0.0
Services	22.9	94.8	95.5	18.3	11.2	97.2
			Row %			
Total %	100.0	4.4	5.9	0.8	85.8	3.1
Agriculture	100.0	0.8	2.9	0.0	96.3	0.0
Manufacturing[c]	100.0	0.4	0.6	1.2	97.4	0.4
Construction	100.0	0.8	3.6	0.3	95.1	0.2
Trade	100.0	0.3	0.1	0.1	99.5	0.0
Transport	100.0	1.1	1.3	16.5	80.9	0.2
Finance	100.0	0.1	0.0	0.1	99.8	0.0
Services	100.0	18.8	25.3	0.6	42.0	13.3

[a]Six major metropolitan areas, authors' processing. Includes all economically active Jews irrespective of work status.

[b]Includes employers and employees.

[c]Includes the mining and electricity sectors, with 205 and 133 employed Jews, respectively.

TABLE 32. ECONOMICALLY ACTIVE JEWS AGED 15 AND OVER, BY TYPE OF EMPLOYER, SEX, AGE, AND MAJOR METROPOLITAN AREA, 1980[a] (PERCENT)

	Total	Central Govt.	Provincial Adminis-tration	Local Author-ity	Public Author. Corp.	Private Business Enterpr.	Non-profit Organi-zation
Total	100.0	4.4	5.0	0.9	0.8	85.8	3.1
Sex							
Males	100.0	4.5	2.7	0.9	1.0	89.6	1.3
Females	100.0	4.3	9.0	1.1	0.4	79.0	6.2
Age							
15–29	100.0	9.4	8.4	0.8	1.3	77.5	2.6
30–44	100.0	3.2	5.0	0.8	0.7	87.1	3.2
45–64	100.0	2.6	3.3	1.2	0.6	88.9	3.4
65+	100.0	2.2	2.3	1.0	0.3	91.1	3.1
Metropolitan area							
Johannesburg	100.0	3.4	4.6	0.8	0.7	87.2	3.3
Germiston	100.0	2.8	4.4	0.3	1.3	89.8	1.4
Cape Town	100.0	5.2	6.6	1.5	0.5	82.9	3.3
Durban	100.0	5.7	4.3	1.0	1.6	84.5	2.9
Pretoria	100.0	19.3	2.9	0.5	1.4	74.3	1.6
Port Elizabeth	100.0	2.5	4.2	0.8	1.0	89.4	2.1

[a]Six major metropolitan areas, authors' processing.

TABLE 33. JEWS AND TOTAL WHITES, BY INCOME, 1980

Income Category in S.A. Rands[a]	Jews	Total Whites
% with income out of population aged 15 +	67.9	67.8
Total no.	63,239	2,238,366
Total %	100.0	100.0
2–1,199	6.5	7.4
1,200–2,399	7.9	10.1
2,400–3,599	7.9	11.3
3,600–5,999	15.2	20.2
6,000–8,399	12.9	17.2
8,400–11,999	10.2	15.0
12,000–17,999	13.9	11.8
18,000–29,999	13.3	5.0
30,000–41,999	4.2	1.2
42,000+	8.0	0.8
Median annual income	8,323	6,139

[a]In 1980 the South African rand was equivalent to about $0.80.

TABLE 34. JEWISH POPULATION AGED 15 AND OVER, BY TYPE AND LEVEL OF JEWISH EDUCATION, 1974[a]

Type of Jewish Education	Jewish Education Level Attained: Total	None	To Bar Mitzvah	Post Bar Mitzvah	Matriculation
			Column %		
Total no.	66,597	13,989	35,270	11,160	6,112
Total %	100.0	100.0	100.0	100.0	100.0
None	18.7	92.0	—	—	—
Heder	52.9	2.2	74.6	60.7	25.2
Day school	10.1	0.9	5.2	14.2	50.9
Other[b]	18.3	4.9	20.2	25.1	23.9
			Row %		
Total %	100.0	21.0	53.0	16.8	9.2
Heder	100.0	0.8	75.4	19.3	4.5
Day school	100.0	1.7	27.7	23.7	46.9
Other[b]	100.0	5.3	59.2	23.2	12.2

[a]South African Jewish Population Study, six largest Jewish communities.
[b]Including private tutorial.

TABLE 35. SELECTED INDICATORS OF JEWISH EDUCATION, 1981-82[a]

Indicators	Total	Johannesburg	Cape Town	Rest of South Africa
Schools				
Total	146	56	22	68
Nursery schools	64	25	15	24
Day schools[b]	24	9	5	10
Of these: primary[c]	14	4	4	6
secondary[d]	10	5	1	4
Hadarim	58	22	2	34
Pupils				
Total	14,300	7,722	3,174	3,404
Nursery schools[e]	3,765	2,164	723	878
Day schools[b]	8,311	4,368	2,289	1,654
Of these: primary[c]	4,360	2,145	1,311	904
secondary[d]	3,951	2,223	978	750
Hadarim	2,224	1,190	162	872
% Enrolled out of 3–17 age group[f]				
Total	55	54	58	57
Nursery and day schools	47	46	55	42
Hadarim	8	8	3	15
Teaching Posts[g]				
Total	991	510	228	253
Nursery schools[h]	235	107	44	84
Day schools[i]	655	368	170	117
Of these: Jewish studies[j]	160	108	23	29
General studies	495	260	147	88
Hadarim[k]	101	35	14	52

[a]Based on results of the First International Census of Jewish Schools in the Diaspora, conducted by the Project for Jewish Educational Statistics, Institute for Contemporary Jewry, the Hebrew University of Jerusalem. The census covered the 1981–82 and 1982–83 school years in the Northern Hemisphere and 1981, 1982, and 1983 school years in the Southern Hemisphere. Coverage of schools in South Africa was close to 100 percent for nursery and day schools. Response for *hadarim* (supplementary schools) was somewhat lower, but certainly not below 90 percent.

[b]Each nursery, primary-, and secondary-level unit was counted as a separate school.

Continued on the next page

TABLE 35.—*(Continued)*

[c]Grades 1 to 6.

[d]Grades 7 to 12.

[e]Excludes 946 non-Jewish pupils, countrywide. The proportion of non-Jewish pupils in day schools was 0.9 percent, and has been disregarded.

[f]Percentage enrollment = (total enrolled in Jewish schools/total Jewish children aged 3–17) × 100. Figures for "Rest of South Africa" were estimated.

[g]Teachers who taught at more than one school were subject to multiple reporting, hence "Teaching Posts" rather than "Teachers." Since several schools did not report on teachers—in particular, Johannesburg *hadarim*—the percentage of schools which did report is noted in each case.

[h]Nursery schools reporting: total—89 percent; Johannesburg—72 percent; Cape Town and rest—100 percent.

[i]Day schools reporting: total—92 percent; Johannesburg and Cape Town—100 percent; rest—80 percent.

[j]Includes 6 teachers who also taught general studies.

[k]*Hadarim* reporting: total—67 percent; Johannesburg—23 percent; Cape Town—100 percent; rest—94 percent.

Review of the Year

UNITED STATES

Civic and Political

Intergroup Relations

MANY OF THE SPECTERS haunting the consciousness of American Jews materialized at some point during 1986. Organized anti-Semitic groups made front-page news, some of them trying to turn economic crisis in the farmlands to their advantage. A Jewish Wall Street financier was caught in some illicit and profitable deals. There were continuing attempts to "Christianize" America. And an American Jewish spy was arrested for turning over valuable American secrets to Israel. By the end of the year, these specters seemed to have receded, but many Jews were left feeling distinctly uneasy.

Extremism

In February ten members of the neo-Nazi gang called the Order were convicted by a U.S. district court in Seattle of a series of violent actions connected with their expressed desire to establish an Aryan society. At least two murders were cited, including the 1984 machine-gun slaying of Alan Berg, a Jewish radio personality in Denver. The group was also charged with raising more than $4 million through armed robberies.

While the Order suffered a severe blow when many of its leaders were given prison sentences ranging from 40 to 100 years, similar groups continued to function. The Aryan Nations, for example, of which the Order was an offshoot, later in the year made the news on its own. In July, when the Aryan Nations World Congress convened in Hayden Lake, Idaho, the media reported an orgiastic display of cross burnings, Nazi salutes, swastikas, and automatic weapons. Although the Aryan Nations was an umbrella for an assortment of neo-Nazi and KKK groups, as an entity it had a special mission of its own. A document titled "Declaring a Territorial Sanctuary" laid out an elaborate plan for assembling American whites, not including Jews, under their own government in the Northwest states, while the rest of the population would be consigned to "the ZOG, the Zionist Occupation Government." Members of the Aryan Nations signed a "Declaration of War Against 'The ZOG.' "

In October 22-year-old Robert Pires, who frequented the Aryan Nations compound in Idaho, was arrested on three counts of bombing. During the previous month, Pires had bombed the home of a Catholic priest, a luggage store, and the federal building in Coeur d'Alene, seven miles from the Idaho headquarters of the Aryan Nations. One of the chief developers of Coeur d'Alene had been placed on the Aryan Nations "hit list" as "one of the ten worst Jews in town," although he was not Jewish; and the priest had been described in Aryan Nations literature as a "rabbi in disguise."

Earlier in the year, a bomb-wielding couple had entered a school in Cokeville, Wyoming, where they held 150 children hostage and demanded several million dollars to finance a white supremacist homeland. One of their bombs exploded, burning a number of the children, and the two kidnappers committed suicide. Among their papers was found material from several of the centers of organized bigotry, notably Posse Comitatus, a long-standing organization which combined bigotry with resistance to the income tax. During the year, eight members were indicted for engaging in illegal paramilitary training near Fresno, California, and one of its founders, a former army colonel who specialized in anti-Semitic diatribes, was charged in Las Vegas, Nevada, with threatening to kill a judge and assorted IRS agents.

The theme of bigoted violence was heightened by reports from the Anti-Defamation League (ADL) that both the U.S. Armed Forces and the prison system had been infiltrated by extremists. In July three marines at Camp Lejeune were discharged for participating in rallies and paramilitary exercises staged by the White Patriot party, formerly known as the Confederate Knights of the Ku Klux Klan. Defense Secretary Caspar Weinberger ordered a crackdown in a September memorandum which said that "military personnel, duty bound to uphold the Constitution, must reject participation in such organizations." The American Civil Liberties Union objected that the Weinberger memorandum violated First Amendment rights, but the Defense Department explained that it was not prohibiting belief or even membership, only such activities as public demonstrations, recruiting, and training.

The ADL reported in June that a number of prison gangs throughout the country, including the widespread Aryan Brotherhood, were linked up with the Aryan Nations. Some objections were voiced that the attempt to make such linkages violated the religious freedom of convicts, some of whom, for example, were members of an Aryan Nations invention, the "Church of Jesus Christ Christian." Illinois prison officials refused to acknowledge the religious legitimacy of such a group, and their decision was upheld by a U.S. district court.

The primary channel through which the Christian religious emphasis penetrated the organized network of bigotry was Christian Identity, another umbrella group with which organizations such as the Aryan Nations, Posse Comitatus, and the Ku Klux Klan were associated. Its underlying theme was Christian white supremacy: white Anglo-Saxons are the lost tribes of Israel, Jews are the children of Satan, and the black, brown, and yellow races are "pre-Adamic" inferiors. As an entity, Christian Identity distinguished itself during the year by attacking Christian fundamentalists for supporting Israel.

LYNDON LAROUCHE

In addition to the groups preaching violence with a Christian religious patina, there were troubling developments in the political arena, mainly in the form of Lyndon LaRouche and his associates. LaRouche had been an obscure figure on the fringes of the American political scene since the end of World War II. At first, he moved in left-wing radical student circles, sometimes as a Trotskyite, and stayed in those environs until the 1970s. At that point he began to shift to right-wing politics, citing the danger of the Soviet threat, and quickly became one of the most fanciful purveyors of conspiracy theories. LaRouche's list of conspiratorial villains was long and bizarre, including Queen Elizabeth as an international drug-dealer, but he blamed most of the world's problems on the Rockefellers and the Jews. One LaRouche watcher, journalist Dennis King, reported to a Jewish meeting that his "grand design is Hitlerism, but reworked to appeal to America in the 1980s." His organizational fronts were chameleonlike, changing names frequently, often including the words "Labor" or "Democratic." He acquired a relatively small but cultishly devoted band of followers, including some of Jewish ancestry.

Without revealing their connection to LaRouche, hundreds of his followers quietly entered the 1986 political campaign lists in two dozen states, most of them as purported Democrats. The nation's media suddenly blossomed with this news in March, after two of his followers won the Democratic party's primary election as nominees for lieutenant governor and secretary of state in Illinois. The Democratic party was shaken by this development, and its gubernatorial candidate, Adlai E. Stevenson III, withdrew from the official ticket to run as an independent. The Jewish community was no less shaken. In the subsequent journalistic investigation it was revealed that there had been well over a hundred LaRouche candidates for congressional and gubernatorial seats and uncounted hundreds for state and local posts.

There was no dearth of explanations for the startling primary victory in Illinois. With voter turnout low, the two LaRouche candidates were able to win the primary with the support of only 6 percent of the state's registered voters. In addition, all LaRouche candidates hid their connections and their agendas, running mainly on the issues of unemployment, crime, and drugs. However, even given the explanations, and even admitting the ignorance of the voters about LaRouche, the results were disturbing. There was, for example, an inescapable ethnic note in the election. LaRouche's candidates in Illinois were named Fairfield and Hart; their opponents in the Democratic primary were Sangmeister and Pucinski. One voter said, "I voted for [the winners] because they had smooth-sounding names."

Many of the extremist groups, including LaRouche's, continued to concentrate their efforts on the economically embattled farmers of the Midwest. In July the president of the Illinois American Agricultural Movement issued a statement to the press, repudiating any relationship with LaRouche. Admitting that the movement had been initially attracted to LaRouche—"In some terms, they can be convincing"—he stated that "deeper study" had rendered LaRouche unacceptable. Still the potential attraction of these groups struck a historic chord. A prime enemy of the farmer struggling with bankruptcy and foreclosure had always been "the banker." Earlier American farm movements had coalesced around opposition to the Eastern banking establishment, and on the edges of those movements had often lurked the age-old image of "the Jewish moneylender." Echoes from that past still reverberated. One candidate for public office in Nebraska, a farmer, recommended in his campaign booklet that voters read *Spotlight,* the durable publication of the anti-Semitic Liberty Lobby. Another Nebraska candidate was associated with a meat-packer who had placed ads claiming that a Zionist-Jewish conspiracy controlled the American economy.

Acknowledging the heightened activity among farmers by extremist groups and the potential danger, the Jewish community mounted some remedial efforts. In the spring, the American Jewish Committee, along with the Catholic diocese, the United Methodist Church, and the Episcopal diocese of the region sponsored a conference of religious leaders in northern Kentucky and southern Ohio. The participants discussed proposals for outreach to farmers and their families and the development of interreligious agencies to aid distressed farmers, as well as issuing public statements against extremist groups. A similar conference was held in Wichita, Kansas, and in Indiana the Indianapolis Jewish Community Relations Council and the Indiana Rural Crisis Inc., comprising local farmers, formed a working coalition. The major objective of these activities was to combat the extremist groups; a secondary goal was to find ways in which the Jewish community could join in easing the farmers' plight, with legal and financial advice and by lobbying for appropriate legislation.

EXTENT OF EXTREMISM

What was the Jewish community to make of the apparent upsurge in extremism? On the one hand, there was plenty of good news by the end of the year, suggesting that the forces of organized bigotry in America had more bark than bite. The membership of the various groups was overlapping and small by usual standards. Law enforcement agencies put the formal membership of the umbrella Aryan Nations at several thousand. The Center for Democratic Renewal in Kansas City, an anti-extremist coalition, estimated that there might be 15,000 followers in an area comprising some 35 million people. And the American Jewish Committee reported in November that the growth rate of these extremist organizations had not risen in several years, although the level of individual violence had increased. The National Jewish Community Relations Council concurred, but warned in a paper prepared for its annual plenary conference in December that "while hate groups continue to decline in numbers, their sense of desperation that has resulted in acts of violence remains a concern."

The degree to which extremist groups are repudiated by the establishment is an important index of their real standing. Throughout 1986 these groups were vehemently and uniformly condemned by a mainstream spectrum of religious representatives. While the Aryan Nations was holding its congress, the governors of the five states designated as the future white homeland all issued strong condemnations. There was support from no significant quarter.

All the extremist candidates for major office were soundly defeated at the polls. Most of the LaRouche candidates received 10 percent or less of the votes. The two Nebraska candidates received less than 5 percent of the votes. After the Illinois primary, the April *New York Times*/CBS News poll found that 1 percent of Americans had a favorable opinion of LaRouche. A Harris poll conducted in rural Iowa and Nebraska at the end of January found that while eight out of ten people blamed Congress for their problems, and as many blamed the banks and the Reagan administration, only about one out of ten was willing to blame "certain religious groups, such as Jews."

Examined clinically, the influence of the organized extremist groups did not finally seem to be substantial or growing. On the other hand, there was an obvious propensity for violence in their ranks, there were LaRouche's political antics, and, as a result, there was much media attention. Consequently, the Jewish community was not at ease, especially since other troubling events were taking place at the same time.

Anti-Semitism

The names of Jonathan Pollard and Ivan Boesky weighed heavily on Jews in late 1986. They were not inventions of the organized bigots but real actors in sordid dramas which many feared would directly affect American attitudes toward Jews.

Jonathan Jay Pollard, an American Jew and former civilian intelligence analyst for the U.S. Navy, had been arrested in November 1985, charged with spying for the State of Israel. His wife, Anne Henderson Pollard, was charged as an accomplice. (See AJYB, vol. 87, 1987, pp. 161–63 and 293–94.) According to federal prosecutors, Pollard had made contact with a high-ranking Israel Air Force officer in the United States in 1984 and offered to supply classified "scientific, technical and military" information that could be useful to Israel's defense. For a year and a half, every two weeks, Pollard delivered secret documents in a suitcase to a secretary at the Israeli embassy in Washington. At the time of his arrest he had received a total of $45,000 from the Israelis and been promised much more to come. In June Pollard pleaded guilty to the charge. Four Israelis, none of them by then in the States, were named as conspirators by the Justice Department but were not indicted. At year's end, Pollard was in a federal prison in Petersburg, Virginia, awaiting sentencing.

When the story first broke, the Israeli government apologized, labeled the operation "rogue," disbanded the unit responsible, and, without precedent, allowed American officials to come to Israel to investigate. President Ronald Reagan publicly announced that he accepted the Israeli explanations, and government and defense attorneys alike made it clear that both sides hoped to avoid a trial. While there was some grumbling in the congressional cloakrooms, the direct political damage to Israeli-American relations seemed under control. Still, there were too many unanswered questions, and too many disturbing implications, for the matter to be swept aside so easily.

While most American Jews condemned Pollard as a criminal, he was not without defenders. They claimed either that his mission had been limited to gaining American intelligence about military matters in the Arab states, which U.S. intelligence had been unwilling to share, such as the Soviet weapons which they held, or simply that spying among friends was not uncommon. Rejecting such claims, the *New Republic,* a journal notably friendly to the State of Israel, struck a note not usually heard when it stated in a June 30 editorial that the relationship between the two countries was "in no way symmetrical." It explained: "Our ties to Israel are based on conviction and preference. Israel's ties to us are based on necessity. . . . The U.S. had been more than understanding and more than supportive of those needs. . . . This American support creates certain prerogatives for the U.S. It also creates certain obligations for Israel, and one of these is that it behave with scrupulous honor and honesty to its friend."

In addition to the question of Israeli-U.S. relations, the fact that Pollard was an American Jew raised fears in many minds that the issue of "dual loyalty" would stir up anti-Semitism. For while Pollard had received $45,000 from Israel in payment for his espionage, he and his wife insisted that their primary motivation was love for Israel.

While it was still too early to gauge accurately, there was some evidence that the Pollard episode had not directly increased the anti-Semitic quotient among Americans. For years the major survey organizations had put the "dual loyalty" question to the American public: "Do you think most American Jews are more loyal to Israel than to the U.S.?" About a quarter of the American people had always responded affirmatively to this question. In June (after Pollard's arrest but before his guilty plea) the Roper poll found that 24 percent answered affirmatively to the "dual loyalty" question, essentially unchanged from 27 percent in 1985 and 25 percent in 1984.

The poll notwithstanding, the possible effect of a derailed American-Israeli relationship on American Jews remained a troubling and largely unexplored question. After all, the American Jewish community was visibly engaged in promoting American support of Israel. The polls showed a significant portion of the American public both aware and tolerant of this activity because it viewed American support of Israel as being in America's best interest. Perhaps the most damaging aspect of the Pollard affair was the implication that the interests of the two countries were at times divergent, in which case "dual loyalty" was not such a benign matter. This concern was aggravated by growing revelations in November and December about Israel's role in secret arms shipments to Iran and the diversion of funds from those sales to Nicaraguan *contras.* As investigations into these matters got under way, it became evident that Israel's foreign-policy objectives were not always the same as those of the United States.

The second major scandal (there were lesser ones, too, during the year, such as corruption among New York City officials, many of them Jews) involving a Jew made the news in November. Ivan Boesky, a New York arbitrager, pleaded guilty to having made huge profits as a result of illegally using corporate "insider" information to which he had been privy. Following a lengthy investigation, the Securities and Exchange Commission announced that Boesky had been banned from professional stock trading in the United States and had agreed to pay $100 million in penalties.

Not only was Boesky Jewish, he was a highly identified Jewish community leader and philanthropist. The *New York Post* ran a three-year-old picture of him, wearing a yarmulke, being held aloft by a rabbi and others, as he was being honored for donating $2 million to the Jewish Theological Seminary. He had also been the U.J.A./Federation campaign chairman in New York for a two-year period ending in 1985, and had pledged over $1 million to Princeton University for a Jewish student center and other purposes.

The case against Boesky grew out of a wider investigation of Wall Street professionals involved in insider trading. A key figure was Dennis B. Levine, an investment banker who had been charged several months earlier with illegal insider trading, and who was in fact Boesky's prime source of information about impending takeovers. Other Jewish names predominated as the investigation widened. *Newsweek*, in its December 1 issue, reported: "Boesky, Levine and others implicated earlier this year are Jewish; so are many now being connected with the investigation. The talk on Wall Street this week included some ethnic jokes along with more disparaging remarks about Jews. . . . 'That's definitely an undercurrent and it's quite disturbing,' says Ira Sorkin, a former SEC official."

Given the "financier" context, many Jews felt that the Boesky trauma was the most harmful the Jewish image sustained during the year, although some maintained that the damage was mainly restricted to those Wall Street circles which had never been too friendly. The affair left many Jews feeling not only uncomfortable but troubled—particularly as more and more Jewish names surfaced—about ethical standards among Jewish business people, including leaders of the community. (See "Jewish Communal Affairs," elsewhere in this volume.)

A minor episode, but one with disturbing overtones, centered on two leading intellectuals, the left-wing novelist and essayist Gore Vidal and neoconservative Norman Podhoretz, editor of *Commentary* magazine. The March 22 issue of the liberal journal *The Nation* carried an attack by Vidal on Podhoretz, which skillfully amalgamated anti-Semitic and anti-Israel sentiment with a "dual loyalty" attack on American Jews. Characterizing Podhoretz as an "Israeli Fifth Column," Vidal wrote: "Over the years [Podhoretz] has, like his employers, the A.J.C., moved from those liberal positions traditionally occupied by American Jews (and me) to the far right of American politics. The reason for that is simple. In order to get Treasury money for Israel (last year $3 billion), pro-Israel lobbyists must see to it that America's 'the Russians are coming' squads are in place so that they can continue to frighten the American people into spending enormous sums for 'defense,' which also means the support of Israel in its never-ending wars against just about everyone." Vidal said he had long recognized that Podhoretz was not planning to become an "assimilated American . . . but rather his first loyalty would always be to Israel." Responding to the attack in a syndicated column in May and in *Commentary* in November ("The Hate That Dare Not Speak Its Name"), Podhoretz labeled the piece "the most blatantly anti-Semitic outburst to have appeared in a respectable American periodical since World War II." Acknowledging that the *Nation* article was part of a long-standing feud between Vidal and himself and his wife, writer Midge Decter, Podhoretz charged that it went far beyond the acceptable "retaliatory strike" by reviving "the two classic themes of anti-Semitic literature—the Jew as alien and the conspiratorial manipulator of malign power dangerous to everyone else." Podhoretz was also troubled by the fact that few liberals came to his defense, even though, as a *New Republic* editorial put it (denouncing Vidal), Vidal's accusations applied not just to neoconservatives but "by extension [to] all American Jews who support Israel."

While the Pollard case, the Iran affair, and, in lesser measure, the Vidal episode, raised questions about the special nature of the American-Jewish relationship with Israel, American public support of Israel, as measured by polls, showed no signs of dwindling. Moreover, general empirical measures of anti-Semitism remained historically low during 1986. In its June poll, Roper asked Americans to name the groups that they thought had too much power, a critical item in the measurement of anti-Semitism. Business corporations, labor unions, and mass media were each named by about 4 out of 10 respondents. Arab interests were named by about 3 out of 10; Orientals, blacks, and the Catholic Church were each named by at least 1 out of 10. Jews were named by less than 1 out of 10—8 percent—unchanged since 1984. Providing support for these findings, the ADL's annual audit found that reported acts of anti-Semitic vandalism against Jews and Jewish property had declined by 7 percent from 1985.

ELECTIONS

One of the most telling measures of active anti-Semitism is the elective political process. In the 1986 congressional elections, all Jewish incumbents were reelected to the Senate and the House of Representatives. Although there was some shift in names as a result of resignations, the proportion of Jews in the two houses remained the same, 7 to 8 percent, or about three times the proportion of Jews in the population.

In light of the poll findings on anti-Semitism, and given the socioeconomic standing of the Jews and their high level of political activism, that percentage is not particularly surprising. More surprising is the fact that almost all of those Jewish congressmen were elected by overwhelmingly non-Jewish constituencies. Of the eight Jewish senators, five were elected by constituencies that were 99 percent or more non-Jewish: Republicans Rudy Boschwitz from Minnesota, Chic Hecht from Nevada, Warren Rudman from New Hampshire, Edward Zorinsky from Nebraska, and Democrat Carl Levin from Michigan. The other three represented constituencies with larger, but still small, Jewish constituencies: Republican Arlen Specter from Pennsylvania (3 percent Jewish) and Democrats Howard Metzenbaum from Ohio (1.3 percent) and Frank Lautenberg from New Jersey (5.6 percent). All eight were identified and identifying Jews.

The hard evidence suggests, then, that there was no noticeable rise in anti-Semitism in 1986—despite Boesky, Pollard, the farmland crisis, or the activity of extremist groups. However, in his 1986 survey of American Jewish attitudes prepared for the American Jewish Committee, Steven M. Cohen found that Jews were more troubled than they had been. Whereas in 1984, 40 percent of American Jews agreed that "anti-Semitism is currently not a serious problem," in 1986 only 26 percent accepted that proposition. Over and above their usual wariness, apparently, Jews had been somewhat traumatized by the events of 1986—and not just by those events which related directly to anti-Semitism.

Christian Fundamentalists

Many Jews continued to be disturbed by various activities of Christian fundamentalists. A chief concern was the appearance of explicitly Christian-oriented sentiments in the political arena. In the fall campaign, the National Republican Senatorial Committee sponsored a radio commercial in several Southern states which referred to the importance of a "relationship with Christ." Theodore Ellenoff, president of the American Jewish Committee, expressed his group's concern at "the exclusionary implications of these commercials." Soon after, the Republican committee announced that it was withdrawing the radio commercial, "after hearing from some of our support groups and Jewish groups."

Two Jewish congressional incumbents were attacked on religious grounds. Congressman Mel Levine of Los Angeles was attacked by his opponent, Rob Scribner, as being opposed to "nearly everything the Lord's church stands for." Scribner urged voters to help "take territory for our Lord Jesus Christ." In Florida, Congressman Larry Smith's positions were attacked by his opponent, Mary Collins, as "the antithesis of what the Christian community would prefer." Both Levine and Smith won their elections handily.

There were a half dozen other reported Christian-oriented campaigns by congressional candidates. Congressman Mark Siljander of Michigan said he should be reelected "to break the back of Satan." Sen. James Broyhill's supporters in North Carolina sent out a letter linking his opponent, Terry Sanford, with the one-world government related to the Antichrist. Congressman William Cobey of the same state described himself as "an ambassador for Christ." A fund-raising letter of candidate Joe Morecraft of Georgia said that "God had provided another man who is willing to serve our Lord in the halls of Congress." Candidate William Costas of Indiana said that he was in the race because of a message from God. Candidate Tom Carter of Texas attacked his opponent, Congressman John Bryant, because he was "rated zero by Christian Voice for his opposition to family and moral issues." In all cases, the explicitly Christian-oriented candidates were defeated.

Concern was aroused, however, as TV evangelist Marion G. (Pat) Robertson talked throughout the year of his probable interest in running for the 1988 Republican presidential nomination. In language chilling to the Jewish community, as well as to many others, TV evangelist Jimmy Swaggart supported a possible Robertson candidacy with these words at a September religious rally: "The possibility definitely exists that the hand that lays on the Bible to take the oath of the highest office of the land will be joined to a shoulder and a head and a heart that's saved by the blood of Jesus and baptized in the Holy Spirit." An NBC News/*Wall Street Journal* survey in July found that among the half of the population who knew Robertson's name, roughly four out of five were opposed to his candidacy.

Among those who attended the fifth annual National Prayer Breakfast, organized in February by Christian evangelical leaders to express support for the State of Israel, were Jerry Falwell, who had just changed the name of the financially ailing Moral Majority to the Liberty Federation, Robertson, and representatives from the Israeli embassy and some of the major American Jewish organizations. In his address, after lauding Israel, Robertson cautioned the Jewish community that "it does not serve your ends to strip the religious symbols [from] the public squares of America, [or to] diminish the faith of evangelical Christians." Thus did he touch on the major bone of contention between many Jews and the fundamentalist Christian leaders.

Church-State Relations

The year 1986 saw a number of fundamentalist initiatives on the church-state front, beyond the failed efforts to introduce sectarian religion in the political campaign.

A group of Christian fundamentalist parents in East Tennessee won an initial victory in a U.S. district court in October, in their attempt to have the public schools accommodate to their religious needs. At issue were some books in a state-approved reading series which these parents found religiously offensive because they included references to "supernatural" telepathy, evolution, and "one-worldism." Also objected to was a first-grade reader in which a little boy cooked, which seemed to suggest that "there are no God-given roles for the different sexes."

After the children of these parents were suspended by the school board for refusing to read the offending texts, a federal judge ruled that they could not be forced to read material that violated their religious beliefs. He suggested that a reasonable solution would be to let them sit out the class and learn to read at home or elsewhere. Later, seven fundamentalist Christian parents were awarded more than $50,000 to cover the cost of private reading instruction for their children.

One constitutional lawyer, William Bentley Ball, supported the judge's action on the basis of parental rights as well as the free exercise of religion, saying, "Suppose that, instead of fundamentalist Christians, these plaintiffs were . . . Jews protesting a book calling the Holocaust a fraud, or black parents, a Shockleyite text?" Opposing the decision, another constitutional lawyer, David H. Remes, warned that the attempt "to eliminate from the public-school curriculum all that is religiously objectionable to some religious sect will leave public education in shreds—or make it hostage to the demands of the dominant religions." It was for the latter reasons that major Jewish organizations expressed concern about the Tennessee decision, which would presumably be subject to further appeal.

The mainstream Jewish community continued to make its own way through the complexities of the First Amendment. Assertively espousing the wall of separation on the one hand, it also sought help for its accommodationist needs, though it sometimes felt that its own "fundamentalist" wing went too far in that pursuit. The prime example of the latter was the matter of religious symbols in public places: Christian crosses and nativity scenes balanced by menorahs, which were reportedly placed by the Lubavitch movement on 50 or 60 government sites in the winter of 1986.

The legal rulings on these religious symbols were mixed. In November the U.S. Supreme Court let stand a lower court ruling that prohibited an illuminated cross from being displayed above a firehouse in St. Charles, Illinois. "We are obviously very delighted," said the American Jewish Congress. But during the same season, a federal judge ruled in favor of a nativity scene on Chicago's city hall grounds, and in Los Angeles, a state court refused to bar the display of a menorah in city hall. To add to the confusion, a federal court refused to allow a menorah to be placed on the grounds of the state capitol in Iowa.

Meanwhile, the major Jewish organizations, which opposed the government-site placement of crosses and menorahs alike, supported government accommodations to religious needs in other areas. For example, they applauded the core of a Supreme Court ruling in November in a case brought by public-school teacher Ronald Philbrick against the school board of Ansonia, Connecticut, which had denied him paid days-off on holy days observed by the Worldwide Church of God. The Supreme Court affirmed that employers must attempt to make "reasonable accommodations" to the religious needs of employees, although it did not spell out the exact nature of such accommodations.

In a case that directly concerned Jews, the Supreme Court ruled in March that the Air Force did not have to alter its dress code to allow a Jewish officer to wear his yarmulke while on duty. The decision was the culmination of five years of litigation by Captain Simcha Goldman, a clinical psychologist who had been informed by the commander of Pease Air Force Base in California that when he testified in a military court wearing a skullcap he was in violation of the dress code. A circuit court of appeals had ruled that the Air Force had complete discretion to decide whether a violation of the dress code would harm its military mission, and the Supreme Court upheld that ruling. The major Jewish agencies mounted a campaign in Congress for legislative relief, but in August the Senate narrowly defeated a measure that would have allowed Jewish members of the military to wear yarmulkes on duty, if it did not interfere with the performance of that duty. Three of the Senate's Jewish members voted against the measure. Jewish agencies vowed to renew their efforts to find a satisfactory solution.

The Satmar Hassidim sought accommodation for their religious needs in two different cases. In Orange County, New York, the Satmar would not permit male students to be driven to their parochial school by the female bus drivers of the school-board transportation system. While the school board initially complied with this request, it reinstated the female drivers after being charged with sex discrimination. The Satmar sued the board, meanwhile providing its own drivers. In the Williamsburg section of Brooklyn, the Satmar demanded that their girls who were receiving remedial instruction in the public schools be physically separated from the rest of the students. The school board initially complied, building a physical barrier, but it was removed after suit was filed by several Hispanic parents alleging sexism and racism.

American society continued to wrestle with the problem of balance between separation and accommodation without a blueprint, as it probably always would. While the major Jewish agencies concerned themselves primarily with legal issues, it was the more subtle "Christianizing" spirit that probably concerned most Jews. They could not but be troubled, for example, by the words of the judge who gave permission for Chicago's nativity scene: "The truth is that America's origins are Christian. . . ." Although America was not "Christianized" by the end of the year, such utterances added to the wary temper of American Jews.

Nazis in the U.S.

The year opened with another revelation about ex-Nazis having been brought to this country after World War II by U.S. intelligence agencies. The *Village Voice* (N.Y.) reported in February that Mykola Lebed, a prominent East European collaborator with the Nazis, had been brought to America in 1948 and given permanent residence by the CIA, under a provision which allowed that agency to import a hundred people a year for national security reasons, regardless of their past. As in the other cases, the CIA had presumably taken this action to improve its intelligence about the Soviet Union.

Meanwhile, the government continued to try to redress its past indifference, or worse, with respect to ex-Nazis living in this country. John Demjanjuk, a retired Cleveland autoworker accused of complicity in sending almost a million Jews to their deaths, became the first alleged war criminal to be extradited to Israel by the United States. Israel had always considered itself a proper venue for trying war crimes against the Jewish people, but none of its requests for extradition had heretofore been honored. Demjanjuk, a Ukrainian by birth, had already been stripped of his citizenship in 1981 for misrepresenting his past when he came to the United States in 1952. The way was cleared for extradition after a federal district judge in Cleveland and an appeals court heard testimony that Demjanjuk had been a guard at Treblinka, known as "Ivan the Terrible," who had personally tortured and maimed camp inmates as they were herded into the gas chambers. Demjanjuk was deported to Israel in February, after failing to obtain a delay of extradition from the Supreme Court.

Demjanjuk steadfastly denied that he was "Ivan the Terrible" and claimed that it was a case of mistaken identity. Some 40,000 Ukrainian-Americans living in the Cleveland area mounted a campaign to support Demjanjuk's claim, through the Ukrainian Orthodox Church in the Free World and the United Ukrainian Organizations. They received support from Patrick Buchanan, White House director of communications and a syndicated columnist, who wrote in October, after Demjanjuk was indicted in Israel, that Demjanjuk was "a victim himself of a miscarriage of justice," and that his case might be "the American Dreyfus case." Former Israeli supreme court justice Haim Cohen said in November that Demjanjuk should not be brought to trial because after 40 years it would be difficult to provide accurate eyewitness identification. Despite such misgivings, Israel proceeded with elaborate preparations for the trial.

The U.S. Supreme Court upheld deportation orders issued against Boleslavs Maikovskis, a Latvian Nazi collaborator, and Karl Linnas, an Estonian who had been sentenced to death in absentia by the Soviet government. A foreshadowing of their fate came in the spring with news that Feodor Fedorenko, the first Nazi collaborator to have been deported by the United States to the USSR, was sentenced to death by the Soviet authorities, and that Andrija Artukovic, the "Butcher of the Balkans," who had earlier been extradited to Yugoslavia, was sentenced to death by that government. It was also learned that Valerian Trifa, who had been deported as an ex-Nazi to Portugal, died in that country.

The Office of Special Investigations of the Department of Justice, which had prosecuted these cases, reported at year's end that 22 naturalized citizens had been deported as ex-Nazis since the office began its operations in 1979. About 30 more cases were in the courts, and more than 500 investigations were active.

Waldheim Affair

In the course of Kurt Waldheim's campaign for the Austrian presidency, which he won in June, questions were raised about what knowledge U.S. intelligence agencies may have had of his wartime activities. The questions were asked both because of the revelations about the use of ex-Nazis by these agencies and because

UN records were reputed to hold information about Waldheim that was available to government agencies. The questions remained unanswered.

As one indication of U.S. displeasure with Waldheim's election, the U.S. ambassador to Austria was conveniently "out of the country" at the time of Waldheim's inauguration. Then, Secretary of State George Shultz made his appearance at an international conference in Vienna contingent upon his not meeting with Waldheim, even casually. The organized Jewish community campaigned for the U.S. government to place Waldheim on its "watch list," which would normally bar his entrance into this country. Attending a rally outside the Department of Justice building toward that end, just days before the Waldheim election, former congresswoman Elizabeth Holtzman said that his election would be part of a "growing trend to deny the Holocaust."

Of some symbolic importance, the international Genocide Convention was finally ratified in February by the U.S. Senate in an 83-11 vote. This came after 37 years of disputation about the possible effect of the measure on American sovereignty. The next step under the treaty process called for passage by Congress of legislation making participation in genocide a crime under American law; however, no action was taken on this during the year.

Interracial and Civil Rights Issues

No overt Jewish-black confrontations occurred in 1986, such as the eruptions of the previous few years involving Jesse Jackson and Louis Farrakhan. In fact, in considering a possible repeat candidacy for the presidency, Jackson seemed bent on healing the breach with the Jewish community that had developed in 1984. He took every opportunity, for example, to stress his active interest in the issue of Soviet Jewry.

The Reverend Louis Farrakhan, who in 1984 had called Hitler "wickedly great" and referred to Judaism as a "gutter religion," held a news conference in October at which he said he hoped to mend his fences with the Jewish community. Before and after his statement, his appearance on college campuses occasioned some minor controversies between Jewish and black students.

Neither did black-Jewish relations visibly heat up over the issue of South Africa. The Union of Orthodox Jewish Congregations of America, at its national convention in December, called for its congregations and all Jewish institutions to divest themselves of South African investments—an action which most Jewish organizations had already adopted.

The chief interracial focus of the year was probably three "affirmative action" rulings of the U.S. Supreme Court. In all three cases, tensions and passions ran high over efforts to redress discrimination in employment through the use of preferential treatment.

A 5–4 decision handed down in May held unconstitutional a Michigan school board's policy of laying off white teachers ahead of minority-group teachers with less seniority. While the case seemed to some to be definitive—seniority could not normally be breached by preferential layoffs—in fact, eight of the nine justices indicated support in general for racial preference in legitimate circumstances. In July, in a 5–4 decision, the Court upheld a specific 29-percent "goal" established by a lower court for minority-group membership in a New York sheet-metal workers' union. At the same time, in a 6–3 decision on a Cleveland fire-fighters' case, the Court upheld the right of lower courts to approve consent decrees that included racial preferences.

With respect to the latter two cases, a *New York Times* headline aptly referred to the "High Court's Ambivalence." In the New York case, the sheet-metal workers' union had been ordered by a lower court in 1964 to engage in some affirmative action program to remedy the fact that there were no black members. In 1975, having found no *bona fide* effort to improve the situation, the lower court ordered a compliance goal which was calculated as the percentage of nonwhites in the relevant labor pool in the New York area. In 1982, the union was found in contempt of court for "willful disobedience" of that earlier order and was fined. In the Cleveland fire-fighter case, the Supreme Court avoided ruling directly on the content of the particular consent decree which had been agreed upon by both sides, and which included a preferential hiring goal. It merely said that a lower court had authority to approve such consent decrees.

In both rulings the Supreme Court clearly rejected the premise put forth by President Reagan's solicitor-general that all racial preferences in hiring and promoting were illegal except to benefit individuals who had been personal and direct victims of discrimination. The NAACP called these two decisions "a tremendous victory for affirmative action." The solicitor-general commented that the Supreme Court had said about quotas, "not never, but hardly ever." Indeed, according to prevailing interpretations, the majority decisions did indicate that the courts should impose specific quotas only as a last-ditch remedy for "egregious" and stubborn discrimination.

These decisions were watched carefully by the organized Jewish community. The major Jewish agencies had all evolved positions which in various degrees supported some "color-conscious" affirmative action to remedy the effects of past discrimination, but opposed rigid quotas. The attempt to find an acceptable accommodation had proved thorny, at times becoming a major item of contention between black and Jewish organizations. As Hyman Bookbinder, Washington representative of the American Jewish Committee, said in January at a Martin Luther King Day celebration: "Needlessly hostile debate has been raging around the issue of quotas. . . . Confusion and conflict over the proper use of arithmetic standards has unfortunately kept us from working as hard as we could for the noncontroversial components of any meaningful package of affirmative action programs."

Pending any future Supreme Court changes in these close-vote decisions, it appeared that some level of reasonable accommodation had been reached. There was at least some satisfaction in most quarters, and no great heat was engendered. In particular, Jewish-black differences on the quota issue had not been aggravated, some Jewish agencies even joining forces with black organizations in presenting briefs on the Cleveland and New York cases.

Catholic-Jewish Relations

It was a more dramatic year for Jewish-Catholic than for Jewish-black relations. On the positive side, Pope John Paul II visited the main synagogue in Rome in April, the first papal visit to a Jewish house of worship in history. While American and world Jewish organizations universally applauded his action, they pointed out that a major barrier to full Jewish-Catholic reconciliation remained: the Vatican's failure to establish diplomatic relations with Israel.

This failure was aggravated in the United States by events surrounding John Cardinal O'Connor, the archbishop of New York. Considered "close" to the New York Jewish community and supportive of its issues, Cardinal O'Connor returned from a visit to Lebanon in June with a list of "preconditions" for Vatican recognition of Israel: Israel's assistance in finding "a Palestine homeland," in achieving peace in Lebanon, and in bringing about "the security of some eight million Christians in Arab countries." Although the Jewish community was critical of his remarks, it also recognized the prelate's desire to take a role in bringing about peace and perhaps influencing the Vatican's position on Israel. Prime Minister Shimon Peres invited O'Connor to visit his country, and a trip was agreed to, for after Christmas, that would take the cardinal to Israel, Jordan, and Egypt. Even before his departure, however, the Vatican enjoined O'Connor from holding any meetings with top Israeli officials in Jerusalem, since they could be construed as formal political recognition of Israel and of its control over Jerusalem. Jewish and Israeli leaders were predictably upset, but the visit was expected to go ahead, with suitable adjustments made.

In November Bishop James Malone, president of the U.S. Catholic Conference, urged the UN General Assembly to reverse its "deplorable" resolution equating Zionism with racism, but he did not address the question of diplomatic recognition by the Vatican.

One other Jewish-Catholic issue lurked in the wings: a perception in the Jewish community that the Catholic Church abroad had not exorcised its record during the Nazi period and still at times remained insensitive to Jewish feelings about the Holocaust. There were protests from American Jewish leaders, for example, when they learned early in the year of a plan to establish a Carmelite convent at the Auschwitz concentration-camp site. A fund-raising drive for the Auschwitz project begun the previous year in Europe had already drawn harsh criticism from European Jewish leaders, who viewed it as an affront to the memory of the Jews who were killed there. A similar reaction was evoked by the discovery in September that a Catholic church had been built at the site of a Nazi torture chamber at the Sobibor death camp in Poland.

EARL RAAB

The United States, Israel, and the Middle East

Relations between the United States and Israel remained close and cordial in 1986, even in the face of the potentially damaging Pollard and Iran/*contra* affairs. The year began with high hopes for progress in the Middle East peace process, based on positive signals from Jordan's King Hussein, but steps forward were only followed by regression in that area. It was a year, too, in which the United States took its strongest stand yet against terrorism—against Libya, specifically—apparently with salutary results.

United States-Israel Relations

The year began with American-Israeli relations at a peak. Since 1983 the Reagan administration had been raising the long-standing "special relationship" between Washington and Jerusalem to new highs. Strategic cooperation was no longer a vague concept but an operational reality. Economic relations were entering a new era, following the passage in 1985 of the Free Trade Area agreement. Aid to Israel was not only at its highest level ever but was now all in the form of grants rather than loans. And U.S. determination to help preserve Israel's economic and strategic strength had been demonstrated by the intense personal involvement of Secretary of State George Shultz in dealing with Israel's economic crisis of 1985. Above all, there was a new willingness by American officials to proclaim the value of the relationship—in effect, taking it out of the closet for all to see, including, and maybe especially, the Arab world.

The factors that had generated these developments were many. Since 1981 oil had declined as a political force, reducing the influence of Saudi Arabia on U.S. policy. Peace between Egypt and Israel, cold as it was, meant that full-scale war in the region was not imminent, thereby reducing the sense of urgency about the Arab-Israeli conflict that had shaped the outlook of the 1970s. Disunity in the Arab world and among Palestinian leadership was greater then ever, making it more difficult to construct policies dependent on Arab decisiveness and coherence. Finally, the recent surge of international terrorism had generated respect for Israel as the model of counterterrorist activity.

By the end of 1986 these fundamental forces continued to dominate the landscape; nevertheless, all was not positive. For one thing, the Jonathan Pollard affair remained an open wound. Then, in November 1986 revelations about U.S. efforts to sell arms to Iran, with Israel's assistance, burst into the headlines. As the year closed, it was certain that Irangate would have an impact on U.S. Middle East policy, but what that would be was uncertain.

STRATEGIC DEFENSE INITIATIVE

American-Israeli strategic and political cooperation branched out into new areas in 1986. One such area was the Reagan administration's major defense project, the Strategic Defense Initiative (SDI). With the administration encouraging Western allies to participate in the plan, early in 1986 Israeli analysts began to consider the possibility of an Israeli role. Arguments for involvement included the belief that it would deepen Israel's strategic partnership with the United States; would enhance Israel's deterrence against its enemies; demonstrate to the United States that Israel was not merely a regional client; and help Israel develop its own missile-interception technology, linking itself to the frontiers of Western technology. The potential negatives of Israel joining were increased hostility from the Soviets and resentment by those in the United States who opposed SDI. For those who argued for an Israeli role, of particular interest was the U.S. statement that the program would "examine technologies with potential against short-range ballistic missiles." Increasingly, Israeli defense experts viewed the coming threat to be Syria's SS-21 surface-to-surface missiles capable of reaching population centers. SDI research offered the possibility of countering this new threat.

On May 6 U.S. defense secretary Caspar Weinberger and Israeli defense minister Yitzhak Rabin signed a memorandum of understanding on Israel's future role in SDI. Israel would be assisted in obtaining SDI contracts, and the way was open for leading defense contractors to work with Israel on SDI research. The *Wall Street Journal* noted on May 7 that the agreement could have a significant effect on the work in that Israel was likely to examine the application of SDI high-technology weapons in tactical warfare rather than in strategic nuclear warfare envisioned by the United States. The *Journal* indicated that Israel was likely to focus on ground-based weapons that could be deployed against short- or medium-range nuclear missiles.

The formal agreement on Israel's participation in SDI was signed on November 5. Israel was the third country to sign on, joining Great Britain and West Germany. The agreement provided that Israel would undertake research on tactical ballistic-missile systems, the funding for which would amount to $5.1 million.

VOICE OF AMERICA

A second agreement reflecting the evolving cooperative relationship was signed in August, this for a Voice of America relay station to be housed in Israel. The story had begun in December 1984, when President Ronald Reagan sent a personal letter to Prime Minister Shimon Peres asking Israel to allow construction of a relay station that would overcome Soviet efforts to jam VOA broadcasts. Peres hesitated because of concern for the impact on Soviet Jewry. In October 1985, on the occasion of a Peres visit to Washington, the president again sought to persuade the prime minister to agree to the relay station. This time Peres said yes, and his accession was attributed to Israel's simple inability to say no to the United States. President Reagan said of Israel that she "is not reluctant and is not neutralistic."

Throughout much of 1986, negotiations took place over technical aspects of the proposal. Finally, in August, an agreement was signed in Israel in the presence of Vice-President George Bush. The station, to be built in the Negev, would take five years to complete, at a cost of $250 million, and would be the largest such installation serving the West. It would be staffed by about 100 technicians, mostly Israelis, and it would employ advanced U.S. technology making it more difficult for the Soviets to jam broadcasts.

NATOIZATION

A third proposal for cooperation, which was still unresolved by the end of the year, was to have Israel treated as a NATO country for purposes of winning U.S. defense contracts. To encourage NATO allies to standardize their weapons systems, Washington did not make them pay for initial, "nonrecurring" research-and-development expenditures, thus making U.S. weapons cheaper and more enticing.

When Defense Minister Rabin visited Washington in May he raised the idea of "NATOization" status for Israel. This would enable Israeli defense industries to compete on equal terms with their European counterparts for lucrative contracts. It also would make Israel eligible to lease military hardware from the United States. In September, on another visit to Washington, Rabin discussed the matter further with Shultz and Weinberger, but at the end of the year the matter was still under consideration.

LAVI PROJECT

The Lavi jet fighter-plane project reflected growing U.S.-Israeli cooperation but also made clear the problems that could surface between the partners. In 1983 Congress had approved the use by Israel of funds from foreign military sales (FMS) funds to finance development of the plane. Although Secretary of Defense Weinberger opposed this decision on the ground that FMS funds were supposed to be used for purchasing weapons and equipment in the United States, the decision by Congress led to the earmarking for the Lavi of $350 million in 1983 and $550 million in 1985, out of the total U.S. military aid package for Israel. Israel estimated that each jet would cost $15 million, but a confidential U.S. Defense Department study, publicized on April 29, concluded that Israel had greatly underestimated the Lavi's price, that each jet would cost $22 million. It concluded that the plane would meet its technological potential but production costs would be far higher than the $550 million a year budgeted by Israel's Defense Ministry, based on the production of 24 planes a year. Israel Aircraft Industries (IAI) disputed these figures, arguing that the basic labor cost of research and development in Israel was significantly less than in the States, which the report did not take into account.

On June 10 it was reported that Shultz and Weinberger had written to Peres urging him to reconsider the project and to buy instead a revamped F-16 using technology developed for the Lavi. On July 21 Israel formally unveiled a prototype of the Lavi; Peres called the plane a "superb achievement" that only "five or six countries all over the world" could hope to match. He said that the Lavi was not only the ideal warplane for Israel's needs but also could be a major export item.

U.S. reaction continued to be ambivalent. On August 11 the Defense Department announced the release of $67 million for contracts involved in the project but said that the U.S. government still expected Israel to consider alternative programs that the Pentagon would develop.

U.S. AID

The U.S. aid package to Israel ran into problems stemming from the budget deficit and the Gramm-Rudman legislation providing for budget cuts. When fiscal year 1986 went into effect on October 1, 1985, Israel was budgeted to receive $1.2 billion in economic aid and $1.8 billion in military aid, all in the form of grants. In addition, a significant part of the money to Israel was to be dispensed at the beginning of the fiscal year, rather than quarterly.

In January 1986, in response to Gramm-Rudman, the Reagan administration announced a 4.3-percent across-the-board budget cut and asked Israel to return $51 million of the 1986 money just received, noting that without the return of the money, aid to other countries would have to be cut by an average of 6.5 percent. On January 21 Israel agreed in principle to return that amount from the economic aid portion, though the Israeli government made clear it was under no legal obligation to do so. On February 24 Israel sent a check of $51.6 million to the Agency for International Development. Meanwhile, the administration proposed freezing aid to Israel and Egypt at 1986 levels for fiscal year 1987. In submitting its package to Congress, the administration praised Israel's economic progress, particularly its steps toward economic reforms and austerity measures, but also said that Israel had a long way to go and needed more comprehensive changes to reduce its dependence on external aid.

On October 16 a House and Senate conference reached an agreement on foreign aid for fiscal 1987. The total was trimmed to $13.37 billion, but that for Israel and Egypt remained the same, Israel getting $3 billion, and Egypt $2.3 billion. In addition to sustaining aid levels, on December 24, following a major effort by Sen. Daniel Inouye (D., Hawaii), the administration proposed a debt-relief plan for Egypt, Israel, and 36 other countries deemed strategically important and pro-America. The plan would give an opportunity to those countries to defer part of their interest payments on military loans and to refinance high-interest loans at current low-interest rates; countries would then make up the difference in interest in a single payment when loans came due. In Egypt's case, it was reported that the plan would allow postponement of as much as $3 billion in interest payments until the year 2009. Israel would save $200 million in payments in 1986 and over four years would save $1 billion.

ARMS SALES

A continuing source of tension between supporters of Israel and the administration was proposed arms sales to Arab countries.

In November 1985 the House of Representatives had pushed through compromise legislation blocking the administration's plan to sell $1.9-billion worth of arms to Jordan until March 1, 1986, unless "direct and meaningful peace negotiations" between Jordan and Israel began before that date. Early in 1986 the administration talked of going ahead with the sale in March; Assistant Secretary of State for Near Eastern Affairs Richard Murphy's visit to see Hussein in Europe in January (see below) was interpreted as an effort to promote the sale. Early in February, however, Shultz informed congressional leaders that the administration had shelved the proposed plan after Senators Robert Dole (R., Kans.) and Richard Lugar (R., Ind.), among others, convinced the administration that at least 80 senators would support a resolution opposing the sale.

On March 11 the administration shifted gears and notified Congress that it planned to sell $354 million in advanced missiles to Saudi Arabia. Congressional opposition to the sale was intense, led by Sen. Alan Cranston (D., Calif.) and Congressman Mel Levine (D., Calif.). On May 6 the Senate voted 73–22 to reject the plan; the House followed suit the next day by 356–62, votes called "veto proof" by opponents of the sale. Although spokesmen indicated that the president would veto the congressional rejection, the overwhelming vote notwithstanding, the administration attempted to reduce the opposition by announcing on May 20 that it was removing from the package the sale of Stinger anti-aircraft missiles, which caused particular concern lest they fall into terrorists' hands. The following day the president cast his veto. On June 5 the revised sale went through, as the Senate failed by one vote to achieve the two-thirds necessary to override the veto. Eight senators switched their vote in favor of the sale, citing the administration's removal of the Stingers and the desire to support the president in his role as Middle East mediator. Opponents of the sale claimed victory despite the vote, Senator Cranston noting that the final package amounted to less than 10 percent of the Saudis' original "wish list" of arms.

Aside from this new arms package, 1986 saw the delivery of the first AWACS to Saudi Arabia promised in 1981. The sale had been made five years earlier, conditional on certification by the administration that the Saudis had made "substantial" efforts to aid the Middle East peace process. While criticism of Saudi Arabia was voiced, Congress decided not to attempt to block the delivery. On June 14 it was announced that Saudi Arabia agreed to prevent AWACS technology and intelligence from falling into hostile hands and from being used to threaten Israel. On June 18 the president took the final step, certifying Saudi Arabian contributions to the peace process. Delivery took place on June 30.

THE POLLARD AFFAIR

The Pollard spy case, which broke on November 21, 1985, was the principal threat to U.S.-Israeli relations in 1986. In December 1985, following the arrest of Jonathan Pollard for transmitting classified intelligence documents to Israelis in the States, Israel maintained that the incident was unauthorized and offered "full cooperation" in the investigation. A joint team from the State and Justice departments, led by State's legal adviser, Abraham Sofaer, visited Israel, received pertinent documents, and interviewed Israeli officials. On December 20 the State Department indicated that it had been given "full cooperation" by the Israelis.

During the early months of 1986 U.S. authorities and Pollard's attorney entered discussions in an attempt to strike a plea bargain and avoid a trial, in the hope, apparently, of minimizing the damage to U.S.-Israeli relations. Complications developed, however, as federal investigators continued looking into the affair. On May 30 unnamed State Department officials indicated that according to new information in their possession other unidentified individuals in the United States and Israel, including an Israeli Air Force official, may have been tied to the espionage operation. Israel did not respond to these new charges but strongly denied reports of a widespread and well-financed Israeli intelligence operation in the United States.

On June 4 Pollard pleaded guilty in district court in Washington to participating in an espionage conspiracy directed by Israeli officials, as agreed upon by his lawyers and federal prosecutors. Federal officials said that Pollard was cooperating in the continuing investigation, and prosecutors indicated they had agreed not to ask for a life sentence but would ask Judge Aubrey E. Robinson to impose a "substantial" prison sentence.

Comments in the days following Pollard's guilty plea spotlighted the conflict between the State Department, seeking to limit the damage caused by the affair, and the Justice Department, complaining about the withholding of information. On the day of the hearing, a Justice official pointed to discrepancies between information obtained from Pollard in recent months, made public in court that day, and what Israeli officials had told the U.S. investigating team the past December. Noted, for example, was the failure to disclose the role of Israeli Air Force colonel Aviem Sella or the fact that a bank account had been set up for Pollard in Switzerland. Citing these new revelations, FBI director William Webster said in an interview on June 6 that despite promises of full cooperation, Israel had given only "selective cooperation." He characterized this as "disappointing," but said, "considering the nature of intelligence gathering, it's really not surprising."

Prime Minister Peres, with the approval of the entire cabinet, responded to these charges on June 8. He denounced attempts by some to "foul the atmosphere" between Israel and the United States. He again said that Israel had "provided full cooperation" and pledged "a continuation of the cooperation." And he strongly denied as "unfounded" suggestions by U.S. officials that the operation was much more extensive than Washington had been told by Israel.

The Israeli reaction set off a sparring match between the State and Justice departments. On June 9, State, which reportedly had cautioned Israel strongly against covering up information, issued a statement supporting Israel. It said that the United States had "no evidence of any espionage ring involving Israeli officials" other than those already named and that the indictment and successful prosecution were "made possible through the cooperation of the Government of Israel." The Justice Department responded that the existence of an Israeli spy ring could not be ruled out, and was reported to be considering revoking the immunity from prosecution that had been granted the Israelis interviewed the previous December, on the ground that they may have misled U.S. representatives.

The White House entered the fray unequivocally on the side of the State Department on June 10. Spokesman Larry Speakes said: "We stand by exactly what the State Department said yesterday and have nothing new to add to it." The support of the White House for State's efforts to minimize the damage to relations quieted things down. During the last months of the year, the affair moved away from center stage. On November 19, Judge Robinson, at the request of both sides, postponed the sentencing for two months.

Irangate

In November 1986 a story erupted that threatened to disrupt a host of U.S. relationships and policies in the Middle East—including the progress made in the preceding months against international terrorism, the friendly state of U.S.-Israeli relations, and U.S. credibility in the Arab world. The story was one that quickly came to be known as Irangate or the Iran-*contra* affair.

FIRST REPORTS

It began with a report on November 3 in the pro-Syrian Lebanese magazine *Al-Shiraa,* quoting senior Iranian sources who claimed that former U.S. national security adviser Robert McFarlane had made a secret trip to Teheran in October and had offered to send arms to Iran in exchange for hostages being held in Lebanon. Only the day before, David P. Jacobsen, an American held hostage in Lebanon for more than 17 months by Shi'ite Muslim extremists, had been freed in Beirut. Jacobsen was the third American hostage to be released from Lebanon in the previous year and a half; Lawrence Jenco had been freed in July 1985 and Rev. Benjamin Weir in September 1985. With the release of Jacobsen, five Americans were still being held in Lebanon. The organization called Islamic Jihad, a Shi'ite group linked to Iran that had held Jacobsen, released a statement saying that it had freed him because of "certain approaches [taken by the U.S.] that could lead, if continued, to a solution of the hostages issue."

On November 4 the Speaker of the Iranian parliament, Hojatolislam Hashemi Rafsanjani, confirmed the *Al-Shiraa* report. Speaking on the anniversary of the takeover of the U.S. embassy in Teheran in 1979, he said that McFarlane and four other men had come to Iran in the fall, posing as a flight crew and carrying Irish passports. They had been expelled after offering U.S. arms supplies in exchange for Iranian cooperation in curbing terrorism. A story also circulated that McFarlane had brought with him as gifts a Bible signed by President Reagan, several Colt pistols, and a key-shaped cake.

McFarlane, on November 6, denied the report and said that it would soon be clear that the Americans had kept to their policy of not selling arms to Teheran as long as it was supporting terrorism. And the president said the same day that "the speculation, the commenting on a story that came out of the Middle East and that, to us, has no foundation—all of that is making it more difficult to get the other hostages out."

The *New York Times,* however, carried a story, also on November 6, which said that American intelligence sources had revealed that the United States *had* sent military spare parts to Iran as part of a secret operation to gain the release of the hostages and to influence policy-making in Teheran. The sources also indicated that the United States had encouraged third parties, particularly Israel, to provide similar shipments.

DETAILS REVEALED

Some details of the story and the decision-making process also began to emerge. According to intelligence sources, McFarlane had worked on the operation with his successor at the National Security Council (NSC), Vice Adm. John M. Poindexter, and with Lt. Col. Oliver North, a member of the NSC who had played a key role in coordinating aid to the *contra* rebels fighting the Nicaraguan government. Secretary of State Shultz and Secretary of Defense Weinberger were said to have strongly objected to the top-secret plan, run by the NSC, when they found out about it. Their objections centered on three points: the operation would undercut the fight against terrorism and would offer incentives for the kidnapping of more Americans; it would frighten the Arabs of the Persian Gulf, who were already fearful of an Iranian victory; and it would antagonize U.S. allies who had been under pressure from Washington to join the Iranian arms embargo.

The administration reacted to these reports by imploring the press to try, for the sake of the remaining American hostages in Lebanon, to put a lid on the story. On November 7, with released hostage David Jacobsen at his side, the president refused to answer questions about the dealings with Iran, saying he could not do so "without endangering the people we're trying to rescue." Jacobsen urged reporters to "just be responsible and back off," saying that all the speculation could endanger the lives of the five Americans still in Lebanon.

REAGAN'S RESPONSE

When the very opposite occurred and stories proliferated, the president was forced to address the issue. On November 12 he met with Senate majority leader Robert Dole, Senate minority leader Robert Byrd (D., W.Va.), House majority leader Jim Wright (D., Tex.), and Congressman Richard Cheney (R., Colo.). For the first time, Reagan admitted that he had authorized the arms shipments. The following day, in a nationally broadcast speech, the president sought to tell his side of the story: "I know you've been reading, seeing and hearing a lot of stories the past several days attributed to Danish sailors, unnamed observers at Italian ports and Spanish harbors, especially unnamed officials of my administration. Well, now you're going to hear the facts from a White House source and you know my name." The president said that the United States had been conducting a "secret diplomatic initiative to Iran" for 18 months with four goals in mind: to renew our relationship with Iran; to bring an end to the Iran-Iraq war; to eliminate state-sponsored terrorism; and to effect the safe return of the hostages. He labeled "utterly false" the charge that Washington had shipped weapons to Iran as ransom payment for the release of hostages in Lebanon. Rather, he had authorized the transfer of "small amounts of defensive weapons and spare parts for defensive systems" to Iran for the purpose of sending a signal that the United States "was prepared to replace the animosity between us with a new relationship."

It had been made clear to Teheran, the president added, that if it sought an improved relationship, the "most significant step" it could take would be to use its influence in Lebanon to secure the release of American hostages. But, he reiterated, "we did not—repeat—did not trade weapons or anything else for hostages."

The speech did little to still the expanding imbroglio. The Arab League on November 14 called the arms shipment to Iran a "flagrant violation" of professed U.S. neutrality in the war. A comment the same day by a spokesman for French premier Jacques Chirac pointed to the impact of the affair on the attempt to build an antiterrorist front: "Those who give morality lessons would do well to sweep in front of their own doors before criticizing others. The French government has neither sold nor exchanged arms to obtain the liberation of its hostages." Representatives at a NATO meeting in Istanbul on November 18 expressed shock and anger at the U.S. action and passed a resolution calling on member governments not to negotiate with "terrorists, their backers or protectors."

On November 19 the president held a press conference, his first since August 12, in which he defended his administration's dealings with Iran but said that "to eliminate the widespread but mistaken perception that we have been exchanging arms for hostages, I have directed that no further sales of arms of any kind be sent to Iran." He defended the action's legality, asserting that arms had been sent to Iran after he signed a secret January 17 intelligence finding to authorize specific exceptions to the Iranian arms embargo.

Much of the reaction to the press conference focused on the president's contradictory remarks, among them Reagan's denial of an arms-for-hostage swap followed by his citing the release of three U.S. captives over the past year as evidence that the Iranian initiative had had some success. Also, the president indicated that the United States had not condoned "the shipment of arms by other countries" to Iran. Soon after the press conference, the president issued a statement of correction: "There was a third country involved in our secret project with Iran." Meanwhile, a nationwide poll conducted November 15–18 (after the president's speech but before the press conference) found that only 20 percent of Americans believed the president's statements on the affair had been "essentially true," while 82 percent disagreed with the decision to sell arms to Teheran.

The period of November 20–24 was marked by public bickering among top administration officials. Ex-adviser McFarlane referred to the arms deal as a "mistake," leading White House chief of staff Donald Regan to say: "Let's not forget whose idea this was. It was Bud's [McFarlane's] idea. When you give lousy advice, you get lousy results." And on November 24, following reports that administration officials were critical of Shultz for distancing himself from the affair, Undersecretary of State John Whitehead distanced State even further. In testimony to the House Foreign Affairs Committee, he said it was time "for the White House to come forward with a positive plan to undo the damage quickly," and indicated that State still did not have a detailed record of what had happened.

THE CONTRA AND ISRAELI CONNECTIONS

Whatever hope the administration had to contain the affair disappeared on November 25 when it became known that between $10 and $30 million in profits from the sale of American arms to Iran had been secretly diverted to help the *contra* rebels fighting the Nicaraguan government. The president himself revealed the findings in a brief announcement, in which he indicated that as a result of the new information he had accepted the resignations of Poindexter and North.

On the same day, Attorney General Edwin Meese filled in the details discovered in the Justice Department's review of the arms-supply policy. The United States, he said, sent arms to Israel, which had agreed to act as middleman in the secret U.S.-Iranian contacts. "Representatives of Israel"—Meese said it was yet to be determined whether these representatives "were specifically authorized by the government or not"—sold the arms to Iran for $10 to $30 million more than cost. He claimed that these extra funds were transferred either by the Israelis or the Iranians, acting with Colonel North's knowledge, to Swiss bank accounts controlled by the *contras.* North was cited by Meese as the only person in the U.S. government who knew precisely about this operation.

ISRAELI REACTION

From the start of the affair, stories appeared about Israeli involvement. An unnamed senior Israeli official was quoted on November 22 in the *New York Times:* "From the very beginning of this operation we have acted on behalf of the United States. Everything we did, including shipping arms to Iran, we did with the explicit approval of Washington. We offered them our good offices and assets, and they used them." But it wasn't until the revelations about diversion of funds raised fears that Washington might scapegoat Israel that Israeli leaders decided to speak. On November 26, after a meeting between now Prime Minister (as a result of the rotation with Peres in October) Yitzhak Shamir, now Foreign Minister Peres, and Defense Minister Rabin, a statement was issued: "The Government of Israel confirms that it helped transfer defensive arms and spare parts from the United States to Iran upon the request of the United States." On the subject of money transfers, however, the government was unequivocal: "These funds did not pass through Israel. The Government of Israel was surprised to learn that supposedly a portion of these funds was transferred to the *contras.* If such a transaction took place, it had nothing to do with Israel and the Government of Israel had no knowledge of it. Israel did not serve and would not have served as a channel for such a transaction."

The denial notwithstanding, an interview with President Reagan in *Time* magazine, published on November 30, seemed to implicate Israel further. After blaming the press for divulging the operation and thus endangering it, he discussed Israel's role in the transfer of funds, going beyond Meese, who had cited involvement of "Israeli representatives," not necessarily officials. The president was clearly referring to Israel, though not by name, in his description of events: "Another country was facilitating the sale of these weapons systems. They then were overcharging and were apparently putting the money into the bank accounts of the leaders of the Contras. It wasn't us funneling money to them. This was another country."

Israeli officials were reported to be baffled and disturbed by the president's comments, and on December 2, Israel again firmly denied the charge. Clearly, the introduction of the *contra* issue had changed the dimensions of the problem for the administration and, if Israel were to be implicated in this aspect, for Israel as well. As long as the issue revolved around arms to Iran, it touched on foreign-policy matters that were not clearly defined or divisive. The *contra* issue, however, was one that had divided the country and Congress, raising critical legal issues and highlighting the struggle between the executive and legislative branches of government.

INVESTIGATIONS BEGIN

In response to the rising tide of criticism, the president took two steps. First, on November 25, he announced the formation of a special review board to probe the activities of the NSC; the next day he appointed John Tower, former Republican senator from Texas, former secretary of state Edmund Muskie, and former national security deputy Brent Scowcroft to the board. Then, on December 2 he asked for the appointment of an independent counsel to investigate charges of illegality.

Meanwhile, reports in the *New York Times* revealed Saudi Arabian involvement in the arms sales to Iran. Saudi businessman Adnan Khashoggi was reported to have introduced two Israelis—Al Schwimmer and Yaacov Nimrodi—to Manucher Ghorbanifar, an Iranian arms dealer. The four men reportedly were the keys to the arms-for-hostages deal. Khashoggi was also reported to have played a central role in financing the purchase of arms by Iran. More significantly, it was said to have been done with the tacit approval of the Saudi government, reflecting Saudi fears of an Iranian victory in the war and the need to reach some accommodation.

On December 4 the investigation broadened as House and Senate leaders agreed that each body would form its own panel to investigate the Iran-*contra* arms deal. In his weekly radio address on December 6, the president admitted mistakes in the "execution" of the policy, but not that the policy itself was a mistake. Signs that the president was suffering politically appeared in a *New York Times*/CBS News poll of December 10, which found that 47 percent of the people thought the president had lied when he said he knew nothing of the diversion of funds to the *contras;* 37 percent said they thought he was telling the truth.

By the end of the year, an independent counsel and the heads of the congressional committees had been named. On December 19 a special panel of three federal judges selected Lawrence Walsh as independent counsel, with a broad mandate to investigate not only the arms sales to Iran and the diversion of funds to the *contras,* but all aid given to the *contras* by anyone in or out of government since 1984. On December 16 Senate leaders named Daniel Inouye, and a day later House leaders chose Lee Hamilton (D., Ind.) to head their respective panels.

Terrorism

The year began with mixed perceptions concerning the West's efforts to combat international terrorism. On the one hand, the United States had demonstrated its resolve to be firm by such actions as intercepting the jetliner carrying the *Achille Lauro* terrorists out of Egypt in October 1985. On the other, the proliferation of terrorist episodes gave the impression that the terrorists were winning the day, and cooperation by U.S. allies was as meager as ever.

FOCUS ON LIBYA

The simultaneous attacks on December 27, 1985, at the Rome and Vienna airports that had left 19 dead, including 5 Americans, were attributed to Abu Nidal, a renegade Palestinian terrorist leader believed to be backed by Libya. On January 7 Washington announced the imposition of economic sanctions against Libya and ordered the 1,000 to 1,500 Americans remaining in Libya to leave immediately. The next day President Reagan followed up with an order freezing all Libyan assets in the United States. So began a four-month campaign to take action against one of the key states held responsible for the spread of terrorism. This effort took political, economic, diplomatic, and, ultimately, military form.

Reagan's appeal for America's allies to join in isolating the regime of Col. Muammar Qaddafi fell on deaf ears, leading analysts to predict that the impact of a solo U.S. boycott would be negligible. The U.S. decision to impose economic sanctions took place only after serious consideration had been given to a military option and then ruled out. As he had in the past, Secretary of State Shultz favored a military response, while Secretary of Defense Weinberger had urged caution. Concern about the loss of civilian life and the prospect that Americans working in Libya might be subject to reprisals reportedly led the president to rule out a military strike for the time being. The decision to order Americans to leave was widely interpreted to mean that the United States was seeking to untie its hands in case it eventually decided to launch a military strike.

In a press conference to the nation announcing the measures, the president prepared the ground for U.S. action. He said there was "irrefutable evidence" of Qaddafi's support for Abu Nidal: "Libya has engaged in armed aggression against the United States under established principles of international law just as if he [*sic*] had used its own armed forces." And the president warned that "if these steps do not end Qaddafi's terrorism, I promise you that further steps will be taken."

EUROPEAN RESPONSE

Western Europeans were cool to the U.S. appeal for solidarity, arguing that economic sanctions would not work, and that the costs to Europe, which carried on much greater trade with Libya than did the United States, would be too high. Only Italy took any concrete action, on January 9 announcing that it was banning weapons sales to Libya and pledging that Italian workers would not take over jobs vacated by Americans. Disappointed by the European response, Shultz indicated on January 9 that the administration would move from public appeals to moral suasion. Between January 15 and 23, Deputy Secretary of State John Whitehead visited various European capitals. Little was accomplished, however, except a pledge by most of the countries not to take commercial advantage of U.S. sanctions against Libya. Even as diplomatic efforts continued, a war of nerves was taking place in the Mediterranean. The Soviet Union stationed the flagship of its Mediterranean fleet in Tripoli and deployed three warships off the Israeli coast to warn Libya against any possible Israeli air strike. On January 15 Secretary Shultz reasserted the American right to carry out military attacks against terrorists or state sponsors. He said the United States "cannot wait for absolute certainty and clarity" before striking at terrorist targets. On January 23 the administration ordered aerial operations from two aircraft carriers, the USS *Coral Sea* and USS *Saratoga,* near Libya. Naval maneuvers were also held off Libya January 23–30 and February 11-14, U.S. forces approaching but not penetrating the disputed Gulf of Sidra, which Qaddafi claimed as Libyan territorial waters.

While the administration was conducting a war of nerves with Libya, on February

4 Israel intercepted a Libyan civilian jet flying from Tripoli to Damascus, which Israeli intelligence suspected was carrying Palestinian terrorist leaders who had attended a two-day conference of radical Arabs and Palestinians. It turned out, however, that the passengers were seven Syrian politicians and two Lebanese militia officials. The Arab League widely condemned Israel's action, and Syria sponsored a resolution in the UN Security Council condemning Israel. On February 6 the U.S. vetoed it, saying that while it deplored the Israeli action, the resolution did not recognize the right of states to intercept aircraft under "exceptional circumstances."

MILITARY ACTIONS

Meanwhile, U.S. activities against Libya expanded. By March a third carrier, the USS *America,* had joined the fleet. The carriers together had approximately 240 planes and were escorted by 27 other warships, an unusually large force. On March 23 the Navy Task Force crossed into the Gulf of Sidra. Over the next two days Libya fired anti-aircraft missiles at American warplanes; U.S. forces responded by attacking a number of Libyan ships and a missile installation on the Libyan coast. On March 27 the U.S. fleet left the gulf. While the stated purpose of the operation had been to challenge Qaddafi's claims concerning the gulf, the administration let it be known that its true aim was to punish Qaddafi for his sponsorship of terrorism.

The administration received strong bipartisan support in Congress for the action, and from Israel and Great Britain abroad. Of the allies, Italy was most critical, Prime Minister Bettino Craxi saying, "Italy does not want war on its doorstep."

During the crisis, there were many suggestions that Qaddafi might retaliate by ordering terrorist assaults either in the United States or against American facilities abroad. These fears appeared to have been realized when a bomb exploded on April 5 in a West Berlin discotheque frequented by Americans. Two people died, including an American serviceman, and 200 were injured, including more than 60 Americans. On April 9 the supreme commander of NATO, Gen. Bernard W. Rogers, said there was "indisputable evidence" of a Qaddafi role.

In response, the United States pressed its allies to expel Libyan diplomats and called on West Germany to close the Libyan mission in Bonn. To support its case, the administration was reported to have provided intercepted messages from Libya to Europe, including a congratulatory message from Tripoli to its mission in East Berlin following the bombing. France and West Germany expelled several Libyan diplomats, but refused to link the action to the West Berlin bombing.

On April 9 President Reagan, in a press conference, described Qaddafi as "this mad dog of the Middle East," but refused to commit the government to military retaliation. On the same day, Qaddafi, in his first press conference since the Gulf of Sidra clashes, warned that if Libya was attacked, he would order Arab and other radical groups to strike at "American targets all over the world."

On April 14 the United States struck. Air force F-111s based in Britain and carrier-based navy bombers bombed targets in Tripoli and Benghazi, Libya. One

F-111 was lost in the attack, which struck five military targets. Numbers of civilians were killed, including Qaddafi's adopted infant daughter.

In a nationally broadcast address announcing the strikes, President Reagan said he had ordered the attack in retaliation for the discotheque bombing and to deter future Libyan terrorism. He alluded to the frustration of seeking international cooperation: "I said that we would act with others if possible and alone if necessary to insure that terrorists have no sanctuary anywhere."

Domestic reaction was overwhelmingly positive. A *New York Times*/CBS News poll released on April 17 found that 77 percent of the public approved and 14 percent disapproved of the attack. The public viewed the administration as having finally backed up its tough rhetoric.

Abroad, the story was different. Not unexpectedly, the Soviets, the Arabs, and other Third World countries vehemently denounced the U.S. action. Only Great Britain and Israel offered strong support. British prime minister Thatcher, who had allowed U.S. bombers to take off from bases jointly controlled by Britain, was outspoken: "It was inconceivable to me that we should refuse U.S. aircraft and U.S. pilots to be able to defend their own people. . . . If one always refused to take any risks because of the consequences, then the terrorist governments will win and one can only cringe before them."

While Britain had allowed the use of planes from its bases, the French had refused to allow U.S. planes to fly over French territory during the mission. Secretary Weinberger noted publicly that the 18 F-111s flew a route of 2,800 nautical miles to avoid flying through the air space of any nation. Had the French granted permission, he said, the distance would have been cut by more than half and would have reduced the risks.

EUROPEAN CHANGE OF HEART

Elsewhere in Europe, although the United States was criticized, the weeks following the attack witnessed a marked change in European attitude. Most significantly, French president François Mitterrand indicated that his country was ready to undertake joint measures, even possibly military action, against terrorists, and was dropping its opposition to discussing terrorism at the upcoming Tokyo economic summit. This changed attitude seemed to confirm reports that Mitterrand and Premier Jacques Chirac were shocked by the strong anti-French feelings that had surfaced. Elsewhere, Libyan diplomats and students were expelled from Britain, West Germany, and Denmark.

The Tokyo economic summit, held May 4–6, saw further action. The leaders of the industrial democracies issued a joint statement condemning terrorism, singling out Libya by name as a target for action, and setting forth six measures that the nations agreed could be taken against nations supporting terrorism. Included were a ban on arms exports, improved extradition procedures, stricter immigration and visa requirements, and the "closest possible" cooperation between policy and security services. President Reagan expressed pleasure with the declaration and said that the leaders had moved "beyond words and rhetoric" in their struggle against terrorism.

Meanwhile, stories circulated of Qaddafi being ill or in a state of shock following the raids. When he gave a speech on June 11, after many weeks outside public view, observers noted that his face was puffy and he spoke haltingly, slurring his words. Eight days later he told a Western interviewer that he was not ill, that he was "very tired" when he gave his June 11 speech because it was the end of Ramadan, the month of fasting, and that his grip on power and the support of the people remained strong.

For several months a quiet settled on U.S.-Libyan relations. Qaddafi remained out of sight, and terrorism associated with Libya seemed to have declined or disappeared. Then, in late August, reports appeared in the press that the two countries were "on a collision course again." The *Wall Street Journal* on August 25 quoted U.S. intelligence officials saying that Qaddafi had renewed his sponsorship of terrorism and that Washington was planning new, more punishing air strikes against key economic targets. The source also spoke of covert activities by the CIA to destabilize Qaddafi's regime and renewed U.S. efforts to get its allies to tighten political and economic sanctions. NATO commander Bernard Rogers talked of using B-52s against Qaddafi the next time around. Special envoy Vernon Walters, U.S. ambassador to the UN, visited Europe September 1-5, stopping in eight Western European nations. Reportedly, he did not hint at any new U.S. military action but instead called for tighter punitive sanctions against Libya, including a cutoff of air traffic and an embargo on Libyan oil.

One month later, the *Washington Post* reported that the brouhaha of late August had been a disinformation campaign by the administration, with the "basic goal of making Qaddafi *think* that there is a high degree of internal opposition to him within Libya, that his key trusted aides are disloyal, that the U.S. is about to move against him militarily." President Reagan said that he had approved a plan in August to make Qaddafi "go to bed every night wondering what we might do" to deter him from supporting terrorism. But he denied the *Post* story of a disinformation campaign. And Secretary Shultz told reporters in New York, "Frankly, I don't have any problems with a little psychological warfare against Qaddafi," but he knew of "no decision to have people go out and tell lies to the media." Assistant Secretary of State for Public Affairs Bernard Kalb resigned on October 8 as the State Department's chief spokesman, in protest of "the reported disinformation program."

POSITIVE OUTCOMES

This controversy aside, by the fall all signs indicated that despite the initial negative reaction in the West to the U.S. attack on Libya, the raid had generated a number of positive developments. The administration's credibility seemed at a high point, its actions now seen as matching its rhetoric. The allies, after an initial negative reaction, were further along the road of cooperation than ever before. And Qaddafi appeared weaker and less willing to support terrorism, despite predictions that the attack would strengthen his control and lead to an increase in terrorism.

Meanwhile, on October 24 a British jury convicted Nezar Hindawi of having plotted to place a bomb on an El Al jet on April 17. Hours later, citing "conclusive evidence" that the Syrian government had trained him, supplied the bomb, and directed the plot, the British government severed diplomatic relations with Syria. In a show of solidarity, the United States and Canada immediately recalled their ambassadors to Damascus, a move one step short of breaking relations.

The Middle East Peace Process

Although the year was not, overall, productive in moving the peace process forward, the factors that had created a sense of movement and dynamism the year before continued to operate. In particular, King Hussein of Jordan spoke and acted like a leader who believed that time was no longer on his side, that a resolution of the conflict was imperative.

HUSSEIN'S ROLE

The evolution in the thinking of Jordan's King Hussein, first evidenced in 1982–1983, offered the main hope that the stalemate of 1986 was only temporary.

Hussein's sense of urgency stemmed from his perception that events in the West Bank were moving in a direction that could, in time, endanger his throne. The fact that more Israelis were settling there raised the fear that growing numbers of Palestinians would leave in the face of increasing Israeli control and move across the Jordan, thereby dramatically increasing the Palestinian majority and threatening the Hashemite dynasty. The imperative for Hussein had become the need to stanch the flow of Palestinians from the West Bank. A peace agreement with Israel seemed the best, though not the only, way to achieve this end.

Hussein's new motivation, however, was tempered by some long-standing realities. The Rabat Conference of 1974 had named the PLO as the representative of the Palestinians. While Hussein had never been particularly pleased by this decision, he remained loyal to the will of the Arab League. Any move by Hussein seemed to demand a legitimacy which could come either from the PLO itself or from Syria, the leader of the rejectionist front. Thus, on February 11, 1985, Hussein had signed an accord with Arafat which seemed to offer the possibility of progress. Early on, however, the accord encountered problems concerning definitions, representation, and other matters.

Hussein's frustration with Arafat had led him, late in December of 1985, to seek a modus vivendi with Arafat's main adversary in the Arab world, Hafez al-Assad, president of Syria. The meeting was the first in six years between the two leaders, who had fallen out in 1979, when Syria accused Jordan of harboring dissidents to topple Assad. Relations remained difficult because the two supported opposing sides in the Iran-Iraq war: Syria being Iran's main ally in the Arab world, Jordan the Arab country most active in assisting Iraq.

Hussein's attempt to get Assad to support his strategy to bring about negotiations failed. Syria was more interested in other matters, particularly its continual war of nerves with Israel. Indeed, ever since his defeat by Israel in 1982, Assad had been focusing on building his strength and blocking American and Israeli moves. He had resisted Israel in Lebanon, sabotaged the Reagan peace plan of 1982, sabotaged Secretary of State Shultz's peace agreement of 1983 between Israel and Lebanon, and was now engaged in sabotaging Hussein's peace offensive. While Assad agreed to meet Hussein because his Saudi benefactors wanted it, because he never felt comfortable about being odd man out in his support of non-Arab Iran in the Gulf war, and because he had an interest in helping to move Hussein away from Yasir Arafat, Assad's hated rival, none of this was enough to move him to support Hussein's diplomacy. A Jordanian official said, "The differences we had were quite fundamental and cannot be resolved in one visit."

MURPHY TRIP TO EUROPE

Meanwhile, the U.S. State Department sought to keep alive the momentum toward peace that had built up in 1985. Assistant Secretary Murphy, who had made six trips to the Middle East in 1985, in mid-January left for Europe for further meetings with Middle East leaders. A particular sense of urgency surrounded the trip because Shimon Peres, viewed by many in Washington as a key to a breakthrough, was scheduled to turn over the reins of power to Yitzhak Shamir in October 1986 under Israel's rotation agreement. Speculation existed that the State Department saw the need for immediate movement if progress were to be made at all.

The Arafat-Hussein agreement of February 1985 had pointed to an international conference with participation of the Soviet Union. Although the administration had long been unenthusiastic about the idea, Prime Minister Peres's statement in October 1985 at the UN that he would be willing to attend an international conference if the Soviets restored relations with Israel and allowed Jewish emigration generated new interest in Washington in the idea. As Murphy embarked on his trip, Secretary Shultz indicated that the United States saw an international meeting as having only a limited role, one that was specifically not intended to intervene in direct Arab-Israeli talks or to block the results of those talks. Murphy, he said, was going to explore attitudes in the region toward the specific powers of such a conference and the question of Palestinian representation. The latter issue had plagued the process throughout the past year, with Jordan saying that members of the PLO must be included. Now, hints of change in that position had surfaced, and Murphy was looking to see if Hussein was ready to consider Palestinians acceptable to Israel.

Reports indicated a second purpose to Murphy's trip: the hope that it would bring enough signs of movement to soften opposition to the administration's proposed

$1.9-billion arms sale to Jordan. Congress had voted in November 1985 to bar the sale before March 1 unless Jordan began "direct and meaningful negotiations with Israel," but the president had promised to bring the sale up even at the prospect of defeat.

With Shimon Peres arriving in the Netherlands on January 19, at the beginning of a 12-day trip to Western Europe, and King Hussein in London, Murphy shuttled between the two for several days. At a press conference on the flight from Israel to Europe, Peres had reiterated his understanding of an international conference: the Soviet Union could attend but its role must be minimal, because the purpose of the conference was to move immediately to direct talks; and, there was to be no PLO participation. Meanwhile, reports circulated that Hussein was not hopeful that the PLO would renounce terror and recognize Israel as the price of admission.

During the course of this three-way diplomacy in Europe, Peres on several occasions reflected on the state of the peace process, offering a mix of optimism and a sense of urgency. At The Hague, on January 20, the Israeli leader said that "more than 50 percent" of the destination had been traversed toward convening an international forum and finding Palestinian representation for direct Arab-Israeli talks. At the Royal Institute of International Affairs in London, on January 23, Peres said: "1986 is a crucial year. It may be the best year for peace. If wasted, the opportunity may never return." On the same day, on NBC's "Today" show, Peres indicated that Hussein was making a final effort to see if Arafat would renounce terrorism, accept UN Security Council Resolutions 242 and 338, and agree to direct negotiations with Israel. The following day, at a London news conference, he talked of important progress having been made over the past month. But, he added, "I don't want to create the impression that we have overcome the difficulties. We are very far from it." He also indicated that he had received assurances from Murphy that Hussein would move toward talks with Israel even if the PLO and Syria withheld approval. Other reports suggested that Murphy was pessimistic about the possibility of Hussein jettisoning the PLO because Arab states would not support such a step.

If there were positive results of the Murphy shuttle, they were not readily evident. He was reported to have discussed with Hussein new names as potential representatives of the Palestinians. During the previous year, Hussein had submitted a list of Palestinian candidates to Washington, but only two—Hana Siniora and Fayez Abu Rahme—were acceptable to Israel. The others were deemed to be too close to the PLO. Hussein then had said he needed at least four Palestinians, but he submitted no new names. Hence, a stalemate had developed on this critical point, which Murphy's trip to London was seeking to break. Discussions did not, however, amount to a breakthrough.

INDIRECT NEGOTIATIONS

Upon Hussein's return to Amman on January 25, direct talks began between the king and Arafat, and indirect talks between the PLO leader and special U.S. envoy Wat Cluverius, carried out through the Jordanian government and non-PLO

Palestinians. The talks, which also involved Cluverius shuttling between Amman and Jerusalem, were an attempt to break the impasse that had developed because the PLO still had not accepted UN Resolutions 242 and 338. After two weeks, on February 8, the talks broke up in failure. The PLO had demanded that the United States accept the principle of "self-determination for the Palestinian people," a code-phrase for a Palestinian state, in return for acceptance of 242 and 338. Washington refused, and the PLO in turn refused to sanction Jordanian peace talks with Israel.

According to a Western diplomatic source, cited in the *Washington Post* on February 10, the Soviets played a negative role throughout this period of indirect talks. The Soviet ambassador to Jordan was said to have met with Arafat on at least three occasions, seeking to persuade him not to accept 242. The Soviets feared that a divided PLO under Arafat would be drawn into a U.S.-sponsored plan which would leave them with a minimal role; in exchange for rejection of 242, the Soviets promised the PLO to throw their weight behind the reunification of the organization. Six days later, senior Reagan administration officials were cited as supporting this reading of Soviet obstructionism.

Reaction to the breakup of the latest talks was mixed. On February 10 the State Department sought to present the situation in a positive light, describing the peace process as still alive and as incremental. At the same time it was reported that Hussein had told Peres, through Cluverius, that because of PLO rejectionism, there would now be a "long hiatus." Peres said on February 18, "We have returned to square one," blaming the failure on Arafat, who, he said, had demonstrated that he was not serious about peace.

HUSSEIN'S TELEVISION ADDRESS

The breakdown became complete on February 19, when Hussein delivered an extraordinary 3 1/2-hour television speech on his talks with Arafat. In harsh terms, Hussein declared that he was ending his effort and accused the PLO leader of breaking his word. He said that Arafat had told Jordanian ministers in August 1985 that he accepted 242 and 338, but Hussein later discovered that Arafat and the PLO Executive Committee had already decided not to accept 242. Hussein also claimed that before he began the final round of talks with the PLO on January 25, he had extracted a key concession from Washington—American agreement to *invite* the PLO to an international conference, once the PLO accepted three points (242 and 338; no terrorism; direct talks with Israel). The prior U.S. position had been only to *talk* to the PLO if it accepted the three points.

Hussein's announcement blaming the PLO reminded some of a similar statement he had made in April 1983, when he attributed his inability to pursue the Reagan Middle East plan to PLO rejectionism. Observers noted one difference, however. In 1983 Hussein said it was up to the PLO to decide how to proceed. In 1986 he hinted that the Palestinian people might do well to consider whether their best interests were being served by the PLO leadership. While paying lip service to the principle of the PLO as representative of the Palestinians, he left open other alternatives. Stressing Jordanian connections to the Palestinians, he indicated that the Jordanian parliament would vote new election laws to give West Bankers more representation and that Palestinians in refugee camps within Jordan would now be enfranchised. He said, "We are unable to coordinate politically with the PLO leadership until such time as their word becomes their bond," and that he was turning over the problem to the Palestinians in the territories and the diaspora, as well as the Arab states, to determine how to proceed.

REACTION TO HUSSEIN'S ADDRESS

Palestinian leadership in the West Bank called Hussein's decision to end PLO participation "a major disappointment." Mustafa Natshe, who had been deposed as mayor of Hebron in July 1983, following the murder of a Jewish settler, echoed the PLO line: there can be no alternative to the PLO and no substitute for self-determination.

Israeli leaders reacted to the Hussein speech with delight. On February 19 Defense Minister Yitzhak Rabin said he saw a historic opportunity without the PLO, though Hussein had offered no concrete hope of entering talks with other Palestinians. Abba Eban expressed pleasure that Hussein had described the PLO as an obstacle to peace.

U.S. State Department spokesman Charles Redman talked the next day of the need for a "period of reflection" on all sides. He confirmed that the United States had told Hussein on January 25 that the PLO could have a spot in an international conference if it agreed to the three points, and that the PLO would be free to propose self-determination once a conference began. He added: "Of course, the PLO's failure to meet the King's conditions makes this a moot question. . . . The PLO has now failed the King's test, and history moves on."

The Arafat-Hussein break effectively put the issue on the back burner. In his State of the Union address on February 4, President Reagan did not mention the Middle East; nor did Secretary of State Shultz the same week in his review of U.S. foreign policy before the House Foreign Affairs Committee. And early in February the administration withdrew its year-old request for the $1.9-billion arms sale to Jordan. As William Quandt, former president Jimmy Carter's National Security Council adviser on the Middle East, wrote shortly after Hussein's speech, Hussein was likely to bypass the PLO only if there were an Arab consensus behind such a move, or if Israel made him an offer he could not ignore, or if there were an assertive American initiative. Not one of these possibilities was in the cards.

The revelation by Washington that it had secretly offered the PLO a place at the conference table evoked a mixed reaction in Israel's divided government. On February 28 Foreign Minister Shamir met with U.S. ambassador Thomas Pickering to protest the fact that Israel had not been informed of the U.S. communication with

Hussein. By contrast, Peres's staff played down the matter, not seeing the move as a major change because, they said, Israel's agreement was still necessary for any PLO role and that would not happen. Meanwhile, senior Israeli officials on February 24 characterized Hussein's refusal to cooperate further with Arafat as a major policy change. They saw the king as trying to become the principal negotiator on the issue of the West Bank, looking for Egyptian backing and Syrian acquiescence.

Hussein continued his frontal assault on the PLO in an interview in March, published in two Kuwaiti papers. He said that he would continue peace discussions if a new Palestinian representation emerged, and accused PLO leaders of "wanting to rule the land, not just restore it." This comment expanded on a theme he had raised in his television speech, in which he seemed to criticize the Rabat decision of 1974 for turning the focus of the Arab world away from regaining the land and toward establishing PLO credibility. By his comments, the king was saying, in effect: to those in the territories to whom return of the land is the priority, I am your man. And to the Israelis and Americans he was saying something that had been implicit all through the years: in exchange for exclusion of the PLO, give me, Hussein, the territories. This was the most direct challenge to the PLO in years.

WEST BANK DEVELOPMENTS

As the peace process itself slowed to a dead stop, attention shifted to creating an environment in which the next surge of peacemaking might have a better chance to succeed. In late February, Peres increasingly talked of devolution on the West Bank, suggesting steps to make it easier for Palestinians in the territories to express their political views and administer their own affairs. He focused as well on economic progress as an essential ingredient for progress toward peace. In January he suggested to West German chancellor Helmut Kohl that the European Economic Community assist the Middle East through major economic cooperation. On March 30 he proposed a Marshall-like plan for the Middle East, calling for a $28-billion program, a third each to be raised from governments, banks, and industry, in the United States, Western Europe, and Japan.

ASSASSINATION OF AL-MASRI

Peres's efforts had hardly gotten off the ground when they encountered a major setback. On March 2 Nablus mayor Zafr al-Masri was assassinated. He had accepted the appointment the previous December because of his perception that municipal conditions had drastically declined since the previous mayor was deposed by Israel in 1982, in an effort to curtail Palestinian nationalist and pro-PLO activities. Al-Masri's death was seen in the context of his support for Hussein over the PLO and in the king's hint that if West Bank leaders were prepared to seek a formula for peace talks, the king might follow.

The Popular Front for the Liberation of Palestine (PFLP) took responsibility for the assassination, saying that it was a warning against cooperating with the Jordanian-Israeli scheme to replace the PLO. While the assassination was condemned not only by Jordan but also by the PLO, which had in fact approved al-Masri's appointment and saw him as a supporter, it was clearly seen as a defeat for Hussein. Al-Masri's funeral on March 3, which was attended by 50,000 people, was the scene of anti-Hussein, pro-Arafat fervor, the biggest demonstration of Palestinian nationalism since 1967.

Most West Bank leaders did not come forward to support Hussein. Following al-Masri's death, other Arabs proposed by Peres for mayoral positions refrained from claiming their positions. One, Nadim Zarou, scheduled to be mayor of Ramallah, fled to Jordan on March 3, while another, Jamil Tarafi, of El Bireh, placed advertisements in three East Jerusalem newspapers on March 4 saying that he would not accept the appointment. A group of moderate Palestinians from the Bethlehem area immediately shelved plans to join a pro-Jordanian group of West Bank political figures going to Amman to express support for Hussein.

Meanwhile, the leadership of the PLO was pursuing a low-key response to Hussein, intended to prevent an even greater rupture. Following the murder of al-Masri, PLO leader Abu Jihad on March 9 condemned the action and blamed the PFLP. On the same day, the PLO Executive Committee meeting in Tunis declared that it had not cut ties with Hussein and had not canceled the February 11, 1985, agreement.

Despite the setbacks, Israel and Jordan each had reasons to continue their efforts in the West Bank: Israel, to improve the quality of life, in the hope of winning cooperation, if not friendship; Jordan, to prevent a mass exodus of Palestinians; and their common goal of encouraging local, moderate leadership at the expense of the PLO.

On June 24 Hussein's government announced a five-year development plan for the West Bank, to be funded to the tune of $150 million a year. Investment was intended to promote job opportunities and permanent employment in the hope of limiting emigration. However, Hussein's development plan appeared to be in trouble even before it began. Anti-Hussein demonstrations occurred almost daily in July, including the burning of pictures of the king. Jordanian representatives tried to separate the plan in the public's mind from its struggle with the PLO. Prime Minister Zaid al-Rifai claimed that the "drive has no political implications" and was not "an attempt on our part to create an alternate leadership on the West Bank." Jordanians insisted that they had developed the plan before the February 19th fallout, and it was intended only to avert a security-threatening mass exodus of Palestinians to Jordan. The PLO, however, saw the plan as part of the king's plot against the organization and encouraged resistance.

On September 28 Israeli military authorities in the West Bank appointed three Arab mayors, Abed el Magid el-Zir in Hebron, Khalil Musa Khalil in Ramallah, and Hassan Mustafa Tawil in El Bireh. All were known to be pro-Jordanian. Local residents actively promoted the appointments, hoping to find solutions to such unmet municipal problems of a nonpolitical nature as garbage, water, and sewage. A further sign of Israeli-Jordanian cooperation was the acceptance by Jordan of a plan to have West Bank physicians complete their training in Israeli hospitals.

On November 3 a Palestinian-owned branch of the Cairo-Amman Bank opened in Nablus, the first Arab bank to open in the territories. It was reported that the Jordanian and Israeli central banks had arrived at a secret agreement providing for joint supervision of the new institution.

Resistance to Hussein, however, remained intense, both in the West Bank and in the Arab world. This was manifest in reports in early November that his plan for West Bank development was sorely lacking in money. At a three-day development conference of 150 Arab and foreign officials in Amman, Hussein asked for financial aid from the international community, but suspicions of his motives caused many to stay away who did not want to be perceived as opposing the PLO.

FURTHER DIPLOMATIC MOVES

In early April, with the United States retreating in its diplomatic efforts and only months remaining before the rotation would take place in Israel, Peres, on an unofficial visit to Washington, met with Secretary Shultz and Vice-President Bush. Although Peres said there was no choice but to push on, since he "didn't see anything else more promising" than the U.S.-backed effort to coax Hussein into peace talks supported by the "Palestinian people," State Department officials indicated a U.S. reluctance to make any moves during this "period of reflection." They said the ball was in the PLO's court, but they didn't expect any movement by the PLO or unilateral steps by Hussein.

While the political discussions seemed to be going nowhere, U.S. leaders talked up economic programs. On April 6 CIA director William Casey, speaking to the American Israel Public Affairs Committee, offered support for Peres's Middle East Marshall Plan. On April 22 the *Wall Street Journal* reported that President Reagan had committed himself to speaking about the Middle East Marshall Plan to his colleagues representing Western governments at their annual meeting to be held May 4–6 in Tokyo. Clearly, the theme of an economic framework had growing appeal as the political framework seemed to be breaking up.

In a speech before the American Enterprise Institute on May 7, Israeli defense minister Rabin stressed the need for patience with regard to the peace process. As long as Hussein was unwilling to move without either the PLO or Syria, Rabin said, the prospects for peace were poor. He stressed the need to develop Palestinian moderates on the West Bank, cultivate pro-Jordanian elements, extend greater autonomy to the residents, and suppress terrorism against moderates. Rabin noted that in the current environment, the most significant relationship was that of Israel with Egypt.

Peres made one more effort to persuade Shultz to come to the Middle East by sending Ezer Weizman, minister without portfolio, to Washington. Meeting with

Weizman on May 21, Shultz expressed his reluctance to return to the region without assurances of real progress. In fact, since Weizman brought no new ideas for breaking the impasse, the administration continued its recent tack of leaving the diplomacy to middle-level officials, based on its feeling that the Arabs and Israelis had to come to negotiations mainly through their own efforts.

The state of the peace process was evident from the low-key nature of Hussein's visit to Washington in June. The main news that emerged from the meetings was Hussein's announcement on June 10 that the foreign ministers of Syria and Iraq, two states long at odds, would meet in three days as a result of his mediation. (On June 13 Assad called off the meeting.) Hussein also urged Washington to pay more attention to Syria; he was described as seeing Syria as crucial to peace efforts and asked that Vice-President Bush visit Syria on his scheduled Middle East trip in July.

THE MOROCCAN INTERLUDE

In the midst of the dog days of summer and depressing days in the peace process, a ray of hope appeared in the form of a visit to Morocco by Shimon Peres on July 21. It was the first official meeting between top Israeli and Arab leaders since the last talks held by Menachem Begin and Anwar Sadat in 1981. King Hassan had foreshadowed the meeting in April when he made a public plea for some Arab leader to meet with an Israeli leader to learn directly of Israel's position on the 1982 Fez plan of the Arab League. He described the meeting as an attempt to get Israel to accept fundamental Arab conditions for peace—acceptance of the PLO and complete withdrawal by Israel from the territories. He indicated that he thought the time was ripe for such a meeting because inter-Arab squabbling had brought a certain paralysis to the process and because Peres, seen by the Arabs as a hope for peace, was scheduled to give up the prime minister's position in October.

The two-day visit was short on substantive achievement but long on symbolic value. In Israel, it was seen as an important step toward acceptance in the Arab world; a second major Arab country had broken Israel's isolation. Criticism of the meeting in the Arab world was far less severe than that directed at Sadat's 1977 Jerusalem visit. Jordan, which insisted it had no prior knowledge of the visit, was reserved but cool toward King Hassan. Other moderate Arab states said little, with the exception of Egypt, which welcomed it. Not unexpectedly, the radical Arab states on July 22 condemned the meeting, but only Syria broke relations with Morocco. On July 27 Hassan resigned as chairman of the Arab League, to allow the convening of an Arab summit meeting to assess his action.

The U.S. government hailed the meeting as a "historic opportunity to further the cause of peace" in the Middle East, but there was much speculation concerning Hassan's motives, including the notion that he was trying to curry favor to gain more U.S. assistance. In the long term, the summit would likely be seen as one small step in the evolution of Arab attitudes toward Israel's place in the Middle East.

GEORGE BUSH'S VISIT

On July 25 Vice-President Bush embarked on an 11-day trip to Israel, Jordan, and Egypt, the most senior U.S. official to visit the region in more than a year. Nothing of substantive importance developed during the trip. Israel and Egypt's dispute over Taba, the slip of land in the Sinai whose status was still in contention, remained near agreement on arbitration but was still not resolved by the time Bush left, and Egypt's request for American help concerning its debt remained unmet. Critics looking at the unfocused character of the Bush trip attributed it to his presidential ambitions.

Among the highlights of his visit were his call on July 29 for direct Hussein and Peres talks; his reiteration the same day of America's terms for meeting with the PLO, in conversation with 18 Palestinians; and a statement of principles, issued on August 5 on his stop in Cairo, which he said Israel, Jordan, and Egypt had agreed upon. Among the principles accepted were the need for Palestinian representation in negotiations; rejection of violence and terrorism; and a growing acceptance of Israel and of Israeli security needs.

On August 2, when Bush was in Jordan, Prime Minister Rifai reiterated his government's perception of the necessity for progress, summing up Jordan's sense of what was necessary for a breakthrough: the need to persuade the PLO to accept 242 and Israel's right to exist; to get Israel to accept the concept of an international conference; and U.S. and Soviet agreement to pave the way for such a conference. Rifai indicated that until the logjam was broken, Jordan would concentrate on assisting the residents of the territories. He noted that a portion of the U.S. monies formerly funneled to the territories through voluntary organizations was now going through Jordan.

SOVIET-ISRAELI TALKS

August brought increasing speculation that the Soviet Union was reevaluating its attitude toward Israel and its role in the peace process. On August 5 the Soviets confirmed earlier reports that Israeli and Soviet representatives would meet in Helsinki on August 11 to discuss consular issues. While the Soviets insisted the discussions were intended simply to deal with Soviet properties in Israel, many in Israel and elsewhere thought more was involved. On August 4 Peres had said that Israel would accept Soviet participation in Middle East peace talks only if the Soviets were to renew ties with Israel. On August 17 Israeli and Soviet representatives met in Helsinki, the first official contact between the two countries since the Soviet Union broke off relations with Israel in 1967. The talks broke up after 90 minutes. The Soviets suggested that a delegation visit Israel to look into what they called "consular matters" and to inspect Soviet-owned property in Israel. But Soviet negotiators brought the meeting to an end after the Israelis asked to send a delegation to Moscow in exchange for a Soviet mission to Israel.

ADDITIONAL U.S. EFFORTS

In Washington, on August 19, the State Department announced that the Hassan-Peres and Soviet-Israeli talks had prompted a review of U.S. policy to determine whether a new diplomatic opening existed to justify a stepped-up U.S. role. Secretary Murphy left on a trip to the Middle East on September 1 to push for a final agreement on Taba and to support the Peres-Hussein efforts to improve the life of the Palestinians on the West Bank. Two days later it was announced that Murphy had not made enough progress to justify a trip to the region by Secretary Shultz. Shultz's unwillingness to commit himself reflected his ongoing philosophy that the United States should not seem more eager for peace than the parties themselves.

Shultz did meet with Peres on September 15 when the Israeli leader was in New York attending the UN General Assembly session. Their discussion centered on an international conference with possible Soviet participation. Shultz told reporters that the Soviets could have a role only if they reestablished relations with Israel and allowed free emigration of Jews soon. Peres said, "I don't anticipate this is going to happen in the near future." He indicated that an international conference could be supportive but could be no substitute for direct negotiations on a bilateral basis. A senior U.S. official briefing reporters following the meeting said that Shultz and Peres had no apparent differences on the subject, which seemed to reflect an evolution in U.S. policy toward a more positive attitude toward the conference idea. On the other hand, Israel's foreign minister and soon-to-be prime minister, Yitzhak Shamir, reacted to efforts by Peres to pursue the conference idea with the words "What do we need this trouble for?"

Peres also met with President Reagan the same day, each making optimistic public statements afterward about the prospects for peace, widely read by the press as rhetoric to cover up the actual lack of progress during the year.

Israel's Relations with Syria and Egypt

The United States found itself in 1986 concerned with two specific problems between Israel and its neighbors Syria and Egypt. In the case of Syria, the problem was to prevent war-scare talk from escalating into the real thing. And in the case of Egypt, the problem was to begin to resolve the dispute over Taba in order to move the Egyptian-Israeli relationship, the foundation of a wider peace, back on track.

SYRIA-ISRAEL

The year opened with talk of potential confrontation between Syria and Israel because Syrian mobile anti-aircraft missiles in Lebanon's Beka'a Valley, as well as longer-range fixed SAM-2 missiles emplaced just inside Syria, were seen by Israel as an intolerable threat to its right to fly reconnaissance missions over Lebanon.

U.S. officials said on January 4, and Israeli sources confirmed the next day, that

Syria had withdrawn its mobile missiles from Lebanon, but the longer-range SAM-2s over the border in Syria remained in place. Early in March temperatures rose following an address by President Assad in which he declared that Syria was still building toward strategic parity with Israel—Assad's goal ever since Sadat's peace left Syria as Israel's main opponent—and threatened that if diplomacy did not lead to the return of the Golan Heights to Syria, then the "Golan will be the center of Syria."

Tensions increased further on April 17 when an Israeli security guard at London's Heathrow Airport discovered a concealed bomb in a bag carried by a pregnant woman about to board an El Al flight to Tel Aviv that had 340 passengers aboard. The next day police arrested an Arab, Nezar Hindawi, whom they accused of tricking the woman, his girlfriend, into carrying the bomb. On May 7 Israeli defense minister Rabin said, "We have reason to believe that [the attempt to blow up the El Al jet] was planned and carried out by part of the established organization of the security and intelligence community of Syria."

The following day CBS News carried a report quoting U.S. and Western European intelligence sources reporting that Israel was preparing a strike against Syria. With tensions increasing, Prime Minister Peres and Chief of Staff Moshe Levy saw fit to issue statements on May 9 denying that the two countries were close to war. On May 12, however, reports surfaced of Syria building a tank and artillery trench system in southern Lebanon, which was seen by some as an effort by Syria to nibble away at Israel's deterrent capacity. On May 14 Secretary of State Shultz, citing the "highly tense situation," cautioned Israel and Syria to avoid conflict; the next day the State Department offered a more soothing assessment, saying there were "no indications that recent tensions" between Israel and Syria would lead to warfare.

Further easing of tensions followed an Assad interview with the *Washington Post* on May 17. In it he denied that either Syria or Israel was engaged in unusual military buildups or movements and indicated that tension appeared to be lessening. He also specifically denied his government's involvement in the El Al plot. Peres on May 18 welcomed Assad's comments on the atmosphere between Israel and Syria, but dismissed Assad's denial of responsibility for the El Al plot, saying he would be "very much surprised if it was done without his knowledge." By the end of May, the war scare had diminished. In June it was reported that U.S. diplomats had been secretly mediating between Israel and Syria and that Assistant Secretary Murphy had made at least one trip to Damascus.

EGYPT-ISRAEL

The dispute over Taba dominated Israeli-Egyptian relations for a good part of 1986. A significant breakthrough was the agreement on January 13 by the Israeli cabinet to commit Israel to arbitration to resolve the dispute, something the Likud had strongly resisted.

Egyptian-Israeli relations were not helped by Mubarak's rejection in January of a proposal by the visiting Ezer Weizman for a summit meeting with Shimon Peres, and by an attack on four Israelis in Cairo resulting in the death of Etti Tabor, wife of an Israeli diplomat, on March 19. Peres indicated the next day that the attack would not dampen efforts by Israel and Egypt to reach a comprehensive Middle East peace agreement. Mubarak expressed his condolences to Avraham Sharir, Israel's minister of tourism, who was in Cairo at the time.

Increasingly, as the larger peace process slowed to a halt, Israeli leaders focused on the need to solidify relations with Egypt. But Egypt continued to reject the new Israeli positions, confirming the suspicion that improving its relations with the rest of the Arab world was more important than improving relations with Israel.

On August 5, after months of speculation about progress and breakthroughs in the talks, it was reported that Israeli and Egyptian negotiators had reached "substantial agreement" on a compromise formula for submitting the dispute to international arbitration. U.S. officials had sought to achieve a final agreement while Bush was in the region, but it was not to be. Assistant Secretary of State Murphy, who had accompanied Bush, stayed behind to work on remaining details.

The last issues were resolved on September 10, worked out in Cairo by Murphy and Egyptian and Israeli negotiators. The arbitration process itself was expected to take 18 months. The resolution of the arbitration issue cleared the way for a summit in Alexandria on September 11, which lasted three hours. Egypt agreed to return its ambassador, and a joint statement was issued calling 1987 "a year of negotiations for peace." Both Peres and Mubarak indicated their support for an international conference, but remained fundamentally apart on a role for the PLO and on Palestinian self-determination, both of which Egypt favored and Israel opposed. The United States welcomed the summit as a "positive step" that it hoped would "pave the way for a broader peace in the region," while the Arab League on September 12 condemned it as a "public relations exercise." On September 23 Egypt's chargé d'affaires in Tel Aviv, Mohammed Bassiouny, promoted to ambassador, presented his credentials.

KENNETH JACOBSON

Communal

Jewish Communal Affairs

THE ISSUE THAT MOST worried American Jewish leaders in 1986 was conflict between the Jewish religious movements. Other developments that attracted attention in the community were revelations of financial crime in Jewish leadership circles, the spread of AIDS among Jews, and disagreements among scholars over the quality of American Jewish life and the long-term potential for survival of American Jewry. American Jews also confronted certain external issues relating to the American political system, the administration in power, and foreign governments. These included strengthening Jewish influence on the domestic political scene, facilitating the emigration of Soviet Jews, and mounting an appropriate and effective response to the election of a former Nazi officer as president of Austria.

Jewish Religious Life

The theme of the annual General Assembly of the Council of Jewish Federations and Welfare Funds (CJF) is usually a reliable guide to the Jewish community's deepest anxieties. In 1986 the theme was "*Klal Yisrael*"—Jewish unity. CJF president Shoshana Cardin opened the proceedings with a reminder that "the agenda that unites us is more compelling than that which divides us." Harold Schulweis, a California Conservative rabbi, delivered an emotional talk decrying what he saw as increasing separation between American Jewish religious movements. "The division," he said, "is no longer between 'them' and 'us,' but within us."

The friction between the Jewish denominations in 1986 was an intensification of strife that went back to the early nineteenth century. At the time, the new Reform Judaism declared itself no longer bound by *halakhah*—Jewish law—while its traditionalist opponents, soon to be known as Orthodox, maintained that law's ongoing validity. Yet it was not till recently—beginning in the 1950s and accelerating ever since—that religious polarization became a serious concern of American Jewry.

There were three related reasons for this. One was the revival of American Orthodox Judaism. Previously assumed to be an immigrant faith destined to disappear in the course of time, Orthodoxy managed to reverse the process, slowing attrition among its youth, attracting *ba'alei teshuvah*—recruits from outside the movement, and developing an assertiveness it never had before.

Another new factor in the equation was the State of Israel, where Orthodoxy was legally recognized as the sole legitimate brand of Judaism. Time after time, disputes over the role of religion in the Jewish state spilled over to poison relations between the movements in the United States. The animosities would then be transferred back across the Atlantic, adding more fuel to the fires in Israel.

Third, resentment over these first two trends led American Reform Judaism to drop earlier inhibitions against overt actions that might shock and alienate the Orthodox. Thus, in 1983, Reform, giving up hope that its conversions would ever be recognized in Orthodox circles, had declared that the child of a Jewish father and non-Jewish mother did not need a formal conversion to be considered a Jew, so long as he or she publicly identified as a Jew. While this step formalized a practice that was already common among Reform rabbis, the issue of "patrilineal descent" became a powerful symbol of Jewish fragmentation.

ISRAEL'S LAW OF RETURN

In 1986 the key Israel-related issue dividing the Jewish religious movements had to do with the Law of Return, which guaranteed citizenship rights upon request to any Jew arriving in Israel. The law defined as Jewish anyone born of a Jewish mother or converted to Judaism. Early in the year the Israeli Knesset considered an amendment that had been attempted several times before, one that would specify that only conversions performed according to *halakhah* rendered an individual Jewish for the purpose of the Law of Return. This change, supported by Orthodox parties in the Knesset, would have effectively delegitimized conversions done by non-Orthodox rabbis. The driving force behind the amendment was the worldwide Lubavitch Hassidic movement, headquartered in New York. Modern Orthodox groups, both in Israel and the United States, doubted that it could pass, and demonstrated little enthusiam for pressing the issue. American Reform and Conservative leaders mobilized against the measure, charging that the great majority of American Jews were not Orthodox and would only be alienated from Israel by any step that strengthened the Orthodox monopoly. The Knesset defeated the amendment in February, to some extent because of fear of American Jewish reaction.

The issue came up in different form in April, when the two Israeli chief rabbis visited the United States and castigated Reform and Conservative Judaism for "creating a new Torah that can divide the Jewish people." The rabbis called on these movements to stop performing conversions. Reform and Conservative leaders retorted that religious pluralism was good for the Jewish people, and that it was the Israeli Orthodox establishment that sowed divisiveness.

In late June, the Shoshana Miller case reignited the controversy over non-Orthodox converts in Israel. Miller, who had undergone a Reform conversion in the United States, moved to Israel in 1985 and requested Israeli citizenship under the

Law of Return. Minister of Interior Rabbi Yitzhak Peretz, a leader of one of the Orthodox parties, granted her wish, but had the word "convert" printed on her identity card. American Reform and Conservative organizations denounced this move as a back-door attempt to nullify the Knesset's recent decision not to amend the Law of Return. Franklin Kreutzer, president of the United Synagogue of America (Conservative), warned of "dire negative consequences" for Conservative *aliyah* to Israel. Rabbi Alexander Schindler, president of the Union of American Hebrew Congregations (Reform), went so far as to compare the "convert" stamp on Miller's identity card to the yellow star that the Nazis had forced Jews to wear.

So volatile did the question of Israeli policy toward non-Orthodox converts become that even American Jewish organizations and leaders not affiliated with denominational movements got involved. For the first time in its history, the Council of Jewish Federations went on record "to inform Israeli leadership of the divisive impact any change in the Law of Return would have on North American Jewry." Kenneth Bialkin, chairman of the Conference of Presidents of Major Jewish Organizations—which had previously steered clear of religious disputes—expressed dismay at the treatment accorded Shoshana Miller. He said that "the mischievous and unacceptable order requiring the legending of Jews according to the quality of their Jewish origin" would undermine Jewish unity.

Israel's Supreme Court soon ruled against Interior Minister Peretz, in part, ironically, because traditional Jewish law forbids shaming a convert. The non-Orthodox movements in America applauded the decision, while warning against possible Orthodox machinations to block its execution. However, Rabbi Moshe Sherer, president of Agudath Israel (Orthodox) in the United States, said that the issue was not closed: "When it comes to identity, there is no compromise. It is not a business deal which can be settled by everyone giving up some points. It goes to the very heart of Jewish survival." Sherer warned that if non-Orthodox forms of Judaism were to transplant themselves to Israel, the Jewish people might split in two, since the Orthodox would never accept non-Orthodox converts as Jews.

The dangers of religious polarization revealed by the Miller case, coinciding with the outbreak of physical violence between Orthodox and secularists in Israel, evoked a peacemaking initiative from the Rabbinical Council of America (RCA), which represented the modern Orthodox rabbinate. In August the council called for a moratorium on any new religious legislation in Israel, presumably including amendments to the Law of Return. It also asked for calm and respectful dialogue between the Orthodox and others. American spokesmen for the other movements, while praising the intentions behind this Orthodox overture, pointed out that the status quo that would be preserved by such a moratorium was inherently unfair to them, since it did not recognize the religious legitimacy of their rabbis.

OTHER ISSUES

There were other interdenominational disputes during the year that were not related to Israel. They involved two American Jewish umbrella organizations that, up to this point, had served as neutral arenas where the movements could address issues of concern to American Jewry as a whole.

The membership of the Synagogue Council of America encompassed synagogue and rabbinic bodies of Orthodoxy, Conservatism, and Reform. The small Reconstructionist movement requested admission into the Synagogue Council, but in April the Orthodox members vetoed the application. This demonstrated, said Reconstructionist leader Rabbi David Teutsch, the "woefully insufficient commitment to pluralism on the part of the Orthodox in the American Jewish community."

The very existence of the JWB Commission on Jewish Chaplaincy was threatened by denominational strife. This body, which had representation from all the movements, collectively certified chaplains for the American armed forces. In June Rabbi Louis Bernstein, the Orthodox representative, announced his movement's withdrawal in protest over a unilateral decision by his Reform counterpart, Rabbi Joseph Glaser, to certify a female rabbi. This step, charged Bernstein, "broke the rules." Glaser, however, was in no mood to apologize. All too aware that the Orthodox would never agree to certify a woman, he explained, he had gone ahead on his own, as a matter of conscience. The crisis was resolved in August when a new system for choosing Jewish chaplains was devised: each movement's rabbinic organization would endorse its own candidates, with no need for the approbation of the other groups.

Did this accumulation of interdenominational disputes endanger the community? Those approaching the question from a scholarly standpoint, viewing current rancor within the broad context of the Jewish historical experience, tended to doubt it. Samuel Heilman, a sociologist at Queens College in New York City, prepared an analysis for the American Jewish Congress entitled "American-Jewish Disunity: An Overview." Heilman did not believe that current strife among Jews was any worse than in the past, and he stressed how united American Jews actually were on such issues as support for Israel, rescuing Soviet Jewry, and fighting anti-Semitism. Gerson Cohen, chancellor of the Jewish Theological Seminary and a noted historian of medieval Jewry, went even further, declaring: "There has never been as much unity in Jewish history."

Others, addressing the situation from a communal-policy vantage point, were more pessimistic. Notable among them was Rabbi Irving "Yitz" Greenberg, founder and president of the National Jewish Center for Learning and Leadership (CLAL). In lectures and articles, Greenberg advanced the thesis that unless denominational differences were bridged—especially on such matters as conversion, patrilineal descent, and divorce procedures—the Jewish people could well divide into two or more sects whose members would not marry anyone outside their own group.

In March, CLAL sponsored a conference in Princeton, New Jersey, on the question "Will There Be One Jewish People by the Year 2000?" It attracted an impressive turnout of rabbis and lay leaders from all the movements. The program featured addresses by leaders of Orthodoxy, Conservatism, Reform, and Reconstructionism—though at Orthodox insistence, the speakers did not appear together on the same platform. Rabbi Alexander Schindler, representing Reform, took the opportunity to apologize publicly for having compared some Orthodox leaders to Nazis, and Rabbi Norman Lamm, president of Yeshiva University (Orthodox), suggested the establishment of a joint *bet din* (religious court) to handle controversial issues of Jewish identity, whose members would be chosen on the basis of scholarship and religious observance, not denominational affiliation. Lamm's idea evoked little support from others in the Orthodox community.

TENSIONS WITHIN EACH MOVEMENT

Conflict between the major movements in 1986 was accompanied by—and surely exacerbated by—factionalism inside the movements. Within Reform and Conservative Judaism, traditionalist and modernist rabbis vied over questions of law and ritual. In the case of Orthodoxy, the focus of internal contention was how much, if any, cooperation and association were appropriate with the official bodies and leaders of non-Orthodox movements.

Three years after its patrilineal-descent decision, some within the Reform movement expressed doubts about its wisdom. Unexpectedly vehement criticism from Conservative rabbis and Reform leaders in Israel led to a few calls for reconsideration. The laity, however, backed by most of the rabbis, opposed reopening the matter.

A new issue, that of personal religious observance, emerged as a potentially divisive force. Reform had long before discarded the Orthodox notion of fixed, codified ritual obligations, stressing instead personal ethics and prophetic social justice. But trends in the broader society in the 1980s made many Reform Jews more receptive to traditional observance patterns. This was especially evident among younger rabbis and rabbinical students. At the 1986 convention of the Central Conference of American Rabbis (CCAR), Peter Knobel, one of those young rabbis, went so far as to suggest that the movement as a whole develop standards of ritual practice which, while not Orthodox, would diminish, to some extent, the personal religious autonomy that Reform had historically championed. CCAR's executive vice-president expressed sympathy for this view. Citing the dictum that Reform granted *halakhah* "a voice but not a veto," Rabbi Joseph Glaser asked, "Who are the other voters? Pressure? Fads? Radical chic? Weakness and despair? Reaction?" Rabbi Alfred Gottschalk, president of Hebrew Union College, which ordained Reform rabbis, decried the call for standards: "We're making an idol out of *halakhah,*" he said. Still, it was clear that interest in ritual practice was on the rise in the movement, and that classical Reform was on the defensive.

Conservative Judaism in 1986 was still seeking to heal the wounds inflicted by its decision two years earlier to ordain women rabbis. Symbolic of the ongoing division among Conservatives over gender roles in religion was the existence at the Jewish Theological Seminary, the training ground for the Conservative rabbinate, of two separate prayer services, one "traditional," where women sat separately and did not lead prayers, and the other "egalitarian," where men and women participated equally.

The struggle over women's ordination had led to the establishment of the Union for Traditional Conservative Judaism (UTCJ), which stayed in existence even after that issue was resolved, pressing for higher standards of religious observance and greater emphasis on *halakhah* within Conservative Judaism. At the 1986 convention of the Rabbinical Assembly (RA), the UTCJ proposed a resolution opposing patrilineal descent and providing for sanctions against any RA member who accepted as a Jew someone neither born of a Jewish mother nor converted according to Jewish law. The measure passed 235 to 92. However, when the UTCJ tried to get the Conservative rabbis to reject the movement's new prayer book for ostensibly deviating from tradition, and sought to guarantee itself a platform at the 1987 convention, it was defeated overwhelmingly.

The retirement on July 1 of Gerson Cohen as chancellor of the Jewish Theological Seminary was expected to ease the tensions between the traditionalist and modernist wings, since Cohen had been an outspoken proponent of women's ordination. His successor, Ismar Schorsch, while insisting that the clock would not be turned back on the women's ordination issue, made immediate efforts to conciliate the traditionalists and restore harmony to the movement.

The debate within Orthodoxy over relations with the non-Orthodox had implications for the very existence of "modern" Orthodoxy, which had long championed such cooperative endeavors. So-called right-wing or yeshivah Orthodoxy, in contrast, took a separatist stand, charging that membership on boards of rabbis or other umbrella organizations together with non-Orthodox rabbis constituted recognition of the other movements, and was therefore banned.

The inherent dynamism of rightist Orthodoxy, combined with the illness and withdrawal from public life of Rabbi Joseph B. Soloveitchik, who had been looked to as a mentor by those who favored working with the non-Orthodox, weakened the position of modern Orthodoxy in the community. Increasingly, rabbis who had called themselves "modern" decided to avoid the stigma associated with the word by denoting themselves "centrists." The Rabbinical Council of America, previously the acknowledged bastion of modern Orthodoxy, was now divided over whether to cooperate with the non-Orthodox movements on religious matters. At the organization's 1986 convention, suggestions to work out joint procedures on conversion with Reform and Conservative rabbis ran into heavy criticism, not because of *halakhic* misgivings, but because many members took the triumphalist position that the other movements would soon fade away and only Orthodoxy would survive.

Demoralization in the ranks of modern Orthodoxy led "Yitz" Greenberg, the president of CLAL and himself an Orthodox rabbi, to attempt a revitalization of this trend within Orthodoxy. Seven people accepted Greenberg's invitation to a preliminary meeting, which dealt with strategies to regain power for the modernists. Despite optimistic predictions by some of those who attended, nothing further came of the initiative.

The Jewish Political Agenda

Most American Jews combined a passionate commitment to the security of fellow Jews around the world—and particularly, after 1948, the security of Israel—with a politically liberal stance on other public-policy issues. Since the time of the New Deal, their political attitudes had been roughly congruent with those of the Democratic party, which consequently won the lion's share of the Jewish vote.

In recent years this picture showed signs of shifting. The election of Ronald Reagan as president in 1980 brought into power a conservative Republican administration which by 1986 had compiled a stongly pro-Israel record, at the same time that elements within the Democratic party seemed to be losing enthusiasm for Israel's cause. But could American Jews in good conscience reward Republicans at the ballot box, given the administration's conservative social and political agenda in domestic and foreign affairs? The 1986 congressional elections provided a focal point for heated Jewish debate over this question.

For one segment of American Jewry, the problem did not exist. Many Orthodox Jews were quite comfortable with the Reagan administration's overall approach to the issues. The Agudath Israel organization, representing this Orthodox element, agreed with the president on opposition to abortion and gay rights and support for tax credits to parents whose children attended nonpublic schools. As one activist put it, the stance of Agudath Israel showed that "the entire Jewish community is not out there attacking the Reagan administration for its abortion policies and then looking for its support on the issue of Israel."

Other American Jews viewed pro-Israel sentiment in Republican ranks as an opportunity to maximize Jewish political clout. Jewish political action committees (PACs) proliferated, almost all of them contributing money to candidates for public office on the basis of their records on Israel and Soviet Jewry, irrespective of their positions on other issues. This strategy was designed to encourage candidates of both parties to vie for Jewish support. The American Israel Public Affairs Committee (AIPAC), a national lobbying organization based in Washington, did not itself participate in distributing funds but did rate candidates on "Jewish" issues, without taking into consideration their liberal or conservative loyalties on other matters.

CONFLICT OVER PACS

Much controversy surrounded these "single-issue" PACs. In the May 26 *New Republic,* Robert Kuttner charged that by concentrating on Israel and tending to favor incumbents over challengers, Jewish PACs were actually providing more help to conservative Republicans, who opposed Jews on church-state and social-justice issues, than to liberal Democrats, whose overall agenda was much more in tune with predominant Jewish sentiments. While Kuttner's facts and figures were debated back and forth, his allegation brought to the surface a serious conflict of values and political strategy within the American Jewish community.

The issue was joined even before the Kuttner article appeared, at the American Jewish Congress biennial in March. Rabbi Arthur Hertzberg, a former president of the organization, and Massachusetts congressman Barney Frank argued passionately for a broad, liberal Jewish agenda. For Hertzberg, traditional Jewish values demanded concern for the poor and underprivileged and opposition to a socially conservative administration. He claimed that "we have a stake in a generous and open America which we helped to fashion and which now is under attack." Congressman Frank argued that there was an American consensus that backed Israel for geopolitical reasons, and that there was therefore "no reason to support right-wingers who oppose abortion, the Equal Rights Amendment for women, and who want prayer in the public schools because this is, they say, a Christian nation—just because they support Israel."

Richard Altman, director of NATPAC, a large pro-Israel PAC, and political analyst Ben Wattenberg argued the other side. Altman asserted that Jewish PACs deserved the credit for bipartisan congressional support of increased American aid to Israel, despite the budget cuts mandated by the Gramm-Rudman Act. Republicans, he said, must be made to feel that pro-Israel activity is appreciated: "We don't have the luxury of supporting only liberal congressmen like Barney Frank." Wattenberg argued the necessity of realistic political trade-offs: "If 90 percent of a congressman's supporters are for school prayer, and he is for Israel, then you shouldn't withhold money because of his position on school prayer."

The debate over single-issue PACs was further complicated by White House efforts to attract Jewish support for funding the *contra* rebels in Nicaragua. Members of the administration told Jews that not only was the Sandinista regime a threat to American security but the *contras* were anti-Semitic and pro-PLO. In a conversation with a delegation from the Conference of Presidents of Major Jewish Organizations, President Reagan himself added the argument that a hostile Nicaragua could very well endanger American supply routes to Israel. The immediate effects of this administration initiative were outrage at the assumption that Jews could only be mobilized on the issue by appeals to parochial Jewish interests and bitter controversy between Jewish leaders over whether the closing of a synagogue in Managua, Nicaragua, constituted anti-Semitism. Expressing the feeling of many Jews, columnist Marvin Schick charged that "if Nicaragua is a Jewish issue, fish ride bicycles. . . . The American public and Congress can arrive at a judgment without the gratuitous benefit of a crude attempt to provoke Jewish reaction." (*Long Island Jewish World,* May 23–29, 1986)

The public discussion about Jewish political options encouraged speculation about the Jewish vote in the fall elections for the Senate and House of Representatives. Would the community's traditional liberal sympathies generate another overwhelming show of support for the Democrats, or would the new single-issue emphasis lead to significant support for conservative Republicans who were pro-Israel? The results were inconclusive. Generally, the Jewish vote went to Democrats, but a few pro-Israel Republican incumbents garnered considerable Jewish backing, even though they ran against liberal Democrats. It was clear that the debate among Jews over appropriate Jewish political behavior would intensify as the Reagan administration entered its final two years.

Soviet Jewry

During the year American Jewry agonized over how best to facilitate the emigration of Soviet Jews. Despite the release of some notable refuseniks, the dismal overall emigration statistics disappointed activists and sharpened debate within the Soviet-Jewry movement over strategy.

The November 1985 summit meeting in Geneva had produced optimism, bordering on euphoria, that Soviet leaders were prepared to liberalize emigration policy. Hopeful that a deal could be struck, World Jewish Congress president Edgar Bronfman, whose business contacts gave him entrée into high Soviet circles, went to Moscow in December 1985 for private negotiations. No massive upsurge in emigration was forthcoming, however, although a number of well-known refuseniks were granted permission to leave the Soviet Union.

The meager results of Bronfman's initiative evoked anger from Morris Abram, president of the National Conference on Soviet Jewry (NCSJ), who, in January, called on the American government to link any future arms-control agreement with the Soviets to human rights. Abram said that if there were no progress on the Soviet Jewry issue by the time Mikhail Gorbachev arrived in the United States for another summit, public anti-Soviet demonstrations would be appropriate.

Abram's hard line drew immediate criticism. Edgar Bronfman rejected linkage on the ground that world peace would benefit all people, including Soviet Jews. Martin Peretz and Leon Wieseltier, editor in chief and literary editor, respectively, of the influential *New Republic,* denounced Abram's suggestion in a letter to the *New York Times* (January 22, 1986), arguing that "if arms control indeed represents an improvement in the security of the United States . . . even the predicament of Soviet Jewry pales before it." The threat of public demonstrations came in for criticism from the Orthodox Agudath Israel organization, which had consistently opposed confrontation with the Soviet Union, preferring quiet diplomacy.

In February this internal Jewish controversy was temporarily drowned out by exultation over the release of Natan (Anatoly) Sharansky, whose years of prominence as a Soviet Jewish activist made him a symbol of the movement in the minds of American Jews. But leaders of the Soviet Jewry cause in the United States warned against any assumption that Soviet authorities had changed their policy. In light of the small number of Jews allowed to leave, said NCSJ executive director Jerry Goodman, the Sharansky episode was a mere public-relations stunt: "There's little doubt that these so-called famous cases are designed to reach American public opinion." Observed Morris Abram, "What we are witnessing is emigration by 'eyedropper'—one Jew at a time."

Meanwhile, Sharansky, who settled in Israel, lent his voice to the hard-line anti-Soviet position. On a visit to the United States in May, he scoffed at "private diplomacy" and called for "open struggle and open pressure," including a massive demonstration upon Gorbachev's arrival in the United States, which was expected to take place sometime in 1986, "so that the American press will write more about the anti-Soviet demonstrations and less about the dress of Mrs. Gorbachev." In the months that followed, Sharansky spoke out against the renewal of Soviet-Israeli consular relations and against cooperation between the American Bar Association and the Association of Soviet Lawyers, in the absence of any change in Soviet emigration policy. On both these issues he dissented from the NCSJ and sided with the more militant Union of Councils for Soviet Jews (UCSJ) and Student Struggle for Soviet Jewry (SSSJ).

The National Conference, for its part, sought to carve out an approach that would combine public pressure on, and private negotiation with, the Soviet Union. It proposed a new look at the Jackson-Vanik Amendment of 1974, which limited Soviet-American trade by barring most-favored-nation status for the Soviet Union until it liberalized emigration. In July the NCSJ proposed a series of calibrated responses to Soviet behavior: any marked increase in the number of Jews allowed to leave would bring a corresponding easing of the trade restrictions.

REAGAN-GORBACHEV SUMMIT

The announcement of a Reagan-Gorbachev summit to be held in October in Reykjavik, Iceland, raised concern that the human-rights agenda would be overshadowed by the arms-control issue. While the leadership of the mainstream Soviet Jewry movement was satisfied by President Reagan's assurances that their cause would not be neglected in Reykjavik, some activists were skeptical. "Nobody wants to challenge the Administration to take a stand on Soviet Jewry," complained Glenn Richter of SSSJ, "although there is plenty of evidence that the Administration will only go so far on this issue."

Both camps within the Soviet Jewry movement sent observers to the summit; predictably, each group had a different assessment of the talks. For the moderate leaders, the very fact that the subject of human rights was on the agenda constituted a triumph. Morris Abram, recently elevated to the chairmanship of the Conference of Presidents of Major Jewish Organizations, commented, "Never before have American leaders gone to a summit meeting so thoroughly briefed on the issue of human rights in the Soviet Union and so thoroughly dedicated to raising it." "Hereafter," according to Jerry Goodman, "it will be difficult for the Kremlin to say that these questions are internal matters that should not be dealt with in an international forum." B'nai B'rith president Seymour Reich added, "We wanted to get world attention. I think we got it." For the UCSJ, however, anything short of an agreement for "the evacuation of all Soviet Jews who wish to leave" spelled failure. The group called for harsh economic sanctions against the Soviet Union and a boycott of Soviet-American cultural and scientific exchange programs.

By year's end it was clear that Reykjavik had not affected Soviet emigration policy. While a few more prominent refuseniks were allowed to leave in the wake of the summit, total emigration remained tiny, and new, restrictive guidelines for the issuance of visas were enacted. Morris Abram, reflecting the American Soviet Jewry movement as a whole, was pessimistic: "If we are forced to assume a confrontational stance toward the Soviet Union it is with reluctance. Yet we are convinced that improved relations are simply impossible so long as the Soviet Union relentlessly crushes its Jewish citizens."

Legacies of the Holocaust

The farther the Nazi Holocaust receded into historical memory, the more insistent American Jews seemed to be about commemorating it. In September thousands of survivors gathered at New York's Liberty Island to remember their liberation from the concentration camps and their first view of the United States, which for many of those present had taken place 40 years earlier at that very spot. Earlier in the year New York's Jewish Museum featured an exhibit on "Justice in Jerusalem Revisited: The Eichmann Trial 25 Years Later." Visitors could view daily continuous videotape screenings of the 165 hours of the trial. Throughout 1986, statements by Jewish leaders on subjects ranging from the Middle East to Soviet Jewry drew frequent parallels to what was done or not done to save the Jews of Europe a generation earlier.

On September 4 the City of New York announced plans to build a $60-million "Museum of Jewish Heritage—A Living Memorial to the Holocaust" on 165,000 square feet of land in lower Manhattan. The museum would include a six-story-high translucent cube illuminated 24 hours a day, symbolizing Jewish survival. The awarding of the Nobel Peace Prize, in October, to Elie Wiesel, Jewry's foremost literary interpreter of the Holocaust, signaled to Jews that their interest in commemorating the Holocaust was legitimate, indeed praiseworthy, in the eyes of the world.

Jewish organizations, without dissent, applauded Justice Department efforts to denaturalize and deport Nazi war criminals who had entered the United States after World War II and criticized those courts and government agencies that delayed the process. In October, when White House director of communications Patrick Buchanan argued that the evidence against one of the deportees—John Demjanjuk—was false, the Jewish community expressed outrage. Rabbi Marvin Hier, dean of the Simon Wiesenthal Center in Los Angeles, was particularly outspoken, accusing Buchanan of a "gross interference in the administration of justice."

WALDHEIM CONTROVERSY

But it was the case of Kurt Waldheim that drew most attention from Jews. Waldheim, who had served as UN secretary-general from 1971 to 1981, was a candidate for the presidency of Austria. In March the World Jewish Congress (WJC) made public information linking Waldheim to Nazi actions against civilians—including Jews—during World War II. When Waldheim admitted that he had known of atrocities but had not actually participated in them, other Jewish organizations entered the fray: the Conference of Presidents of Major Jewish Organizations called on the UN to open its files on accused Nazi war criminals, the Synagogue Council of America asked the world body to investigate whether Waldheim's Nazi past had influenced his conduct as secretary-general, and the American Jewish Congress canceled its popular tour stop in Austria.

The aggressive anti-Waldheim campaign unleashed by the WJC drew heavy fire from Simon Wiesenthal, the veteran Nazi-hunter. In Wiesenthal's view, by inflaming passions without offering any hard evidence of Waldheim's "crimes," the Congress had insulted Austrian national pride and set the stage for an anti-Semitic backlash against Jews in that country, not to mention enhancing Waldheim's electoral prospects. Rabbi Alexander Schindler, president of the Union of American Hebrew Congregations, agreed that the WJC had handled the Waldheim matter in a heavy-handed, counterproductive way.

Waldheim won the election in June. As the WJC continued to release additional bits of evidence about his whereabouts and conduct during the war, many in the American Jewish community called on their government to place Waldheim on the "watch list" of suspected Nazi war criminals who were barred from entering the United States.

An American Jewish Committee initiative in Austria sparked controversy. In August a Committee delegation visiting Vienna concluded an agreement with the Austrian government for a joint program aimed at reduction of anti-Semitism in that country. The plan called for a scientific survey of Austrian attitudes toward Jews and academic conferences and symposia on the subject. According to Committee officials, this was the first time that Austria had cooperated with a non-Austrian Jewish organization. The delegation carefully avoided meeting with the newly elected President Waldheim.

The WJC lost no time in attacking the Committee, going so far as to accuse Marc Tanenbaum, its international affairs director, of serving "as public relations agent of the Austrian government." The Committee's executive vice-president, David Gordis, responded, "The problem with standing on the sidelines sniping at Austria is that it only exacerbates the situation and creates further problems for Austrian Jews." Nathan Perlmutter, national director of B'nai B'rith's Anti-Defamation League, praised the Committee's strategy of distinguishing between Waldheim the individual and the Austrian people, saying, "I don't think any real obstacle exists to greater understanding between Austria and the Jewish community."

With Kurt Waldheim installed as the president of Austria for a six-year term, there was no end in sight to the controversy that still swirled over his role as a Nazi officer during World War II, or to the internal Jewish debate over how to address it.

The Boesky Affair

American Jewish organizational life, which is entirely voluntary, depends heavily on large contributors—the "big givers." Some of these individuals attain leadership positions in the Jewish community solely on the basis of their wealth and generosity. In 1986 American Jews discovered how risky this could be.

Ivan Boesky was a legend on Wall Street. The son of Russian immigrants, he made millions in risk arbitrage, buying the stock of companies that were about to be taken over by other companies. Boesky gave huge sums to Jewish causes and was appropriately honored by them. He contributed several million dollars to New York UJA-Federation and was its campaign chairman from 1984 until July 1986. Several million more Boesky dollars went to the Jewish Theological Seminary, two million of it for the seminary library, named for him and his wife. Boesky was also on the boards of Yeshiva University and the United States Holocaust Memorial Council. In 1986 he pledged the initial "leadership gift" for a new center of Jewish life at Princeton University. Boesky was politically well connected as the Republican National Committee's special adviser on Jewish affairs and finance chairman of the National Jewish Coalition, a pro-Republican group.

In November the Boesky myth disintegrated: the Securities and Exchange Commission fined him $100 million for insider trading, with a criminal investigation to follow. Boesky immediately resigned from all his positions in Jewish communal life, and the organizations he had supported moved quickly to distance themselves from him. "He is no longer our campaign chairman," a senior UJA-Federation professional reminded the media, "but simply a contributor." Students at the Jewish Theological Seminary rushed to have their pictures taken in front of the sign that said "Ivan F. and Seema Boesky Family Library" before it was removed.

Shock waves rippled through the American Jewish community. It quickly became known that Boesky had for some time been cooperating with the authorities, even allowing his phone conversations to be tapped. Others in the financial world were sure to be implicated, among them, undoubtedly, more wealthy Jewish philanthropists. Organization heads worried that some big givers might no longer be in a position to donate large sums.

Another concern was potential anti-Semitism. Earlier in 1986 New York City had been rocked by political scandals involving Jewish officeholders. There was fear that Boesky's downfall, by attracting even more attention to Jewish dishonesty in the metropolis, might provide potent ammunition to bigots, especially in the South and West, who were predisposed against big cities, Jews, and Wall Street.

The Boesky case also raised the sensitive issue of Jewish business ethics. What kind of a community was it, many asked, that could allow a Boesky to virtually buy his way into prominence? What had happened to Jewish moral values? Rabbis of all the movements expressed chagrin. Walter Wurzburger (Orthodox): "We are too ready to accord all kinds of honors and distinctions to people for no other reason than that they have a lot of money and are willing to make contributions to Jewish causes. . . . Before a Jewish institution accepts a large gift, they should carefully examine the propriety of the donor." Alexander Schindler (Reform): "The personal morality of the present generation of Jews has deteriorated." Wolfe Kelman (Conservative): "The brightest and best young Jews have been going into investment banking instead of medicine or law. That is a symptom of something that is a distortion of Jewish values." David Teutsch (Reconstructionist): "We no longer do what the Jewish community has customarily done: We do not teach each other about morality."

While just as appalled by Boesky as the rabbis, Jewish lay leaders were far less judgmental about the Jewish community as a whole. Kenneth Bialkin, a former national chairman of the ADL and the immediate past president of the Conference of Presidents of Major Jewish Organizations, accused the critical rabbis of "group libel . . . a terrible exaggeration which only plays into the hands of our enemies." The great bulk of Jews on Wall Street, he asserted, were honest. While Bialkin agreed that organizations should investigate the backgrounds of proposed honorees, he said that there was no way that Jewish leadership could have known the truth about Boesky before the SEC ruling was made public. Harvard law professor Alan Dershowitz, who was active in Jewish causes, denied that there was any great ethical weakness in the Jewish community, pointing out that "crime is largely a function of opportunity." It just so happened that many Jews worked in the stock market, which was where the chance to do insider trading existed.

A Jewish Response to AIDS

American Jews began to shape a specifically Jewish response to the rapid spread of Acquired Immune Deficiency Syndrome (AIDS). Many in the Jewish community argued that Jews suffering from this fatal disease faced special difficulties because of their religious affiliation.

Because intravenous drug use and homosexual activity—the two primary ways AIDS was contracted—were condemned by the Jewish tradition, it was charged, parents and friends often shunned the victims or tried to cover up the nature of the illness. Bitter accusations surfaced about rabbis and Jewish hospital chaplains refusing to visit AIDS patients, and Jewish funeral homes declining to conduct funerals for AIDS victims. There was also some fear that the spread of the disease would precipitate an antihomosexual backlash targeted at Jews, since a number of leading representatives of the gay community were Jewish. Analogies were drawn to the Black Plague of the fourteenth century, when Jews became scapegoats for a deadly disease that no one understood.

The Union of American Hebrew Congregations (Reform)—which included four gay synagogues in its membership—was the first Jewish religious body to assert officially that AIDS research should be a national priority and that discrimination against those suffering from the disease was contrary to Jewish values. In December a special UAHC committee on AIDS recommended that every Reform congregation set up counseling programs for victims and their families and that rabbis deliver sermons on the topic.

The UAHC also joined with national organizations of the Conservative and Reconstructionist movements, as well as the Council of Jewish Federations, B'nai B'rith, the Association of Jewish Family and Children's Services, and Jewish gay groups, to create a National Jewish AIDS Project. This was to serve an educational purpose, raising the consciousness of rabbis, Jewish agencies, Jewish funeral-home directors, and the general Jewish population about the need for sensitivity and compassion toward AIDS victims.

Congregation Beth Simchat Torah—a predominantly homosexual synagogue in New York City, 60 of whose members and friends had died of AIDS—published a brochure on Jewish funeral and burial practices, giving particular attention to the problems confronted by the families of AIDS victims who wished to follow traditional Jewish practice.

The Community Assesses Its Prospects

Many American Jews spent time in 1986 pondering the future of their community. This interest in collective introspection grew directly out of Charles Silberman's book *A Certain People,* which had appeared the year before. Silberman became a sought-after speaker before Jewish audiences, for whom he elaborated upon his optimistic view of American Jewish life.

The Silberman thesis had a number of parts. He argued, first, that anti-Semitism, while still alive, had ceased to be a problem for most American Jews. This allowed Jews to rise high in the American economic, social, and political structure. And unlike previous examples of successful Jewries, Silberman said, American Jews did not have to abandon their Jewishness in order to "make it." Silberman even found grounds on which to mitigate the potential demographic challenges to the community of a low birthrate and substantial intermarriage: women were postponing, not abandoning, motherhood, he said, and the large number of children of intermarriage who affiliated Jewishly, particularly when the non-Jewish spouse converted, could actually be increasing the Jewish population. All in all, American Jews had good reason for satisfaction, if Silberman was correct.

Students of American Jewish life differed over his findings. Brown University sociologist Calvin Goldshcheider published a book in 1986, *Jewish Continuity and Change,* which provided scholarly backing for many of the points that Silberman had formulated in his popularly written volume. Goldscheider claimed that while there certainly had been a drop in traditional indexes of Jewishness in the United States—ritual observance, for example—structural Jewishness remained strong: Jews tended to enter "Jewish" occupations, associated overwhelmingly with other Jews, and lived in predominantly Jewish neighborhoods. While differing in form from the past, concluded Goldscheider, Jewish identification persisted.

Others were dubious. Social scientists Nathan Glazer and Samuel Heilman and communal leader Arthur Hertzberg, among others, suggested that the "Jewishness" celebrated by the optimists was superficial and of questionable authenticity and was no substitute for the "Judaism" of the tradition. Interestingly, Silberman found that lay audiences took greatest umbrage at his view that anti-Semitism was no longer a serious problem, the one aspect of his book that drew general assent from the scholarly community.

The American Jewish Committee convened a conference of experts in May to deal in depth with the issues arising out of this controversy. What emerged was a recognition that the questions were much more complex than simply whether Jewish life in the United States was thriving or declining. It became clear that demographic data were hard to interpret and even harder to project into the future, and that any assessment of the "quality" of Jewish culture was inescapably subjective. One thesis that drew considerable attention was that, while certain parts of American Jewry were indeed deepening their Jewishness, others were on an accelerated assimilatory course out of the Jewish community.

LAWRENCE GROSSMAN

Demographic

Counting Jewish Populations: Methods and Problems

THE COUNTING OF JEWISH populations has been reported since the time of the Exodus from Egypt. From the very outset, the question of method has been almost as significant as the question of substance. Not only how many Jews are there, but how is the number determined? Who should be counted? Should all Jews be counted or only men of war or only taxpayers? What of those who, though not themselves Jewish, are part of Jewish households? What of those who once were Jewish (and remain so by Jewish law) but who have since renounced their Jewishness through conversion or simple drift away from the community? The question of counts presupposes that we know "who is a Jew," but that question is bedeviling elements of the Jewish community at this very time. There is, too, the matter of how to conduct the count. Shall we count individuals or households? And what kinds of information are available—at what cost in dollars and effort and with what degree of accuracy?

For the United States, the only Jewish population number of which we can be certain is that of the 23 Jewish refugees from the Inquisition who landed in New Amsterdam (New York) in 1654. For more than two centuries after that we have only speculation as to the number of Jews in the United States as a whole and in particular cities. The first set of estimates to which scholars have given serious credence is that published by the Board of Delegates of American Israelites and the Union of American Hebrew Congregations in 1880.[1] Fortuitously, since the 1880 estimates came right at the beginning of the mass migration from Eastern Europe, particularly Russia, they provide a fixed point that was found useful for making later estimates.

For much of this century, Jewish population estimates were often speculative. Using one or another ingenious method, sometimes with great sophistication,

[1]Board of Delegates of American Israelites and the Union of American Hebrew Congregations, *Statistics of the Jews of the United States* (Philadelphia, 1880), cited in Stephen G. Mostov, "Migration Patterns of America's German Jews," in U.O. Schmelz, P. Glikson, and S. DellaPergola, *Papers in Jewish Demography 1981* (Jerusalem, 1983).

sometimes with incredible naiveté, estimates of major centers were arrived at. In many of the smaller communities, the "estimate" was often merely the guess of a communal leader. For years certain entries remained the same simply because no one could be motivated to compute a new, perhaps more accurate, estimate. With a mixture of annoyance and relief, one scholar commented, " . . . not until 1948, following three decades of grossly exaggerated estimates, did a reasonable calculation of the American Jewish population gain acceptance."[2]

The U. S. and Other Censuses

Jews as Jews have never been enumerated in the national decennial census. The decennial census has never had a religion question, and even the ethnic identity question on the 1980 census did not allow for a Jewish response. As far as the decennial census is concerned, therefore, Jews (and Protestants and Catholics) do not exist. While popular wisdom has it that the absence of a religion question reflects the constitutional ban on the establishment of religion, this notion is not supported either by judicial decision or legislation.[3]

The absence of good official statistics, necessitating resort to various ingenious procedures, is attributable as much to Jewish concerns as it might be to fundamental church-state issues. For example, the recording of Jews as Jews at ports of entry, the official practice from 1899 through 1943, was decried by some of the very people and groups that engaged in Jewish population estimating and was not viewed happily by Jewish communal bodies and leaders.[4] The author of the Jewish population article in the first volume of the *American Jewish Year Book* described the enumeration of Jewish immigrants as " . . . a discrimination which has been properly condemned, but is held by the officials to be expedient."[5] Just a few years earlier, Jews in Germany correctly viewed the inclusion of a religion question in the census as the government's acquiescence to the demands of organized anti-Semitic groups.[6] During the hearings of the U.S. Immigration Commission (1907–1910), Jews actively opposed the enumeration of Jews as an ethnic group. They wanted to be counted as either of Jewish faith or of Russian or Polish (as appropriate) birth. Their sense of themselves as Jews was that they were members of a confessional

---

[2]Ira Rosenwaike, "The Utilization of Census Mother Tongue Data in American Jewish Population Analysis," *Jewish Social Studies* 33, nos. 2–3 (Apr.-July 1971): 156.

[3]Dorothy Good, "Questions on Religion in the United States Census," *Population Index* 25, no. 1 (Jan. 1959): 3–16.

[4]For a history and analysis of the issue, see Nathan Goldberg, "Forty-Five Years of Controversy: Should Jewish Immigrants Be Classified as Jews?" in Nathan Goldberg, Jacob Lestchinsky, and Max Weinreich, eds., *The Classification of Jewish Immigrants and Its Implications* (New York, 1945), 90–105.

[5]Abram S. Isaacs, "The Jews of the United States," AJYB, vol. 1, 1899–1900, 14–15.

[6]See Solomon Neumann, *Zur Statistik der Juden in Preussen von 1816 bis 1880* (Berlin, 1884), 6, cited in Jack Wertheimer, *Unwelcome Strangers: East European Jews in Imperial Germany* (New York, 1987), 32, 210 n.18.

community, like Protestants and Catholics. They denied that the Jews were a people or nation (particularly in exile), convinced that affirmation of Jewish peoplehood would threaten their status as members of the American nation.[7]

Once, in March of 1957, the Bureau of the Census did ask about religion on its monthly Current Population Survey, a sample survey rather than a full population enumeration. That 1957 estimate of Jewish population is extremely valuable in its own right and valuable too as an aid to other inquiries.[8] From 1850 through 1936, the federal government conducted a Census of Religious Bodies. Based on the reports of ecclesiastical officials rather than direct enumeration of the population, the Census of Religious Bodies reported the number of members or communicants a religious group had in various areas and in the nation as a whole. While this series cannot be used for developing precise estimates of Jewish population, it can be used to assess trends in Jewish population geography.[9]

State and local governments have conducted censuses as well, usually halfway between two decennial censuses. Less inhibited by church-state issues and also less constrained by demands for privacy, these nonfederal censuses have been valuable sources of information. Both the state of Iowa and Hamilton County, Ohio (Cincinnati), conducted censuses with a religion question in 1935. The manuscript censuses of the states of New York and Michigan have been made available to investigators. In these instances, Jewish households are identifiable through a variety of "markers," including name and national origin.[10]

Other nations with substantial Jewish populations do identify and enumerate Jews, in some instances as an ethnic group, in others as a religious group, and in the Canadian case, as both. Among these are the Soviet Union, Australia, New Zealand, and Switzerland.[11] The similarity of Canadian and American Jewish

---

[7]Charles A. Price, "Methods of Estimating the Size of Groups," in Stephan Thernstrom, ed., *Harvard Encyclopedia of American Ethnic Groups* (Cambridge, 1980), 1041.

[8]Good, "Questions on Religion."

[9]Uriah Zvi Engelman, "Jewish Statistics in the U.S. Census of Religious Bodies (1850–1936)," *Jewish Social Studies* 9, no.2 (Apr. 1947): 127–74.

[10]For use of the New York State manuscript census as an aid in reconstructing Jewish household structure and economic role in comparative perspective, see Herbert G. Gutman, *The Black Family in Slavery and Freedom* (New York, 1976), 521–30; for use of the 1925 New York State census in the course of a New York City Jewish population estimate, see Samuel A. Goldsmith, *Jewish Communal Survey of Greater New York; First Section: Studies in the New York Population* (New York, 1928), 13–19. The Jewish responses to the 1935 Iowa State census may be found in Rosenwaike, "Utilization of Census Mother Tongue Data": 141–59; on the Hamilton County Jewish responses, see Ira Rosenwaike, "The Utilization of Census Tract Data in the Study of the American Jewish Population," *Jewish Social Studies* 35, no.1 (Jan. 1963): 42–56.

[11]For a useful discussion of Jewish populations as represented in recent official censuses, see Ivor I. Millman, "Data on Diaspora Jewish Populations from Official Censuses," in U. O. Schmelz, P. Glikson, and S. J. Gould, *Studies in Jewish Demography Survey for 1972–1980* (New York, 1983), 33–120.

populations makes the Canadian census particularly valuable to the student of American Jewry. Among other reasons, it sheds light on discrepancies between ethnic and religious modes of Jewish identification. For example, in the 1971 Canadian census, among those reported as Jews by ethnicity were 7,825 Protestants and 3,340 Roman Catholics.[12] In part this is likely to occur by way of the census practice of ascribing ethnic identity through the paternal line, while Jewish tradition ascribes Jewish identity through the maternal line. In all, the 1971 Canadian census found 7 percent more people identified as being Jewish by ethnicity than were found by religion. Since the American Jewish community experiences many of the same social processes as the Jewish community of Canada, the availability of Canadian census data compensates in part for its absence in the United States.[13]

Census Proxy Indicators

On the American decennial census, through the census of 1980, three questions have been of special interest for the study of ethnic populations generally and Jewish populations particularly. These are race (white, black, other), country of origin, and mother tongue. Each of these questions entered the census schedule in response to a political concern and serves as a full or partial proxy for the identification and enumeration of Jewish populations. (By proxy we mean an accessible and valid substitute indicator. Thus, while Jews as such are not found in the census, any attribute enumerated in the census that is largely or uniquely held by Jews can be used as a substitute.)

RACE

The question of race was asked in the first American census in 1790 so that blacks might be enumerated for the population base required for representation in the House of Representatives. This is what led to the "three-fifths of a man" compromise in the U. S. Constitution. Since Jews are overwhelmingly white, the student of Jewish population can take into account broader ethnic succession from white to black as a context for studying Jews. For example, one study was based on the assumption that Jews were a stable proportion of the white non-Hispanic population of New York City. An estimate of the Jewish population of the city for 1970 was computed using the Jewish percentage as of 1957 and the number of white non-Hispanics as of 1970. While estimates on the level of the tract and even the county

[12] J. A. Norland, "Canadian Jewish Population, 1971," *Canadian Jewish Population Studies* 3, no. 4 (1974): 2–3.

[13] Joseph Norland and H. Freedman, "Jewish Demographic Studies in the Context of the Census of Canada," in U. O. Schmelz, P. Glikson, and S. DellaPergola, *Papers in Jewish Demography 1973* (Jerusalem, 1977), 59–78; Louis Rosenberg, "Births, Deaths and Morbidity Among Jews in Montreal in 1950," *Jewish Social Studies* 15, no. 2 (Apr. 1953): 101–12.

were flawed, for the city as a whole the assumption was valid and the resulting estimate was within the correct range.[14]

COUNTRY OF ORIGIN

The question on country of origin was introduced in 1850 in response to the large wave of immigration from the German states and Ireland in the 1840s. America wanted to know where its new residents were coming from, where in the United States they were residing, and other facts about the new "foreign" population. Two decades later, when the children of the migrants of the 1840s were old enough to be counted as adults, the census broadened its questioning to include not only the country of origin of the non-American-born but the country of origin of the parents of the American-born whose parents were born abroad. The two generations, parents born abroad and their native-born children, were designated as "foreign stock."[15]

The use of the decennial census for Jewish population counts was introduced for the census of 1900 by Dr. Walter Laidlaw, founder of the New York Federation of Churches and a major figure behind the development of the census-tract system. Laidlaw's motive was practical. He wanted his and other religious bodies to be able to use the census as a planning tool for the delivery of religious-based services. He appealed "to the churches and synagogues not to allow the social and civic agencies to distance them in deriving and bestowing benefit through it [i.e., the census]."[16]

Laidlaw's workers interviewed thousands of households, determining both their religion and their country of origin. Based upon his interviews he estimated that 90 percent of persons from Russia were Jews, 70 percent from Austria were Jews, and so on. In principle, Laidlaw's method was sound. His error was in generalizing to a population other than that from which his sample of interviews was drawn. He did no interviewing in Brooklyn and Queens but generalized to the entire city, including those two boroughs. However, the relationship between country of origin and religion was not the same in the areas in which he interviewed as in the areas in which he did not interview. The result was that Laidlaw overestimated the Jewish population by over 20 percent for 1900 and 1910. In subsequent years, i.e., 1920 and 1930, Laidlaw's estimates became more credible as his methods improved and Jewish population became more evenly distributed across the city.[17]

The Russian-stock indicator has been a useful proxy for the study of Jewish population *characteristics* and *geography* but has been less useful for the study of

---

[14]Abraham C. Burstein, "Estimates of Jewish Population, New York City" (1974, mimeo), cited in Jack Diamond, "A Demography of the Jews of New York City: A Preliminary Survey" (American Jewish Committee, Aug. 1976, typescript), 8.

[15]Price, "Methods of Estimating the Size of Groups," 1033–44.

[16]Rosenwaike, "Utilization of Census Tract Data": 43.

[17]Ira Rosenwaike, *Population History of New York City* (Syracuse, 1972), 122–25.

Jewish population *size,* primarily because it neglects Jews of Poland, Hungary, Rumania, and elsewhere in Eastern Europe. However, since the socioeconomic characteristics of Russian Jews at the time of the great migration were largely the same as those of other East European Jews, studies of educational and occupational attainment and of population segregation and centralization based upon census data have usually understood Russian to mean Jewish.[18] More recently the country-of-origin question has become useful in the study of the new Soviet Jewish immigration to the United States as well as for the study of Israeli immigrants.[19]

MOTHER TONGUE

By the beginning of the twentieth century, need was felt to supplement the country-of-origin question with one that would identify more precisely the ethnicity of immigrants from southern and Eastern Europe, particularly those from multiethnic areas like the Russian and Austro-Hungarian empires. The mother-tongue question, then, was introduced into the census in 1910 to develop a more refined picture of the population.[20]

The mother-tongue question has proved to be more useful than country of origin in computing Jewish population numbers. While the wording of the language question has changed from one decade to the next, it can be assumed safely that all those who report Yiddish facility, childhood memory, or use in their parental households are themselves Jews.[21] In 1910, the first year of its use, 1,676,762 persons (both native and foreign-born), an estimated 82 percent of American Jewry, reported Yiddish as their mother tongue.[22] In 1970, two generations later, 1,600,000 persons reported at least some familiarity with Yiddish. While the more recent number constitutes a much smaller segment (approximately 27 percent) of the American Jewish population, it is still substantial.[23] The Yiddish-language census sample has

---

[18]Erich Rosenthal, "The Equivalence of United States Census Data for Persons of Russian Stock or Descent with American Jews: An Evaluation," *Demography* 12, no. 3 (May 1975): 275–90; Nathan Kantrowitz, *Ethnic and Racial Segregation in New York City* (New York, 1973), see particularly 31. For a historical perspective, see Stephan Thernstrom, *The Other Bostonians* (Cambridge, 1973), 111–75.

[19]Paul Ritterband, "Israelis in New York," *Contemporary Jewry* 7 (1986): 113–26.

[20]Price, "Methods of Estimating the Size of Groups," 1033–44.

[21]The language question was included in every census from 1910 through 1980, with the exception of 1950. Unfortunately, the wording of the question and the definition of the responding population were not consistent over the 70-year period.

[22]Joseph Jacobs, "Jewish Population of the United States," AJYB, vol. 16, 1914–1915, 339.

[23]The comparability of the U.S. Census Yiddish mother-tongue population and the 1971 National Jewish Population Study Yiddish-competent population has been established in Frances E. Kobrin, "National Data on American Jewry, 1970–71; A Comparative Evaluation of the Census Yiddish Mother Tongue Subpopulation and the National Jewish Population Study," in U.O. Schmelz, P. Glikson, and S. DellaPergola, eds., *Papers in Jewish Demography 1981* (Jerusalem, 1983), 129–43.

been used to estimate local Jewish population size, Jewish economic activity, and Jewish fertility.[24] In one of its earliest uses, by virtue of establishing a well-grounded minimum number, the Yiddish-language statistic was able to show that a 1910 estimate of Jewish population was too low.[25] More recently, for a 1970 estimate, a ratio was computed based on Jewish population as estimated in the 1957 Current Population Survey and the number of Yiddish mother-tongue respondents in 1970. Using this ratio, the number of Jews and their geographic distribution was successfully calculated for several metropolitan areas.[26]

Noncensus Proxy Indicators

The basic logic has been established. Where the number of Jews is not known from the census, either one develops an estimate through a proxy indicator (e.g., mother tongue), or, as we will describe in the next section, one conducts a community survey, or both. In this section we discuss another method, the use of noncensus proxies. The three that are commonly used are death rates, Yom Kippur absences, and distinctive Jewish names.

DEATH RATE

The death-rate method is premised on two assumptions: first, that Jewish deaths can be identified unequivocally, and second, that a Jewish death rate can be established. The first of these turns out to be simple. In study after study, from the beginning of this century to this decade, investigators have reported that death certificates supply as a matter of course the name of the decedent along with country of birth, the funeral home, and the cemetery of internment. Each of these entries is an indicator of Jewishness. One finds very few misclassifications in the direction of over- or underestimating the number of Jewish deaths.

---

[24]Barry Chiswick, "The Labor Market Status of American Jews: Patterns and Determinants," AJYB, vol. 85, 1985, 131–53; Ronald K. Watts, "Jewish Fertility Trends and Differentials: An Examination of the Evidence from the Census of 1970," *Jewish Social Studies* 40, nos. 3, 4 (1980): 293–312.

[25]Joseph Jacobs, "The Jewish Population of New York, *American Hebrew* 90, no.13 (Jan. 26, 1912); Henry Chalmers, "The Number of Jews in New York City," *Publications of the American Statistical Association,* 14, 1914–15 (1916): 74. In this instance the Jacobs estimate was significantly off. It is the case, however, that in retrospect he was a major pioneer in the development of Jewish population statistics in the United States, publishing his results in this yearbook and various journals. An accomplished medieval historian, Jacobs first attempted these methods in London, where he was employed by the Board of Deputies of British Jews as secretary of the Russo-Jewish Committee and edited the British *Jewish Year Book.* His estimates, even when wrong, are not rank speculation but are based on thoughtful method. Jacobs tried to extend the death-rate method (described in the next section) by securing mortality statistics from various part of the country. Unfortunately, the effort was not successful.

[26]Ira Rosenwaike, "Estimating Jewish Population Distribution in U.S. Metropolitan Areas in 1970," *Jewish Social Studies* 36, no. 2 (1974): 106–17.

The first death-rate study of which we are aware is one of Parisian Jewry for 1780, published in 1878. The first contemporary death-rate study we know of was conducted in turn-of-the-century Baltimore and was immediately followed by studies in New York, London, Chicago, Detroit, and elsewhere in the United States and abroad, ultimately developing into one of the basic methods of Jewish population estimation.[27] The Baltimore study laid out the issues clearly.[28] To calculate the number of Jews, the number of Jewish deaths (326 in this instance) was divided by the death rate. As a first approximation, the Baltimore white death rate was used (18 per thousand), yielding an estimated Jewish population of 18,000, i.e., 326/.018 = 18,111, rounded to 18,000. The problem is that while we have confidence in the number of Jewish deaths, the same is not true of the death rate. The Baltimore study and all studies that followed it recognize that the Jewish death rate cannot be assumed to be the same as the local white death rate. On the contrary, because of differences in age structure, the sex ratio, immigration status, socioeconomic conditions, and life-style associated with being Jewish, Jewish death rates are very much unlike those of the populations among whom Jews live. This was as true in late czarist Russia as in contemporary Providence, Rhode Island.[29]

As is clear from the algorithm, the lower the death rate, the larger the population that is computed. Similarly, if the death rate employed is an overestimate, the result will be an underestimate of the Jewish population. In the instance at hand, the death rate was too high, thus producing an underestimate of the number of Jews in Baltimore. The investigator, George Barnett, proceeded to divide the Baltimore Jewish population into two major elements, the well-established German Jews and the recent Polish and Russian immigrants. Through a sophisticated use of late nineteenth-century census-collected Jewish vital statistics, along with vital statistics of Jews in Germany (analyzed and published by Arthur Ruppin), Barnett computed a death rate and then a size estimate for the German Jewish population. For the East European Jews, Barnett computed a death rate for census-identified Russians,

---

[27]Isidore Loeb, *Biographie d'Albert Cohen* (Paris, 1878), 27, cited in Zosa Szajkowski, "The Growth of the Jewish Population of France," *Jewish Social Studies* 8, no. 3 (July 1946): 179–96; George E. Barnett, "The Jewish Population of Maryland," AJYB, vol. 4, 1902–1903, 46–62; Joseph Jacobs, "The Jewish Population of New York," *The Jewish World*, Aug. 17, 1902: 8; S. Rosenbaum, "A Contribution to the Study of Vital and Other Statistics of the Jews in the United Kingdom," *Journal of the Royal Statistical Society* 68 (1905): 526–56, cited in Steven Haberman, Barry A. Kosmin, and Caren Levy, "Mortality Patterns of British Jews 1975–79: Insights and Applications for the Size and Structure of British Jewry," *Journal of the Royal Statistical Society* 146, no. 3 (1983): 294–310. For references to other American studies, see below.

[28]Interestingly enough, the impetus for carrying out a death-rate study in Maryland came not from a social scientist or statistician but from a rabbi in a small town in the state. The actual work of combing through the death records and establishing the basic facts was done by Henrietta Szold, secretary of the Jewish Publication Society and an editor of the AJYB, who later became the founder of Hadassah and Youth Aliyah.

[29]Alice Goldstein, "Patterns of Mortality and Causes of Death Among Rhode Island Jews, 1979–1981," *Social Biology* 33, nos. 1–2 (1987): 87–101.

whom he assumed to be Jews (see above), borrowing his data from New York. He then had the number of deaths, the death rates, and the population size of the major elements in the Jewish community and was able to compute a total Jewish community size of 25,000 persons, well above the estimate computed using the white death rate.[30]

In the 1902 New York study conducted by Joseph Jacobs, the number of Jewish deaths was collected as it was in Baltimore.[31] The Jewish death rate was taken areally; that is, the death rate was computed for specific wards known to be populated overwhelmingly by immigrant Jews. It was then reasoned that since the living conditions in these wards were such as to lower life expectancy, the overall death rate had to be adjusted downward to compensate. To check his results, Jacobs examined data on Jewish immigration to New York, natural increase (the surplus of births over deaths), and marriage rates and found that the estimates from death rates were consistent with those from marriages and natural increase.

Over time, the death-rate method became increasingly sophisticated. The Detroit study computed and published several population estimates (for 1940) using different death rates. The results based on death rates of Detroit Jewish tracts and upper-income tracts (in which Jews and non-Jews lived) and constructed Canadian Jewish death rates were extraordinarily close. By contrast, the use of general white Detroit or Canadian death rates resulted in much lower population estimates (on the order of one-third lower).[32]

The Chicago study for 1930 also computed population estimates using more than one set of death rates—in this instance one based on known Jewish tracts and the other on white middle-class tracts. The results of the two sets of calculations differed by approximately 7 percent, a small number but large enough to make the investigator check the outcome. Abram Jaffe examined the internal demographic characteristics of each group and concluded that despite socioeconomic similarities, the Jewish death rate was in fact different and produced more plausible results.[33]

YOM KIPPUR-ABSENCE METHOD

The logic of the proxy procedure as laid out in the discussion of the death-rate and other proxy methods is the same. One counts the proxy indicator, computes the proportion of the larger population which members of the proxy population represent (the appropriate rate), and then computes a ratio of the two. In the case at hand, that means counting the number of pupils absent on Yom Kippur and then dividing

---

[30]Barnett, "Jewish Population of Maryland."

[31]Jacobs, "Jewish Population of New York."

[32]S. Joseph Fauman and Albert J. Mayer, "Estimation of Jewish Population by the Death Rate Method," *Jewish Social Studies* 18, no. 4 (Oct. 1955): 315–22. "Constructed" rates are calculated from life tables rather than from direct observation of mortality.

[33]Abram Jaffe, "A Study of Chicago Jewry (1930) Based on Death Certificates," in Sophia M. Robison, *Jewish Population Studies* (New York, 1943), 131–51. See particularly 146.

that number by the proportion of the Jewish population eligible for inclusion among the absentees, i.e., the Jewish school population. The major advantage of the Yom Kippur method over the death-rate method is that school records are kept centrally. The investigator does not have to go through the arduous task of reading, classifying, and coding thousands of records. Perhaps it was its simplicity that encouraged early investigators to employ the method in London in 1892 and in Philadelphia in 1904.[34]

As with the death-rate method, the Yom Kippur method stands on the investigator's ability to secure accurate counts, in this case, of Yom Kippur absences, and to know what percentage of the Jewish population is in school. The latter is usually represented by the proportion of the Jewish population that is of primary-school attending age.[35] The ratio of the two gives the estimate of the number of Jews in the community. Various objections have been expressed about this method. For one, in schools that are largely Jewish, non-Jewish pupils also absent themselves on the holy day. Investigators using the method respond that where Jews are a small minority, parents may well send their children to school on Yom Kippur, so that the resulting underestimate balances out the overestimate. To determine if his Yom Kippur-absence count was accurate, one early researcher supplemented that number with an actual count of Jewish pupils, identified by name, in the central school records, concluding that the results " . . . are in close agreement."[36]

A second major source of error is the misestimation of the Jewish age distribution. Studies conducted in Pittsburgh and Minneapolis comparing the Yom Kippur method with other procedures conclude that the Yom Kippur method undercounts Jews. Closer examination reveals that the undercounts result from not adequately taking into account lower Jewish fertility, which leads to both a smaller proportion of Jews in the school-age cohort and smaller household size.[37] What this error demonstrates is that the various parameters used in calculating population by means of proxies cannot be taken mechanically from either prior studies or general census populations. Jews have had distinctive birthrates and death rates, and therefore age structures, through most of this century. With the wrong initiating figures, the outcomes will inevitably be wrong.

---

[34]C. Morris Horowitz and Lawrence J. Kaplan, "The Jewish Population of the New York Area" (New York, 1959, mimeo), 85. See, too, Charles Seligman Bernheimer, *The Russian Jew in the United States* (Philadelphia, 1905).

[35]In at least one instance the local school system is reported to have recorded pupils' religion, making it unnecessary to gather Yom Kippur absence statistics. See Maurice Taylor, "A Sample Study of the Jewish Population of Pittsburgh, 1938," in Robison, *Jewish Population Studies,* 81–108. See particularly 88.

[36]Alexander M. Dushkin, "A Statistical Study of the Jewish Population of New York," in *The Jewish Communal Register of New York City, 1917–1918* (1918), 75–88. See particularly 78–80.

[37]Taylor, "Sample Study of Jewish Population of Pittsburgh"; Sophia M. Robison, "The Jewish Population of Minneapolis, 1936," in Robison, *Jewish Population Studies,* 152–59. See particularly 155–56.

THE DISTINCTIVE JEWISH NAME METHOD

While what has been called the Distinctive Jewish Name (DJN) method is usually associated with the work of Samuel C. Kohs during the 1940s, we can trace its use in the United States at least as far back as 1912 to the work of Joseph Jacobs in New York.[38] Jacobs, calling the procedure the " 'Cohen' method," realized that Jews had a name distribution unlike that of non-Jews. Thus, names could serve as proxies for Jews in the same way as deaths, Russian origin, Yiddish language, Yom Kippur absence, and the like. The procedure, reduced to its simplest terms, is the same: determine the proportion of Jews who bear distinctive Jewish names (from a source such as a synagogue membership list or list of Federation donors). In a general population source that includes Jews and non-Jews (such as a city directory or telephone book) count the number of DJN entries. Knowing what proportion of Jews have DJNs, using simple division, compute an estimate of the total number of Jews in that source. Problems with this method arise from biases in the lists and sources that are not known or accounted for, such as unlisted telephones. Jacobs, for example, underestimated the Jewish population using the " 'Cohen' method." In computing the proportion of Jews who bore distinctive Jewish names, he inadvertently constructed a list of distinctive German Jewish names. His source was the contributors' roster of the predominantly German Jewish United Hebrew Charities, a list that underrepresented the large and increasing population of Russian Jews. When corrected for this bias, the " 'Cohen' method" did give a reasonable estimate of the Jewish population, approximating that produced by the death-rate method.

There is a special irony in the use of distinctive names to identify and enumerate Jews. When the 1924 National Origins Act was being put into force, the law mandated that the manuscript censuses from 1790 through 1890 be searched, the names collected and classified by ethnicity, and calculations made of mortality and fertility, to determine the ethnic composition of the American population as of 1890. The purpose of this law, of course, was to exclude or minimize the number of "undesirables" from southern and Eastern Europe, including Jews, who had been entering the country. Be that all as it may, the name method has proven useful.[39]

More recently, debate has arisen over the accuracy of the method. One scholar noted that the DJN method grossly overestimated the number of Jews in the area he was studying. He used what he believed to be "standard" parameters, but the proportion of Jews bearing one of the names on his DJN list proved to be too small. Since this fraction is the denominator of the ratio, too small a fraction leads to too

---

[38]Jacobs, "Jewish Population of New York"; Fred Massaryk, "A Changing Era in U.S. Jewish Population Research: Multiple Research Strategies—Indexes and Heuristics," in Schmelz, Glikson, and DellaPergola, eds., *Papers in Jewish Demography 1981,* 105–27; Stanley Waterman and Barry Kosmin, "Mapping an Unenumerated Ethnic Population: Jews in London," *Ethnic and Racial Studies* 19, no. 4 (1986): 484–501.

[39]William S. Bernard, "Immigration: History of U.S. Policy," in Thernstrom, *Harvard Encyclopedia of American Ethnic Groups,* 486–95. See particularly 493.

large a population estimate. In actuality, the proportion of Jews bearing DJNs varies significantly by area of the country. Some of this may be due to the simple random variation one finds in any population or sample. The variation also reflects regional differences in treatment of immigrants at ports of entry, degrees of assimilation, and differences in national origins.[40] The general point to be made is that with all of the proxy measures, the investigator cannot assume an invariant relationship between his proxy indicator and the number of Jewish households or persons. The number of deaths per 1,000 Jewish population in a retirement area is different from that in a suburb populated by young families. The DJN method requires knowledge of the Jewish age structure and the Jewish name distribution. Each of these methods has proven to be extremely useful, but unless used conservatively can be misleading.

Sample Surveys

JEWISH COMMUNAL AND GENERAL DATA COLLECTIONS

The various proxy methods are intriguing, at least in part because of their ingenuity, but it is this very ingenuity that makes some uncomfortable. Would it not be more accurate to go out and count Jews directly, the way the Bureau of the Census enumerates the population of the United States? The answer is yes, but! Since the Jews are a subpopulation, and one whose members are not identified as such by the U.S. Census, it has fallen to Jewish communal agencies to conduct their own counts. Again, the direct approach would be to visit every residence in town or call every phone in town to locate Jews. The number of Jews in the town would then equal the number of persons who say they are Jews along with the number of (Jewish?) people in their households. Unfortunately, this kind of total enumeration of individuals is too expensive to carry out.

Where the town and the Jewish community to be studied are both small, it is possible to make a master list of all known Jewish households and then, through personal contacts, to identify others who do not appear on the master list. In larger communities, however, those which contain the vast majority of America's Jews,

---

[40]Mark Abrahamson, "The Unreliability of DJN Techniques," *Contemporary Jewry* 7 (1986): 93–98; Bernard Lazerwitz, "Some Comments on the Use of Distinctive Jewish Names in Surveys," ibid., 83–91. One must take great care in using the DJN technique to note the degree of acculturation of the local Jewish community and its "ethnic" mix. Recent Russian Jewish immigrants to the United States retain more Russified spellings of their names than do those who came to the United States at the turn of the century. Other Jewish ethnic groups have distinctive Jewish-name patterns that do not appear Jewish to the outsider but make sense to the insider. For Italian Jews, see Rosalba Davico, "Les isolats" Israélites en Piémont (XVIIIe-début XIXe s.): structure des familles et mémoire généalogique," in Schmelz, Glikson, and DellaPergola, *Papers in Jewish Demography 1981,* 61–70. For German Jews, see Rudolf Glanz, "German Jewish Names in America," *Jewish Social Studies* 23, no. 2 (Apr.1961): 143–69.

some form of population sampling must be employed. The main prerequisite of a sample is that it appropriately reflect the population it claims to represent. Thus, a sample drawn from lists of Jewish charitable contributors or synagogue members will not accurately represent the larger Jewish community in terms of demographic characteristics or social and religious attitudes and behaviors. (The oft-cited classic example of bad sampling is that of the *Literary Digest* in 1936. The magazine predicted that Franklin Roosevelt would lose the election, based on a sample drawn from phone books. This apparently biased the investigation in favor of those who could afford telephones—in the midst of the Depression—who were, presumably, more likely to be Republicans.)

Since drawing a Jewish sample is no simple matter, some investigators have found ways to avoid it. One method is to piggyback on a larger study of the total population. For example, the Gallup Organization, one of the major polling firms, introduced a routine question about religion on its interview schedules in 1939 and one on national origin in 1941. Using Gallup surveys aggregated over several years, one investigator developed a credible estimate of national Jewish population during the mid-1970s.[41] Aggregated sequences of the General Social Survey of the National Opinion Research Center offer another opportunity to study national Jewish population characteristics. Large-scale general surveys in New York City in 1935 and 1950 produced both stable and valid population estimates and data for describing and analyzing Jewish characteristics.[42] Local political polls can be used to estimate Jewish population and to serve as a check on other estimates.[43]

Where a sample is drawn, the investigator is subject to two opposing constraints. These are cost and representativeness. For a random sample—one in which every household has the same probability of being contacted—if Jews are 10 percent of the population, the investigator has to contact 100 households to reach 10 Jewish households. In areas where Jews are a smaller proportion of the population, the number of "screening contacts" would, of course, increase. Assuming Jews to be 2.5 percent of the American population, obtaining a random sample of 1,000 Jewish

---

[41]Alan M. Fisher, "The National Gallup Polls and American Jewish Demography," AJYB, vol. 83, 1983, 111–26.

[42]Nettie Pauline McGill, "Some Characteristics of Jewish Youth in New York City," *Jewish Social Service Quarterly* 14, no. 2 (1937): 251–72; Neva R. Deardorf, "The Religio-Cultural Background of New York City's Population," *Milbank Memorial Fund Quarterly* 33, no. 2 (Apr. 1955): 152–60; Ben B. Seligman, "The Jewish Population of New York City: 1952," in Marshall Sklare, ed., *The Jews: Social Patterns of an American Group* (Glencoe, Ill., 1960); Morey J. Wantman, Morton Israel, and Leonard S. Kogan, *Estimates of Population Characteristics New York City, 1964–65–66–68–70* (New York, 1972); Henry Cohen, "Jewish Population Trends in New York City, 1940–1970" (Federation of Jewish Philanthropies of New York, Jan. 1956, typescript); Nathan Glazer, Herbert Hyman, and S.M. Lipset, "Characteristics of New York City Jews" (American Jewish Committee, Nov. 1952, typescript).

[43]Paul Ritterband and Steven M. Cohen, *The Jewish Population of Greater New York: A Population Profile* (New York, 1984), 77–78.

households across the United States would require contacting 40,000 American households—a costly procedure. To keep costs down, investigators find various ways of "enriching" the pool of households to be contacted so that Jews will be a larger proportion of the pool than in fact they are in the city or town at large. One way of doing this is to increase phone calls in telephone exchanges that have higher-than-average proportions of distinctive Jewish names, producing a "stratified" sample. Within these areas or phone exchanges, households are contacted randomly, giving a "stratified random" sample.

Some studies use a list sample along with a random sample. The list sample, consisting of members of synagogues, contributors to the local federation, and other Jewish communal lists, gives access to households at minimal cost. The list sample is supplemented by a random sample and the two are merged, with the list sample weighted down. That is, each case on the list sample is worth less statistically than one in the random sample. When properly weighted, the combined sample should *approximate* the results of a pure random sample, and at less cost. To estimate the Jewish population from a random sample, the investigator computes a ratio of all completed household calls in the denominator and completed calls to Jewish households in the numerator. This gives the proportion of all households in the area that are Jewish. The household figures are multiplied by average Jewish household size; Jewish population size is then estimated as a percentage of total population size.

Both the stratified sample and the list sample introduce bias in that not all Jews will have an equal probability of being interviewed. With appropriate statistical procedures, much of the bias can be handled. The investigator must decide how much bias or distortion the study can tolerate, a question for which there is no simple *a priori* answer. Precision is sought but is balanced against costs.

The sample survey is by far the most common mode of Jewish population estimation currently used. Though expensive, the survey collects information on a wide variety of issues in addition to population size. What are the characteristics of Jews who belong to synagogues? Who gives to the federation campaign and why? Who is intermarried and what is happening to the children? The number of questions asked is limited only by the imagination of the investigator, the patience of the respondent, and the budget of the sponsor. Interviews of 30 to 45 minutes are not uncommon.

In reviewing recent population studies using Jewish communal survey methods, the authors identified several problems that require additional discussion.

WHO IS A JEW?

The basic issue for this and other methods is determining who is a Jew. Studies done during the immigrant period had relatively little to worry about in this regard. There were few "patrilineal" Jews, few Jews who would not be buried as Jews, few intermarriages, few Jews who would not keep their children out of school on Yom

Kippur, few Jews for whom Jewish identity was not of primary salience. As acculturation took its course, the question of Jewish identity arose, not just as a religious or communal concern but as a practical research matter. The Pittsburgh study (data collected in 1938) explicitly stated:

> A Jew was defined as one born of Jewish parents or of a mixed marriage. In addition, a gentile married to a Jew or related by marriage to a Jewish person in the same household and identifying with the Jewish group was included in the count. No one, born a Jew or not, who was unwilling to be so identified was included in the count. Children of mixed marriage not being brought up as Jews and not so considered by the parent or parents were likewise not counted.[44]

A recent study in Denver attempted to deal with some absurdities of self-definition by excluding persons who were

> Jews for Jesus, individuals who have no Jewish parents or grandparents but who identify with the Jewish community, and children or grandchildren of intermarriage who do not currently identify as Jewish (these actually disqualified themselves). But including "Jewish Buddhists". . . who continue to identify as Jews.[45]

In these and other surveys a Jew is someone who thinks of him/herself as a Jew or is thought of as a Jew by the interviewed respondent, who is usually a head of household. Thus, persons who by traditional Jewish law are not regarded as Jews might well be counted as Jews, if they are married to Jews and identify with the Jewish people or are children of a Jewish father and non-Jewish mother. Most investigators have accepted this definition or something like it for their own surveys. Some have gone one step further and have included in the Jewish population counts spouses and children who are not Jewish and show no "identification," however defined, with Jews or Judaism. The logic of this procedure leads to a paradox and an irony. Since one Jew is enough to make an entire household Jewish, the more intermarriage there is, the larger the Jewish population! In Great Britain, with its centralized religious structure (in emulation of the Church of England), the authorities have been able to legislate a single definition of a Jew. For purposes of enumeration, the Research Unit of the Jewish Board of Deputies defines Jews as " . . . those who are born of a Jewish mother or have been formally converted by an Orthodox or progressive (Reform or Liberal) Beth Din."[46]

Defining who is a Jew, which necessarily entails including or excluding individuals, is by no means a new problem. In his plan for Jewish territorial autonomy in Eastern Europe, Simon Dubnow, the great Russian Jewish historian, proposed that Jews who had been baptized could still be members of the Jewish people and be

---

[44]Taylor, "Sample Study of Jewish Population of Pittsburgh," 83.

[45]Bruce Phillips and Eleanor P. Judd, *The Denver Jewish Population Study 1981* (Allied Jewish Federation of Denver, 1982), vii.

[46]B. A. Kosmin, "Demography and Sampling Problems," in D. Bensimon, ed., *Communautés Juives (1880–1978), sources et méthodes de recherche* (Paris, 1978), 263.

counted as Jews if they so wished.[47] For some purposes, e.g., asserting its electoral strength, the community wants to cast the widest net possible. Thus, people are included who are Jews by some definitions and not others as well as individuals who are Jewish by no one's definition at all.

UNCOUNTED JEWS

The survey method is based on calling households and asking if there is anyone in the household who is Jewish. Usually, the caller identifies him/herself as someone who is associated with a university and calling on behalf of the local Jewish federation. A number of persons who are Jews do not respond affirmatively to the questioner. Some simply do not believe that the call is not for fund-raising purposes. Others do not want to be bothered, though they may well be committed Jews. Still others are uncommitted Jews who no longer wish to identify with the Jewish community, even to the point of responding to questions on the phone. Studies have determined that 4 to 5 percent of Jews who are affiliated with the Jewish community refuse to acknowledge being Jewish when called in a Jewish community survey.[48]

One researcher reports that, in his experience, Jews are more active outside the home than non-Jews and are therefore more difficult to reach by phone. While this is probably not a major source of undercount, it is a source nevertheless.[49]

Since Jewish communal surveys are surveys of households, they almost always miss institutional populations of particular interest to the Jewish community, namely, students in dormitories and residents of nursing homes and geriatric facilities. (We estimate from various national sources that about 1.5 percent of the American population is in geriatric/nursing facilities.) Since only some residents of institutions have individual telephone lines and are accessible to Jewish community surveys, various characteristics of these people as well as their numbers are missing from many surveys. Some studies, but not all, use the Bureau of Census definition of households, excluding from enumeration dependent members of the household who are living elsewhere in student housing.

Improving Methodology

It is amply clear that we do not know with exactitude the number of Jews in the United States as a whole, not even in any given state, city, town, or village—not for lack of trying on the part of either the researchers or the communal lay leadership

[47]Reported in Robert M. Seltzer, "Jewish Liberalism in Late Tzarist Russia," *Contemporary Jewry* 9, no.1 (1988): 57.

[48]Michael Rappeport and Gary A. Tobin, *A Population Study of the Jewish Community of Metro West* (East Orange, N.J., 1987), 12; Gary A. Tobin, *Jewish Population of Greater Baltimore* (Baltimore, 1986), 29.

[49]Ira Sheskin, *The Jewish Federation of Palm Beach County Demographic Study* (1987), 15.

but simply because the issues are complex and uncertainty is built into the research process. One procedure that might lead to greater precision in estimates is triangulation, i.e., the use of multiple methods. Many of the studies we cited, particularly those up to the 1940s, used multiple methods. They compared results achieved by methods that were independent of one another. At times these methods gave significantly discrepant results. One scholar noted that discrepancies arose, not because of the methods but because of the ways in which Jews thought of themselves.

> Many who would admit being Jewish when so questioned would keep their children out of school on the holidays and would bury their dead according to Jewish ritual. Some, however, might send their children to school on the holidays and retain only the Jewish burial ceremony. On the other hand, some persons, although buried as Jews, might not have admitted being Jewish if questioned during their lifetime. Thus it is that three somewhat different populations would be arrived at according to three somewhat different definitions.[50]

A multimethod procedure built into a study design from the beginning does not add significantly to the cost but does add significantly to the quality of the estimates. Some of these "second opinions" are free for the asking, such as the use of general surveys that have large enough sample sizes to warrant their use in Jewish population estimation. The early Chicago study that we cited above examined discrepant results by comparing age and sex distributions generated by two different assumptions. This procedure could easily be adopted by other investigators irrespective of method. Social facts uncovered by the survey can be compared with external sources that are well documented. While these will vary by community, they may include the number of recent Soviet immigrants, the number of Israeli-born, the number of pupils enrolled in Jewish day schools, and other relevant data. It is up to the local community to choose its "validators," but they do exist.

The "time series" is one of the most interesting and useful sources of validation. Where there is a good estimate at one point in time and an independent estimate made at a second point in time, a test estimate can be constructed for the second point by using the estimate for time one, the volume of in- and outmigration between the two points, and the number of births and deaths. The federal government's record of Jewish immigrants into the United States between 1899 and 1943 and other sources are available for domestic Jewish migration, as are sources for birth and death rates.[51]

There is not even the hint of a possibility that the U.S. government will include a religion question in the 1990 census. The Yiddish-language and Russian-origin items will clearly be of less use in the 1990 census than they were in the past. Some

---

[50]A.J. Jaffe, "The Use of Death Records to Determine Jewish Population Characteristics," *Jewish Social Studies* 1, no. 2 (Apr. 1939): 144.

[51]For a superb use of the immigration data for describing and analyzing American Jewish population, see Simon Kuznets, "Immigration to the United States: Background and Structure," *Perspectives in American History* 9 (1975): 35–124.

of our other proxies are also becoming a bit worn about the edges. In light of these facts, the community's obligation to create and maintain good population records is all the greater.

PAUL RITTERBAND
BARRY A. KOSMIN
JEFFREY SCHECKNER

Jewish Population in the United States, 1987

THE JEWISH POPULATION OF the United States in 1987 was estimated to be 5,944,000. While this figure is somewhat higher than that reported for 1986, it may not signify an actual increase in the Jewish population. Rather, a combination of factors led to the new figures. First, several growing communities recently completed demographic studies and thus reported significant population gains. Second, we have expanded our list of communities to include a number of places that had never before reported a Jewish population. Finally, we have adjusted population estimates to meet some of the problems described in the preceding essay.

While the Jewish federations are the chief reporting bodies, their service areas vary in size and may represent several towns, one county, or an aggregate of several counties. In some cases we have subdivided federation areas to reflect the more natural geographic boundaries. Some estimates, from areas without federations, have been provided by local rabbis and other informed Jewish community leaders. In still other cases, the figures that have been updated are from past estimates provided by UJA field representatives.

The state and regional totals shown in Appendix tables 1 and 2 are derived by summing the individual estimates shown in table 3 and then making three adjustments. First, communities of less than 100 are added. Second, duplicated counts within states are eliminated. Third, communities whose populations reside in two or more states (e.g., Kansas City and Washington, D.C.) are distributed accordingly.

The reader should be aware that population estimating is not an exact science and that collection procedures can result in annual fluctuations in community or state totals. It is also important to note that the results of a completed local demographic study often change the previously reported Jewish population figure, even where there has been no actual demographic change. Thus, even though the 1987 totals for Pennsylvania and Wisconsin show Jewish population increases over 1986, these new higher figures are solely the result of adjustments of previous data.

In determining Jewish population, communities count both affiliated and nonaffiliated residents. In most cases, counts are made by households, with that number multiplied by the average number of self-defined Jewish persons per household. Most communities also include those born and raised as Jews but who at present consider themselves of no religion. Non-Jews living in Jewish households, primarily the non-Jewish spouses and any non-Jewish children, are not included in the 1987 estimates presented in the appendix below.

Where non-Jews have been included in the local population count and the number of Jews (minus non-Jews in the household) has not been reported, we have reduced the Jewish population count by 7 percent, which is the average proportion of non-Jews we have found in such surveys. In surveys which have not included Jews who publicly deny being Jews (see "Uncounted Jews" section of previous article), we have adjusted upward for this source of error. Regarding institutionalized Jews: where the local community has not included this population in its count we have augmented the estimate by approximately 1.5 percent. This includes nursing homes and the population living in student dormitories, some of which were not included heretofore. Some areas, such as in the Sunbelt region, often include part-time residents in their totals. In the interest of accuracy and consistency, adjustments have been made for such overcounts.

In analyzing those communities that show increases, several distinct patterns emerge. The continued growth of the Sunbelt and West Coast communities, particularly those in coastal Florida and northern California, seems unabated. College towns, state capitals, and resort areas show similar growth patterns. The exurbs, those small towns and rural areas just beyond the traditional boundaries of a metropolitan area, are also experiencing significant growth.

The community reporting the largest numerical Jewish population gain since the last estimate was completed was the San Francisco–Oakland–San Jose Consolidated Metropolitan Statistical Area, whose increase exceeded 50,000 persons. Additionally, six communities that had no prior enumeration of a Jewish population each report a Jewish population of at least 500 for 1987: Fairfield and Chico, California; Naples, Pasco County, and Stuart–Port St. Lucie, Florida; and Medford, Oregon.

Since the 1986 estimates were provided, 15 communities have reported more than doubling the size of their Jewish populations. These include: Anchorage, Alaska; Napa, Redding, and San Luis Obispo, California; Aspen, Colorado; Vero Beach, Florida; Augusta, Maine; Harford County, Maryland; Greenfield and Cape Cod, Massachusetts; Hoboken, New Jersey; Las Cruces, Los Alamos, and Santa Fe, New Mexico; and Myrtle Beach, South Carolina.

Other communities showing significant Jewish population increases over the 1986 estimates include Phoenix, Arizona; Antelope Valley, Bakersfield, Eureka, Modesto, Salinas, and San Bernardino, California; Colorado Springs, Colorado; New Haven and New Milford, Connecticut; Washington, D.C.; Ft. Pierce, Orlando, Palm Beach County, and Tampa, Florida; Atlanta, Georgia; Iowa City, Iowa; Aurora and Rockford, Illinois; Baltimore and Frederick, Maryland; Worcester, Massachusetts; Ann Arbor, Michigan; Rochester, Minnesota; Laconia, New Hampshire; Ithaca, Poughkeepsie, and Rochester, New York; Eugene, Oregon; Greenville, South Carolina; Austin and Beaumont, Texas; Burlington, Vermont; Norfolk and Roanoke, Virginia; and Tacoma, Washington. It should be noted that some of these increases may have occurred over a period of time and are just now being substantiated. In contrast, declines are reported more regularly and tend to be less dramatic.

The footnotes detailing the areas included in particular communities have been expanded and grouped by state. Also: one asterisk indicates that the population includes the entire county; two asterisks indicate a two-county area; three asterisks indicate that the Jewish population figure has not been updated for several years.

BARRY A. KOSMIN
PAUL RITTERBAND
JEFFREY SCHECKNER

TABLE 1. JEWISH POPULATION IN THE UNITED STATES, 1987

State	Estimated Jewish Population	Total Population*	Estimated Jewish Percent of Total
Alabama	10,000	4,021,000	0.2
Alaska	2,600	521,000	0.5
Arizona	69,200	3,187,000	2.2
Arkansas	2,000	2,359,000	0.1
California	868,200	26,365,000	3.3
Colorado	49,000	3,231,000	1.5
Connecticut	113,300	3,174,000	3.6
Delaware	9,500	622,000	1.5
District of Columbia	25,400	626,000	4.0
Florida	549,200	11,366,000	4.8
Georgia	62,500	5,976,000	1.0
Hawaii	8,000	1,054,000	0.8
Idaho	400	1,005,000	0.1
Illinois	259,800	11,535,000	2.2
Indiana	19,900	5,499,000	0.4
Iowa	6,700	2,884,000	0.2
Kansas	15,200	2,450,000	0.6
Kentucky	12,200	3,726,000	0.3
Louisiana	16,800	4,481,000	0.4
Maine	8,800	1,164,000	0.8
Maryland	209,700	4,392,000	4.8
Massachusetts	286,600	5,822,000	4.9
Michigan	84,600	9,088,000	0.9
Minnesota	31,400	4,193,000	0.8
Mississippi	2,400	2,613,000	0.1
Missouri	63,600	5,029,000	1.3
Montana	450	826,000	0.1
Nebraska	7,300	1,606,000	0.5
Nevada	19,500	936,000	2.1
New Hampshire	7,000	998,000	0.7
New Jersey	427,700	7,562,000	5.7
New Mexico	6,400	1,450,000	0.4
New York	1,891,400	17,783,000	10.6

State	Estimated Jewish Population	Total Population*	Estimated Jewish Percent of Total
North Carolina	15,300	6,255,000	0.2
North Dakota	850	685,000	0.1
Ohio	136,000	10,744,000	1.3
Oklahoma..........	5,500	3,301,000	0.2
Oregon	12,500	2,687,000	0.5
Pennsylvania	347,000	11,853,000	2.9
Rhode Island	17,500	968,000	1.8
South Carolina......	8,300	3,347,000	0.2
South Dakota.......	450	708,000	0.1
Tennessee..........	19,700	4,762,000	0.4
Texas	97,800	16,370,000	0.6
Utah	2,700	1,645,000	0.2
Vermont...........	4,600	535,000	0.9
Virginia............	65,300	5,706,000	1.1
Washington	22,700	4,409,000	0.5
West Virginia.......	3,300	1,936,000	0.2
Wisconsin..........	37,000	4,775,000	0.8
Wyoming	450	509,000	0.1
U.S. TOTAL	**5,943,700	238,740,000	2.5

N.B. Details may not add to totals because of rounding.
*Resident population, July 1, 1985. (*Source:* U.S. Bureau of the Census, *Current Population Reports,* series P-25, No. 957.)
**Exclusive of Puerto Rico and the Virgin Islands, which recently reported Jewish populations of 1,500 and 350, respectively.

TABLE 2. DISTRIBUTION OF U.S. JEWISH POPULATION BY REGIONS, 1987

Region	Total Population	Percent Distribution	Jewish Population	Percent Distribution
Northeast	49,859,000	20.9	3,103,900	52.2
New England	12,660,000	5.3	437,800	7.4
Middle Atlantic	37,199,000	15.6	2,666,100	44.9
North Central	59,197,000	24.8	662,800	11.2
East North Central ..	41,642,000	17.4	537,300	9.0
West North Central ..	17,555,000	7.4	125,500	2.1
South	81,859,000	34.3	1,114,900	18.8
South Atlantic	40,227,000	16.8	948,500	16.0
East South Central...	15,122,000	6.3	44,300	0.7
West South Central ..	26,510,000	11.1	122,100	2.1
West	47,826,000	20.0	1,062,100	17.9
Mountain...........	12,789,000	5.4	148,100	2.5
Pacific	35,037,000	14.7	914,000	15.4
TOTALS.............	238,740,000	100.0	5,943,700	100.0

N.B. Details may not add to totals because of rounding.

TABLE 3. COMMUNITIES WITH JEWISH POPULATIONS OF 100 OR MORE, 1987 (ESTIMATED)

State and City	Jewish Population
ALABAMA	
***Anniston	100
*Auburn	100
*Birmingham	5,100
Decatur (incl. in Florence total)	
*Dothan	150
Florence	150
Gadsden	180
Huntsville	750
**Mobile	1,000
**Montgomery	1,650
Selma	210
Sheffield (incl. in Florence total)	
Tuscaloosa	315
Tuscumbia (incl. in Florence total)	
ALASKA	
**Anchorage	2,000
***Fairbanks	210
Juneau	100
Ketchikan (incl. in Juneau total)	
ARIZONA	
*Flagstaff	250
*Phoenix	50,000
*Tucson	18,500
Yuma	100
ARKANSAS	
Fayetteville	120
***Ft. Smith	160
Hot Springs (incl. in Little Rock total)	
**Little Rock	1,250
Pine Bluff	100
***Wynne-Forest City	110
CALIFORNIA	
Alameda County (listed under San Francisco Bay area)	
Antelope Valley	700
Bakersfield (incl. in Kern County)	
Berkeley (incl. in Contra Costa County total)	
*Chico	500
Contra Costa County (listed under S.F. Bay area)	
***El Centro	125
***Elsinore	250
*Eureka	500
Fairfield	800
Fontana (incl. in San Bernardino total)	
*Fresno	2,000
Kern County	1,400
Lancaster (incl. in Antelope Valley)	
Long Beach (also incl. in Los Angeles total)[N]	13,500
Los Angeles Metro area	501,000
Merced	170
*Modesto	450
Monterey Peninsula	1,500
Napa	450
Oakland (incl. in Alameda County)	
Ontario (incl. in Pomona Valley)	
Orange County	80,000
Palmdale (incl. in Antelope Valley)	
Palm Springs[N]	9,500
Palo Alto (incl. in South Peninsula)	
Pasadena (also incl. in L.A. Metro Area)	2,000
Petaluma (incl. in Sonoma County)	
Pomona Valley[N]	3,500
Redding	145
Riverside	1,325
Sacramento[N]	10,000
Salinas	500
San Bernardino area	2,800
*San Diego	37,000
San Francisco Bay area[N]	196,000
San Francisco	45,500
North Peninsula	22,000
South Peninsula	19,500
San Jose	32,000
Alameda County	30,500
Contra Costa County	21,000

[N]See Notes below. *Includes entire county. **Includes all of 2 counties. ***Figure not updated.

State and City	Jewish Population
Marin County	17,000
Sonoma County	8,500
*San Jose (listed under San Francisco Bay area)	
*San Luis Obispo	1,000
*Santa Barbara	3,800
*Santa Cruz	1,200
Santa Maria	200
Santa Monica (also incl. in Los Angeles total)	8,000
Santa Rosa (incl. in Sonoma County)	
*Stockton	1,600
***Sun City	800
Tulare & Kings County	500
Vallejo	400
*Ventura County	7,000
COLORADO	
Aspen	250
Boulder (incl. in Denver total)	
Colorado Springs	1,500
Denver[N]	45,000
*Ft. Collins	1,000
Grand Junction	100
***Greeley	100
Loveland (incl. in Ft. Collins total)	
Pueblo	375
Vail	100
CONNECTICUT	
Bridgeport[N]	18,000
Bristol	200
Colchester	575
Danbury[N]	3,500
Danielson	130
Greenwich	3,900
Hartford[N]	28,000
Hebron (incl. in Colchester total)	
Lebanon (incl. in Colchester total)	
Lower Middlesex County[N]	1,475
Manchester (incl. in Hartford)	
Meriden	1,400
Middletown	1,300
New Britain (incl. in Hartford)	
New Haven[N]	28,000
New London[N]	4,000
New Milford	400
Newtown (incl. in Danbury)	
Norwalk[N]	4,000
Norwich	1,800
Putnam	110
Rockville (incl. in Hartford)	
Shelton (incl. in Valley area)	
Stamford/New Canaan	12,000
Storrs (incl. in Willimantic total)	
Torrington	560
Valley area[N]	550
Wallingford	500
Waterbury	2,700
Westport (also incl. in Norwalk)	2,800
Willimantic area	700
***Winsted	110
DELAWARE	
Dover[N]	650
Wilmington (incl. rest of state)	9,500
DISTRICT OF COLUMBIA	
Greater Washington	165,000
FLORIDA	
Boca Raton-Delray Beach (listed under Southeast Fla.)	
Brevard County	2,250
*Crystal River	100
Dade County (listed under Southeast Fla.)	
**Daytona Beach	2,000
Fort Lauderdale (listed under Southeast Fla.)	
Fort Pierce (listed under Southeast Fla.)	
Gainesville	1,200
Hollywood (listed under Southeast Fla.)	
**Jacksonville	7,000
Key West	170
*Lakeland	800
Lee County (incl. Ft. Myers)	3,500
*Miami (incl. in Dade County)	
Naples	750
*Ocala	100
Orlando[N]	15,000
Palm Beach County (listed under Southeast Fla.)	
**Pasco County	1,000
**Pensacola	775
***Port Charlotte	150
**Sarasota	9,000
***St. Augustine	100
*St. Petersburg (incl. Clearwater)	9,500
Southeast Florida	481,500
Dade County	241,000
Hollywood[N]	60,000

State and City	Jewish Population
Ft. Lauderdale[N]	85,000
Boca Raton-Delray Beach	52,000
Palm Beach County (excl. Boca Raton-Delray Beach)	55,000
Stuart-Port. St.Lucie	3,000
Fort Pierce	500
Tallahassee	1,000
*Tampa	12,500
*Vero Beach	300
Winter Haven (incl. in Lakeland total)	
GEORGIA	
Albany	400
Athens	250
Atlanta Metro area	55,000
Augusta[N]	1,400
Brunswick	100
**Columbus	1,000
**Dalton	225
Fitzgerald-Cordele	125
Macon	900
*Savannah	2,600
*Valdosta	110
HAWAII	
Hilo	320
Honolulu (includes all of Oahu)	7,300
Kauai	110
Maui	250
IDAHO	
**Boise	220
Lewiston	100
Moscow (incl. in Lewiston total)	
ILLINOIS	
Aurora area	500
Bloomington-Normal	170
Carbondale	100
*Champaign-Urbana	2,000
Chicago Metro area	248,000
**Danville	130
*Decatur	225
East St. Louis (incl. in So. Ill.)	
Elgin[N]	600
Galesburg	120
*Joliet	850
Kankakee	200
*Peoria	1,000
Quad Cities[N]	1,650
**Quincy	125
Rock Island (incl. in Quad Cities)	
Rockford[N]	1,300
Southern Illinois[N]	900
*Springfield	1,100
***Sterling-Dixon	110
Waukegan	1,200
INDIANA	
Anderson	105
Bloomington	300
Elkart (incl. in South Bend total)	
***Evansville	1,200
Ft. Wayne	1,170
Gary (incl. in Northwest Ind. Calumet Region)	
**Indianapolis	10,000
Kokomo	100
Lafayette[N]	600
***Marion	170
*Michigan City	435
***Muncie	175
Northwest Indiana-Calumet Region[N]	3,000
Richmond	110
***Shelbyville	240
South Bend[N]	1,900
*Terre Haute	325
IOWA	
Ames (also incl. in Des Moines total)	200
Cedar Rapids	430
Council Bluffs (also incl. in Omaha total)	150
Davenport (incl. in Quad Cities, Ill.)	
*Des Moines	3,000
*Iowa City	1,200
***Muscatine	120
**Sioux City	655
Waterloo	235
KANSAS	
Kansas City (incl. in Kansas City, Mo.)	
Lawrence	175
Manhattan	100
*Topeka	500
Wichita[N]	1,000
KENTUCKY	
Covington/Newport (incl. in Cincinnati, Ohio total)	
Lexington[N]	2,000
*Louisville	9,200
***Paducah	175
LOUISIANA	
Alexandria	350
Baton Rouge[N]	1,400
Lafayette	100
Lake Charles	300
Monroe	525

State and City	Jewish Population
**New Orleans	12,000
*Shreveport	1,100
South Central La.[N]	720
Tallulah (incl. in Vicksburg, Miss. total)	
MAINE	
Augusta	500
Bangor	1,250
Biddeford-Saco (incl. in So. Maine)	
Brunswick-Bath (incl. in So. Maine)	
***Calais	135
Lewiston-Auburn	500
Portland	3,900
Rockland	100
Southern Maine (incl. Portland)[N]	5,500
Waterville	300
MARYLAND	
*Annapolis	2,000
**Baltimore	93,000
Cumberland	265
Easton Park area[N]	100
*Frederick	600
*Hagerstown	300
*Harford County	1,000
Howard County	7,200
Montgomery and Prince Georges counties	104,500
Salisbury	400
Silver Spring (incl. in Montgomery County)	
MASSACHUSETTS	
Amherst	750
Andover[N]	3,000
Athol area	250
Attleboro	200
Beverly (incl. in Lynn total)	
Boston Metro Region[N]	228,000
Brookline (also incl. in Boston total)	26,000
Cape Cod (incl. all of Barnstable County)	2,900
Fall River	1,780
Falmouth (incl. in Cape Cod)	
Fitchburg	300
Framingham[N]	10,800
Gardner (incl. in Athol total)	
Gloucester (also incl. in Lynn total)	450
Great Barrington	105
*Greenfield	900
Haverhill	1,500
Holyoke	1,100
*Hyannis (incl. in Cape Cod)	
Lawrence (incl. in Andover total)	
Leominster	750
Lowell	2,000
Lynn-North Shore area[N]	26,200
*Martha's Vineyard	260
New Bedford[N]	2,700
Newburyport	280
Newton (also incl. in Boston total)	34,000
North Adams (incl. in N.Berkshire total)	
North Berkshire County	750
Northampton	700
Peabody (incl. in Lynn total)	
Pittsfield (incl. all Berkshire County)	3,100
Plymouth	500
Provincetown (incl. in Cape Cod)	
Salem (incl. in Lynn total)	
Southbridge	105
Springfield[N]	11,000
Taunton area	1,200
Webster	125
Worcester[N]	12,000
MICHIGAN	
*Ann Arbor	4,500
Battle Creek	245
Bay City	280
Benton Harbor	500
**Detroit	70,000
*Flint	2,000
*Grand Rapids	1,500
Jackson	375
*Kalamazoo	1,030
*Lansing	2,100
*Marquette County	150
Midland	200
***Mt. Clemens	420
Mt. Pleasant[N]	120
Muskegon	235
*Saginaw	200
***South Haven	100
MINNESOTA	
***Austin	125
**Duluth	800
***Hibbing	155
*Minneapolis	22,000
Rochester	400
**St. Paul	7,700
Winona (incl. in LaCrosse, Wis. total)	
MISSISSIPPI	
Biloxi-Gulfport	150
Clarksdale	100
**Cleveland	120
**Greenville	480

State and City	Jewish Population
**Hattiesburg	180
**Jackson	700
***Natchez	140
**Vicksburg	105
MISSOURI	
Columbia	350
Hannibal (incl. in Quincy, Ill. total)	
Joplin	100
Kansas City Metro area	22,100
***Kennett	110
Springfield	285
*St. Joseph	300
**St. Louis	53,500
MONTANA	
*Billings	200
Butte	110
Helena (incl. in Butte total)	
NEBRASKA	
Grand Island-Hastings (incl. in Lincoln total)	
Lincoln	800
Omaha[N]	6,500
NEVADA	
Carson City (incl. in Reno total)	
*Las Vegas	18,000
**Reno	1,400
NEW HAMPSHIRE	
Bethlehem	100
Claremont	200
Concord	450
Dover	450
Hanover-Lebanon	360
***Keene	105
***Laconia	270
Littleton (incl. in Bethlehem total)	
Manchester	3,000
Nashua	480
Portsmouth area	1,100
Salem (also incl. in Andover, Mass. total)	150
NEW JERSEY	
Asbury Park (incl. in Monmouth County)	
*Atlantic City (incl. Atlantic County)	15,800
Bayonne (incl. in Hudson County)	
Bergen County	100,000
***Bridgeton	375
Bridgewater (incl. in Somerset County)	
Camden (incl. in Cherry Hill total)	
Cherry Hill[N]	28,000
Edison (incl. in Middlesex County)	
Elizabeth (incl. in Union County)	
Englewood (incl. in Bergen County)	
Essex County[N]	78,300
North Essex	16,000
East Essex	11,200
South Essex	20,800
Livingston	12,900
West Orange-Orange	17,400
Flemington	900
Freehold (incl. in Monmouth County)	
Gloucester (incl. in Cherry Hill total)	
Hoboken (incl. in Hudson County)	
Hudson County	14,250
Bayonne	5,000
Jersey City	3,500
Hoboken	750
North Hudson	5,000
Jersey City (incl. in Hudson County)	
Lakewood (incl. in Ocean County)	
Livingston (incl. in Essex County)	
Middlesex County[N]	40,000
Millville	135
Monmouth County	33,600
Morris County	34,600
Morristown (incl. in Morris County)	
Mt. Holly (incl. in Cherry Hill total)	
Newark (incl. in Essex County)	
New Brunswick (incl. in Middlesex County)	
Northeastern N.J.[N]	320,650
Ocean County	9,500
Passaic-Clifton (also in Passaic County total)	8,000
Passaic County[N]	18,700
Paterson (incl. in Passaic County)	
Perth Amboy (incl. in Middlesex County)	
Phillipsburg (incl. in Easton, Pa. total)	
Plainfield (incl. in Union County)	
Princeton	2,600
Salem	100
Somerset County[N]	4,800

State and City	Jewish Population
Somerville (incl. in Somerset County)	
Sussex-Warren counties	4,600
Toms River (incl. in Ocean County)	
Trenton[N]	8,500
Union County[N]	30,000
Vineland[N]	2,450
Wayne (incl. in Passaic County)	
West Orange (incl. in Essex County)	
Wildwood	425
Willingboro (incl. in Cherry Hill total)	
NEW MEXICO	
*Albuquerque	4,500
Las Cruces	525
Los Alamos	250
Santa Fe	900
NEW YORK	
*Albany	12,000
Amenia	140
Amsterdam	450
***Auburn	315
***Batavia	165
Beacon (incl. in Dutchess County)	
*Binghamton (incl. all Broome County)	3,000
Brewster (also incl. in Danbury, Conn.)	300
*Buffalo	18,500
Canandaigua (incl. in Geneva total)	
Catskill	200
***Corning	125
Cortland	440
Dunkirk	120
Ellenville	1,600
Elmira[N]	1,100
Fleischmanns	115
Geneva	300
Glens Falls[N]	800
***Gloversville	535
***Herkimer	185
Highland Falls (incl. in Orange County)	
Hudson	470
*Ithaca	1,250
Jamestown	185
Kingston[N]	4,500
Lake George (incl. in Glens Falls total)	
Liberty (also incl. in Sullivan County total)	2,100
***Massena	140
Middletown (incl. in Orange County)	
Monroe (incl. in Orange County)	
Monticello (also incl. in Sullivan County total)	2,400
New York Metro area[N]	1,718,000
Bronx	85,000
Brooklyn	429,000
Manhattan	282,000
Queens	329,000
Staten Island	34,000
Nassau County	320,000
Suffolk County	112,000
Westchester County	127,000
New Paltz	150
Newark (incl. in Geneva total)	
Newburgh (incl. in Orange County)	
Niagara Falls	425
***Norwich	120
Olean	120
**Oneonta	250
Orange County	8,950
Oswego	100
Pawling	105
Plattsburg	275
Port Jervis (also incl. in Orange County total)	560
Potsdam	250
*Poughkeepsie	6,500
**Rochester	23,000
Rockland County	60,000
Rome	205
Saratoga Springs	500
**Schenectady	5,400
***Sharon Springs	165
South Fallsburg (incl. also in Sullivan County total)	1,100
Sullivan County	7,425
Syracuse[N]	9,000
Troy area	900
Utica[N]	2,000
Walden (incl. in Orange County)	
Watertown	170
NORTH CAROLINA	
Asheville[N]	2,100
**Chapel Hill-Durham	2,400
Charlotte[N]	4,000
*Fayetteville	500
Gastonia	240
Goldsboro	120
*Greensboro	2,700
Greenville	300
Hendersonville	135
**Hickory	100
High Point (incl. in Greensboro total)	
Raleigh	1,375
Whiteville Zone[N]	160

State and City	Jewish Population
Wilmington	500
Winston-Salem	440
NORTH DAKOTA	
Fargo	500
Grand Forks	130
OHIO	
**Akron	6,000
Athens	100
Bowling Green (also incl. in Toledo total)	120
**Canton	2,500
Cincinnati[N]	22,000
**Cleveland	70,000
*Columbus	15,000
**Dayton	6,000
East Liverpool	200
Elyria	250
Fremont (incl. in Sandusky total)	
Hamilton	560
*Lima	365
Lorain	600
***Mansfield	600
***Marion	150
Middletown	150
New Philadelphia (incl. in Canton total)	
**Newark	105
Norwalk (incl. in Sandusky total)	
Oberlin (incl. in Elyria total)	
**Sandusky	130
Springfield	250
*Steubenville	165
Toledo[N]	6,300
Warren (also incl. in Youngstown total)	400
Wooster	125
Youngstown[N]	4,500
***Zanesville	350
OKLAHOMA	
Norman (also incl. in Oklahoma City total)	350
**Oklahoma City	2,300
*Tulsa	2,750
OREGON	
***Corvallis	240
Eugene	2,300
**Medford	500
Portland	9,000
***Salem	250
PENNSYLVANIA	
Allentown	5,000
*Altoona	520
Ambridge[N]	350
Beaver Falls (incl. in Upper Beaver County)	
Bethlehem	810
*Bradford	120
***Brownsville	100
*Butler	300
**Chambersburg	470
Chester (incl. in Phila. total)	
Chester County (also incl. in Phila. total)	4,000
Coatesville (incl. in Chester County total)	
***Connellsville	110
Delaware Valley (Lower Bucks County)[N]	14,500
***Donora (incl. in Pittsburgh total)	
Easton area	1,200
*Erie	800
Farrell (incl. in Sharon total)	
Ford City (incl. in Kittaning total)	
Greensburg (also incl. in Pittsburgh total)	425
**Harrisburg	6,500
Hazleton area	425
Homestead (incl. in Pittsburgh total)	
Indiana	135
Jeanette (incl. in Greensburg total)	
Johnstown	410
***Kittanning	175
*Lancaster	2,100
*Lebanon	400
Lewisburg	125
Lock Haven (incl. in Williamsport total)	
McKeesport (incl. in Pittsburgh total)	
Monessen (incl. in Pittsburgh total)	
***Mt. Pleasant	120
New Castle	350
New Kensington	380
Norristown (incl. in Philadelphia total)	
**Oil City	145
Oxford-Kennett Square (incl. in Chester County)	
Philadelphia area[N]	250,000
Phoenixville (incl. in Chester County)	
Pike County	150
Pittsburgh[N]	45,000
Pottstown	700
***Pottsville	500
*Reading	2,800
***Sayre	100
*Scranton	3,200
Sharon (also incl. in Youngstown, Ohio total)	260
State College	550
Stroudsburg	410
Sunbury	120

State and City	Jewish Population
Tamaqua (incl. in Hazleton total)	
Uniontown	290
Upper Beaver County	200
**Washington (also incl. in Pittsburgh total)	250
Wayne County	210
Waynesburg (incl. in Washington total)	
West Chester (also incl. in Chester County)	300
Wilkes-Barre[N]	4,000
**Williamsport	415
York	1,600
RHODE ISLAND	
Providence (incl. rest of state)	17,500
SOUTH CAROLINA	
*Charleston	3,500
**Columbia	2,000
Florence	210
Georgetown (incl. in Myrtle Beach total)	
Greenville	800
Kingstree (incl. in Sumter total)	
**Myrtle Beach	425
***Orangeburg County	105
Rock Hill (incl. in Charlotte, N.C. total)	
*Spartanburg	320
Sumter[N]	175
SOUTH DAKOTA	
Sioux Falls	115
TENNESSEE	
Bristol (incl. in Johnson City total)	
Chattanooga	2,000
Jackson	100
Johnson City	210
Kingsport (incl. in Johnson city total)	
Knoxville	1,350
Memphis	10,000
Nashville	5,450
Oak Ridge	240
TEXAS	
Amarillo[N]	190
*Austin	5,000
Baytown	300
Beaumont	800
*Brownsville	325
College Station	400
*Corpus Christi	1,400
**Dallas	24,500
De Witt County[N]	150
El Paso	4,800
*Ft. Worth	4,100
Galveston	800
Harlingen (incl. in Brownsville total)	
**Houston	42,000
Kilgore (incl. in Longview total)	
Laredo	420
Longview	200
***Lubbock	350
Lufkin (incl. in Longview total)	
Marshall (incl. in Longview total)	
*McAllen	475
Midland-Odessa	150
Paris (incl. in Sherman-Denison total)	
Port Arthur	260
San Angelo	100
*San Antonio	9,000
Sherman-Denison	125
Tyler	450
Waco[N]	500
Wharton	170
Wichita Falls	260
UTAH	
Ogden	100
*Salt Lake City	2,350
VERMONT	
Bennington	100
Brattleboro	150
**Burlington	3,000
Montpelier-Barre	500
Newport (incl. in St. Johnsbury total)	
Rutland	450
**St. Johnsbury	100
VIRGINIA	
Alexandria (incl. Falls Church, Arlington, & Fairfax counties)	35,100
Arlington (incl. in Alexandria total)	
Blacksburg	300
Charlottesville	950
Chesapeake (incl. in Norfolk total)	
Danville	180
Fredericksburg	140
Hampton (incl. in Newport News)	
Harrisonburg (incl. in Staunton total)	
***Hopewell	140
Lynchburg	275
**Martinsville	130
Newport News (incl. Hampton)[N]	2,500
Norfolk (incl. Virginia Beach)	15,000
Petersburg	740
Portsmouth-Suffolk (also incl. in Norfolk total)	1,100

State and City	Jewish Population
Radford (incl. in Blacksburg total)	
Richmond[N]	8,000
Roanoke	1,050
Staunton[N]	375
Williamsburg (incl. in Newport News total)	
Winchester[N]	145
WASHINGTON	
***Bellingham	120
Longview-Kelso (incl. in Portland, Ore. total)	
***Olympia	145
Pullman (incl. in Moscow, Idaho total)	
*Seattle[N]	19,500
Spokane	1,000
*Tacoma	1,100
Tri Cities[N]	240
Vancouver (incl. in Portland total)	
WEST VIRGINIA	
Bluefield-Princeton	250
*Charleston	1,025
***Clarksburg	205
Huntington[N]	380
Morgantown	200
***Parkersburg	155
***Weirton	150
**Wheeling	500
WISCONSIN	
Appleton	250
Beloit	120
Green Bay	260
*Kenosha	200
LaCrosse	150
*Madison	4,500
Milwaukee[N]	30,000
Oshkosh	150
*Racine	375
Sheboygan	190
Superior (also incl. in Duluth total)	100
Waukesha (incl. in Milwaukee total)	
Wausau[N]	240
WYOMING	
Casper	100
Cheyenne	230
Laramie (incl. in Cheyenne total)	

Notes

CALIFORNIA

Long Beach–includes in L.A. County, Long Beach, Signal Hill, Cerritos, Lakewood, Rossmoor, and Hawaiian Gardens. Also includes in Orange County, Los Alamitas, Cypress, Seal Beach, and Huntington Harbor.

Palm Springs–includes Palm Springs, Desert Hot Springs, Cathedral City, Palm Desert, and Rancho Mirage.

Pomona Valley–includes Alta Loma, Chino, Claremont, Cucamonga, La Verne, Montclair, Ontario, Pomona, San Dimas, Upland.

Sacramento–includes Yolo, Placer, El Dorado, and Sacramento counties.

San Francisco Bay area–North Peninsula includes northern San Mateo County. South Peninsula includes southern San Mateo County and towns of Palo Alto and Los Altos in Santa Clara County. San Jose includes remainder of Santa Clara County.

COLORADO

Denver–includes Adams, Arapahoe, Boulder, Denver, and Jefferson counties.

CONNECTICUT

Bridgeport–includes Monroe, Easton, Trumbull, Fairfield, Bridgeport, Stratford, and part of Milford.

Danbury–includes Danbury, Bethel, New Fairfield, Brookfield, Sherman, Newtown, Redding, Ridgefield, and part of Wilton; also includes Brewster and Goldens Bridge in New York.

Hartford–includes most of Hartford County and Vernon, Rockville, Ellington, and Tolland in Tolland County.

Lower Middlesex County–includes Branford, Guilford, Madison, Clinton, Westbrook, Old Saybrook. Portion of this area also included in New London total.

New Haven–includes New Haven, East Haven, Guilford, Branford, Madison, North Haven, Hamden, West Haven, Milford, Orange, Woodbridge, Bethany, and Cheshire.

New London–includes central and southern New London County. Also includes part of Lower Middlesex County and part of Windham County.

Norwalk–includes Norwalk, Weston, Westport, East Norwalk, part of Darien, part of New Canaan, and part of Wilton.

Valley Area–includes Ansonia, Derby-Shelton, Oxford, Seymour, and Beacon Falls.

Waterbury–includes Middlebury, Southbury, Naugatuck, Watertown, Waterbury, Oakville, and Woodbury.

DELAWARE

Dover–includes most of central and southern Delaware.

DISTRICT OF COLUMBIA

Greater Washington–includes Montgomery and Prince Georges counties in Maryland; Arlington County, Fairfax County, Falls Church, and Alexandria in Virginia.

FLORIDA

Ft. Lauderdale–includes Ft. Lauderdale, Pompano Beach, Deerfield Beach, Tamarac, Margate, and other towns in northern Broward County.

Hollywood–includes Hollywood, Hallandale, Dania, Davie, Pembroke, and other towns in southern Broward County.

Orlando–includes all of Orange and Seminole counties, and part of Lake County.

GEORGIA

Augusta–includes Burke, Columbia, and Richmond Counties and part of Aiken County, South Carolina.

ILLINOIS

Elgin–includes Northern Kane County, Southern McHenry County, and western edge of Cook County.

Quad Cities–includes Rock Island, Moline (Ill.), Davenport, Bettendorf (Iowa).

Rockford–includes Winnebago, Boone, and Stephenson counties.

Southern Illinois–includes lower portion of Illinois below Carlinville, adjacent western portion of Kentucky, and adjacent portion of southeastern Missouri.

INDIANA

Lafayette–includes Clinton, Montgomery, and Tippecanoe counties.

Northwest Indiana–includes Crown Point, East Chicago, Gary, Hammond, Munster, Valparaiso, Whiting, and the Greater Calumet region.

South Bend–includes St. Joseph and Elkhart counties and part of Berrien County, Mich.

KANSAS

Wichita–includes Sedgwick County and towns of Salina, Dodge City, Great Bend, Liberal, Russel, and Hays.

KENTUCKY

Lexington–includes Fayette, Bourbon, Scott, Clark, Woodford, Madison, Pulaski, and Jessamin counties.

LOUISIANA

Baton Rouge–includes E. Baton Rouge, Ascencion, Livingston, St. Landry, Iberville, Pt. Coupee, and W. Baton Rouge parishes.

South Central–includes Abbeville, Lafayette, New Iberia, Crowley, and Opelousus.

MAINE

Southern Maine–includes York, Cumberland, and Sagadahoc counties.

MARYLAND

Easton Park Area–includes towns in Caroline, Kent, Queen Annes, and Talbot counties.

MASSACHUSETTS

Andover–includes Andover, N. Andover, Boxford, Lawrence, Methuen, Tewksbury, Dracut, and town of Salem, New Hampshire.

Boston Metropolitan Region–includes 14 towns in Essex County, 34 towns in Middlesex County, 21 towns in Norfolk County, 15 Towns in Plymouth County, 1 town in Bristol County, and all of Suffolk County.

Framingham–includes Maynard, Stow, Hudson, Marlborough, Framingham, Southborough, Ashland, Hopkinton, Holliston, Milford, Medway, Millis, Medfield, Billingham, and Franklin. Portion also included in Boston total.

Lynn–includes Lynn, Saugus, Nahant, Swampscott, Lynnfield, Peabody, Salem, Marblehead, Beverly, Danvers, Middleton, Wenham, Topsfield, Hamilton, Manchester, Ipswich, Essex, Gloucester, and Rockport. Portion also included in Boston total.

New Bedford–includes New Bedford, Dartmouth, Fairhaven, and Mattapoisett.

Springfield–includes Springfield, Longmeadow, E. Longmeadow, Hampden, Wilbraham, Agwam, and West Springfield.

Worcester–includes Worcester, Northborough, Westborough, Shrewsbury, Boylston, West Boylston, Holden, Paxton, Leicester, Auburn, Millbury, and, Sutton.

MICHIGAN

Mt. Pleasant–includes towns in Isabella, Mecosta, Gladwin, and Gratiot counties.

NEBRASKA

Omaha–includes Douglas and Sarpy counties. Also includes Pottawatomie County, Iowa.

NEW HAMPSHIRE

Laconia–includes Laconia, Plymouth, Meredith, Conway, and Franklin.

Manchester–includes Manchester, Hookset, Merrimac, Amherst, Goffstown, Auburn, Derry, and Londonderry.

NEW JERSEY

Cherry Hill–includes Camden, Burlington, and Gloucester counties.

Essex County–East Essex includes Belleville, Bloomfield, East Orange, Irvington, Newark, and Nutley in Essex County and Kearney in Hudson County. North Essex includes Caldwell, Cedar Grove, Essex Fells, Fairfield, Glen Ridge, Montclair, North Caldwell, Roseland, Verona, and West Caldwell. South Essex includes Maplewood, Millburn, Short Hills, and South Orange in Essex County and Springfield in Union County.

Middlesex County–includes in Somerset County, Kendall Park, Somerset; in Mercer County, Hightstown.

Northeastern N.J.–includes Bergen, Essex, Hudson, Middlesex, Morris, Passaic, Somerset, and Union counties.

North Hudson County–includes Guttenberg, Hudson Heights, North Bergen, North Hudson, Secaucus, Union City, Weehawken, West New York, Woodcliff.

Passaic County–includes all towns in Passaic County. Previous estimates for North Jersey have been distributed between Passaic, Bergen, and Morris counties.

Somerset County–includes most of Somerset County and a portion of Hunterdon County.

Trenton–includes most of Mercer County.

Union County–includes all of Union County except Springfield. Also includes a few towns in adjacent areas of Somerset and Middlesex counties.

Vineland–includes most of Cumberland County and towns in neighboring counties adjacent to Vineland.

NEW YORK

Elmira–includes Chemung, Tioga, and Schuyler counties. Also includes Tioga and Bradford counties in Pennsylvania.

Glens Falls–includes Warren and Washington counties, lower Essex County and upper Saratoga County.

Kingston–includes eastern half of Ulster County.

New York Metropolitan Area–includes the 5 boroughs of New York City, Westchester, Nassau, and Suffolk counties. For a total Jewish population of the New York Metropolitan Region, include southwestern Connecticut, Rockland, Putnam, and Orange counties in New York and northeastern New Jersey.

Syracuse–includes Onondaga County, Western Madison County, and most of Oswego County.

Utica–Southeastern third of Oneida County.

NORTH CAROLINA

Asheville–includes Buncombe, Haywood, and Madison County.

Charlotte–includes Mecklenberg County. Also includes Lancaster and York counties in South Carolina.

Whiteville Zone–includes Elizabethtown, Fairmont, Jacksonville, Lumberton, Tabor City, Wallace, Warsaw, and Loris, S. Carolina.

OHIO

Cincinnati–includes Hamilton County. Also includes Boone, Campbell, and Kenton counties in Kentucky.

Toledo–includes Fulton, Lucas, and Wood counties. Also includes Monroe and Lenawee Counties, Michigan.

Youngstown–includes Mahoning and Trumbull counties. Also includes Mercer County, Pennsylvania.

PENNSYLVANIA

Ambridge–includes lower Beaver County and adjacent areas of Allegheny County.

Delaware Valley–includes Bensalem Township, Bristol, Langhorne, Levittown, New Hope, Newtown, Penndel, Warrington, Yardley, Richboro, Feasterville, Middletown, Southampton, and Holland.

Philadelphia–includes Philadelphia City, Montgomery, Delaware County, and central and upper Bucks County. For a total Jewish population of the Philadelphia Metropolitan Region, please include lower Bucks County, Chester County, and Cherry Hill area of New Jersey.

Pittsburgh–includes all of Allegheny County and adjacent portions of Washington, Westmoreland, and Beaver counties.

Wilkes-Barre–includes all of Lucerne County except southern portion, which is included in Hazleton totals.

SOUTH CAROLINA

Sumter–includes towns in Sumter, Lee, Clarendon, and Williamsburg counties.

TEXAS

Amarillo–includes Canyon, Childress, Borger, Dumas, Memphis, Pampa, Vega, and Hereford in Texas, and Portales, New Mexico.

De Witt County–includes communities also in Colorado, Fayette, Gonzales, and La Vaca counties.

Houston–includes Harris, Montgomery, and Ft. Bend counties and parts of Brazoria and Galveston counties.

Waco–includes Mclellan, Coryell, Bell, Falls, Hamilton, and Hill counties.

VIRGINIA

Newport News–includes Newport News, Hampton, Williamsburg, James City, York County, and Poquosson County.

Richmond–includes Richmond City, Henrico County, and Chesterfield County.

Staunton–includes towns in Augusta, Page, Shenendoah, Rockingham, Bath, and Highland counties.

Winchester–includes towns in Winchester, Frederick, Clark, and Warren counties, Virginia, and Hardy and Jefferson counties, West Virginia.

WASHINGTON

Seattle–includes King County and adjacent portions of Snohomish and Kitsap counties.

Tri Cities–includes Pasco, Richland, Kennewick, and Yakima.

WEST VIRGINIA

Huntington–includes nearby towns in Ohio and Kentucky.

WISCONSIN

Milwaukee–includes Milwaukee County, Eastern Waukesha County, and Southern Ozaukee County.

Wasau–includes Stevens Point, Marshfield, Antigo, and Rhinelander.

Review of the Year

OTHER COUNTRIES

Canada

National Affairs

ALTHOUGH CANADA IN 1986 ENJOYED continued economic expansion and a modest decline in the unemployment rate, the governing Progressive Conservative (PC) party of Prime Minister Brian Mulroney did not fare well politically. Beset by an image of bungling and incompetence, it also saw some of its leading members become involved in scandal. As a consequence, by the end of the year the Conservatives trailed both the Liberals and the New Democrats (NDP) in public-opinion polls. The most surprising political development of the year was the surge in popularity of the NDP, whose socialist outlook had previously consigned it to also-ran status but which now emerged—largely because of the personal appeal of its leader, Ed Broadbent—as a serious contender against the other two parties.

One of the most difficult issues for the government was refugee policy. Canada's generally humanitarian approach had made it a popular destination for growing numbers of refugees, especially from South Asia, including many who entered the country illegally and then claimed refugee status. Canadians seeking to stem this flow sought to distinguish those who were genuine refugees from political persecution from those who were simply seeking a better life, but this distinction was not universally accepted. The issue was dramatized in August, when 155 Tamils were found in a small boat off Canada's Atlantic coast, after having been brought from West Germany by freighter. The question of admitting the fugitives proved divisive in the country, with Jews, mindful of the hostile posture of Canada toward Jewish refugees during the Nazi period, generally supportive of the Tamil case. The striking contrast between public attitudes in the present and those of the 1940s was noted by many observers. In 1940, Jews, desperate for a haven, were refused admission to the country; in 1986, Tamils—also desperate—entered illegally and were permitted to stay.

The Tamil case served to highlight the changes that had taken place in Canadian society generally over the previous 45 years, changes that for Jews had been nothing less than monumental. Whereas before World War II they suffered from innumerable forms of discrimination, especially in education, employment, and housing, by 1986 they enjoyed complete equality in all areas. Human rights had become the policy of the federal and provincial governments, and Jews were active in the debates over refugee and other civil-libertarian issues. One of the most outspoken voices on general refugee policy was Rabbi W. Gunther Plaut of Toronto, who chaired the Canadian Commission on Refugees.

A number of Jews ran for office in municipal elections in Winnipeg and Montreal. In Winnipeg, councillors Larry Fleisher and Helen Promislow were reelected. Montreal voters surprised everyone by electing the reform-minded Montreal Citizens Movement (MCM) in virtually a clean sweep of the mayoralty and 58 city council seats. Among the veteran MCM councillors who were reelected were Michael Fainstat, Arnold Bennett, Marvin Rotrand, Sam Boskey, and Abe Limonchik. Fainstat was appointed chairman of the executive committee, the second most important post in the city government. Saulie Zajdel became the first Lubavitcher to be elected to the city council.

In the federal cabinet, Gerry Weiner was appointed minister of state for immigration. Weiner, who represented a suburban Montreal constituency for the PCs, had served as mayor of Dollard des Ormeaux, Quebec, before entering federal politics.

Canadians of all faiths joined Jews in mourning the victims of the September massacre at Istanbul's Neve Shalom Synagogue and in voicing their outrage. Memorial services were held in Toronto, Montreal, and Ottawa, the last of which was addressed by Deputy Prime Minister Don Mazankowski.

Fear of terrorism prompted Toronto filmmaker Simcha Jacobovici to sue the government in order to force it to remove an entry for birthplace from Canadian passports. Jacobovici argued that such information might result in the holder being singled out by terrorists, with people born in Israel especially at risk but members of other national groups vulnerable as well. Subsequently, Secretary of State for External Affairs Joe Clark announced that passports without country of origin would be available on an optional basis.

The federal government named its first honorary citizen, Raoul Wallenberg, in recognition of his heroic efforts to save Jews in Budapest in 1944.

Relations with Israel

Relations between Canada and Israel remained good, despite some differences of opinion over the occupied territories and related matters. In April External Affairs Minister Clark included Israel in a Middle East itinerary. In his meetings with Israeli officials, Clark stressed his support for Israeli security but also endorsed a homeland for the Palestinian Arabs in the West Bank and the Gaza Strip. He indicated, too, that Canada would maintain low-level contacts with the Palestine Liberation Organization (PLO), although it would not recognize the PLO until that body officially accepted Israel's existence.

Prime Minister Shimon Peres of Israel paid a successful visit to Canada in September, stopping in Ottawa, Toronto, and Montreal. He discussed commercial and political issues with Prime Minister Mulroney and also met with various opposition politicians. In Montreal he addressed a Jewish community rally, attended a reception tendered by the Sephardic Jewish community, and had lunch with leading Quebec businessmen and political leaders. Throughout his trip he was received with enthusiasm.

Political efforts in Israel's behalf were the focus of the annual parliamentary dinner of the Canada-Israel Committee (CIC) in November. Joe Clark addressed the conference, adding little to stated positions of the government but stressing Canadian opposition to international terrorism and a willingness to undertake bilateral or multilateral action to combat the threat. There was also some discussion at the meeting of the government's policy toward PLO members who applied for admission to Canada for various purposes, whose applications were treated on an individual basis and generally granted. Government spokesmen declined to endorse Jewish community demands that Canada cut off ties to the PLO and bar PLO members from entering the country on the grounds that they belonged to a terrorist organization.

An important development was the inauguration of direct Toronto–Tel Aviv air service by El Al Israel Airlines, previously limited in Canada to Montreal. There was also expansion of trade between the two countries, especially in the area of Israeli exports to Canada.

Anti-Semitism

Although the trials of James Keegstra of Alberta and Ernst Zundel of Ontario had concluded in 1985, with both men convicted under separate provisions of the criminal code of anti-Semitic actions, debate continued over the ultimate benefits and costs of the process. (See AJYB, vol. 87, 1987, pp. 197–99.) While there was a certain degree of satisfaction within the Jewish community regarding the outcomes, there was also unhappiness over the extensive publicity given the two men and their Holocaust-denying and anti-Semitic views. Countering the pessimistic view, Carleton University political science professor Conrad Winn argued, based on his study of Canadian public opinion (see "Publications," below), that the Zundel trial was worthwhile because people learned about the Holocaust from it and developed greater sympathy for the Jews as a result. He claimed that approximately half of the Canadian population knew about the trial, of whom some 37 percent changed their views about Jews, generally becoming more positive.

Winn's contentions were supported by a study of Canadian newspaper coverage of the Keegstra trial conducted by Sol Littman, who represented the Simon Wiesenthal Center in Canada. Virtually all of the editorials and opinion columns that he examined condemned Keegstra and what he represented, and many of the newspapers expressed approval of the conviction. Those who questioned the wisdom of bringing charges against Keegstra believed either that freedom of speech should take precedence over antihate laws or that the best way to deal with types like Keegstra was to relegate them to obscurity. In an analysis of both trials, Manuel Prutschi, director of community relations for the Canadian Jewish Congress (CJC), found encouragement in the decisive way in which the hatemongers were dealt with, despite the pain aroused by the trials. The support of Canadians at large was seen as a gratifying by-product of the two cases.

Keegstra and Zundel both appealed their convictions, on the grounds of free-speech rights and various procedural questions. The hearing on the Keegstra appeal was delayed beyond the end of the year. The Zundel appeal was heard late in 1986, with the decision still pending at year's end.

Other incidents of anti-Semitism came to light during the year. In New Brunswick, Malcolm Ross, a teacher and official of a right-wing Christian group, was charged under the criminal code with wilfully promoting hatred against Jews, the same charge under which Keegstra had been convicted in Alberta. The charges, which were filed by a retired Jewish professor, were based on a number of anti-Semitic booklets written and distributed by Ross, in which he promoted Holocaust denial and the notion of a Jewish conspiracy to dominate the world. After a year of investigating the matter, the provincial attorney general decided not to prosecute, citing technical reasons. Despite subsequent evidence of official foot-dragging and fresh accusations based on newspaper articles written by Ross, no action had been taken by year's end. Some Jewish organizational representatives were hesitant to press the matter, based on their assessment of the likelihood of acquittal and the effects of such an outcome.

A more dramatic and less ambiguous episode occurred in Alberta, where an avowedly racist group that operated on both sides of the U.S.-Canadian border, the Aryan Nations, became active and announced plans to set up a training camp. A coalition of opponents of the group gave wide publicity to its anti-Semitic and white-supremacist teachings, thereby arousing public antagonism to the group. As a result, all the political parties in the Alberta legislature unanimously condemned the Aryan Nations and its activities. The camp was set up but proved to be an insignificant venture.

General levels of anti-Semitism were measured in a survey conducted by the League for Human Rights of B'nai B'rith. Prof. Taylor Buckner of Concordia University in Montreal, who analyzed the data, said that about 16 percent of the total Canadian population could be considered anti-Semitic, but that the proportion was higher in Quebec, at about 22 percent. In a survey of Jewish attitudes in Toronto, conducted by public-opinion specialist Martin Goldfarb for the *Toronto Star,* 85 percent of the respondents believed that there was prejudice against Jews, and 55 percent said they had personally experienced prejudice or discrimination.

Holocaust-Related Issues

The Deschenes Commission, established in 1984, continued to study the situation regarding alleged Nazi war criminals living in Canada and to consider recommendations for legislation to allow their investigation and prosecution. The commission's report was expected early in 1987. Even as its investigation was under way, however, the commission became a source of controversy when several Eastern European ethnic groups accused it of engaging in a witch-hunt. Representatives of the Jewish community, which strongly supported the inquiry, pointed out that individuals would be investigated not because of membership in particular ethnic groups but because of their own actions during World War II. Regarding the role of the Canadian government in the matter of war criminals, lawyer David Matas, representing B'nai B'rith's League for Human Rights, described a historical "record of inactivity, of obstruction of justice, of obfuscation of the law, of destruction of documents" that needed to be rectified by immediate and vigorous action and the pursuit of justice.

The international controversy over Austrian president Kurt Waldheim's past spilled over into Canada, where Waldheim had served as ambassador from 1960 to 1962. CJC legal counsel Irwin Cotler charged that the government had known about allegations of his involvement in war crimes at the time that he was accredited but had failed to act. According to Cotler, Canada had signed a 1948 UN document in which Waldheim was identified as a suspected war criminal. Notwithstanding various protests during and after the Austrian election, as well as calls for an international investigation of Waldheim and for barring him from entering Canada, the Canadian ambassador in Vienna attended Waldheim's inaugural ceremony in July and an official congratulatory telegram was sent by the governor-general.

JEWISH COMMUNITY

Demography

The Jewish population of about 310,000 was essentially stable, its low growth rate typical of an industrial society but exacerbated by a higher proportion of older people than the Canadian population as a whole. The growing concentration of Jews in metropolitan Toronto, enhanced by the move of nearly 10,000 Montreal Jews during the Parti Québécois era (1976–1985), seemed likely to continue. Younger people drifting away from small communities in the eastern half of the country contributed to the growth in Toronto. Together, Montreal and Toronto accounted for about three-quarters of the country's Jews.

The Jewish community of Vancouver, with about 20,000 members and still growing, had surpassed Winnipeg in size. The latter community continued to decline; a significant proportion of its youth had moved away, and its population of about 15,000 had an overrepresentation of older people. The two Alberta communities, Edmonton and Calgary, with Jewish populations respectively of about 5,560 and 4,300, had grown rapidly during the boom in the oil patch in the 1970s; however, the decline in economic opportunity during the glut period of the 1980s arrested the growth of both cities and their Jewish communities.

The major sources of Jewish immigration during the previous two decades were North Africa and Israel. It was estimated that about 11,000 Canadian Jews had been born in North Africa, mainly Morocco, and another 7,000 in Israel. Over 2,000 Soviet Jewish families had settled in Canada during the preceding 15 years. Finally, some 2,000 South African Jews had arrived during the 1970s, settling mainly in Toronto.

In both Montreal and Toronto, the Sephardic communities were becoming more visible and more active in the affairs of the entire Jewish community. This was especially true in Montreal, where the Sephardim constituted as much as 25 percent of the Jewish population.

Demographic analysis of the Jewish community would henceforth be more difficult because of a decision by Statistics Canada to drop the religion question from the mid-decade 1986 census. However, the ethnicity question, which included Jewish ethnicity as a possible response, was retained on the long form administered to a 20-percent sample of the population. Authorities indicated that efforts would be made to reinstate the religion question for the 1991 census.

Community Relations

Relations with various levels of government were a major concern to Jews, either because of community needs that only government could respond to or because of government regulations that impinged on minority or individual rights. Several current issues, such as Sunday closings, school prayer, and government aid to parochial schools appeared similar to ones fought over in the United States; in Canada, however, with its more tolerant view of the relationship between church and state, the issues were framed quite differently.

The lack of provincial government financial support for Jewish day schools in Ontario continued to be a source of disappointment to the community. While Catholic schools were supported, and that support had recently been extended to the final three years of high school, Jewish schools received no government aid. Moreover, long-term efforts by community leadership to change the policy had not borne fruit. In February, in a major legal decision, the Ontario Court of Appeals ruled 3–2 that the extension of government funding to the Catholic high schools was constitutional and, further, that the omission of other private schools, such as the large Jewish system in Toronto, was not unconstitutionally discriminatory. In its decision the court upheld the traditional preferential treatment accorded the Protestant and Roman Catholic religions in Ontario and Quebec schools and rejected Jewish arguments based on the concept of equality for other religions under the new Charter of Rights and Freedoms. Jewish groups found some consolation in the fact that the dissenting opinions responded positively to the equality argument. The Ontario Jewish Association for Equity in Education pledged to continue the fight for funding in both the legal and political arenas.

Jewish groups sought government aid to deal with the perennial problem of ensuring that Jewish women received a *get* (a religious divorce decree) when they were divorced. The passage in January of Ontario's Family Law Reform Act, which contained a provision that parties to a civil divorce would have to certify that they had "removed all barriers . . . that would prevent the other spouse's remarriage" in order for the civil divorce to be granted, represented a major breakthrough in Canadian law. It was anticipated that the new law would reduce the power of husbands to demand a favorable property settlement in exchange for a Jewish divorce. The broad coalition of Jewish organizations that had pushed for the provincial legislation vowed to press for comparable amendments to the federal Divorce Act, and Justice Minister John Crosbie promised "sympathetic and careful consideration" of the Jewish proposals.

Problems arose for Jews in several areas in which religious observance came into conflict with existing laws. Ontario's strict law curtailing Sunday shopping—which hampered Jewish Sabbath observers—was challenged in the Supreme Court of Canada by merchants who claimed that it violated constitutional guarantees of freedom of religion. The cases before the court were bound to set precedents because they were the first to test certain provisions of the Charter of Rights and Freedoms, which had come into effect in April 1985. While the decision of the Supreme Court was still pending, a provincial court in Toronto, ruling on another case, declared the Ontario law unconstitutional. However, in December the Supreme Court upheld the constitutionality of the Ontario law by a 6-1 vote. The court essentially concluded that individual assertions of freedom of religion in such matters had to defer to a compelling state interest in providing a uniform day of rest.

In a related issue, Justice Minister Crosbie announced the government's intention to accommodate employees whose religious holidays kept them away from work on regular working days; however, he declined to offer specific legislation for achieving that objective.

Quebec Jews pressed their provincial government to eliminate provisions of the law that prevented people other than Catholics and Protestants from voting in school-board elections. (The boards in Quebec were not neutral; they were either Catholic or Protestant.) Both Premier Robert Bourassa and Education Minister Claude Ryan promised the necessary changes in the law, and these were in fact made during the year.

Another troubling issue was that of bilingual labeling of kosher food products. Although food products made in Canada routinely carried labels in English and French, many kosher products imported from the United States used English only, and their sale violated Quebec's language law. Since strict enforcement of the law reduced the choices available to the kosher consumer, it was seen by some as interference with religious practice. However, because the language question in Quebec was extremely sensitive, and also because there was a substantial minority of Francophones in the Jewish community, efforts to seek an exemption from the law for kosher products were promoted cautiously. The election of the Liberal government in Quebec in late 1985 was viewed as an opportunity to reopen the issue in a friendlier environment than existed under the Parti Québécois, which was strongly opposed by Jews. In fact, the minister in charge of the language law, Lise Bacon, agreed to look into the matter.

Segments of the Jewish community came into conflict with government over other issues which, while seemingly narrow, nevertheless held broad significance. Two such issues were municipal taxation laws and zoning. In Montreal, the national headquarters of the CJC was the subject of a dispute with significant financial implications. Congress authorities contended that the building was exempt from property tax because it was owned and used by a nonprofit charitable organization. The city argued differently and assessed back taxes for three years. The YM-YWHA was the subject of a similar dispute. Between the two organizations, the amount of back taxes claimed totaled nearly $1 million. While an appeal to the Quebec Municipal Commission was pending, the city put the Congress building on the bailiff's block for a tax sale; however, attorneys for the CJC were able to forestall the sale pending a final determination of the tax liability in the courts.

Zoning issues involving synagogues arose as new congregations attempted to operate in residential neighborhoods over the opposition of local homeowners. In Toronto a group of Russian immigrants purchased a former electricity substation with the intention of converting it into a synagogue. Neighbors opposed a proposed zoning variance before the Ontario Municipal Board, arguing that the synagogue would bring about congestion and noise. Although the board disregarded the objections and authorized the change, the borough of North York, in which the dispute occurred, began considering passage of a by-law that would prohibit religious institutions on residential streets in the future.

A bitter zoning dispute took place in Cote St. Luc, a Montreal suburb, when a new congregation of Moroccan immigrants purchased a home for use as their synagogue. Although the city turned down a request for a zoning change to permit the use of the building as a house of worship, the Groupement Sepharade de Cote St. Luc continued to hold religious services there. Opposition from some residents of the area led to heated debates in city council meetings, as a result of which the congregation was charged in municipal court and a trial was planned.

An internal dispute in another Cote St. Luc Sephardic synagogue resulted in a landmark decision in Quebec Superior Court, the first instance of civil intervention in an internal synagogue matter. The judge ruled that the newly elected president had to resign because he was not qualified under the congregation's own by-laws. The legal case was the outcome of intense conflict within the congregation, during which the board member who brought charges against the president was physically barred from attending the service. An appeal was planned.

Communal Affairs

Canadian Jewry's central body, the Canadian Jewish Congress, met in its triennial plenary assembly in Toronto in May. Delegates from across the country gathered to elect the leadership and set policy directions. A spirited fight for the presidency ensued between Dorothy Reitman of Montreal and Moshe Ronen of Toronto. Reitman, a woman in her 50s who had served Congress for many years, including nine as a national officer, was the candidate of the Congress veterans, while Ronen, only 27, was perceived as a youth candidate and an insurgent, challenging the established way of doing things. Reitman, who stressed her experience and the importance of continuity in the organization, won the election and became the first female president of CJC. Both candidates highlighted the need to broaden participation in Jewish community affairs, with Ronen emphasizing the benefits of active student input. Ronen also called for a more activist stance on Israel-related issues, a greater stress on Jewish education, and more intense efforts to deal with the problems of the Jewish poor. Reitman urged greater involvement in broader Canadian social issues, such as capital punishment.

Although Ronen lost the race for the presidency, 24-year-old Alan Feld of Toronto was elected associate chairman of the national executive, running on an activist and youth-oriented platform. Mira Koschitzky of Toronto won the post of chairwoman of the national executive.

Jewish education remained a major issue of concern in the community, particularly its financial aspects. In a most significant development, the Montreal federation—Allied Jewish Community Services (AJCS)—agreed to a substantial increase in funding for Jewish day schools. This followed a campaign by parents and educators concerned about the fact that even with funding from the Quebec government the schools confronted large deficits, and the resulting sharp tuition increases threatened to affect enrollments. The elevation of Jewish education to a high community financial priority represented a major shift from past practices, which tended to favor health and welfare activities. In practical terms, the intention of AJCS was to offset a major portion of the schools' scholarship needs.

At the Jewish National Education Conference, held in Montreal in March, Stephen Lipper, an AJCS officer and former president of the Association of Jewish Day Schools, questioned the benefits of government subsidies in Quebec, characterizing the experience of 18 years as a mixed blessing at best. Lipper argued that the linguistic strings attached to the grants had a negative effect on the quality of education at the elementary level. (Schools were required to teach at least 14 hours per week in French, which for Jewish day schools meant lengthening the already long day and cutting back Hebrew and English instruction. The law also limited attendance at English-language schools to children who had at least one parent educated in English schools in Quebec, with nearly all others—including newcomers—required to attend French-language schools.) Critical views of the present system were also expressed by Harold Waller, a former day-school president, who argued that the long-term implications of the subsidy system had not been analyzed sufficiently. He called on the community to support schools that would operate without government grants.

A new source of funding for certain types of community projects came into being with the establishment of the CRB Foundation, named for its benefactor, Charles R. Bronfman. With an initial capitalization that made it one of the five largest foundations in Canada, the fund planned to make grants in two main areas, Canadian affairs and international Jewish affairs. In the latter area the foundation planned to support projects dealing with Israel-Diaspora relations or with overcoming polarization within the Jewish community. The foundation was headed by Stephen Cohen, former professor of social psychology at CUNY, and was based in Montreal.

A training program that had existed in the United States for over 15 years, whose purpose was to develop executives for Jewish community federations, was expanded this year to include Canada. The Federation Executive Recruitment Program, operating in affiliation with the University of Toronto, offered courses in social work and Judaic studies. A major motivation for extending the program to Canada was to encourage more home-grown talent to staff key federation positions, which were often filled, of necessity, by Americans.

The Canadian Zionist Federation (CZF) was caught up in a conflict over the application for membership of Tehiya Canada, which had been pending since 1981, when the organization was founded. The organization claimed that its application had been subjected to bureaucratic stalling, due to political opposition within the Labor-dominated CZF. Eventually the federation relented and Tehiya was admitted to membership—in time to contest the elections for the 1987 World Zionist Congress.

The elections themselves became the subject of controversy within the CZF, the question being whether they were needed at all or whether the number of delegates could simply be allocated among the constituent organizations by consensus. Although there was some opposition to the holding of elections on the ground of cost, several constituent organizations—in particular Kadima, the Reform Zionist body—insisted that elections be held, and that view prevailed.

Soviet Jewry

Since the plight of Natan Sharansky had been a major focus of efforts in behalf of Soviet Jews for years, Canada's Jews rejoiced at the news of his release from Soviet prison in February. Human rights lawyer Irwin Cotler, who played a major role as Sharansky's attorney, was present at Ben-Gurion Airport in Israel to join in the welcome.

In a major effort to publicize the plight of Soviet Jews, the Jewish Students' Network Caravan for Soviet Jewry traveled across Canada in May, from Halifax to Vancouver, ending the two-week journey at the international exposition in Vancouver, where there was a Soviet pavilion. The 50 student participants organized demonstrations in many cities along the route.

Canadian Jewish leaders participated in the International Council of the World Conference on Soviet Jewry in Paris in September. Canadian Jewry was appointed to the executive of the organization and played a central role in the formulation of policy. Barbara Stern and Martin Penn of the CJC led the delegation.

Religion

Two of the largest congregations in Canada celebrated significant birthdays this year: Congregation Shaar Hashomayim in Montreal its 140th and Beth Tzedec in Toronto its 100th. The Beth Jacob Synagogue in Hamilton also observed its centenary.

Toronto was the site of a meeting of the World Union for Progressive Judaism in April. At this first international conference of the body to be held in North America, delegates discussed patrilineal descent, the place of Reform in Israel, and other key issues. Later in the year Canadian Reform congregations met in a biennial conference in Montreal to consider such matters as the funding of non-Orthodox institutions in Israel by the Jewish Agency, relations with Israel, and involvement in the Canadian Zionist Federation.

A disappointment to Canadian Reform Jews was the departure of Rabbi Kenneth Segel from the pulpit of Montreal's Temple Emanu-El-Beth Shalom after only two years. Rabbi Segel disclosed his frustration with the lack of acceptance of Reform Judaism in Montreal, which he attributed to the community's strong traditional leanings. Another Reform rabbi who left Canada after a fairly short stay was Tracy Klirs of Winnipeg, Canada's first woman rabbi.

In other developments: shifts in population led to the sale of Congregation Beth David in Portage La Prairie, Manitoba, the last rural synagogue in that province, and of Congregation Beth Aaron in Montreal; in Toronto, an egalitarian Conservative congregation, Kehillat Ahavat Hesed, began functioning; an *eruv* was established to enclose the Montreal suburbs of Cote St. Luc and Hampstead, thus enhancing the towns' attractiveness to Orthodox families; and locally produced kosher wines went on sale in Toronto.

Culture

Both Toronto and Montreal supported lively Yiddish theatrical groups, as well as other activities in Yiddish. In Montreal, audiences saw such plays as *The Megillah, In My Father's Court, The Agunah,* and *The Rothschilds,* while the Toronto group produced *Kuni Leml.* Additional evidence of the vitality of Yiddish culture in Canada was found in the outdoor concerts held in Toronto, Winnipeg, and Montreal during the summer. Several thousand people attended the concerts, which were annual events. Much of the impetus for Yiddish cultural activity came from the National Committee on Yiddish of the CJC, which stimulated the creation of Yiddish groups, consisting mainly of Canadian-born Jews, in Ottawa and Winnipeg as well as in the two major cities. Over 700 people participated in an evening of Yiddish culture held at Montreal's Concordia University in November. Noted writer Yehuda Elberg chaired a program that included dramatic performances and readings.

Montreal playwright Mike Gutwillig's first play, *The Special,* was staged professionally in New York. The story concerned a relationship between a Jewish man and a French Canadian woman during the period of intense political activity in Montreal around 1980.

Habimah, Israel's national theater company, performed during the biennial drama festival in Quebec City, the Quinzaine Internationale du Théatre Québec. The troupe presented the first North American performance of director Steven Berkoff's adaptation for stage of *The Trial* by Franz Kafka.

In Toronto, Jewish writers helped to observe Jewish Book Month by reading from their own works at a public gathering. Among the writers who participated were Carol Libman, Leo Orenstein, and Helen Weinzweig. Montreal writers Irving Layton and Mordecai Richler were the subjects of two of three films made by the National Film Board in a series entitled "Life Transformed: Montreal Writers on Film." After premiering in Montreal, the series was shown in cities from coast to coast.

Montreal hosted its fourth annual International Jewish Film Festival, at which over 20 films were screened.

Harry Rasky's film *Homage to Chagall: The Colours of Love* won an Emmy International Award for its television showing in the United States. It had previously won numerous other honors.

Publications

Canadian Jewish writers published a number of notable books during the year, two of particular relevance to Canadian life. In *Hate on Trial: The Zundel Affair, the Media, and Public Opinion in Canada,* Gabriel Weimann and Conrad Winn conclude that the trial publicity hurt Zundel's cause and generally increased sympathy for the Jews. *Juifs et Québécois Francais: 200 ans d'histoire,* by Jacques Langlais and David Rome, analyzes the situation of the Jews in Quebec in the period 1880–1980, attempting to explain the presence and nature of anti-Semitism in that province.

In *The Christian Problem: A Jewish View,* Stuart Rosenberg explores the religious foundation of anti-Semitism. Rosenberg argues that the traditional notion of the rejection of Jesus by Jews should be turned around, that it was the Christians who rejected Judaism, and that the reasons for their departure from rabbinic Judaism antedated the birth of Jesus. The persistence of anti-Jewish attitudes after the Enlightenment is explored in *The Image of Jews and Judaism in the Prelude to the French Enlightenment* by Arnold Ages, covering the period 1685–1715.

Community and the Individual Jew: Essays in Honor of Lavy M. Becker, edited by Ronald Aigen and Gershon Hundert, is a festschrift marking the 80th birthday of a leading Montreal personality and the moving force behind the establishment of Reconstructionism in Canada. The Canadian contributors include Rabbi W. Gunther Plaut, Michael Brown, and Morton Weinfeld. Bernard Avishai's *The Tragedy of Zionism* is a critical study of recent developments in Israel. *The Unwanted* by Michael Marrus is a comprehensive study of European refugees—Jewish and non-Jewish—in the twentieth century.

David Mendel Harduf published a paperback English-Yiddish, Yiddish-English dictionary—believed to be the only such dictionary available in the pocketbook format. Another new Yiddish publication was *A Drop of Consolation in My Misery,* a collection of poems by Moishe Shaffir.

Other noteworthy books published during the year were *Nazi Germany* by Allan Hux and Frederick Jarman, the first high-school textbook for the Canadian market to provide an extensive treatment of the Holocaust; *6,400 Questions About Judaism and the Jewish People* by Edmond Lipsitz; *Essential Words: An Anthology of Canadian Jewish Poetry,* edited by Seymour Mayne; *The Letter,* a novel by Rabbi W. Gunther Plaut; *Working Without a Net: My Intimate Memoirs,* the autobiography of Toronto actress Lynne Gordon; *Dance with Desire,* a collection of poetry by Irving Layton; *Ancient Judaism* by Irving M. Zeitlin; and *The Dimensions of Orthodox Judaism* by Rabbi Reuven Bulka.

Personalia

A number of Jews were appointed to the prestigious Order of Canada, including leaders of the Jewish community. The new members were Dr. Phil Gold, Dr. Samuel Freedman, Victor Feldbrill, Joseph Shoctor, Mitchell Franklin, Anne G. Ross, Milton Harris, Ben Kayfetz, Alan Rose, Moshe Safdie, Dr. Arthur Vineberg, and Samuel Berger. Mira Spivak was appointed to the Senate, bringing to eight the number of Jews in the 104-member upper house of Parliament. Joseph Rabinovitch became the first non-Protestant director-general of the Protestant School Board of Greater Montreal. Dr. Phil Gold garnered another award, designation as a "Great Montrealer." William Miller was appointed to the federal government's Human Rights Tribunal; R. Lou Ronson was appointed vice-chairman, and Jack Diamond, a member, of the Ontario Human Rights Commission. Albert Hershkovitz retired as vice-president of the Ontario Federation of Labor, and Elinor Caplan resigned from the Ontario cabinet, amid allegations of conflict of interest involving her husband.

The first endowed chair in Jewish studies in Canada was established at McGill University, and Prof. Ruth R. Wisse was appointed to occupy it. Prof. Barry Glickman of York University was awarded a prestigious E. W. Steacie Memorial Fellowship for his work in cell mutations. Tom Beck was elected president of the Toronto Symphony Orchestra, and Tevie Miller became chancellor of the University of Alberta.

Within the Jewish community, major appointments included: Andrea Stringer, president of the Hamilton Jewish Federation; Judge Irving Halperin, member of the board of governors of the Jewish Telegraphic Agency; Leon Oziel, president of the Canadian Sephardic Federation; Sidney Spivak, chairman of the Canada-Israel Committee; Marjorie Blenstein, president of the Winnipeg Jewish Community Council; Ronald Appleby, president of the Toronto Jewish Congress; David Azrieli, president of the Canadian Zionist Federation (CZF); Rabbi Meyer Krentzman, executive director of the CZF; Jack Rose, chairman of the Canadian Committee of the Council of Jewish Federations; Martin Levine, president of the United Israel Appeal; Michael Davis, president of the Canadian Friends of Hebrew University; Phil Granovsky, chairman of the board of Bank Hapoalim (Canada); and Tom Beck, president of Canadian Friends of Weizmann Institute.

Among leading Jews who died in 1986 were the following: World War II flying ace Albert Cohen, in January, aged 69; Joe Zuken, longtime Winnipeg city councillor, in March, aged 74; Henry Papernick, veteran Toronto community leader, in March, aged 88; Nathan Urbach, Toronto Hebrew teacher, synagogue president, and community activist, in March, aged 85; actress Tony Robins, in March, aged 55; Rabbi Yisroel Weber of Hamilton, in April, aged 53; Alan Borden, past president of B'nai B'rith, in May, aged 44; Dr. Wilfrid Yaphe, McGill University microbiologist, in May, aged 65; Bert Baruch Migicovsky, retired government biochemist, in May, aged 71; Jacob Monbaz, former Israeli consul-general in Montreal and Toronto, in May, aged 72; Montreal restaurateur Lou Kirsch, in May, aged 62; actor David Ellin, in June, aged 61; singer Charles Jordan, in July, aged 71; Mark Levy, Toronto community leader, in August, aged 82; Imrich Yitzhak Rosenberg, former Jewish community leader in Czechoslovakia, who was instrumental in the rescue of Jews from the Nazis, in August, aged 73; Moshe Waxman, Hamilton synagogue leader, in September, aged 108; Bert Pearl, radio personality, in September, aged 73; Moshe Sambatyon, Talmud scholar, in September, aged 73; Hillel Michaels, Yiddish journalist, in September, aged 99; Morris Moscovitch, Montreal businessman and community worker, in September, aged 71; Rabbi Abraham Feinberg, rabbi emeritus of the Holy Blossom Temple in Toronto, in October, aged 87; Michael Franklin, the first Jewish senior Crown prosecutor in Quebec, in October, aged 87; Roy Matas, judge of the Manitoba Court of Appeal, in November, aged 66; Gerald Bronfman, philanthropist and community leader, in December, aged 74; Rabbi Neil Rosenbloom of Toronto, killed by a gunman during a holdup while visiting in Pittsburgh, in December, aged 23.

HAROLD M. WALLER

Western Europe

Great Britain

National Affairs

THE YEAR 1986 WAS marked by sharply contrasting trends in political and economic affairs. Notable improvement took place in labor-industrial relations, with the total of working days lost through strikes the lowest in over 20 years. By contrast, the total of 3.2 million unemployed—about 11 percent of the working population—represented only a slight decline over the previous year.

Politically, Prime Minister Margaret Thatcher's Conservative government made a remarkable late-year recovery, following some early disasters. The year began with two cabinet resignations, first that of Defense Secretary Michael Heseltine, soon after that of Secretary of Trade and Industry Leon Brittan. The two ministers had clashed over conflicting plans for saving the ailing Westland helicopter company. Following this controversy, the government retreated, in the face of opposition on patriotic grounds, on plans to sell Leyland Trucks to the General Motors Corporation and Leyland Cars to the Ford Motor Company. Another threat to the government was the drop in the price of North Sea oil from $20 a barrel in January to $10 in the summer, although it recovered to $15 by the end of the year.

Early in the year, public-opinion polls showed the Conservatives having 33 percent support, compared to Labor's 38 percent, and the Social Democratic/Liberal Alliance's 28 percent. By the end of the year the respective percentages were 41, 39, and 18. Although several Tory victories in local elections in September and October appeared to signal an upward trend, the recovery was perhaps due less to the Conservative party's achievements than to opposition to the defense policies of Labor and the Social Democratic/Liberal Alliance. Labor's call for unilateral nuclear disarmament had proven consistently unpopular with the electorate, and the differences over defense issues between various factions of the Social Democrats and the Liberals left them vulnerable to Tory attack. Moreover, because the subject of defense claimed so much attention, areas of Conservative weakness—unemployment, poverty, and the uneven regional pattern of prosperity—were left unexploited by the opposition.

Relations with Israel

Highlights of the year were visits by Prime Minister Shimon Peres of Israel to Britain in January and by Prime Minister Thatcher to Israel in May. The "introduction of an air of trust and closeness between Israel and Britain and more understanding on the peace process" were the most important outcomes of his meetings, Peres told the *Jewish Chronicle.* During the five-day visit, Peres received a full ceremonial welcome and had talks with Thatcher and Foreign Secretary Sir Geoffrey Howe on proposals for ending the Middle East stalemate. On the practical level, the British government agreed to end its practice of authenticating documents related to the Arab boycott of Israel. On another issue in contention, however, Britain's embargo on sales of arms and North Sea oil to Israel, the government was unyielding. Soon after, in February, Britain signed a $5-billion arms-for-oil deal with Saudi Arabia.

During Thatcher's successful three-day trip, the first by a British prime minister to Israel, she toured southern Israel, visited several institutions, including Yad Vashem, and held talks with Peres, Foreign Minister Yitzhak Shamir, and Defense Minister Yitzhak Rabin. Prime Minister Thatcher continued to pursue two chief policy aims: countering Arab terrorism and encouraging King Hussein, Prime Minister Peres, and moderate Palestinians to embark on peace negotiations.

Britain's strong stand on terrorism was demonstrated on two particular occasions. In April Mrs. Thatcher allowed the United States to send planes from American bases in Britain to bomb Libya. In October Britain broke off diplomatic relations with Syria, following the conviction of Jordanian journalist Nezar Hindawi for attempting to blow up an El Al airliner the previous April. Sir Geoffrey Howe told Parliament that there was clear evidence of Syrian involvement in the bomb plot.

In the area of peace negotiations, London talks between Thatcher and Hussein in April concentrated on practical steps aimed at persuading West Bank and Gaza Palestinians to participate in negotiations. In April two Palestinian Arab leaders—Hanna Siniora, editor of the East Jerusalem Arabic-language newspaper *Al-Fajr,* and Fayez Aby Rahmeh from Gaza—discussed with Tim Renton, minister of state at the Foreign Office, in London, the possibility of forming a Palestinian delegation for peace talks.

Even though Foreign Office officials and Labor party leaders met the PLO's "foreign minister," Farouk Kaddoumi, at a March reception hosted by Denis Walters, MP, chairman of the Conservative Middle East Council, Mrs. Thatcher insisted during her May visit to Israel that British leaders would not meet Yasir Arafat or other PLO figures unless they renounced terrorism, accepted UN Resolution 242, and specifically recognized Israel's right to exist in security. Failing acceptance of these terms, she said, alternative Palestinian leadership should be sought, possibly by holding local elections in the West Bank and Gaza. Mrs. Thatcher reiterated Britain's concern for the legitimate rights of the Palestinian Arabs and her belief that the best chance of a solution lay in the context of a Jordanian federation, not in the creation of a separate Palestinian state.

A curious and possibly damaging episode occurred in the fall, when Mordechai Vanunu, a former Israeli nuclear technician, vanished from Britain after having sold to the *Sunday Times* of London a detailed description, with photographs, of Israel's nuclear facility. After weeks of press speculation that Vanunu had been abducted from British soil by Israeli security agents, Israel acknowledged, on November 9, that Vanunu was "under lawful detention" in Israel. Israel denied, however, that he had been "kidnapped" or that Prime Minister Peres had been in contact with Mrs. Thatcher over the matter. Later that month, David Waddington, minister of state in the Home Office, rejected demands from several MPs for an inquiry into the alleged abduction, but did acknowledge that the Israeli government's silence about the circumstances of Vanunu's disappearance only fueled speculation and damaged Israel's interests.

Labor party leader Neil Kinnock, who was criticized by the Board of Deputies of British Jews over his meeting in March with Farouk Kaddoumi, told the board that his party's long-standing friendship with Israel "is inviolable, that our commitment to the existence of the State of Israel is unconditional and that our condemnation of terrorism and violence is absolute." Nevertheless, Palestinians Siniora and Rahmeh were invited to the September Labor party conference, where the PLO's London representative, Faisal Oweida, attended a caucus of the pro-Arab Labor Middle East Council.

Members of the executive of the Transport and General Workers' Union (TGWU) met in February with members of the Palestine Trade Union Federation, in the West Bank, following an earlier meeting with Histadrut representatives. "We should talk to both sides," TGWU general secretary Ron Todd said. Five of the union's 11 regions were affiliated with the Trade Union Friends of Israel (TUFI).

The National Union of Journalists' annual conference at Sheffield in April voted to establish contact with the Palestine Trade Union Federation and the Union of Palestinian Writers. TUFI's display stand at the National Association of Local Government Officers' annual conference in Bournemouth in June was seized and held by PLO members after an ugly confrontation between the two groups.

In the first issue of an Arab League quarterly journal published in London, *Arab Affairs,* Liberal party leader David Steel wrote that Britain should recognize in deeds and words that no progress toward a settlement of the Palestinian issue was possible without PLO involvement. Without an Israeli withdrawal and the establishment of a Palestinian national entity, the author asserted, there was no hope of long-term peace.

In an opinion poll carried out for the Zionist Federation (ZF) by NOP Market Research Ltd., between January 29 and February 3, of the total nationally representative sample of 815 adults, 18 percent sympathized with Israel, 7 percent with the Arabs, 18 percent with both, 41 percent had sympathy with neither side, and the remainder had no opinion. Among that portion of the sample that took a position on the Arab-Israeli conflict, 71 percent were sympathetic to Israel, 29 percent to the Arabs. Among all respondents, 64 percent said that the Lebanon war made no difference to their sympathies; 86 percent thought there was no justification for terrorism against civilians. Those holding no opinion tended to be young and less educated, the ZF reported. Conservative voters supported Israel more than Labor voters; older people more than younger.

In July Tel Aviv University awarded Prime Minister Thatcher an honorary degree; in August she agreed to join the board of trustees of the Ben Gurion Centennial Fund, which provided financial support for Ben Gurion University in Beersheba.

Anti-Zionism and Anti-Semitism

Pro-Arab and Jewish students came into conflict on several campuses during the year. At London's South Bank Polytechnic, at Thames Polytechnic, and at York University, Jewish students protested the public playing of taped anti-Semitic speeches of American Black Muslim leader Louis Farrakhan. At South Bank Polytechnic, the Jewish Society protested in March when the student union proposed a policy calling for the expulsion of "any society which supports or condones any form of racism, Zionism or sexism." At its April conference, the National Union of Students (NUS) condemned the Polytechnic for anti-Semitism; in November, following appeals by the Board of Deputies and the Inner London Education Authority, the Polytechnic's student representative council ratified the Jewish Society's constitution.

Anti-Zionist motions, often instigated by the Socialist Workers' Group and the National Organization of Labor Students, were debated on several campuses. In June Jewish students from all parts of Scotland demonstrated outside NUS's Edinburgh offices against an NUS conference on Palestine held in Glasgow in conjunction with the General Union of Palestinian Students.

JEWISH COMMUNITY

Demography

The Jewish population of Great Britain was estimated at 330,000. Leading Jewish population centers were London (201,000), Manchester (30,000), Leeds (14,000), Glasgow (11,000), and Brighton (10,000).

The Board of Deputies' research unit reported a continuing drop in the number of synagogue marriages, from 1,153 in 1984 to 1,144 in 1985 (less than 60 percent of the 1961 figure). Of the 1985 total, 101 marriages took place under right-wing Orthodox auspices (as compared with 110 in 1984); 736 under modern Orthodox (743); 54 under Sephardi (49); 169 under Reform (179); and 84 under Liberal auspices (72 in 1984).

Burials and cremations performed under Jewish religious auspices numbered

4,844 in 1985, against 4,945 the previous year. The 1985 total comprised 3,905 Orthodox burials (3,869 in 1984); 551 Reform (580); and 388 Liberal (496 in 1984).

According to the board's research unit, although Anglo-Jewry had traditionally been associated with 15 cities or towns, the recent trend was toward concentration in four or five centers. Thus, two out of every three Jews lived in London, while several former major centers showed considerable decline. Liverpool had dropped from 11,500 in 1918 to 5,000 in 1985; Edinburgh from 2,800 to 1,000; Sheffield from 2,300 to 1,000; and Leeds from 15,600 to 14,000.

British Jewry in the Eighties: A Statistical and Geographical Guide, compiled by Stanley Waterman and Barry Kosmin and issued in June, revealed British Jewry to be a declining population, with more people over the age of 55 and fewer under 45 than the national average. In a discussion of Jewish occupational structure, the authors point out that considerable change occurred over the previous century, and that Jews experienced more rapid upward mobility than the general population. More Jews than would be expected were to be found in medicine, accountancy, and university teaching; they were also overrepresented among London's famed cabdrivers, approximately one-third of whom were Jewish. At the same time, the number of Jewish shopkeepers had declined over recent decades, because of the demise of many small family businesses. Jewish representation was below average in unskilled and manual jobs.

Although the divorce rate among Jews was not as high as in the general population, it had been rising steadily, with the 1980 figure more than double that of 1965. By 1985, an estimated 400 Jewish couples were divorcing annually, involving some 450 children. Community concern over the increase was reflected in the opening in April of a West Central counseling and research group, and the reorganization, in October, of the Jewish Family Mediation Service, so as to provide improved services to divorced parents and their children.

Communal Activities

After announcing in March that the fund raising and staffing of the 46 welfare agencies under the Central Council of Jewish Social Services would be centralized within four months, council leaders bowed to the objections expressed by smaller agencies and in June offered a more flexible and gradual approach to coordination. In August the four major welfare organizations—the Jewish Welfare Board (JWB), Norwood Child Care, Ravenswood Foundation for the Mentally Handicapped, and the Jewish Blind Society (JBS)—began a program of joint activities involving extended cooperation between their respective professionals. The change was designed to bring about improved service to the community as well as substantial financial savings. In October ten North-West London Orthodox congregations formed their own social and welfare body, the Coordinating Board of North-West London Communities.

In November the council embarked on a campaign to expand its role in the community and improve its public image. Measures included restructuring the council to give member agencies a wider role in deliberations, establishing a board of trustees, creating an advisory unit and planning committee, developing a leadership training program, and introducing a Jewish social-service element in training programs for rabbis.

Significant change was reported at Ravenswood, Britain's second-largest and fastest-growing Jewish welfare agency. Whereas five years earlier, all its mentally handicapped clients had been in residential care, Ravenswood was currently helping handicapped members of 500 families, including 300 children, to live either at home or in hostels. For its 175 institutionalized residents, aged 5 to 55, the agency sought to provide maximum integration of adults and children in order to create a family-type atmosphere.

In July JWB announced a five-year plan to decentralize its services, in order to minimize delays and bureaucracy. Administration of its homes and day centers, social work, and home-support services would be moved from the Golders Green, North-West London, headquarters to three regional centers in North-West London, North-East London, and Redbridge.

Despite the severe financial problems that plagued all Jewish social agencies, several new facilities for elderly and handicapped Jews were opened during the year: a JBS home in North-West London for 35 visually impaired residents, their average age 87; a B'nai B'rith Housing Society accommodation project in Willesden, North London, for 85 residents; and a Haven Foundation group home in Finchley, North-West London, for mentally handicapped young adults. In addition, JBS announced plans for a home for the young elderly, with renovation of newly acquired North-West London premises to commence in spring 1987. B'nai B'rith was involved in a scheme approved by Brent Council to convert part of Cricklewood Synagogue into 36 apartments for the elderly.

Community Relations

Chief Rabbi Sir Immanuel Jakobovits became involved in controversy when he published his views on the problem of poverty in the inner city in a long article in the *Jewish Chronicle* in January, which was later reprinted as a pamphlet and widely distributed. Jakobovits was responding to a report of the Archbishop of Canterbury's Commission on Urban Priority Areas that urged greater government action to alleviate poverty, which was most acute among black immigrants. The chief rabbi's article, titled "From Doom to Hope," essentially held up Jewish religious teachings and the Jewish historical experience as models of a "self-help" approach to unemployment and deprivation. While the rabbi's views had many supporters, they also evoked criticism—for being condescending, for falsely equating the experiences of blacks and Jews, and even for being—albeit unintentionally—racist, as when he expressed regret that others did not share "the Jewish work ethic."

In February Greville Janner, MP, warned of potential discord between Jews and blacks. One factor was the chief rabbi's pamphlet. A second, greater point of conflict was the decision in January by the British government to bar Louis Farrakhan, the American Black Muslim leader, from entering England because of his public anti-Semitic remarks. In polls conducted in two London boroughs, over 80 percent of the blacks questioned blamed the ban on a "strong Jewish lobby," and about 70 percent felt that Farrakhan stood for black economic independence, not anti-Semitism.

The Council of Hackney, North London, an area with a sizable Orthodox population, in January refused Farrakhan the use of council premises. In July the council launched a major campaign that included distributing leaflets in Yiddish and six other languages, to alert its multiracial population to the problems of racism. Nearly 2,000 cases of racial harassment were reported in the district in 1985, against Jews as well as against blacks.

Various actions were taken by the Jewish community to try and reduce overall racial tensions. In May the chief rabbi began a series of visits to different London immigrant communities, where he spoke about the values of Judaism as they related to the immigrant experience. In the London borough of Tower Hamlets, for example, he met with Jews, Bangladeshis, West Indians, and Somalis. In November the Board of Deputies issued a statement urging Jews to contribute to "solving inner city problems as citizens"; it also agreed to coordinate the work of Jewish welfare organizations that helped Jews living in racially mixed, deprived areas.

The Jewish Social Responsibility Council, which changed its name to the Jewish Council for Community Relations, worked to increase awareness in the Jewish community about racial issues. The Board of Deputies convened a meeting of Jewish and West Indian leaders to try to strengthen relations and improve mutual understanding. A multiracial branch of Labor Friends of Israel was formed, also with the goal of improving intergroup relations.

The Board of Deputies welcomed the government's new Public Order Act, passed in November, which was said by Home Secretary Douglas Hurd to "include the strongest provisions ever brought forward by any government against the evil of incitement to racial hatred." One of the most important changes, according to Jacob Gewirtz, executive director of the board's defense and group relations committee, made it an offense to possess literature "likely to stir up racial hatred," if it could be proved that the material was intended for public distribution. (In April four members of the British National party were fined by Plymouth Crown Court for distributing racist leaflets to schoolchildren. In July British National party chairman John Tyndall and John Morse, editor of the right-wing *British Nationalist* newspaper, were jailed for inciting racial hatred.) The Board of Deputies failed to persuade the government either to inquire into Kurt Waldheim's wartime activities or to refrain from sending a British representative to his inauguration as Austrian president, in July. The government's position was, on the first matter, that it had no evidence of Waldheim's alleged misconduct, and, on the second, that he was the democratically elected head of a country with which Britain had friendly relations.

Despite pressure from the Board of Deputies, in November the government rejected calls for a parliamentary debate into allegations by the Simon Wiesenthal Center in Los Angeles that 17 known Nazi criminals were currently living in Britain. In November a new all-party parliamentary war crimes committee was launched in the House of Commons, its purpose to press the government for a response on this issue and to increase awareness of the problem.

Soviet Jewry

Following the announcement of Natan (Anatoly) Sharansky's release in February, the National Council for Soviet Jewry organized a demonstration outside London's National Theater at which celebrities read a roll call of 10,000 refuseniks still in the Soviet Union. A mammoth meeting in the Albert Hall, under the auspices of the Women's Campaign for Soviet Jewry, was a highlight of Sharansky's visit to Britain in September, during which he also appeared on national television, addressed major bodies engaged in the Soviet Jewry movement, and met parliamentary leaders.

The government's official response, in July, to a foreign affairs committee report on British-Soviet relations stated: "The lack of progress over human rights remains a serious obstacle to public perception of the Soviet Union. It is legitimate and important to continue to bring our concern to the attention of the Soviet authorities at every suitable opportunity." Several such opportunities arose during the year. In June Liberal party chief whip David Alton visited refuseniks while on a fact-finding visit to Russia. In November Deputy Prime Minister Lord Whitelaw reported on his talks with Soviet leader Mikhail Gorbachev about the release of refuseniks. All political leaders raised questions of human rights when Soviet foreign minister Eduard Shevardnadze visited Britain in July.

At its annual conference in April, the NUS voted to affiliate with the Student and Academic Committee for Soviet Jewry. The conference program included a roll-call of 500 names of Jewish student refuseniks, in which most factions participated. In November 49 campuses throughout Britain joined in an NUS-sponsored day of solidarity with Soviet Jewry; they also sent representatives to a mass demonstration outside Aeroflot's London offices. The Social Democrats launched a campaign of students and professors in behalf of Soviet Jewry.

Appeals to Soviet authorities in behalf of refusenik mathematician Vladimir Lifshitz were made by a parliamentary group, as well as by the International Committee of Scientists for Soviet Refuseniks. Activities in behalf of other individuals included birthday celebrations for Sharansky in January by the Brighton and Hove Committee for Soviet Jewry, the Michael Sobell Sinai School, Kenton, Middlesex, and the Cambridge Students' Campaign for Soviet Jewry. A demonstration was held for Ida Nudel, outside London's Soviet embassy, by the National Council for Soviet Jewry, on National Solidarity Day in April. In June the Open University conferred an honorary doctorate in absentia on Victor Brailovsky, scientist and longtime refusenik.

Religion

The year saw a number of organizational changes in British Jewry's main religious bodies.

Seeking to expand its program and achieve wider influence in the community, the United Synagogue (US), the Orthodox coordinating body, appointed its first chief executive, whose functions would include helping to formulate and implement policies, establishing a sound fiscal framework, and serving as liaison between the lay leaders of the US and its funded organizations, such as the London Board for Jewish Religious Education. (A reorganization of the London Board for Jewish Religious Education was announced in December. The new board would incorporate all US educational activities as well as its Youth and Community Services division.)

Day-to-day administration of the Kashrus Commission, which previously functioned independently, was taken over by the US, under the judicial authority of its London Beth Din.

Long-standing differences between the *kashrut* bodies of the US and the Federation of Synagogues (which had its own Beth Din and did not recognize the authority of the chief rabbi) erupted into open conflict which lasted some six months. It reached a climax in August when four leading butchers, including Blooms—a major restaurant and kosher-food supplier—relinquished their London Board licenses and changed to the Federation of Synagogues' wholesaler. The problem was resolved by the chief rabbi in December: the two separate bodies were dissolved and a new joint rabbinical authority comprising rabbinical judges of the London Beth Din and the *batei din* of the Federation of Synagogues and of the Sephardi community was formed to supervise the *kashrut* of all London slaughtering.

Feelings ran high when Rabbi Isaac Bernstein of Finchley, North-West London, publicly insulted Progressive Judaism. One outcome was that US rabbis received guidelines urging them not to use "abuse, invective, and rancor" in respect of the Progressive movement. In December, as a result of a campaign by the Association of US Women, US council president Victor Lucas announced that the chief rabbi, the *dayanim* of London's Beth Din, and the association had agreed to a formula giving women a greater say in running US congregations.

Membership in the Reform Synagogues of Great Britain (RSGB) rose 1 percent in the past year, executive director Raymond Goldman announced in June; 16 congregations had grown, 11 were stable, and 6 declined. RSGB's youth wing, with 1,500 members, was the second largest Jewish youth movement in the country, after B'nei Akiva.

The Union of Liberal and Progressive Synagogues (ULPS), announced plans to move its offices in 1989 from the Montagu Center in London's West End to the new complex being built at the St. John's Wood Liberal Synagogue, North-West London; the group reported a slight decline in membership, to 12,000.

As of November the Masorti Assembly of Synagogues (Conservative), formed in September 1985, had 2,500 members in five congregations, all in the London area, including Rabbi Dr. Louis Jacobs's New London Synagogue.

Education

As part of a specially designated "Year of Jewish Education," which opened in September, the Board for Jewish Religious Education offered a series of events designed to stimulate synagogue members' interest in education and also to raise funds to meet the board's estimated expenditure of £1 million. The chief rabbi's Jewish Educational Development Trust appointed a program director as its first full-time employee in June, to recruit personnel into Jewish education and supervise projects carried out as part of the year's special program.

Demand for places still exceeded supply at the new £2-million Harry and Abe Sherman Rosh Pinah Primary School, which opened in Edgware, North-West London, in September: 120 applications were received for 60 places. In September, too, a new branch of the Menorah Primary School opened in Golders Green.

In February it was announced that Jews' College, under US auspices, would add a counseling course to its new practical rabbinics program. The number of students had risen to 36 in July, according to director Simon Caplan, who predicted an increase to 45 the following year. In July Rabbi John Rayner reported that Leo Baeck College, the postgraduate training school for Progressive rabbis, had ordained 83 rabbis serving 80 communities worldwide during its 30 years' existence. Current enrollment in the five-year rabbinic program averaged 20 students, male and female.

A course for the unemployed and the retired was launched in September by the RSGB's new Center for Jewish Education, which combined its former education and youth department and the extension division of Leo Baeck. The center, which also offered services in the areas of teacher training, programming, and religious-school development, was directed by Rabbi Michael Heilbron. The RSGB voted to establish a special trust to support its educational work. In December the ULPS council decided to bring its schools under the Reform center's umbrella.

Leeds University renewed its fellowship in Jewish Studies for a further four years, though the university's Semitics Department was renamed the Department of Arabic Studies. University College, London (UCL), and the Hebrew University of Jerusalem agreed to a joint program in which Jonathan Frankel, associate professor of contemporary Jewry at the Hebrew University, would spend six months every two years at UCL, and UCL students would spend a year at the Hebrew University. Kent University announced that it would offer courses in Jewish law. The Oxford Center for Postgraduate Hebrew Studies made three appointments in the field of historical anti-Semitism. A senior research fellowship in anti-Semitism and racial incitement was established at London's City University, which awarded the chief rabbi an honorary degree in December.

In April the Chief Rabbi's Office, the Board of Deputies, and the Lubavitch Foundation launched "Operation Judaism," to fight missionary activities on campus.

In August Board of Deputies president Lionel Kopelowitz expressed concern that from an estimated Jewish university student body of 10,000, only 3,500 took part in Jewish campus activity, and no more than 10 percent of Jewish academics showed interest in the religious and cultural life of Jewish students. In September, the board, in association with B'nai B'rith, launched the Year of the Jewish Student, designed to increase Jewish students' identification with Jewish campus groups and activities.

Publications

A prize was endowed by the family of the late George Webber, former reader in English law at University College, London, to encourage a wider readership of contemporary Hebrew literature in English translation. The first award was made in June. Jonathan Israel received one of the two Wolfson awards in general history for his *European Jewry in the Age of Mercantilism, 1550–1750,* the first time the prize had been given for a Jewish book.

Books on Jewish history published during the year included *Anglo-Jewry in Evidence,* a collection of documents, edited by Rabbi Jonathan Romain; *Leo Baeck Institute Year Book,* vol. 31; *The Mythmaker: Paul and the Invention of Christianity* by Hyam Maccoby; *The Early Days of Sheffield Jewry, 1760–1900* by Neville David Ballin; and *Jewish Policies and Right-Wing Politics in Imperial Russia* by Hans Rogger.

Works on Israel and the Middle East included *The Siege: The Saga of Zionism and Israel* by Conor Cruise O'Brien; *After the Last Sky: Palestinian Lives* by Edward Said; *Between Washington and Jerusalem: A Reporter's Notebook* by Wolf Blitzer; *Semites and Anti-Semites* by Bernard Lewis; *The War of Desperation: Lebanon 1982–85* and *Know the Middle East* by John Laffin; and *Inside the Promised Land* by Gerald Kaufman.

Among new books on the Holocaust and its survivors were *Strangers in Their Own Land: Young Jews in Germany and Austria Today* by Peter Sichrovsky; *The Holocaust: The Jewish Tragedy* by Martin Gilbert; *The Psychological Problems of Refugees,* essays compiled and edited by Ron Baker; and *The Secret Hunters* by Anthony Kemp, describing the activities of a war-crimes investigation team.

New works on Judaism included *Judaism* by Myer Domnitz; *Judaism* by Nicholas de Lange; *Horizons of Jewish Prayer* by Jeffrey M. Cohen; *Aspects of British Judaism* by Lewis Glinert; and *Studies in Eastern Jewish Mysticism* by Joseph Weiss. Books on Bible and archaeology included *Secrets of the Bible Seas: An Underwater Archaeologist in the Holy Land* by Alexander Flinder; and *Megiddo* by Graham I. Davies.

Noteworthy new autobiographical and biographical works were *Churchill and the Jews* by Michael J. Cohen; *And There My Trouble Began: Uncollected Writings, 1945–85* by T.R. Fyvel; *Spirit of Stoke Mandeville: The Story of Sir Ludwig Guttman* by Susan Goodman; *The Human Province* by Elias Canetti; *All in a Lifetime* by Edward Isaacs; *Growing Up in the Gorbals* by Ralph Glasser; and *Shcharansky, Hero of Our Time* by Martin Gilbert.

Fiction published during the year included *So Long As They're Cheering* by Sue Krisman; *Can't Buy Me Love* by Michael Estorisck; *Casualties* by Lynne Reid Banks; *The Unloved* by Arnost Lustig; *The Story So Far* by David Nathan; and *Images* by Maisie Mosco.

Two new works on Jewish artists were *The Circle of Montparnasse: Jewish Artists in Paris, 1905–1945,* edited by Kenneth Silver and Romy Golan; and *The Vision of Simeon Solomon* by Simon Reynolds, the painter. Collections of photographs included *Israel, a First View* by Lord Snowdon; *High Above the Holy Land* by Sonia Halliday and Laura Lushington; and *The Land of Israel* by Hilla and Max Jacoby.

Two works on literature were *A Short Digest of Jewish Literature in the Middle Ages* by Armin Krausz; and *Frankenstein's Island: England and the English in the Writings of Heinrich Heine* by S.S. Prawer.

Poetry published this year included *Footsteps on a Downcast Path* by Jon Silkin, poems relating to events in Jewish history; and *Ask the Bloody Horse* by Dannie Abse, who also published *Journals from the Ant-Heap,* a collection of his newspaper writings.

What's the Joke? A Study of Jewish Humour Through the Ages, by Chaim Bermant, was in a category of its own.

Personalia

Knighthoods went to Ralph Halpern, chairman and chief executive of the Burton group; Alan Greengross, Tory politician; Roy Calne, professor of surgery at Cambridge University; Geoffrey Rudolph Elton, regius professor of modern history at Cambridge; and Dr. Walter Bodmer, director of research at the Imperial Cancer Research Fund. Sir Sigmund Sternberg was invested Knight Commander of the Equestrian Order of St. Gregory the Great, one of the highest honors conferred by the Roman Catholic Church. Sir Keith Joseph, retiring minister of education, was named a Companion of Honor, one of the highest honors Britain can bestow.

Among British Jews who died in 1986 were Donald Samuel, communal worker, in January, aged 82; Lily Bernstein, violinist, in January; Sidney Harrison, pianist, teacher, and broadcaster, in January, aged 82; Gerald Schneider, prominent Orthodox rabbi, in January, aged 55; Walter Schindler, psychotherapist, in February, aged 89; Samuel Klein, *Jewish Chronicle* employee for over 70 years, in February, aged 86; Ilse Joseph, violinist, in February, aged 65; Heinz Kiewe, textile expert, in February, aged 79; Emmanuel Levy, artist, in March, aged 86; Marcel Lorber, musician, in March, aged 85; Tony Robins, actress, in March, aged 55; Morris

Davidson, rabbi emeritus of the South-West London Synagogue, in March, aged 78; Marcus Shloimovitz, campaigner for Jewish rights in Manchester, in April, aged 86; Thea Doniach, painter, in April; David Franklin, banker and philanthropist, in April, aged 67; Simon Lyons, retailer, in April, aged 75; Adele Reifenberg, artist, in April, aged 93; Emanuel Lord Shinwell, Labor party elder statesman, in May, aged 101; Kurt Maschler, publisher, in May; Frederick Kormis, sculptor, in May, aged 91; Michael Kennedy Leigh, philanthropist, in May, aged 89; Rev. Aryeh Garbacz, spiritual leader of the Southend and Westcliff Hebrew Congregation for over 50 years, in May, aged 87; Emanuel Raffles, Manchester rainwear manufacturer and philanthropist, in May, aged 93; Jakob Jascha Rabinowitch, radiologist, in June, aged 73; Michael Sacher, leading businessman and Zionist, in July, aged 68; Archie Sherman, property developer and philanthropist, in July, aged 74; Joseph Ellis Lord Stone, personal physician to Harold Wilson, in July, aged 83; Joan Bennett, Cambridge English scholar, in August, aged 90; Rabbi Eliezer Simcha Rabinowitz, after a rabbinic career of over 50 years, in August, aged 73; Richard Barnett, archaeologist and Sephardi historian, in August, aged 77; Stuart Young, chairman of the British Broadcasting Corporation and a leading communal figure, in September, aged 52; Imanuel Bergman, scientific officer for health and safety, Sheffield University, in September, aged 58; Moshe Sanders, bookseller, in September, aged 81; Lord Bearsted, philanthropist, in October, aged 77;' Elias Bloch, physicist, in Glasgow, in October; Louis Minski, psychiatrist, in November, aged 84; Kurt Hirsch, professor of pure mathematics, Queen Mary College, London, in November, aged 80; Fanny, Lady Brodie, widow of the late chief rabbi, in November, aged 93; Harold Price, professor of mathematics, Leeds University, in November, aged 69; Hermann Fechenbach, artist, in December, aged 89; Sydney Torrance, research chemist, in December, aged 74; Eileen Ellenbogen, teacher, writer, and translator, in December, aged 74; Ben Shaw, Liverpool civic personality, in December, aged 80; Deborah Rowland, first Jewish woman judge, in December; Louis Gerhard Graf, rabbi of the Cardiff Reform congregation for over 30 years, in December, aged 74; Florrie Passman, Jewish youth club leader, in December, aged 98; David Goodkin, for 35 years editor of the *Birmingham Jewish Recorder,* in December, aged 71.

LIONEL & MIRIAM KOCHAN

France

National Affairs

ELECTIONS IN MARCH RESULTED IN the expected victory for the Right, thus ending five years of Socialist control of the National Assembly. This produced the unprecedented situation of a conservative legislature having to share power with a Socialist president, François Mitterrand—whose term would not end until 1988—creating the potential, at least, for conflict and instability. Although the new government, led by neo-Gaullist Jacques Chirac as prime minister, moved quickly to undo various Socialist economic measures and to deal with the problem of immigration—one of the most explosive issues in France—it was forced to put most of its energies in 1986 into crises caused by terrorist activity: a series of kidnappings of French citizens in Lebanon and a wave of bombings that swept Paris during a good part of the year.

The new conservative governing coalition, composed of the Rally for the Republic (RPR) party, headed by Jacques Chirac, and the Union for French Democracy (UDF), the party of former president Valéry Giscard d'Estaing, jointly garnered only 40 percent of the vote, less than an absolute majority, necessitating the support of rightist independents for control of the legislature. The Socialists, with 32 percent of the vote, actually finished as the largest single party in Parliament and thus were in a stronger position than expected. The election results confirmed the continuing decline of the Communist party and the rise of Jean-Marie Le Pen's ultraright, racist National Front (FN), each of which won a little less than 10 percent of the vote. The latter's success seemed to indicate that its 11-percent win in the 1984 European Parliament elections was no one-time phenomenon, as its opponents had hoped.

Regional elections produced roughly the same results as in the National Assembly. The coalition's weak majority gave added influence to the FN, particularly in some of the regional councils, where the Front held the balance between Right and Left. Although on the national level coalition leaders had promised no cooperation with the FN, local agreements between the coalition and the FN in several cases prevented a Socialist from being elected to head a regional council. Taking an active part in parliamentary life, FN representatives tried to press their views on limiting immigration and expelling illegal residents and to seek legitimacy for their discriminatory approach to "foreigners." At the same time, the moderate Right tried to win over FN voters by adopting part of its program (on immigration, naturalization, public security, etc.). It was left to the Socialists, in an effort to destabilize the moderates, to remind them continually of the ethical contradictions inherent in their uneasy partnership with the extreme Right. (See below, "Racism, Anti-Semitism, Historical Revisionism.")

Although public debate was heated on the main points of the new majority's legislative program—privatization of state-owned industries and banks and economic liberalization—it remained on the whole muted, at least until the last months of the year. One reason was President Mitterrand's desire to preserve the status quo as long as possible and avoid an institutional crisis. Another was the general awareness that neither the Left nor the Right had been able to find a solution to France's most serious social problem, unemployment, which in November reached 2.6 million out of a total population of some 55 million. To bring about any improvement in this situation, it was felt, required a minimal degree of national unity. Finally, the threat posed by terrorist activity, abroad and at home, also tended to foster national consensus.

Hostages Abroad, Terrorism at Home

One of the most difficult problems faced by the new government of Jacques Chirac was that of the French hostages in Lebanon. By the beginning of the year, four French citizens had been kidnapped; on March 5, the Islamic Jihad announced that one of them had been killed. Between March and December the number of French hostages in Lebanon ranged between nine and five, as new kidnappings took place and some prisoners were freed. Under the pressure of this situation, French policy on the Middle East aimed almost exclusively at having the hostages released. While the government openly played the Syrian card, acknowledging that country's supremacy in Lebanon, that tactic met with limited success, since most of the hostages were detained by pro-Iranian groups which were out of Syrian control.

A wave of terrorist bombings plagued Paris throughout much of the year, creating tension and wariness among its residents. The sequence of bombings and their toll was as follows: February 3—bomb in a shopping arcade on the Champs Elysées, 7 wounded; another unexploded bomb was discovered in the Eiffel Tower and defused. February 4—bomb in a bookstore in the Latin Quarter, 3 wounded; February 5—bomb in a big sporting goods store in Les Halles, 9 wounded; March 17—bomb in the fast train between Paris and Lyons, 9 wounded; March 20—bomb in a luxury shopping mall on the Champs Elysées, 2 killed, 28 wounded; September 4—unexploded bomb found in a crowded subway train; September 8—bomb in the post office of city hall, 1 killed, 18 wounded; September 12—bomb in the cafeteria of a supermarket in the Paris suburb of La Défense at lunchtime, 1 killed, 42 wounded; September 14—bomb found in a popular café in Champs Elysées, two policemen killed while trying to dismantle it, one person wounded; September 15—bomb at police headquarters, 1 killed, 51 wounded; September 17—bomb thrown from a car in the Rue de Rennes, outside a crowded store, 7 killed, 51 wounded.

Responsibility for the bombings was claimed by a Lebanese group, the Committee for Solidarity with Arab and Middle Eastern Political Prisoners (CSPPA), whose exact identity was not clear. The group demanded the release of three Middle Eastern terrorists who had been convicted and imprisoned in France, among them

Georges Ibrahim Abdallah, presumed head of the Lebanese Armed Revolutionary Faction (FARL), who was implicated in the murder of Israeli and American diplomats in 1982.

French responses to terrorism at home and abroad reflected the contradictions in French foreign policy. Since the 1960s, French governments had sought both to protect the country against terrorism and to maintain friendly relations with the Arab states, thereby continuing France's historic role as a major power in that part of the world. On the one hand, therefore, the government adopted a firm public stance, refusing to meet the terrorists' demands. This line was supported by a majority of the French people: in the middle of September, during the worst period of bombings, 70 percent of those polled felt that the government should not release Abdallah, while only 10 percent supported his release. Still, France seemed ready to use any diplomatic means possible to obtain the release of French hostages and an end to the bombings on French soil. For example, the government allowed a pro-PLO Greek Orthodox cleric, Bishop Hilarion Capucci, who had been convicted in Israel in the early 1970s of smuggling explosives to Palestinians, to meet with Abdallah in September, presumably because of the priest's contacts in the Arab world. French ambivalence was evident, too, in the government's willingness to supply arms to Iraq for its war with Iran, at the same time that it was carrying on secret negotiations with Iran for release of French hostages.

The reign of terror in Paris did galvanize the government into taking measures against terrorism. In February France ratified the European Convention on extradition; in June the National Assembly adopted more stringent measures against terrorism; and in September a temporary regulation introduced visas for all foreigners entering France, except persons from EEC countries or Switzerland. (It seems likely, however, that in this case terrorism was used as a convenient pretext for a measure that was aimed mainly at illegal immigration.) At the same time, France did not allow American planes to fly over France during the U.S. April raid on Libya.

In general, not only did the government hesitate to take a firm stand against the very regimes which probably controlled the terrorists, it openly courted Syria and Iran, two of the prime offenders. Although Chirac could claim for his policy the release of two hostages, at year's end six French citizens were still being held in Lebanon.

In addition to violence carried out by foreigners, terrorist acts were perpetrated by domestic radicals. The extremist movement Direct Action, a small group composed mainly of "*enfants perdus*" of the post 1968 generation, whose organization had been legally dissolved in 1982, was unusually active in 1986. Unlike Middle Eastern terrorism, which hit indiscriminately in busy public places, Direct Action carefully chose symbols of "capitalist oppression" as its targets, murdering or attempting to murder executives of major companies (e.g., the president of Renault, who was killed in November), and attacking selected buildings (e.g., the Interpol office in a suburb of Paris). The trial in December of members of Direct Action who had been apprehended highlighted a fundamental problem faced by the legal system. Because of intimidation and threats, the appointed members of the jury refused, under a variety of pretexts, such as health, to appear in court. As a consequence, a law was adopted instituting special courts in which terrorists would be tried only by professional judges, who were presumably less vulnerable to pressure.

Relations with Israel

French policy continued the line of quiet reconciliation with Israel begun by President Mitterrand, at the same time recognizing the PLO and supporting Palestinian nationalist aspirations. Meetings between French and Israeli officials took place throughout the year on a variety of topics. In an October meeting in Paris between outgoing Israeli prime minister Shimon Peres and Prime Minister Chirac, the latter agreed to increase exchanges of intelligence information but rejected more active forms of cooperation, because of French ties to the Arab world. None of this differed significantly from the policies pursued by the Socialists after they came to power in 1981, though toward the end of the year opposition forces in Parliament were becoming openly critical of the government's less than forceful handling of terrorism.

The contradictions in French policy resulted in some confusion, particularly in interviews given by Prime Minister Chirac to the foreign press. In August the Israeli journalist Ben Porath asserted in *Yediot Aharonot* that Chirac had come out against a Palestinian state, thereby implying the possibility of a drastic change in French policy in the Middle East. In an atmosphere of near scandal, Chirac denied having made any statement to that effect. In November the prime minister was caught in another embarrassing situation. In an interview with American journalist Arnaud de Borchgrave of the *Washington Times* (which Chirac's press office may have confused with the *Washington Post*), Chirac apparently declared "off the record" that Israel might have been involved in the aborted attack in April on an El Al plane in London, as a provocation to embarrass Syria. The unauthorized publication of this startling charge forced the prime minister into a new series of partial and awkward denials. The Israelis avoided aggravating the problem by stating that they knew Chirac to be a good friend of Israel.

Racism, Anti-Semitism, Historical Revisionism

The growing appeal of the National Front could be attributed to large-scale frustration over France's weak economy and unemployment, which found a convenient scapegoat in the four million or so foreigners settled in the country. (After World War II, France began importing large numbers of migrant workers, to relieve a labor shortage. A large proportion of that wave of immigration, which was stopped in 1974, came from former French colonies in North Africa and black Africa.) Among various manifestations of racist feeling during the year was a series of arsons in buildings occupied by immigrant families in Paris. In two months alone (November-December), 19 immigrants were killed in fires whose perpetrators were never found.

The tendency to xenophobia and racism was undoubtedly heightened by attitudes bred during France's colonial past and as a consequence of unemployment. Seeking to attract FN voters back to the traditional parties, the government played to some of these feelings, strengthening identity controls for foreigners and drafting a new law that would bar the naturalization of youngsters born in France to foreign parents (*jus soli*). What emerged from the controversy surrounding these issues was a sense that the very terms of the debate over foreigners had changed. Whereas in the early eighties it had been between advocates of a multiracial, multicultural society and advocates of assimilation and integration, by 1986 it was between those who believed that immigrants could become fully integrated into French society and those who claimed that the largely non-European immigrants could not be integrated and should therefore be sent back to their countries of origin, together with their children born in France, "who will never be really French." Actively fighting the growing open racism were such nonpartisan antiracist movements as SOS-Racisme, which again drew an audience of some 100,000 to its annual June street concert in Paris.

Overt anti-Semitism, on the other hand, remained rather limited. In January the Ligue Internationale Contre la Racisme et l'Antisémitisme (LICRA, International League Against Anti-Semitism and Racism) instituted suit against FN leader Jean-Marie Le Pen because, in a meeting in October 1985, he had cited four journalists with typically Jewish names as examples of "all the liars of the press in this country." Still, Le Pen remained cautious in his public attacks, not out of love for the Jews, but in order to avoid charges of anti-Semitism which might damage his career.

THE ROQUES AFFAIR

One significant incident involving apparent anti-Semitism was the "*Affaire Roques,*" which aroused anew the debate over historical revisionism, specifically, denial of the Holocaust. The story in fact began in June 1985, when a retired engineer and student of literature, Henri Roques, submitted a dissertation to the University of Nantes for a doctoral degree. His subject was a critical analysis of the posthumous confessions of Kurt Gerstein, the former SS officer who described the atrocities he had witnessed in extermination camps, including the operation of the gas chambers. In his dissertation, Roques pointed out contradictions and improbabilities in the various versions of Gerstein's work, alleging that what was presented as a main piece of evidence for the existence of the gas chambers was worthless. Since the academic jury was composed of sympathizers of the extreme Right, Roques had no difficulty getting his degree.

When the story was disclosed in the local press in the spring of 1986, it caused an immediate furor. On May 20, some 60 academic personalities from around the country signed a petition protesting the dissertation, its subject matter, and the conditions under which it was accepted. On the 29th, a protest demonstration called by the pro-Communist, antiracist Mouvement Contre le Racisme et pour l'Amitié entre les Peuples (MRAP, Movement Against Racism and for Friendship Among Peoples) and the pro-Communist Union des Juifs pour la Résistance et l'Entraide (UJRE, Union of Jews for Resistance and Mutual Help) was held near the Memorial of the Unknown Jewish Martyr in Paris. After several weeks of public uproar and after an administrative hearing found that the dissertation had not been accepted according to the university's own regulations, Minister of Research Alain Devaquet announced on July 2 that Roques's degree would be rescinded.

JEWISH COMMUNITY

Demography

According to most sources, the number of Jews in France was 550,000–600,000. Some 50 percent of them lived in Paris and its suburbs; 30 percent in the south (the Mediterranean coast, including the cities of Marseilles and Nice) and southwest (including Toulouse); 7 percent in the Lyons area; and 6 percent in the east (Alsace and Lorraine).

Communal Affairs

Jewish communal bodies remained extremely concerned about the activities of the National Front. In a statement published immediately after the elections to the National Assembly, Théo Klein, president of the Conseil Représentatif des Institutions Juives de France (CRIF, Representative Council of French Jewish Institutions), noted that while the Jewish community as such did not identify itself with any political party, it regretted the fact that so many voters were attracted by the demagogic slogans of the FN. On March 22 he sent a letter to the secretaries-general of the governing coalition parties, urging them against making agreements with the FN in regional councils. At every opportunity, CRIF drew public attention to the dangers of ignoring the rise of prejudice in France. Chief Rabbi René Sirat raised the issue in an internal Jewish context, for example, bringing it up at the Conference of European Rabbis in June, and called for opening up religious dialogue between Islam and Judaism, similar to that between Christianity and Judaism.

In February CRIF protested to the government over recent French votes against Israel in the UN. In meetings with the prime minister (in June and on November 9, when CRIF welcomed him to its general assembly) and with President Mitterrand (in May), the question of improving French-Israeli relations was discussed. Because there was relatively little diplomatic activity relating to the Middle East this year, the Jewish community had less motive for intervention than in previous years.

Protests were lodged, however, over a meeting between Minister of Police Robert Pandraud and PLO leader Farouk Kaddoumi as well as the visit to France of Bishop Capucci.

There was little interest in France, even in the Jewish community, in the case of William Nakash, the French citizen who fled to Israel after murdering an Arab in 1983 and was later convicted *in absentia* and given a life sentence. France's request for extradition was rejected by Israeli authorities on grounds of anti-Semitism in French prisons—a charge strongly denied by French Jewish leaders.

Holocaust-Related Matters

The preparations for the trial of Klaus Barbie (scheduled to begin in 1987) and the debate over the Roques affair served to keep public attention on the events of World War II. Another event linked to the Holocaust took place on July 18, marking the anniversary of the mass arrest of Parisian Jews by the Nazis in July 1942. At a ceremony renaming the square near the stadium where the Jews of Paris had been detained before deportation "Square of the Jewish Martyrs of the Winter Velodrom," Prime Minister Chirac delivered a speech expressing the commitment of the French people to preserving the memory of the Holocaust.

After several years of legal proceedings, a notorious Nazi collaborator, Jean Leguay, who served as secretary-general of the Vichy national police during the war, which took part in the round-up of Jews, was indicted in October for crimes against humanity. A trial date had not been set.

The year saw intense activity directed against the proposed convent of Polish Carmelite nuns at the site of the Auschwitz-Birkenau extermination camp in Poland. The organizers of the campaign in France against erection of the convent were Chief Rabbi Sirat, the leaders of CRIF, Prof. Ady Steg, president of the Alliance Israélite Universelle, and such notable Catholic personalities as the archbishop of Lyons and the head of the French episcopal committee on relations with Judaism. On March 23 a special committee on the convent was constituted, chaired by Prof. Steg and including representatives of the consistories, CRIF, the Alliance, and the French section of the World Jewish Congress (WJC). In April a delegation met with Josef Cardinal Glemp, head of the Polish Church, to express its views. In July, at the initiative of the president of CRIF and the bishop of Lyons, a Jewish-Christian meeting took place in Geneva, Switzerland, with participants from France, Belgium, Poland, and Italy. The meeting resulted in a joint declaration titled "*Zakhor*" (Remember), which did not mention the convent issue per se but stressed the need to honor the memory of the Holocaust victims. In September a group of 185 Jews and Christians took part in a pilgrimage to Auschwitz, organized by the Mouvement Libéral Juif de France (the Reform movement) and Serge Klarsfeld, World War II historian and Nazi-hunter.

An international meeting on the plight of Syrian Jewry took place in February in Paris, called by the International Committee for the Freedom of Syrian Jewry, and attended by more than 200 delegates.

Although not directly a French issue, the creation of the European Jewish Congress (EJC), which was announced at the WJC General Assembly in Jerusalem in January, had significant repercussions in the French Jewish community. Traditionally jealous of its independence, and opposed to what it viewed as American interference, France had always refused to join the European branch of the WJC. However, because the newly constituted EJC was affiliated with the WJC but structured so as to be free of American influence, CRIF—the umbrella organization comprising some 50 Jewish groups—was persuaded to join. On November 1, Théo Klein, president of CRIF, was elected president of the EJC. Although the EJC question was debated at length, CRIF's constituent organizations could not reach unanimity on membership. On November 6, the president of the Central Consistory (the main religious body of French Jewry, created in 1808 by Napoleon), Jean-Paul Elkann, announced the decision of the consistory to suspend its participation in CRIF, as a protest against affiliation with the EJC. Elkann was supported in this by the president of the Paris Consistory, Emile Touati. The decision of the consistory did not mean a total rupture, but it definitely weakened CRIF's standing as the chief representative of the community.

The year saw new initiatives for developing closer ties between French-speaking Jewish groups in the world. In May the Reform congregations of French-speaking European countries held a conference in Paris. In June French Jews and French-speaking Israelis took part in an encounter in Jerusalem, out of which came a program of action for improving communication. And in July a group of French Jewish academics (among them Alain Finkielkraut and Roland Goetschel) met with French-speaking Israeli academics in Tel Aviv, in the framework of the Israel Diaspora Institute of Tel Aviv University, for the same purpose. These developments showed a new willingness among French Jews to open themselves to contacts and exchanges outside the borders of France.

Culture

The continued blossoming of Jewish culture could be seen in the growing acceptance of aspects of Jewish culture by the French public at large. Examples of this phenomenon included performances by a Yiddish cabaret in September in the much frequented Georges Pompidou Center; the addition of a course on modern Jewish history to the regular offerings of the prestigious Ecole des Hautes Etudes en Sciences Sociales (the American George Mosse and the Israeli Zeev Sternhell were guest lecturers in 1986); a run of the play *Ghetto,* by Israeli playwright Joshua Sobol, at the Creteil Theater (in the suburbs of Paris); showings of films on Jewish subjects; an exhibition of paintings by Russian-born Bencjon Benn at the Carnavalet Museum; the by-now traditional Yiddish festival, in June, in the center of the city; and the performance of four original French plays on Jewish-related themes in the Avignon theater festival. More than a few observers noted the irony that even as many Jews were becoming personally de-Judaized, French society was becoming culturally Judaized.

Various innovative educational programs were offered, such as the "Month of Judaism" at the Rashi Center in Paris. Over the course of several weeks, hundreds of participants attended lectures, round-table discussions, and workshops on the theme "Judaism and Human Law." The month ended with a three-day symposium, organized in cooperation with the Sorbonne, on the subject of "The Return to Judaism." Participants included novelist Marek Halter, philosopher Bernard-Henri Lévy, and writer Alain Finkielkraut (who in May was awarded the prize of the Foundation of French Judaism), as well as leading non-Jewish figures, such as novelist Françoise Sagan and historian Emmanuel Le Roy Ladurie. A similar "Month of Jewish Culture" was organized in July in the city of Nice.

With the support and help of philosopher Shmuel Trigano, the Alliance Isráelite Universelle opened a college of Jewish studies (Collège d'Etudes Juives-Bet ha-Midrash), an instructional institution as well as a center for research and creativity in history, philosophy, Hebrew, Talmud, and other fields. Summer programs in Jewish studies were offered in July and August at the universities of Aix en Provence, Cannes, and several other locations.

The fifth international festival of Jewish film was to have taken place in the second half of September, but had to be postponed because of the wave of terrorist attacks. It finally opened at the end of October in the Rashi Center and ran for more than a month.

Claude Lanzmann's film *Shoah* was awarded prizes by the Rotterdam film festival and LICRA (the League Against Anti-Semitism and Racism). The film also won an honorary "*César*" (the French "Oscar"). Michel Boujenah, a Jewish actor of Tunisian origin, was awarded a *César* for best supporting actor for his performance in *Trois hommes et un couffin.*

A video magazine called Judeotel became available this year, a program of Jewish news and culture transmitted via computer and telephone to subscribers whose fees covered the cost of the program. This was not the case, unfortunately, with the daily bulletin of the Jewish Telegraphic Agency, which, although regarded as an incomparable information tool, had too few subscribers to cover its costs. Because the Fonds Social Juif Unifié (FSJU, United Jewish Philanthropic Fund) was unable to continue its support, the last issue of the bulletin was published December 1.

It was announced in January that the projected new museum of Jewish art and culture would be housed in the Hôtel de Saint-Aignan, one of the finest seventeenth-century mansions in the once aristocratic area of Le Marais in Paris. Sponsored by the French Jewish community, the mayor of Paris, and the French Ministry of Culture, the museum was scheduled to open in several years.

Publications

Among works on basic Judaism published this year were the translation by Maurice Hayoun of Hermann L. Straik's classic *Introduction to Talmud and Midrash* (based on the Günter Sternberger edition); and *Kabbale, vie mystique et magie*

("Kabbalah, Mystical Life and Magic") by Haim Zafrani. An original scholarly work was *Inscriptions hébraïques et juives dans la France médiévale* ("Hebraic and Jewish Inscriptions in Medieval France") by Gérard Nahon. New works of fiction that were well received were *Un été à Jérusalem* ("A Summer in Jerusalem"), whose young author, Chochana Boukobza, was awarded the Prix Méditerranée, and the French translation of Israeli author Amnon Shamosh's *Michel Ezra Safra and Sons.* A new work about Jews in France was *David et Marianne* by Freddy Eytan ("Marianne" being the symbol of the French Republic). The June issue of the quarterly *Pardes,* published by a group of young intellectuals around Shmuel Trigano, was on the theme "Jews in France: Individual Adventure or Collective Fate?"

Other noteworthy works of nonfiction were *Les Nations Unies au Moyen-Orient* ("The UN in the Middle East") by Israel's ambassador to France, Ovadia Soffer; the translation from English of Nelly Wilson's *Bernard Lazare;* and Victor Malka's *Les Juifs sépharades* ("The Sefardi Jews"), a concise portrait of a group that was increasingly prominent in the Jewish community.

The proceedings of the International Symposium on Nazi Germany and the Genocide of the Jews, held in 1982 in the Ecole des Hautes Etudes en Sciences Sociales, were published at the end of the 1985. Another work on the World War II period was by Annette Wiewiorka on the fate of Jewish Communist resistance members (*Ils étaient juifs, résistants, communistes*). Francine Kauffmann wrote a reevaluation of André Schwarz-Bart's novel *The Last of the Just* (*Relire le Dernier des Justes*). Poet and polemist Jacques Givet, author of an earlier work on Israel and the European Left, published a fierce attack against Klaus Barbie's lawyer, Jacques Vergès, in *Le cas Vergès.*

The awarding of the Nobel Peace Prize to Elie Wiesel was greeted with enthusiasm in France, where the writer was extremely popular and respected. Wiesel lived in France for a number of years after his liberation from Auschwitz and all his works were originally written in French.

Personalia

Former minister of justice Robert Badinter was appointed president of the Constitutional Council in February, in which position he replaced Daniel Mayer. Gerard Israel, secretary-general of the Alliance Israélite Universelle, was appointed to the newly created consultative committee on human rights in the prime minister's office. The committee was chaired by Jean Pierre-Bloch, president of LICRA and a member of CRIF.

Théo Klein was reelected president of CRIF in April for a second term of two years. In July CRIF elected two new vice-presidents: Nicole Goldmann, vice-president of FSJU, and Henry Bulawko, chairman of CRIF's Holocaust Commemoration Committee.

Former cabinet minister Lionel Stoleru was elected president of the France-Israel Chamber of Commerce. Marc Bitton, a member of the national board of SOS-

Racisme, was elected president of the Union of Jewish Students of France (UEJF). Simon Wiesenthal, a citizen of Austria, was appointed to the Legion of Honor, in a ceremony on September 29 at the French embassy in Vienna.

Among prominent Jews who died in 1986 were Dr. Benjamin Ginsbourg, in January, one of the founders of the Bernard Lazare Circle (a left-wing Zionist group that attracted many intellectuals), an officer of the Legion of Honor, and an active resistance fighter during World War II; and Edmond Tenoudji, in April, vice-president of the Central Consistory, officer of CRIF and of the FSJU, president of the movie production company Marceau-Cocinor, and founder of two Jewish schools.

Several writers died in 1986: Jacques Sabbath, author of short novels and former editor in chief of the Jewish community monthly *L'Arche;* David Malki, born in Lodz in 1899, whose books in Yiddish on the sages of the Talmud had been translated and published in French; Roger Ikor, the controversial author of *Les Fils d'Avrom* ("The Sons of Avrom"), the second part of which, *Les Eaux Mêlées* ("Mixed Waters"), was awarded the Goncourt Prize in 1955.

NELLY HANSSON

The Netherlands

National Affairs

THE 1986 QUADRENNIAL ELECTIONS for Parliament left the ruling coalition of Christian Democrats (CDA) and Liberals (VVD) in power, with a total of 81 seats in the 150-member Second Chamber. The CDA victory was attributed largely to the personal appeal of its leader, Premier Ruud (Rudolph) Lubbers, whose forceful approach to existing economic problems inspired widespread confidence.

The Labor party (PvdA) gained five seats—giving it 52 seats to the CDA's 54—largely at the expense of the smaller, more radical, left-wing parties, such as the Communists, who, for the first time since 1918, were not represented at all in the Second Chamber. On the other side of the political spectrum, the right-wing Centrum party, which opposed the large-scale presence of immigrants from countries such as Surinam, Turkey, and Morocco, and which had been described for several years as an extreme danger to democracy, lost its only seat, partly owing to internal party strife.

Foreign policy played practically no role in the election campaign. The main issues were social and economic, such as unemployment, the size of government benefits, the length of the work week, women's rights, euthanasia, the placement of 48 American cruise missiles on Dutch territory, and the use of nuclear power.

Countrywide elections for municipal councils in March saw the first-time participation of approximately 300,000 members of ethnic minorities (aliens who had been legally resident in the Netherlands for at least five years) and 150,000 Surinamese and Antillans, most of them Dutch subjects and recent immigrants. Some 20 of the new arrivals were elected to municipal office in various parts of the country. By contrast, Amsterdam, Rotterdam, and The Hague—with ethnic concentrations reaching as high as 20 percent—each elected one candidate of the anti-alien Centrum party. Overall, in these local elections, Labor made some notable gains, while the other large parties remained more or less stable.

The number of individuals seeking political asylum in Holland rose considerably in 1986, swelled by the arrival of some 3,500 Tamils—of whom 1,200 still remained at the end of the year—as well as refugees from Afghanistan, Pakistan, and Bangladesh. Under Dutch law, persons claiming political asylum had the right to stay in the country as long as their claim had not been definitely rejected—which could take several years—and were entitled to public assistance for the duration of their stay.

Despite a drop in revenues from natural gas of over $5 billion in 1986, the Dutch economy continued to show growth. Seeking to cut the budget deficit of over 8 percent, the government introduced drastic cuts in education, public health, welfare, and other public services, which led to numerous protest demonstrations throughout the year. While unemployment decreased by some 100,000 to about 700,000 at the end of 1986, at 15 percent it was one of the highest unemployment rates in Europe and remained a major government concern.

Relations with Israel

The Netherlands government continued to support the view that peace in the Middle East depended on recognition by the Arab states and the Palestine Liberation Organization (PLO) of Israel's right to exist within secure, recognized, and guaranteed borders and Israel's recognition, on the other hand, of the legitimate rights of the Palestinians.

Premier Shimon Peres of Israel paid a three-day official visit to the Netherlands in January, during which he also signed an agreement on full diplomatic relations with Premier Felipe Gonzalez of Spain, who had come to The Hague for the occasion. Peres, accompanied by Premier Lubbers, addressed a Jewish meeting in Amsterdam. Despite the stringent security precautions necessary because of recent terrorist attacks in Rome and Vienna, the hall was filled to capacity and the meeting judged a great success.

Following a decision in February by the Conference of Foreign Ministers of the European Economic Community (EEC) to pursue a more vigorous course of behind-the-scenes diplomacy in the Middle East, Foreign Minister Hans van den Broek of the Netherlands, as chairman of the conference, paid visits to a number of countries, including Syria, Jordan, and Tunisia. In Tunisia he met with Yasir Arafat and with the secretary-general of the Arab League.

In November the Netherlands and Israel signed an agreement for technological cooperation in joint ventures in developing countries.

In mid-October Princess Juliana, the former queen, and her husband, Prince Bernhard, paid a semiofficial visit to Israel as guests of the Jewish National Fund, among other reasons to dedicate a Queen Beatrix Forest in Lower Galilee. Though Dutch foreign policy prevented the princess from making an official visit to the Old City of Jerusalem, she managed to do so privately, including a stop at the Western (Wailing) Wall, only two days after a terrorist attack there. She also met with settlers from Holland during her stay.

Holocaust-Related Issues

A major cause célèbre developed in November over revelations that the widow of a former Nazi, Flora Rost van Tonningen, herself an acknowledged neo-Nazi, was receiving a generous government pension. The late Meinout Rost van Tonningen had been one of four members of the Dutch Nazi party in Parliament from 1937 to 1941 and from then on had served as president of the German-controlled

Netherlands State Bank. Arrested and imprisoned immediately after the liberation of the Netherlands, he died in prison in 1946, allegedly a suicide. Mrs. Rost van Tonningen's subsequent application for a parliamentarian widow's pension was granted in 1950; originally covering only the four years that her husband had been a member of Parliament, it amounted to a relatively modest annual sum. In 1956 it was increased, through a general amendment to the pensions law, and by 1986, thanks to additional across-the-board increases, it amounted to Dfl. 25,000 ($12,500) a year. Public indignation was fueled by the knowledge that Mrs. Rost van Tonningen—an acknowledged Nazi even before her marriage—continued to express neo-Nazi attitudes. Her villa in Velp, near Arnhem, was a distribution center for neo-Nazi literature imported from West Germany, and neo-Nazis from various European countries occasionally met there. The fact that Mrs. Rost van Tonningen—now a woman in her 70s—had been receiving a state widow's pension since 1950 was by no means a secret, but its publication in a Dutch weekly in November caused a great commotion.

Following widespread protests, and on the eve of a parliamentary debate scheduled for November 27, a parliamentary hearing took place on November 24 in which representatives of wartime resistance groups, former concentration-camp inmates, and Jewish organizations voiced strong opposition to continuation of the pension. The emotional full-day hearing was shown in its entirety on television, as was the parliamentary debate on November 27, which lasted for nine hours, including many adjournments. The dividing line between those opposing and those not opposing continuation of the pension—they were about equally divided—cut across political lines. An important question was whether the pension could be discontinued by simple ad hoc legislation or whether it required an amendment to the constitution, dependent on a two-thirds majority, which most probably could not be obtained. A special parliamentary commission was appointed to study the legal problem; however, no early report, let alone a parliamentary decision, was expected.

The WUV, the law providing for permanent payments to victims of the Nazis (and of the Japanese in the Japanese-occupied Dutch East Indies) during the years 1940–1945, whose earning capacity was reduced by their wartime experiences, was extended to persons who did not live in Holland before 1945 but arrived there between 1945 and August 15, 1955, and subsequently acquired Dutch citizenship—mostly former Displaced Persons. Earlier the WUV had been extended to persons who moved from Holland after 1945 to another country and acquired a new nationality. It was now also made applicable to persons over 65, who would continue to receive old-age pensions as well.

Claude Lanzmann's documentary film *Shoah* was shown on Dutch television by the progressive broadcasting company V.P.R.O., in two segments of 4½ hours each, on January 5 and 12. A viewer survey found that some 23 percent of the Dutch population 18 years of age and over watched the program for one hour or more; of this group, 4 percent watched the full nine hours. Sixty-six percent did not watch at all, and 11 percent watched for less than one hour. Telephone numbers of Jewish and other relevant organizations were shown on the screen, for those who wanted to express reactions to the program. A total of 739 phone calls were received, including 109 from Jews—mostly persons who had become emotionally agitated—and 45 callers with anti-Semitic messages.

THE JEWISH COMMUNITY

Demography

The number of Jews in the Netherlands was estimated at about 25,000. Of these, some 11,000 were officially considered to be members of the Ashkenazi community (Nederlands Israelitisch Kerkgenootschap, NIK), distributed among 42 local congregations throughout the country; about 2,500 belonged to the Liberal community, with six congregations; and about 1,000 were members of the Sephardi community, with one congregation, in Amsterdam. At least half of all Jews in the Netherlands were not affiliated with the organized Jewish community at all. Moreover, of those officially registered as Jews by the NIK, quite a number had long ceased to pay membership dues.

Emotions continued to run high over the announcement in December 1985 that the Jewish Social Welfare Foundation (Joods Maatschappelijk Werk, JMW) was preparing to make a demographic survey of Jews in the Netherlands. Earlier surveys carried out in 1954 and 1966 were regarded as no longer adequate for assessing future communal needs and had been criticized on methodological grounds. Some opponents of the new survey claimed that the counting of Jews was reminiscent of Nazi methods and that the registration of persons as Jews might endanger them if the Nazis came to power again. Such fears could not even be allayed by assurances about the secrecy of the data and their destruction after processing. Another objection concerned the criterion to be used in determining who was Jewish. A member of the survey commission, herself a member of a Liberal congregation, caused great indignation with a statement in the Dutch-Jewish weekly *Nieuw Israelitisch Weekblad* that in her view the criterion should "no longer be Jewish law—*halakhah*—but rather the standard applied by Hitler, i.e., having at least two Jewish grandparents." Other opponents feared that the new criterion would be simply a loosely defined "feeling of attachment," or sense of Jewish identity. Still other opponents asserted that for planning purposes, changing social patterns were as important as demographic data. They pointed to the fact that whereas people once entered old-age homes when they turned 65, they now remained independent much longer, often into their 80s. One result of this change was a surfeit of empty rooms in existing homes.

Those in favor of the survey noted that many persons who objected to it were already registered officially as Jews in other ways, for example, as recipients of WUV payments. As things turned out, in the midst of the controversy, first the Liberal community and then the Ashkenazi community, which were to have subsidized the survey, withdrew their cooperation. In January the JMW decided to put it aside indefinitely.

Communal Affairs

In Amsterdam, the long-standing conflict with Chief Rabbi Meir Just over his retirement was at long last resolved, in part owing to the mediation of the Ashkenazi Chief Rabbinate of Israel. On January 19 an agreement was signed by the rabbi, the NIK, and the Amsterdam Ashkenazi Congregation canceling the rabbi's contract but allowing him to retain the title of chairman of the Netherlands Chief Rabbinate for three years, during which he would continue to issue certificates of *kashrut* for export and receive a salary. Rabbi Just, in turn, agreed to give up his claims to the positions of either chief rabbi or communal rabbi in Amsterdam, thus paving the way for replacements to be selected.

After considering a number of candidates, on July 7 the Amsterdam Ashkenazi District Council appointed two communal rabbis: the ultra-Orthodox Shmuel E. Roth of Gateshead, England, and Dutch-born Isaac Vorst, who had already served for many years as spiritual head of the Amstelveen congregation near Amsterdam. The chief rabbi's position was offered to a Mizrachi supporter living in Jerusalem, but for various reasons he decided against coming to Amsterdam. At the end of the year there was still no chief rabbi, and no new candidate was in sight.

On September 30, the eve of Rosh Hashanah, the Ashkenazi congregation in The Hague inaugurated its new synagogue, in the presence of Queen Beatrix and many official guests. The synagogue was located on the ground floor of a new apartment building, erected to replace the previous synagogue structure, which had proved too costly to maintain for the small congregation of 450 members. (See AJYB, vol. 87, 1987, p. 236.)

In the southeastern province of Limburg, the four existing congregations—Maastricht, Heerlen, Roermond, and Venlo—each of which had become too small to survive independently, united to form one congregation.

Considerable publicity was given in the press, general as well as Jewish, to a lawsuit brought by a Jewish man against the Maimonides Lyceum, for refusing to admit his 12-year-old son as a pupil. The Orthodox day school claimed that the boy was not eligible because his mother was not a Jew according to *halakhah.* The presiding judge of the Amsterdam lower district court dismissed the father's suit on the ground that a religious school had a right to its own admission policy. The father appealed to the higher district court, which was still considering the case at year's end.

The retiring principal of the 170-pupil Maimonides Lyceum, Louis Evers, was succeeded by Dr. Henry Markens, a chemist, who had been chairman of the Amsterdam Ashkenazi Council since 1984—a post which he now resigned—and vice-chairman of the executive of the NIK.

Jewish-Christian Relations

The Consultative Council for Jews and Christians (OJEC) observed its fifth anniversary in November with a study conference addressed by, among others, Chief Rabbi Sir Immanuel Jakobovits of Great Britain. In September the council organized its second annual weekend for young Christians and Jews, to enable them to become better acquainted with each other's faiths. It also maintained interfaith "Houses of Learning" throughout the country—which were attended largely by Christians—and continued to publish educational pamphlets.

One of its publications, *The Goeree Affair,* concerned the Protestant gospel-preaching couple Lucas and Jenny Goeree, who had been enjoined by the district court in Zwolle in 1985 from distributing publications in which they charged that the Jews brought the Holocaust upon themselves by rejecting Jesus as the Messiah. Despite the guilty verdict, the couple continued distributing their pamphlets and appealed to a higher court. At the same time, the case—still open at year's end—led to a continuing controversy in church circles about the authority of a civil court to interfere in matters of religious conviction.

Soviet Jewry

In a speech delivered during an official visit to Moscow in October, Premier Lubbers advocated a more liberal emigration policy for Soviet Jews. This passage was omitted, however, in the official account of his remarks in *Pravda.*

Natan Sharansky paid a visit to Amsterdam in September, where he addressed the annual demonstration in behalf of Soviet Jewry and met with Premier Lubbers. His visit received considerable attention in the Dutch media.

Anti-Semitism

Although no physical attacks on Jews or Jewish property took place during the year, Jewish institutions continued to take security precautions. In July the government gave a one-time subsidy of Dfl. 650,000 ($325,000) to the Jewish foundation *By Leven en Welzijn* (By Life and Well-being), which was responsible for guarding Jewish buildings and meeting places.

An incident with anti-Semitic overtones took place on August 27, when supporters of the Hague soccer club FC Den Haag, marching through Amsterdam on their way to a match with the Amsterdam Ajax club—considered a Jewish club though it had few Jewish members—shouted anti-Semitic slogans and demonstrated the Hitler salute. (The Amsterdam club at one time had more Jewish, or half-Jewish, players and for many years a Jewish chairman.) Disturbing as the incident was, most observers felt that it had to be viewed in the context of violence and vandalism typically practiced by European soccer fans and not as a sign of growing anti-Semitism.

Israel and Zionism

The centennial of the birth of David Ben-Gurion, one of the year's highlights in the program of the Netherlands Zionist Organization, featured a visit by Yitzhak Navon, Israel's former president and current minister of education.

Freddy (Frederika) Markx, longtime chairwoman of the Women's Zionist Organization, WIZO, retired upon reaching the age of 65 and was succeeded by Betty Heertje. Perla (Keller) van Rijk retired as chairwoman of the Friends of Youth Aliyah in Holland, a position she had occupied for 25 years.

Culture

An exhibition entitled "The Changing Role of the Jewish Woman in Judaism" was shown at the Jewish Historical Museum from April to the end of October. It was the museum's last exhibit before its move from the Waag building to new quarters in the former complex of Ashkenazi synagogues in Jonas Daniel Meyer Square, scheduled to take place in April 1987. The show was organized by a guest curator, American-born Judith Frishman van Voolen, the wife of the Liberal Dutch rabbi Edward van Voolen. The show focused on the changing role of women in the Reform movement in the United States.

The Fourth Symposium on the History of Dutch Jewry took place in Israel in December, with most of the 120 participants from Israel and from Holland—the latter including non-Jews—and a few from other countries. These symposia had been held every two years since 1980, the meeting site alternating between Holland and Israel. The symposium, at which some 25 papers were presented, was organized by the Institute for the History of Dutch Jewry in Jerusalem, headed by Dr. Joseph Michman (Melkman), formerly of Amsterdam.

Publications

After nearly six years of work on the project, the Netherlands State Institute for Documentation on the Second World War (RIOD) published a scientific edition of the *Diaries of Anne Frank,* edited by staff members David Barnouw and Gerrit van der Stroom. The work's lengthy introduction contained a detailed analysis by experts of the handwriting in the original notebooks, the paper, and the ink. These findings were presented to refute claims by neo-Nazis in various countries that the work was a forgery. The volume also contained all the passages that had been omitted in the edition edited by Anne Frank's father, the late Otto Frank, because he felt they were too personal. The first copy of the scientific edition was presented at a press conference on May 12 to Elfriede (Markowitz) Frank, Otto Frank's second wife, who lived in Basel, Switzerland.

This year also saw the posthumous publication of additional writings by Etty Hillesum, whose wartime diaries had been published in 1983. The new volume, which ran to 874 pages, contained the originally published diaries, additional writings, and a collection of letters written by her in Amsterdam, between August 1942 and May 1943, to a friend in Westerbork, Osias Kormann. The letters had only recently come to light.

In December the firm of Christie's Amsterdam held its second auction of Judaica, its first auction having taken place a year earlier. Buyers were mostly Orthodox Jews from abroad.

In November a privately sponsored monument was unveiled in the so-called Rivers quarter of Amsterdam-South, commemorating one of the "Jewish markets" that existed there in the years 1942–1943, a place where Jews could buy and sell food and other provisions, which they were barred from doing in regular stores and markets.

Personalia

Among prominent Jews who died in 1986 were Dr. David Heymans, aged 82, for many years chairman of the Haarlem Jewish community and a member of the executive of the Netherlands Ashkenazi community, in July; Mozes M. Poppers, for many years chairman of the Society for Jewish Scholarship and a member of many other Jewish boards, in December, aged 80; and Erwin Juhl, one of the founders and longtime board members of the Amsterdam Liberal community, in December, aged 81.

HENRIETTE BOAS

Italy

THE PERIOD 1981–1986 GAVE rise to several important developments related to the legal status and internal organization of the Italian Jewish community. This half decade was marked,too, by a number of dramatic events, chief among them the terrorist attack on the Rome synagogue in 1982 and, four years later, the historic visit by Pope John Paul II to that same synagogue. Demographically, the Italian Jewish community continued to experience losses due to deaths and assimilation, but these were partly offset by immigration.

National Affairs

From July 1983 until July 1986 Italy enjoyed rare political stability, with only one government in office, a five-party coalition headed by Socialist Bettino Craxi as prime minister, the Christian Democrat Giulio Andreotti as foreign minister, and Republican Giovanni Spadolini as minister of defense. In June 1985 Christian-Democrat Francesco Cossiga was elected to replace Socialist Sandro Pertini as president of the Republic, in the traditional alternation of the position between Catholics and secularists. Cossiga, highly regarded as a liberal, invited representatives of Italy's minorities to his inauguration, including leaders of the Jewish community.

The period of relative calm ended in the summer of 1986, when Italy found itself with the kind of cabinet crisis that had been common in pre-Craxi days. Craxi regained his position after a month with no government in office, but only after making concessions to the Christian Democrats (DC)—the largest party in the coalition and the party that had governed Italy during most of the postwar years. By the end of the year, it was questionable whether Craxi could long maintain his position against the growing DC challenge.

The temporary political unrest did not appear to have harmed either the social or the economic stability that Italy had been enjoying under its recent leadership. As of the fall of 1986, Italy had surpassed Great Britain in gross national product, reaching fifth place among the industrial powers, after the United States, Japan, Germany, and France.

Relations with Israel

Italy's relations with Israel, which could fairly be termed uneven over the years, essentially continued as such. These ups and downs reflected the differing attitudes of each new political coalition that came to power. Italian governments tended to fall into one of four ideological matrixes: the "classic" Right, the Catholic, the liberal-secular, and the Marxist-socialist. Among these, only the liberal-secular group (Republicans, Liberals, Social Democrats) displayed a consistently pro-Israel position, while the others were sharply critical of Israel in response to particular events. The outbreak of the 1982 Israeli war in Lebanon, in particular the Sabra and Shatilla massacre which occurred during the hostilities, evoked a spate of anti-Israel, and even anti-Semitic, pronouncements. In this period, Palestine Liberation Organization (PLO) head Yasir Arafat was invited to Italy by Giulio Andreotti, a prominent leader of the Christian Democratic party and at the time chairman of the Interparliamentary Union. Arafat was also received with honor by President Sandro Pertini, Foreign Minister Emilio Colombo, and, in private audience, by Pope John Paul II.

Coverage of the war by the Italian media was one-sided and extremely hostile to Israel, including explicit calls to Diaspora Jews to dissociate themselves from Israel. Supporters of Israel blamed the media for creating an atmosphere in which subsequent actions against Jews were regarded as legitimate.

On October 9, 1982, at the end of religious services in observance of the holiday of Shemini Atzeret, a terrorist unit threw hand grenades into a crowd of Jewish congregants gathered outside the main synagogue in Rome. Two-year-old Stefano Tachè was killed and 40 people were wounded. Although the attackers escaped, they were identified as Palestinian extremists who had been helped by local underworld members. The attack was a major trauma for Rome's Jewish community, which, sensing a threat to its very existence and status, reacted by closing itself off from contact with the outside world, even refusing to receive the public condolences of Italian authorities. Eventually, mutual understanding was achieved, largely due to the efforts of Chief Rabbi Elio Toaff of Rome, who convinced his community to accept the participation of President Pertini and other Italian politicians in the child's funeral. The rabbi's actions and the presence of leading officials at such a significant gathering helped to restore open dialogue between the Jewish community and Italy's intellectual and political sectors.

Relations cooled again following a meeting between Prime Minister Craxi, Foreign Minister Andreotti, and PLO leader Arafat in Tunis in December 1984. Andreotti had already made his sentiments clear, when he voted in support of an anti-Zionist motion at the Interparliamentary Conference in Geneva the previous April. These steps were counterbalanced by Italy's action within the Common Market in support of a new trade agreement between Israel and the EEC. (Italy felt, in fact, that the presence of Israeli products on the European market could reduce competition between Italy and Spain, which had just entered the EEC.)

A succession of reciprocal visits also led Italian and Israeli governments to renew in 1985 the cultural agreement that had been in effect since 1971 and to draw up an extensive program for the succeeding three years. The plan provided for exchanges and collaboration between scholars and specialists from the two countries and incorporated a long list of activities, including art exhibitions, theatrical presentations, lectures on literature, language courses, art workshops, sporting and youth events, joint ventures between universities, scholarship awards, and exchanges of archivists. The agreement also covered the important work being done by Italian architects and archaeologists in the Israeli town of Acre and by Israeli experts at the site of the ancient Jewish catacombs in Rome. Among the diplomatic visits that helped bring about the agreement was that of Prime Minister Shimon Peres to Italy in February 1985 and that of Defense Minister Spadolini and Minister of Tourism Lelio Lagorio to Israel in the spring of 1985.

ACHILLE LAURO

On the political front, the Israeli bombing of PLO headquarters in Tunis in October 1985 was strongly condemned by the Italian government. Only a few days later, a deeper crisis was provoked by the tragic episode of the *Achille Lauro,* the Italian cruise ship that was hijacked by four Arab terrorists, who murdered an American Jewish passenger, Leon Klinghoffer. In the aftermath of the incident, after the passengers were freed, the four terrorists and their leader, Arafat-supporter Mohammed Abu al-Abbas, were apprehended and brought to Italy by an American military plane. After taking custody of the Palestinians, however, and despite urgent requests from the United States that he be held, Italian authorities allowed Abbas to go free, claiming insufficient evidence against him. This event and the government's overall handling of the episode sparked a series of political crises, including the temporary collapse of the Craxi government. Craxi initially condoned the PLO's "resort to arms" as a "legitimate" means of gaining national liberation. Later he expressed a more moderate position, supporting Israel's right to exist, urging peace negotiations, and stressing the "uselessness" of violence. Meanwhile, Italian authorities began preparing the legal case against the four hijackers and more than a dozen other Palestinians, including the fugitive Abu Abbas, all of whom were charged with involvement in either planning or carrying out the hijacking.

In an attempt to repair the damaged relations caused by the *Achille Lauro* incident, Defense Minister Spadolini paid a visit to Jerusalem in February 1986, bringing greetings to the World Jewish Congress meeting there at the time. Spadolini was a sharp critic of his own government and what he regarded as appeasement of the PLO. In May Foreign Minister Andreotti paid an official visit to Israel, during which he made it clear that Italy sought complete reconciliation with the Jewish state and stressed the two countries' shared goal of combating terrorism.

When the trial of the 15 *Achille Lauro* suspects began in June 1986, only five were in custody; the rest, including Abu Abbas, were tried in absentia. The case ended three weeks later, with six of the defendants convicted of terrorist crimes: Abu Abbas and two associates were given life sentences for organizing the hijacking, but it was thought extremely unlikely that they would be apprehended. A controversial sentence was given to the confessed murderer of Leon Klinghoffer—30 years in prison, instead of life, as requested by the prosecution. Both the judge and the jury seemed to accept the defense's claim of "extenuating circumstances," namely, the fact that the defendants "had grown up in tragic conditions."

Of the remaining nine defendants, five were found guilty of lesser crimes and four were acquitted. The U.S. State Department announced itself pleased "that persons responsible for the death of an American citizen and injury and damages to others have been convicted" but expressed regret that Klinghoffer's murderer was not treated more severely. The United States reserved the right to seek extradition of the hijackers once all Italian legal proceedings, including appeals, had ended.

The convictions handed down in the *Achille Lauro* case signaled a change in the official attitude, many observers believed. In the aftermath of the sentencing, the press extensively criticized the authorities' handling of the affair and acknowledged that its own coverage had tended to be both anti-Israel and anti-Jewish. In actuality, the tensions in Italy-Israel relations had already begun to ease up at the end of 1985, when the government retreated from its pro-PLO position. Prime Minister Craxi's policy of friendship toward Arafat and Libyan leader Muammar Qaddafi—in the express hope of encouraging moderation on their part—was placed under severe strain by the December 1985 Arab terrorist attack at El Al counters in the Rome and Vienna airports.

Following charges by the United States that Libya was behind the airport attacks, and a call by President Ronald Reagan for economic sanctions against Libya, Italy reluctantly announced a ban on weapons sales to that country. This came amidst growing recognition that Italy's sympathy for the PLO was not only jeopardizing its relations with Israel and the United States but was arousing the ire of anti-Arafat Palestinian groups like the Abu Nidal faction. The matter was complicated by the strong ties that existed between Italy and Libya, its former colony, involving trade, Italians resident in Libya, and Libya's 15-percent share in Fiat, Italy's biggest auto maker, which it had acquired during the economic recession of 1976.

Concerned though Rome was about the apparent increase in terrorism on its own soil and elsewhere, it was cautious about retaliating against Libya, partly because of the limited evidence concerning Libya's role, and partly for fear of igniting further hostilities in the Mediterranean region. Still, in the months that followed, Italy expelled a number of Libyan diplomats and reduced its oil imports from that country. In October the Agnelli family, the owners of Fiat, announced a decision to buy back Libya's 15-percent interest in their company, a decision that was warmly approved both by Israel and by the Jewish community of Italy.

The Italian government took a harder line against Syria as well, based on increasing evidence of that country's role in international terrorism, and signed an agreement in June 1986 with the U.S. government for cooperation in the fight against terrorism.

Evidence that anti-Israel feeling had softened was seen only a few months later, in September, following the brutal Arab terrorist attack on the synagogue in Istanbul, Turkey, in which some tens of unarmed Jews were killed. The tragedy elicited strong expressions of sympathy and condemnations of terrorism, with leading public and political figures attending the crowded memorial gathering organized by the Jewish community of Rome. Yet another sign of improved relations between the Italian government and the Jewish community was the attendance, for the first time, of a president of the Republic of Italy—in this instance, Francesco Cossiga—at the quadrennial national congress of the Union of Italian Jewish Communities, held in Rome in November.

In that same month Italy and Israel were briefly linked in a bizarre spy incident. Mordechai Vanunu, an Israeli employee of the nuclear plant at Dimona, who revealed nuclear secrets to the *Sunday Times* of London, was spirited out of England by Israeli secret agents and apparently taken to Israel by way of Rome. Details of the incident were still unknown at the end of the year.

Church-State Relations

In February 1984 the signing of a historic new "concordat" between Italy and the Vatican abolished Roman Catholicism as the state religion of Italy and established new regulations governing relations between church and state. Among the terms of the agreement, two directly affected Jews: one took away control of the ancient Jewish catacombs in Rome from the Vatican, giving it to the government (see below, "Culture"); the second provided for the continuation of Catholic religious instruction in public schools, but changed it from a compulsory to an elective subject.

As part of the process of working out new agreements (*intese*) between the government and the non-Catholic religions, a special commission composed of legal experts and Jewish communal representatives had been meeting for several years; at the end of 1986 it was preparing a final draft to submit to the government. The draft agreement would have to be voted on first by the Union of Italian Jewish Communities and eventually by the Italian Parliament. Among the terms being proposed by the Jewish community were rights for Jews to be absent from work on Saturday and to observe *kashrut* in public institutions (army, hospitals, prisons), as well as the official commitment of the State of Italy to protect the Jewish historic, artistic, and cultural heritage.

JEWISH COMMUNITY

A change in Italian law in this period had significant implications for the Jewish community. In July 1984, the Corte Costituzionale (Supreme Court) repealed the fourth article of the law pertaining to the Italian Jewish communities, promulgated in 1930. According to that article, all Jews were required to affiliate with the organized Jewish community wherever they lived and to pay a tax for the support of communal institutions. With the repeal of this article, membership in a Jewish community became wholly voluntary. The great majority of Italian Jews gave an immediate positive response to the appeal for affiliation, with only a few hundred disassociating themselves from their communities. Thus, the transition from a compulsory to a voluntary system was effected smoothly.

Demography

The 1986 Jewish population of Italy (including all Jews except immigrants in transit, such as Russian and Persian Jews) was estimated at 31,800—mainly concentrated in Rome (15,000) and Milan (8,500). The figures reflected the continuing high rates of aging and assimilation that characterized the Italian Jewish population. These rates had been partially offset in the 1970s by immigration—from Iran, for example. After the 1978–79 revolution, several hundred Iranian Jewish families, comprising some 1,350 individuals, settled in Milan. A group of several thousand Jewish emigrants from the Soviet Union temporarily sojourned in Ostia (Rome), but eventually received visas to the United States and left Italy. Several hundred Israeli students were enrolled in Italian universities, primarily in medical studies.

The demographic crisis was felt most keenly in the small communities. In 1985, for instance, the community in Alessandria officially closed down as an independent entity, its few remaining members being absorbed administratively by the nearby community in Turin. Between 1984 and 1985, Jewish schools closed both in Genoa and in Leghorn, although the kindergarten continued to function in the latter.

The Persian (Iranian) Jewish community in Milan was well integrated within the existing community structure, where it played an active role. At the same time, it managed to maintain its distinctive character and traditions and supported a large synagogue and community center. The Persians were not the only non-Italian Jewish group in Italy. A community of some 2,500 Libyan Jews lived in Rome, most of them having arrived before 1967 and by now well integrated into Italian society. A 1986 community survey sponsored by the Milan Jewish community and the Center for Contemporary Jewish Documentation (CDEC) revealed about 37 different ethnic origins just among the Jews of Milan.

Communal Activities

In January 1983 there was a change in the leadership of the Unione delle Comunità Israelitiche Italiane (Union of Italian Jewish Communities, UCII), the body representing the local communities to the Italian government and the central authorities, as provided by the law of 1930. Tullia Zevi of Rome, a journalist and author, was elected to succeed Vittorio Ottolenghi as the new president; she was reelected in 1986. A woman of wide-ranging professional and personal experience—she had lived in the United States for many years, had been active in the World Jewish Congress, and was fluent in several languages—she was viewed as an ideal representative of the community. She believed in the crucial role of a strong Diaspora and advocated close contact between world Jewish communities.

In 1986 the Jewish community focused its attention on three main areas: strengthening Jewish education, developing Jewish cultural projects, and concluding the agreement with the Italian government that would henceforth regulate Jewish communal affairs.

The most difficult and controversial issue in the new accord was that of education. Although the new concordat had decreed that Catholicism was no longer the state religion, the traditional system of teaching Catholic doctrine in public schools would continue, ostensibly as an elective. The Ministry of Education did permit non-Catholic groups to arrange religious instruction for pupils of other faiths, but opponents of the system argued that any sectarian religious teaching violated the constitutional principle of equality and was inherently discriminatory. The UCII joined with other non-Catholic groups in fighting for the secularization of public education.

The UCII also faced a worrying decrease in enrollment in Jewish schools, as a result of population decline. Jewish schools existed in only five communities: Rome and Milan both had elementary and secondary schools; Turin had an elementary and a junior high school; and Trieste and Florence each had an elementary school. In the academic year 1985–1986 the total number of children attending Jewish day schools was 2,014, or 40–45 percent of the Jewish school-age population. Talmud Torah (supplementary) schools in Rome and Milan enrolled an additional few hundred pupils.

Rabbinical studies were offered at the Orthodox Rabbinical College in Rome, where a complete course of study was attended by a dozen students.

The Pope Visits the Synagogue of Rome

The highlight of 1986 for the Jewish community of Italy was undoubtedly the visit of Pope John Paul II to the central synagogue of Rome on April 13. Before an enthusiastic congregation of 1,000, the pope and the spiritual head of the Rome Jewish community, Chief Rabbi Elio Toaff, after greeting each other warmly, took part in a ceremony that included choral renditions, readings from the Psalms by the two spiritual leaders, and speeches. The occasion was termed "historic" because no pope had ever before entered a Jewish house of worship. Also, since the visit had been initiated by the Vatican, it seemed to imply a desire for formal reconciliation with the Jews of Rome, who had suffered over the ages at the hand of the Church. At the same time, it showed a willingness on the part of the Jews to move beyond the past.

"Twenty years after Pope John XXIII and the Second Vatican Council," stated Rabbi Toaff, in his address to the congregation, "one historical period has been closed and a new one is finally to be opened under the banner of equality, respect, and esteem for the people among whom Christianity originated." In his remarks, Pope John Paul reaffirmed the legacy of John XXIII and the declaration "Nostra Aetate," which, he noted, condemned every kind of discrimination, including anti-Semitism. He referred to the Jews as "our older and favorite brothers" and said they were "beloved of God." The ceremony in the synagogue was broadcast live around the world.

An immediate echo of the visit was a ceremonial meeting between the Bishop of Florence and the Florentine Jewish community one month later, with the Florentine community represented by its president, Edoardo Vitta, professor of international law at the University of Florence. While Jews were dismayed over the absence of any reference by the prelates to the State of Israel, optimists interpreted the visits as a hopeful sign that recognition of Israel might soon follow.

Apart from the issue of Israel, relations between Christians and Jews in Italy reached a peak of good feeling in 1986. At the end of October, Chief Rabbi Toaff and five other rabbis participated in an ecumenical religious gathering for world peace, held in Assisi, to which Pope John Paul II had invited representatives of 50 world religious groups. Each group conducted separate prayer services according to its own rites.

Twelfth UCII Congress

Because the signing of a new agreement with the government of Italy was imminent, the 12th quadrennial congress of the UCII, held in November 1986, possessed special importance. With the UCII on the threshold of major organizational change, including a host of new regulations that would govern the internal life of the community and the nature of its relationship to Italian society at large, the union's leadership felt the need both to prepare the community for the coming changes and to discuss some of the more urgent issues to be covered in the final agreement. Among these were Jewish education, cultural preservation, and respect for all aspects of Jewish life in Italy.

In addition to its purely internal purposes, the congress provided an opportunity for the Jewish community to gain public recognition for its activities and institutions and to cement ties with the non-Jewish world. The gala opening session heard a report from President Zevi on the UCII's activities and aims. It also heard a review of the history and contributions of the Jews of Italy presented by the Italian Jewish scientist Rita Levi-Montalcini, who only a month earlier had been awarded a Nobel Prize in Medicine. Among the Italian ministers and politicians who attended sessions of the congress were President of the Republic Cossiga, Foreign Minister Andreotti, and Under Secretary of State Giuliano Amato. Their presence was seen not simply as a formal gesture but as expressing the genuine interest of Italy's establishment in the small but influential Jewish community.

Anti-Semitism

A number of anti-Semitic incidents were reported in 1986. Although no single one was considered particularly serious, their cumulative occurrence in the context of a generally friendly society was viewed as significant. Jewish cemeteries were vandalized in Pisa, Trieste, Leghorn, and Verona, and severe damage was done to the remains of the ancient synagogue in Ostia (Rome), the oldest known synagogue in Europe. In the autonomous region of Alto Adige, bordering Austria, neo-Nazi groups daubed anti-Semitic slogans. In the same area, anti-Jewish views published in the local press were strongly denounced by the Jewish community of Merano. A translation of the anti-Semitic and revisionist French book *La vérité sur le procès de Auschwitz,* by Jean Pierre Bermont, which claimed that Auschwitz was a fabrication of the Jews, was published in Italy. Although the book did not find a wide audience in Italy, its very appearance contributed to the popularization of historical revisionism relating to the Holocaust, which was widespread in both France and Germany.

Culture

A project to collect and preserve the libraries and archives of Jewish communities throughout Italy—many of which were defunct or without resources—and to centralize the materials in Rome, was inaugurated by the UCII in 1984, with the aid of a generous grant from the government. By 1986 the Italian National Jewish Library and Heritage Center had taken possession of the community libraries of Ancona, Ferrara, Firenze, Pisa, and Pitigliano; the Jewish communal archive of Senigaglia; the valuable library of the Italian Rabbinical School; and the vast archives of the UCII itself, already housed in Rome. In 1986 the center began to benefit from the help of specialized Israeli staff who were sent to Italy under the provisions of the 1985 cultural agreement between Italy and Israel. The center's quarters, an elegant restored palace on the bank of the River Tiber, across the bridge from the Great Synagogue of Rome, were scheduled to open to the public in 1990.

In September 1986 the Olivetti industrial group announced its willingness to finance the cataloging of the cultural treasures of the Jews of Italy. Strengthened by this offer, the center announced that it would enlarge its range of projects beyond the bibliographic collection to include the care of Jewish archaeological remains, the preservation of Jewish historical landmarks, and the restoration of old synagogue structures.

One such project, begun in 1984, was the reconstruction of the ancient synagogue in Pitigliano, in Tuscany, which had been almost completely destroyed by an earthquake in the 1960s. Another synagogue, a particularly beautiful structure in Gorizia, in the northern district of Friuli, reopened to the public after a long period of renovation. The main synagogue of Rome, constructed in 1904, underwent major repairs.

In July 1985, following the signing of the new concordat with the Vatican, the UCII acquired guardianship of the ancient Jewish catacombs of Rome from the government, which now controlled them. Situated beneath property belonging to wealthy Roman Catholic families, the catacombs had been entrusted for decades to the Holy See. In 1986, after Jewish scholars had had a chance to study the underground network of tombs, the site was opened to the public for the first time.

In January 1986 archaeologists uncovered the remains of a synagogue dating from the fourth century CE in Bova Marina in southern Italy. Historians hoped the excavations would shed new light on the Jewish diaspora in the Roman period.

A key institution devoted to protecting the Italian Jewish cultural heritage was the Center for Jewish Contemporary Documentation (Centro Documentazione Ebraica Contemporanea, CDEC) in Milan, which had an extensive collection of documents on the Jews of Italy during the Holocaust as well as a number of important private archives pertaining to contemporary Jewish history, Italian Zionism in particular. In December 1984 the CDEC was added to the list of Italian cultural institutions eligible for government financial aid. Two years later the center was awarded a special medal from the Province of Milan "for its intensive and serious activity in gathering precious historical and bibliographic material and also for encouraging interest in and study of the history of Italian Jews."

Interest in Italian Jewish affairs was demonstrated in a number of congresses and meetings. Of particular importance was the "Italia Judaica" program, which brought together Italian and Israeli scholars to seek out material relating to Italian Jewry in Italian archives. The results of this research were presented and discussed in series of meetings. The first two, held in Italy in 1981 and in 1984 (in Bari and in Genoa, respectively), were on the Medieval, Renaissance, and Baroque periods; a third congress took place in Tel Aviv in June 1986, covering Jewish life in Italy from late Renaissance to the 1st Emancipation; and a fourth Italia Judaica congress was scheduled for June 1989 in Siena, Italy, on "The Jews in Italy, 1870–1945." Promoters and organizers of this project were Prof. Vittore Colorni (University of Ferrara), Fausto Pusceddu (Italian Ministry of Cultural Affairs, Rome), Prof. Giuseppe Sermoneta (Hebrew University, Jerusalem), and Prof. Shlomo Simonsohn (Tel Aviv University).

Interest in the history of Italian Jewry also extended across the Atlantic Ocean to the United States, where two congresses on that subject were held in the fall of 1986. The first, which took place in Boston in November, focused on the period of the Holocaust and was entitled "Italians and Jews: Rescue and Aid During the Holocaust." Organized by the National Italian American Foundation, in collaboration with Boston University, the American Jewish Committee, and the U.S. Holocaust Memorial Council, the conference brought together experts such as Paul Bookbinder, Andrea Canepa, Lynn Gunsberg, Meir Michaelis, Klaus Voigt, and Susan Zuccotti. Several Jews who had been rescued by Italians during the war presented moving testimony about their experiences to the conference.

The second conference, held in New York in December, was organized by Brooklyn College and cosponsored by the Foreign Ministry of Italy and the Italian Cultural Institute of New York. It too dealt with the wartime period, offering a four-day program of historical lectures, personal testimonies, photographic exhibitions, film showings, and lively discussions. Among the participants were Tullia

Zevi, head of the Union of Italian Jewish Communities; Furio Colombo, journalist; Denis Mack Smith, Oxford University; Mario Toscano, University of Rome; and Sergio Minerbi, Hebrew University of Jerusalem.

The year 1986 saw a flourishing of cultural and artistic activity, largely initiated by young Jewish artists. Especially noteworthy were the theater group created by Roman actor Vittorio Pavoncello, which performed works on traditional and modern Jewish themes; the concerts and recordings of Miriam Meghnagi, a Libyan-born singer of international Jewish songs; and the Jewish cultural television program "*Sorgente di vita*" (Source of Life), directed by Dani Toaff and Emanuele Ascarelli.

Publications

Two important memoirs published in 1986 were *Storia di un ebreo fortunato* by Dan Vittorio Segre (published in English as *Memoirs of a Fortunate Jew*) and *Racconti di vita ebraica* ("Tales of a Jewish Life") by Augusto Segre. Two noteworthy festschrifts, containing historical essays on individuals and on Italian Jewry as a whole, were *In memoria di Yoseph Colombo,* issued by the Italian Jewish monthly review *La Rassegna Mensile d'Israel,* and the *Scritti in memoria di Nathan Cassuto,* published in Jerusalem. Colombo was a Hebrew scholar, educator, and editor of *La Rassegna Mensile.* Cassuto, son of the eminent Judaica scholar Umberto Cassuto, was a physician and surgeon as well as a rabbi. Appointed chief rabbi of Florence in 1943, he remained with his community until deported by the Nazis to a concentration camp in Poland, from which he never returned.

The widely acclaimed novelist, essayist, and poet Primo Levi published a new work, *I sommersi e i salvati* ("The Drowned and the Saved"), a reconsideration of his Holocaust experiences and their aftereffects. Nicola Caracciolo's *Gli ebrei e l'Italia durante la guerra 1940–45* ("The Jews and Italy During the War") recounts Italian efforts to rescue Jews from the Holocaust. The book was based on interviews of both Italian and non-Italian Jews that were conducted for a television program broadcast in the fall of 1986.

Other new works relating to Jewish life in Italy included a collection of photographs by Salvatore Fornari, *Roma del ghetto* ("Rome of the Ghetto"); a historical novel by Riccardo Calimani, *Storia del ghetto di Venezia* ("History of the Venice Ghetto"); and a guidebook by Annie Sacerdoti and Luca Fiorentino, *Guida all'-Italia ebraica* ("Guide to Jewish Italy").

Among new publications on the subject of Israel were: *Le origini del sionismo e la nascita del kibbutz 1881–1920* ("The Origins of Zionism and the Birth of the Kibbutz") by Lorenzo Cremonesi; *Israele 40 anni di storia* ("Israel's 40-Year History") by Fausto Coen; and Marco Paganoni's *Dimenticare Amalek* ("To Forget Amalek"), an analysis of the complex attitudes of the Italian leftist parties toward Israel. Also worthy of mention is the 1986 annual volume of the bimonthly *Storia Contemporanea* ("Contemporary History"), edited by Renzo De Felice, containing eight essays by Italian and Israeli experts on the subject of Jews and Arabs in the strategy of Italian fascism.

A work about Jews in opera was *Mille voci una stella* ("A Thousand Voices, a Star") by Luciano Di Cave, portraits of Jewish opera singers.

The review of studies on Italian Jewry, *Italia,* edited by Professors Giuseppe Sermoneta and Roberto Bonfil of the Hebrew University of Jerusalem and published in Israel, issued its seventh volume in 1986.

Personalia

Italian Jewish biologist Rita Levi-Montalcini was co-winner of the 1986 Nobel Prize in Medicine. Giacomo Sabban, Turkish-born professor of mathematics at the University of Rome, was elected president of the Jewish community of Rome. Rabbi Menachem Emanuel Artom of Israel was appointed religious head of the Jewish community of Turin.

A leading Italian Jew who died in 1986 was Augusto Segre, in November, aged 71. Born in 1915, the son of the rabbi of Casale Monferrato (in Piedmont), he was one of the outstanding Italian Jews of his generation. A rabbi and a teacher at the Rabbinical College of Rome, he dedicated his life to spreading Jewish education and culture, particularly among the young. Secretary for many years of the Union of the Italian Jewish Communities and editor of its popular publication *La Rassegna Mensile d'Israel,* he was the author of works on Jewish thought and on the history of the Italian Jews. In later years he was professor of Jewish thought at the Catholic Lateranense University. An active member of the Zionist movement from his youth, Segre made important contributions to the Italian Zionist Federation. During World War II he served in the Italian resistance in the mountains near Casale Monferratos. In 1979 he and his wife settled in Israel, joining a son and daughter in Jerusalem. He died in Rome while on a visit to friends and his former community.

Sergio Tagliacozzo, who died in December, aged 52, was for many years head of the Rome Jewish community. A well-known merchant and popular figure in that city, he was working on a book about his life at the time of his final illness. Cesare Polacco, a popular Jewish actor, died in March, aged 85.

SIMONETTA DELLA SETA

Central Europe

Austria

National Affairs

TWO EVENTS DOMINATED THE Austrian political scene in 1986. One was the election of Kurt Waldheim as the country's president, which stirred up controversy within the country and abroad, forcing Austrians to confront a painful, largely unexamined past, and catapulted Austria's small Jewish community into a state of crisis. The second event was the election to Parliament later in the year, in which surprising losses by the two leading parties seemed to reflect a mood of growing uncertainty in the country.

Elections

Kurt Waldheim, former minister of foreign affairs and two-term secretary-general of the United Nations, was presented to the public as the presidential candidate of the People's party (Conservatives) as early as October 1985. The Conservatives, who had been in opposition since 1971, believed that the nomination of such a distinguished figure virtually assured their victory. Their confidence was bolstered by the declining popularity of the Socialist party—in power for 16 years running—as a result of various scandals and unpopular decisions. In addition, the Socialist candidate, Kurt Steyrer, minister of environmental affairs, had come under fire in December 1985 for calling out the police to remove young demonstrators by force from a proposed electric-plant site near the Danube River. In contrast to Steyrer, Waldheim was not only popular but was touted as "the man trusted by the world." In short, the Conservatives were certain that Waldheim would become the first non-Socialist in postwar Austria to hold the largely ceremonial but prestigious post of president.

Public discussion of Waldheim's wartime past started early in March. The weekly news magazine *Profil* (and independently, in the United States, the *New York Times*) reported that German military documents newly discovered in various archives showed Waldheim linked to Nazi activity in the Balkans between 1942 and

1945. This was in startling contrast to his own claim in his published autobiography, *In the Eye of the Storm,* and elsewhere, that an injury received on the Russian front ended his military service in 1941 and that he spent the rest of the war in Vienna, writing his doctoral thesis in law.

Various sources were credited with bringing the relevant documents to light, chief among them the World Jewish Congress (WJC). It was also rumored that Socialists in the Foreign and Justice ministries had passed incriminating material to the press. The original impetus for investigating Waldheim appears to have been a controversy over a memorial plaque for Gen. Alexander von Löhr, a key figure in the creation of the Austrian Air Force in World War I. During World War II, as commander of German Army Group E in the Balkans, Löhr was responsible for brutal retaliatory campaigns against Yugoslav partisans. He was also charged with ordering the aerial bombardment of Belgrade, although Germany had not made an official declaration of war, an action for which he was executed in 1947 by the Yugoslavs as a war criminal. In the controversy over the memorial plaque, investigators of Löhr's past turned up the name of Kurt Waldheim as a member of the general's staff. At first the information met with disbelief, but it aroused sufficient interest at the WJC, *Profil,* and the *Times* to send them searching for corroborating evidence.

The documents uncovered by investigators revealed, for one thing, that Waldheim had been affiliated with two Nazi student organizations, though the significance of this was unclear. They also revealed that far from being discharged from the military in 1942, he had been assigned to General Löhr's staff, serving in Yugoslavia and Greece. Although there was no evidence of his having committed atrocities, German army documents made clear that as an intelligence officer he was involved in a wide range of activities, including participation in high-level staff meetings at which he often reported on the situation in the Balkans. Despite his repeated assertions, therefore, that he knew nothing of the operations against partisans and Jews, it seemed amply clear that at the very least he was familiar with the brutal reprisals carried out against partisans and the deportation of over 40,000 Jews from Saloniki, when he was stationed just outside that city.

Most Austrians failed to understand the attacks against Waldheim. The fact that he had been elected UN secretary-general twice, his past at no time being raised as an issue, seemed a powerful argument against the charges. In their eyes, too, he was seen not as a war criminal but rather as something of an opportunist, at worst a Nazi sympathizer. Some thought Waldheim even lacked enough character to have been a war criminal. For the most part he was considered a fellow-traveler, someone who always accommodated, who played the game, wherever he was. In the UN, too, according to this view, his actions were geared to pleasing the majority, in the hope of being reelected secretary-general. Even Waldheim's opponents did not all regard him as a war criminal. Many simply felt that 40 years after the war, with 70 percent of Austrians having been born after 1938, the country should be led by someone who was not incriminated in any way in those troubling events. Moreover, many felt that Waldheim had lost his moral authority because of his "carefree relations with the truth."

Austria's own complicity in the events of the Nazi period was something most Austrians preferred not to face. After the war, Austrian politicians kept pointing out that Austria had in fact been Hitler's first victim, abandoned by the world, getting help from no one. The 1943 Moscow Declaration of the Allies affirmed this as a historical fact, by implication exonerating Austria of any guilt. As a result, in the postwar years, Austrians, unlike Germans, never paid reparations and never engaged in any serious assessment of their own role in the events of the war.

While presenting a face of innocence to the outside world, internally Austrians seemed to hold a different view of things. In 1949, in the first postwar election in which former Nazis were allowed to vote, both major parties, the Socialists and the Conservatives, courted ex-Nazi voters. And in 1986, as Waldheim's alleged wartime activity continued to make headlines around the world, scandal-weary Austrians objected less to the fact that he had blatantly lied than to what they felt was foreign interference in their domestic affairs. With Waldheim and Austria itself under attack, the slogan on Waldheim posters—"Now more than ever"—(he was managed by an American public relations firm) reflected the defiant mood of the population.

For the first time since 1945 strong anti-Semitic sentiments were openly expressed. The majority of the press, most notably the daily *Kronenzeitung,* with a circulation of 1.5 million, joined the anti-Semitic chorus. The exceptions were few. The charges and evidence against Waldheim were said to have been initiated by the World Jewish Congress and thus dismissed as worthless. The opposition to the anti-Semites—a minority of the press and the public and, officially, at least, the Socialist party—was unable to stem the tide.

Waldheim's repeated denials of having taken part in anything reprehensible and his claim of only "having done his duty" aroused indignation among former members of the resistance movement, anti-Nazis, and of course Jews. One moderate voice was that of Simon Wiesenthal, a central figure in the Jewish community of Vienna, besides having distinguished himself in the pursuit of Nazi criminals, who expressed the view that while Waldheim had surely known of the deportations of Jews from Greece, he was probably not a war criminal in any legal sense. It was pointless to go after Nazi sympathizers after a lapse of 40 years, he asserted, since there had been some 600,000 Nazi party members in Austria in 1945 (proportionately many more than in Germany). The still living real murderers should be brought to justice, he urged. Wiesenthal further claimed that the WJC's repeated threats to disclose new evidence that never materialized only served to awaken dormant anti-Semitic attitudes. (Conflict between Wiesenthal and both the Socialists and the WJC was nothing new. In 1975, then chancellor Bruno Kreisky accused Wiesenthal of having collaborated with the Germans during the war. Although Wiesenthal received strong support from many quarters, nothing was heard from the WJC or its president, Nahum Goldmann, a friend of Kreisky.)

Waldheim actually gained a certain amount of credibility thanks to the outgoing Austrian president, Socialist Rudolf Kirschläger, a former judge, who agreed to examine the WJC's file and UN documents on Waldheim. In an eagerly awaited address to the nation on April 23, the president said that Waldheim must have known about German reprisals against partisans in the Balkans but that the documents contained no actual evidence of war crimes. The impact of Kirschläger's statement, which Waldheim's supporters took as a virtual acquittal, was decisive.

In the May 3rd voting, Waldheim won slightly less than a majority (49.6 percent against Steyrer's 43.7 percent), necessitating a runoff election a month later. The June 8th voting gave Waldheim a 54-percent victory, which many observers credited to a patriotic backlash stirred by the campaign against him.

Reaction abroad to Waldheim's election was predictable: Western countries reacted coolly; Soviet-bloc and Arab countries acclaimed the event as a victory over Zionism. No Israeli was present at the presidential oath-taking ceremony. The United States was represented by a junior diplomat, Ambassador Ronald Lauder having excused himself on grounds of urgent personal business.

The Socialists drew personal conclusions from Waldheim's victory. Acknowledging his own eroded popularity, Chancellor Fred Sinowatz resigned and was replaced by Finance Minister Franz Vranitzky, a man with broad banking experience, regarded as a more pragmatic, moderate Socialist. Vranitzky formed a new coalition of Socialists and members of the rightist Freedom party, but in September the coalition collapsed. This happened when the Freedom party, whose official program was liberal but whose voters traditionally came from German nationalist and rightist quarters, elected Jörg Haider, an extreme nationalist, as their leader. His views were too much for Vranitzky, who ended the partnership and called an early election for November. Political observers predicted that a broader coalition of Socialists and Conservatives would be formed after the elections, one that could more effectively tackle such economic problems as losses in state-owned industries, rising unemployment, and a significant trade deficit.

Believing themselves on a political upswing as a result of Waldheim's victory, the Conservatives again emphasized patriotic themes during the election campaign. This time, however, it proved a miscalculation. Many voters who had voted for Waldheim now supported either the Freedom party or the Environmentalists, the Greens. In what was considered a significant upset, both major parties lost votes, the Freedom party gained enormously, and the Environmentalists, presided over by Freda Meissner-Blau, won seats for the first time. The final distribution of seats in Parliament was as follows: Socialists, 80; Conservatives, 77; Freedom party, 18; Environmentalists, 8. The anticipated broad coalition was formed, headed by Vranitzky.

Contrary to popular expectation, the furor surrounding Waldheim's election did not abate, either in Austria or abroad. Many intellectuals and artists, as well as average citizens, could not accept Waldheim as president. He was rarely invited to cultural or civic events and seldom appeared in public. Against normal custom, he did not preside at the opening of the Conference on Security and Cooperation in Europe (CSCE) in November, and only a few delegates, in most cases from the Eastern-bloc countries, paid him official visits. Immediately after the election, Simon

Wiesenthal proposed the formation of an international commission of historians to investigate the facts about Waldheim's past, but Waldheim objected. There was concern that Austria might now find itself dangerously isolated abroad and torn by unbridgeable gaps among the various political factions at home.

The Waldheim Affair and the Jewish Community

While almost no Jews voted for Waldheim, many criticized the actions of the World Jewish Congress in the affair. Resentment centered on that body's failure either to inform the Jewish community in advance or to discuss with its leaders possible consequences for the Jews of Austria, which almost any community member could have foretold. Emotions ran high when WJC officials promised imminent publication of documents proving Waldheim's war crimes, but these documents never appeared. Many believed that the WJC should have allowed some other organization to take the lead, preferably a neutral public body or a newspaper. At a meeting of the WJC in Geneva, in May, Paul Gross, representative of Austria to that body, tried to explain the point of view of the Jewish community in Austria, but it was too late. Once having started, the affair developed its own momentum, beyond anyone's control, with the predicted negative effects on the Jewish community.

Since 1945, the Jewish community of Vienna, consisting in the main of refugees from Soviet-bloc countries and Holocaust survivors and their children, had not experienced anything like the wave of anti-Semitism that now engulfed them. Viennese Jews were inundated with hate mail. Jewish tombstones and Jewish-owned buildings were defaced. For Jewish children who met with insulting remarks in schools, it was usually their first direct confrontation with anti-Semitism. The worst moment occurred in May, when activist Beate Klarsfeld arrived in Vienna from Germany to speak at an anti-Waldheim rally, and Orthodox Jews were physically attacked. The community as a whole was in a state of agitation and confusion and divided over the question of its own stance, with a noticeable generation gap. The younger generation urged a self-assured, assertive bearing, while older members, in most cases Holocaust survivors, pleaded for moderation and prudence. The president of the community, Ivan Hacker, took a position similar to Wiesenthal's, not supporting Waldheim but trying not to inflame the situation. An Auschwitz survivor himself, Hacker was a longtime B'nai B'rith president who had worked hard to foster dialogue between Jews and non-Jews and now saw his efforts to achieve mutual understanding threatened.

The community was uncertain about how to represent itself but felt it could not ignore the spate of anti-Semitic remarks made by campaigning politicians or the overt anti-Semitic attitudes of some newspapers, especially the *Kronenzeitung,* the most popular Austrian tabloid, and the *Presse,* a liberal-conservative journal. Still, it was only after the election that representatives of the Jewish community made public statements advising caution against the upsurge in anti-Semitism, which "disquieted the Jewish community and also endangered democracy."

While the official Jewish community tried to keep a low profile, many individual members served on public protest committees. One such body was Neues Osterreich (New Austria), a group composed of intellectuals, many of them Jews, which organized demonstrations, lectures, and symposia, and published a booklet documenting Waldheim's years in the Balkans.

Many Jews, shaken by events, began questioning whether they should even remain in the country. Over the previous ten years the community had developed a degree of self-confidence and security; now suddenly it underwent a collective emotional crisis. Young people in particular searched for answers to the dilemma of their status and their future. The situation calmed down somewhat after the presidential election, but it left Jews alert and fearful. Austrian officials tried to ease tensions through various actions, but many Jews doubted that the wounds could ever be healed.

Anti-Semitism

Several incidents in recent Austrian history had revealed the depth and persistence of anti-Semitism in the country, extending into the highest levels of society. In 1975 Simon Wiesenthal was severely attacked by the then chancellor, Bruno Kreisky, himself a Jew, for disclosing the SS past of Friedrich Peter, chairman of the Freedom party, with whom the Socialists formed a government in later years. By attacking Wiesenthal, Kreisky secured for himself the general approval of the population, and, however unintentionally, opened the way to public expression of anti-Semitism. The acquittals handed down in a number of war-crimes cases met with popular approval, and in 1985 Defense Minister Friedhelm Frischenschlager won support when he went to Graz to welcome home Walter Reder, a convicted war criminal released from a life sentence in Italy.

However, prior to the Waldheim affair, no major political party had openly appealed to voters' anti-Semitic sentiments, certainly not in such blatant fashion. When the secretary-general of the conservatives, Michael Graff, spoke of the "dishonorable fellows" (a medieval insult against Jews) from the WJC and said that "feelings wished by nobody were aroused," his words were viewed as provocative. Any attacks against Waldheim were characterized as "Mafia tactics" by world Jewry. Although Austrians generally differentiated between Jews and Israelis, this year saw increasing use of the phrase "world Jewish conspiracy," especially by journalists and diplomats who felt that Waldheim was being punished for his policies as secretary-general of the UN by a united front of Israelis, Jews, and Americans. In discussing the topic, the term "American" was usually used as a synonym for "Jew." The preferred wording was actually "certain groups on the East Coast," which everyone understood referred to the Jews. Waldheim himself never stopped pointing out how the American people had loved him when he was at the

UN, except the Jewish press on the East Coast, which started a campaign against him. In the same breath, he assured the "suffering Austrian Jews of his protection from the understandable rage of the Austrian population."

In an attempt to gauge the actual prevalence of anti-Semitism in the country, a number of public-opinion surveys were conducted during the year. Based on these surveys, it was possible to conclude that 15–20 percent of the population harbored strong anti-Semitic feelings. Depending on how each survey defined anti-Semitic attitudes, the figures ranged from a low of 10 percent to a high of 25 percent. The overall assessments were arrived at on the basis of responses to specific items such as these: 15 percent said they would prefer to have no Jews in Austria; approximately 17 percent thought that things went better for Austria after the Nazis carried out the "final solution of the Jewish problem"; 23 percent wanted Jews barred from public office; 22 percent regarded Jews as "unsympathetic"; 38 percent believed that Jews were responsible for their own persecution; 48 percent believed that Jews had a disproportionate amount of economic and political influence; and 7 percent experienced physical revulsion when shaking hands with a Jew. (The figures are from polls conducted by the Gallup, Fessel, Ifes, and Imas Institute.)

In all the surveys, older people expressed more anti-Semitism than younger ones; university graduates displayed less general prejudice and the lowest level of hatred of Jews. Geographically, Vienna showed up more positively than the provinces. Although comparisons of surveys over time show a steady, if slow, decline in anti-Semitism, a distinct upsurge occurred following Waldheim's election. It seemed to calm down a bit by the end of the year, but was still a worrisome phenomenon.

Relations with Israel

The Waldheim affair threatened a breach in relations with Israel, which had improved considerably since Chancellor Bruno Kreisky, an outspoken critic of Israeli policies, left office in 1983. Chancellor Sinowatz related to Israel much more even-handedly than his predecessor, though the government continued its support of the Palestinian cause.

Despite the urging of the WJC and others, President Chaim Herzog and Prime Minister Shimon Peres of Israel both advocated a noncommittal, moderate course with regard to Waldheim. Foreign Minister Shamir, however, was blunt in his approach, telling an interviewer in May—after the first vote—that the election of Waldheim would be "a tragedy" and making other statements that many Austrians viewed as undue interference in their country's affairs. Following the election, Israel recalled Ambassador Michael Elizur, who in any case was due to retire, but replaced him with a lower-level official, a chargé d'affaires. In protest, Austria called back Ambassador Otto Pleinert from Tel Aviv for consultation. He returned to his post in Israel after a few weeks, but his term of office was nearing its end and it was uncertain whether Austria would replace him. Meanwhile, the absence of an Israeli ambassador in Vienna was a source of regret to many Austrians.

Apart from these diplomatic difficulties, contacts in other areas were numerous and mutually gratifying. Prominent non-Jewish and Jewish Austrians, including government officials, served on the boards of various societies supporting institutions in Israel, such as Tel Aviv University, Tel Hashomer Hospital, the Technion in Haifa, and the Weizmann Institute.

Austria was especially interested in new technologies being developed in Israel and helped to finance a number of joint projects. The Technion in Haifa and the Vienna Technical University undertook joint research in nuclear reactor safety and organic manure yields. Future plans included the participation of Israeli scientists in conferences on laser technology, inorganic chemistry, and mechanics. Tel Aviv University planned joint projects on solar energy and reactor safety with the Vienna Technical University.

In the aftermath of the presidential election, efforts were made by various groups to improve relations between the two countries. Christian-Jewish associations stood out in this effort, organizing pilgrimages to Israel, followed up with discussions and lectures about their experiences. A group of Israeli journalists visited Austria at the time of the elections to parliament. Noted Austrian authors Helmut Butterweck, Gunter Seidl, H.C. Artmann, and J. Kaiser lectured in Israel on their own works and works of other Austrian writers. Labor unions arranged group tours to Israel for teenagers, enabling them to become familiar with the country. Asher Ben Nathan, former Israeli ambassador to France and Germany, lectured on Israeli foreign policy at the Renner Institute in Vienna to a large and appreciative audience. The Linz municipal theater presented the play *Ghetto,* by Israeli playwright Yehoshua Sobol, performed by a company from Haifa.

The Austria-Israel Association organized various events in 1986, though the Waldheim affair cast a definite shadow on its mood. The association's president, Walter Schwimmer, a member of the Conservative party, vehemently defended Waldheim and his behavior, which naturally created tensions within the organization. Schwimmer also found fault with Israel's failure to appoint a new ambassador to Austria and made critical remarks about the actions of the WJC. All of this contributed to a sense of discomfort among Jewish members of the association.

Despite the strain of the situation, Austrian politicians, artists, scientists, and journalists attended the traditional Independence Day reception given by the Israel embassy in May.

Christian-Jewish Relations

Following the various election campaigns, Christian bodies in Austria made concerted efforts to improve relations with the Jewish community. The Cartellverband (CV, Confederate Association), a conservative Christian association of university graduates, organized a "Jewish Week," with the goal of educating its members about Jews and Judaism. The program featured lectures, discussions, and a comprehensive book exhibition. A highlight of the week was a panel discussion including former CV president Rudolf Kirchschläger, E. Ludwig Ehrlich, executive director of B'nai B'rith, and a group of Catholic and Jewish students. Kirschläger warned that the centuries-old tradition of anti-Semitism in the Church could not be wiped out in a generation, noting that efforts in this direction had begun only after the Holocaust. The young speakers deplored anti-Semitism as well as urging closer contact with Jews and increased learning about Jews and Judaism. The program was shown on TV and drew considerable attention.

Another significant interfaith event was the "joint hour of meditation" held on the eve of Yom Kippur, in which the newly appointed archbishop of Vienna, Hermann Cardinal Groer, participated with Chief Rabbi Paul Chaim Eisenberg and other dignitaries. The program was initiated by the Laymen's Council and Catholic Action. The latter's new president, Paul Schulmeister, a leading figure in the movement for Christian-Jewish reconciliation, had been an active fighter against anti-Semitism for many years.

Cardinal Groer accepted an invitation to visit the Jewish Community Center, which was the first visit ever by a churchman of his rank. That evening, Franz Cardinal König, former archbishop of Vienna, speaking at a ceremony at the Jewish Community Center at which a group of Righteous Gentiles were honored by the Israeli institution Yad Vashem, expressed his solidarity with the Jewish people. Meetings and events for the promotion of Christian-Jewish dialogue took place not only in large public settings such as the above, but also in smaller, less formal frameworks. Hedwig Wahle, for example, of the Sisters of Sion, was very active in this field. Also, numerous adult education courses offered opportunities for increasing knowledge about Judaism.

Several exhibitions mounted during the year were on themes related to Jews in Austria, Judaism, or anti-Semitism. The opening of an Anne Frank exhibit in September drew many visitors from abroad as well as prominent Austrians. Unfortunately, police had to be called because of a disturbance by neo-Nazi groups. A program of discussions and lectures on Judaism and anti-Semitism was offered in conjunction with the exhibit. In a show titled "Quiet Answer—Early Warning," the well-known Austrian painter George Chaimovitz exhibited paintings and drawings relating to neo-Nazism.

CSCE Meeting

Vienna was host to the Third Conference on Security and Cooperation in Europe (CSCE) beginning in November. This follow-up meeting to the 1975 Helsinki accords was attended by representatives of the 33 European countries, the United States, and Canada who were the signatories to the Helsinki Final Act. The conference, which was expected to continue until July 1987, if not longer, focused on security questions in Europe, on cooperation in economic, scientific, cultural, and other fields, and on human rights issues.

Activities outside the official plenum drew more popular attention and interest than the official program's lengthy speeches and diplomatic maneuvering. Among the many groups that arrived from all parts of Europe to plead for specific causes, Jewish activists for human rights in the Soviet Union were especially visible. Fifty Jewish students from England joined with Austrian Jewish students to stage an "anti-conference" at which they demanded the release of Jewish prisoners in the USSR and the right of emigration for Soviet Jews. The high point of the event was a press conference of the "International Resistance Movement," attended by such personalities as the French playwright Eugene Ionesco, the French Jewish writer and painter Marek Halter, Soviet dissident Yuri Orlov, and many more. In addition to the distinguished panel, the audience heard long-distance telephone conversations with Yves Montand in France and Natan Sharansky in Israel.

Participants in this conference were impressed and moved by the pleas of Soviet Jewish émigrés who came from Israel to speak in behalf of relatives in the USSR: mothers of children who had been waiting for up to 15 years for emigration permits; fathers like Vladimir Magarik, whose son had been sentenced to 3 years in a labor camp; sons like Alexander Slepak, whose father, Vladimir, one of the founders of the Moscow Helsinki group, had been waiting 17 years for an exit permit, 5 of them as a prisoner in Siberia. In addition to calling international attention to their plight, the émigrés also sought direct contact with Soviet officials. This time, in contrast to earlier conferences, Soviet delegates to the CSCE were more amenable to conversation. Thus, Ilana Friedmann, Ida Nudel's sister, succeeded—after a two-day hunger strike—in gaining a meeting with the Soviet delegation.

The Vienna Jewish community arranged its own press conference on the situation of Soviet Jewry on November 3. The participants were the leaders of Soviet Jewry movements in a number of countries, among them: Avraham Harman of Israel; Claude Kelman and Annemarie Revco of France; Barbara Stern of Canada; Lynn Singer of the United States; Werner Rom of Switzerland; and Stephen Roth and June Jacobs of Great Britain. The Austrian representatives were Chief Rabbi Paul Chaim Eisenberg and Heinz Kienzl, director general of the Austrian National Bank.

The Soviets, understandably eager to present their own side of the picture, arranged a press conference at which four Soviet emigrants expressed their wish to return to the Soviet Union. The Soviets also announced that new emigration regulations would go into effect in 1987, though what their impact would be was not immediately clear. (See the article on the Soviet Union elsewhere in this volume.)

JEWISH COMMUNITY

Demography

An estimated 12,000 to 15,000 Jews lived in Austria—mostly in Vienna—of whom 6,200 were registered in the Israelitische Kultusgemeinde, the organized Jewish community. An additional 4,000 Jews were émigrés from the Soviet Union, some of whom had gone to Israel and returned to Austria, others persons who had arrived in Austria in transit to other destinations but who never left the country. There was also a sizable population of assimilated Jews married to non-Jewish partners. Most of the Jews living in Vienna had themselves come from Hungary and other Eastern-bloc countries, or their parents had done so, in the 50s and 60s. Although they too considered Vienna a transit country when they arrived, they ended up settling there permanently. Jews who had lived in Austria prior to 1938 and returned after the war accounted for only a tiny fraction of the community.

Communal Activities

The executive council of the Kultusgemeinde was composed of 24 members, representing varying backgrounds and ideologies. The strongest faction, with eight seats, the so-called Alternatives, was a coalition of disparate groups, including Herut, Mapam, and the Union of Jewish Victims of Nazi Regimes, the Wiesenthal group. Poale Zion, the Labor Zionists, had five seats, and the Younger Generation, a politically mixed group of professionals and artists, mostly under 40, had four seats. The Union of Sephardic Jews, chaired by Galibov Gregori, had one seat. Its members were mainly Georgian Jews from the USSR, most of whom lived in poor circumstances. The group helped its members with funds that came partly from the community treasury and partly as donations from wealthy individuals. Orthodox Jews were represented on the council by four groups: Mizrachi, headed by Rabbi Izhak Ehrenberg and Prof. Josef Grunberger (three seats); Kehal Israel (Agudah), led by Rabbi Chaim Grünfeld and Simon Moskowits (one seat); Mahsike Hadat and Ohel Moshe (one seat each).

The Jewish community in Salzburg had somewhat more than 100 members, Graz, 80; Innsbruck and Linz, 70 members each. The five communities formed the Federal Board of Jewish Communities in Austria, which met once a year in a general assembly. The president of the board was Ivan Hacker; the vice president, Anton Winter. The Jewish community maintained excellent relations with Austrian authorities, as evidenced, for example, by the presence of both Chancellor Vranitzky and the vice mayor of Vienna, Erhart Busek, at the Kol Nidre service in Vienna's main synagogue.

Vienna's chief rabbi was Chaim Paul Eisenberg, whose father held the office from 1948 to his death in 1983. Among other functions, the chief rabbi delivered regular talks on state television on the occasion of Jewish holidays. In addition to the main synagogue there were nine Jewish prayer houses in Vienna, including a Sephardic one. Recently, one of the older prayer houses that had been badly damaged in November 1938, on *Kristallnacht,* was restored and began serving the Agudah community.

Part of the community tax paid by Viennese Jews was used for the care of 700,000 graves in the two Jewish sections of Vienna's central cemetery. The larger and older of these, which had its first Jewish burial in 1879, was the final resting place of many illustrious figures, among them playwright Arthur Schnitzler and novelist Friedrich Torberg. From 1917 on, with a few exceptions, Jewish funerals took place in the new section. Since the Jewish community was unable to look after all the graves, many of which were badly neglected, the municipality of Vienna had assumed responsibility for their maintenance.

The communal old-age home, which had an adjoining acute-care facility, housed approximately 100 persons. Upkeep of the home was a heavy burden on the community, since many of the residents were on social welfare and needed supplementary support.

While the Jewish community was small in number, it had a busy organizational life and a varied program of cultural and social activities. Among the many organizations, the Zionists were particularly visible, and in the Zionist Federation, the Shomer Hatzair and B'nai Akiva youth groups, which arranged frequent joint excursions to Israel, were the most active. The Union of Jewish Students was vigorous in organizing political protest. Members of B'nai B'rith's youth division, the Maimonides Lodge, established in 1985 by the Zwi Perez Chajes Lodge, also took part in protests against anti-Semitism during this critical year.

Among the associations whose activities enlivened cultural and social life in Vienna was the Keren Hayesod, presided over by Anton Winter, and its youth division, chaired by Victor Wagner. Keren Kayemet (JNF), led by Friedrich Wiesel, who also headed B'nai B'rith in Austria, offered regular lectures on topics of the day. WIZO, the Women's Zionist Organization, arranged regular afternoon teas accompanied by artistic performances. Other active groups, with their presidents, were the following: Friends of Tel Aviv University—Hella Gertner; Friends of Tel Hashomer Hospital—Jadzia Gertner; Friends of the Haifa Technion—Simon Moskovits; Friends of the Hebrew University of Jerusalem—Prince Schwarzenberg; Friends of Alyn—Sara Moskovits.

Education and Culture

Of the approximately 1,200 Jewish children aged 3–18 living in Vienna, fewer than half were receiving a Jewish education. The Zwi Perez Chajes School, one of two state-recognized Jewish all-day schools, had 180 pupils, 25 percent of them of Russian or Sephardic origin. School fees for these children had to be reduced in many cases or were paid either by the parents' association or by the community. (This school, by the way, when faced with the dilemma of having to hang a framed photograph of the new president of Austria in every classroom—the standard practice throughout the country—or risk appearing unpatriotic, found a Solomonic solution: it decided to display the coat of arms of the Republic of Austria instead.)

Talmud Torah Mahsike Hadat had an enrollment of 120 children up to age 14, mostly from Orthodox families. It offered a business course for girls as well as a kindergarten and a *heder*. The organization had also established four kindergartens elsewhere and three Talmud Torah schools.

The Lubavitch organization, headed by Rabbi Yakov Biderman, was actively engaged in caring for the needs of Russian Jews living in Vienna, among other things running a community center, two kindergartens, and four day nurseries for children of school age, with a total enrollment of nearly 100 children.

The Judaica Institute of the University of Vienna had approximately 300 students, most of them non-Jews interested in Jewish affairs and history. Regarded as one of the most important centers of Jewish teaching and research in Europe, the department's courses included Talmud and rabbinic literature, Jewish philosophy, Bible and biblical archaeology, European Jewish history, Yiddish, modern Hebrew, and Jewish art. The institute was directed by Prof. Kurt Schubert and listed on its faculty such renowned scholars as Jacob Allerhand, G. Stemberger, and N. Vielmetti.

The Jewish Museum, established in 1982 and directed by Professor Schubert, was located in Eisenstadt, some 80 kilometers east of Vienna. Among the year's visitors to its displays on Jewish history in Austria was German president Richard von Weizsäcker. The annual symposium sponsored by the museum in cooperation with the Vienna University Judaica Institute was on the subject of Jewish identity.

The 3,000 objects in the Max Berger Judaica Collection, located in Vienna, made it the most comprehensive private collection of Judaica in Europe. The handsome apartment in which the collection was housed also contained an extensive library, a manuscript collection, and an archive of prewar Central European photo-documents.

Simon Wiesenthal's Documentation Center in Vienna was the primary source of information on Nazism and neo-Nazism. Hundreds of journalists from around the world visited Wiesenthal in 1986 in search of information relating to the Waldheim affair.

The Jewish Welcome Center, a branch of the Austrian Tourist Office, helped Jewish tourists from abroad to become acquainted with Jewish life in Vienna. The center's director was Leon Zelman.

The varied life of the community was reflected in its range of publications. *Die Gemeinde* was the official community monthly, sent to every member. *Illustrierte Neue Welt,* founded in 1897 by Theodor Herzl, was a monthly devoted to strengthening ties between Austria and Israel and between Jews and non-Jews. Edited by journalists Joanna Nittenberg and Marta Halpert, the periodical was read by many non-Jews as well as by Austrians living abroad. Individual organizations published their own organs, mostly on a quarterly basis: Heruth (affiliated with the Israeli Herut party); the Union of the Working Class (Poale Zion); the Union of Jewish Victims (Simon Wiesenthal group); the General Zionists; and Mizrachi (Religious Zionists). *Schomernik* was published by Hashomer Hatzair, from time to time. *Nudnik,* a newspaper produced by university students, was published whenever events warranted it. *Das Jüdische Echo,* an annual edited by Leon Zelman, contained articles from Austria and abroad on cultural subjects.

Personalia

Among prominent Austrian Jews who died in 1986 were Siegfried Lazar, director of the Jewish community and member of Poale Zion, aged 64; Heinz Wagner, Keren Hayesod leader and member of the community board, aged 62; Gerhard Coron, industrial entrepreneur, active in various organizations, especially Keren Hayesod, aged 82; Lily Goldfinger, active in the old-age home, aged 72; Stella Klein-Löw, Socialist delegate to the communal general assembly, teacher, and author, aged 82; Moses Löw, Socialist party leader, aged 87; Chanan Reem, director of Keren Hayesod, aged 63; and Heinrich Sussmann, well-known painter, a member of the resistance in France during World War II, aged 82.

JOANNA NITTENBERG

Federal Republic of Germany

National Affairs

OUTWARDLY, AT LEAST, 1986 WAS a year of relative political calm and economic stability for West Germany, holding out the prospect that in 1987 Chancellor Helmut Kohl would easily win reelection to a second term. Still, several controversial issues simmering just below the surface threatened to upset the equilibrium: nuclear energy and environmental concerns, domestic terrorism and violence, and the direction of German foreign policy, specifically, relations with the United States and Eastern Europe. There were also some lingering political scandals, and the Nazi chapter in German history became an issue as academics and politicians debated opposing views of that period.

Responding to concern about pollution of the environment due to a growing number of accidents in chemical plants, the government appointed its first federal minister of environment, Frankfurt mayor Walter Wallmann. In December the cabinet agreed to take legal action against chemical-plant violations. Thousands of people took part in public protests throughout the year against nuclear power projects.

The two-year-old scandal concerning tax breaks given to corporations and prominent individuals for political contributions remained in the news, though there were no new dramatic revelations. In May Chancellor Kohl was cleared of a perjury charge arising from a parliamentary inquiry into party financing. The most significant development, however, came in July, when the West German supreme court ruled unconstitutional the law making corporate donations to political parties tax deductible. The ruling embarrassed Kohl's Christian Democratic Union (CDU) and the allied Christian Social Union (CSU) and Free Democratic party (FDP), parties that had supported enactment of the law the year before, amid a scandal involving donations by the Flick industrial concern. The scandal had led to the prosecution of two former economics ministers and a former Flick general manager, and the trial was still in progress at year's end.

Kohl's conservative CDU maintained its position in state and local elections. The second half of the year saw the parties gearing up for the general elections set for January 1987. As the CDU and CSU made increasing use of anti-Communist, patriotic, and nationalist themes to attract conservative voters, critical observers termed this a "*Wende,*" a turn in the government's basic policy and attitude in the direction of a patriotic and nationalist revival. In their public pronouncements, representatives of the three national coalition parties stressed the need to increase awareness of German national values, to step from the shadows of the Nazi past, and to restore strong national pride, without which the nation was said to have no chance of meeting future challenges.

Chancellor Kohl, who was 56 years old, had repeatedly used the phrase "the blessing of late birth," and earned public criticism for it. The phrase was understood to exclude personal responsibility for Nazi crimes and to imply that the new Germany was not to be blamed for the crimes of the old. As he explained in the Bundestag (federal parliament) in December, what he actually intended was to dramatize to the young his generation's commitment, because of their own experience as children with state barbarity, to preventing a recurrence.

The question of state indemnification for individual victims of Nazi persecution who had received inadequate payments or none at all under existing law was debated by the federal parliament in June. The Social Democrats (SPD) and the Greens demanded the establishment of a special fund to satisfy legitimate claims, including those of Gypsies, slave workers, euthanasia and sterilization victims, homosexuals, and handicapped persons, as well as the "Mengele twins," the victims of Josef Mengele's medical experiments at Auschwitz. At the request of the Bundestag, the government prepared a comprehensive report on individual indemnification payments and reparations effected by the state up to that time. It showed that as of the end of 1985 a total of DM 77 billion had been paid, including about 60 billion marks under the federal indemnification law, 3.9 billion under the restitution law, and 3.5 billion under the reparations pact with the State of Israel, and that over DM 100 billion would be paid by the end of the century.

The government concluded that no new legislative action was required, that in fact the state had taken pains to guarantee satisfactory payments to all groups of Nazi victims, including the Mengele twins. (The latter, the report even suggested, had not been used by the physician for criminal pseudomedical experiments but only for "measurements.") The SPD and the Greens voiced profound disappointment with the report, and even the FDP, a coalition partner, was critical. The SPD renewed its demand that an initial fund of DM 250 million be created for payments to underprivileged Nazi victims, but no action had been taken by year's end. Independently, since it did not fall under federal German jurisdiction, the West Berlin House of Representatives (parliament) decided in June to establish a special hardship fund to aid victims of Nazi injustice in that city who had not received adequate compensation under existing laws. In September the Bonn parliament adopted an amendment to the federal law on social security making Nazi victims eligible for public assistance on the same terms as war victims.

In a related matter, early in the year Deutsche Bank, after taking over the Flick industrial concern, paid $2 million to the Conference on Jewish Material Claims Against Germany, as restitution to wartime Jewish slave workers.

The slight upward trend in the West German economy continued over the year. The gross national output rose by 2.5 percent, as it had in 1985, and national income rose by 6.3 percent, the highest since 1979. Unemployment figures showed an overall drop of 76,000 to 2.22 million, or from 9.3 to 9.0 percent of the total work force.

Reappraisal of the Nazi Past

Debate over interpretations of the Nazi era intensified, possibly aroused by the previous year's observance of the 40th anniversary of Germany's defeat in World War II. Christian Democratic leaders continued to express unhappiness with the speech delivered by President Richard von Weizsäcker, himself a CDU member, on May 8, 1985, the anniversary of Germany's defeat. In that address, the president urged Germans not to forget Nazi crimes and asserted that by the end of the war many Germans knew about the mass killings of Jews and others. To the government's dismay, over 1.5 million copies of von Weizsäcker's speech had been sold or otherwise circulated within a year, and it had been translated into 12 languages. Social Democratic leaders, on the other hand, declared the speech to be one of outstanding importance, expressing what they believed should be the basic outlook of every German.

Campaign oratory was not the only forum for this debate. The government's movement rightward and its attempt to dissociate itself from the Nazi past received support from rightist German historians, as part of a "*Historikerstreit,*" or dispute of the historians. A leader of the revisionist school, Ernst Nolte, 61, a renowned German historian and researcher on fascism, published an article in June in the leading daily *Frankfurter Allgemeine Zeitung* in which he accused critics of Nazism of ignoring the simple fact that what the Nazis had done others had done before—"with the sole exception of the gassing procedures." Asserting that the uniqueness of the Holocaust was questionable, he attempted to compare the Stalinist labor camps and Nazi concentration camps. "Didn't the Gulag Archipelago precede Auschwitz? Did not Auschwitz, in its roots, perhaps stem from a past which had not actually been past?" Nolte asked. Perhaps, he suggested, Auschwitz resulted from the Nazis' fear of the Soviets, and "the so-called extermination of Jews during the Nazi Reich" may in fact have been a defensive response to the continued Bolshevist threat of annihilation. Nolte also referred to the alleged "declaration of war" made by Chaim Weizmann and world Jewry against the Nazi Reich in 1939, and Jewish support of Great Britain in her battle against Hitler, suggesting that Hitler had been justified in treating the Jews as "prisoners-of-war."

In a similar vein, historian Andreas Hillgruber, in a volume of essays titled *Two Kinds of Destruction: The Shattering of the German Reich and the End of European Jewry,* drew parallels between "the annihilating capacity of Communism" and Nazism, and voiced respect for the Nazis' desperate battle on the eastern front to preserve the German Reich and prevent Russian revenge orgies. The fact that the extermination camps in the east continued to operate until the very end of the war was viewed as incidental.

Among critics of the newly expressed views was Frankfurt philosophy professor Jürgen Habermas, a liberal sociologist, who denounced the apologetic tendencies and what he regarded as "questionable revisionism." Bielefeld history professor Jürgen Kocka decried the suggestion that the Holocaust could be viewed as a logical, if preemptive, act of self-defense against an alleged threat from the Bolshevist east. Historian Hans Mommsen saw the dispute as an expression of a latent crisis in the German people's feelings about their own political legitimacy, brought on by the involuntary confrontation with the Nazi past in 1985, on the 40th anniversary of their country's defeat. Conservative circles were trying to straighten the nation's back by stressing positive national traits, Mommsen suggested. At the same time, they were trying to come to grips with the Nazi past by separating it from the rest of German history and presenting it as an unavoidable disaster.

Terrorism and Extremism

Several significant acts of politically motivated violence were committed in West Germany in 1986, the work of both left-wing domestic groups and Arab radicals. While Chancellor Kohl maintained that West German and other European terrorists were receiving training and weapons in the Middle East, the government was unable to offer proof of direct links between European and Arab terrorist activity in West Germany.

In March a bomb exploded in the West Berlin offices of the German-Arab Friendship Society (Deutsch-Arabische Gesellschaft), injuring nine persons and causing considerable damage. In November two Jordanians of Palestinian origin were convicted of the crime: Ahmed Hasi was sentenced to 14 years in prison; Farouk Salameh to 13 years. When the court also concluded that the Syrian embassy in East Berlin had supplied the bomb, the Bonn government promptly downgraded its political ties with Syria, ordering Syrian diplomats to leave the country, refusing to appoint a new German ambassador to Damascus when the incumbent's term ended, and freezing economic aid to that country.

Hasi had actually been arrested the previous April in connection with the bombing of a West Berlin discotheque frequented by U.S. troops, but the police failed to find enough evidence for his conviction. An American serviceman and two non-American civilians were killed in the disco attack, and 230 persons, many of them U.S. citizens, were injured. An anonymous caller to a news agency in West Berlin said the bombing was the work of the German left-wing extremist Rote Armee Fraktion (RAF, Red Army Faction), but a caller to another news agency claimed the attack for an Arab anti-Western group calling itself "Inshallah." In London, in November, Hasi's brother, Nezar Hindawi, was found guilty of a bomb attempt on an El Al passenger plane the previous April. West Berlin police claimed to have evidence that he had also been involved in planning the attack on the German-Arab center in Berlin.

Based on intelligence reports that the Libyan People's Bureau was somehow involved in the terror, the United States asked the Bonn government to carry out reprisals against Libya. West Germany, however, like other European allies, had thus far resisted U.S. pressure to join in economic sanctions against Libya, initiated by President Reagan after terrorist attacks on the Rome and Vienna airports late in 1985. Bonn had also been reluctant to approve the American air attack on Libya in April, following which thousands of West Germans—mobilized by various peace groups and the Greens—gathered in a number of cities to protest the American operation.

The left-wing domestic terrorist group RAF was behind the car-bombing murder, in July, of a senior executive of the German Siemens electronics group, Karl-Heinz Beckurts, and his driver, near Munich. Police said the name of the victim, a nuclear physicist, appeared on a list of RAF "targets" seized in 1984. The assassination was seen as part of a war of intimidation aimed at shaking up the country's power elite and damaging the "imperialist system." In October a senior official of the West German foreign ministry, Gerold von Braunmühl, was shot dead outside his home in Bonn. Again, the RAF claimed responsibility, as it did for most of a series of bomb attacks carried out against arms and electronics firms, power lines, courthouses, and other public buildings in the summer and fall, which caused considerable damage. Several RAF members were brought to trial and sentenced to long prison terms. In December the Bundestag voted for new measures designed to prevent and punish terrorist activities.

Neo-Nazi groups were also active during the year. A "Rudolph Hess Liberation Commando," believed to belong to the militant right, claimed responsibility in October for a bomb attack on a building outside Spandau prison in West Berlin, where Hitler's deputy was serving a life sentence.

The most active and militant neo-Nazi group was the Freiheitliche Deutsche Arbeiterpartei (FAP, Free German Labor party), which was founded in 1970 and had about 400 full members nationwide in 1986. Almost unknown before the outlawing of the Action Front of National Socialists (ANS) in 1983, the FAP subsequently attracted many former ANS members and set up new branches in various parts of the country. Although the group's attempts to win seats in a number of municipal and state legislatures had met with no success to date, its activities—including dissemination of stickers and leaflets with antidemocratic, anti-Jewish, and racist contents, anti-Semitic graffiti, and the use of violence against political opponents—increasingly alarmed state agencies. While the government declined to outlaw the group, local courts convicted a number of FAP members for illegal propaganda activities, possession of small arms, and violence. Trade unions, the Communist party, Young Socialists, the Greens, and the Union of Nazi Victims were among those joining in public demonstrations against FAP rallies.

Anti-Semitism

The extent of anti-Semitism in West Germany continued to be a subject of dispute, with rightists generally minimizing its existence and leftists and many Jews claiming that both latent anti-Semitism and open anti-Jewish attitudes had intensified.

The subject was debated in the Bundestag in February, though only a few dozen of the more than 500 deputies were present. CDU and CSU speakers said the debate was unnecessary, that there had only been a few isolated incidents of anti-Semitism. Chancellor Kohl denied any revival of the problem, even claiming that the vast majority of the German people, particularly the young, were immune to anti-Semitism. By contrast, spokesmen for the SPD, the FDP, and the Greens voiced deep alarm over growing anti-Jewish expressions, calling for increased vigilance and determined counteraction.

In April the chairman of the West Berlin Jewish community, Heinz Galinski, said during a Warsaw Ghetto commemoration that not since 1945 had Jews in Germany encountered as much hostility as in the recent past. What he found most disturbing, he said, was that while there had always been latent anti-Semitism, anti-Jewish attitudes were now being voiced openly, often by political figures. Galinski was alluding to a series of incidents that had only recently occurred. Early in the year, Hermann Fellner, a CSU deputy in the Bundestag, commented that Jews who had been slave laborers in Nazi enterprises had "neither a legal nor a moral basis for their claims," and that Jews were "quick to step forth whenever money starts to jingle in German cash registers." The response of Fellner's CSU party was merely to chide him for his "unhappy" choice of words, echoed by Chancellor Kohl calling Fellner's statement "foolish." To Galinski and other Jews, however, the words represented "the most monstrous insult to Jews ever voiced by a member of the federal parliament."

The CDU mayor of the Rhenish provincial town of Korschenbroich, Count Wilderich von Spee, 58, told the town's finance committee in January that he would have to "kill a few rich Jews" in order to balance the local budget. The mayor subsequently resigned under pressure, but the public prosecutor failed to act on charges of insult and incitement of hatred brought by the Jewish community, instead ordering the mayor to pay a fine of DM 90,000. CDU officials in other towns supported him and warned that overreaction to the mayor's words could breed new anti-Semitism. The Korschenbroich episode was followed by one in Frankfurt, where Günter Dürr, a leading Social Democrat in the Frankfurt city council, called former Israeli prime minister Menachem Begin a "murderer, terrorist, and fascist." Dürr later apologized, but Jewish leaders saw the statement as yet more evidence of the loosening of restraints.

Leading FDP Bundestag deputy Hildegard Hamm-Brücher revealed that she had received piles of hate mail after presenting the Theodor Heuss Foundation's Heuss Prize to Jewish community leader Werner Nachmann. She had also received letters after the Fellner and von Spee incidents, supporting the politicians for telling the truth.

Public debate continued on Rainer Werner Fassbinder's controversial play *Garbage, the City, and Death.* After its performance was prevented in Frankfurt in 1985, following primarily Jewish protests, attempts were made in 1986 to stage readings in Cologne and elsewhere, but these too were halted. The Frankfurt supreme court ruled in April that the play contained "clearly derogatory and stereotype-like anti-

Semitic tendencies," after suit was brought by ten Jewish citizens on the ground that they had been insulted by its contents. Performance of another anti-Jewish play, *The Sages of Ararat,* which denounced Jews both as communists and capitalists and charged them with the murder of their own brothers during the Nazi era, was called off before its premiere at Aachen University, following pressure by Nazi victims, Christian-Jewish cooperation groups, and local political parties.

Another manifestation of anti-Semitism was the reappearance, after several years, of a board game in which players send Jews to the gas chamber. The game was reportedly produced by an American neo-Nazi group and mailed to schools and student groups by neo-Nazis in various parts of Germany. In addition, numerous Jewish cemeteries and memorial sites were desecrated, some of them by vandals identified as militant neo-Nazis. Gravestones were overturned or destroyed and anti-Jewish slogans smeared on them. A number of Jewish communal centers and synagogues were similarly defaced.

A public-opinion survey was carried out in March by the Institute for Demoscopy at Allensbach, on behalf of the illustrated weekly *Stern,* to answer the question "How anti-Semitic are the Germans?" Fifteen percent of those surveyed professed anti-Jewish sentiments, and 6 percent were openly anti-Semitic. While the responses to a series of wide-ranging questions were interpreted by the researchers as showing no increase in anti-Semitism over previous years, and perhaps even a slight decline, the survey revealed that most Germans wanted to forget the past and not be reminded of Nazi crimes any longer. Jewish community leaders were not reassured by the survey findings. In their view, so long as any anti-Semitism existed, more needed to be done to counteract it, by legal means as well as through education.

Nazi Trials

According to the annual report of the Central Agency for the Investigation of Nazi Crimes at Ludwigsburg (established in 1958), some 1,300 cases were pending before West German courts and 100 or so cases awaited preliminary investigation. The agency was still searching for a dozen or so persons accused of major crimes, but the average age of these individuals was 75, and at least six of them were believed to be living in South America. Files on several new suspects were opened in the course of the year, mainly as a result of documents provided by Polish authorities, but it was doubtful that further trials would result. In general, because of the death and aging of both suspects and witnesses, and difficulties in obtaining reliable evidence, fewer cases ended in convictions. An agency spokesman noted that eventually the public prosecutors would be forced to stop investigating "on biological grounds," and after that the agency would serve strictly as a center of research and documentation on Nazi crimes. In recent years, in fact, an increasing number of scholars, historians, and students from Germany and abroad had visited the agency to examine its files and documents.

The summary report issued by the agency indicated that between the end of

World War II and January 1986 West German public prosecutors had investigated a total of 90,921 persons suspected of Nazi crimes, of whom 6,479 had been convicted and sentenced: 12 to death, 160 to life imprisonment, 6,192 to varying prison terms, and 114 to payment of fines. Proceedings against 83,140 suspects had been closed without convictions.

A report on the prosecution of Nazi criminals in West Germany compiled by the federal justice ministry in Bonn and published in August essentially confirmed the figures released by the Central Agency in Ludwigsburg but also included trials of Nazi criminals conducted by non-German legal authorities. Thus, American, British, and French military courts had sentenced 5,025 suspects in the immediate postwar years, including 806 to death, of whom 486 had been executed. Soviet courts had convicted virtually thousands for involvement in Nazi crimes, in many cases using mere membership in certain army units or the SS as a basis for conviction, regardless of individual guilt or innocence. Courts in the former Nazi-occupied countries had also sentenced numerous Nazi suspects, particularly in Poland, and Israel had tried and executed Adolf Eichmann.

The report noted that immediately following the war, allied military authorities had restricted West German courts to trying only persons charged with offenses against fellow Germans; not until 1952 was the prosecution of all Nazi suspects placed under German jurisdiction. In the early fifties, however, the number of proceedings fell considerably, with the judiciary and the population at large being of the opinion that the whole complex of Nazi crimes had already been dealt with sufficiently. Interest in the subject only reawakened with the return of the last German prisoners of war, among them many eyewitnesses to Nazi crimes in the east, and the opening of Allied archives to German investigators. This in turn led to the creation of the Central Agency, whose work produced an enormous increase in proceedings.

In October the public prosecutor of West Berlin terminated proceedings against former judges and attorneys of the Nazi People's Court (*Volksgerichtshof*) who had been accused of handing down excessive death sentences. The decision, which was based on presumed lack of malicious intent as well as the infirmity of the suspects, was widely criticized by Jews and others.

Legal actions during the year included the following:

West Berlin: In December former concentration-camp prisoner and guard Otto Heidemann, 74, was sentenced to ten years in prison for the murder of a fellow prisoner. He died in a prison hospital ward a few days after sentencing.

Frankfurt: In January a new trial opened in the case of three physicians, Dr. Aquilin Ullrich, 71, Dr. Heinrich Bunke, 71, and Dr. Klaus Endruweit, 72, who were charged with complicity in murder in connection with the Nazi mercy-killing program. The three had already been acquitted of the same charge in 1967, on the ground that they had been unaware of the criminal nature of their role in euthanasia, but that verdict was annulled by the West German supreme court. At a retrial in December, former SS captain Friedrich Paulus, 81, was sentenced to four years in prison, as an accomplice in the murder of 161 Polish civilians. An earlier decision to stop his trial on the ground of excessive duration was quashed by the supreme court.

Krefeld: In May former SS sergeant Wolfgang Otto, 74, was sentenced to four years in prison for the murder of a concentration-camp prisoner, one-time chairman of the German Communist party Ernst Thälmann, in 1944.

Wuppertal: In October the trial opened of former SS sergeant and concentration-camp guard Gottfried Weise, 65, who was charged with the murder of six prisoners at Auschwitz.

Foreign Affairs

The Kohl government played a significant role in an East-West spy exchange in February that resulted in the release of Natan (Anatoly) Sharansky from the USSR, for which it was warmly thanked by U.S. president Ronald Reagan and Israeli prime minister Shimon Peres. In March Bonn agreed to participate in research on the Strategic Defense Initiative, the U.S. space-based missile defense program.

Foreign Minister Hans-Dietrich Genscher visited Moscow in July for lengthy discussions with Communist party chief Mikhail Gorbachev and Foreign Minister Eduard Shevardnadze on arms reduction and issues relating to nuclear-reactor security and to sign an agreement for scientific cooperation. Later in the year, West German–Soviet relations were strained by mounting anti-Communist statements made by Bonn government speakers, including Chancellor Kohl's comment in an interview with *Newsweek* comparing Gorbachev's political skills to those of Nazi propaganda leader Josef Goebbels. Kohl subsequently told the Bundestag that his remarks had been misinterpreted, but he refused to apologize and relations remained at a low ebb.

On a state visit to Great Britain in July, President von Weizsäcker met with Jewish emigrants from Nazi Germany and presented the Goethe Medal to literary translator Michael Hamburger, son of a Jewish physician who had fled from his home in Berlin in 1933. During a visit to Norway in September, von Weizsäcker was received at the parliament in Oslo by its president, Jo Benkow, a Norwegian Jew who had survived Nazism in Swedish exile, and whose his entire family had perished in the gas chambers of Auschwitz. In one of his addresses, the West German president thanked Norway for having given refuge to emigrants from Nazi Germany, among them Max Tau, the Jewish author, and Willy Brandt, who later became West Germany's chancellor. Von Weizsäcker's visit to a memorial symbolizing Norwegian resistance to Nazi occupation, where he laid a wreath, was seen as a highlight of his stay and a significant contribution to German-Norwegian reconciliation. In an effort to achieve similar reconciliation with Poland, in November the Bonn parliament approved a motion initiated by the Greens to establish a permanent West German memorial exhibition at Auschwitz.

West Germany's Middle East policy continued along the course set by the

European Community member states. Essentially this meant support for Israel's right to exist in peace within safe borders and for the Palestinian people's right to self-determination, neither to be achieved at the expense of the other, however. The Federal Republic favored the participation of the Palestine Liberation Organization in all negotiations but expected the PLO to unequivocally recognize Israel's right of existence and renounce the use of violence. Government spokesmen reiterated the Federal Republic's commitment to neutrality in the Middle East conflict, which included the decision not to supply arms to either side. Opposing this view, CSU leaders favored arms exports to such "moderate" Arab states as Saudi Arabia, arguing that this would help stabilize the region and not harm anyone.

German relations with Syria were frozen during the fall, after evidence was presented of Syrian complicity both in a bomb attempt on an Israeli passenger plane in London and of planned bombings in West Berlin. The scheduled signing of an agreement on West German economic aid was canceled, and West German state agencies stepped up control of Syrian institutions and personnel in the Federal Republic.

The Bonn government disclosed that it had rejected a request in 1985 by the Munich aerospace company Messerschmitt-Bölkow-Blohm to sell $1 billion-worth of transport aircraft to Teheran, on the ground that the deal could not be approved until the Iran-Iraq war ended. On the subject of arms deliveries to Arab states, it was revealed during court proceedings against leading employees of the Rheinmetall arms plant at Düsseldorf—indicted for illegal arms exports—that a variety of arms produced by Rheinmetall had been sold to Saudi Arabia in the past years in violation of West German export restrictions.

In a debate on human rights at the beginning of the year, the Bundestag denounced violations, mainly those in Third World and Communist countries, and called on the Soviet Union to allow the free emigration of Jews and ethnic Germans. An international meeting devoted to the plight of the German and Jewish minorities in the Soviet Union took place in Bonn in March. The conference was arranged by the Institut für Ostrecht of Cologne University, in conjunction with the American Jewish Committee, financed by the Elson Foundation and the Volkswagen Foundation, with participants from West Germany, the United States, and Austria. It was the first instance of Germans and American Jews cooperating on a strictly foreign-policy issue.

Relations with Israel

A highlight of the year was the visit to Bonn in January of Israeli prime minister Shimon Peres, who was on a tour of European capitals. Peres held extensive talks with West German political leaders and visited the memorial site at the former Bergen-Belsen concentration camp to pay tribute to the victims of Nazi persecution.

In an eight-hour meeting, Peres and his German counterpart, Helmut Kohl, exchanged views on topics of mutual interest, political and practical. In the latter area, they agreed on the formation of a joint research foundation to carry out civilian projects in the sciences. Kohl assured Peres that reports of rising anti-Semitism in West Germany were unjustified and reiterated his government's commitment to the support of Israel, not only in bilateral relations but also in the European and United Nations frameworks.

In October, on the occasion of the 100th anniversary of the birth of David Ben-Gurion, Chancellor Kohl recalled the speech given by Israel's first premier in the Knesset in 1959, in which he declared that "the Germany of today is not the Germany of yesterday." Despite the shadow of the past, Kohl noted, Ben- Gurion had stretched out his hand in friendship to West Germany.

A two-volume work listing the names of 128,000 German Jews who perished in Nazi camps, which had been compiled by the West German Federal Archives over the previous 25 years, was presented to Yad Vashem, the Holocaust Memorial Institution in Jerusalem, in October. Absent from the work were the names of Jewish victims who had lived in the present territory of the East German Democratic Republic (DDR), since the necessary cooperation could not be obtained.

The agreement on the establishment of a German-Israeli research foundation was signed in Bonn in July by West German research minister Heinz Riesenhuber and Israeli science minister Gideon Patt. Jointly funded with an initial capital investment of DM 150 million, the foundation was intended to finance a variety of projects in science and technology. Quite apart from this new venture, Israeli-West German scientific cooperation continued to thrive. All important Israeli research institutes had links with West German research bodies and scientists, and the West German research ministry was spending about DM 20 million per year on joint projects.

Over the year West Germany imported DM 1.2 billion-worth of Israeli goods, 9.7 percent less than in 1985, and exported DM 2.4 billion-worth of goods to Israel, 5.2 percent more than the year before. Agricultural products and textiles ranged first among imported goods; machinery, motorcars, chemical, and electrotechnical products headed the export list.

Among visitors from Israel to West Germany during the year were Amnon Rubinstein, Israeli minister of posts and telecommunication, who inspected West German postal installations and discussed German assistance in the modernization of Israeli postal systems, and Ezer Weizman, the Israeli cabinet minister, who met with Chancellor Kohl for an exchange of views. A delegation of the Israeli Labor party—six of whose nine members were Arabs—visited the Federal Republic at the invitation of the SPD's Friedrich Ebert Foundation, for talks with Social Democratic representatives. It was the first official Israeli delegation traveling abroad to have an Arab majority.

The most prominent West German visitor to Israel in 1986 was Bundestag president Philipp Jenninger in May, accompanied by his four vice-presidents representing the major West German parties. Youth exchanges between the Federal Republic and Israel were the subject of a visit to Israel in September by the Bonn minister of youth, family, women, and health affairs, Rita Süssmuth. She reported that an average 10,000 youths of school age participated: some 7,000 Germans to Israel and 3,000 Israelis to Germany. Süssmuth discussed plans to increase the latter figure with Israeli minister of cultural affairs Yitzhak Navon. Johannes Rau, head of the North Rhine–Westphalian state government and SPD candidate for chancellor, visited Israel in April. He placed a wreath at the Yad Vashem memorial site, met with President Chaim Herzog, Prime Minister Peres, and other Israeli leaders, and received an honorary doctorate from Haifa University.

A group of 24 German and Israeli historians convened at the Hebrew University in Jerusalem to discuss German-Israeli relations, the social history of German Jews, German-Jewish symbiosis in pre-Nazi Germany, and Jewish emigration from Nazi Germany. The conference was sponsored jointly by the Hebrew University and Hamburg University.

West German tourism to Israel recovered from the 1985 slump that followed a spate of terrorist attacks on international air traffic, including the bombing of El Al installations in Rome and Vienna. Some 150,000 Germans visited Israel in 1986. The federal agency for political education (*Bundeszentrale für politische Bildung)* in Bonn, which since 1963 had organized and financed visits to Israel by over 4,000 West German opinion-makers—mainly educators, politicians, journalists, and church representatives—sent its 100th group to the Jewish state in November. More German and Israeli towns concluded partnership agreements, among them Worms and Tiberias, Nuremberg and Haderah.

Israeli artist Dani Karavan designed a square in front of the new museum center in Cologne named after the late German writer and Nobel Prize laureate Heinrich Böll.

President von Weizsäcker awarded the Great Service Cross with Star and Sash of the Federal Order of Merit to former Israeli ambassador to Bonn Yohanan Meroz, and the Great Service Cross to Tel Aviv mayor Shlomo Lahat. Other Israeli citizens to receive the Service Cross were physicians Dr. Eli Mayer and Dr. Max Sachs; the former mayor of Binyaminah, Peter Lauer; the director-general of ORT occupational schools in Israel, Israel Goralnik; and Henry Klausner, conductor, educator, and Histadrut musical director.

Israel's Yad Vashem again honored as Righteous Gentiles a number of German citizens who had aided and rescued Jewish victims of Nazi persecution. Among them were Dr. Paul Kerner, Hugo Armann, Gitta Bauer, Maria Schwelien (posthumously), Fritz Müller (posthumously), Gerhard Müller (posthumously), Maria Müller, Christian Pütz and Christina Pütz (both posthumously), Adele Köh, Elfriede Stichnoth, and Prof. Fritz Strassmann (posthumously). Over 180 Germans were among the 1,800 or so Righteous Gentiles of many nations who had received Yad Vashem honors to date.

JEWISH COMMUNITY

Demography

As of January 1, 1986, the 65 local Jewish communities in the Federal Republic and West Berlin had 27,538 members—13,990 males and 13,548 females. A year later, they registered 27,533 members—13,998 males and 13,535 females, with an average age of 44.0 years. The age distribution of registered Jews was as follows: 0–15 years—3,533; 16–30—4,517; 31–40—4,269; 41–60—7,013; 61–70—3,977; and over 70—4,224. In addition to the above, 25,000 or so Jews who were not affiliated with the organized community were estimated to be living in the country.

In 1986 the Central Welfare Agency of Jews in Germany, located in Frankfurt, recorded 569 immigrants and 275 emigrants, as well as 122 births, 477 deaths, and 59 conversions to Judaism. The largest communities, as of January 1, 1987, were those of West Berlin (6,002), Frankfurt (4,909), and Munich (4,030), followed by Düsseldorf (1,579), Hamburg (1,390), and Cologne (1,245).

Communal Activities

Continuity of the community and the transmission of Jewish traditions to younger generations continued to occupy the leaders of the Central Council of Jews in Germany (Zentralrat der Juden in Deutschland), as did problems of anti-Semitism.

The Central Council's board met with Prime Minister Shimon Peres during his visit to Bonn in January and accompanied him to the memorial site at the former Bergen-Belsen concentration camp. Peres also visited the Jewish community in West Berlin, which presented him with 20 computers to be used for traffic education among children of new immigrants in Israel.

The weekly *Allgemeine jüdische Wochenzeitung,* the only national Jewish newspaper in West Germany, celebrated its 40th anniversary in April. The paper was founded by Jewish publisher and editor Karl Marx in Düsseldorf in 1946 and taken over by the Central Council in 1973.

An important event took place in November when the Hesse state government signed an agreement with the Union of Jewish Communities in that state, guaranteeing financial assistance for the communities' religious, cultural, and social activities. It was the first such pact concluded in a West German state and corresponded to similar agreements existing with the Christian churches.

A new Jewish community center opened in Frankfurt in September, the largest in West Germany. Made possible by financial assistance from the Hesse state government and the Frankfurt municipality, the center housed offices, an assembly hall, a Jewish day school, kindergarten, home for the aged, kosher restaurant, youth center, and gymnasium. The cornerstone for a new Jewish community center was laid in Heidelberg. In Darmstadt, where a new synagogue was planned, violinist Yehudi Menuhin gave a concert to help finance the project.

The Jewish community of the northern port city of Bremen celebrated the 25th anniversary of the opening of its New Synagogue. The synagogue on Pestalozzistrasse in West Berlin was dedicated after undergoing extensive reconstruction. A Jewish day school, the first in West Berlin since the war, was opened on Bleibtreustrasse in the Charlottenburg district in August, with 25 children enrolled in the first grade. The I.E. Lichtigfeld Jewish Day School in Frankfurt celebrated the 20th anniversary of its opening, its student body having grown from 30 to 120.

The Academy of Jewish Studies in Heidelberg, whose enrollment had risen from 16 students in 1979 to 86, remained the only Jewish institution of higher learning in the country. It maintained cooperative agreements with Heidelberg University and the Hebrew University of Jerusalem as well as with the Jewish Theological Seminary in New York, the Hebrew Union College in Cincinnati, and other schools abroad. The school's function was to train Jewish communal leaders and teachers, to prepare those wishing to pursue advanced studies abroad as cantors and rabbis, and to acquaint interested non-Jews with Jewish culture. In addition to its academic program, the academy housed Europe's largest collection of transparencies of Jewish art, comprising some 10,000 slides, as well as a collection of over 12,000 photographs of Jewish cemeteries and gravestones in southwest Germany.

Culture

A "Jewish Theater in Germany" was founded in Heidelberg in February, to present professional performances of plays by Jewish and Israeli authors to Jewish and non-Jewish audiences in all parts of the country. The group also hoped to present works by Jewish authors that had disappeared during the Nazi period and been recently discovered. Young members of the Jewish community in Frankfurt formed a dance company, "Paamey Machol," directed by Beersheva-born Shaul Shani, which performed locally, in other cities, and abroad. Similar groups were started in Düsseldorf and West Berlin. The Old Opera at Frankfurt and the local Jewish community cosponsored a Week of Jewish Culture titled "Shalom," featuring performances by the Israel Philharmonic Orchestra, Israel's National Folklore Dance Company, and Jewish and non-Jewish singers.

An international seminar on "German Jews and Liberalism," arranged by the FDP's Naumann Foundation and the Leo Baeck Institute of London, was held near Bonn, with scholars from the United States, Britain, Israel, and West Germany participating. The Lessing Academy at Wolfenbüttel sponsored an international symposium on Moses Mendelssohn, with participants from both Germanys, the United States, Israel, and several European countries.

Exhibitions relating to Jews and Jewish life opened in a number of locations. The new city-financed Jewish Museum in Frankfurt opened with a display of about 160 paintings, drawings, letters, and other documents left by German-Jewish artists, politicians, and writers, including items from the Leo Baeck Institute in New York that had earlier been shown in other West German centers. A show entitled "Once at Home in Hamburg: Jewish Life in the Grindel District" was mounted at the Museum for the History of Hamburg. "Weissensee—A Cemetery Mirrors Jewish History in Berlin" was the title of an exhibition shown in that city. A permanent exhibit depicting the history of local Jewish families opened at Koblenz. The city of Kassel arranged a display relating to the life and work of the late Jewish theologian Franz Rosenzweig, a native son, and to local Jewish history. To mark the 100th anniversary of his birth, the city sponsored an international conference on Rosenzweig, with participants from the United States, Israel, Britain, Holland, France, Italy, and Germany.

A documentary on the liberation of Auschwitz, based on film sequences shot by a Soviet cameraman, was shown on West German television. Copies of the program, which was produced by West Berlin's Chronos Film Company, were donated to Yad Vashem in Jerusalem and the Diaspora Museum in Tel Aviv. Another documentary, this one about the liberation of the Nazi extermination camp at Majdanek, was produced by Chronos from film footage found in Allied archives and was also shown to West German audiences. The producers hoped to counteract charges that reports of Nazi brutalities were exaggerated.

Author Elie Wiesel paid his first visit to Germany since World War II in January. In the course of his visit, which was in behalf of the U. S. Holocaust Memorial Council, he addressed a group of West German public figures on the subject "Remembrance and Reconciliation." A congratulatory message was sent by Chancellor Kohl to Wiesel on his receipt of the Nobel Peace Prize in December. Eighty-three deputies of the West German parliament had written to the Swedish Academy recommending Wiesel for the award, praising his contributions to reconciliation and international understanding.

The city of Frankfurt's Goethe Medal went to German-born French Jewish historian, political scientist, and publicist Alfred Grosser for his contributions to French-German reconciliation. The federal state of Baden-Württemberg bestowed an honorary professorship on German-born Israeli scholar and author Schalom Ben-Chorin, who was presented with the Bavarian state's Order of Merit for his part in Christian-Jewish dialogue. David Stern, German-born linguistics professor at the University of Toronto, received an honorary doctorate from Hamburg University. Trier University bestowed an honorary degree on 95-year-old Yiddish professor and researcher Salomo A. Birnbaum, of Toronto's Maimonides College.

By paying DM 120,000 to a Paris art collector, the city of Wuppertal regained possession of a portrait of Wuppertal-born Jewish poet Else Lasker-Schüler by Jankel Adler. The painting had been removed from a local museum by the Nazis in 1937.

An international symposium on methods of researching and preserving Jewish cemeteries in Germany was arranged by Duisburg University and the Catholic Academy of Aachen. Some 70 representatives of Jewish communities, West German universities, and communal authorities, as well as private researchers, attended the meeting, held at Krefeld. The regional government of Württemberg allocated DM

328,000 to the Jewish communities in this southwest German region for the maintenance of 54 old Jewish cemeteries.

Christian-Jewish Relations

The German Coordinating Council of Associations for Christian-Jewish Cooperation, representing 55 local branches in all parts of the Federal Republic and West Berlin, continued its active program of lectures, discussion groups, and other events. The group was headed by Prof. Eckhard von Nordheim, for the Evangelical Church; Prof. Lorenz Weinrich, for the Catholic Church; and Rabbi Henry G. Brandt, for the Jewish community. The council's theme for 1986, "*Bewährung liegt noch vor uns—Vom Vorurteil zur Partnerschaft*" (The Hour of Trial Still Lies Ahead of Us—From Prejudice to Partnership), was also the motto of the nationwide Brotherhood Week in March. Speaking at the opening ceremony, in Duisburg, in an atmosphere overshadowed by recent anti-Semitic occurrences, Catholic Council representative Hans Hermann Henrix observed that the motto appeared to signify a skeptical evaluation of Christian-Jewish relations 40 years after Auschwitz. The year's Buber and Rosenzweig Medal of the Coordinating Council was presented at the ceremony to Heinz Kremers, professor of evangelical theology at Duisburg University, a leading figure in Christian-Jewish dialogue over the years.

Thousands of Catholics, most of them young people, attended sessions devoted to Jews and Judaism at the 89th German Catholic Congress, in Aachen. Rabbis and other Jewish representatives took part in the meetings, and the Aachen Jewish community hosted a reception welcoming congress participants. During a one-week visit to New York and Washington in March, members of the board of the Central Committee of German Catholics held extensive talks with leaders of Jewish organizations there, including the World Jewish Congress, American Jewish Committee, National Conference of Christians and Jews, American Jewish Congress, Anti-Defamation League of B'nai B'rith, and the International Jewish-Catholic Liaison Committee of the Synagogue Council of America. Among the subjects discussed were the Vatican's policy toward Israel, the planned erection of a Catholic monastery at Auschwitz, the Passion Play at Oberammergau, and anti-Semitism in Germany.

On a visit to the Union of Jewish Communities in Hesse, the president of the Evangelical Church in Hesse and Nassau, Helmut Spengler, expressed the view that the Christian-Jewish relationship was marred by Christian missionizing among Jews and deplored the fact that "we as Christians have not offered more determined resistance to anti-Semitism but have, in part, even supported it in the course of history."

Jews and Christians held joint memorial services for the victims of Nazi terror at the former Nazi concentration camps of Bergen-Belsen and Dachau. Ceremonies were also held, in November, in a number of towns, to mark the anniversary of the Nazi pogroms in 1938. In Worms, an interreligious gathering commemorated the

800th anniversary of the construction of the ritual bath, which was still in use, near the old synagogue in that city.

An international youth center was inaugurated near the former extermination camp of Auschwitz in December. The center, erected at the initiative of the Christian German group "Aktion Sühnezeichen" (Symbol of Atonement Project), was financed with the help of the federal government and most of the states. West German and Polish political leaders, victims of Nazi persecution, and former concentration camp prisoners, among them the head of the West Berlin Jewish community, Heinz Galinski, himself a survivor of Auschwitz, attended the inauguration.

Memorial stones and plaques dedicated to Jewish victims of Nazism and former Jewish communities were unveiled in a number of towns, including Hennef-Geistingen, Eppertshausen, Würzburg-Heidingsfeld, Tailfingen, Lingen, Ludwigshafen, Düsseldorf, Hamburg, Lübbecke, Freiburg, Salzkotten, Fürth, Regensburg, Hammelburg-Paffenhausen, Hessloch, and Aschaffenburg. The former synagogues of Hohenlimburg, Hechingen, and Gelnhausen were reopened to the public, after being restored by local citizens to serve as museums, cultural centers, and meeting places. The chapel at the old Jewish cemetery in Hildesheim was restored and reopened as an archive and information center on Jews and Nazism. A plaque commemorating Jewish teacher and cantor Naphtalie Bamberger, who died in 1938, was unveiled at the municipal museum of Kitzingen, which once housed the local Jewish elementary school.

A town in the state of Hesse, Hessisch Lichtenau-Hirschhagen, arranged a reunion for about a hundred or so former slave laborers in a local Nazi ammunition plant—citizens of various Nazi-occupied countries, including Hungarian Jewish women—with local Germans who had befriended and helped them.

The government once again presented the Service Cross of the Federal Order of Merit to German citizens who had aided and rescued persecuted Jews during the Nazi regime. Among this year's recipients were Hildegard Arnold and Berta Zimmermann, of Berlin. The annual Peace Prize of the West German Booksellers Union went to Polish Catholic historian and author Wladyslav Bartoszewski, for his role in the wartime rescue of Polish Jews and in postwar Polish-German reconciliation.

Publications

New publications relating to the Nazi era included: Claude Lanzmann, *Shoah. Mit einem Vorwort von Simone de Beauvoir* ("Shoah: With a Foreword by Simone de Beauvoir"; Claassen); Adam Czerniakow, *Im Warschauer Ghetto. Tagebuch 1939–1942* ("In the Warsaw Ghetto: A Diary"; Beck); David S. Wyman, *Das unerwünschte Volk. Amerika und die Vernichtung der europäischen Juden* ("The Abandonment of the Jews"; Hueber); Adolf Diamant, *Ghetto Litzmannstadt. Bilanz eines nationalsozialistischen Verbrechens. Mit Deportations-und Totenlisten der aus dem Altreich stammenden Juden* ("The Litzmannstadt Ghetto. Balance Sheet of a National Socialist Crime. With Deportation and Death Lists of Jews from the

German Reich"; Central Council of Jews in Germany); Hermann Hermes, *Deportationsziel Riga. Schicksale Warburger Juden* ("Deportation Destination Riga. The Fate of Jews from Warburg"; Hermes); Ulrike Migdal, ed., *Und die Musik spielt dazu. Chansons und Satiren aus dem KZ Theresienstadt* ("And the Music Plays On: Songs and Satire from the Theresienstadt Concentration Camp"; Piper); Herbert Schultheis, *Die Reichskristallnacht in Deutschland nach Augenzeugenberichten* ("The Reich Crystal Night in Germany as Described by Eyewitnesses"; Rotter); Lotte Adolphs, *Kinder in Ketten. Kinderschicksale in Ghettos und Konzentrationslagern* ("Children in Chains: The Fate of Children in Ghettos and Concentration Camps"; Braun); Andreas Hillgruber, *Zweierlei Untergang. Die Zerschlagung des Deutschen Reiches und das Ende des europäischen Judentums* ("Two Kinds of Destruction: The Defeat of the German Reich and the End of European Jewry"; Siedler); Wladyslav Bartoszewski, *Uns eint vergossenes Blut. Polen und Juden in der Zeit der 'Endlösung'* ("We Are Linked by Shed Blood. Poles and Jews at the Time of the 'Final Solution' "; Fischer); Simon Wiesenthal, *Krystyna. Die Tragödie des polnischen Widerstands* ("Krystyna: The Tragedy of Polish Resistance"; Nymphenburger); Arnold Paucker, ed., *Die Juden im nationalsozialistischen Deutschland 1933–1943* ("The Jews in Nazi Germany"; Mohr); Lucy S. Dawidowicz, *Der Krieg gegen die Juden 1933–1945* ("The War Against the Jews"; Fourier).

Among new books on Judaism, Jewish history, and religion were: Walter Grab/ Julius H. Schoeps, eds., *Juden in der Weimarer Republik* ("Jews in the Weimar Republic"; Burg); Wilma Iggers, ed., *Die Juden in Böhmen und Mähren. Ein historisches Lesebuch* ("The Jews of Bohemia and Moravia: A Historical Reader"; Beck); Peter Melcher, *Weissensee. Ein Friedhof als Spiegelbild jüdischer Geschichte in Berlin* ("Weissensee: A Cemetery Mirrors Jewish History in Berlin"; Haude & Spenersche); Walter Kickel, *Das Gelobte Land. Die religiöse Bedeutung des Staates Israel in jüdischer und christlicher Sicht* ("The Promised Land: The Religious Meaning of the State of Israel in the Eyes of Jews and Christians"; Kösel); W. Breuning/H. Heinz, eds., *Damit die Erde menschlich bleibt. Gemeinsame Verantwortung von Juden und Christen für die Zukunft* ("That the Earth May Stay Humane: Jews and Christians' Joint Responsibility for the Future"; Herder); Joseph Walk, *Biographisches Handbuch zur Geschichte der Juden in der Weimarer Republik* ("Biographical Handbook for the History of Jews in the Weimar Republic"; Saur); Schalom Ben-Chorin, *Was ist der Mensch. Anthropologie des Judentums* ("What Is Man: Anthropology of Judaism"; Mohr); Mordechai Breuer, *Jüdische Orthodoxie im Deutschen Reich 1871–1918;* ("Jewish Orthodoxy in the German Reich 1871–1918"; Athenäum); Trude Maurer, *Ostjuden in Deutschland 1918–1933* ("East European Jews in Germany 1918–1933"; Christians).

New works of biography, memoir, and fiction included: Simcha Naor, *Krankengymnastin in Auschwitz. Aufzeichnungen des Häftlings Nr. 80574* ("Physical Therapist in Auschwitz. Notes of Prisoner No. 80574"; Herder); Primo Levi, *Wann, wenn nicht jetzt? ("If Not Now, When?"*; Hanser); Bruno Kreisky, *Zwischen den Zeiten. Erinnerungen aus fünf Jahrzehnten* ("Between Eras: A Memoir of Five Decades";

Siedler); Wilhelm von Sternburg, *Lion Feuchtwanger—ein deutsches Schriftstellerleben* ("Lion Feuchtwanger: A German Author's Life"; Athenäum); Barbara Honigmann, *Roman von einem Kinde. Sechs Erzählungen* ("Novel of a Child: Six Stories"; Luchterhand); Manès Sperber, *Der schwarze Zaun* ("The Black Fence"; Europaverlag); Jurek Becker, *Bronsteins Kinder. Roman* ("Bronstein's Children: A Novel"; Suhrkamp); Yohanan Meroz, *Meine Jahre in Bonn. Ein israelischer Botschafter erinnert sich* ("My Years in Bonn: An Israeli Ambassador Remembers"; Ullstein); Gerhard Zwerenz, *Die Rückkehr des toten Juden nach Deutschland* ("The Return of the Dead Jew to Germany"; Hueber); Minna Lachs, *Flucht und Geborgenheit. Erinnerungen 1907–1941* ("Flight and Rescue: Memoirs 1907–1941"; Europaverlag).

Other new works of nonfiction included: *Alphons Silbermann/Julius H. Schoeps, eds., Antisemitismus nach dem Holocaust* ("Anti-Semitism After the Holocaust"; Wissenschaft und Politik); Henryk M. Broder, *Der ewige Antisemit. Über Sinn und Funktion eines beständigen Gefühls* ("The Eternal Anti-Semite: On the Meaning and Functioning of a Permanent Emotion"; Fischer); Paul W. Massing, *Vorgeschichte des politischen Antisemitismus* ("The Early History of Political Anti-Semitism"; Europäische Verlagsanstalt); Günther B. Ginzel, ed., *Antisemitismus. Erscheinungsformen und Motive des Judenhasses gestern und heute* ("Anti-Semitism: Manifestations and Motivations of Hatred Against Jews Yesterday and Today"; Schneider); Christhard Hoffmann/Bernd Passier, eds., *Die Juden. Vorurteil und Verfolgung im Spiegel literarischer Texte* ("The Jews: Prejudice and Persecution Reflected in Literature"; Reclam); Heiner Lichtenstein, ed., *Die Fassbinder-Kontroverse oder Das Ende der Schonzeit* ("The Fassbinder Controversy, or, the End of the Closed Season"; Athenäum); Gershon Shaked, *Die Macht der Identität. Essays über jüdische Schriftsteller* ("The Power of Identity: Essays on Jewish Writers"; Athenäum); Herbert A. Strauss/Christhard Hoffmann, eds., *Juden und Judentum in der Literatur* ("Jews and Judaism in Literature"; Deutscher Taschenbuch-Verlag).

Personalia

The 1986 Theodor Heuss Prize of the Theodor Heuss Foundation in Bonn (named for the first postwar West German president) was presented to Werner Nachmann, chairman of the board of directors of the Central Council of Jews in Germany, for his contributions to German-Jewish reconciliation. Marcel Reich-Ranicki, Frankfurt Jewish publicist and literary critic, received the Great Service Cross of the West German Order of Merit, for promoting the works of young German authors. Hans Chaim Schafgans, leading representative of the Jewish community in Bonn; Jakob Nussbaum, president of the Jewish sports organization Maccabi Deutschland; and Kate Kemper, a successful Jewish businesswoman, all received the Service Cross. The Order of Merit of the State of North Rhine-Westphalia was presented to Alexander Ginsburg, secretary-general of the Central

Council of Jews in Germany; Kurt Neuwald, a leading representative of postwar German-Jewish organizations and chairman of the Jewish communities in Northern Rhineland; and Hedvika Hornstein, of Düsseldorf, a leader in the WIZO organization and Christian-Jewish activities.

Ernst Gottfried Lowenthal, German-Jewish historian and author, received the Dr. Leopold Lucas Prize of the Eberhard Karls University at Tübingen, for his role as a chronicler of German-Jewish history. Poet Rose Ausländer, of Düsseldorf, received the Book Prize of the German Union of Evangelical Libraries, and Gerty Spies, a poet from Munich, was awarded the Literature Prize of Schwabingen. The Fritz Bauer Prize of the West German Humanistic Union was given to Berlin scholar Ossip K. Flechtheim. The Honorary Prize for Television Entertainment of the West German Broadcasting Station at Cologne went to German-Jewish radio and television star Hans Rosenthal, who was chosen West Germany's most popular entertainment personality by readers of the country's leading TV magazine.

The city of Wuppertal named a street after a local Jewish physician, Eugen Rappoport, who perished in the Theresienstadt ghetto in 1942. The city of Cologne named a street after Herbert Lewin, a local Jewish physician and postwar leader of German-Jewish groups, who died in 1982. The city of Duisburg named a square in memory of a local Jewish lawyer, Harry Epstein. Max Willner, a postwar Jewish leader who headed the Union of Jewish Communities in the State of Hesse, was awarded the Medal of Honor of Tel Aviv University on the occasion of his 80th birthday.

Emil Davidovic, a rabbi in North Rhine-Westphalia, died in January, aged 73. Rudolf Pick, noted Jewish lawyer and communal leader, of Düsseldorf, died in September, aged 81.

FRIEDO SACHSER

German Democratic Republic

A TOTAL OF 382 JEWS were registered in the eight organized communities in East Germany (German Democratic Republic, GDR) in 1986. Of these, 187 lived in East Berlin, 50 in Dresden, 48 in Leipzig, 31 in Erfurt, 29 in Magdeburg, 14 in Halle, 12 in Karl-Marx-Stadt, and 11 in Schwerin. An additional 2,000 to 3,000 nonaffiliated Jews were estimated to be living in the country as well.

The East Berlin community, headed by Dr. Peter Kirchner, a physician, was the center of Jewish activity and the only place where regular religious services were held. Although the community was still without a permanent rabbi, Rabbi Ernst M. Stein came from West Berlin on occasion to help out, and Rabbi Ernst Lorge of Chicago officiated during the High Holy Days, under the auspices of the American Jewish Committee.

The East German government agreed to allocate the sum of 40 million marks for the reconstruction of the New Synagogue on Oranienburger Strasse, which had been desecrated during *Kristallnacht* in 1938 and destroyed in a bombing raid in 1943. Once rebuilt, the building would house a Jewish museum and offer facilities for the community's religious and cultural events.

After extensive renovation, the old cemetery of the Conservative Jewish Congregation Adass Yisroel, founded in 1870, was reopened during the summer. The inaugural ceremony was attended by delegations of former Berlin Jews from Israel and other countries, who also witnessed the affixing of a plaque at the building on Tucholskystrasse 40, in East Berlin, which had once housed the synagogue, rabbinical seminary, and offices of the Adass Yisroel community.

The government allocated GDR-M 2.5 million for the erection of a new wall surrounding the Weissensee cemetery, in existence since 1880, and with 115,000 burial sites the largest Jewish cemetery in Europe. Plans to build a highway across the remaining unused areas were canceled by East German state and Communist party chief Erich Honecker, following protests from the Jewish communities of both East and West Berlin.

The government contributed GDR-M 170,000 to support the East Berlin community's functioning, plus 150,000 marks for cemetery maintenance. In all, 140 Jewish cemeteries existed in the GDR, but most were no longer in use. Maintenance work was carried out at many of the sites by Christian volunteer groups, primarily the Evangelical Church's Sign of Atonement Project.

Outside East Berlin, Jewish communal life was confined to religious occasions and commemoration of anniversaries, with Jewish representatives participating in ceremonies honoring victims of anti-Fascist resistance.

Community leaders met with state and government representatives to discuss problems of mutual concern, such as the restoration of the Oranienburger Strasse Synagogue and other houses of worship and maintenance of cemeteries. No serious tensions existed between Jews and the government, not even over the subject of Israel. Despite its differing views, the Jewish community accepted government policy and issued no statements of its own on the Middle East situation, although it did protest occasional media comments with anti-Jewish undertones or excessive attacks on Israel and its policies.

Possibly as a result of growing political stability, both inside and outside the country, the state relaxed some of its restrictions. Representatives of the Jewish community were allowed to attend international Jewish gatherings, and many Jews from abroad came to visit their coreligionists in East Germany. In January an official delegation of the Union of Jewish Communities in the GDR attended the World Jewish Congress jubilee meeting in Jerusalem. In April Kurt Goldstein, secretary-general of the World Organization of Anti-Nazi Underground Movements, traveled to Jerusalem to attend the presentation of the Ka-Zetnick Literary Award to Mezei Andras of Hungary and Jerzy Ficowski of Poland, for their writings on the Holocaust. East German Jewish representatives attended a European Jewish Congress meeting in Geneva and a conference of the International Council of Christians and Jews in Spain; they also met during the year with West German Jewish representatives.

Over 60 former students of the Jewish private school on Rykestrasse in East Berlin, which opened in 1904 and closed in November 1938, after *Kristallnacht,* came from Israel, the United States, and South Africa to attend a reunion in June. The building, which was restored after the war and rented by the organization People's Solidarity, currently served as a cultural and social center. Other visitors to the country included a group of Israeli writers, in May, who were received by the Union of East German Authors. East German travelers to Israel included conductor Kurt Masur, as guest conductor of the Israel Philharmonic Orchestra, and actor Ekkehard Schall, who performed at the Jerusalem Festival.

Gertrud Zeiner, a leading member of the Jewish community in Karl-Marx-Stadt, received DDR's Distinguished Service Medal. Ludwig Geiger's *History of the Jews in Berlin,* first published between 1871 and 1889, was reprinted by the DDR Zentralantiquariat of Leipzig. *The Diary of Anne Frank* ran as a serial in *Junge Welt,* the daily organ of the DDR youth organization.

The GDR's hard-line anti-Israel position remained unchanged (though the government did, for the first time, permit Jews of retirement age to visit relatives in Israel for up to three months a year). Leaders of the Palestine Liberation Organization (PLO) were frequent visitors in East Berlin, and the PLO office there, which held the status of an embassy, was regarded as an operational center for Al-Fatah activities.

East German lawyer Wolfgang Vogel played a central role in the negotiations that led to the freeing of Natan (Anatoly) Sharansky as part of a spy swap between East and West in February.

The district court of Karl-Marx-Stadt, in March, sentenced two former members of Nazi police battalion No. 41, Eberhard Täschner and Kurt Brückner, to life imprisonment, for their part in the persecution, deportation, and murder of hundreds of Polish citizens, including many Jews. East German courts had so far sentenced a total of 12,876 persons on war-crime charges, according to the DDR attorney general. An editorial in *Nachrichtenblatt,* the quarterly news bulletin of the Union of Jewish Communities in the GDR, reiterated the official community view that the victims of Nazism regarded the trials not as revenge but as justice and as deterrents of future crimes. A congratulatory message to Austrian president Kurt Waldheim on his election, sent by GDR state and party chief Erich Honecker, was published in the East German press without any mention of Waldheim's alleged Nazi wartime activity.

FRIEDO SACHSER

Eastern Europe

Soviet Union

Domestic Affairs

DURING 1986 IT BECAME increasingly apparent that Communist party leader Mikhail Gorbachev was intent on reforming the Soviet system, though how and to what extent was not clear. Taking advantage of the fact that many Soviet officials were elderly and had occupied their posts for a long time, Gorbachev set about to change Leonid Brezhnev's policy of "stability of cadres." In the course of the year, some 30 government ministers and heads of state committees were replaced. Several first secretaries of republic party organizations and about one-third of the provincial (*oblast'*) party secretaries were removed, as were the heads of the Moscow and Leningrad party organizations. However, since the officials who replaced them were similar to their predecessors in background, there was presumably no fundamental change in outlook to be expected.

In Gorbachev's major address to the 27th congress of the Communist party in February, almost a year after becoming general secretary, he criticized the lack of dynamism and reluctance to change which, he claimed, pervaded the Soviet system, and called for a "radical reform" of the economy, including a flexible price system and the possibility of allowing some private enterprise in the service sector. He repeated his call for "*glasnost'* " (openness) and called upon Soviet citizens to confront the shortcomings in the system and try to remedy them. In their speeches to the congress, party secretary Yegor Ligachev and former foreign minister Andrei Gromyko, now ceremonial head of state, indicated less enthusiasm for *glasnost'* and reform than Gorbachev.

Nevertheless, the Soviet media clearly reflected the public interest in *glasnost'*. Newspaper articles and a popular play dealt with the theme of privileges for party members and corruption among the country's elite; the new head of the filmmakers' union, Elem Klimov, announced the formation of a commission to review censored films; lively debate at a national writers' congress saw Andrei Voznesensky and Evgenyi Evtushenko, among the country's best-known poets, call for the publication of all of Boris Pasternak's works and for the establishment of a Pasternak museum.

In July Voznesensky published a poem, "The Ditch," in which he lashed out at grave robbers who had desecrated the mass grave of Jews shot by the Nazis in the Crimea in 1941 and criticized the authorities who tolerated these crimes, implying that such degenerate acts were permitted because the victims were Jews.

Discussion in historical journals became bolder and more lively, shedding new light on some of the more obscure areas in Soviet history. For the first time in about a decade, data on infant mortality and on alcohol consumption were published. These data showed that infant mortality rates in the USSR were about twice the rate in the United States, and the average per capita consumption of alcohol was 8.5 liters. As part of the campaign against alcoholism, the price of vodka was increased twice during the year. Gorbachev announced that sales of alcohol had fallen 35 percent in the first half of 1986. The size of the grain harvest in 1985 was also revealed, in contrast to recent years when such information was not published. The press published articles on drug abuse, hitherto said not to be a problem, and on prostitution, until then claimed to have been eliminated after the revolution. Increasingly, the media reported mishaps such as an earthquake in Moldavia and a fatal mine blast in the Ukraine, events which once would have been passed over in silence. A major catastrophe, the collision of two ships and the sinking of one of them in the Black Sea, leaving 398 dead, was widely reported within 48 hours of the accident. Attacks on official corruption continued, and the idea of elections in which there would be more than one candidate for each office was openly discussed.

A fire that broke out on April 26 in a nuclear power plant in Chernobyl, Ukraine, was reported only on the 29th, after Swedish monitors detected a sudden rise in radiation levels in the atmosphere, traced the source to the Soviet Union, and demanded an accounting. At first reporting only two dead as a result of the accident, by July Soviet authorities admitted that 28 people had died and "the health of many others was impaired." By August at least 12 high-ranking officials were dismissed in connection with the accident, but no major shake-ups occurred in the highest echelons of the party. Because of fallout over large areas of the continent, several Western European governments banned food imports from the USSR and Eastern Europe. An offer of American government help to the USSR was declined, but a few physicians, including an Israeli citizen working in New York, spent several weeks treating radiation victims. While the long-term health and environmental effects of the accident were not immediately ascertainable, the Soviet leadership managed to contain the potential domestic and international political damage fairly well.

Dissidents

There were some signs of limited political liberalization during the year, but no institutional or other fundamental reforms were undertaken. Dissident Yuri Orlov, who had spent seven years in labor camps, was released in October and permitted to leave for the United States. The poet Irina Ratushinskaya, whose poetry included religious themes and who was highly regarded by Western literary critics, was freed after three years in labor camps.

The most dramatic development was the approval of scientist Andrei Sakharov's request to be released from his exile in Gorky. When Sakharov returned to Moscow, from which he had been banished in 1980, joining his wife Elena Bonner, who had returned to the USSR after several months in Italy and the United States, he condemned the Soviet military presence in Afghanistan and called on Soviet leaders to free dissidents who were in jails and labor camps. At the same time, he expressed "great respect" for Gorbachev's attempts to reform the system, leading some observers to interpret Gorbachev's bold step as an attempt to split the dissident movement and win at least part of it over to his reformist program.

Foreign Affairs

Displaying a new sensitivity to its international image, the Soviet Union adopted a generally conciliatory posture in foreign affairs. Soviet representatives tended to be more open and patient in their dealings with foreign journalists and others than they had been under the previous Soviet administration. Gorbachev himself was reported to make a highly favorable impression on visiting foreign dignitaries, who were undoubtedly influenced by his intelligence, command of the facts, and charm.

Relations with the United States improved, though there were some reverses. Cultural exchanges, halted in 1980 following the invasion of Afghanistan, were resumed. The United States was said to be ready to remove most export controls on oil and gas equipment and technology. The Soviet Union, for its part, allowed at least nine Soviet spouses of Americans to join the latter in the United States, and promised to resolve 36 other cases of divided spouses by allowing 117 people to emigrate.

On the other hand, tensions between the superpowers rose after the Soviet authorities arrested Nicholas Daniloff, an American correspondent for *U.S. News and World Report,* when he accepted a package from a Soviet acquaintance. The package turned out to contain classified Soviet material, and Daniloff was charged with espionage. Shortly before, Gennadi Zakharov, a Soviet citizen employed by the UN, had been arrested and indicted on espionage charges in New York. In mid-September both Zakharov and Daniloff were given into the custody of their respective embassies, awaiting trial. After considerable diplomatic maneuvering, Daniloff was released and left for the United States at the end of September. Zakharov was freed a day later, amid denials by U.S. officials that his release was part of an exchange.

In December the Soviets announced that four American companies had signed formal agreements to enter into joint ventures in the USSR, something made possible by a new Soviet law. Another seven companies were said to have signed preliminary letters of intent.

A summit meeting between Secretary Gorbachev and President Ronald Reagan of the United States took place in Reykjavik, Iceland, in mid-October. Reagan stated before the meeting that human-rights issues would receive equal priority at the talks with arms-control matters. However, inability to reach agreement on arms control apparently made human rights a secondary issue. The main sticking points seemed to be Soviet opposition to the Strategic Defense Initiative ("Star Wars") insisted upon by President Reagan, and some uncertainty about the American position on nuclear disarmament. The USSR proposed revising the 1972 Anti-Ballistic Missile Treaty between the two countries in order to delay the American SDI program, but this was not accepted.

At the request of Secretary of State George Shultz, a large package of information on 11,000 people who had been waiting longer than five years to emigrate from the Soviet Union was prepared for the meeting; however, no agreement on these refuseniks was reached at Reykjavik. A month after the meeting the Soviet Union proposed that an international conference on human rights be held in Moscow. Soviet spokesmen, now willing to entertain questions on human rights and emigration, claimed that as of January 1, 1987, applications for emigration would be acted on within a month, except for "unusual cases."

Relations with Israel

There was improvement in Soviet relations with Israel, foreshadowed by statements by Poland and Hungary that they would move to establish "interest sections" in Israel and allow Israel to do the same in their countries. The Soviet Union took even more measured steps. In August Prime Minister Shimon Peres of Israel stated that he would not object to Soviet participation in an international conference on the Middle East, on condition that the USSR establish "full diplomatic relations" with Israel. On August 4 the Soviet foreign ministry announced that it would open discussions with Israel on consular matters and on Soviet church properties in Jerusalem. Soviet newspapers emphasized that discussions would be limited to those two items, but there was public demand in Israel to put the issue of Soviet Jewish emigration on the agenda. *Izvestiia,* on August 13, explained that the absence of diplomatic relations with Israel was due to "Tel Aviv's aggressive policy in the Middle East. That cause has not been eliminated, and therefore there is no reason at present for the Soviet position to change."

Soviet-Israeli talks began on August 17 in Helsinki and lasted only 90 minutes. It was reported that the Soviet delegation had discussed their representation in the Finnish embassy in Israel, the status of Soviet citizens living in Israel, and their properties there. The Israelis were said to have raised the issues of Jewish emigration and of Jewish prisoners held for Zionist activity. Indications were that the door was not closed to future discussions.

On September 22 Prime Minister Peres met at the UN with Foreign Minister Eduard Shevardnadze for more than an hour. This was said to be the highest-level meeting between Soviet and Israeli officials since 1967.

JEWISH COMMUNITY

Demography

The Jewish population of the USSR was estimated at 1.8 million, with the largest concentration in the Russian republic (700,651) and the second largest in the Ukraine (634,154), where Jews were the third largest nationality.

Emigration and Emigration Activists

In 1986 only 914 Jews emigrated from the Soviet Union, down from 1,140 in the previous year and the lowest total in 20 years. In August the Council of Ministers announced amendments to regulations governing departure from the USSR, scheduled to take effect January 1, 1987. The most important provisions were that Soviet citizens could leave "on private matters, regardless of origin . . . race, nationality, sex, education, language or attitude toward religion"; applications to leave "for reunion with family members" would be considered only when an invitation was presented from a parent, spouse, child, or sibling living abroad; those "conversant with state secrets" would not be allowed to leave, nor would they "if there are other reasons affecting the security of the state." Soviet Jewish and foreign observers pointed out that these regulations codified what had been Soviet practice in recent years when emigration levels declined precipitously. The restriction of invitations to first-degree relatives was seen as shrinking considerably the pool of potential applicants. Moreover, since there was no specification of what constituted being "conversant with state secrets," this provision could continue to be used to deny emigration even to those who had not been involved in secret work, according to their own understanding, or who had in the past had access to material then considered confidential but long since rendered innocuous.

Before the 27th Communist party congress in February, 142 refuseniks sent an appeal to it requesting the release of those imprisoned for Zionist activities, the fixing of a maximum five-year waiting period for those refused emigration on grounds of "regime considerations," and the publication of hitherto secret regulations on emigration. Only the latter request was met in part.

In February a seminar commemorating the 850th anniversary of the birth of Maimonides was organized in Moscow by 42 refusenik scientists and scholars, the largest such gathering since 1980.

The most dramatic event involving refuseniks came in the same month, when Anatoly Shcharansky was released from prison and allowed to leave the country. (Soon thereafter he adopted the Hebrew name Natan and simplified the spelling of his last name.) Sharansky had been sentenced in 1978 to 13 years on charges of treason, espionage, and anti-Soviet agitation. In December 1985 his living conditions were improved, and he was given medical treatment and an improved diet. On

February 11 he was exchanged in Berlin, along with three others accused of being NATO spies, for five people from Warsaw Pact countries. His wife, Avital, who had campaigned tirelessly all over the world for his release, flew to meet him, and both arrived in Israel a short time later to a tumultuous welcome. Sharansky was greeted by Prime Minister Peres and other high government officials and was congratulated on his release in a phone call from U.S. president Reagan. In August, Sharansky's mother, Ida Milgrom, her son Leonid, and his family were permitted to leave for Israel.

Shortly before Sharansky's release, teacher Ilya (Eliyahu) Essas was permitted to go to Israel after many years in refusal. Essas had been one of the moving spirits behind a religious revival in Moscow and had organized a network of religious study groups there. Toward the latter part of the year some other well-known and long-term refuseniks were allowed to leave. They included Yaakov Mesh of Odessa, Boris Kalendarov, Yaakov Gorodetsky, and Isaac Kogan of Leningrad, and the Goldstein brothers of Tbilisi. Boris Gulko, a chess champion, Vladimir Brodsky, and Veniamin Bogomolny, who claimed to be the refusenik of longest standing, were also allowed to leave with their families. David Goldfarb, an elderly and ill refusenik, joined his son in New York after American industrialist Armand Hammer obtained permission to fly him out in his private plane. Alexander Yakir was released from a labor camp after serving two years for draft evasion, and two refusenik mathematicians were allowed to participate in an international meeting held in Tashkent.

By contrast, Alexei Magarik, a 27-year-old cellist and Jewish activist, was arrested in Tbilisi on charges of drug possession and sentenced to three years. Vladimir Lifshitz in Leningrad was sentenced to a similar term in prison for "defaming the Soviet state." In August, after many months of waiting for word on her request, and after going on a hunger strike, Inessa Flerov was granted permission to go to Israel in order to donate bone marrow to her critically ill brother. Her husband, who was initially denied an exit visa, won his release shortly after the summit meeting in Reykjavik.

In the United States, Alexander Slepak, son of longtime refusenik leaders Vladimir and Masha Slepak, was allowed to speak with a Soviet consul in Washington about his parents. He and Ludmilla Alexeeva, a former dissident, were allowed to plead the cases of the Slepaks and dissident prisoner Anatoly Marchenko. The meeting apparently came about after the younger Slepak spoke with the Soviet ambassador to the United States when they returned to Washington from the Reykjavik meeting on the same plane.

It was noted in the fall that no Jewish activists were being kept under arrest for more than 15 days, nor were there any trials of such people. By the end of the year, the number of Jewish activists in prison was said to have declined from over two dozen to 14. Yet there was no indication that any substantial emigration was in the offing.

In October and November about 17 Soviet immigrants to the United States returned to the Soviet Union, and about 50 more went back in December, by which time five of the original group had left the USSR and once again entered the United States. Both Soviet and American newspapers featured this development.

Culture

Sovetish haimland, the only Yiddish journal published in the Soviet Union, celebrated its 25th anniversary in October. During the quarter century of its publication, 285 issues had appeared. According to the editors, *Sovetish haimland* had published in its pages 76 novels, 109 long stories, 1,478 short ones, 6,680 poems, 28 plays, and 1,628 articles of literary and artistic criticism. During the same quarter century, 127 books were published in Yiddish and 122 in Russian translation by the Sovetskii Pisatel' publishing house. According to Georgi Markov, chairman of the Union of Soviet Writers, 132 Yiddish titles had been published in translation in languages other than Russian.

A week-long series of events was held in Moscow to mark the magazine's anniversary, during which it was awarded the Order of Friendship of Peoples. The 25th-anniversary issue featured 31 writers born after World War II, whose professions included engineering, archaeology, computers, music, history, and the military. Three were identified as graduates of the special course for Yiddish writers at the Gorky Literary Institute who were employed full time as writers. The average age of the contributors was 35. Six of them were born in areas annexed by the USSR in 1939–1940 and two were from Birobidzhan.

Sovetish haimland (no. 3) reported receiving suggestions from readers that, in order to reach a wider audience, the journal be divided into a Yiddish section and a section of Russian translations from Yiddish. The editor replied, "Regarding the linguistic format of the journal we would not hasten to declare our solidarity with [the proposed change]." He added, "We will take up the question of who reads *Sovetish haimland,* and probably more than once. We will also not be able to avoid the question of the creative future of our magazine. In any case, no matter what difficulties there might be, there are reserves—the mail of *Sovetish haimland* and the new names of authors in the journal testify to that."

The editor of *Sovetish haimland,* Aron Vergelis, was elected to the board of the Union of Soviet Writers at its national congress, the first Yiddish writer since 1949 to be so honored. Six Jews were elected to the secretariat of the union's board. At the writers' congress, Ekaterina Sheveliova criticized the main report given by union chairman Markov for not mentioning the Jewish writers Ilya Ehrenburg and Samuil Marshak. She pointed out that "the report says not a word about Yiddish literature, which now, together with all Soviet literature, is at the forefront of the ideological struggle."

A report on Soviet publishing in the years 1981–1985 mentioned that in 1985 eight Yiddish books had been published in editions of 7,000 copies. In addition, 12 volumes were published as translations from Yiddish, 11 of them into Russian, in a total of 2,432,200 copies. *Sovetish haimland* was listed as printing 5,000 copies. (In the early years of its publication it was published in editions of 25,000; more recently it was said to have declined to 7,500.) The newspaper *Birobidzhaner shtern* was said to publish 12,000 copies.

To mark the 150th anniversary of the birth of Yiddish and Hebrew writer Mendele Mocher Sforim, a collection of his works was published in Russian. Several other works of Jewish content were published during the year, including a book of medieval Hebrew poetry translated into Georgian by Dzhemal Adzhashvili; an anthology of Soviet Yiddish poetry in Russian translations by such noted Russian writers as Akhmatova, Antokolsky, and Marshak; and a new publication, *Year by Year,* which was a collection of material from *Sovetish haimland* translated into Russian. The latter volume, containing 368 pages, was published in an edition of 30,000.

The Moscow Jewish Dramatic Theater Studio, formerly the Dramatic Ensemble, began its summer season in July with a repertoire of five plays, two in Russian, two in Yiddish, and one using both languages. The Stanislavsky Theater in Moscow continued to feature Arkady Stavitsky's *40 Sholem Aleichem Street,* a play about the adverse effects on an Odessa Jewish family of the sons' decision to emigrate. The Jewish Chamber Musical Theater of Birobidzhan opened a summer season in Moscow with a four-play repertoire. The Freilichs Show Ensemble appeared in several cities in Belorussia and Siberia, and the Vilnius Yiddish Folk Theater staged Avrom Kahan's *The Brody Singer* for an audience of 700 in the Lithuanian capital.

Some modest activities in Judaic scholarship were reported. Igor Krupnik, a Candidate of Historical Sciences at the Institute of Ethnography of the Academy of Science, surveyed some of these activities in an article published in the November issue of *Sovetish haimland.* Concentrating on the younger generation of scholars, Krupnik mentioned two dissertations on contemporary Hebrew that were defended at the G.V. Tsereteli Oriental Institute of Tbilisi University in 1982 and a third that was defended in 1985. Alexandra Eikhenvald and Yuri Kornienko coauthored a book on linguistic policy in the contemporary Middle East. "Unfortunately," Krupnik observes, "far less attention is paid to the study of other [than Hebrew] Jewish languages. For example, thus far I am unable to identify even a single younger researcher who is specializing in Yiddish" (p. 73). According to Krupnik, in the previous four or five years, an average of about 20 publications (books, articles) a year on Judaica had been published in the USSR. Most of them were "brief and modest," and there were several areas identified by Krupnik in which no scholarly work was being done. Among the researchers mentioned were Maria Veinshtain, a graduate of the Leningrad Conservatory of Music, who had been writing on Ashkenazic folk music, as had Vladimir Bitkin of Kishinev.

One of the younger scholars was Shimon Yakirson, born in Leningrad in 1956 and a graduate of the Leningrad Cultural Institute, where he specialized in the "history of the book." He studied Hebrew for one year at Leningrad State University. Since 1980 he had been curator of the Hebrew and Yiddish collection of the Leningrad section of the Institute for Oriental Studies. Yakirson said that while his grandparents spoke Yiddish, he felt that his own knowledge of the language was inadequate for his professional responsibilities. He noted that the collections contained some 50–60,000 items, about one-sixth in Yiddish, exclusive of the Hebrew and Yiddish newspapers, as well as 63 Hebrew incunabula and about 500 Hebrew manuscripts. A catalogue of the latter was being prepared by Igor Naftuliev. Yakirson himself was preparing a catalogue of Hebrew incunabula in all Soviet libraries. There was also, in Leningrad, a collection of literature in other Jewish languages, including Ladino, Judaeo-Persian, and the Iranian dialect Tat.

According to Tatiana Helfman, curator of Judaica, the Leningrad State Museum for the History of Religion and Atheism had 1,050 Judaica items, "mostly collected during the Soviet period." (In the late 1920s and 1930s many such items were confiscated from synagogues.) The items included 300 Torah scrolls, works of art, and *ketubot,* among others. Some 74 Judaica items, such as bridal canopies and prayer shawls, were part of other collections in the museum, as were about 200 Judaica-related photographs and a collection of antireligious newspapers and posters. Helfman reported that the Lvov (Ukraine) Museum for the History of Religion and Atheism had "rich Judaica collections" and that the Pecherska Lavra monastery in Kiev had Judaica silver items.

Religion

Konstantin Kharchev, chairman of the Council on Religious Cults, visited an Orthodox Jewish day school in New York, where he asserted that "a revolutionary process of democratization" was under way in the USSR that would affect religion positively.

Despite protests, the *mikvah* (ritual bath) in the Moscow suburb of Marina Roshcha was closed by the authorities. In recent years, newly religious young women had been using the facility.

Personalia

Honors were awarded to several Soviet Jews during the year. Among them was Academician Alexander Efimovich Sheindler, who received the title of Hero of Socialist Labor with the Order of Lenin and the Hammer and Sickle gold medal on his 70th birthday, "for great services in the development of science and in the training of science personnel." Academician Mark Mitin, a philosopher and ideologist, received the Order of Friendship of Peoples on his 80th birthday. Yiddish writer Note Lurie was awarded a certificate of honor on his 80th birthday by the presidium of the Supreme Soviet of the Ukrainian Soviet Socialist Republic.

Among Soviet Jewish public figures who died during the year were Moishe

Itkovich, essayist, critic, and translator into Yiddish, aged 84; and Yiddish poets Misha Mogilevich, aged 66; Bronia Sinelnikova, aged 77; and Pinie Krichevsky, aged 65. Berl Roizin, literary critic and Yiddish translator, died in an automobile accident, aged 73. Leonid Kantorovich, co-winner of the Nobel Prize for Economics in 1975, died at the age of 74.

ZVI GITELMAN

Soviet Bloc Nations

POLITICAL LEADERS IN Eastern Europe watched developments in the Soviet Union carefully as they tried to determine what changes would be made under Secretary Mikhail Gorbachev and how they would affect Eastern Europe. As Gorbachev's reform ideas began to emerge, leaders in Bulgaria, Poland, and Hungary seemed to endorse them, while those in Czechoslovakia, the German Democratic Republic, and Rumania displayed lack of enthusiasm in one way or another.

Those countries that seemed to align themselves with reform also took modest steps toward improving relations with Israel. Foreign Minister Yitzhak Shamir of Israel met the foreign ministers of Bulgaria, Hungary, and Poland at the UN in October. In Bulgaria, Foreign Minister Petar Mladenov hosted a dinner for Shulamit Shamir, wife of Yitzhak Shamir, who was on a visit to her native country. However, no other steps were taken toward resumption of relations with Israel, broken off by Bulgaria in 1967.

Hungary

Hungarian officials indicated that they would discuss with the Israeli government the possibility of opening interest sections in their respective countries. Hungarian party activists, led by Jozsef Gyorke, deputy head of the Hungarian Socialist Workers party's foreign affairs department, visited Israel as guests of the Israeli Communist party.

JEWISH COMMUNITY

With no firm data available on the size of the Hungarian Jewish population, estimates ranged from 35,000 to 100,000.

A new synagogue, the first to be built in Hungary since 1945, was opened in Siofok, on the shores of Lake Balaton, a popular resort area. Chief Rabbi Alfred Schoner, who replaced the deceased Rabbi Laszlo Salgo, officiated at the opening ceremony.

The choir of the Rabbinical Seminary in Budapest visited and performed in Israel.

Poland

In September an Israeli interest section, dealing primarily with Polish applicants for Israeli visas, opened in Warsaw. The section was headed by veteran diplomat Mordechai Paltzur.

The year was marked by stepped-up exchanges with Israeli cultural groups and by an increase in the number of cultural events with Jewish themes. The first visit by an Israeli cultural group since 1967 occurred when the Bat Dor dance company gave six performances in Poland. The Mazowsze dance company of Poland toured Israel for three weeks in May, and Minister of Culture M. Kuszynski visited the International Folklore Festival in Haifa in July. Several groups of Israeli youth toured the country at the invitation of Polish authorities. These were the first Israeli youth groups to visit Poland in over 20 years.

A conference on Polish Jewish history was held at the Jagellonian University in Krakow in September, in which Israeli scholars took a prominent part. One of them, the distinguished linguist Moshe Altbauer, was honored in an impressive ceremony in which his doctorate, conferred 50 years earlier by the Jagellonian, was "confirmed" by university authorities. The same university announced the establishment of an institute for the study of the history and culture of Polish Jews.

Poland's Catholic hierarchy came under increasing pressure from European and U.S. Jewish leaders, as well as from other Catholics and Protestants, over the Carmelite convent at Auschwitz. The matter dated back to 1984, when eight to ten nuns, with the approval of Church and government authorities, moved into an abandoned building on the site of the former concentration camp, intending to establish a convent. The project became known in late 1985, when a support group began raising funds for the convent in Belgium. Polish authorities, taken aback by the vehemence of Jewish opposition, at first reacted defensively.

In a series of meetings that took place throughout 1986, involving, in various combinations, officials of the World Jewish Congress and leaders of various European Jewish communities with Cardinal Macharski, whose diocese encompassed Auschwitz, the Polish primate, Cardinal Glemp, and other Church officials, both sides sought to clarify their positions. To Poles, the convent represented a memorial to the martyrdom of Father Maximilian Kolbe and the convert Edith Stein, both killed by the Nazis, as well as a place for "expiation and prayer for peace, justice, and freedom." To Jews, for whom Auschwitz was the prime symbol of the Holocaust, the convent was an insult to the memory of millions of victims and an attempt to preempt the special place occupied by Auschwitz in Jewish history and sentiment. A meeting on July 22 in Geneva between high-level Jewish and Catholic leaders resulted in agreement by Cardinal Macharski to halt work on the convent while negotiations continued.

JEWISH COMMUNITY

The Jewish population of Poland was estimated at 5,000, of whom nearly 2,000 were registered with the religious community.

A kosher canteen, funded by the American Jewish Joint Distribution Committee, opened in Warsaw. It was intended for local residents as well as tourists from abroad. A festival of films on Jewish themes, held in Krakow, featured more than a dozen works. Also shown in Warsaw were four prewar Yiddish films. A Judaica exhibit opened at the State Archaeological Museum in the presence of the minister of culture, and in Bialystok and Tykocin an exhibit was mounted of over 400 photographs of remaining Jewish cemeteries in Poland. An exhibition of tapestries was shown in the restored synagogue in Wlodawa.

The Catholic University of Lublin organized a "week of Jewish culture," featuring lectures on the history and culture of Polish Jewry. It was inaugurated by a mass in the university church at which the Hebrew *kaddish* prayer was recited. A modern art gallery in Warsaw showed 40 paintings by Urszula Grabowska on Jewish and biblical themes. An anthology of modern Hebrew poetry in Polish translation, edited by Jewish writer Alexander Ziemny, was published in Warsaw.

Rumania

The destruction continued of a major part of historic Bucharest, including an area with important Jewish sites. The Spanish synagogue, the last Sephardic synagogue in Eastern Europe, was razed, despite protests by the U.S. government and Israeli ambassador Yosef Govrin. The matter was raised in the U.S. Senate when the issue of renewing most-favored-nation privileges for Rumania was discussed, but to no avail.

In July President Nicolae Ceausescu met with Uzi Baram, secretary-general of Israel's Labor party, and in the following month a Rumanian party secretary was received by Prime Minister Shimon Peres and Foreign Minister Yitzhak Shamir in Israel.

JEWISH COMMUNITY

The Rumanian Jewish population, estimated at 26,000 in 1985, continued to decline as a result of emigration and the high mortality rate of an aged population.

A small synagogue in Buhusi was burned down and its Jewish janitor stabbed to death. Police arrested four young men. There were reports that two synagogues still in use in Iasi, where the largest Jewish population in the country once resided, had been destroyed, apparently by vandals.

Yugoslavia

JEWISH COMMUNITY

The Yugoslav Jewish community numbered about 5,000, including many intermarried families.

In December the Jewish community of Zagreb (Croatia) celebrated its 180th anniversary. The Jewish population of the city, about 11,000 before World War II, now numbered about 1,150. Rabbi Zadik Danon, the only rabbi in the country, officiated at Sabbath services for the occasion. The president of the Croatian parliament, as well as the deputy mayor of Zagreb, participated in the festivities, as did leading Catholic and Muslim clergy.

Zvi Gitelman

Australia

THE DECADE OF THE 1980s SAW Australia playing an increasingly self-confident role on the international scene, in marked contrast to its near-isolationism of earlier years. Domestically, the country struggled to expand its population and strengthen its economy. At the same time, it confronted the issue of justice for the dispossessed aborigines and the integration of a society second only to Israel in its mix of ethnic and cultural subgroups.

For Jews, Australia continued to offer a congenial home, largely free of discrimination, though anti-Zionism showed a worrying increase in recent years. The community's ranks were growing through immigration, and it supported a thriving array of religious, educational, and cultural institutions.

National Affairs

The election in March 1983 of a new Labor government under former trade-union leader—and Rhodes Scholar—Bob Hawke led to a generally pragmatic economic policy that included concessions to industry and big business, despite Labor's theoretical orientation toward the working class, and an even stronger internationalist stance. Hawke believed Australia was vital to U.S.interests in the Pacific region. He also saw the country generally as a leader, with Japan and China, in the Pacific basin, which he and his advisers perceived as of vital geopolitical importance in the future. Despite a minor recession and some concern over free-trade policies because of cheap imports from the region, Australia nurtured strong trading relations with Japan and strengthened relations with China.

The Hawke government strongly encouraged Australia's new image as a multicultural country. The movement toward multiculturalism had begun, reluctantly, with the acceptance of refugees before, during, and after World War II, although they were barely tolerated by the largely Anglo-Celtic majority of the period. In the 1950s, however, mass importation of workers from southern Europe began a flow which increased to a flood, so that by the mid-80s at least one in five Australians was foreign-born or had foreign-born parents. The tensions resulting from mass immigration were addressed vigorously by succeeding governments since the 1970s, with measures ranging from intensive English-as-a-second-language programs to antidefamation laws in many states.

Relations with Israel

Hawke's elevation to Labor party leadership and election as prime minister presented Australian Jewry with a dilemma. Like former prime minister Malcolm Fraser, Hawke was considered to be a firm supporter of Israel. However, while trusting Hawke personally, the Jewish community had reservations about the influence of the Labor party's left-wing pro-Arab minority. These reservations were underlined by a major policy shift perpetrated by the Hawke government only six months after taking office: permission was granted for an Arab League office to be established in Australia and for Australian ambassadors to have diplomatic contacts with PLO representatives. Although the former did not come to pass—the Arabs apparently thought better of it—and the latter proved to be less significant than at first thought, at the time these decisions shook the community badly.

Australia's relations with Israel since 1981 can best be described as uneven. While there was general overall support for Israel, it was marred by periodic troubling issues. On the negative side, Australia's voting record at the United Nations showed only patchy support for Israel. In addition, with Gough Whitlam—former left-wing prime minister—as Australian ambassador to UNESCO for several of these years, that agency was able to win Australian support for many anti-Israel policies. In 1984, when Australia was elected to a seat in the Security Council, where its vote assumed even greater significance, Jewish leaders won a promise from Hawke that he would personally keep a close watch on Middle East issues and keep a stronger hand on Australia's votes on specific resolutions. Also problematic for Jews was Australia's "controversial visitors policy," which allowed prominent Palestinians and American Black Muslim leaders to come on speaking tours. By contrast, a proposed Australian venue for a UN conference on Palestine was diplomatically sidestepped.

On the positive side, there was the state visit to Australia of President Chaim Herzog of Israel at the end of 1986 (and the return visit to Israel of Hawke in early 1987). Herzog's Australian tour, the first by an Israeli president, was well received; he met most of the significant political power brokers, won relatively positive media coverage, and, not surprisingly, endeared himself to Australian Jewry. Foreign Minister Bill Hayden had visited Israel in January 1984, to check on Australia's contingent in the Sinai MFO (Multinational Force and Observers). Several parliamentarians and some of the public were against Australian participation in the force, but such dissension as there was largely died down. Premier Neville Wran of New South Wales and, independently, NSW opposition leader Nick Greiner, visited Israel in 1985.

Another positive development was the unanimous vote by the Australian Parliament in late 1986 to condemn UN Resolution 3379 equating Zionism with racism. This was achieved largely through the efforts of Zionist Federation leader Mark Leibler and because there was general bipartisan understanding of the gross offensiveness of the equation. The Australian government also moved to end the citizenship problem of Australian immigrants to Israel, so that they would no longer lose their Australian passports upon becoming Israelis under the Law of Return, but could maintain dual citizenship. Given the high percentage of Australian *olim,* the issue had become a thorn in the Australian Zionist side.

Australian-Israeli exchanges of scientific and agricultural technology continued. Israel was teaching Australia about arid-land farming, especially modern irrigation techniques, cotton-growing, and advances in desalination, while Australia sent experts in microsurgery and other specialized medical procedures to Israel. These exchanges were sometimes brought about through Jewish sponsorship of exchange professorships or scholarships.

Australia's trading links with the Arab world, concentrating as they did on primary exports from Australia, with the trade balance very much in Australia's favor, continued to outstrip Australian-Israeli trade relations. Two-way trade between Israel and Australia was at about the $100-million mark, around 60 percent of it Israeli exports of manufactured goods, industrial machinery, irrigation equipment, plastics, fertilizer, and high technology. Australian exports to Israel were principally primary produce, largely coal, wool, and rice.

The shocking introduction of Middle East-linked terrorism into the South Pacific region began with a bomb blast in December 1982, which severely damaged the Israeli consulate general in Sydney and injured an employee. A second bomb, planted in the parking lot of the Hakoah soccer-social club in Sydney's Bondi district, was defused in time. Libyan influence in the South Pacific, largely within emergent island nations like Vanuatu, was beginning to be of concern.

Nazi War Criminals

As a result of submissions made by the Australian Jewish community, and based on parallel activity being carried out in the United States and Canada, in June 1986 the Australian government commissioned senior civil servant Andrew Menzies to conduct an investigation into charges that Nazi war criminals had found sanctuary in Australia after World War II. Menzies' report, presented to Parliament at the end of 1986, recommended the establishment of a special unit, similar to the U.S. Office of Special Investigations. He proposed that it examine, initially, the 70 individuals whose cases were presented in a closed section of the report. The report also recommended passage of an amendment to the Australian War Crimes Act of 1945 to allow civil (as opposed to military) prosecution for war crimes.

Soviet Jewry

Through Soviet diplomatic channels in Canberra and by way of its own envoys to the USSR, Australia continued to plead the overall cause of human rights in the USSR and the specific case of Soviet Jews.

An Australian parliamentary delegation to the Soviet Union in 1986, led by Australia's first female Speaker, Joan Child, expressed the government's interest in the plight of Jewish refuseniks by presenting a list of cases to Soviet authorities. Prime Minister Hawke had a long-term interest in the issue of Soviet Jewry, dating from a visit to the USSR in 1979, when he tried to have some refuseniks released and was badly let down and embarrassed because the Kremlin reneged on what he believed was a final agreement. The issue remained an emotional one for Hawke.

Anti-Semitism and Anti-Zionism

Australia was in many ways the fabled "*goldineh medinah*" for Jews: there was no institutionalized anti-Semitism, Jews had over the years held high government positions (including, twice, the highest appointed office, that of governor general), and Jewish communal life was allowed to flourish. The populist anti-Semitism prevalent before the 1940s had pretty much died away, partly out of shock over the horror of the Holocaust but also because of Australia's own transformation into the world's second most multicultural nation (after Israel). By the 1980s ethnicity had even become fashionable, and antidiscrimination policies and legislation were established and accepted.

Multiculturalism was not without problems, however, among them the importation to Australia of ancient feuds and modern political antipathies. On several occasions the Australian Jewish community took various Arabic-language newspapers before the Press Council for condemnation, not only for virulently anti-Israel stands but for grossly offensive anti-Semitic articles, including extracts from the notorious *Protocols of the Elders of Zion.*

"Traditional" anti-Semitic acts such as daubings, synagogue thefts, and, in one case, arson, showed signs of increasing, though not to really troubling levels. Right-wing anti-Semitism, although not significant and largely discredited, persisted, primarily among less educated and sophisticated Australians, particularly those living in rural areas. These were the natural targets of the League of Rights, a group that produced and distributed Holocaust revisionist literature and was known to circulate the *Protocols of the Elders of Zion.* Regarded as being on the lunatic fringe by most Australians, its activities were carefully monitored by the Jewish community and its propaganda usually successfully countered through friendly non-Jewish sources.

More worrying for the Jewish community was the continuing transmutation of anti-Semitism into anti-Zionism, with Israel berated by its critics in unreasonable terms, singled out for abuse that went beyond simple political disagreement. In Australia as elsewhere, Israel's incursion into Lebanon in 1982 produced an outpouring of anti-Israel media coverage disproportionate to the event. Succeeding years saw periodic expressions of anti-Zionism, largely from the left and often expressed as pro-PLO attitudes. The problem was particularly acute on college campuses throughout Australia, where Jewish students worked hard to block periodic pro-PLO student activities. By 1986, however, the press and electronic media had largely moderated their anti-Israel stance.

Of far greater concern to the Jewish community was the anti-Zionism and, in one case at least, the overt anti-Semitism, of elements within the Christian churches. The community was shocked when the Anglican dean of Perth, David Robards, spoke publicly about Jewish vengeance and the "genocidal God of the Old Testament." Despite attacks from Jewish communal representatives and members of his own church, he remained unrepentant. Anti-Israel sentiment, expressed openly or subtly, was evident in various Protestant denominations, in particular in the Australian Council of Churches.

JEWISH COMMUNITY

Demography

As the census question on religion was not compulsory, Australian Jewish population figures were always more a matter for sociologists and demographers than statisticians. The 1981 census, adjusted upward to allow for those who did not answer the question, showed an Australian Jewish population of around 70,000, roughly divided between Sydney and Melbourne, with small numbers in other areas. The 1986 census figures had not yet been processed, but it was thought likely that a new question on "ethnic origin" would help to clarify Jewish statistics. Some Jewish scholars were using a working figure of between 80,000 and 100,000 for the total Jewish population. Whatever the absolute numbers turned out to be, however, the proportion of Jews in Australia was likely to remain at around 0.4 percent.

Plans were being made to undertake major demographic surveys of the Jewish community in 1987, based on the 1986 census and local tabulations of Jewish births, marriages, and deaths. This effort would be part of the international Jewish demographic survey for the year 1990, which had been launched by demographic experts in Israel.

Jewish immigration to Australia from South Africa was estimated to have been around 10,000 during the previous 10 years and was still continuing. From the Soviet Union it had diminished radically, and from other sources, including Israel, it remained constant.

With Jews concentrated so heavily in the two major capital cities of Sydney and Melbourne, the viability of the small communities elsewhere was a matter of concern. As a result, largely, of South African immigration, Perth and Adelaide's Jewish populations had stabilized and even increased; Brisbane, however, remained a small and fragile community, while Hobart had a minuscule Jewish population.

A demographic trend of great concern to communal planners was the rising proportion of Jews at the aged end of the spectrum, twice as high as that of the general population. The growing need for such services as welfare and old-age homes inevitably competed with other demands on communal resources, in particular capital funds for expansion in education.

The intermarriage rate was steady but low, and seemed to affect primarily the fringes of what was still largely an immigrant and traditional community. The divorce rate, however, was high, reflecting the general trend in the middle class, in which Australian Jewry was firmly located.

Community Relations

The Jewish community, as the oldest and most entrenched of all "ethnic" groups in Australia, was looked to by many of the newer arrivals as a model for minority-group organizing strategies. In the main, the Jewish community was well protected by custom and its own efforts, and many of the antagonisms once directed at Jews were now deflected onto newcomers, particularly Asians. If anything, a certain complacency had seen Jewish representation in Parliament, for example, once quite strong on the federal and state levels, diminish almost to nothing. Sen. Peter Baume, who had been a minister in the government of Malcolm Fraser, and Barry Cohen, a minister in the Hawke government, were the only two Jews on the federal scene, while Joe Berinson, the West Australian attorney general, was the only significant Jewish figure in state politics. New South Wales (NSW) Jewry was proud when Paul Landa became that state's attorney general in 1983, and his premature death after two years was a blow. Another Jewish political figure no longer on the scene was Sir Zelman Cowan, the second Jewish governor general in Australian history, who served from 1975–1980. Cowan was highly successful as a conciliatory figure who diffused the passions generated when his predecessor, Sir John Kerr, dismissed the Whitlam government in November 1975. Sir Zelman subsequently took up the posts of provost of Oriel College at Oxford University and president of the British Press Council, as well as filling certain roles in Israel, including serving on the board of the Van Leer Institute.

Despite the sometimes wavering stance of the Labor party toward Israel and increasing internal fragmentation in the Liberal party, individual politicians maintained extremely friendly relations with the Jewish community. Prime Minister Hawke, for example, launched the Hebrew University's Golda Meir Fellowship Fund in Australia. He also delivered the first in a series of memorial orations following the death of Prof. Julius Stone, a major figure in the field of international law, and negotiated with the Soviet government for the release of Soviet Jews. State premiers and opposition leaders were always to be seen at major Jewish communal gatherings.

For a community its size, Australian Jewry was remarkably visible and influential. On the local front, the Jewish community was in the forefront of the fight to have Anti-Discrimination and Incitement to Racial Hatred legislation introduced into state and federal parliaments. It also succeeded in creating and maintaining bipartisan support for the State of Israel in the various parliaments and in keeping press criticism of Israel within generally acceptable bounds. It fought for government funding for day schools—an issue which also affected Catholic and major Protestant schools—and was producing a stream of academic and popular histories about Jews in Australia in preparation for the upcoming bicentenary.

Christian-Jewish Relations

A Council of Christians and Jews was established in 1985 in Melbourne, and moves began to form a similar group in Sydney, as forums for discussing mutual concerns, including, but not limited to, the Protestant churches' attitudes to Israel. Leaders of these groups hoped thereby to reduce divisive actions and pronouncements.

Relations between Jewry and the Catholic Church in Australia, by contrast, were cordial, reflecting the general Catholic-Jewish rapprochement begun with Vatican II. Pope John Paul II's visit to Australia at the end of 1986 included a meeting, at his request, with Australian Jewish leaders, in which the pontiff declared that anti-Semitism was "sinful."

Communal Activities

The vibrancy of Australian Jewish life continued to surprise visitors from abroad. Australian Jewry was a very committed community, the vast majority of its members identifying with one organization or another, even if only nominally. Since a growing proportion of Jewish families had at least one child in a Jewish day school, that identification seemed likely to be strengthened.

The Australian Jewish community was structured on basically British lines, with accommodations made for the vast size of the country and its federal system of government. Thus each state had its own board of deputies, and all the boards were grouped under the roof Executive Council of Australian Jewry. The Zionist movement was similarly structured, with state Zionist councils and the Australian Zionist Federation. The two roof bodies worked in parallel, following different agendas. Occasional overlap resulted in conflict, especially on the issue of which body should represent the interests of Israel to government.

Among the many organizations and institutions that had been established over the years, a number celebrated significant anniversaries in the period under review. Among them were the National Council of Jewish Women (60 years), WIZO (50 years), B'nai B'rith (40 years), and the Brisbane Hebrew Congregation (100 years).

Australian Jewry continued to be almost totally Zionist—in the broad sense of providing moral and financial support for the State of Israel—and its financial contributions to Israel were proportionately large. Ties between the two countries were strengthened with the combining, in May 1985, of the *Jerusalem Post* International Edition with the *Australian Jewish Times,* the country's leading Jewish newspaper, allowing the broad Australian Jewish public, and significant elements of non-Jewish Australia, access to Israel's only English-language newspaper.

One notable development of recent years, reflecting world trends, was an increase in activities relating to the Holocaust. A gathering of Holocaust survivors was held in Sydney in May 1985, attended by international luminaries, including Beate Klarsfeld. A Holocaust museum was established in Melbourne and an institute of Holocaust studies in Sydney. A traveling Holocaust exhibition presented by B'nai B'rith toured major cities in Australia and New Zealand, and a Holocaust teaching kit for use in public high schools was developed by the New South Wales Jewish Board of Deputies.

A steady flow of prominent Jews and Israelis visited the country, usually invited by communal organizations as speakers. They provided intellectual refreshment for a community keenly aware of its isolation at "the end of the world."

Australian Jewry assumed a leading role in fostering Jewish communal life in the Asian and Pacific regions. The brainchild of Isi Leibler, president of the Executive Council of Australian Jewry for part of this period and head of the World Jewish Congress Asia-Pacific section, the Asia-Pacific Jewish Association was formed in May 1980 to bring together the small Jewish communities of the region for mutual assistance and the sharing of ideas and problems. The countries involved were New Zealand, Singapore, Japan, Taiwan, Thailand, India, Korea, the Phillipines, and Hong Kong, with smaller affiliates such as New Caledonia and Sri Lanka.

Another Leibler-inspired project was the introduction of a periodic Asian Jewish Colloquium; the first was held in Singapore in 1984 and the second in Hong Kong in 1987. This academic forum for Asian scholars and their Jewish counterparts from Israel and the Diaspora quickly proved effective in helping to improve Israel's relations with countries in the region.

The historic Sydney-Melbourne communal rivalry—often no more than a series of thinly disguised personality conflicts—and a more recent conflict between the Zionist Federation and the Executive Council over issues related to lobbying the government, had eased considerably toward the end of the period.

On the world Jewish scene, partly through the personal force of Jewish leaders like the Leibler brothers, Australia had a significant presence in the World Jewish Congress, the Jewish Agency, and the World Zionist Organization, where it was seen as a highly successful Zionist community that contributed both funds and *olim* to Israel far in excess of what might be expected of it.

Religion

The perennially simmering religious divisions—between Reform and Orthodox and between centrist (modern) Orthodox and right-wing or ultra-Orthodox—occasionally flared up, but the fires were eventually tamped down, through the exercise of leadership, the passage of time, or just the indifference of most Jews to the issues.

Flare-ups tended to occur over Orthodox and Reform rabbis sharing a platform at communal functions, such as Yom Hashoah commemorations or rallies for Israel during the Lebanon War.

There was no Conservative movement in Australia, and the mainstream or modern Orthodox synagogues were very Anglo-Jewish in custom and ritual. Of the various Hassidic sects, only the Lubavitch-Chabad movement was represented in strength in Australia, while the Adass Yisroel was the most visible of the "*mitnagdish*" ultra-Orthodox groups. Most Australian Jews belonged to or identified with one synagogue or another, even if their identification consisted only of Rosh Hashanah or Yom Kippur attendance. Membership in the Reform Jewish stream was growing, as was adherence to ultra-Orthodoxy, but the overwhelming majority of Australian Jews were "traditional," which usually meant belonging to a modern Orthodox congregation.

Both the modern Orthodox and Reform movements showed signs of a growing traditionalism. For example, many Reform rabbis were observing Jewish Sabbath laws and introducing more Hebrew and traditional practices into synagogue ritual. Modern Orthodox rabbis, too, were reemphasizing traditional practice, encouraging daily *shul* going where the Sabbath alone had sufficed in the past, or being more rigorous about Sabbath laws, where once they may have, say, turned a blind eye toward congregants driving to synagogue.

There was some divisiveness over the issue of *kashrut* in Sydney, where the procedures of the modern Orthodox *batei din* were challenged, especially by the Chabad. Melbourne avoided such conflict by virtue of having several *kashrut* authorities, including the Chabad and the Adass.

Education

The Jewish day-school movement continued to flourish in Australia, with eight schools in Melbourne, five in Sydney, one each in Adelaide and Perth, and a kindergarten in Brisbane. Several of these, including Carmel College in Perth, offered all grades through high school. An estimated 80 percent of Jewish children in Melbourne attended day schools; in Sydney the figure was around 50 percent and growing. Apart from the Liberal movement's two schools in Sydney and Melbourne, the Jewish day schools were all Orthodox. Government funding for private schools was provided but occasionally threatened; communal leaders made it clear that cessation of state aid would cause a fundamental crisis for the Jewish schools.

Jewish education outside the day-school system and adult Jewish education, until recently poor relations, were both expanding. Jewish community efforts to have Jewish studies offered at the college level were increasingly successful, with modern and classical Hebrew, Jewish history, and Holocaust-related courses offered in several major universities. The problem of training Jewish studies teachers for the day schools was addressed by having special courses introduced into government-controlled teacher-training programs. Preparations were still being made to open the Mandelbaum College at the University of Sydney, which, on completion, would be a postgraduate center for Jewish and related studies. A Jewish residential college for undergraduates already existed at the University of NSW. The country's one rabbinical college, a *kollel* located in Melbourne, trained Orthodox rabbis. Informal adult education, largely conducted by synagogues, seemed to thrive, though most Australian Jews remained depressingly illiterate in their own heritage.

Personalia

A number of Australian Jews received state honors—from the British Queen (under Liberal governments) or the Australian government (under Labor governments). Sir Asher Joel, a prominent public relations expert and media owner who stage-managed such events as visits by the Queen to Australia, the opening of the Sydney Opera House, and the first tour of Australia by Pope John Paul II, remained the most highly decorated Australian Jew. Many Jews were prominent in the legal world; at one time the Law Reform Commissioners in Sydney and Melbourne were both Jews—Ronald Sackville and Louis Waller, respectively. Professor Waller also headed a Victorian government study into the medical ethics of *in vitro* fertilization. Marcus Einfeld was named a federal court judge, and other Jews sat on the bench at all judicial levels and in most states.

The death of Prof. Julius Stone in 1985 meant the loss of both a great legal mind and a renowned champion of Israel. The great Zionist pioneer Max Freilich, who was instrumental in swaying Australian government opinion to support the creation of the State of Israel, died in 1986. Other prominent Jews who died in recent years were Melbourne communal leader Arnold Bloch (1985) and Sydney leaders Hilary Pryor (1982) and Hannah Kessler (1984).

SUSAN BURES

Israel

THE FOCUS OF ISRAELI affairs in 1986 was predominantly internal: the conduct of the national unity government, which managed to hold together and function despite alternating states of warfare and paralysis in the cabinet; the Shin Bet affair—the aftermath of a 1984 terrorist episode that had potentially serious political implications; the controversy over the conversion of an American Reform Jew, Shoshana Miller; and continuing debates over the "who is a Jew" question, economic policy, and the Lavi jet-fighter project. Two new matters involving national security burst onto the scene during the year: the alleged publication of Israeli nuclear secrets by a former technician, Mordechai Vanunu, and Israel's involvement, on behalf of the United States, in the sale of arms to Iran. No progress of any consequence was seen in the peace process, though Prime Minister Peres held a surprise meeting with Morocco's King Hassan. While there was no official change in the status of the occupied territories, there were signs of growing unrest among the inhabitants of those areas.

Political Affairs

With Prime Minister Shimon Peres and Vice Premier and Foreign Minister Yitzhak Shamir scheduled to swap jobs in mid-October—under the terms of the power-sharing agreement their two parties, Labor and Likud, respectively, had entered into following the deadlocked 1984 general election—virtually every topic under the public-sector sun seemed to be handled as much with an eye toward rotation day as on its own merits. Peres came under growing pressure throughout the year from within his own party to abort the rotation scheme and either remain in power or call an early election, if the Likud did not play ball according to Labor's rules. Although Peres himself did not threaten to renege on the rotation plan, the fact that others in Labor were not so reticent caused most ranking Likud figures to tread carefully.

In Herut, the major component of the Likud, the uncertainty about rotation was an underlying, if publicly unacknowledged, factor in a challenge mounted against party leader Yitzhak Shamir at the party's convention in March. Although previous efforts had been made by factions within Herut to wrest control of the leadership from the Shamir group, the intensity manifested in the 1986 convention was unusual even by Herut standards. Despite the endorsement of Shamir's candidacy as party leader by titular party head Menachem Begin, who issued a rare public message, Deputy Prime Minister and Housing Minister David Levy declared that he and not Shamir was Begin's true political heir. In an on-again off-again alliance with Levy was Ariel Sharon, who had transformed his ranking portfolio in the national unity government—minister of industry and trade—into a lever for political rehabilitation, following his resignation as defense minister in the wake of the Kahan Commission report on the 1982 massacre at two Beirut refugee camps.

The Levy challenge to Shamir, combined with a sense of destabilization caused by the shifting alliances within the party, brought about the total breakdown of the convention into fistfights, chair-throwing, and verbal and physical brawling. Although fitful efforts were made throughout the remaining prerotation period to restore harmony in Herut and renew the convention, these proved unavailing; certainly Shamir had nothing to gain from such a move before he became premier.

In striking contrast to the Herut fiasco, the Labor party convention held in early April was a paradigm of unity. Party leader Shimon Peres, firmly in the driver's seat and riding high in public esteem—a Smith Research Center poll published in the *Jerusalem Post* around this time gave him a 74-percent approval rating as prime minister—parlayed the occasion into an opportunity to oust Finance Minister Yitzhak Modai, a highly popular minister and former ally in pushing through the 1985 economic stabilization plan. Modai had publicly accused Peres of masking his intent to bail out ailing Histadrut (Federation of Labor) enterprises under the guise of a proposed new "economic growth" program. When Peres announced at the opening of the Labor party convention on April 8 that he intended to sack Modai, Likud spokesmen threatened to resign from the coalition; however, Modai spared his party the almost certain embarrassment of having to make good on its threat by announcing (April 9) that he would resign "if Prime Minister Peres so desires."

The result, decided upon at the weekly cabinet meeting of April 13 (and formally approved by the Knesset two days later), was a switch in portfolios between Finance Minister Modai and Justice Minister Moshe Nissim (both from the Likud's Liberal party component). But Peres wanted more. He insisted that Modai be barred from holding the finance portfolio not only until rotation but for the entire duration of the national unity government. For his part, the volatile Modai appeared embarked on a course of political self-destruction when a second major clash with Peres just three months later eventuated in his resignation as justice minister (July 24). This time the Liberal party decided to entrust Tourism Minister Avraham Sharir with the vacant portfolio, leaving Modai out in the cold, though he continued to serve as a Knesset member.

A second major challenge to Peres emanated from Ariel Sharon. In the wake of the massacre of 22 worshipers in an Istanbul synagogue on September 6, Sharon released a statement that same evening asserting that the "baseless peace plans" of Prime Minister Peres were debilitating Israel and thereby all but inviting terrorist attacks in the country and on Jewish targets abroad. The following day Peres suspended the weekly cabinet meeting, at which the principal topic on the agenda was to have been the Istanbul outrage, until Sharon apologized for his remarks publicly and in writing. With just over a month to go before rotation, some observers thought Sharon was seeking to torpedo the Peres-Shamir switch, hoping to replace Shamir as Likud leader in the event an early election was called. If so, he soon found he had miscalculated, as he came under intense pressure from his own party to dispatch the desired letter of apology.

All of these disputes, however, were only the prelude to the squabbling and bickering that marred the implementation of the rotation itself. In the public perception, the Labor party, and Shimon Peres in particular, lost points by unabashedly taking advantage of the rotation to alter the original agreement and to extract concessions from the Likud, which was now effectively at Labor's mercy.

The area of major dispute was cabinet and other appointments. The Alignment refused to countenance Yitzhak Modai's return to the government. Shamir rejected Yossi Beilin, the cabinet secretary and Peres's closest aide, as the candidate for Israel's next ambassador to the United States, a post that would fall vacant in mid-1987. Peres dropped his demand that Ezer Weizman continue to serve in the Prime Minister's Office as minister in charge of Arab affairs, while the Likud agreed to a Labor appointee as chairman of Israel Aircraft Industries, in return for which the Likud could name the chairman of the advisory committee to the Bank of Israel.

On October 10, following a two-day visit to Paris, his final official state visit as prime minister, Peres tendered his resignation to President Chaim Herzog under the terms of the coalition agreement and in accordance with the Basic Law on the Government. At the same time, the Alignment announced its refusal to take part in a joint delegation with the Likud to the president—in order to recommend that he name Yitzhak Shamir to form the new government—until Peres's demands were met.

By October 14, the date originally scheduled for the rotation, everything seemed to hinge on Shamir's consent to the appointment of Yossi Beilin as ambassador to Washington, but neither side would budge. When Peres insisted that the Knesset session scheduled for October 14 be canceled, he was reprimanded by members of his own party for behaving "more like a politician than a national leader."

By October 16, at least 61 MKs, sufficient for a parliamentary majority, had recommended to President Herzog that he name Yitzhak Shamir to form a new government—this, even without the Alignment. On October 18 Peres and Shamir signed a ten-point agreement enabling the formation of the new government. Among the agreement's key elements (according to the text published in *Ma'ariv* on October 19): areas of ministerial responsibility would be transferred only with joint Peres-Shamir consent; topics of special importance would be placed on the cabinet agenda within 21 days of a request by Peres; Yitzhak Modai would serve as a minister without portfolio, and any change in his status would require prior agreement between Peres and Shamir; a ministerial committee would see to "appropriate representation by both sides" (meaning Likud and Labor) on the boards of directors of government corporations; Peres would chair the ministerial committees on

Jerusalem and the Negev; the Alignment would have ongoing input where economic issues were concerned; Peres would submit the names of candidates for the post of ambassador to the United States, and the prime minister would give his consent to one of them within three months. An annex to the agreement stated that four Labor appointees in departments attached to the Prime Minister's Office—including the adviser on counterterrorism, Amiram Nir, whose name was soon to figure prominently in the Iran-*contra* affair—would not be replaced "at this time."

Thus, on October 20, one week after the appointed time, Yitzhak Shamir was able to present his government in the Knesset, Shamir resuming the premiership two years after his previous tenure in that post. The only personnel changes in the 25-person cabinet were the return of Yitzhak Modai and the cooption of Labor's Shoshana Arbelli-Almoslino as minister of health, replacing Mordechai Gur, who had previously announced that in the wake of the Shin Bet affair (see below), he would resign from the government rather than serve under Yitzhak Shamir.

In his policy statement to the Knesset, Shamir elevated the utilitarian need for a national unity government into an ideological platform: "National unity," he declared, "is not just a matter of parliamentary convenience" but could forge "true cooperation" at all levels in the country. On foreign policy, Shamir said his government would "continue to initiate and seek ways to peace," though "not . . . out of weakness" and not through the agency of an "international forum," which could never serve as a substitute for "direct, face-to-face discussions." Shamir assured the "Arab residents of Judea, Samaria and the Gaza District" a "life of dignity" and of "peaceful coexistence with their Jewish neighbors," provided only that they dissociated themselves entirely from the terrorist organizations. This was also the *sine qua non* for "these Arab residents [being] able to run their own affairs."

Once the new government was installed, the interparty front grew calm, but strife erupted within the two major parties, where ranking figures had been frustrated in their aspirations because of the Peres-Shamir compromise agreement. Thus, Shamir was unable to delegate responsibility for Soviet Jewry affairs to Moshe Arens without Peres's—unforthcoming—assent, while in Labor, Peres, blocked in his desire to name Yossi Beilin ambassador to Washington, now found himself stymied as well in his wish to name him deputy minister of foreign affairs (because Beilin was not a Knesset member). When Peres decided to appoint Beilin director-general of the Foreign Ministry, he came up against his own previous pledge to Avraham Tamir, the outgoing director-general of the Prime Minister's Office and a close associate of Ezer Weizman, to appoint him to that post. In a move that riled the Weizman group and drew considerable public scorn, Peres kept his promise to Tamir by naming him director-general, but then went ahead and appointed Beilin "political director-general" and ruled that he outranked Tamir. Aggravating the issue in the eyes of the public was the fact that the person who was being ousted from the position of director-general, David Kimche, was universally respected as a model civil servant of the highest professionalism.

National Security

THE SHIN BET AFFAIR

Repercussions of the April 12, 1984, terrorist hijacking of Bus No. 300 bound from Tel Aviv to Ashkelon continued to make themselves powerfully felt in 1986. Questions had been raised after the incident about the two terrorists who were captured alive and killed before they could be brought to trial; accusations were subsequently made of an official cover-up. In 1985 the key army and police figures involved in storming the bus and capturing the terrorists were exonerated by military and police tribunals, but that by no means ended the matter. (For more detailed background, see AJYB, vol. 86, 1986, pp. 333–34, and AJYB, vol. 87, 1987, p. 305.) What was soon dubbed the "Shin Bet affair," referring to the part played by the General Security Service, or Shin Bet, in the episode, threatened to evolve into a full-blown political crisis, as allegations were made that the country's top leaders were implicated, or at least knew of, the events in question. This did not happen, largely because the principals involved cast aside their political differences and banded together in a virtuoso display of damage control.

As the affair unfolded, deeper questions came to the fore than just the disputed facts, such as ministerial responsibility for the actions of subordinates and possible violations of Israeli law by the country's highest officials. Perhaps most important, the affair led to a national debate on the subject of "state security," a concept that had been universally accepted as justifying virtually any action—for understandable reasons—since the establishment of the state. Israelis were now forced to contemplate the full implications of the concept for the life of the polity and the possible need to set limits on it. Like much else in Israeli life of the 1980s, some of the roots of the problem were traceable to the Six Day War in 1967, after which, as a result of Israel's capture of Arab territories, the Shin Bet found itself in the vanguard of a no-holds-barred fight against terrorism. Now, for the first time, the vaunted and ultrasecret security service, whose chief reported directly to the prime minister, found itself under unaccustomed, and unwelcome, public scrutiny.

On May 24 Israel Televison reported that Attorney General Yitzhak Zamir wished to initiate a police investigation against a "senior official," but that heavy pressure was being brought to bear on him by, among others, Prime Minister Peres, to desist from this course. It was then revealed (by ABC-TV, in flagrant disregard of Israeli military censorship) not only that the official in question was the chief of the Shin Bet but that his name was Avraham Shalom—the first time in Israeli history that the name of a serving head of that agency had been made public—and that the allegations against him related to his part in the Bus No. 300 incident.

Essentially, the story that soon emerged was that Shalom, who was at the scene when Israeli troops stormed the hijacked bus at dawn on April 13, 1984, had ordered the killing, on the spot, of the two terrorists who were taken off the bus alive. When official inquiries were launched into the manner of their deaths—following heavy pressure by the Israeli press—Shalom organized a cover-up. This was effected principally by way of a senior Shin Bet official (later named as Yossi Ginossar), whom Shalom arranged to have serve on the state attorney's investigative commission. After Ginossar briefed Shalom daily on the progress of the inquiry, the two, with the aid of two legal advisers, fabricated and falsified evidence in order systematically to mislead the commission. One immediate result of this was that an Israeli army brigadier general was very nearly wrongly accused of murder.

Peres's involvement went back at least to October 29, 1985, when the then deputy Shin Bet chief, Reuven Hazak, met with the prime minister (with Shalom's knowledge) and told him the entire story. According to what Peres was to tell the Knesset (on June 30, 1986), he met with Hazak again about a week later and informed him that his "conclusion," after giving the matter thought, was "I believe in the GSS chief." Peres also suggested that Hazak take study-leave. (Ultimately, Hazak, along with two other senior officials who supported him in his struggle, was forced out of the service.) At all events, by mid-February 1986, Attorney General Zamir, who had by then learned about the alleged cover-up but had been prevented by Peres from meeting with the Shin Bet personnel who were demanding an inquiry, approached Peres with a request that he act on the matter. By the time the story became public knowledge, Zamir had in fact already directed Israel Police Inspector-General David Kraus to launch an investigation. Kraus, however, received the attorney general's directive just before going on vacation abroad, and filed it in his safe, intending to deal with it when he returned.

Since Israel's political hierarchy was preoccupied with the historic visit of British prime minister Margaret Thatcher when the story broke in May, some days passed before it began to respond and to coordinate a strategy for defusing the potentially explosive issue. Thus, Foreign Minister Shamir—prime minister at the time of the bus hijacking in 1984 and as such responsible for the Shin Bet—said on May 29 that the entire matter should be dropped from the public agenda because of its adverse effects on the security service. This was an approach which Shamir, a former longtime senior official in Israel's Mossad intelligence agency, was to voice consistently throughout the affair. As for what he had known at the time of the incident, Shamir, pleading "considerations of state security," would say only: "I knew what a prime minister should know, and I acted accordingly." Speaking the same day, Prime Minister Peres also enunciated some of the themes that were to characterize his posture in the coming period: No proof existed that Shin Bet actions during the bus hijacking incident had been sanctioned by the political echelon; he, Peres, had not been informed that anything was amiss when he took over as prime minister, and in any case it was inappropriate for a prime minister to investigate the actions of his predecessors in office; moreover, if Shin Bet personnel were placed on trial they would be unable to defend themselves properly because of the bar on them against revealing secret matters; and finally, Peres said, to pursue the matter further would harm state security.

That the matter was, nevertheless, being pursued further behind the scenes by those with vested interests soon became public knowledge. On June 1, the cabinet, at its weekly meeting, appointed a new attorney general to replace Zamir—a largely unknown 63-year-old Tel Aviv district court judge named Yosef Harish. The appointment would take effect June 4. According to the cabinet communiqué, the move was based on a previous announcement by Zamir (in February) "that he had decided to conclude his term of office and would resign upon the appointment of a new attorney general." Coming, however, as the Shin Bet affair gathered momentum under Zamir's watchful prodding, the appointment of Harish was widely viewed as a dismissal of Zamir because of his refusal to yield to Peres and Shamir on the investigation. Zamir himself was informed of the decision only minutes before the cabinet meeting, and most of the ministers had no inkling of what was afoot, although Harish had been "vetted" by Peres, Shamir, and Justice Minister Yitzhak Modai. One of Harish's first acts on assuming office was to order the police to defer the Shin Bet investigation until he could master the material.

On June 25 the outcome of more behind-the-scenes machinations was revealed when Cabinet Secretary Yossi Beilin issued the following statement:

> The prime minister was today informed that the president of Israel has accorded the head of the General Security Service amnesty in the events of Bus No. 300. The president acted on his full authority, following the recommendation of the minister of justice, based on prior consultations with the [inner] cabinet and with the attorney general.
>
> The head of the General Security Service informed the prime minister that he wishes to be discharged from his post, as publication of his identity will not enable him to continue to function as head of the GSS.

The statement went on to say that at the attorney general's recommendation, the prime minister would set up a committee "to set future procedures and modes of action for the GSS, based on the lessons of the past."

This communiqué was more than a little disingenuous. For one thing, Prime Minister Peres had in fact been present at the gathering—at his own residence—the previous night, where the deal was conceived by which Shalom would resign in return for being granted a presidential pardon and hence immunity from prosecution. According to the daily *Ha'aretz,* the chief concocters of the arrangement were two leading Israeli lawyers, Ram Caspi and Ya'acov Ne'eman (the latter a partner of Chaim Herzog in his former law office), together with Justice Minister Modai. Herzog, who was apprised of the plan by the two lawyers in the course of the late-night meeting at the prime minister's residence, gave his agreement in principle. He requested, however, that the matter be coordinated with the attorney general and that the inner cabinet vote its approval.

This was duly done and the president was so informed by Justice Minister Modai and Cabinet Secretary Beilin the following morning, June 25. (Interviewed on Israel Radio that day, Attorney General Harish said that he himself had favored a continuation of the police investigation, "which was set in motion by my predecessor." Harish also confirmed reports that he had learned about the original approach to the president only "after the fact"—although he supported the deal once it was consummated. Legal commentators noted that the very fact that private lawyers had been called in was a slap in the face to Harish personally and, more important, to the institution of the attorney general in Israel.)

The second unlikely point made in the cabinet secretary's statement was that Shalom had asked to be relieved of his duties as Shin Bet head due to "the exposure of his identity." Although this may well have been a consideration, Shalom's position had become untenable primarily because he was a *prima facie* accomplice to the murder of helpless prisoners and had lent a hand to the obstruction of justice. The communiqué also failed to mention that one of those involved in the "prior consultations" was Shalom himself; and that three other senior Shin Bet personnel had been granted amnesty together with Shalom. They turned out to be Yossi Ginossar and the two legal advisers.

However, the president's desire to put an end to the "devil's dance" around the affair, as he told the nation via Israel TV, went unrealized. A group of lawyers, acting in concert with MK Yossi Sarid (Citizens' Rights and Peace Movement, CRM), outraged at what they considered the flaunting of the rule of law in the country and suspecting that the true motivation for the pardon was to block a formal inquiry that could reveal the culpability of ranking politicians, petitioned the High Court of Justice to overturn Herzog's pardon. At the same time, Prime Minister Peres came under heavy fire from within the Labor party for his part in arranging the presidential pardons; particularly vocal in their criticisms were Minister Without Portfolio Ezer Weizman (the only member of the inner cabinet to vote against the arrangement) and Energy Minister Moshe Shahal.

On June 30 Peres replied in the Knesset to five no-confidence motions concerning the presidential pardons. While defending his own actions since having learned about the cover-up nine months earlier, he indicated that he would not be averse to the formation of a "legally constituted commission"; as a representative of the "political echelon," he said, he had "nothing to hide."

Although the no-confidence motions were handily defeated by the coalition, the Likud charged that Peres, by expressing his willingness to have a commission of inquiry appointed, was trying to dissociate himself from Shamir—who was adamantly opposed to such a course—and was, by inference, trying to pin the blame on him. This impression was strengthened on July 1, when the text of the letter from Shin Bet chief Shalom to President Herzog requesting a pardon was made public. According to Shalom, "All my actions with respect to the '300 incident' were carried out with authority and permission, in order to maintain state security and to prevent the exposure of [the state's] deepest secrets." Since Shalom's direct superior at the time of the event was Prime Minister Shamir, he was the only feasible source for any "authority and permission" which may have been given. (In an interview in the monthly *Monitin,* Shamir denied having issued a general directive to the Shin Bet in 1983, under which any terrorist apprehended on a hostage-taking mission was to be killed.)

As public and institutional pressure mounted for the attorney general to act—on July 1 the High Court of Justice ordered Harish to show cause why a formal investigation of the Shin Bet affair should not be conducted—Harish on July 13 recommended the formation of a judicial commission of inquiry. However, when the full 25-person cabinet met the next day, it voted 14–11 against the establishment of such a commission—a victory for the Likud, backed by all the religious ministers. At the same time, Peres named a three-man committee, headed by former director of military intelligence Maj. Gen. (res.) Aharon Yariv, to set operational guidelines for the Shin Bet. (The committee submitted its recommendations, which were, naturally, classified, on July 31.) On July 17 Harish met with police chief Kraus to discuss details of the police probe, the way for which had now been cleared by the cabinet decision.

On August 6 the High Court of Justice, in a split decision (2–1), upheld President Herzog's pardon for the Shin Bet chief and three senior officials of the service. In a 161-page decision, the Supreme Court president, Justice Meir Shamgar, was joined by Justice Miriam Ben-Porat for the majority, while Justice Aharon Barak dissented. Although the legal point at issue was whether the president of Israel had the authority to grant a pardon before the person concerned had been duly convicted in a trial, the High Court's judgment all but guaranteed that the affair was as good as dead, even if the final death throes were to be protracted. Less than three weeks after the court's ruling, President Herzog pardoned another seven Shin Bet agents who had been involved in the bus hijacking episode and its aftermath. Herzog explained that he had been moved to take this course in order to prevent "discrimination against officials of a certain rank in the GSS as compared with officials of a different rank." Thus, this was not "a new decision, but [the] direct and logical continuation of the previous" amnesty decision.

Although all the potential felons had been pardoned, the police went through the motions of a secret investigation, questioning Peres, Shamir, the Shin Bet men involved, and others. On September 18 the police team submitted its findings to the attorney general, and on December 29 Harish issued a statement, together with a legal opinion on the findings of the police, in which he concluded, *inter alia:* "The investigation material contains nothing on which to base evidence of [the political echelon's] involvement. . . ."

If there was nothing on which to ground evidence of culpability, neither was there anything to praise in the conduct of the political echelon, according to the legal opinion written by staff members of the state attorney's office. The authors of the document rebuked Prime Minister Shamir and Vice Premier and Foreign Minister Peres (as they were in the postrotation era), if not for their commissions, then undoubtedly for their omissions:

> If the attorney general thinks there is *prima facie* material which warrants an investigation into extremely serious offenses committed by a person in the

executive branch, the rule of law obligates an investigation and an examination. . . . Security considerations call for no other [course of action]. There is no security without law. The rule of law is a component of national security.

Both Shamir and Peres expressed their satisfaction that the "devil's dance" had ended; both declared that they regarded the affair as closed. According to press reports, the pardoned chief of the Shin Bet, Avraham Shalom, resigned from the service, as did Yossi Ginossar; the two legal advisers were reported to have been transferred to other posts in the agency. On December 31 the Knesset debated four motions for the agenda on the Harish report; not a single cabinet minister was present during the debate.

THE VANUNU CASE

On October 5, 1986, the London *Sunday Times* published a sensational two-page spread entitled "Inside Dimona, Israel's Nuclear Bomb Factory." The report, complete with photographs and diagrams purporting to depict the Dimona Nuclear Research Center, claimed that Israel, with a "projected arsenal of 100–200 [nuclear] weapons," was "the sixth most powerful nation on earth." The source for this at-once startling and long-suspected information was named by the paper as Mordechai Vanunu, a 31-year-old former technician at the Dimona installation. According to the *Times,* the Moroccan-born Vanunu was said to have been dismissed from his position at Dimona in November 1985 after working there for over nine years, because of the "left-wing tendencies" that came to the fore when he began taking part-time courses at Ben-Gurion University in Beersheba. Vanunu then made his way to Australia, where he met a "mercurial" Spanish journalist to whom he told his story, and through whom the *Times* learned about it. After satisfying themselves of the story's authenticity, the paper's editors went ahead and printed it.

On October 6, the day after the piece appeared, a communiqué from the Israeli cabinet stated that "the government is used to sensational reports about the Nuclear Research Center at Dimona, and does not make a practice of commenting on them." It went on to reiterate Israel's official nuclear position: "Israel's policy has not changed, and it will not be the first to introduce nuclear weapons into the region."

In the meantime, the story had taken a bizarre twist: Vanunu himself had disappeared from his London hotel on September 30 and had not been seen since. An Australian clergyman, John McKnight, then turned up in Israel, saying Vanunu had converted to Christianity and had been a member of his church in Sydney. McKnight said he was in Israel to try and locate Vanunu, but was being given the runaround. McKnight left Israel at the end of October, amid rumors that Israel's Mossad intelligence agency had kidnapped Vanunu illegally on British soil and brought him to Israel secretly, where he was now imprisoned. Official comment, however, was limited to "We do not know anything about this matter" (a spokesman in the Prime Minister's Office) and "[Vanunu] is not being held in a jail of the Prisons Service" (a Prisons Service spokesman).

There followed a week of intense diplomatic pressure, notably from England, combined with the threat of a petition to the High Court of Justice, as well as press speculation and sleuthing by Israeli journalists to discover Vanunu's whereabouts. (As the *Jerusalem Post* put it in a scathing editorial entitled "When Government Lies": "Every knowledgeable Israeli already knew for a fact that Mr. Vanunu was being held in a prison cell somewhere in Israel.") Finally, on November 9, the cabinet secretary issued the following statement:

> Mordechai Vanunu is under lawful detention in Israel, in the wake of a court order which was issued following a hearing at which the lawyer he chose was present. Due to *sub judice* regulations, no further details will be published. All the rumors to the effect that Vanunu was "kidnapped" on British soil are totally without foundation, and it follows that there is likewise no basis for the report that Mr. Peres contacted Mrs. Thatcher to inform her about something that never took place.

The reference to British prime minister Margaret Thatcher was intended to refute press reports purporting to spell out the manner in which Vanunu had been brought to Israel—reports that were becoming a diplomatic embarrassment for both Jerusalem and London.

On November 28 Vanunu was brought to the Jerusalem district court, where unprecedented security measures were in force, and in a closed-door hearing was formally charged under the "State Security, Foreign Relations and Official Secrets" section of the Penal Code. Although the details of the indictment itself were barred for publication, one of the articles under which Vanunu was charged—treason ("assistance to an enemy in war")—carried with it a maximum death penalty. Vanunu was also accused of having committed "aggravated espionage," which bore a maximum sentence of life imprisonment. Earlier in the month, Foreign Minister Peres had spelled out the Israeli position during a visit to Chicago. According to a Reuters report, Peres said that even though Vanunu was lying when he claimed Israel had manufactured nuclear warheads, he had to face prosecution in Israel because he did "not have the right" to talk about this topic. Vanunu had broken the law, Peres said, by revealing matters "which are considered state secrets, or pretending to."

Vanunu himself found a novel way to inform the world about his strange odyssey. On December 21, as he was being taken into the Jerusalem district court for a remand hearing, he suddenly pressed the palm of his hand—which was covered with writing—against the window of the police van bringing him to the court. Before the security guards could react, the press photographers and TV cameramen at the scene went into action, recording the event for posterity. When the guards did manage to overcome Vanunu, he began shouting to the reporters present, until he was gagged. What Vanunu had written on his palm (in English) was: "Vanunu M. was hijacked in Rome Itl. 30.9.86, 2100, came to Israel by BA FLY 504." (Mordechai Vanunu was kidnapped in Rome, Italy, on September 30, 1986, at 9:00 P.M., and was brought to Israel via British Airways flight No. 504.) The possible adverse effect of the episode on Israeli-Italian relations occasioned concern. In Rome, Prime

Minister Bettino Craxi stated that no "satisfactory response" had been forthcoming from Israel, and "we will insist that this be provided." Even Craxi admitted, however, that the most Italy could do would be to lodge an official protest.

If Vanunu's purpose, as was suggested in some quarters, had been to trigger a public debate in Israel about the country's nuclear policy, this objective went almost entirely unrealized. Aside from a few scattered articles in the press, one or two of them calling for a revision of the deliberately vague Israeli nuclear posture, the traditional silence on this subject was scrupulously maintained.

Mordechai Vanunu's trial opened on December 28,1986, in the Jerusalem district court before a panel of three judges. He pleaded not guilty to all the charges and was ordered remanded in custody until the conclusion of the proceedings against him.

Peace Initiatives

Throughout 1986 Prime Minister Peres pursued the peace initiatives he had helped set in motion the previous year, his efforts focused principally on furthering the idea of an international conference as an "opening" or "accompaniment" to direct talks with Jordan and a Palestinian delegation. From the very outset of the year, when he undertook a "peace mission" to Western Europe (January 12–31), which included meetings with Assistant Secretary of State Richard Murphy of the United States in London and The Hague, to the very end of his tenure as prime minister, when he and President Hosni Mubarak of Egypt declared 1987 the "year of peace" at the conclusion of a historic summit meeting in Alexandria (see "Foreign Relations: Egypt"), Peres hammered home his theme: "It is peace that we seek—based on dignity and mutual respect; achieved by negotiations and compromise."

Early in the year the possibility of a breakthrough seemed to present itself when Jordan's King Hussein announced (February 19) that he was breaking off his year-long dialogue with Arafat about possible Middle East peace moves. For the Labor party especially, which had consistently espoused a "Jordanian option" and (in common with the Likud) rejected the PLO as a negotiating partner, the derailing of the Hussein-Arafat talks seemed to hold out genuine prospects. Defense Minister Yitzhak Rabin urged the Arab residents in the territories "to stand up on their own, on their own authority, . . . [and] join [King] Hussein in a move of peace negotiations with Israel, without the PLO." However, events such as the assassination of the moderate mayor of Nablus, Zafr al-Masri (March 2), and the outpouring of sympathy for the PLO at his funeral (see "The Administered Areas"), did not augur well either for the practicability of the Jordanian option or for the participation of Palestinians from the territories in peace moves. That no dramatic breakthrough was imminent was further confirmed during another round of talks with Richard Murphy, who was in Israel from March 11–13 as part of a regional swing.

Not even Prime Minister Peres's declaration on April 8 to the opening of the Labor party's convention that Israel recognized the Palestinians "as a nation" caused much of a stir. And even though Peres said in a television interview at the end of that month that "quiet diplomacy" was under way with Jordan, the United States continued to play a cautious game in the region—following the fiascoes of the recent past—even canceling Secretary of State George Shultz's previously announced visit to the Middle East.

The single most dramatic peace-related event of 1986 was undoubtedly Prime Minister Peres's surprise visit to Morocco for talks with King Hassan II. On July 21, Peres, together with Alignment Knesset faction chairman Rafi Edri (himself of Moroccan extraction) and several close aides, flew secretly to Morocco. During their 48-hour stay, Peres and Hassan met three times, including one private session, at the king's summer palace at Ifrane, in the Atlas Mountains. According to a joint communiqué issued simultaneously in Rabat and Jerusalem on July 24, following Peres's return home, the talks were "marked by frankness" and were "devoted essentially to the study of the Fez Plan." (Adopted at the Arab summit conference held at Fez, Morocco, in September 1982, this "plan" was actually a set of eight principles of which the seventh—referring to "guarantees of peace for all the states of the region"—was generally held to constitute implicit recognition of Israel.) Yet the communiqué also stressed that "the meeting was of a purely exploratory nature, aiming at no moment at engaging in negotiations." Hassan pledged to inform Arab leaders "of the points of view developed during the talks" while Peres would do likewise *vis-à-vis* the Israeli government.

Although Hassan, in a speech to the Moroccan nation delivered while Peres was on his way back to Israel, seemed to deflate the significance of the meeting, Peres professed to view the talks as "an important turning point in the history of the peace efforts in the entire region." Speaking in the Knesset on July 25, Peres stressed that by hosting him publicly, Hassan had shown that "the traditional 'barrier of shame' " which prevented Arab leaders from meeting openly with Israeli figures could be circumvented with no adverse effects. In an interview on Israel Radio (July 25), Foreign Minister Yitzhak Shamir pooh-poohed the significance of the event, averring that "we've already passed that barrier about Israel being a pariah in the region." In fact, whatever long-term processes the Peres-Hassan talks may have set in motion, in the immediate perspective the visit appeared to have occurred in its own time warp, as it were, outside the framework of ongoing events in the region.

A more substantive boost to the peace process seemed to ensue from the Peres-Mubarak summit meeting at Alexandria (September 11–13), which produced a joint statement asserting that Israel and Egypt "should now concentrate their efforts on reviving the comprehensive peace process." Concerned about a continuing "stalemate," the two leaders gave their assent to the convening of an international conference as a framework for talks, differing, however, with respect to the role the superpowers, and especially the Soviet Union, should play in such a conference. Both Peres and Mubarak were at odds with Yitzhak Shamir and the Likud, who bitterly rejected the entire concept of an international conference.

Nevertheless, according to the communiqué released after the weekly meeting of the Israeli cabinet on September 14, Prime Minister Peres informed the ministers that "the international conference is not intended to replace direct negotiations but to advance them. It is self-evident that it [will have] no authority to impose solutions or to annul agreements. After the opening of the conference, negotiations will be conducted in bilateral geographical committees without international intervention." Shamir, however, indicated that he was unimpressed by Peres's insistence that such a conference would constitute no more than a "framework" for direct talks. Returning from a visit to the United States at the beginning of October, Shamir said that the two governments were agreed that the only way to advance the peace process was via direct talks without any form of "international accompaniment." Shamir also pledged that his term of office as prime minister would see "many initiatives" with respect to the peace process.

A peace initiative of a different sort took place in November, when a delegation of 22 Israelis, led by Latif Dori, a Mapam activist, met in Constanza, Rumania, with 15 members of the PLO, headed by Abed al-Razak Ahye, a member of the organization's executive. Beyond the occurrence of the dialogue itself, which lasted for several hours, and the participation in the talks of Israelis of Middle East extraction, what riveted public attention was the Israeli contingent's blatant defiance of the recently passed amendment to the Prevention of Terrorism Ordinance banning contacts between Israelis and members of terrorist organizations—a category which, under formal Israeli definition, included the PLO. The fact that at the working session the Israeli and PLO delegations were separated by both their Rumanian hosts and a partition of plants—this at the suggestion of the Israeli delegation's legal adviser—did not prevent the police from serving summonses on four of the group's members upon their return to Israel on November 7. A week later the four were formally questioned, and in mid-December the police, following consultation with the attorney general, recommended that they be brought to trial.

Israel—U.S. Relations

Relations with the United States continued on an even keel for most of the year. The Reagan administration continued to express itself effusively about Israel's economic recovery program, and a midyear visit by Vice-President George Bush afforded the opportunity for some traditional rhetoric about the bonds between the two countries, notably on the level of strategic cooperation. Ironically, however, those events which tended to inject a jarring note into the prevailing harmony cropped up precisely in the strategic realm: these included Washington's growing doubts about the feasibility of the Lavi jet-fighter project, new accusations hurled at Israel concerning alleged espionage activities in the States, and the revelations of Israel's apparent involvement in the so-called Iran-*contra* affair. The State Department continued to be closely involved in furthering Israeli-Egyptian relations, particularly in the protracted negotiations over Taba, but remained chary of plunging into the cold waters of comprehensive Middle East peacemaking.

In a visit to the States at the beginning of April, Prime Minister Peres was commended by Secretary of State Shultz for his "bold and farsighted leadership," which had enabled Israel to cope with its economic problems "in a forthright and constructive way." Shultz was referring specifically to the impressive results of Israel's economic stabilization plan, introduced in July 1985. At the same time, Washington continued to caution Israel about the long-term economic situation. As Under Secretary of State Allen Wallis, in Israel in June for talks within the framework of the Israel-U.S. Joint Economic Development Group, pointed out, certain external factors that had contributed to the revival of the Israeli economy, such as the shortfall in world oil prices and a weak U.S. dollar, were likely to prove temporary phenomena; moreover, emergency U.S. aid amounting to $1.5 billion during the year following adoption of the economic recovery plan would no longer be available.

The first anniversary of the establishment of the Free Trade Area agreement (FTA) between the two countries was marked at a September meeting of the Israel-American Chamber of Commerce in Tel Aviv. U.S. ambassador to Israel Thomas Pickering described the agreement as a "unique milestone" for both countries. Industry and Trade Minister Ariel Sharon, however, noted that the 10-percent increase in Israeli exports to the States from 1985 to 1986 was only one-third the increase that had been registered in 1985 over 1984. Nevertheless, Sharon said, the FTA pact had offset some of the deleterious effects of the weakened dollar for Israeli exporters. Putting matters into broader perspective, U.S. trade representative Clayton Yeutter said in November, following discussions held in Israel by the joint follow-up committee on the FTA, that a single year, or even a five-year-period, was insufficient to judge the worth of a trade accord.

The ongoing strategic cooperation between the two countries was deepened by a meeting of the Joint Political/Military Group in Tel Aviv in March. Two months later (May 6), Defense Minister Rabin and Secretary of Defense Caspar Weinberger initialed an agreement committing Israel to take part in the development of the U.S. Strategic Defense Initiative, or "Star Wars." (Israel followed Britain and West Germany in this regard.) The initial Israeli windfall from this move was an agreement, worth $6 million, signed in Israel on November 5, under which the Defense Ministry was to conduct a study on defensive systems against tactical ballistic missiles—a subject of special interest to Israel in light of various Soviet-made missiles deployed in Syria.

Strategic cooperation was also a major subject of discussion in the visit to Israel by Vice-President George Bush (July 27–30). Two agreements were signed during the visit, a memorandum aimed at increasing tourism between the two countries and a draft accord for the construction of a Voice of America relay station in the Arava desert. When he left Israel for the remaining stops on his Middle East junket—Jordan and Egypt—Bush was carrying messages from Prime Minister Peres to King Hussein and President Mubarak. However, any desire Bush may have had to leave the region with a concrete accomplishment in the realm of peacemaking remained unfulfilled—notwithstanding Peres's assertion that he was "convinced that as a result of the vice-president's visit, the peace process will gain momentum."

In a press conference he held to sum up his visit, Bush was asked about the impact the Pollard affair was having on Israeli-U.S. relations. (Jonathan Pollard, a U.S. Navy civilian intelligence analyst, was arrested on November 21, 1985, and charged with spying for Israel; Jerusalem subsequently dismantled the unit involved and issued a formal apology. Both Pollard and his wife were awaiting trial in Washington.) According to the vice-president, "There was a feeling in some quarters [in Jerusalem] that there was a vendetta against Israel, but after this visit I think it's understood that there is none."

In fact, less than two months before the Bush visit, the American media had carried new allegations to the effect that Pollard was only part of a far larger Israeli espionage ring in the United States. At about the same time, FBI director William Webster told the *New York Times* that only "selective cooperation" had been forthcoming from Israel in the Pollard investigation—prompting Defense Minister Rabin to charge (June 7) that some circles in Washington were "out to get Israel." The cabinet added its voice to the fray the following day, when the communiqué issued following its weekly meeting said that Israel viewed "with concern" a "wave of unfounded reports [in the United States] regarding supposed espionage episodes and Israeli arms deals." The "arms deals" reference concerned a separate case in which a retired Israeli brigadier general, Avraham Baram, had been arrested, together with two other Israelis and two Americans in connection with an alleged scheme to sell U.S. arms to Iran. Where the Pollard case was concerned, the communiqué stated, Israel had evinced "sincere cooperation" in its investigation, "in the spirit of the close relations between the two countries."

Nevertheless, exactly one month later the Defense Ministry was constrained to issue another denial, once more describing as "unfounded" reports in the American press—this time to the effect that Israel had unlawfully exported weapons technology from the United States. What was especially "grave," the Defense Ministry added, was that "this matter has been published before the facts have been clarified." Although the State Department expressed regret at the "unauthorized disclosures," it did not escape notice that, following past patterns (which predated the Pollard episode), the entire affair had blown up while a ranking Israeli defense figure—in this case the chief of staff, Lt. Gen. Moshe Levy—was visiting the United States.

LAVI PROJECT

A subject of ongoing concern was the Lavi jet-fighter project, of which the development stage was being financed almost entirely by the U.S. government. In February a report by the U.S. deputy under secretary of defense for planning and resources, Dov Zakheim, which estimated that the Lavi's final production costs would far exceed the Israeli figures, was conveyed to the Defense Ministry. Although Israeli officials contested the conclusions of the Pentagon report, in May

Ambassador Thomas Pickering told Israel TV that the costing disparities between Israel and the United States should be "ironed out" before Israel moved from the development to the production stage of the project. In June, following a visit to Israel by a Pentagon team under Zakheim, Defense Minister Rabin declared that the project would continue. July 21 saw the Lavi's first public "rollout" in a ceremony at Israel Aircraft Industries, attended by some 2,000 persons, including a congressional delegation and representatives of American firms subcontracted to manufacture key systems for the aircraft. Despite its reservations, the Pentagon in August sent Israel a positive signal by releasing some $69 million earmarked by Congress for the Lavi which it had been holding up. In an interview with the *Jerusalem Post* in September, on the eve of a visit to Washington, Defense Minister Rabin enunciated Israel's stand on the Lavi: "We see the Lavi as an economic-technological-military project essential to Israel's overall military infrastructure at all levels, and not just as a weapons system." On the very last day of 1986, the Lavi prototype made its maiden flight, a 26-minute performance. This came almost seven years after its inception and an investment, to date, of $1.2 billion.

IRAN-CONTRA AFFAIR

In the waning days of the year Israel found itself involved in what came to be known as the Iran-*contra* affair, yet another episode with profound political-security implications—for itself and for the United States. In this tangled web of arms-for-hostages deals with Iran and the diversion of the profits to the antigovernment forces in Nicaragua known as the *contras,* Israel acted, certainly in the initial stages, at the request of senior American officials possessing ostensible presidential sanction. However, repeating its initial response to the Pollard affair, Jerusalem once more opted for an information policy that proved counterproductive. For a full three weeks, from November 4, when a Lebanese paper reported that the United States had shipped arms to Iran, and speculation ran rife about Israel's part in the operation, until November 25, when U.S. attorney general Edwin Meese revealed that profits from the arms deals with Iran had been rerouted to the *contra* rebels in Nicaragua, with Israel supposedly acting as some sort of conduit, the Israeli leadership engaged in stonewalling. The inevitable impression, as Jerusalem moved from a posture of blanket silence to denial to less unequivocal denial, as evidence of Israeli complicity mounted, was that the Israeli leadership—in particular the so-called prime minister's forum of Yitzhak Shamir, Shimon Peres, and Yitzhak Rabin—had something to hide.

Indeed, in an interview with Israel TV, recorded hours before Meese exploded his bombshell but broadcast, embarrassingly, two hours afterward, Prime Minister Shamir was asked about the Israeli connection in the U.S. arms deals with Khomeini's Iran and replied categorically: "There is no secret Israeli connection with Khomeini's Iran. Period." Yet even as the interview was being screened, Shamir, Peres, and Rabin were closeted in a frantic effort to formulate a reaction that would take into account the Meese revelations. Manifestly aimed less at the Israeli public than at the evening network news programs in the United States, the statement that was finally released—at approximately 1:00 A.M. local time—acknowledged a partial Israeli role but dissociated Israel from any connection with the explosive *contra* aspect of the affair:

> The Government of Israel confirms that it helped transfer defensive arms and spare parts from the U.S. to Iran at the request of the U.S. The payment for this equipment was made directly by an Iranian representative to a Swiss bank in accordance with instructions from the American representatives. These funds did not pass through Israel. The Government of Israel was surprised to learn that supposedly a portion of these funds was transferred to the *contras.* If such a transaction took place, it had nothing to do with Israel, and the Government of Israel had no knowledge of it. Israel did not serve and would not have served as a channel for such a transaction.

With the cat out of the bag, the Shamir-Peres-Rabin "triumvirate," as they were dubbed by the Israeli press, launched a campaign of damage control. Besides possible injurious effects on Israel's traditionally good relations with Congress, the government faced mounting domestic criticism over the possibility that arms funneled to Iran by Israel might have found their way to the Iranian-controlled Hezbollah group in Lebanon and been employed against Israeli soldiers. Addressing this criticism, Prime Minister Shamir said on November 28, "We found this risk tolerable." Former Foreign Ministry director-general David Kimche told Israel TV (December 12) that Israel's objective in acceding to the U.S. request for assistance in the operation was to bolster pro-Western elements in Iran and forge contacts in that highly strategic country with a view to the post-Khomeini period—a tactic that was assailed by various Israeli experts.

Other Foreign Relations

EGYPT

Like other seemingly unrelated matters, Israeli-Egyptian relations in 1986 were affected by the schism at the heart of the national unity government. Although those relations were given a shot in the arm in the form of a Peres-Mubarak summit meeting in September, the fact that the summit was delayed until the eve of the rotation meant that Peres had no opportunity to use it as a lever for further Middle East peace moves prior to his replacement as prime minister by Yitzhak Shamir.

What caused the delay was the unresolved issue of ownership of Taba, a tiny coastal strip south of Eilat containing an Israeli five-star hotel and holiday village, which was also claimed by Egypt and had been a major bone of contention between the two countries ever since the signing of the peace treaty between them in 1979. Following Israel's withdrawal from Lebanon in 1985, resolution of the Taba issue was the only remaining unmet condition set by Egyptian president Mubarak for a summit meeting with the Israeli prime minister and the return of an Egyptian ambassador to Tel Aviv (where a chargé d'affaires had been in residence ever since the Beirut refugee-camp massacre in 1982). Progress was slow, however, because the Likud insisted that the dispute be resolved through "conciliation" (nonbinding arbitration), the first stage stipulated in the peace treaty, while the Labor Alignment maintained that conciliation had already been tried and found wanting, and that international arbitration, the next step set forth in the peace treaty, was now called for.

Under Peres's prodding, a marathon 12-hour inner cabinet meeting on January 12 hammered out a 14-point resolution, of which the first and most important clause was that "the Taba issue and the other disputed points along the international border between Israel and Egypt will be resolved by means of an arbitration process." At Shamir's insistence, several clauses were added to the original draft resolution, referring to Israeli demands concerning the aftermath of the Ras Burka massacre of October 1985; the need for a reaffirmation of the peace treaty and the Camp David accords; and commitments by the two countries to prevent terrorist activity and "hostile propaganda" against each other. According to another key clause, "The return of the Egyptian ambassador, the signing of the arbitration *compromis* [as the arbitration agreement was formally termed] and the process of normalization will commence simultaneously."

President Mubarak, however, was opposed to settling all outstanding matters simultaneously, with the result that the Taba talks once more bogged down. Matters were not helped by the fatal terrorist shooting, on March 19, of a member of the Israeli delegation to the Cairo Trade Fair, Eti Tal-Or, aged 23; three other Israelis were wounded by gunfire.

It was not until early August, following intervention by the United States—both Assistant Secretary of State Richard Murphy and State Department legal adviser Abraham Sofaer were dispatched at various stages to help bridge the remaining gaps—that Israeli and Egyptian delegations, meeting in Cairo, finally came up with a draft agreement on a Taba arbitration document. On August 13, following a seven-hour meeting, the inner cabinet decided by a vote of 8–2 (Sharon and Arens), to approve the draft *compromis.* With a Peres-Mubarak summit meeting now tentatively scheduled for September 11, Israeli and Egyptian negotiators, urged on by the State Department's Richard Murphy, worked almost around the clock from the beginning of September to tie up the loose ends and thereby allow the summit to proceed. In fact, it was not until 2:30 A.M. on September 11, less than 12 hours before Peres's scheduled arrival in Egypt, that the *compromis* agreement was at last signed.

The chief accomplishment of the Alexandria summit meeting itself—the first in five years between an Israeli premier and an Egyptian president and the first ever at this level in which Israel was represented by the leader of the Labor party—was the fact that it took place at all. Both sides hoped that the encounter, in the words of the joint communiqué issued at the conclusion of the talks, would herald "a new era in the bilateral relations between Egypt and Israel as well as in the search for a just and comprehensive peace in the Middle East." Egyptian foreign minister Esmat Abdel-Meguid announced that Mohammed Bassiouny, who had served as chargé d'affaires in the Egyptian embassy in Tel Aviv for six years and as ambassador in all but name since 1982, was being appointed ambassador to Israel. (Bassiouny formally presented his credentials to President Herzog on September 23.)

On November 30 the full cabinet ratified the Taba *compromis* document, and on December 10 the international arbitration process—expected to last for at least a year—got under way at Geneva.

EUROPE

A moving and historic event in 1986 was the establishment of diplomatic ties between Israel and Spain—nearly 500 years after the expulsion of the Jews from Spain in 1492. In February Israel's first ambassador to Spain, Shmuel Hadas, presented his credentials to King Juan Carlos; a month later Spain's first envoy to Israel, Pedro Lopez Aguirregengoz, presented his credentials to President Herzog. In September a three-day visit to Israel by Spanish foreign minister Francisco Fernandez Ordonez produced a decision to set up a joint committee to examine possible cooperation between the two countries in a number of areas, including tourism, technology, and culture.

The most important European visit of the year was that of Prime Minister Margaret Thatcher of Great Britain (May 24–27), the first such visit by an incumbent British premier and another event redolent with history. The drama of the visit was symbolized by Mrs. Thatcher's entry into the King David Hotel in Jerusalem, where she and her entourage were lodged. Just 40 years earlier, the Irgun, the prestate Jewish underground organization headed by former prime minister Menachem Begin, had blown up the wing of the hotel that housed British headquarters at the time, with the loss of 91 lives. Israelis were deeply moved when Mrs. Thatcher knelt on the floor at the Yad Vashem Holocaust Memorial—her very first official act in the country—and when she laid a wreath at the tomb of Israel's first prime minister, David Ben-Gurion, at Kibbutz Sde Boker in the Negev. More substantively, the British leader had some strong words to say in support of the struggle of Soviet Jewry to emigrate and against appeasement of terrorists.

On the Middle East situation, which dominated Thatcher's talks with the Israeli political leadership, she declared that "Britain is committed to a stable, peaceful and secure future for the people of Israel." At the same time, she was forthright in stating her belief that Israel "will only find the security [it] seeks[s] by recognizing the legitimate rights of the Palestinian people and their just requirements." Thatcher, who also met with a delegation of leading Palestinians from the territories, called on Israel to take "practical steps" to ameliorate the lot of the Palestinians there. More controversially, she also urged that they be allowed to elect their own representatives—a notion to which most Israeli leaders were not amenable—in order to enable the creation of an "alternative" Palestinian leadership that could replace the PLO as a dialogue partner in talks with Israel and Jordan, with the ultimate goal of establishing a Jordanian-Palestinian "federation."

Another first-time visit was that of a serving West German defense minister. During his four-day stay in Israel in April—made solely for "information-gathering" purposes, according to the German embassy in Tel Aviv—Manfred Woerner held talks with his host, Defense Minister Rabin, and other ranking defense establishment officials on Israel's security posture and the Middle East picture as a whole, as well as visiting a number of military sites and defense plants. Prime Minister Peres had visited West Germany during his January swing through Western Europe.

The year saw expanded bilateral Franco-Israeli activity, a state of affairs that undoubtedly pleased Prime Minister Peres, an inveterate Francophile ever since his days in the Defense Ministry under Ben-Gurion, when Paris was Israel's chief arms supplier. Peres himself was in France twice: in April, to address the parliamentary assembly of the Council of Europe, where his theme was the need for talks between Israel and a Jordanian-Palestinian delegation, followed by a lightning visit to Paris for a meeting with President François Mitterrand; and again in October—his final official visit abroad as prime minister—for a 48-hour stay during which he met again with Mitterrand, held talks with Premier Jacques Chirac on methods of combating international terrorism, and tendered a reception at Versailles as part of the celebrations marking the centenary of David Ben-Gurion's birth.

Relations with Italy received a boost in the form of a visit by Foreign Minister Giulio Andreotti in May, with the talks focusing on the need for greater international cooperation in the war against terrorism. This common desire by the two countries was given formal expression on December 4, when visiting Interior Minister Oscar Luigi Scalfaro and Minister of Police Haim Bar-Lev signed an agreement by which a "bilateral committee" was to be formed, to be headed by the two ministers and to meet at least once a year. The two countries agreed to enhance their cooperation in fighting terrorist organizations, illicit drug dealing, and organized crime.

Israel's traditionally solid ties with the Netherlands were further cemented in a visit to that country by Prime Minister Peres in January on his Western European mission. High on the agenda of Peres's talks with Premier Ruud Lubbers was Holland's continued representation of Israeli interests in the Soviet Union. In mid-October Princess Juliana and Prince Bernhard of the Netherlands paid a six-day visit to Israel as guests of the Jewish National Fund, during which the former queen dedicated a forest in Galilee named in honor of her daughter Queen Beatrix (in whose favor she abdicated the throne in 1980).

An area of Europe that seemed to play a marginal role in Israeli foreign relations received some top-level attention in 1986 when Defense Minister Rabin paid a week-long visit to Scandinavia in November, including a rare visit to Finland, where he met with President Mauno Koivisto and other leading figures. Much closer to home, Israel's relations with Greece—since the establishment of Israel-Spain ties, the only EEC member-state that did not recognize Israel—underwent perceptible improvement during the year. In May Tourism Minister Sharir met for one hour with Foreign Minister Karolos Papoulias in Athens; in July, MK Shulamit Aloni (CRM) became the first Israeli member of parliament to pay an official visit to Greece, also as the guest of Foreign Minister Papoulias; and on November 27 Israel and Greece signed a tourism cooperation agreement during a two-day visit by Deputy Minister of Economics and Tourism Panaglotis Roumeliotis, the highest-ranking Greek official ever to visit Israel.

Against the backdrop of the highly positive picture of Israeli-Western European ties, the case of Austria stood out starkly. Israel's relations with Vienna deteriorated sharply in 1986, as evidence mounted of the alleged Nazi background of Kurt Waldheim, the former UN secretary-general who was elected Austria's president. Initially the Israeli government sought to distance itself from the campaign against Waldheim spearheaded by the World Jewish Congress, out of reluctance to be seen interfering in the internal affairs of another country and apprehension about possible adverse consequences for Austrian Jewry. In May, however, Foreign Minister Shamir told the *New York Times* that a Waldheim election victory would have a negative effect on Israeli-Austrian relations—drawing an immediate charge by Austrian foreign minister Leopold Gratz of unconscionable Israeli meddling in Austrian affairs. Following Waldheim's victory, Israel recalled its ambassador to Austria, Michael Elitzur, and in November (now) Foreign Minister Peres told the Knesset that Israel would not be dispatching an ambassador to Vienna "at this stage." Austria responded by recalling Ambassador Otto Pleinert from Tel Aviv "for consultations."

Some movement was registered in Israel's relations with Eastern European countries, notably in the form of the first official meeting between Israeli and Soviet representatives since the USSR severed its diplomatic ties with Israel in 1967. Prior to the meeting, which was held in Helsinki on August 18, Israeli spokesmen had been at pains to play down its significance. Thus, on August 16 Prime Minister Peres told Israel Radio that in agreeing to the meeting Moscow had taken a "small step" whose importance should not be overestimated, although it did hold out "possibilities" vis-à-vis the future. In the event, this cautious approach proved justified, as the low-level talks (the Israeli team was led by Yehuda Horam, head of the Foreign Ministry's Eastern Europe desk), which were to have lasted two days, were broken off after just 90 minutes. The Soviets contended that by raising the issue of Soviet Jewry, Israel had gone beyond the agreed parameters of the meeting, which they maintained had been convened solely to make arrangements for the visit to Israel of a Soviet consular delegation, ostensibly to examine Russian property holdings there. In response, Prime Minister Peres said Israel would countenance no compromises where Soviet Jewry was concerned; Foreign Ministry director-general David Kimche attributed the Russians' sudden cold feet to their desire to placate the Arab world.

Moscow did agree, however, to talks on September 13 between the Israeli and Soviet ambassadors to Washington, and to a meeting, the second in two years, between Prime Minister Peres and Foreign Minister Eduard Shevardnadze of the USSR at the UN on September 22. Their topics of discussion included the convening of an international peace conference on the Middle East and the question of Soviet Jewry.

Later that week Foreign Minister Shamir met at the UN (separately) with the foreign ministers of Bulgaria (Bulgarian-born Shulamit Shamir, the prime minister's wife, had paid a week-long visit to that country earlier in September, as the guest of the Bulgarian Foreign Ministry), Hungary, and Poland. In the latter, an Israeli "interests section" was already functioning informally, and the two ministers discussed the progress made in furthering relations between the two countries since the previous October, when a similar meeting was held at the UN.

OTHER COUNTRIES

The most spectacular foreign relations mission during the year was undoubtedly President Chaim Herzog's visit, lasting nearly three weeks, to the South Pacific and the Far East. The 59,000-kilometer trip, made in an Israel Air Force Boeing 707 with the accompaniment of a large entourage of advisers, Foreign Ministry personnel, and journalists, was designed, as the president explained on his return, to get across the Israeli position on various issues, open up "new possibilities of trade and contact," and improve "the good relations that already exist between [Israel] and most of these countries." Another major goal of the trip was to tighten Israel's bonds with some far-flung Jewish communities. Herzog's junket covered Australia, New Zealand, Fiji, Tonga, Hong Kong (a stopover not on the original itinerary but necessitated by the cancellation of a planned visit to the Phillipines due to internal unrest there), Singapore, and Sri Lanka.

In July a government delegation from the Philippines was in Israel to request technical aid in agriculture and solar energy. A rare high-level visitor from Japan was the deputy foreign minister, Shinichi Yanai, who was in Israel for four days at the end of September, following Foreign Minister Shamir's visit to Tokyo the previous year.

Israel's slow but steady renewal of relations with countries of black Africa continued apace in 1986, with the Ivory Coast and Cameroon becoming the third and fourth African states—following Zaire and Liberia (whose foreign minister, J. Bernard Blamo, paid a week-long visit to Israel in June)—to restore relations with Israel since 1982. Besides issuing verbal declarations against South Africa's apartheid system, on June 16 Jerusalem joined countries of the West in shutting down its embassy in Pretoria for 24 hours, in memory of the Soweto uprising and massacre ten years earlier and to protest the imposition of a "state of emergency" by the South African government on the country. However, Israel's essentially ambivalent posture toward Pretoria was manifested in August when an Israeli economic delegation visited South Africa in order to renew long-term contracts for Israel's importation of coal and to extend an agreement under which South African Jews could invest funds in Israel.

Israel's traditionally good relations with Latin America were boosted when Foreign Minister Shamir made a ten-day visit to Costa Rica, Guatemala, and Honduras in May. Uruguayan president Julio Maria Sanguinetti was in Israel that month as the guest of President Herzog, and July saw a week-long and first-ever visit by the prime minister and minister of finance and defense of Belize, Manuel Esquivel. Other ranking visitors from Latin America in 1986 included Ecuador's foreign minister, Edgar Teran (November), who signed an economic cooperation agreement on behalf of his country; the Argentine minister of labor and energy (March), who signed a memorandum of understanding on scientific-technological cooperation—the first of its kind between the two countries; and the president of the Costa Rica Legislative Assembly (December).

Lebanon

Although the three-year war in Lebanon, which grew out of "Operation Peace for Galilee," officially came to an end in mid-1985 with the completion of the phased withdrawal of most of the Israeli troops from that country, Lebanon continued to exact a toll from Israel. However, as Defense Minister Rabin said in mid-January, marking the first anniversary of the government's decision to withdraw the IDF (Israel Defense Forces) from Lebanon, the price Israel was now paying, "though dear, cannot be compared to the human and economic price we paid while we were deployed there."

The very first week of the year saw the firing of 14 Katyusha rockets at the town of Kiryat Shemona and other settlements in upper Galilee, prompting calls by Likud figures for an expansion of the "security zone" in southern Lebanon—a buffer area, adjacent to the Israel-Lebanon border, maintained jointly by the IDF and the Israeli-backed South Lebanon Army (SLA). Defense Minister Rabin would not countenance this idea, nor the opposite proposal, put forward from time to time by UN spokesmen or by countries participating in UNIFIL (UN Interim Force in Lebanon)—namely, to eliminate the security zone altogether and permit UNIFIL troops to deploy along the international border.

Instead, Israel continued to employ its traditional retaliatory and preemptive measures against terrorist and guerrilla targets in Lebanon—air strikes, reinforced by ongoing ground and sea patrols in the immediate border area, and occasional sweeps north of the security zone as well. Determined to defend and protect the northern border, yet unwilling to commit Israeli troops on a large scale to the anarchic land to the north, Israel found itself confronting the growing strength both of Palestinian organizations that were reestablishing themselves after the debacle of 1982, and, more ominously, the radical Iranian-backed Shi'ite organization Hezbollah (Party of God). Speaking in Kiryat Shemona on January 13, Defense Minister

Rabin warned that if the normal course of life were disrupted on the Israeli side of the border, Israel would employ means "to show the other side concretely that there will be no one-sided terror." Rabin also had occasion to note that the one threat that Israeli policymakers had feared in the wake of the IDF's pullback had not materialized: the Syrians, far from endeavoring to encroach on the security zone, had actually removed about half of their forces from Lebanon and had made no attempt to move southward.

In the course of the year, half a dozen Israeli soldiers were killed or captured in clashes north of the border; the upper Galilee was hit almost monthly by Katyusha rockets, causing injuries, some severe, and property damage, with almost every incident followed by retaliatory attacks by Israel Air Force planes on terrorist posts in Lebanon. The Israel Navy several times intercepted boats sailing for Lebanon carrying arms for the PLO. The kidnapping of two Israeli soldiers on February 17 in an ambush led to an extensive search mission through Shi'ite villages; subsequent diplomatic efforts to secure the soldiers' release were to no avail. On October 16 an Israeli Phantom warplane crashed during an attack on terrorist bases near Sidon. The pilot was rescued in a daring helicopter operation but the navigator was taken captive.

By year's end, according to a press briefing by Israeli military sources, some 7,000 Palestinian fighters were deployed in Lebanon, including 2,500 in and around Sidon (1,500 of them affiliated with Yasir Arafat's Fatah organization) and 2,300 in Beirut.

The Administered Areas

Under Defense Minister Rabin, who bore ministerial responsibility for activities in the territories, Israeli policy there remained virtually unchanged in 1986. At the same time, the government's pro-Jordan orientation was given a boost by the falling-out between King Hussein and Yasir Arafat. Indeed, largely as a result of that development, the fact of the evident but previously not formally acknowledged collaboration between Israel and Jordan in the territories—both eager to usurp the PLO's standing there—was spelled out in plain language by Rabin himself.

In an interview with the *Jerusalem Post* on the eve of the premiership rotation in October, the defense minister explained that Israel had set itself two interrelated goals in the territories: the eradication of terrorism using "every legal means available," and the improvement of "the quality of life" of the local residents. Within the context of the latter objective, Rabin pointed out, Israel wished to forge an "authoritative" and moderate leadership in the West Bank. This, he said, was now feasible, thanks to Jordan's reorientation following its rift with the PLO, making it possible for Israel to work "with Jordan" in order to "creat[e] an infrastructure upon which we hope to build a better future." The single greatest threat to these positive developments was internecine Palestinian terrorism—not only against "Palestinians who are openly pro-Zionist, but against any Palestinian who dares speak about the possibility of a political settlement," Rabin said.

A case in point was the violent aftermath to the appointment of Zafr al-Masri as mayor of Nablus in November 1985. The Civil Administration's proclaimed intention of installing pragmatic, moderately inclined Arabs as mayors in West Bank towns where PLO-affiliated mayors had been deposed by the Israeli authorities sustained a serious blow on March 2 when the 44-year-old al-Masri was gunned down by two assailants. Responsibility for the killing was claimed by George Habash's Popular Front for the Liberation of Palestine (PFLP); condemnation came from Jordan and the PLO alike, both of which were reported to have tacitly approved al-Masri's appointment. The funeral procession was seized upon by thousands of young Palestinian nationalists to stage a boisterous demonstration of their support for Yasir Arafat and the PLO and to vent their disdain for Jordan and King Hussein.

The al-Masri slaying forced Israel to shelve temporarily its declared intention to install additional notables as mayors in West Bank towns, since the candidates for those positions withdrew their names for fear of suffering a similar fate. Evidently their apprehensions were allayed in the course of the coming months, however, for on September 28 three pro-Jordanian local dignitaries (though none with the stature of al-Masri) took over as mayors in Hebron, Ramallah, and El-Bireh. Yet the true state of affairs was perhaps best depicted in a Reuters photograph, published in the *Jerusalem Post,* showing the newly named mayor of El-Bireh, Hassan a-Tawil, standing in the doorway of the municipality building flanked, bodyguard-fashion, by two armed Israeli soldiers.

At about the same time as the new mayors took over, Israeli-Jordanian cooperation in the West Bank found expression in another sphere. On September 17 Coordinator of Activities in the Territories Shmuel Goren announced that a Jordan-based bank had been granted a permit to reopen its Nablus branch, thus becoming (on November 3) the first Arab bank to open for business in the territories since 1967.

Much of the unrest in the territories, and in the West Bank in particular, continued to originate in the local colleges and universities. On Independence Day (May 14) several persons were wounded in Nablus, including two by gunfire from Israeli troops, as students from that city's An-Najah University rioted to protest a massive Gush Emunim demonstration in Nablus urging the government to allow Jewish settlement in the city. About two weeks later Israeli security forces, in an unusual move, entered the An-Najah campus, where they impounded what military sources described as "nationalist material" and detained 20 students for questioning.

A more sustained wave of unrest, which began at the end of November with the by now almost traditional demonstrations marking the UN vote for the partition of Palestine (November 29, 1947), persisted through the entire month of December. The situation was aggravated by the desire of West Bankers to show solidarity with PLO forces in Lebanon who were engaged in an armed conflict with various Shi'ite groups there. On December 4, two students (both from the Gaza Strip) were killed and 12 others were wounded when Israeli troops opened fire on a demonstration at Bir Zeit University. Two days later a 12-year-old boy was killed at the Balata refugee camp in Nablus when an Israeli patrol was stoned. On December 8 the Israeli authorities closed down the old campus of Bir Zeit University for one month and ordered An-Najah University shut for a week. The unrest spread to East Jerusalem and the Gaza Strip as well.

The normally quiescent Golan Heights was the scene of a serious demonstration in late February during a visit there by Prime Minister Peres. Three policemen were injured and 18 local Druze were arrested when demonstrators stoned Peres's car and tried to prevent him from entering the local-council building in the village of Majdal Shams. Peres told the Druze notables that "the Golan Heights is part of Israel," but the riotous demonstrators chanted "The Golan belongs to Syria!" and burned an Israeli flag.

Israeli activity against burgeoning Palestinian nationalism in the territories was directed increasingly at the East Jerusalem press. In addition to the occasional barring of distribution of various papers in the territories for periods of up to two weeks, usually under the rubric of "censorship violations" (East Jerusalem papers had to submit all or most of their material for prior military censorship), the major occurrence in this sphere was the expulsion of the editor of the East Jerusalem daily *A-Sha'ab,* Akram Haniye. The deportation order, issued at the beginning of November, was not implemented for almost two months, due to Haniye's appeal to the High Court of Justice against the move. At one hearing the O/C Central Command, Maj. Gen. Ehud Barak, told the High Court that Haniye was a leading Fatah activist who had served as a conduit for PLO instructions regarding terrorist attacks in the territories. On December 16 Israeli authorities conveyed to the High Court over 300 classified documents said to prove Haniye's PLO affiliation. However, the court did not get the chance to rule on the case; Haniye himself asked his lawyers to drop the appeal proceedings because the court refused to allow him or his lawyers to see the secret material offered in evidence against him by Israel. On December 28 Haniye was put on a plane for Geneva. He was the second West Bank journalist to be deported in 1986, following the expulsion (January 31) of Mahmoud Abd al-Jawad, a staffer for the Palestine Press Service and the newspaper *Al Mithaq.*

A survey of Arab public opinion released in September seemed to indicate that Israel was fighting a rearguard battle in its effort to contain Palestinian nationalism and that its hope of fuller collaboration with Jordan was unrealistic. The poll results showed fully 93.5 percent of the population of the territories believing that "the PLO is the sole and legitimate representative of the Palestinian people." Although Yasir Arafat himself received somewhat less support as the preferred Arab leader (71.1 percent), the second-place finisher, Jordan's King Hussein, scored a paltry 3.4 percent. Moreover, 77.9 percent said that their "preferred permanent solution to the Palestinian problem" was "the establishment of a democratic Palestinian state in *all of Palestine*" (emphasis added). Most disquieting were the results pertaining to the use of violence as a means to achieve the Palestinians' goals: 78.4 percent of the respondents said that "acts of force are justified in the pursuit of the Palestinian cause." In an evident rejection of the much vaunted Israeli policy aimed at bettering the standard of living in the territories, an overwhelming majority, 84.5 percent, averred that living conditions had "become worse" in the preceding five years.

The poll, which covered about 1,000 persons in 42 towns and villages and 8 refugee camps in the West Bank and the Gaza Strip, was jointly sponsored by the New York newspaper *Newsday,* the Australian Broadcasting Corporation, and the East Jerusalem daily *Al Fajr.* Although, as Meron Benvenisti, director of the West Bank Data Base Project, told the *Jerusalem Post,* the poll's sample population group may have been biased in favor of the more politically aware (over 37 percent of those interviewed were either students or professionals), the survey was—taking into account the constraints imposed by a military occupation—the most comprehensive attempt yet undertaken to determine where the residents of the territories stood politically.

The reaction of the Israeli authorities went beyond the perhaps expectable dismissal of the poll's results as biased and unreliable. According to a press statement issued on November 21 by An-Najah University and not denied by Israeli authorities, the poll's director, Mohammed Shadid, a political-science lecturer at An-Najah since 1980, was summoned to the office of the Nablus military governor on November 4 and asked to publish a "revised version" of the poll's results in a pro-Jordanian East Jerusalem daily. When Shadid refused, he was issued an order on November 13 barring him from teaching anywhere in the West Bank.

Jewish settlement activity in the territories continued in 1986 in unspectacular but steady fashion. According to an Israel Radio report in late September, the virtual freeze on the establishment of new settlements had not stemmed the growth of the already existing West Bank Jewish communities. Some 60,000 Jews resided there, according to the report, constituting an increase of about 50 percent since the Peres government took office in 1984. Over two-thirds of the settlers resided in "bedroom communities" that were effectively suburbs of Jerusalem and Tel Aviv—fully 20 percent of them, 12,000 persons, in Ma'aleh Adumim, just outside Jerusalem on the road to Jericho. Over 50 percent of the Jewish settlers were not religious.

Even though the "hard-core" ideological settlers affiliated with Gush Emunim and residing largely in the Samarian hills constituted a distinct minority among the Jewish residents in the West Bank, it was they who continued to set the tone. On April 14, persons traveling to a Peace Now meeting in Hebron, including two MKs from the Citizens Rights Movement (CRM), were physically assaulted by Jewish settlers who tried to prevent their passage. Army troops had to be called in to clear the road. Two weeks later some 10,000 persons visited Hebron to show solidarity with Gush Emunim and the settler movement. Three CRM MKs made an appearance at the rally as a counterdemonstration, and Kach leader MK Meir Kahane was forcibly removed from the site by soldiers for incitement.

The settlers continued their efforts to penetrate the Arab towns of Nablus and Jericho. In August a group of 15 activists, led by Tehiya MK Geula Cohen and Gush Emunim leader Rabbi Moshe Levinger, managed to evade army roadblocks and reach the ancient synagogue in Jericho. A day earlier, army troops opened fire at a Gush Emunim vehicle that was en route to Jericho after having disregarded soldiers' orders to halt at a roadblock. No one was hurt, but the incident touched off a spate of mutual recriminations between Gush Emunim and the IDF, aggravating already strained relations stemming from the settlers' long-standing contention that Israeli troops in the territories were not doing enough to protect them. In October the military government evicted 15 settlers from "Joseph's Tomb" in Nablus, after they had refused to leave the site following the completion of morning prayer services. In the Gaza Strip, Jewish settlers began operating their own armed "civil guard" to counter growing local unrest there.

The demographic picture continued to cause concern. Speaking at a press conference at the end of January, Dr. Benvenisti said that the Arab population in the West Bank was approaching 800,000, an increase of nearly one-third since 1967. Moreover, the rate of population growth in the territories was once more on the rise, the result of declining emigration due to the diminished demand for foreign workers in the oil-producing Arab states. The upshot was an acceleration of the long-term trend that was closing the gap between the Jewish and Arab populations in the area of former Mandatory Palestine (Israel plus the territories). The 1986 ratio of 63 percent Jews to 37 percent Arabs (1984 figure: 65:35) was expected to stand at no more than 58:42 by the year 2000, Benvenisti said.

Another Benvenisti report, dealing with the Gaza Strip, painted an appalling picture. According to the study released at the end of May, the Gaza Strip's 525,000 persons constituted a population density of over 2,000 persons per square kilometer, a figure matched only by Hong Kong. Moreover, the population of Gaza, which included some 40 percent of all the Palestinians in the territories, most of them residing in eight huge refugee camps, was doubling every generation and would total as many as 900,000 by the year 2000. Gaza, according to Benvenisti, was "the Soweto of the State of Israel," and the situation there was nothing short of "explosive."

Terrorism

ISRAEL AND THE TERRITORIES

Although 1986 saw a falloff of some 40 percent in overall terrorist attacks in Israel and the territories, stabbings, one of the main forms of the "personal terrorism" that had been rampant in 1985, showed a considerable increase. Paradoxically, both developments were attributable in large measure to the increased presence of the Shin Bet (General Security Service) in the territories, its success in apprehending suspected terrorists, and the limitations placed on access to firearms.

A number of serious terrorist incidents occurred in Jerusalem, especially in or around the Old City. On April 8 ten persons were wounded, one seriously, when a gasoline bomb was thrown through the window of a crowded bus in north

Jerusalem. Five days later a 59-year-old Jewish woman who ran an insurance office in East Jerusalem was murdered at her place of business. On April 27 a British tourist was murdered near the Garden Tomb in East Jerusalem, not far from the site of the earlier slaying. Two other tourists, one American and one German, were also shot and wounded in the Old City around the same time. Demonstratively touring the Old City following these attacks, Jerusalem mayor Teddy Kollek declared that East Jerusalem was safer than Central Park but that fear of terrorism had caused a 40-percent falloff in tourism to the city. (In early May the security forces uncovered a major terrorist cell made up of largely East Jerusalem residents and affiliated with the Syrian-backed Fatah breakaway group led by Abu Mussa. Three of its members were among the terrorists released in the prisoner exchange a year earlier. Following their trial, on September 14 two of the gang's members received life imprisonment and five others were sentenced to prison terms of 8–25 years for their parts in the Jerusalem murders and attempted murders.)

The year's worst single outrage occurred on October 15, when terrorists launched a grenade attack just outside the Dung Gate in the Old City, following a ceremony in which new IDF recruits were sworn in at the Western Wall. In the attack, which came as the soldiers and members of their families were boarding buses to return them to their bases or homes, one person was killed and 70 were wounded. (Although at least four different Palestinian organizations claimed responsibility for the attack, four suspects, members of a local Islamic Jihad group, were arrested within two days of the incident. Their interrogation brought about the arrest of a six-man Fatah cell which was charged with planting a bomb on a Jerusalem bus in December 1983 that claimed six lives and wounded 50 persons; one of the cell's members, who also supplied the grenades for the Dung Gate attack, was sentenced to life imprisonment on December 30.)

On November 15, a 22-year-old student at the Shuvu Banim yeshivah in the Old City, Eliahu Amedi, was stabbed to death while walking to the yeshivah. The assailants, who were caught by security forces as they tried to flee, turned out to be three young men from Jenin, affiliated with George Habash's PFLP. (Sentenced to life imprisonment on December 23, the three were quoted by the *Jerusalem Post* as saying they had chosen their victim at random and that "any Jew" would have done just as well.) Soon after, Jewish hotheads and fanatics, with Kach members prominent among them, rampaged against Arab property in the Old City, forcing nine Arab families living adjacent to the yeshivah in the Moslem Quarter to vacate their homes. They also assaulted passing Arab vehicles in the city's Shmuel Hanavi neighborhood, a disadvantaged area situated on the former border with Jordan, where Amedi had lived.

When MK Ran Cohen of the Citizens Rights Movement sought to pay a condolence visit to the Amedi family, he was attacked by religious extremists. Condemnation of the anti-Arab rioting came from President Herzog, Knesset Speaker Shlomo Hillel, and Mayor Kollek, who criticized the yeshivah students for inflaming passions in the Old City. Subsequently a conciliation meeting was arranged between the heads of the yeshivah and local Arab residents, and the Jerusalem municipality paid compensation to Arabs whose property had been damaged.

The year's final terrorist knifing in Jerusalem occurred on December 12, when a 66-year-old man was stabbed in the stomach as he walked home through the Old City after Friday-evening worship at the Western Wall. The following day a group of about 20 prominent Palestinians in the territories and East Jerusalem issued an unusual statement deploring the attack. "We consider this act to directly contravene the civilized context of our legitimate Palestinian struggle to realize our just demands, and we also consider it to be in complete contradiction to the humanistic principles and religious laws in which we believe," the statement said.

Other victims of terrorist attacks in Israel and the territories in 1986 included: a 40-year-old taxi driver from Ramle shot dead in his cab near Lod (January 2); a border policeman shot and killed while shopping with his family and a friend in the Nablus marketplace (January 11); a bus driver mortally wounded in an attack while en route from the settlement of Neve Zuf in Samaria to Tel Aviv (April 12); a new immigrant from Ethiopia stabbed and lightly wounded while walking in the Hebron marketplace (June 6); 14 persons wounded, two seriously, when a grenade was thrown at a group of Carmiel high-school pupils and their adult escorts on an outing in Jericho (July 24); a 35-year-old Ashkelon man stabbed to death while shopping in Gaza (September 27). Violent demonstrations broke out in Ashkelon the following day as the city's main intersection was being renamed in honor of King Mohammed V of Morocco (father of the current monarch, Hassan II), in a ceremony presided over by Prime Minister Peres. On October 7 a second Ashkelon man was murdered in Gaza, his throat slit from behind. Heavy police and Border Police reinforcements were stationed in Ashkelon as anti-Arab feeling ran high. Defense Minister Rabin, visiting the murder sites, warned Israelis against going alone "to certain places." A third Ashkelon man was lightly wounded in Gaza on November 12 when he was stabbed in the neck. (On December 25 Israeli security authorities announced the uncovering of an Islamic Jihad terrorist cell in Gaza, to which the knifings were attributed.)

Some of the members of the Jewish underground who had been sent to prison in 1985 were granted clemency by President Chaim Herzog, at the recommendation of the minister of justice, and released. In February Boaz Heinemann and his nephew Ya'acov Heinemann were freed: the former, convicted of attempted manslaughter and other crimes, had been slated for release in April; the latter, who was involved in the 1980 attack on the West Bank mayors and the plot to blow up Muslim shrines on the Temple Mount, had been scheduled to be freed in July. Three more of the Jewish terrorists—Yitzhak Novik, Haggai Segal, and Natan Nathanson, sentenced to three-year prison terms for their roles in the attack on the mayors—were released on May 3 after serving two-thirds of their terms (which dated from the time of their arrests, a full year before their convictions). On the eve of Independence Day, President Herzog commuted the sentences of two additional members of the Jewish terrorist organization, Gilad Peli and Yeshua Ben-Shushan, thus leaving 7 of the original 25 members of the group still in prison, including 3 serving life sentences.

In June the trial concluded of the two officers of the Judea-Samaria Civil Administration who were charged with failing to warn a Border Police demolition expert that a car he was about to examine was booby-trapped (the car belonged to one of the West Bank mayors targeted by the Jewish underground). The two were found guilty of breach of trust, failure to prevent a crime, and causing bodily harm through negligence. The sapper, a Druze, was blinded when the bomb exploded in his face. In June one of the officers received a 15-month prison term and the other 3 months.

Two wanted Jewish men returned from the United States to face trial for anti-Arab actions. On December 23, Ira Rappaport, who was convicted, following plea bargaining, of causing grievous bodily harm in the attack on the mayors, was sentenced to 30 months in prison. Rappaport, an American citizen, was in the States on behalf of Gush Emunim in 1984 when the Jewish terrorist group was rounded up but finally returned to Israel voluntarily in 1986 to stand trial. (His extradition was never sought by Israel.) The second case involved Craig Leitner, a member of Meir Kahane's Kach organization, who along with several other Kach activists was involved in a series of attacks against Arabs in 1983, including the ambush of an Arab bus near Ramallah in which six persons were wounded by gunfire. Leitner, who fled to the States in 1984 when he was about to testify as a state's witness in the trial of the group's members, returned to Israel in August and in September was sentenced to 30 months in prison following plea bargaining.

On December 3, three young Israelis—two men (a soldier and a policeman) and a woman student—who were convicted in the April 1985 murder of an Arab taxi driver in Jerusalem, were sentenced to life imprisonment.

ANTI-ISRAEL TERROR ABROAD

On February 4, Israel intercepted a Libyan executive jet bound for Syria from Tripoli, in the wake of intelligence information indicating that one or more top terrorists, including Ahmed Jibril, were on the aircraft. However, when the plane was forced down in Israel, none of the persons Israel sought was among the passengers, who were returning to Syria from a gathering of radical Arab and Palestinian organizations in Libya. Syria, which vowed to retaliate, in the meantime made do with submitting a complaint to the UN Security Council, but the United States vetoed a draft resolution condemning Israel for the operation. When U.S. planes bombed Libya on April 15, to deter Qaddafi from backing terrorism abroad, Israeli leaders welcomed the move enthusiastically. Defense Minister Rabin termed the American raid "an act of self-defense" that would hamper international terrorism.

Two days later a major disaster was averted when an El Al security guard at London's Heathrow Airport discovered a bomb in the hand luggage of a 32-year-old Irish woman who was about to board a Tel Aviv-bound El Al jumbo jet. The woman had been given the booby-trapped handbag by her boyfriend, a 35-year-old

Jordanian, Nizar Hindawi, whose child she was carrying and who had promised to meet her in Israel and marry her. Hindawi surrendered to police in London after the bomb was discovered. The explosive device his girlfriend unknowingly carried in her handbag would have ripped the plane apart in midair, almost certainly killing all 400 persons aboard. When London broke off diplomatic relations with Syria after Hindawi was sentenced to 45 years' imprisonment in October, Jerusalem welcomed the action as "a major step against state-sponsored terrorism."

One of the worst terrorist outrages in recent years—an attack on the Neve Shalom synagogue in Istanbul, Turkey, on Saturday, September 6, in which 22 worshipers were massacred—provoked fierce condemnation from Israeli leaders as well as a minor internal political crisis (see "Political Affairs").

Economic Developments

If Israel's economic situation in 1986 could be summed up in a single word, that word would be stabilization. The overriding goal of the country's economic planners in 1986 was to preserve the accomplishments of the Emergency Economic Stabilization Program introduced on July 1, 1985, notably the drastic reduction in inflation from 150 percent in the first seven months of 1985, to a total of 14 percent in the last five months. The size of the state budget for the fiscal year beginning April 1, as presented by Finance Minister Yitzhak Modai in the Knesset on January 20—NIS 30.8 billion (approximately $19.5 billion)—represented a real cut of 5.3 percent as compared with the previous year.

According to Modai, the budget was geared to achieve several goals: stabilize the balance-of-payments posture and increase the country's foreign-currency reserves by up to $750 million (the amount of the special U.S. emergency aid for 1986); maintain stabilization of inflation at a low level; reduce public-sector employment as part of an effort to effect an overall change in the structure of employment in Israel; forge an economic atmosphere in which the public's expectations would be for continuing stabilization and calm; and create conditions enabling economic growth.

In practice, these targets were achieved only in part, if at all. Thus, inflation was slashed from the 185 percent of 1985 to 19.7 percent in 1986, yet for all that this marked the first time in years that the consumer price index was confined to double digits, it was still in excess of what the Treasury's economists had set their sights on. A main cause of the inflationary decline was the 11.4-percent fall in public consumption (following a 3.2-percent rise in 1985). However, in a virtual reverse of the trends in 1985, this cutback in public consumption was almost exactly offset by an increase of 12 percent in personal spending, following a decline of 0.4 percent in 1985. Purchases of household durables (such as refrigerators, washing machines, televisions, and videos) were up by 55 percent as compared with 1985, and purchases of automobiles increased by 51 percent. Tourism abroad was up by 30 percent in 1986. Unfortunately, the massive foreign-currency outlay by Israelis going abroad was actually aggravated by a decline of 13 percent in incoming tourism to Israel, generating a shortfall of about $200 million as compared with the previous year.

It was in the more fundamental economic statistics that the lingering malaise of the Israeli economy could be seen. In the chronically problematic balance-of-payments sector, Israel ran up a deficit of $4.1 billion in 1986; exports were up by only 5 percent, as compared with increases of 9 percent and 14 percent in 1985 and 1984, respectively. Moreover, investments in fixed capital formations (construction, equipment, transportation) shrank by 6 percent, continuing the pattern of the previous two years. Another long-term adverse trend, reflecting the low level of immigration to Israel in recent years, was the decline (by a sharp 18 percent) in investment in residential housing. By the end of 1986, housing investment was actually almost 40 percent below the 1982 level, and the 14-percent decrease in the number of persons employed in construction was a major contributor to the growth in unemployment. The total of 7.1 percent of the work force unemployed in 1986, up somewhat from 1985, marked the fourth consecutive year of a rise in unemployment. Overall, the Gross Domestic Product was up by a paltry 2 percent during the year, showing no gain (though also no loss) as compared with the previous three years, while the Gross National Product, reflecting no more than isolated pockets of growth in the private sector, including industry, climbed by a minuscule 1.1 percent—tantamount to stagnation.

The question of economic growth spilled into the political arena to become one of the most bitterly contested issues of 1986. In mid-February Prime Minister Peres began urging the adoption of an economic-growth policy to prime the economy as a means to trigger investment and offset rising unemployment. Finance Minister Modai objected that Peres's program would not only refuel inflation, thus undoing all the work of the stabilization measures, but that Peres actually had an ulterior motive: to beef up Alignment-controlled ministries (especially health, education, and agriculture) and, worse, to prop up financially ailing and debt-ridden Histadrut (i.e., Labor) enterprises, specifically the huge Solel Boneh construction company, the Kupat Holim health-insurance fund, and the cooperative settlements. With the ministers already under pressure from the Treasury to agree to cuts within the framework of the 1986–87 state budget (the final size and structure of which was then being fought over in the Knesset's Finance Committee), the injection of the economic-growth issue into the weekly cabinet meeting of February 16 produced the single most vituperative session in Peres's entire tenure as prime minister, which broke down into a near free-for-all. In the crunch, when the continued survival of the government itself was at stake and the rotation was palpably threatened, the leaders of the two major parties were able to abandon their rhetoric and come up with a novel agreement permitting industrial plants in both the private and Histadrut sectors to raise $450 million via the capital market. And, at the 11th hour, on March 30, the cabinet, in a rare show of harmony and unanimity, gave its approval to an aid package totaling some $350 million for Solel Boneh and Kupat Holim and for the cotton and construction industries.

At the same time, the ministers, having failed to reduce the budget by a further $300 million (ironically, almost the same sum as the assistance doled out), took the traditional, and easier, route of imposing new taxes on the public: a levy on education, a tax on old-age pensions, and a surcharge on automobiles. Although these developments cleared the way for the Knesset's approval of the state budget the following day, public pressure led the Knesset to balk at sanctioning the levies on education and on pensions, and they were officially dropped by the government in May, leaving only the levy on cars. One result of this was that the government was forced to implement a genuine series of budget cuts, totaling NIS 320 million, in August.

On December 17, the Finance Ministry formally unveiled an "economic growth and stabilization program" for 1987–88, aimed at creating an "open economy, without undue intervention." Under the proposed plan, the country's taxation structure would be radically altered, wages would remain effectively stable, government involvement in the capital market would be reduced, some foreign-currency restrictions would be lifted, incipient privatization of government corporations would be introduced, and the public-service sector would be cut. However, the modalities of the tax-reform program, which appeared to confer the greatest benefits on the country's highest income groups, were unacceptable to the Histadrut and various groups in the Labor party—as well as to the Likud's David Levy, the populist housing minister, who delivered himself of a furious tirade against the program. The outcome was in the best Israeli tradition: the creation of two ministerial committees, one to decide on the size of the 1987–88 budget and the other to hold talks with the Histadrut and the employers' association on the mooted taxation and the capital-market reforms.

The shekel underwent a linkage change in 1986. Effective August 1, it was linked to a "currency basket" composed of the U.S. dollar (60 percent), the West German mark (20 percent), the British pound sterling (10 percent), and the French franc and Japanese yen (5 percent each). Since the adoption of the economic recovery plan in July 1985, the shekel had been pegged informally to the dollar only. September 3, one year after the introduction of the new shekel, marked the final day on which business transactions could be conducted using the old shekel.

THE BEISKY REPORT

On April 20 the judicial commission of inquiry into the regulation of bank shares, chaired by Supreme Court justice Moshe Beisky, issued its report. (For the background, see AJYB, vol. 87, 1987, p. 283.) In a series of sweeping and devastating conclusions, the commission asserted that the governor of the Bank of Israel and the directors of the country's major banks should resign voluntarily from their posts within 30 days or, failing this, be removed by administrative means. In addition, the commission singled out for blame nine senior officials who no longer held the posts they held in 1983, when the collapse of the bank shares occurred; these included two former directors-general of the Finance Ministry, and a former director of the

Tel Aviv Stock Exchange. The commission also urged that Israel's financial markets undergo a total overhaul and that the attorney general act to determine whether criminal charges should be brought against those involved in the scandal.

It was perhaps not surprising that the heads of three of the four banks named stalled as long as they could before finally resigning, or being forced to do so by public pressure. Only the two directors of Bank Hapoalim tendered their resignations as recommended by the commission; those of Bank Leumi, Bank Discount, and United Mizrahi Bank tried to brazen it out, with Discount's Raphael Recanati not stepping down until mid-July, after the cabinet authorized the new governor of the Bank of Israel to suspend him. As for the latter post, Moshe Mandelbaum tendered his resignation as Bank of Israel governor to the cabinet on June 8, and one week later, after considerable infighting in both major parties, a nonpolitical figure, Hebrew University professor Michael Bruno, a highly respected economist, was named to the post. He was officially sworn in by President Herzog on June 18.

Political and Religious Extremism

Efforts continued to pass legislation to limit the phenomenon known as "Kahanism"—so named after MK Rabbi Meir Kahane, who espoused an anti-Arab, antisecular, and antileftist stance—but the snags that had held up passage of an amendment to the Penal Code in 1985 persisted through a good part of 1986 as well. The chief problem continued to be the insistence of the religious parties that the amendment prohibiting incitement to racism contain a declaration stating explicitly that it did not refer to the *halakhah* (Jewish religious law). As MK Rabbi Haim Druckman (Morasha) put it, under the proposed amendment, "maintaining the *halakhah* will make us all criminals." (The point at issue was that Kahane himself grounded everything he did or said in pronouncements from the Torah and other Jewish religious writings, whereas his denigrators replied that he was quoting such passages out of context.) On top of this, the Likud continued to pursue its "symmetry" notion, requiring simultaneous passage of a bill barring unauthorized meetings, for whatever purpose, between Israelis and "terrorists," meaning, effectively, members of the PLO. The result of these pressures and counterpressures was that not until August 5, 1986, well over a year after its original submission to the Knesset, did the antiracism bill—and its anti-PLO twin—finally come up for a vote in the Knesset.

The antiracism amendment passed (by 57 to 22, with 7 abstentions), but its provisions had by then been so diluted that Kahane himself voted in favor. The PLO bill also passed, with most of the Alignment MKs voting against it or absenting themselves from the vote.

The results of a study by a Haifa University sociologist, Sammy Smooha, released in January, indicated that much remained to be done in the area of changing Jewish attitudes toward the Arab citizens of Israel. According to the research, which was made public in a study day sponsored by the Jewish-Arab Council for Peace Education and the Coexistence Project of Israel's network of community centers, over one-fifth (22 percent) of the Jewish population thought "getting rid of Arabs [was] the most appropriate solution" to the Arab minority problem. Sixty-one percent thought that surveillance over the Arabs should be increased; 24 percent advocated their disenfranchisement; 42 percent wanted the state to encourage them to leave the country; 59 percent averred that it is "impossible to trust" most Israeli Arabs, and 46 percent believed that "Arabs in Israel will never reach the level of development Jews have reached." However, in Smooha's analysis the problem lay less in racism as such than in a growing Jewish intolerance of political dissent. Thus, 61 percent of the Jews polled by Smooha said they would also disenfranchise "Zionist Jews" who favored the establishment of a Palestinian state on the West Bank and Gaza Strip headed by the PLO, while fully 72 percent would strip "non-Zionists," Arabs or Jews, who took such a stand, of their citizenship.

As in past years, extremist behavior thrust Jerusalem into the headlines. A major focal point of Jewish challenge and Arab reaction was the highly sensitive Temple Mount area, administered by the Waqf (Muslim religious trust). On January 8 a minor riot broke out when a delegation of MKs from the Knesset's Interior Committee, led by committee chairman Dov Shilansky (Likud-Herut), visited the site on the Temple Mount known as Solomon's Stables, the declared purpose being to look into allegations of illegal building activity there. Swelling the ranks of the 25-person delegation (which was boycotted by all but one of its Alignment members) were, among others, two MKs from the ultranationalist Tehiya party, neither of them on the committee, and the leader of the extremist Temple Mount Faithful group, which periodically sought to demonstrate an organized Jewish presence on the Temple Mount. A more serious riot erupted a week later, when a group of MKs again ascended the Temple Mount—to demonstrate Israeli sovereignty over the site—and Tehiya MK Eliezer Waldman recited from a book of Psalms and then began chanting the *kaddish* (prayer for the dead). Some 600 police and Border Police were needed to subdue the Arabs protesting the MKs' presence.

On June 6, the last Friday of the Muslims' holy Ramadan month, security guards had to use force to prevent a group of Gush Emunim activists from entering the Temple Mount in the midst of the Muslim prayer services there. The Jewish group was part of a march commemorating the 19th anniversary of the reunification of Jerusalem. Toward the end of October, 300 policemen were on hand to protect some 50 members of the Temple Mount Faithful who were permitted, following coordination with the Supreme Muslim Council, to pay brief visits to the Temple Mount. Ostensibly this was in order to carry out the Sukkot precept of pilgrimage, but the leader of the group, Gershon Solomon, added, "Beyond this, by our presence we have come to say that we are here and that no one in the world can move us."

OTHER RELIGIOUS ISSUES

The control of the Orthodox over matters of personal status became an issue in the case of an American woman immigrant, a convert to Judaism, claiming her right as a Jew to automatic citizenship. Shoshana (Susan) Miller, who was converted to Judaism in the United States by a Reform rabbi, came to Israel in October 1985 and received a certificate under the Law of Return as an *olah* (a new immigrant). However, when she applied to the Interior Ministry for a permanent identity card and showed her conversion certificate, she was told she must first show confirmation of her conversion by a rabbinical court. Responding to a parliamentary question on the matter in the Knesset from Mapam MK Yair Tsaban, Interior Minister Rabbi Yitzhak Peretz, of the ultra-Orthodox Sephardi Torah Guardians party (Shas), touched off a furious exchange when he used the expression "to distinguish between the holy and the profane" in reference to Orthodox and Reform rabbis, respectively.

In mid-April Miller took her case to the High Court of Justice, aided by the Movement for Progressive Judaism and Arza, the Organization of Reform Zionists in the United States. The court ordered Rabbi Peretz to show cause within 45 days why the ministry he headed should not register Shoshana Miller as a Jew. Peretz generated another storm in June when he proposed, as a means for resolving the case, that all converts to Judaism should have this fact indicated in their ID cards; this notion drew fire not only from the secular public but also from such leading religious figures as former chief rabbi Shlomo Goren, who labeled it a "disgraceful" idea because it would shame converts and therefore contravene *halakhah.* Peretz himself, on July 7, spoke in defense of his proposal when he replied in the Knesset to five motions for the agenda on the issue (all of which were referred to committee), maintaining that no discrimination or offense was intended and that the status of the convert had a lengthy and honorable history in the Jewish tradition.

On December 2 the High Court of Justice ruled unanimously that Shoshana Miller must be registered as a Jew, explaining that to insert the word "convert" in her ID card would cause rifts within the Jewish people that would divide those living in Israel "into two peoples, Jews and Israelis," and would thereby "run counter to the national aspirations for which the state was established." In reaction, Rabbi Peretz maintained that the Interior Ministry did not consider the ruling a precedent. Miller hardly helped her own cause by returning to the States just five days after the court's judgment, saying that her father was ill and she would return when he was better. Because of her sudden departure, MK Tsaban's urging that the Interior Ministry issue Miller a normal ID card was in practice something of an empty gesture. Nevertheless, Peretz himself on December 31 told the Knesset that he would resign rather than lend a hand to registering Shoshana—or Susan, as he pointedly insisted on calling her—Miller as a Jew.

Just ten months prior to the High Court ruling in the Miller case, the year's only attempt by the Knesset's religious parties to have the so-called who-is-a-Jew amendment passed was defeated by an absolute majority. The February 5 tally was 61–47 against passage of the codicil, which, by barring non-Orthodox converts from gaining automatic entry to Israel under the Law of Return, would have obviated the Shoshana Miller case. Speaking in the debate, Prime Minister Peres declared: "Restrained and tolerant pluralism—not the imposition of world views—is today required for the survival of the Jewish people and for the realization of content-filled *aliyah.*"

However, as in past years, "restrained and tolerant pluralism" was hardly the motto of religious-secular relations in 1986. Another perennially contentious issue, the introduction of daylight saving, or summer, time, flared up in March, when Interior Minister Peretz, citing the findings of a special committee he had appointed, announced his opposition to the move on the grounds that it would produce no savings in power consumption or reduce the road-accident rate, but would adversely affect observant Jews and would lead to Sabbath desecration on Saturday evenings. The result was a petition to the High Court of Justice by Alignment MK Micha Harish and six industrial firms, arguing that they could save energy and heighten productivity via summer time. In the meantime, seven private members' bills were submitted to the Knesset, seeking to make summer time obligatory under the law, and a kind of grass-roots revolt sprung up, with various sectors of the country declaring that they would adopt summer-time schedules on a unilateral basis. Finally, on April 20 the cabinet plenum preempted both Peretz and the High Court by voting 11–6 to implement summer time in Israel from May 17 to September 6.

March and April also saw a renewal of bus-shelter vandalizings and burnings in Jerusalem, ostensibly to protest advertisements depicting "immodestly clad" women. In mid-April residents of Jerusalem's ultra-Orthodox Me'ah She'arim quarter went on the rampage, smearing a movie theater with paint and then blocking traffic at a major intersection and torching garbage bins. The apparent cause of the riots was the arrest of two members of the small but highly visible Neturei Karta sect, including its leader, 60-year-old Rabbi Uri Blau, on suspicion of vandalizing bus shelters. Blau, who admitted having defaced an "obscene" advertising poster, was sentenced to ten days' imprisonment and a fine of NIS 1,000. Since he had been held in custody for ten days prior to sentencing, he was released. On June 10 Jerusalemites passing by the city's central bus station were shocked to find that no fewer than six bus shelters had been torched overnight. Outraged, Jerusalem mayor Teddy Kollek termed the campaign by the ultra-Orthodox a "civil rebellion" and urged the government to back the city's efforts to "put down" the rebellion as "in any modern state."

Retaliation by secular activists, as expressed in the budding summer-time revolt, now took on more serious dimensions. On the night of June 10 a Tel Aviv synagogue was set ablaze—according to an anonymous call to the Army Radio Station, by a group that was out to combat "ultra-Orthodox terror." On June 14, a Sabbath, prayer books were destroyed and other damage done at a Tel Aviv yeshivah, while that evening a burial-society vehicle was attacked near Me'ah She'arim in Jerusalem. On June 12 Prime Minister Peres had convened a meeting of cabinet ministers, MKs, mayors, the chief rabbis, the police, and the media in an effort to calm tempers and put a halt to the escalating violence. A "council for the discussion of controversial matters" was created, and a statement was issued deploring the use of violence as a means of protest.

The ongoing construction of the Jerusalem Center for Near Eastern Studies, a branch of the Mormons' Brigham Young University in Utah, continued to irk religious sensibilities. On April 28 some 8,000 Orthodox and ultra-Orthodox persons, including Interior Minister Rabbi Peretz and several MKs, gathered across from the site of the new center to protest its construction. On the other side of the Atlantic a smaller but perhaps no less powerful lobby was at work on behalf of the Church of Jesus Christ of Latter-day Saints (the Mormons' official name): every Israeli MK received a letter signed by 154 members of the House of Representatives urging the Israeli authorities to allow construction of the center to proceed unhindered. The letter said pointedly that a key factor in motivating American support for Israel was Israel's "commitment to democracy and pluralism."

In May the special interministerial committee on the Mormon center was informed by Deputy Attorney General Yoram Bar-Sella that no legal grounds existed for halting construction of the complex. In August the committee, which was chaired by Religious Affairs Minister Yosef Burg (NRP), voted 5–3 against Rabbi Peretz's motion that construction be halted, although it did unanimously recommend that the lease for the site be reworded so as to bar missionary activity. On August 17 the cabinet approved the committee's recommendation.

Israel and World Jewry

SOVIET AND ETHIOPIAN JEWS

The single most dramatic and moving event of the year was the arrival in Israel of one of the towering figures of the Jewish and human rights movement in the Soviet Union, Anatoly Shcharansky—who in his homeland took the Hebrew name of Natan and simplified his last name to Sharansky. Released on February 11 in Germany by the Soviets as part of an East-West prisoner exchange, the 38-year-old Sharansky landed at Ben-Gurion airport that evening to a tumultuous welcome by a virtual "who's who" of Israeli politics, a large group of Soviet activists, and the world media. He had already been reunited in Germany with his wife, Avital, who for nearly 12 years, since the day after their marriage in July 1974, had campaigned relentlessly for his release, and the two had flown to Israel together. To those at the airport Sharansky said: "Brothers and sisters, the Israeli nation: During the time that I was in prison there were very difficult days. I was in total isolation. For years I received no word from Israel. But there was not one day, not one moment, that I did not feel a bond with you all. And even when I was in a solitary cell, I sang an Israeli song." On August 25 Sharansky's mother, Ida Milgrom, along with his brother, Leonid, and his wife and two children arrived in Israel. For Sharansky, who flew to Vienna to be reunited with his family, it was the first time he had seen his mother in nearly two years and his first meeting with his brother in six years. On

November 6 Avital Sharansky gave birth to a girl, whom the Sharanskys named Rachel.

Natan Sharansky was not the only refusenik to arrive in Israel in 1986. Others included Rabbi Eliahu Essas, leader of the religious Jewish activist movement in the USSR, who arrived in January with his wife and three children; mathematician Yasha Gorodetzky, who was suddenly allowed to leave the Soviet Union in February after a 6-year struggle; in April, after a 15-year wait, two activist brothers, Grigory and Isai Goldstein, who had renounced their Soviet citizenship following the Munich Olympics massacre of Israeli athletes in 1972 to protest Soviet complicity in the deed; in August, 10-year refusenik Alexander Kushnir, a construction engineer, who was reunited in Israel with his mother, who had come to Israel 13 years earlier; prisoner of Zion Dr. Vladimir Brodsky, an anesthetist, who was released from a prison sentence for "malicious hooliganism" in October; and, in November, Yitzhak Kogan, the "Tzadik (righteous one) of Leningrad," an electronics engineer who became the only qualified ritual slaughterer in his native city. A tragic case was that of Inessa Flerova, who was finally allowed out of the USSR after worldwide pressure was exerted in the hope that a transplant of her bone marrow could save her brother, Michael Sherman, who had immigrated to Israel six years earlier and was suffering from leukemia.

Despite this impressive array of famous arrivals, the total number of immigrants from the Soviet Union was a dismal 202, down even from the previous year's poor showing. Pressure on Moscow to allow more Jews to leave thus continued throughout the year, peaking in a huge rally on June 6 at Jerusalem's outdoor Sultan's Pool, attended by 10,000 persons. The rally, at which Natan Sharansky spoke and France's Yves Montand sang, was the climax of a monthlong campaign of Israeli solidarity with the struggle of Soviet Jewry.

Speaking in the Knesset on November 4, Prime Minister Shamir noted that despite "various rumors" about a change for the better in the Soviets' attitude toward the Jewish population, "the [true] solution will only come about when the gates of the Soviet Union will be opened to the immigration of all Soviet Jews who long to come to their homeland, Israel." Shamir was also critical of those Soviet Jews who were given exit permits for Israel but then settled elsewhere, terming such behavior an "aberration" that was harmful to the *aliyah* movement. The solution was for the Soviets "to allow direct flights of Soviet Jews to Israel," he said.

The massive media attention focused on the Ethiopian Jews who arrived in 1985 via "Operation Moses" inevitably waned in 1986, as the drama of the secret project gave way to more mundane problems of absorption. One of the major problems confronting Ethiopian Jews, their very status as Jews in the eyes of Israel's Orthodox rabbinical establishment, remained not fully resolved. In April, Ethiopian *kessim*, or priests, conducted a marriage ceremony for 15 Ethiopian couples whom the rabbinate refused to marry, due to their refusal to undergo a ritual immersion ceremony to symbolize their "conversion" to Judaism. In October the High Court of Justice had to order the Religious Affairs Ministry to create forthwith the

"Institute for the Heritage of Ethiopian Jewry," whose establishment had been agreed on a year earlier as part of an arrangement by which Ethiopians would not necessarily have to undergo ritual immersion before being permitted to marry. In December a report drafted by the Immigrant Absorption Ministry noted that since 1978 some 16,000 Ethiopian immigrants had arrived in Israel, about half of them before November 1984 and the rest in "Operation Moses" and its adjuncts. The report said that about 2,100 of the recently arrived 3,500 Ethiopian family units were living in permanent housing. The Ethiopians were heavily dependent on social-welfare services, one reason being that fully 38 percent of the families were headed by single parents, as compared with 6 percent of such families in Israel overall.

THE DEMJANJUK CASE

On February 28, Ukrainian-born John Demjanjuk arrived in Israel from the United States, accompanied by U.S. marshals, and was promptly arrested on suspicion of having committed offenses under the Nazis and Nazi Collaborators Punishment Law.

Demjanjuk, 66 years old, was alleged to be the notorious "Ivan the Terrible" of the Treblinka death camp. Israel had been seeking Demjanjuk's extradition since October 1983 (he had lost his U.S. citizenship in 1981), and it was finally granted after legal appeals in U.S. courts had been turned down. The law under which he was arrested, which carried a maximum death penalty, had last been implemented in the trial of Adolf Eichmann, who in 1961, exactly 25 years earlier, was tried and convicted of crimes against the Jewish people and executed.

From the airport Demjanjuk was taken to the nearby Ayalon Prison where he was placed in a maximum-security cell with 24-hour closed-circuit television surveillance. On March 2 he was brought to magistrate's court in Jerusalem, where a judge was asked to remand him in custody for 15 days. In his first appearance in an Israeli court, Demjanjuk stuck to the version of events from which he had not wavered since legal proceedings were begun against him in the United States in 1979, and which he continued to maintain during his interrogation in Israel: "I was never in the place you call Treblinka and I never served the Nazis. I myself was a prisoner of war." Demjanjuk insisted that he was the victim of a case of mistaken identity and that the KGB, the Soviets' secret service, had forged documents allegedly identifying him with the actual "Ivan the Terrible" from Treblinka. Demjanjuk was remanded into custody until a formal indictment was submitted by the State Attorney's Office in September. In April Justice Minister Moshe Nissim formally approved the request of Demjanjuk's American lawyer, Mark O'Connor, to represent his client in an Israeli court, and in July Demjanjuk's family arrived in Israel and visited him in his cell.

On September 29, a 26-page indictment was filed against Demjanjuk in the Jerusalem district court, formally charging him on four counts under the Nazi and Nazi Collaborators Punishment Law of 1950: crimes against the Jewish people, crimes against humanity, war crimes, and crimes against persecuted persons. On November 17, the judges ruled that the trial would open on January 19, 1987, turning down a request from O'Connor for a three-month postponement. However, on December 29, following a request by O'Connor's newly appointed Israeli colleague for the defense, Yoram Sheftel, for a further postponement of two months, the date was finally set for February 16. Sheftel declared that the defense accepted all the facts regarding the Treblinka death camp and the crimes of Ivan the Terrible, but would seek to prove that John Demjanjuk, lately of Cleveland, Ohio, was not that man.

A number of international Jewish gatherings took place in Israel during the year. Of particular interest were the 50th-anniversary meeting of the World Jewish Congress and the First International Colloquium of the Jewish Press, which was attended by about 150 Jewish journalists from Israel and over 20 other countries. Both events were held in Jerusalem in January.

Culture

THE ARTS

A major development in 1986 was the renewal of cultural exchanges between Israel and Eastern Europe, notably with Poland, as a by-product of the developing thaw in Israel's relations with the Communist bloc. Representatives of Israeli theatrical companies visited the Soviet Union in January, the 12-day visit organized by the Israel-USSR Friendship Movement. In March the Bat Dor dance company became the first Israeli cultural troupe to perform in Poland since that country severed relations with Israel in 1967. At the annual Israel Festival/Jerusalem (May 24-June 15), Israelis were able to see two Polish theater works, the Polish Chamber Orchestra, and the renowned Mazowse folk-dance company. Foreign representation at the festival also came from East Germany (Ekkehard Schall of the Berliner Ensemble), West Germany, Argentina, Britain, Spain, Italy, Austria, France, Switzerland, and the United States. The works of two individuals, Spain's poet-playwright Federico García Lorca and West German playwright Franz Xavier Kroetz, were singled out for special presentations.

Israeli filmmaking took some important strides in 1986, including one from a wholly unexpected direction, the Israeli army. *Ricochets,* a feature-length film produced by the Israel Defense Forces' film unit, told the story of an infantry unit seeing combat duty in Lebanon. It was shot on location in that country shortly before the IDF's final withdrawal. Originally intended as an educational vehicle for dramatizing ethical and tactical problems posed by a war situation, it was later released commercially and was a major box-office success. It was also chosen as Israel's official entry at the Cannes Film Festival.

The film became the center of dispute when it failed to be selected as the Israeli candidate for the U.S. Academy Awards. *Ricochets*' commercial distributor went to court in an effort to block the nomination of a very different Israeli war—or antiwar—film, *Avanti Populo,* as the country's official entry for the 1986 Academy Awards' "best foreign film" category. Made on a shoestring budget by 30-year-old writer-director-producer Rafi Bukaee, *Avanti Populo* was set against the backdrop of the 1967 Six Day War and told the story of two Egyptian soldiers (played by Israeli Arab actors) fleeing across the Sinai Desert toward the Suez Canal and home. The dark comedy won first prize at the Lucarno Film Festival and was then selected as Israel's Oscar nominee.

The court prevailed upon the *Ricochets* distributor to drop its suit, at which point Industry and Trade Minister Ariel Sharon lashed out at the choice of *Avanti Populo*—even though it had been selected by a unit in his own ministry—and castigated it and other recent well-received Israeli films as reflecting "defeatist attitudes" espoused by "bleeding-heart left-wing intellectuals." One of the films Sharon may have had in mind was *Smile of the Lamb,* directed by Shimon Dotan from a novel by David Grossman, concerning Arab-Jewish relations against a West Bank setting. The film was highly acclaimed at the 1986 Berlin Film Festival (where actor Tuncel Curtiz received a Silver Bear award) and in March 1986 was named best Israeli film of 1985 at the Israel Festive Film Awards evening held at the Jerusalem Cinematheque.

The year saw some major musical events, including the fifth Arthur Rubinstein International Piano Master Competition, held triennially. Disappointingly, the judges decided not to select a first-prize winner from among the 34 contestants from 14 countries, principally because of the poor level of the contestants' playing with the full orchestra in the final stages.

On December 26, exactly 50 years after its premier performance, Zubin Mehta led the Israel Philharmonic Orchestra in a star-studded jubilee concert at Tel Aviv's Mann Auditorium to mark the occasion. The soloists were three generations of great Jewish and Israeli violinists—Isaac Stern, Itzhak Perlman, and Shlomo Mintz—in appreciation of the fact that the IPO's founder, the late Bronislaw Huberman, was a violinist by training.

Another 1986 jubilee was celebrated by the Israel Broadcasting Authority, marking 50 years of Hebrew broadcasts. Events included nostalgic replays of famous radio moments on Israel Radio and a special exhibition at the Israel Museum.

One of the year's major literary events was the publication of a novel entitled *Arabesques,* written in flawless Hebrew by Anton Shammas, an Arab Israeli. The book depicted the experience of Israel's Arabs in such a way as to challenge stereotypical thinking about them and make their experience more accessible to Israeli Jews. The year's most talked-about book was *Ayen Erekh: Ahavah* ("See Under 'Love' "), by David Grossman, a sweeping novel with a Holocaust background, which generated a furor, not so much because of its controversial contents as for its publisher's resort to American-style hype to sell it—an affront to much of Israel's somewhat staid publishing and literary community. The year's top seller, however, was *Tzipor Hanefesh* (Soul Bird), by Michal Snunit. Originally published in 1984, it was ostensibly a children's book, but one read as avidly by parents as by children.

ARCHAEOLOGY

Some 600 items from the antiquities collection of the late Moshe Dayan went on exhibit in April at the Israel Museum in Jerusalem. The museum drew fierce criticism from some quarters for paying $1 million for the collection to Dayan's second wife, Rachel, since it was no secret that Dayan had acquired many of the pieces through questionable, if not illegal, methods. While the museum issued a statement "fully supporting" a call by the Israel Association of Archaeologists to put a halt to "archaeological looting," it rejected allegations that the exhibit in effect legitimized Dayan's methods, adding that if it had not stepped in, the collection would have been sold piecemeal to private collectors and institutions abroad. The exhibit itself, one of the most popular in recent years at the museum, featured a number of striking and unique objects, including a 9,000-year-old stone mask and anthropoid clay burial sarcophagi of the Canaanite period.

Also on display at the Israel Museum during the year were two tiny silver amulets on which were etched the oldest biblical text ever found—predating the Dead Sea Scrolls by some 400 years—a passage from the Book of Numbers dating to the seventh century BCE. It took Israel Museum experts three years to open the rolled-up cylinders, which were originally excavated in Jerusalem's Hinnom Valley in 1979 by a Tel Aviv University archaeologist, Gabriel Barkai, in a First Temple-period family tomb. The text so far deciphered corresponded to Numbers 6:24–26, *birkat hakohanim,* the priestly blessing, and was nearly identical to the later Masoretic text.

In May an archaeological team led by the Hebrew University's Eilat Mazar and Leen Ritmeyer announced that it had tentatively identified a gateway to the First Temple, the first ever discovered. Elsewhere in Israel, one of the year's most spectacular finds was a 2000-year-old boat, uncovered in February beneath the waters of Lake Kinneret (the Sea of Galilee). The first ancient vessel ever to be retrieved in the country, the boat was encased in sheets of plastic before being removed from its two-millennia-old resting place and taken to nearby Kibbutz Ginossar to undergo rigorous preservation processes. In December underwater archaeologist Shelly Wachsmann, of the Antiquities Department, who was in overall charge of the Kinneret boat, announced that the wreck of a vessel discovered a year earlier off the Mediterranean coast near Kibbutz Ma'agan Michael was probably the first remains of a Phoenician ship found anywhere. The vessel was dated to the late fifth or early sixth century BCE, according to pottery found on it.

Other Domestic Matters

In 1986 Israel's Jewish population grew by 1.3 percent, while the country's Muslim population increased by 3 percent; overall, there were some 4.3 million Israelis, of whom about 3.5 million were Jews, accounting for approximately 82 percent of the population. According to the Central Bureau of Statistics, if present demographic trends continued, this figure would shrink to 76 percent within 20 years (not including the territories). For the first time, the fertility rate among Jewish women aged 20–24 was lower than that for the 30–34-year-old female population, reflecting the ongoing trend toward later marriage. In 1986 the average birthrate for Jewish women was 2.85 children, as compared with a 4.6 average for Muslim women (down from 9 births in the early 1970s). Average life expectancy was 73.5 years for men and 77.2 years for women. Over 37 percent of the country's population resided in the metropolitan Tel Aviv area, while Jerusalem accounted for 10.8 percent of Israel's population (470,000 persons) and Haifa for 9.1 percent. Taken together, Israel's three large urban areas housed over 57 percent of the country's population in 1986. The year saw a rise of 14 percent in road accidents, with 415 persons killed and nearly 21,000 injured in 14,576 accidents.

IMMIGRATION AND EMIGRATION

Only 9,500 new immigrants and potential immigrants arrived in Israel during the year, a falloff of 11 percent over 1985. The steepest decline came in immigration from the African continent, from which 1,000 immigrants arrived, a decline of 58 percent from 1985. Immigration from the United States was more or less stable, at about 1,900 persons. Sharply contrasting with these numbers were the data on emigration issued in October by the Central Bureau of Statistics. According to this report, approximately 380,000 Israelis were living abroad, including at least 262,700 who had been out of the country for four years or more and were therefore officially considered emigrants. Another 50,000 persons who had registered as potential immigrants upon their arrival in Israel subsequently left.

In an attempt to ease the absorption of new immigrants, the Ministry of Defense reduced the period of compulsory military service for new-immigrant males aged 24–48 from 12 to 3 months and abolished all army service for those aged 48 or above. The new regulations, which took effect on April 1, applied also to the children of Israeli emigrants under certain conditions.

In the meantime, a poll commissioned by the Immigration and Absorption Ministry, released in December, found that while 90 percent of Israelis said they would never emigrate, no fewer than 19 percent of those in the 19–28 age group said they might contemplate emigration. The fact that 57 percent of those polled agreed that *yordim* (emigrants: "those who descend") "were *not* people who betray their homeland" was viewed as a significant shift in attitude on this subject.

Two sectors of Israeli society generally regarded as deprived staged strikes during the year. In April the entire Negev "development" town of Yeroham went on strike for eight days, breaking off the action after the government agreed to aid the depressed town, chiefly by moving the Negev Phosphates plant there. In July Arab local councils went on strike for two weeks before they were promised $1.1 million of the $4 million pledged them to help defray accumulated debts of $15 million. The Arab councils were also seeking a massive funding hike to place them on the same development footing as equivalent Jewish local councils.

On July 22 Ben-Gurion International Airport celebrated its operating jubilee, the first aircraft having touched down at Lod Airport (its earlier name) on a flight from Cairo on that date in 1936. On October 20 the Knesset held a special ceremony to honor David Ben-Gurion, one of Israel's founders and its first prime minister and defense minister. The VIP gathering signaled the opening of a yearlong celebration to mark the centenary of Ben-Gurion's birth. The opening ceremony, held at the Jerusalem Theater, was broadcast live over Israel TV. On December 8 an official memorial ceremony was held at the graveside of David and Paula Ben-Gurion at Kibbutz Sde Boker in the Negev, and on the same day the army's general staff held a special session at Sde Boker in honor of the man who led the country through the War of Independence and was largely responsible for creating the Israel Defense Forces.

One of the oddest headline-making events of the year was the case of William Nakash, sought by France after his 1984 conviction *in absentia* for the February 1983 murder of an Arab in the town of Besançon. Nakash was sentenced to life imprisonment for what the French police said was a killing related to a dispute between nightclub owners. According to Nakash's lawyer, however, the man gunned down was a pro-PLO activist, and Nakash had been out to persuade local Arabs to stop pestering Jews—hence the killing was a political act and Nakash was not extraditable. Nakash had in the meantime immigrated to Israel, where he was arrested in 1985 in connection with an armed robbery.

After lengthy delays, the Supreme Court ruled on September 9 that Nakash was in fact extraditable and ordered him returned to France within 60 days. The following day an obviously well-orchestrated campaign, with lobbyists ranging from the two chief rabbis to the ultranationalist Tehiya party to Meir Kahane's Kach party, went into high gear in an effort to block the extradition. Apparently motivated by Nakash's newfound religiosity (he had taken to wearing a skullcap in his court appearances) and by the fact that the victim was an Arab, these groups contended that Nakash's life would be endangered in a French prison. Leading Israeli jurists, such as Hebrew University professor emeritus S.Z. Feller, were aghast at what they regarded as an affront to the rule of law in the country. Justice (and Tourism) Minister Avraham Sharir initially stalled, then announced his decision on December 4 not to extradite. When ordered by the Supreme Court to show cause within seven days why he should not revoke his decision, Sharir submitted an affidavit explaining that the decision was motivated by his sincere belief that Nakash's life would be imperiled in a French prison. On December 22, five Supreme Court justices sharply criticized Sharir for not offering any proof to back up his claims concerning the situation in French prisons. The hearing was deferred to a later date.

The AIDS syndrome gained official recognition in Israel in 1986: in March the Health Ministry announced that all donated blood would be examined for the presence of antibodies to the disease and that seven centers would test people free of charge. Fewer than 30 cases of AIDS had been diagnosed in Israel by year's end.

Personalia

A number of senior appointments were made in the Israel Defense Forces. Among them: Maj. Gen. Ehud Barak was named O/C Central Command on January 19; Maj. Gen. Uri Saguy took over as O/C Southern Command on February 23 from Maj. Gen. Moshe Bar-Kochba; Maj. Gen. Yossi Peled replaced Maj. Gen. Ori Orr (who went on study leave) as O/C Northern Command on June 10; and, on August 24, Maj. Gen. Yitzhak Mordechai relieved Maj. Gen. Saguy, who in turn replaced Maj. Gen. Amir Drori (subsequently named deputy chief of staff) as head of the Ground Corps Command.

On October 6 the cabinet named MK Zevulun Hammer of the NRP minister of religious affairs, in place of Yosef Burg (NRP), who resigned from the cabinet (though not from the Knesset) after 35 consecutive years of holding ministerial posts. On November 11, following the premiership rotation, Elyakim Rubinstein succeeded Dr. Yossi Beilin as cabinet secretary. On December 1, Dedi Zucker, 38, took up his duties as an MK on behalf of the Citizens Rights Movement, replacing Mordechai Bar-On, who resigned from the House. In a ceremony on December 10, former attorney general Yitzhak Zamir was awarded the Emil Grunzweig Prize for his civil-rights activity.

Personalities who died during the year included Yosef Klarman, a founder of Betar and a former head of Youth Aliyah, on January 1, aged 76; Israel Galili, commander of the Haganah in the prestate period, later a minister without portfolio and influential adviser to two prime ministers, Yitzhak Rabin and Golda Meir, on February 8, aged 75; Moshe Pearlman, Israel's first army spokesman, first Government Press Office director, and later a well-known author, on April 5, aged 75; Israel Goldstein, American Zionist leader who settled in Israel and served as world chairman of Keren Hayesod-United Israel Appeal, on April 11, aged 89; Seif e-Din Zuabi, prominent Israeli Arab leader who served in nine consecutive Knessets, on June 26, aged 73; Dan Pagis, noted poet and medievalist, on June 29, aged 56; and Moshe Baram, longtime Labor-party activist, MK (1959–77), and minister of labor (1974–77), December 5, aged 75.

RALPH MANDEL

World Jewish Population, 1986

Updated Estimates

THIS ARTICLE PRESENTS updates, as of 1986, of the Jewish population estimates for the various countries of the world.[1] The estimates reflect some of the results of a prolonged and ongoing effort to study scientifically the demography of contemporary world Jewry.[2] Data collection and comparative research have benefited from the collaboration of scholars and institutions in many countries, including replies to direct inquiries regarding current estimates. It should be emphasized, however, that the elaboration of a worldwide set of estimates for the Jewish populations of the various countries is beset with difficulties and uncertainties. The reader has been given some information on the quality of the estimate for each country by an accuracy rating, using a simple scale explained below.

Over 95 percent of world Jewry is concentrated in nine countries, with approximately 100,000 or more Jews each. The aggregate of these nine major Jewish population centers virtually determines the assessment of the size of total world Jewry. The figures for 1986 have been updated from those for 1984 in accordance with the known or estimated changes in the interval—vital events (i.e., births and deaths), identificational changes (accessions and secessions), and migrations. In addition, some corrections have been introduced in the light of newly accrued information from Jewish sources. Where necessary, corrections have also been applied retrospectively to the 1984 figures, which appear below in revised summary (see table l), so as to allow for comparison with the 1986 estimates.

Jewish Population Trends

Diaspora Jews are highly dispersed. In most countries their number is now rather small and they constitute no more than a minute fraction of the entire population.

[1]The previous estimates, as of 1984, were first published in AJYB, vol. 86, 1986, 350–64, and reprinted in a condensed version in AJYB, vol. 87, 1987, 331–38.

[2]Many of these activities have been carried out by, or in coordination with, the Division of Jewish Demography and Statistics at the Institute of Contemporary Jewry, the Hebrew University of Jerusalem.

Consequently, though Jews tend to cluster in large cities, they are greatly exposed to assimilation. While the assimilatory process leads to demographic losses for the Jewish population, there may also be gains through accession of persons who were born as non-Jews. It is the net balance of the identificational changes that matters demographically; in the longer run, the cohesion of a Diaspora population may be affected as well.[3]

The Jews in most countries of the Diaspora are demographically characterized by very low fertility, considerable outmarriage (which may involve losses of children to the Jewish population),[4] some other net assimilatory losses, and great aging. Since an increased proportion of elderly in the population usually implies not only many deceased but also a reduced proportion of persons of reproductive age—and therefore relatively fewer births—the aging of a population has the effect of reducing the birthrate and raising the death rate. There are differences in the levels of these demographic factors among the Jews in various regions and countries. In all major Diaspora populations the joint balance of the natural and identificational changes is now close to nil or outrightly negative, with the Jewish deceased frequently outnumbering newborn Jews. These negative tendencies have been taken into account in updating the estimates of Jews in many countries.

With regard to the balance of external migrations, there is no regularity among the various Diaspora populations or even in the same population over time. Where the migratory balance is positive—e.g., in North America—it counteracts or even outweighs any numerically negative influence of internal demographic developments. Where the migratory balance is negative, it may cause, or aggravate, the decrease of a Jewish population. In 1985–1986, the overall volume of international migrations of Jews was rather restricted, primarily because of the virtual cessation of Jewish emigration from the Soviet Union.

In contrast, Jews in Israel incur virtually no outmarriages and direct assimilatory losses. Moreover, until the early 1980s they tended to have a positive migration balance. They have a younger age structure than Diaspora Jews and the general populations of the developed countries and exhibit a fairly high level of fertility. The previously substantial fertility differentials between Jews in-gathered in Israel from Asia-Africa and Europe-America are no longer in evidence. Remarkably, European Jews in Israel have not participated in the drastic fertility decline that has characterized the developed nations and Diaspora Jews during the last few decades, but have actually raised their fertility. In recent years, both major origin groups among Israel's Jews have displayed a fertility level surpassing not only the vast majority of Diaspora Jewry but also the general populations in the developed countries.

In the overall demographic balance of world Jewry, the natural increase of Israel has, so far, made up for losses in the Diaspora. But such compensation will not be

---

[3]A fuller discussion of the subject can be found in U. O. Schmelz, "Jewish Survival: The Demographic Factors," AJYB, vol. 81, 1981, 61–117.

[4]If less than half of the children of the outmarried are themselves Jews.

possible for much longer. As a consequence of the intensifying demographic deficit in the Diaspora, a trend for some reduction in the total number of the world's Jews may soon be setting in.[5]

Difficulties in Estimating Jewish Population Size in the Diaspora[6]

Some of the difficulties involved in estimating the size of Jewish Diaspora populations are common to all aspects of the study of Diaspora demography. They are mainly due to the great geographical scattering of Jews (a factor that makes multiple data collection mandatory but also hinders its feasibility); to their unusually strong demographic dynamics in many respects— migrations, social mobility, family formation patterns (including outmarriage), etc.; and to lacunae of available demographic information, which is deficient in both quantity and quality.

More specific difficulties in estimating the up-to-date size of Jewish populations are due to conceptual and measurement problems.

When mixed couples and households are not infrequent, it is necessary to distinguish between the "actually Jewish population" and the "enlarged Jewish population." The latter comprises also the non-Jewish household members (spouses, children, etc.) of the Jews. However socially significant the non-Jewish household members (and more distant non-Jewish relatives) of the Jews may be, they should not be included in a count of Jews. The paradoxical situation that exists is that growth of an enlarged Jewish population may be associated with contraction of the respective actually Jewish population.

Another vexing problem is identificational changes among Jews. Under present conditions, there are Jews who have not formally embraced another religion, yet are either very estranged ("marginal") or have even become resolutely alienated from Judaism and the Jewish community and, if questioned, disclaim being Jews any longer. When a census or survey is taken which inquires into religion or ethnicity, these individuals have an opportunity to define their current status subjectively.[7] In general, the practice of self-determination is followed in all relevant censuses and surveys. This applies to marginal individuals, converts to Judaism (although some of the conversions may be contested between the various ideological trends—Orthodox, Conservative, and Reform), and to all other persons who claim to be Jews. In estimating the size of a Jewish population, it is usual to include, in principle, all marginal individuals who have not ceased to be Jews.[8]

---

[5]*Aliyah* and *yeridah*—immigration to, and emigration from, Israel—obviously constitute only internal transfers within the global Jewish framework.

[6]Reliable figures are currently forthcoming for the Jews of Israel from official statistics.

[7]Misreporting of Jews in official censuses is a different issue; see below.

[8]Even persons who disclaim being Jews at some stage of life may change their minds later.

Not a few Jews (like other persons) have some residential status in more than one country.[9] This may be due to business requirements, professional assignments in foreign countries, climatic differences between countries, migrants staying temporarily in prolonged transit, etc. The danger of double-counting or omissions is inherent in such situations. As far as possible we have tried to account for such persons only once, giving precedence to the usual country of residence.

Figures on Jews from population censuses are unavailable for most Diaspora communities. Even where census statistics on Jews are forthcoming, they are usually scant, because the Jews are a small minority. There have been instances where detailed tabulations on Jews have been undertaken, through Jewish initiative, from official census material; examples are Canada, South Africa, and Argentina. In some countries serious problems exist, or are feared to exist, in the reporting of Jews as such: individuals may prefer not to describe themselves as Jews, or non-Jews may be erroneously included as Jews (as has happened in Latin American countries). These problems require statistical evaluation whose feasibility and conclusiveness depend on the relevant information available.

Surveys are the only way of obtaining comprehensive information on Jewish populations in the absence of official censuses. Jewish-sponsored surveys have the additional advantage of being able to inquire into matters of specifically Jewish interest, e.g., Jewish education, observances, and attitudes. However, since they address themselves to a small and scattered minority with identification problems, they are not easy to conduct competently and may encounter difficulties with regard to both coverage and response, especially with regard to marginal Jews. Again, these aspects require evaluation. Countrywide surveys have been undertaken in the United States, South Africa, France, Italy, Netherlands, etc. Local surveys have been carried out in many U.S. cities, in the United Kingdom, Latin America, Australia, etc. However, these local initiatives have so far been uncoordinated with regard to content and method.

In certain countries or localities, Jewish community registers include all or the largest part of the Jewish population. Often the same communities keep records of Jewish vital events—especially marriages performed with a Jewish ceremony and Jewish burials. However, communal registers tend to cover mixed households insufficiently. Also, although the amount and quality of updating vary from place to place, community registers generally lag behind the actual situation of the respective Jewish populations.

Many estimates of Jewish populations for which no solid data from censuses or surveys exist are regrettably of unspecified or dubious source and methodology.

Besides the conceptual and measurement difficulties affecting the figures for a

---

[9]The problem is even more acute with regard to residential status in more than one locality of the same country, but in principle this does not affect the population estimates for entire countries.

Jewish population at any base date, similar problems recur with regard to the updating information which should account for all the various types of changes in the time elapsed since that base date. For vital events and identificational changes, age-sex-specific models can be of use; these may be applied after studying the evolution of the respective or similar Jewish populations. With regard to the migratory balance in any updating interval, concrete information must be gathered, because of the above-mentioned irregularity, over time, in the intensity of many migratory streams.

Presentation of Data

The detailed estimates of Jewish population distribution in each continent (tables 2–6 below) refer to residents in countries with at least 100 Jews. A residual estimate of "other" Jews living in smaller communities, or staying temporarily in transit accommodations, supplements some of the continental totals. For each of the reported countries, the four columns in the table provide the United Nations estimate of mid-year 1986 total population,[10] the estimated end-1986 Jewish population, the proportion of Jews per 1,000 of total population, and a rating of the accuracy of the Jewish population estimates.

There is wide variation in the quality of the Jewish population estimates for different countries. For many Diaspora countries it would be best to indicate a range (minimum-maximum) rather than a definite figure for the number of Jews. It would be confusing, however, for the reader to be confronted with a long list of ranges; this would also complicate the regional and world totals. Yet, the figures actually indicated for most of the Diaspora countries should be understood as being the central value of the plausible range. The relative magnitude of this range varies inversely with the accuracy of the estimate.

The three main elements which affect the accuracy of each estimate are the nature of the base data, the recency of the base data, and the method of updating. A simple code combining these elements is used to provide a general evaluation of the reliability of the Jewish population figures reported in the detailed tables below. The code indicates different quality levels of the reported estimates: (A) base figure derived from countrywide census or relatively reliable Jewish population surveys; updated on the basis of full or partial information on Jewish population movements in the intervening period; (B) base figure derived from less accurate but recent countrywide Jewish population investigation; partial information on population movements in the intervening period; (C) base figure derived from less recent sources, and/or

---

[10]These were the latest official estimates available at the time of writing. See United Nations, Department of International Economic and Social Affairs, Statistical Office, *Population and Vital Statistics Report: Data Available as of 1 July 1987.* Statistical Papers, ser. A, vol. 39, no. 3 (New York, 1987).

unsatisfactory or partial coverage of Jewish population in country; updating according to demographic information illustrative of regional demographic trends; and (D) base figure essentially conjectural; no reliable updating procedure. In categories (A), (B), and (C), the years in which the base figures or important partial updates were obtained are also stated.

For countries whose Jewish population estimate of 1986 was not only updated but also revised in the light of improved information, the sign "X" is appended to the accuracy rating.

Distribution of World Jewish Population by Major Regions

Table 1 gives an overall picture for 1986 as compared to 1984. For 1984 the originally published estimates are presented along with somewhat revised figures that take into account, retrospectively, the corrections made in 1986 in certain country estimates, in the light of improved information. These corrections resulted in a net reduction of world Jewry's estimated size by 9,300, or less than 0.1 percent. Some explanations are given below for the relevant countries.

The size of world Jewry is assessed at slightly below 13 million. According to the revised figures, the estimated growth between 1984 and 1986 was negligible—about three per 10,000 annually. Despite all the imperfections in the estimates, it is clear that world Jewry is in the state of "zero population growth," with the natural increase in Israel compensating for the demographic losses in the Diaspora.

The number of Jews in Israel rose from a figure of 3,471,700 in 1984 to 3,562,500 at the end of 1986, or by 1.3 percent annually. In contrast, Diaspora Jewry declined from 9,482,700 (according to the revised figures) to approximately 9,401,400, or by 0.5 percent annually. These changes were almost entirely due to internal demographic evolution, since the migratory balance between the Diaspora and Israel amounted to no more than 9,200 during these two years and was positive for the Diaspora (Israel lost migrants on balance). By the end of 1986, Israel's Jews constituted about 27.5 percent of total world Jewry.

About half of the world's Jews reside in the Americas, with 46 percent in North America. Twenty-eight percent live in Asia (excluding the Asian territories of the USSR and Turkey), nearly all of them in Israel. Europe (including the Asian territories of the USSR and Turkey) accounts for 21 percent of the total. The proportions of the world's Jews who live in Africa and Oceania are very small.

Among the major geographical regions listed in table 1, the number of Jews in Israel—and, in consequence, in total Asia—increased by more than 2 percent in the two-year span 1984–1986. The total number of Jews estimated for North America virtually did not change. The total estimate for Oceania increased by over 2 percent. Most other regions sustained decreases in Jewish population size.

World Jewry constitutes about 2.6 per 1,000 of total world population. One in about 385 people in the world is a Jew.

TABLE 1. ESTIMATED JEWISH POPULATION, BY CONTINENTS AND MAJOR GEOGRAPHICAL REGIONS, 1984 AND 1986

Region	1984			1986		% Change
		Revised				
	Original	Abs. Nos.	Percent	Abs. Nos.	Percent	1984–1986
Diaspora	9,491,600	9,482,700	73.2	9,401,400	72.5	−0.9
Israel	3,471,700	3,471,700	26.8	3,562,500	27.5	+2.6
World	12,963,300	12,954,400	100.0	12,963,900	100.0	+0.1
America,						
Total	6,469,000	6,461,100	49.9	6,454,700	49.8	−0.1
North[a]	6,015,000	6,010,000	46.4	6,010,000	46.4	0.0
Central	47,300	46,300	0.4	45,500	0.3	−1.7
South	406,700	404,800	3.1	399,200	3.1	−1.4
Europe, Total	2,758,600	2,755,800	21.3	2,685,900	20.7	−2.5
West	1,048,900	1,048,600	8.1	1,043,300	8.0	−0.5
East & Balkans[b]	1,709,700	1,707,200	13.2	1,642,600	12.7	−3.8
Asia, Total	3,509,300	3,509,300	27.1	3,597,000	27.8	+2.5
Israel	3,471,700	3,471,700	26.8	3,562,500	27.5	+2.6
Rest[b]	37,600	37,600	0.3	34,500	0.3	−8.2
Africa, Total	147,400	149,100	1.1	145,200	1.1	−2.6
North	16,700	16,700	0.1	15,200	0.1	−9.0
South	119,100	119,100	0.9	116,200	0.9	−2.4
Rest[c]	11,600	13,300	0.1	13,800	0.1	+3.8
Oceania	79,000	79,100	0.6	81,100	0.6	+2.5

[a]U.S.A. and Canada.
[b]The Asian territories of USSR and Turkey are included in "East Europe and Balkans."
[c]Including Ethiopia.

Individual Countries

THE AMERICAS

In 1986 the total number of Jews in the American continents was somewhat less than six and a half million. The overwhelming majority (about 93 percent) reside in the United States and Canada, less than 1 percent live in Central America (including Mexico), and about 6 percent live in South America, where Argentina and Brazil have the largest Jewish communities (see table 2).

The balance of Jewish population changes in the United States as a whole must now be close to nil. Several local surveys taken in recent years provide evidence of very low birthrates and of increasing aging among the Jewish population. Thus, it is possible that the influence of internal evolution on the size of U.S. Jewry may be negative, though there is no consensus with regard to this assessment. Any negative internal balance in U.S. Jewry was more than offset several years ago by an undoubtedly positive balance of external migrations. This latter has been greatly reduced, however, by the virtual cessation of Soviet Jewish immigration.

Our 1986 estimate of 5,700,000 Jews in the United States essentially repeats the figures reported for the previous years, and is consistent with the new estimates prepared by the research team of the North American Jewish Data Bank which are reported elsewhere in this volume.[11] Actually, the new figure is 5,814,000 for 1986, but it includes an estimated "under 2 percent" of non-Jewish members of Jewish households. After deducting the latter from 5,814,000, one arrives at the round figure of approximately 5,700,000 Jews in the United States.

In Canada an official population census held in 1981 enumerated 296,425 Jews according to religion. If the persons are added who responded "Jewish" (as a *single* reply) to the census question on ethnic groups, while not indicating any religion (i.e., they were not Christians, etc.), the figure rises to 306,375. There were additonal persons who did not indicate religion but mentioned "Jewish" as part of a *multiple* response to the question on ethnic groups. It is likely that some of them were merely thinking in terms of ancestry but did not actually consider themselves as Jews at the time of the census. By including a reasonable proportion of those who were identified in the census as Jews by multiple ethnicity only, a round total of 310,000 is arrived at for 1981. The figure of 310,000 was also adopted for 1986, as a

---

[11]The new U.S. Jewish population estimates first appeared in B. Kosmin, P. Ritterband, and J. Scheckner, "Jewish Population in the United States, 1986," AJYB, vol. 87, 1987, 164–91. See also U. O. Schmelz, *World Jewish Population: Regional Estimates and Projections* (Jerusalem, 1981), 32–36; U. O. Schmelz and Sergio DellaPergola, "The Demographic Consequences of U.S. Jewish Population Trends," AJYB, vol. 83, 1983, 141–87; U.O. Schmelz and Sergio DellaPergola, *Basic Trends in U.S. Jewish Demography,* Jewish Sociology Papers, American Jewish Committee (New York, 1988).

TABLE 2. ESTIMATED JEWISH POPULATION DISTRIBUTION IN THE AMERICAS, 1986

Country	Total Population	Jewish Population	Jews per 1,000 Population	Accuracy Rating
Canada	25,612,000	310,000	12.1	A 1981
United States	241,596,000	5,700,000	23.6	B 1986 X
Total Northern America		6,010,000		
Bahamas	236,000	300	1.3	C 1973 X
Costa Rica	2,666,000	2,000	0.8	C 1986 X
Cuba	10,246,000	700	0.1	D
Dominican Republic	6,416,000	100	0.0	D
Guatemala	8,195,000	800	0.1	A 1983
Jamaica	2,372,000	300	0.1	B 1986
Mexico	79,563,000	35,000	0.4	C 1980
Netherlands Antilles	261,000	400	1.5	D X
Panama	2,227,000	3,800	1.7	C 1986
Puerto Rico	3,502,000	1,500	0.4	C 1986 X
Virgin Islands	107,000	300	2.8	C 1986 X
Other		300		D
Total Central America		45,500		
Argentina	31,030,000	224,000	7.2	C 1960–86
Bolivia	6,547,000	600	0.1	C 1986
Brazil	138,493,000	100,000	0.7	B 1980
Chile	12,327,000	17,000	1.4	C 1986
Colombia	29,188,000	6,500	0.2	C 1986
Ecuador	9,647,000	1,000	0.1	C 1982
Paraguay	3,807,000	900	0.2	C 1984
Peru	20,207,000	4,000	0.2	B 1985 X
Suriname	380,000	200	0.5	B 1986
Uruguay	2,983,000	25,000	8.4	D X
Venezuela	17,791,000	20,000	1.1	D
Total Southern America		399,200		
Total		6,454,700		

migratory surplus may have roughly offset the probably negative balance of internal evolution since the census.

The estimate for Mexico has been kept unchanged at 35,000. While the official Mexican censuses have given widely varying figures—17,574 in 1950; 100,750 in 1960; 49,277 in 1970; 61,790 in 1980—it is generally admitted that the last three censuses erroneously included many thousands of non-Jews among the Jews.

The Jewish population of Argentina is marked by a negative balance in internal evolution. In the past, the balance of external migrations was strongly negative, but since the present democratic regime came to power, emigration has diminished and there has been some return migration. Assuming a migratory balance close to nil, the estimate has been reduced from 228,000 in 1984 to 224,000 in 1986.

The official population census of Brazil in 1980 showed a figure of 91,795 Jews. Since it is possible that some Jews failed to declare themselves as such in the census, a corrected estimate of 100,000 was adopted for 1981 and has been kept unchanged for 1986, assuming that the overall balance of vital events and external migrations was close to zero.

On the strength of fragmentary information that is accumulating, the admittedly quite tentative estimate for Uruguay has been revised downward, while those for Chile and Venezuela have not been changed.[12]

EUROPE

Of Europe's estimated 2,686,000 Jews, 39 percent live in Western Europe and 61 percent in Eastern Europe and the Balkan countries (including the Asian territories of the USSR and Turkey).

France has the largest Jewish population in Western Europe, estimated at 530,000. Monitoring of the plausible trends in the internal evolution and the external migrations of Jews in France renders it likely that there has been little net change since the major survey that was taken in the 1970s.[13]

A reestimation of the size of British Jewry was carried out by the research unit of the Board of Deputies, based on an analysis of Jewish deaths during 1975–1979. The revised population figure for 1977 was 336,000 with a margin of error of +/− 34,000.[14] Allowing for an excess of deaths over births, some assimilatory losses, and emigration, the update for 1984, as elaborated by the board's research unit, came to 330,000. The update for 1986 is 326,000.

---

[12]For a more detailed discussion of the region's Jewish population trends, see U. O. Schmelz and Sergio DellaPergola, "The Demography of Latin American Jewry," AJYB, vol. 85, 1985, 51–102.

[13]Doris Bensimon and Sergio DellaPergola, *La population juive de France: socio-démographie et identité* (Jerusalem and Paris, 1984).

[14]S. Haberman, B. A. Kosmin, and C. Levy, "Mortality Patterns of British Jews 1975–79: Insights and Applications for the Size and Structure of British Jewry," *Journal of the Royal Statistical Society,* ser. A., 146, pt. 3 (1983): 294–310.

West Germany, Belgium, Italy, and the Netherlands each have Jewish populations ranging around 30,000. There is an internal tendency toward shrinkage of all these Jewries, but in some instances this is offset partly by immigration. Up to 1984 Jews in Italy were legally obliged to register with the local Jewish communities.

TABLE 3. ESTIMATED JEWISH POPULATION DISTRIBUTION IN EUROPE, 1986

Country	Total Population	Jewish Population	Jews per 1,000 Population	Accuracy Rating
Austria	7,565,000	6,400	0.8	A 1986
Belgium	9,913,000	32,000	3.2	D
Bulgaria	8,959,000	3,200	0.4	D
Czechoslovakia	15,534,000	8,200	0.5	D
Denmark	5,121,000	6,600	1.3	C 1984
Finland	4,918,000	1,200	0.2	A 1986
France	55,392,000	530,000	9.6	C 1972–78
Germany, East	16,624,000	500	0.0	C 1986 X
Germany, West	61,048,000	32,700	0.5	B 1986
Gibraltar	29,000	600	20.7	A 1981
Great Britain	56,763,000	326,000	5.7	B 1986
Greece	9,966,000	5,000	0.5	B 1986
Hungary	10,627,000	60,000	5.6	D
Ireland	3,537,000	2,000	0.6	A 1986
Italy	57,221,000	31,800	0.6	B 1986
Luxembourg	363,000	700	1.9	C 1970
Netherlands	14,563,000	26,000	1.8	C 1986
Norway	4,169,000	1,000	0.2	A 1982
Poland	37,456,000	4,400	0.1	D
Portugal	10,291,000	300	0.0	B 1986 X
Rumania	23,174,000	21,500	0.9	B 1986 X
Spain	38,668,000	12,000	0.3	D
Sweden	8,370,000	15,000	1.8	C 1982
Switzerland	6,504,000	19,000	2.9	A 1980
Turkey[a]	50,301,000	20,000	0.4	C 1986
USSR[a]	280,144,000	1,515,000	5.4	C 1979
Yugoslavia	23,271,000	4,800	0.2	C 1986
Total		2,685,900		

[a]Including Asian regions.

Since then, membership in the community has become voluntary. Although most Jews did reaffirm their membership, the new community framework may have repercussions both on the degree of completeness of the communal registers and, in the long run, on the cohesion of the community.

Switzerland's Jews are estimated at below 20,000, on the strength of the 1980 census. While there is evidence of a negative balance of births and deaths (connected *inter alia* with great aging) and of frequent outmarriage, immigration may have offset the internal losses.

Eastern European Jewry is characterized by particularly low levels of effectively Jewish fertility, connected with a frequent and prolonged practice of outmarriage, and by heavy aging. Therefore the shrinking of the Jewish population there must be comparatively rapid.

By far the largest Jewish population in Eastern Europe is concentrated in the Soviet Union, including its Asian territory. Only about 2,000 Jews were permitted to emigrate during 1985–1986, but the heavy deficit of internal population dynamics must have continued and even intensified, due to the great aging that is known to have prevailed.[15] Under these circumstances the estimate has been reduced from 1,575,000 in 1984 to 1,515,000 in 1986.

The Jewish populations in Hungary and Rumania and the small remnants in Czechoslovakia, Poland, East Germany, and Bulgaria are all reputed to be very overaged. Their inevitable numerical decline is reflected in reduced estimates. For Rumania, considerable emigration of Jews is taking place; in addition, a correction was made in the 1986 estimate, omitting non-Jewish members of Jewish households that had been previously included in the figures reported from that country.

The size of Hungarian Jewry—the largest in Eastern Europe outside the USSR—is insufficiently known. Our estimate only attempts to reflect the declining trend that prevails there too, according to the available indications.

The Jewish population of Turkey is estimated at about 20,000, and a deficit of births over deaths is reported.

ASIA

Israel accounts for 99 percent of all the Jews in Asia, excluding the Asian territories of the USSR and Turkey. Israel's Jewish population grew over 1985–1986 by about 90,000. All this growth was due to natural increase, since the migration balance was negative (−9,200) in 1985–1986.

It is difficult to estimate the Jewish population of Iran for any given date, but it continues to dwindle.

---

[15]U. O. Schmelz, "New Evidence on Basic Issues in the Demography of Soviet Jews," *Jewish Journal of Sociology* 16, no. 2 (1974): 209–23.

TABLE 4. ESTIMATED JEWISH POPULATION DISTRIBUTION IN ASIA, 1986

Country	Total Population	Jewish Population	Jews per 1,000 Population	Accuracy Rating
Hong Kong	5,533,000	1,000	0.2	C 1980
India	766,135,000	4,200	0.0	C 1971
Iran	45,914,000	22,000	0.5	D
Iraq	16,450,000	200	0.0	D
Israel[a]	4,333,100[a]	3,562,500	822.2	A 1986
Japan	120,492,000	1,000	0.0	C 1986
Lebanon	2,707,000	100	0.0	D
Philippines	56,004,000	100	0.0	C 1982
Singapore	2,586,000	300	0.1	C 1984
Syria	10,612,000	4,000	0.4	D
Thailand	52,094,000	300	0.0	C 1980
Yemen	7,046,000	1,000	0.1	D
Other		300		D
Total		3,597,000		

[a]End 1986.

TABLE 5. ESTIMATED JEWISH POPULATION DISTRIBUTION IN AFRICA, 1986

Country	Total Population	Jewish Population	Jews per 1,000 Population	Accuracy Rating	
Egypt	49,609,000	200	0.0	D	
Ethiopia	44,927,000	12,000	0.3	D	X
Kenya	21,163,000	100	0.0	B 1986	
Morocco	22,476,000	12,000	0.5	D	
South Africa	33,221,000	115,000	3.5	B 1980	
Tunisia	7,234,000	3,000	0.4	D	
Zaire	80,850,000	400	0.0	D	X
Zambia	6,896,000	300	0.0	D	
Zimbabwe	8,406,000	1,200	0.1	B 1986	
Other		1,000		D	
Total		145,200			

AFRICA

About 145,000 Jews are estimated to remain now in Africa. The Republic of South Africa accounts for 80 percent of total Jews in that continent.

According to the 1980 census of the Republic of South Africa, the final figure for Jews (by religion, among the white population) was 117,963. Since then, Jewish population size there has been reduced by a negative migratory balance.

According to recent reports, the number of Jews remaining in Ethiopia may be very roughly estimated at 12,000. The remnant of Moroccan Jewry continued to shrink through emigration. It should be pointed out, though, that not a few Jews have a foothold both in Morocco (or Tunisia) and in France, and their geographical attribution is uncertain.

OCEANIA

The major country of Jewish residence in this geographical region is Australia, where 95 percent of the estimated total of somewhat over 80,000 Jews live. Australian Jewry is being reinforced by immigration.

TABLE 6. ESTIMATED JEWISH POPULATION DISTRIBUTION IN OCEANIA, 1986

Country	Total Population	Jewish Population	Jews per 1,000 Population	Accuracy Rating
Australia	15,974,000	77,000	4.8	C 1981
New Zealand	3,248,000	4,000	1.2	B 1981
Other		100		D X
Total		81,100		

Dispersion and Concentration

Table 7 demonstrates the magnitude of Jewish dispersion. The individual countries listed above as each having at least 100 Jews are scattered over all the continents. More than half (43 out of 74 countries) have fewer than 5,000 Jews apiece.

In relative terms, too, the Jews are now thinly scattered nearly everywhere in the Diaspora. There is not a single Diaspora country where they amount even to 3 percent of the total population. In most countries they constitute a far smaller fraction. Only three Diaspora countries have 10–25 Jews per 1,000 of total population; and only nine countries have more than 5 Jews per 1,000 of population. The respective nine countries are, in descending order of the proportion—but regardless of the absolute number—of their Jews: United States (23.6), Gibraltar (20.7), Canada (12.1), France (9.6), Uruguay (8.4), Argentina (7.2), Great Britain (5.7), Hungary (5.6), USSR (5.4). This list includes all the Diaspora countries with Jewries of 100,000 or more, except for South Africa and Brazil (in the latter's large population

TABLE 7. DISTRIBUTION OF THE WORLD'S JEWS, BY NUMBER AND PROPORTION (PER 1,000 POPULATION) IN VARIOUS COUNTRIES, 1986

Number of Jews in Country	Total	Jews per 1,000 Population: Below 1	1–5	5–10	10–25	25 and over
	Number of Countries					
Total	74[a]	49	15	6	3	1
Below 1,000	23	18	4	—	1	—
1,000–5,000	19	17	2	—	—	—
5,000–10,000	5	4	1	—	—	—
10,000–50,000	16	9	6	1	—	—
50,000–100,000	2	—	1	1	—	—
100,000–1,000,000	6	1	1	3	1	—
1,000,000 and over	3	—	—	1	1	1
	Jewish Population Distribution (Absolute Numbers)					
Total	12,963,900	373,700	337,100	2,680,000	6,010,600	3,562,500
Below 1,000	10,400	8,100	1,700	—	600	—
1,000–5,000	48,300	40,500	7,800	—	—	—
5,000–10,000	32,700	26,100	6,600	—	—	—
10,000–50,000	353,000	199,000	129,000	25,000	—	—
50,000–100,000	137,000	—	77,000	60,000	—	—
100,000–1,000,000	1,605,000	100,000	115,000	1,080,000	310,000	—
1,000,000 and over	10,777,500	—	—	1,515,000	5,700,000	3,562,500
	Jewish Population Distribution (Percent of World's Jews)					
Total	100.0	2.9	2.6	20.7	46.3	27.5
Below 1,000	0.1	0.1	0.0	—	0.0	—
1,000–5,000	0.4	0.3	0.1	—	—	—
5,000–10,000	0.2	0.2	0.0	—	—	—
10,000–50,000	2.7	1.5	1.0	0.2	—	—
50,000–100,000	1.1	—	0.6	0.5	—	—
100,000–1,000,000	12.4	0.8	0.9	8.3	2.4	—
1,000,000 and over	83.1	—	—	11.7	43.9	27.5

[a]Excluding countries with fewer than 100 Jews.

TABLE 8. COUNTRIES WITH LARGEST JEWISH POPULATIONS (100,000 JEWS AND ABOVE), 1986

			% of Total Jewish Population			
			In the Diaspora		In the World	
Rank	Country	Jewish Population	%	Cumulative %	%	Cumulative %
1	United States	5,700,000	60.6	60.6	43.9	43.9
2	Israel	3,562,500	—	—	27.5	71.4
3	Soviet Union	1,515,000	16.1	76.7	11.7	83.1
4	France	530,000	5.6	82.3	4.1	87.2
5	Great Britain	326,000	3.5	85.8	2.5	89.7
6	Canada	310,000	3.3	89.1	2.4	92.1
7	Argentina	224,000	2.4	91.5	1.7	93.8
8	South Africa	115,000	1.2	92.7	0.9	94.7
9	Brazil	100,000	1.1	93.8	0.8	95.5

the Jews form only 0.7 per 1,000). In the State of Israel, by contrast, the Jewish majority amounted to 82.2 percent in 1986.

While Jews are widely dispersed, they are also concentrated to some extent (table 8). In 1986 over 95 percent of world Jewry lived in the nine countries with the largest Jewish populations, each comprising about 100,000 Jews or more; 83 percent lived in the three countries that have at least a million Jews each (United States, Israel, Soviet Union). Similarly, the United States alone accounted for over 60 percent of total Diaspora Jewry; two countries (United States and Soviet Union) for 77 percent; and the eight Diaspora countries with 100,000 Jews or more together comprised 94 percent of the Diaspora Jewish population.

U. O. SCHMELZ
SERGIO DELLAPERGOLA

Directories
Lists
Obituaries

National Jewish Organizations[1]

UNITED STATES

Organizations are listed according to functions as follows:

Note also cross-references under these headings:

COMMUNITY RELATIONS

AMERICAN COUNCIL FOR JUDAISM (1943). 298 Fifth Ave., NYC 10001. (212)947-8878. Bd. Chmn. Clarence L. Coleman, Jr.; Pres. Alan V. Stone. Seeks to advance the universal principles of a Judaism free of nationalism, and the national, civic, cultural, and social integration into American institutions of Americans of Jewish faith. *Issues of the American Council for Judaism; Special Interest Report.*

AMERICAN JEWISH ALTERNATIVES TO ZIONISM, INC. (1968). 501 Fifth Ave., Suite 2015, NYC 10017. (212)557-5410. Pres. Elmer Berger; V.-Pres. Mrs. Arthur Gutman. Applies Jewish values of justice and humanity to the Arab-Israel conflict in the Middle East; rejects nationality attachment of Jews, particularly American Jews, to the State of Israel as self-segregating, inconsistent with American constitutional concepts of individual citizenship and separation of church and state, and as being a principal obstacle to Middle East peace. *Report.*

AMERICAN JEWISH COMMITTEE (1906). Institute of Human Relations, 165 E. 56 St., NYC 10022. (212)751-4000. Pres. Theodore Ellenoff; Exec. V.-Pres. Ira Silverman. Seeks to prevent infraction of civil and religious rights of Jews in any part of the world; to advance the cause of human rights for people of all races, creeds, and nationalities; to interpret the position of Israel to the American public; and to help

[1]The information in this directory is based on replies to questionnaires circulated by the editors.

American Jews maintain and enrich their Jewish identity and, at the same time, achieve full integration in American life. Includes Jacob and Hilda Blaustein Center for Human Relations, William E. Wiener Oral History Library, William Petschek National Jewish Family Center, Jacob Blaustein Institute for the Advancement of Human Rights, Institute on American Jewish-Israeli Relations. AMERICAN JEWISH YEAR BOOK (with Jewish Publication Society); *Commentary; Present Tense; AJC Journal; Capital Update.* Published in Israel: *Tefutsot Yisrael,* a quarterly, and *Alon Yedi'ot,* a monthly bulletin of the Institute on American Jewish-Israeli Relations.

AMERICAN JEWISH CONGRESS (1918). Stephen Wise Congress House, 15 E. 84 St., NYC 10028. (212)879-4500. Pres. Theodore R. Mann; Exec. Dir. Henry Siegman. Works to foster the creative cultural survival of the Jewish people; to help Israel develop in peace, freedom, and security; to eliminate all forms of racial and religious bigotry; to advance civil rights, protect civil liberties, defend religious freedom, and safeguard the separation of church and state. *Congress Monthly; Judaism; Boycott Report; National Report.*

ANTI-DEFAMATION LEAGUE OF B'NAI B'RITH (1913). 823 United Nations Plaza, NYC 10017. (212)490-2525. Chmn. Burton S. Levinson; Dir. Abraham H. Foxman. Seeks to combat anti-Semitism and to secure justice and fair treatment for all citizens through law, education, and community relations. *ADL Bulletin; Face to Face; Fact Finding Report; International Reports; Law Notes; Rights; Law; Research and Evaluation Report; Discriminations Report; Litigation Docket; Dimensions; Middle East Notebook; Nuestro Encuentro.*

ASSOCIATION OF JEWISH CENTER WORKERS (1918). c/o JCC, 3505 Mayfield Rd., Cleveland Heights, OH 44118 (216)382-4000. Pres. Allan Just. Seeks to enhance the standards, techniques, practices, scope, and public understanding of Jewish Community Center and kindred agency work. *Kesher; Viewpoints.*

ASSOCIATION OF JEWISH COMMUNITY RELATIONS WORKERS (1950). 443 Park Ave. S., 11th fl., NYC 10016. Pres. Jerome Levinrad. Aims to stimulate higher standards of professional practice in Jewish community relations; encourages research and training toward that end; conducts educational programs and seminars; aims to encourage cooperation between community relations workers and those working in other areas of Jewish communal service.

CENTER FOR JEWISH COMMUNITY STUDIES (1970). 1017 Gladfelter Hall, Temple University, Philadelphia, PA 19122. (215)787-1459. Jerusalem office: Jerusalem Center for Public Affairs. Pres. Daniel J. Elazar. Worldwide policy-studies institute devoted to the study of Jewish community organization, political thought, and public affairs, past and present, in Israel and throughout the world. Publishes original articles, essays, and monographs; maintains library, archives, and reprint series. *Jerusalem Letter/Viewpoints; Survey of Arab Affairs.*

COMMISSION ON SOCIAL ACTION OF REFORM JUDAISM (1953, under the auspices of the Union of American Hebrew Congregations). 838 Fifth Ave., NYC 10021. (212)249-0100. Chmn. Harris Gilbert; Dir. Albert Vorspan; Assoc. Dir. Rabbi David Saperstein. Develops materials to assist Reform synagogues in setting up social-action programs relating the principles of Judaism to contemporary social problems; assists congregations in studying the moral and religious implications in social issues such as civil rights, civil liberties, church-state relations; guides congregational social-action committees. *Briefings.*

COMMITTEE TO BRING NAZI WAR CRIMINALS TO JUSTICE IN U.S.A., INC. (1973). 135 W. 106 St., NYC 10025. (212)866-0692. Pres. Charles H. Kremer; Treas. Albert Sigal; Sec. Paul Schwarzbaum. Compiles and publicizes records of Nazi atrocities and labors to bring to justice the perpetrators of those crimes. Remains committed to preserving the memory of all victims of the Holocaust, and actively opposes anti-Semitism wherever and however it is found.

CONFERENCE OF PRESIDENTS OF MAJOR AMERICAN JEWISH ORGANIZATIONS (1955). 515 Park Ave., NYC 10022. (212)-752-1616. Chmn. Morris B. Abram; Exec. Dir. Malcolm Hoenlein. Coordinates the activities of 44 major American Jewish organizations as they relate to American-Israeli affairs and problems affecting Jews in other lands. *Annual report; Middle East Memo.*

CONSULTATIVE COUNCIL OF JEWISH ORGANIZATIONS-CCJO (1946). 135 William St., NYC 10038. (212)349-0537. Cochmn. Clemens Nathan, Joseph Nuss, Adolphe Steg; V.-Chmn. Arnold Franco; Sec.-Gen. Moses Moskowitz. A nongovernmental organization in consultative status with the UN, UNESCO, ILO, UNICEF, and the Council of Europe; cooperates and consults with, advises and renders assistance to the Economic and Social Council of the UN on all problems relating to human rights and economic, social, cultural, educational, and related matters pertaining to Jews.

COORDINATING BOARD OF JEWISH ORGANIZATIONS (1947). 1640 Rhode Island Ave., NW, Washington, DC 20036. (202)857-6545. Pres. Gerald Kraft (B'nai B'rith), Leonard Kopelowitz (Board of Deputies of British Jews), David K. Mann (South African Jewish Board of Deputies); Exec. V.-Pres. Daniel Thursz (U.S.); Dir. Internatl. Council Warren Eisenberg. As an organization in consultative status with the Economic and Social Council of the UN, represents the three constituents (B'nai B'rith, the Board of Deputies of British Jews, and the South African Jewish Board of Deputies) in the appropriate UN bodies for the purpose of promoting human rights, with special attention to combating persecution or discrimination on grounds of race, religion, or origin.

COUNCIL OF JEWISH ORGANIZATIONS IN CIVIL SERVICE, INC. (1948). 45 E. 33 St., Rm. 604, NYC 10016. (212)689-2015. Pres. Louis Weiser. Supports merit system; encourages recruitment of Jewish youth to government service; member of Coalition to Free Soviet Jews, NY Jewish Community Relations Council, NY Metropolitan Coordinating Council on Jewish Poverty, Jewish Labor Committee, America-Israel Friendship League. *Council Digest.*

INTERNATIONAL CONFERENCE OF JEWISH COMMUNAL SERVICE (*see* World Conference of Jewish Communal Service)

JEWISH LABOR COMMITTEE (1934). Atran Center for Jewish Culture, 25 E. 21 St., NYC 10010. (212)477-0707. Pres. Herb Magidson; Exec. Dir. Martin Lapan. Serves as a link between the Jewish community and the trade union movement; works with the AFL-CIO and others to combat all forms of racial and religious discrimination in the United States and abroad; furthers labor support for Israel's security and Soviet Jewry, and Jewish communal support for labor's social and economic programs; supports Yiddish cultural institutions. *JLC Review.*

———, NATIONAL TRADE UNION COUNCIL FOR HUMAN RIGHTS (1956). Atran Center for Jewish Culture, 25 E. 21 St., NYC 10010. (212)477-0707. Chmn. Sol Hoffman; Exec. Sec. Martin Lapan. Works with trade unions on programs and issues affecting both labor and the Jewish community.

———, WOMEN'S DIVISION OF (1947). Atran Center for Jewish Culture, 25 E. 21 St., NYC 10010. (212)477-0707. Natl. Chmn. Eleanor Schachner. Supports the general activities of the Jewish Labor Committee; provides secondary-school and college scholarships for needy Israeli students; participates in educational and cultural activities.

———, WORKMEN'S CIRCLE DIVISION OF (1939). Atran Center for Jewish Culture, 25 E. 21 St., NYC 10010. (212)477-0707. Promotes aims of, and raises funds for, the Jewish Labor Committee among the Workmen's Circle branches; conducts Yiddish educational and cultural activities.

JEWISH PEACE FELLOWSHIP (1941). Box 271, Nyack, NY 10960. (914)358-4601. Pres. Rabbi Philip Bentley; Sec. Naomi Goodman. Unites those who believe that Jewish ideals and experience provide inspiration for a nonviolent philosophy and way of life; offers draft counseling, especially for conscientious objection based on Jewish "religious training and belief"; encourages Jewish community to become more knowledgeable, concerned, and active in regard to the war/peace problem. *Shalom/Jewish Peace Letter.*

JEWISH WAR VETERANS OF THE UNITED STATES OF AMERICA (1896). 1811 R St., NW, Washington, DC 20009. (202)265-6280. Natl. Comdr. Edwin Goldwasser; Natl. Exec. Dir. Steven Shaw. Seeks to foster true allegiance to the United States; to combat bigotry and prevent defamation of Jews; to encourage the doctrine of universal liberty, equal rights, and full justice for all; to cooperate with and support existing educational institutions and establish new ones; to foster the education of ex-servicemen, ex-servicewomen, and members in the ideals and principles of Americanism. *Jewish Veteran.*

———, NATIONAL MEMORIAL, INC; NATIONAL SHRINE TO THE JEWISH WAR DEAD (1958). 1811 R St., NW, Washington, DC 20009. (202)265-6280. Pres. Norman D. Tilles; Museum Dir. Mark Dreyfuss. Maintains a national archives and museum commemorating the wartime service of American Jews in the armed forces of the U.S.; maintains *Golden Book* of names of the war dead; *Routes to Roots.*

NATIONAL CONFERENCE ON SOVIET JEWRY (formerly AMERICAN JEWISH CONFERENCE ON SOVIET JEWRY) (1964; reorg. 1971). 10 E. 40 St., Suite 907, NYC 10016. (212)679-6122. Chmn. Morris B. Abram; Exec. Dir. Jerry Goodman. Coordinating agency for major national Jewish organizations and local community groups in the U.S., acting on behalf of Soviet Jewry through public education and social action; stimulates all segments of the community to maintain an interest in the problems of Soviet Jews by publishing reports and special pamphlets, sponsoring special programs and projects, organizing public meetings and forums. *Newsbreak; annual report; action and program kits; Wrap-Up Leadership Report.*

———, SOVIET JEWRY RESEARCH BUREAU. Chmn. Charlotte Jacobson. Organized by NCSJ to monitor emigration trends. Primary task is the accumulation, evaluation, and processing of information regarding Soviet Jews, especially those who apply for emigration.

NATIONAL JEWISH COALITION (1979). 415 2nd St., NE, Suite 100, Washington, DC 20002. (202)547-7701. Hon. Chmn. Max M. Fisher; Natl. Chmn. Richard J. Fox. Promotes Jewish involvement in Republican politics; sensitizes Republican leaders to the concerns of the American Jewish community; promotes principles of free enterprise, a strong national defense, and an internationalist foreign policy. *NJC Bulletin; NJC for the Record.*

NATIONAL JEWISH COMMISSION ON LAW AND PUBLIC AFFAIRS (COLPA) (1965). 450 Seventh Ave., Suite 2203, NYC 10001. (212)563-0100. Pres. Allen L. Rothenberg; Exec. Dir. Dennis Rapps. Voluntary association of attorneys whose purpose is to represent the observant Jewish community on legal, legislative, and public affairs matters.

NATIONAL JEWISH COMMUNITY RELATIONS ADVISORY COUNCIL (1944). 443 Park Ave. S., 11th fl., NYC 10016. (212)-684-6950. Chmn. Michael A. Pelavin; Sec. Barry Ungar; Exec. V.-Chmn. Albert D. Chernin. National coordinating body for the field of Jewish community relations, comprising 11 national and 113 local Jewish community relations agencies. Promotes understanding of Israel and the Middle East; freedom for Soviet Jews; equal status for Jews and other groups in American society. Through the NJCRAC's work, its constituent organizations seek agreement on policies, strategies, and programs for effective utilization of their resources for common ends. *Joint Program Plan for Jewish Community Relations.*

NEW JEWISH AGENDA (1980). 64 Fulton St., #1100, NYC 10038. (212)227-5885. Cochmn. Bria Chakofsky, Rabbi Marc Gruber; Exec. Dir. David Coyne. Founded as "a progressive voice in the Jewish community and a Jewish voice among progressives." Works for nuclear disarmament, peace in Central America, Arab-Jewish reconciliation, feminism, and economic justice, and against anti-Semitism and racism. *Quarterly newsletter.*

SHALOM CENTER (1983). Church Rd. and Greenwood Ave., Wyncote, PA 19095. (215)886-1510. Pres. Ira Silverman; Bd. Chmn. Viki List; Exec. Dir. Arthur Waskow. National resource and organizing center for Jewish perspectives on preventing nuclear holocaust and ending nuclear arms race. Trains community organizers, holds conferences, assists local Jewish committees and coalitions on nuclear weapons issues. Sponsors Sukkat Shalom. Provides school curricula, sermon materials, legislative reports, adult-education texts, and media for Jewish use. *Shalom Report.*

STUDENT STRUGGLE FOR SOVIET JEWRY, INC. (1964). 210 W. 91 St., NYC 10024. (212)799-8900. Natl. Dir. Jacob Birnbaum; Natl. Coord. Glenn Richter; Chmn. Avraham Weiss. Provides information and action guidance to adult and student organizations, communities, and schools throughout the U.S. and Canada; assists

Soviet Jews by publicity campaigns; helps Soviet Jews in the U.S.; aids Rumanian Jews seeking emigration; maintains speakers bureau and research documents. *Soviet Jewry Action Newsletter.*

UNION OF COUNCILS FOR SOVIET JEWS (1970). 1819 H St., NW., Washington, DC 20006. (202)775-9770. Pres. Pamela Braun Cohen; Washington Rep. Micah H. Naftalin. A confederation of 45 grass-roots organizations established in support of rescuing Soviet Jewry. Works on behalf of Soviet Jews through public education, representations to the administration and Congress, letter-writing assistance, tourist briefing, speakers bureau, Adopt-A-Family, Adopt-A-Prisoner, Bar/Bat Mitzvah twinning, Tarbut, congressional vigil, congressional briefings, and publications programming; affiliations include Soviet Jewry Legal Advocacy Center and Medical Mobilization for Soviet Jewry. *UCSJ Quarterly Report; Refusenik Update.*

WORLD CONFERENCE OF JEWISH COMMUNAL SERVICE (1966). 15 E. 26 St., NYC 10010. (212)532-2526. Pres. Irving Kessler; Sec.-Gen. Solomon H. Green. Established by worldwide Jewish communal workers to strengthen their understanding of each other's programs and to communicate with colleagues in order to enrich the quality of their work. Conducts quadrennial international conferences in Jerusalem and periodic regional meetings. *Proceedings of international conferences; newsletter.*

WORLD JEWISH CONGRESS (1936; org. in U.S. 1939). 1 Park Ave., Suite 418, NYC 10016. (212)679-0600. Pres. Edgar M. Bronfman; Chmn. N. Amer. Branch Leo Kolber (Montreal); Chmn. Amer. Sect. Rabbi Wolfe Kelman; Sec.-Gen. Israel Singer; Exec. Dir. Elan Steinberg. Seeks to intensify bonds of world Jewry with Israel as central force in Jewish life; to strengthen solidarity among Jews everywhere and secure their rights, status, and interests as individuals and communities; to encourage development of Jewish social, religious, and cultural life throughout the world and coordinate efforts by Jewish communities and organizations to cope with any Jewish problem; to work for human rights generally. Represents its affiliated organizations—most representative bodies of Jewish communities in more than 70 countries and 32 national organizations in Amer. section—at UN, OAS, UNESCO, Council of Europe, ILO, UNICEF, and other governmental, intergovernmental, and international authorities. Publications (including those by Institute of Jewish Affairs, London): *Christian Jewish Relations; Coloquio; News and Views; Boletín Informativo OJI; Batfutsot; Gesher; Patterns of Prejudice; Soviet Jewish Affairs.*

CULTURAL

AMERICAN ACADEMY FOR JEWISH RESEARCH (1920). 3080 Broadway, NYC 10027. (212)678-8864. Pres. Isaac Barzilay; V.-Pres. David Weiss Halivni; Treas. Arthur Hyman. Encourages Jewish learning and research; holds annual or semiannual meeting; awards grants for the publication of scholarly works. *Proceedings of the American Academy for Jewish Research; Texts and Studies; Monograph Series.*

AMERICAN BIBLICAL ENCYCLOPEDIA SOCIETY (1930). 24 W. Maple Ave., Monsey, NY 10952. (914)352-4609. Exec. V.-Pres. Irving Fredman; Author-Ed. Rabbi M. M. Kasher. Fosters biblical-talmudical research; sponsors and publishes *Torah Shelemah* (Heb., 39 vols.), *Encyclopedia of Biblical Interpretation* (Eng., 9 vols.), *Divrei Menachem* (Heb., 4 vols.), and related publications. *Noam.*

AMERICAN JEWISH HISTORICAL SOCIETY (1892). 2 Thornton Rd., Waltham, MA 02154. (617)891-8110. Pres. Morris Soble; Dir. Bernard Wax. Collects, catalogues, publishes, and displays material on the history of the Jews in America; serves as an information center for inquiries on American Jewish history; maintains archives of original source material on American Jewish history; sponsors lectures and exhibitions; makes available historic Yiddish films and audiovisual material. *American Jewish History; Heritage.*

AMERICAN JEWISH PRESS ASSOCIATION (1943). c/o St. Louis Jewish Light, 12 Millstone Campus Dr., St. Louis, MO 63146. (314)432-3353. Pres. Robert A. Cohn. Natl. Admin. Off.: 11312 Old Club Rd., Rockville, MD 20852-4537. (301)881-4113. Staff Coord. L. Malcolm Rodman. Seeks the advancement of Jewish journalism, the attainment of the highest editorial and business standards for members, and the maintenance of a strong Jewish press in the U.S. and Canada. *Membership bulletin; roster of members.*

AMERICAN SOCIETY FOR JEWISH MUSIC (1974). 155 Fifth Ave., NYC 10010. (212)-533-2601. Pres. Paul Kavon; V.-Pres. David Lefkowitz; Sec. Hadássah B. Markson. Seeks to raise standards of composition and performance in Jewish liturgical and secular music; encourages research in all areas of Jewish music; publishes scholarly journal; presents programs and sponsors performances of new and rarely heard works and encourages their recording; commissions new works of Jewish interest. *Musica Judaica.*

ASSOCIATION FOR THE SOCIAL SCIENTIFIC STUDY OF JEWRY (1971). City University of New York, 33 W. 42 St., NYC 10036. (212)642-1600. Pres. Egon Mayer; V.-Pres. Morton Weinfeld; Sec.-Treas. Esther Fleishman. Arranges academic sessions and facilitates communication among social scientists studying Jewry through meetings, newsletter, and related materials. *Contemporary Jewry; ASSJ Newsletter.*

ASSOCIATION OF JEWISH BOOK PUBLISHERS (1962). 838 Fifth Ave., NYC 10021. (212)-249-0100. Pres. Charles D. Lieber. As a nonprofit group, provides a forum for discussion of mutual problems by publishers, authors, and other individuals and institutions concerned with books of Jewish interest. Provides national and international exhibit opportunities for Jewish books. *Combined Jewish Book Catalog.*

ASSOCIATION OF JEWISH LIBRARIES (1965). c/o National Foundation for Jewish Culture, 122 E. 42 St., NYC 10168. (212)427-1000. Pres. Edith Lubetski; V.-Pres. Marcia Posner. Seeks to promote and improve services and professional standards in Jewish libraries; serves as a center for the dissemination of Jewish library information and guidance; promotes publication of literature in the field; encourages the establishment of Jewish libraries and collections of Judaica and the choice of Judaica librarianship as a profession. *AJL Newsletter; Judaica Librarianship.*

B'NAI B'RITH KLUTZNICK MUSEUM (1956). 1640 Rhode Island Ave., NW, Washington, DC 20036. (202)857-6583. Chmn. Museum & Art Comm., Murray H. Shusterman; Dir. Linda Altshuler. A center of Jewish art and history in nation's capital, maintains temporary and permanent exhibition galleries, permanent collection of Jewish ceremonial and folk art, B'nai B'rith International reference archive, outdoor sculpture garden, and museum shop. Provides exhibitions, tours, educational programs, research assistance, and tourist information. *Semiannual newsletter; exhibition brochures.*

CENTER FOR HOLOCAUST STUDIES, DOCUMENTATION & RESEARCH. (1974). 1610 Ave. J, Brooklyn, NY 11230. (718)338-6494. Dir. Yaffa Eliach. Collects and preserves documents and memorabilia, oral histories, and literary works on the Holocaust period for purposes of documentation and research; arranges lectures, exhibits, drama and music performances, and exhibitions of Holocaust art; conducts outreach programs to schools; maintains speakers bureau, oral history publication series, and audiovisual department. *Newsletter.*

CENTRAL YIDDISH CULTURE ORGANIZATION (CYCO), INC. (1943). 25 E. 21 St., 3rd fl., NYC 10010. (212)505-8305. Mgr. Jacob Schneidman. Promotes, publishes, and distributes Yiddish books; publishes catalogues.

CONFERENCE ON JEWISH SOCIAL STUDIES, INC. (formerly CONFERENCE ON JEWISH RELATIONS, INC.) (1939). 2112 Broadway, Rm. 206, NYC 10023. (212)724-5336. Hon. Pres. Salo W. Baron. Publishes scientific studies on Jews in the modern world, dealing with such aspects as anti-Semitism, demography, economic stratification, history, philosophy, and political developments. *Jewish Social Studies.*

CONGREGATION BINA (1981). 600 W. End Ave., Suite 1-C, NYC 10024. (212)873-4261. Pres. Elijah E. Jhirad; Exec. V.-Pres. Joseph Moses. Serves the religious, cultural, charitable, and philanthropic needs of the Children of Israel who originated in India and now reside in the U.S. Works to foster and preserve the ancient traditions, customs, liturgy, music, and folklore of Indian Jewry and to maintain needed institutions. *Kol Bina.*

HEBREW ARTS SCHOOL (1952). 129 W. 67 St., NYC 10023. (212)362-8060. Chmn. Lewis Kruger; Pres. Alvin E. Friedman; Dir. Lydia Kontos. Offers instruction in music, dance, art, and theater to children and adults, combining Western culture with Jewish heritage. Presents in its Merkin Concert Hall and Ann Goodman Recital Hall frequent performances of Jewish and general music by leading artists. *Newsletter.*

HEBREW CULTURE FOUNDATION (1955). 515 Park Ave., NYC 10022. (212)752-0600. Chmn. Milton R. Konvitz; Sec. Herman L. Sainer. Sponsors the introduction and strengthening of Hebrew language and literature courses in institutions of higher learning in the United States.

HISTADRUTH IVRITH OF AMERICA (1916; reorg. 1922). 1841 Broadway, NYC 10023. (212)581-5151. Presidium: Boris Shteinshleifer, Matthew Mosenkis, Rabbi Joseph P. Sternstein; Exec. V.-Pres. Aviva Barzel. Emphasizes the primacy of Hebrew in Jewish life, culture, and education; aims to disseminate knowledge of written and spoken Hebrew in the Diaspora, thus building a cultural bridge between the State of Israel and Jewish communities throughout the world. *Hadoar; Lamishpaha.*

HOLOCAUST CENTER OF THE UNITED JEWISH FEDERATION OF GREATER PITTSBURGH (1980). 242 McKee Pl., Pittsburgh, PA 15213. (412)682-7111. Dir. Edie Naveh; Chmn. Dr. Sidney N. Busis; Pres. UJF Leon L. Netzer. Develops programs and provides resources to further understanding of the Holocaust and its impact on civilization. Maintains a library, archive; provides speakers, educational materials; organizes community programs.

HOLOCAUST MEMORIAL RESOURCE & EDUCATION CENTER OF FLORIDA (1981). 851 N. Maitland Ave., Casselberry, FL 32751. (305)628-0555. Pres. and Exec. Dir. Tess Wise. An interfaith educational center devoted to teaching the lessons of the Holocaust. Maintains a library of books, videotapes, films, and other visuals to serve the entire educational establishment. *Newsletter.*

JEWISH ACADEMY OF ARTS AND SCIENCES, INC. (1926). 888 Seventh Ave., Suite 403, NYC 10106. (212)757-1628. Pres. Abraham I. Katsh; Sec. Bernard B. Cohen. An honor society of Jews who have attained distinction in the arts, sciences, professions, and communal endeavors. Encourages the advancement of knowledge; stimulates scholarship, with particular reference to Jewish life and thought; recognition by election to membership and/or fellowship; publishes papers delivered at annual convocations.

JEWISH MUSEUM (1904, under auspices of Jewish Theological Seminary of America). 1109 Fifth Ave., NYC 10028. (212)860-1888. Dir. Joan H. Rosenbaum; Chmn. Bd. of Trustees Morris W. Offit. Repository of the largest collection of Judaica—paintings, prints, photographs, sculpture, coins, medals, antiquities, textiles, and other decorative arts—in the Western Hemisphere. Includes the National Jewish Archive of Broadcasting and the Tobe Pascher Workshop for the design and creation of ritual and ceremonial art objects. Tours of special exhibitions and permanent installations; lectures, film showings, and concerts; special programs for children. *Special exhibition catalogues.*

JEWISH PUBLICATION SOCIETY (1888). 1930 Chestnut St., Philadelphia, PA 19103. (215)564-5925. Pres. Edward E. Elson; Exec. V.-Pres. Richard Malina; Editor Sheila Segal. Publishes and disseminates books of Jewish interest for adults and children; titles include contemporary literature, classics, art, religion, biographies, poetry, and history. AMERICAN JEWISH YEAR BOOK (with American Jewish Committee).

JUDAH L. MAGNES MUSEUM—JEWISH MUSEUM OF THE WEST (1962). 2911 Russell St., Berkeley, CA 94705. (415)849-2710. Pres. Jacques Reutlinger; Exec. Dir. Seymour Fromer. Serves as museum and library, combining historical and literary materials illustrating Jewish life in the Bay Area, the Western states, and around the world; provides archives of world Jewish history and Jewish art; repository of historical documents intended for scholarly use; changing exhibits; facilities open to the general public. *Magnes News; special exhibition catalogues.*

JUDAICA CAPTIONED FILM CENTER, INC. (1983). P.O. Box 21439, Baltimore, MD 21208-0439. Voice (301)922-4642; TDD (301)655-6767. Pres. Lois Lilienfeld Weiner. Developing a comprehensive library of captioned and subtitled films and tapes on Jewish subjects; distributes them to organizations serving the hearing-impaired, including mainstream classes and senior adult groups, on a free-loan, handling/shipping-charge-only basis. *Quarterly newsletter.*

JWB JEWISH BOOK COUNCIL (1943). 15 E. 26 St., NYC 10010. (212)532-4949. Pres. Abraham J. Kremer; Dir. Paula Gribetz Gottlieb. Promotes knowledge of Jewish books through dissemination of booklists, program materials; sponsors Jewish Book Month; presents literary awards and library citations; cooperates with publishers of Jewish books. *Jewish Book Annual; Jewish Books in Review; Jewish Book World.*

JWB JEWISH MUSIC COUNCIL (1944). 15 E. 26 St., NYC 10010. (212)532-4949. Chmn. Leonard Kaplan; Coord. Paula Gribetz Gottlieb. Promotes Jewish music activities nationally; annually sponsors and promotes the Jewish Music season; encourages participation on a community basis. *Jewish Music Notes* and numerous music resource publications for national distribution.

JWB LECTURE BUREAU (1922). 15 E. 26 St., NYC 10010-1579. (212)532-4949. Dir. Sesil Lissberger. Provides, and assists in the selection of, lecturers, performing artists, and exhibits for local Jewish communal organizations; advises on program design; makes booking arrangements. *The Jewish Arts; Learning for Jewish Living—A Listing of Lecturers; Available Lecturers from Israel; Lecturers on the Holocaust.*

LEAGUE FOR YIDDISH, INC. (1935). 200 W. 72 St., Suite 40, NYC 10023. (212)787-6675. Pres. Sadie Turak; Exec. Dir. Mordkhe Schaechter. Promotes the development and use of Yiddish as a living language. *Afn Shvel.*

LEO BAECK INSTITUTE, INC. (1955). 129 E. 73 St., NYC 10021. (212)744-6400. Pres. Yosef Haim Yerushalmi; Sec. Fred Grubel. A library, archive, and research center for the history of German-speaking Jewry. Offers lectures, exhibits, faculty seminars; publishes a series of monographs, yearbooks, and journals. *LBI Bulletin; LBI News; LBI Year Book.*

MARTYRS MEMORIAL & MUSEUM OF THE HOLOCAUST (1963; reorg. 1978). 6505 Wilshire Blvd., Los Angeles, CA 90048. (213)651-3175. Chmn. Jack I. Salzberg; Dir. Michael Nutkiewicz. Seeks to commemorate the events and victims of the Holocaust and to educate against future reoccurrences; maintains permanent and traveling exhibits, sponsors public lectures, offers school curricula and teacher training. West Coast representative of Israel's Yad Vashem; affiliated with the Jewish Federation Council of Greater Los Angeles.

MEMORIAL FOUNDATION FOR JEWISH CULTURE, INC. (1964). 15 E. 26 St., NYC 10010. (212)679-4074. Pres. Philip M. Klutznick; Exec. Dir. Jerry Hochbaum. Through the grants that it awards, encourages Jewish scholarship and Jewish education, supports communities that are struggling to maintain their Jewish identity, makes possible the training of Jewish men and women for professional careers in communal service in Jewishly deprived communities, and stimulates the documentation, commemoration, and teaching of the Holocaust.

NATIONAL FOUNDATION FOR JEWISH CULTURE (1960). 330 Seventh Ave., 21st fl., NYC 10001. (212)629-0500. Pres. George M. Zeltzer; Exec. V.-Pres. Abraham Atik. Provides consultation and support to Jewish community organizations, educational and cultural institutions, and individuals for Jewish cultural activities; awards fellowships and publication grants to individuals preparing for careers in Jewish scholarship; presents awards for creative efforts in Jewish cultural arts and for Jewish programming in small and intermediate communities; publishes guides to national Jewish cultural resources, traveling exhibitions, and plays; serves as clearinghouse of information on American Jewish culture; administers Joint Cultural Appeal on behalf of national cultural organizations; administers Council of Archives and Research Libraries in Jewish Studies, Council of American Jewish Museums, and Council of Jewish Theaters.

NATIONAL HEBREW CULTURE COUNCIL (1952). 14 E. 4th St, NYC 10003. (212)-674-8412. Cultivates the study of Hebrew as a modern language in American public high schools and colleges, providing guidance to community groups and public educational authorities; annually administers National Voluntary Examination in Hebrew Culture and Knowledge of Israel in the public high schools, and conducts summer seminar and tour of Israel for teachers and other educational personnel of the public school system, in cooperation with Hebrew University and WZO. *Hebrew in Colleges and Universities.*

NATIONAL YIDDISH BOOK CENTER (1980). PO Box 969, Old Southeast Street School, Amherst, MA 01004. (413)256-1241. Pres. Penina Glazer; Exec. Dir. Aaron Lansky. Collects used and out-of-print Yiddish books to distribute to individuals and libraries; provides resources to make Yiddish culture accessible to a new generation. *Yiddish Book News; Der Pakn-treger/The Book Peddler.*

NEW YORK HOLOCAUST MEMORIAL COMMISSION (1981). 342 Madison Ave., Suite 717, NYC 10017. (212)687-5020. Cochmn. George Klein, Hon. Robert M. Morgenthau; Exec. Dir. David L. Blumenfeld. Seeks to create a major "living memorial" center in New York City, consisting of a museum, library, archives, and lecture/conference facilities which will commemorate the lives of the Jewish victims of Nazi Germany by creating a record of their cultural and societal lives in Europe, restoring to memory the close affinity between the Jews of Europe and the large Jewish immigrant population of New York City, educating future generations on the history and lessons of the Holocaust, and providing appropriate commemoration honoring the memory of those who died in the Holocaust.

RESEARCH FOUNDATION FOR JEWISH IMMIGRATION, INC. (1971). 570 Seventh Ave., NYC 10018. (212)921-3871. Pres. Curt C. Silberman; Sec. Herbert A. Strauss. Studies and records the history of the migration and acculturation of Jewish Nazi persecutees in the various resettlement countries. *International Biographical Dictionary of Central European Emigrés, 1933–1945; Jewish Immigrants of the Nazi Period in the USA.*

ST. LOUIS CENTER FOR HOLOCAUST STUDIES (1977). 12 Millstone Campus Dr., St. Louis, MO 63146. (314)432-0020. Chmn. Henrietta Freedman; Dir. Rabbi Robert Sternberg. Develops programs and provides resources and educational materials to further an understanding of the Holocaust and its impact on civilization. *Audio Visual and Curriculum Resources Guide.*

SEPHARDIC HOUSE (1978). 8 W. 70 St., NYC 10023. (212)873-0300. Exec. Dir. Janice Etzkowitz; Chmn. Bd. Rabbi Marc D. Angel. Works to foster the history and culture of Sephardic Jewry by offering classes, programs, publications, and resource people; works to integrate Sephardic studies into the curriculum of Jewish schools and adult education programs; offers advice and guidance to individuals involved in Sephardic research. *The Sephardic House Newsletter.*

SKIRBALL MUSEUM, Los Angeles, CA (*see* Hebrew Union College-Jewish Institute of Religion)

SOCIETY FOR THE HISTORY OF CZECHOSLOVAK JEWS, INC. (1961). 87-08 Santiago St., Holliswood, NY 11423. (718)468-6844. Pres. Lewis Weiner; Sec. Joseph Abeles. Studies the history of Czechoslovak Jews, collects material and disseminates information through the publication of books and pamphlets.

YESHIVA UNIVERSITY MUSEUM (1973). 2520 Amsterdam Ave., NYC 10033. (212)-960-5390. Chmn. Bd. of Govs. Erica Jesselson; Dir. Sylvia A. Herskowitz. Collects, preserves, interprets, and displays ceremonial objects, rare books and documents, synagogue models, paintings, and decorative arts expressing the Jewish religious experience historically, to the present. Changing exhibits of contemporary artists, ceremonial objects, and historical subjects; programs for adults and children. *Special exhibition catalogues.*

YIDDISHER KULTUR FARBAND—YKUF (1937). 1123 Broadway, Rm. 305, NYC 10010. (212)691-0708. Pres. Itche Goldberg. Publishes a monthly magazine and books by contemporary and classical Jewish writers; conducts cultural forums; exhibits works by contemporary Jewish artists and materials of Jewish historical value; organizes reading circles. *Yiddishe Kultur.*

YIVO INSTITUTE FOR JEWISH RESEARCH, INC. (1925). 1048 Fifth Ave., NYC 10028. (212)535-6700. Cochmn. Mendl Hoffman, Joseph Greenberger. Exec. Dir. Samuel Norich. Engages in social and humanistic research pertaining to East European Jewish life; maintains library and archives which provide a major international, national, and New York resource used by institutions, individual scholars, and laymen; trains graduate students in Yiddish, East European, and American Jewish studies; offers exhibits, conferences, public programs; publishes books. *Yedies fun Yivo—News of the Yivo; Yidishe Shprakh;*

Yivo Annual of Jewish Social Science; Yivo Bleter.

———, MAX WEINREICH CENTER FOR ADVANCED JEWISH STUDIES (1968). 1048 Fifth Ave., NYC 10028. (212)535-6700. Act. Dean Marvin I. Herzog; Assoc. Dean Jack Kugelmass. Provides advanced-level training in Yiddish language and literature, ethnography, folklore, linguistics, and history; offers guidance on dissertation or independent research. *The Field of Yiddish; Jewish Folklore & Ethnology Newsletter.*

OVERSEAS AID

AMERICAN ASSOCIATION FOR ETHIOPIAN JEWS (1969). 2028 P St., NW, Washington, DC 20036. (202)223-6838. Pres. Nathan Shapiro; Dir. William Recant. Informs world Jewry about the plight of Ethiopian Jews; advocates rescue of Ethiopian Jewry as a major priority; provides relief in refugee areas and Ethiopia; and helps resettlement in Israel. *Release; Newsline.*

AMERICAN FRIENDS OF THE ALLIANCE ISRAÉLITE UNIVERSELLE, INC. (1946). 135 William St., NYC 10038. (212)349-0537. Pres. Henriette Beilis; Exec. Dir. Jack Kantrowitz. Participates in educational and human rights activities of the AIU and supports the Alliance System of Jewish schools, remedial programs, and teacher training in Israel, North Africa, the Middle East, and Europe. *Alliance Review; AF Notes.*

AMERICAN JEWISH JOINT DISTRIBUTION COMMITTEE, INC.—JDC (1914). 711 Third Ave., NYC 10017. (212)687-6200. Pres. Heinz Eppler; Exec. V.-Pres. Ralph I. Goldman. Organizes and finances rescue, relief, and rehabilitation programs for imperiled and needy Jews overseas; conducts wide range of health, welfare, rehabilitation, education programs and aid to cultural and religious institutions; programs benefiting 600,000 Jews in over 30 countries overseas. Major areas of operation are Israel, North Africa, and Europe. *Annual report; Reports from the Field.*

AMERICAN JEWISH PHILANTHROPIC FUND (1955). 386 Park Ave. S., NYC 10016. (212)OR9-0010. Pres. Charles J. Tanenbaum. Provides resettlement assistance to Jewish refugees primarily through programs administered by the International Rescue Committee at its offices in Western Europe and the U.S.

AMERICAN ORT FEDERATION, INC.—ORGANIZATION FOR REHABILITATION THROUGH TRAINING (1924). 817 Broadway, NYC 10003. (212)677-4400. Pres. David B. Hermelin; Exec. V.-Pres. Donald H. Klein. Provides vocational/technical education to over 158,000 students at ORT schools and training centers in 18 countries, with the largest program in Israel serving 92,000 students. Teaching staff numbers 5,200. Annual cost of program is about $119 million. *American ORT Federation Bulletin; ORT Yearbook.*

———, AMERICAN AND EUROPEAN FRIENDS OF ORT (1941). 817 Broadway, NYC 10003. (212)677-4400. Pres. Simon Jaglom; Chmn. Exec. Com. Jacques Zwibak. Promotes the ORT idea among Americans of European extraction; supports the Litton ORT Auto-Mechanics School in Jerusalem and the ORT School of Engineering in Jerusalem. Promotes the work of the American ORT Federation.

———, AMERICAN LABOR ORT (1937). 817 Broadway, NYC 10003. (212)677-4400. Chmn. Sam Fine. Promotes ORT program of vocational training among Jews through activities of the ILGWU and the Amalgamated Clothing & Textile Workers Union. Promotes the work of the American ORT Federation.

———, BUSINESS AND PROFESSIONAL ORT (1937). 817 Broadway, NYC 10003. (212)-677-4770. Pres. Rose Seidel Kalich. Promotes work of American ORT Federation.

———, NATIONAL ORT LEAGUE (1914). 817 Broadway, NYC 10003. (212)677-4400. Pres. Judah Wattenberg; First V.-Pres. Tibor Waldman. Promotes ORT idea among Jewish fraternal *landsmanshaften* and individuals. Promotes the work of the American ORT Federation.

———, WOMEN'S AMERICAN ORT (1927). 315 Park Ave. S., NYC 10010. (212)505-7700. Pres. Gertrude S. White; Exec. V.-Pres. Nathan Gould. Represents and advances the program and philosophy of ORT among the women of the American Jewish community through membership and educational activities; materially supports the vocational training operations of World ORT; contributes to the American

Jewish community by encouraging participation in ORT campaigns and through general education to help raise the level of Jewish consciousness among American Jewish women; through its American Affairs program, cooperates in efforts to improve the quality of education and vocational training in the U.S. *Facts and Findings; Highlights; Insights; The Merchandiser; Women's American ORT Reporter.*

A.R.I.F.—ASSOCIATION POUR LE RÉTABLISSEMENT DES INSTITUTIONS ET OEUVRES ISRAÉLITES EN FRANCE, INC. (1944). 119 E. 95 St., NYC 10028. (212)-876-1448. Pres. Baroness Robert de Gunzburg; Sec.-Treas. Simon Langer. Helps Jewish religious and cultural institutions in France.

CONFERENCE ON JEWISH MATERIAL CLAIMS AGAINST GERMANY, INC. (1951). 15 E. 26 St., Rm. 1355, NYC 10010. (212)-696-4944. Pres. Israel Miller; Sec. and Exec. Dir. Saul Kagan. Monitors the implementation of restitution and indemnification programs of the German Federal Republic (FRG) arising from its agreements with FRG. Administers Hardship Fund, which distributes DM 400,000,000 appropriated by FRG for Jewish Nazi victims unable to file timely claims under original indemnification laws. Also assists needy non-Jews who risked their lives to help Jewish survivors.

HIAS, INC. (HEBREW IMMIGRANT AID SOCIETY) (1880; reorg. 1954). 200 Park Ave. S., NYC 10003. (212)674-6800. Pres. Robert L. Israeloff; Exec. V.-Pres. Karl D. Zukerman. International Jewish migration agency with headquarters in the U.S. and offices, affiliates, and representatives in Europe, Latin America, Canada, Australia, New Zealand, and Israel. Assists Jewish migrants and refugees from Eastern Europe, the Middle East, North Africa, and Latin America. Via U.S. government-funded programs, assists in the resettlement of Indo-Chinese and other refugees. *HIAS Annual Report; HIAS Reporter; Quarterly Statistical Abstract.*

JEWISH RESTITUTION SUCCESSOR ORGANIZATION (1947). 15 E. 26 St., Rm. 1355, NYC 10010. (212)696-4944. Sec. and Exec. Dir. Saul Kagan. Acts to discover, claim, receive, and assist in the recovery of Jewish heirless or unclaimed property; to utilize such assets or to provide for their utilization for the relief, rehabilitation, and resettlement of surviving victims of Nazi persecution.

RE'UTH WOMEN'S SOCIAL SERVICE, INC. (1937). 240 W. 98 St., NYC 10025. (212)-666-7880. Pres. Ursula Merkin. Maintains in Israel subsidized housing for self-reliant older people, old-age homes for more dependent elderly, Lichtenstadter Hospital for chronically ill, subsidized meals, Golden Age clubs. *Annual journal.*

THANKS TO SCANDINAVIA, INC. (1963). 745 Fifth Ave., Rm. 603, NYC 10151. (212)-486-8600. Natl. Chmn. Victor Borge; Pres. and Exec. Off. Richard Netter. Provides scholarships and fellowships at American universities and medical centers to students and doctors from Denmark, Finland, Norway, and Sweden in appreciation of the rescue of Jews from the Holocaust. Informs current and future generations of Americans and Scandinavians of these singular examples of humanity and bravery; funds books about this chapter of history. *Annual report.*

UNITED JEWISH APPEAL, INC. (1939). 99 Park Ave., NYC 10016. (212)818-9100. Natl. Chmn. Martin F. Stein; Chmn. Bd. of Trustees Alexander Grass; Pres. Stanley B. Horowitz. The annual UJA/Federation Campaign is the primary instrument for the support of humanitarian programs and social services for Jews at home and abroad. In Israel, through the Jewish Agency, campaign funds help absorb, educate, and settle new immigrants, build villages and farms in rural areas, support innovative programs for troubled and disadvantaged youth, and promote the revitalization of distressed neighborhoods. UJA/Federation funds also provide for the well-being of Jews and Jewish communities in 33 other countries around the world through the American Jewish Joint Distribution Committee. Constituent departments of the UJA include the Rabbinic Cabinet, University Programs Department, Women's Division, Young Leadership Cabinet, the Young Women's Leadership Cabinet, and the Business and Professional Women's Council. *UJA Life.*

RELIGIOUS AND EDUCATIONAL

AGUDATH ISRAEL OF AMERICA (1922). 84 William St., NYC 10038. (212)797-9000.

Pres. Rabbi Moshe Sherer; Exec. Dir. Rabbi Boruch B. Borchardt. Mobilizes Orthodox Jews to cope with Jewish problems in the spirit of the Torah; sponsors a broad range of projects aimed at enhancing religious living, education, children's welfare, protection of Jewish religious rights, outreach to the assimilated, and social services. *Jewish Observer; Dos Yiddishe Vort, Coalition.*

———, AGUDAH WOMEN OF AMERICA–N'SHEI AGUDATH ISRAEL (1940). 84 William St., NYC 10038. (212)363-8940. Presidium Esther Bohensky, Aliza Grund. Organizes Jewish women for philanthropic work in the U.S. and Israel and for intensive Torah education. Seeks to train Torah-guided Jewish mothers.

———, CHILDREN'S DIVISION—PIRCHEI AGUDATH ISRAEL (1925). 84 William St., NYC 10038 (212)797-9000. Pres. Yosef Simha; Dir. Rabbi Joshua Silbermintz. Educates Orthodox Jewish children in Torah; encourages sense of communal responsibility. Branches sponsor weekly youth groups and Jewish welfare projects. National Mishnah contests, rallies, and conventions foster unity on a national level. *Darkeinu; Leaders Guides.*

———, GIRLS' DIVISION—BNOS AGUDATH ISRAEL (1921). 84 William St., NYC 10038. (212)797-9000. Natl. Dir. Devorah Pollack. Sponsors regular weekly programs on the local level and unites girls from throughout the Torah world with extensive regional and national activities. *Newsletters.*

———, YOUNG MEN'S DIVISION—ZEIREI AGUDATH ISRAEL (1921). 84 William St., NYC 10038. (212)797-9000. Pres. Avrohom Biderman; Dir. Rabbi Labish Becker. Educates youth to see Torah as source of guidance for all issues facing Jews as individuals and as a people. Inculcates a spirit of activism through projects in religious, Torah-educational, and community-welfare fields. *Zeirei Forum; Am Hatorah; Daf Chizuk; Yom Tov Publications; Torah Lodaas; Ohr Hakollel.*

AGUDATH ISRAEL WORLD ORGANIZATION (1912). 84 William St., NYC 10038. (212)-797-9000. Cochmn. Rabbi Moshe Sherer, Rabbi Yehudah Meir Abramowitz. Represents the interests of Orthodox Jewry on the national and international scenes. Sponsors projects to strengthen Torah life worldwide.

AMERICAN ASSOCIATION OF RABBIS (1978). 350 Fifth Ave., Suite 3308, NYC 10001. (212)244-3350. Pres. Rabbi Jacob Friedman; Sec. Rabbi Robert Chernoff. An organization of rabbis serving in pulpits, in areas of education, and in social work. *Bimonthly newsletter; quarterly journal.*

ANNENBERG RESEARCH INSTITUTE (formerly DROPSIE COLLEGE FOR HEBREW AND COGNATE LEARNING) (1907; reorg. 1986). 250 N. Highland Ave., Merion, PA 19066. (215)667-1830. Dir. Bernard Lewis; Assoc. Dir. David M. Goldenberg. A center for advanced research in Judaic and Near Eastern studies at the postdoctoral level. *Jewish Quarterly Review.*

ASSOCIATION FOR JEWISH STUDIES (1969). Widener Library M., Harvard University, Cambridge, MA 02138. Pres. Ruth R. Wisse; Exec. Sec. Charles Berlin. Seeks to promote, maintain, and improve the teaching of Jewish studies in American colleges and universities by sponsoring meetings and conferences, publishing a newsletter and other scholarly materials, setting standards for programs in Jewish studies, aiding in the placement of teachers, coordinating research, and cooperating with other scholarly organizations. *AJS Review; newsletter.*

ASSOCIATION OF HILLEL/JEWISH CAMPUS PROFESSIONALS (1949). 6300 Forsyth Blvd., St. Louis, MO 63105. (314)726-6177. Pres. Rabbi James S. Diamond; Exec. Off. Judith Schwartz. Seeks to promote professional relationships and exchanges of experience, develop personnel standards and qualifications, safeguard integrity of Hillel profession; represents and advocates before National Hillel Staff, National Hillel Commission, B'nai B'rith International, Council of Jewish Federations. *AHJCP Bulletin.*

ASSOCIATION OF JEWISH CHAPLAINS OF THE ARMED FORCES (1946). 15 E. 26 St., NYC 10010. (212)532-4949. Pres. Rabbi Selig Salkowitz; Sec. Rabbi Myron Geller. An organization of former and current chaplains of the U.S. armed forces which seeks to enhance the religious program of Jewish chaplains in the armed forces and in Veterans Administration hospitals.

ASSOCIATION OF ORTHODOX JEWISH SCIENTISTS (1948). 1373 Coney Island Ave., Brooklyn, NY 11219. (718)338-8592. Pres. Sheldon Kornbluth; Bd. Chmn. Nora Smith. Seeks to contribute to the development of science within the framework of Orthodox Jewish tradition; to obtain and disseminate information relating to the interaction between the Jewish traditional way of life and scientific developments—on both an ideological and practical level; to assist in the solution of problems pertaining to Orthodox Jews engaged in scientific teaching or research. Two main conventions are held each year. *Intercom; Proceedings; Halacha Bulletin; newsletter.*

BETH MEDROSH ELYON (ACADEMY OF HIGHER LEARNING AND RESEARCH) (1943). 73 Main St., Monsey, NY 10952. (914)356-7065. Bd. Chmn. Emanuel Welder; Treas. Arnold Jacobs; Sec. Yerachmiel Censor. Provides postgraduate courses and research work in higher Jewish studies; offers scholarships and fellowships. *Annual journal.*

B'NAI B'RITH HILLEL FOUNDATIONS, INC. (1923). 1640 Rhode Island Ave., NW, Washington, DC 20036. (202)857-6560. Chmn. B'nai B'rith Hillel Comm. Edwin Shapiro; Assoc. Internatl. Dirs. Rabbi Samuel Z. Fishman, Rabbi William D. Rudolph. Provides cultural, social, community-service, educational, and religious activities for Jewish college students of all denominational backgrounds on more than 400 campuses in the U.S., Canada, and overseas. Sponsors seminars in Israel, annual Washington Public Policy Conference, National Jewish Law Students Association, Academic Associates, Student Secretariat; cosponsors Washington Soviet Jewry Lobby. *Jewish Life on Campus: A Directory of B'nai B'rith Hillel Foundations and Other Jewish Campus Activities; Igeret; National Jewish Law Review; NJLS Newsletter.*

B'NAI B'RITH YOUTH ORGANIZATION (1924). 1640 Rhode Island Ave., NW, Washington, DC 20036. (202)857-6633. Chmn. Youth Comm. Edward Yalowitz; Internatl. Dir. Sidney Clearfield. Helps Jewish teenagers achieve self-fulfillment and make a maximum contribution to the Jewish community and their country's culture; helps members acquire a greater knowledge and appreciation of Jewish religion and culture. *BBYO Advisor; Monday Morning; Shofar; Hakol; Kesher.*

BRAMSON ORT (1977). 304 Park Ave. S., NYC 10010. (212)677-7420. Dir. Ira L. Jaskoll. A two-year Jewish technical college offering certificates and associate degrees in high technology and business fields, including computer programming and technology, electronics technology, business management, word processing, and ophthalmic technology. Houses the Center for Computers in Jewish Education.

BRANDEIS-BARDIN INSTITUTE (1941). 1101 Peppertree Lane, Brandeis, CA 93064. (818)348-7201. Pres. John Rauch. A pluralistic Jewish institution offering Brandeis Camp Institute (BCI), a leadership program for college-age adults; Camp Alonim for children 8–16; House of the Book shabbat weekends for adults 25+, at which scholars-in-residence discuss current, historical, cultural, and spiritual aspects of Judaism. *Brandeis-Bardin Institute News; BCI Alumni News.*

CANTORS ASSEMBLY (1947). 150 Fifth Ave., NYC 10011. (212)691-8020. Pres. Solomon Mendelson; Exec. V.-Pres. Samuel Rosenbaum. Seeks to unite all cantors who adhere to traditional Judaism and who serve as full-time cantors in bona fide congregations to conserve and promote the musical traditions of the Jews and to elevate the status of the cantorial profession. *Annual Proceedings; Journal of Synagogue Music.*

CENTRAL CONFERENCE OF AMERICAN RABBIS (1889). 192 Lexington Ave., NYC 10016. (212)684-4990. Pres. Rabbi Eugene J. Lipman; Exec. V.-Pres. Rabbi Joseph B. Glaser. Seeks to conserve and promote Judaism and to disseminate its teachings in a liberal spirit. *Journal of Reform Judaism; CCAR Yearbook.*

CLAL (*see* National Jewish Center for Learning and Leadership)

CLEVELAND COLLEGE OF JEWISH STUDIES (1964). 26500 Shaker Blvd., Beachwood, OH 44122. (216)464-4050. Pres. David Ariel; Bd. Chmn. Dan Polster. Provides courses in all areas of Judaic and Hebrew studies to adults and college-age students; offers continuing education for Jewish educators and administrators; serves as a center for Jewish life and culture; expands the availability of courses in Judaic studies by exchanging faculty, students, and credits with neighboring academic institutions; grants bachelor's and master's degrees.

COALITION FOR THE ADVANCEMENT OF JEWISH EDUCATION (CAJE) (1976). 468 Park Ave. S., Rm. 904, NYC 10016. (212)-696-0740. Chmn. Betsy Katz; Dir. Eliot G. Spack. Brings together Jews from all ideologies who are involved in every facet of Jewish education, and are committed to transmitting Jewish knowledge, culture, and experience; serves as a channel of communication for its membership to share resources and methods, and as a forum for exchange of philosophical and theoretical approaches to Jewish education. Sponsors programs and projects. *Bikurim; Crisis Curricula; Mekasher; CAJE Jewish Education News.*

COUNCIL FOR JEWISH EDUCATION (1926). 426 W. 58 St., NYC 10019. (212)713-0290. Pres. Bernard Ducoff; Exec. Dir. Philip Gorodetzer. Fellowship of Jewish education professionals, comprising administrators and supervisors of national and local Jewish educational institutions and agencies, and teachers in Hebrew high schools and Jewish teachers colleges, of all ideological groupings; conducts annual national and regional conferences in all areas of Jewish education; represents the Jewish education profession before the Jewish community; cosponsors, with the Jewish Education Service of North America, a personnel committee and other projects; cooperates with Jewish Agency Department of Education and Culture in promoting Hebrew culture and studies; conducts lectureship at Hebrew University. *Jewish Education; Sheviley Hahinnukh.*

DROPSIE COLLEGE FOR HEBREW AND COGNATE LEARNING (*see* Annenberg Research Institute)

FEDERATION OF JEWISH MEN'S CLUBS, INC. (1929). 475 Riverside Dr., Suite 244, NYC 10115. (212)749-8100. Pres. Jerome Agrest; Exec. Dir. Rabbi Charles Simon. Promotes principles and objectives of Conservative Judaism by organizing, sponsoring, and developing men's clubs or brotherhoods; supports OMETZ Center for Conservative Judaism on campus; promotes Home Library of Conservative Judaism and the Art of Jewish Living series; sponsors Hebrew literacy adult education program; presents awards for service to American Jewry. *Torchlight.*

GRATZ COLLEGE (1895). 10th St. and Tabor Rd., Philadelphia, PA 19141. (215)329-3363. Bd. Chmn. Stephen Sussman; Pres. Gary S. Schiff. Offers a wide variety of bachelor's, master's, teacher-training, continuing-education, and high-school-level programs in Judaic, Hebraic, and Middle Eastern studies. Grants BA and MA in Jewish studies, Bachelor and Master of Hebrew Literature, MA in Jewish education, MA in Jewish music, certificates in Judaica librarianship, Sephardic studies, Jewish chaplaincy, and other credentials. Joint bachelor's programs with Temple University and Beaver College. Gratz College's Division of Community Services serves as the central agency for Jewish education in Greater Philadelphia, providing consultation and resources to Jewish schools, organizations, and individuals. *Various newsletters, a yearbook, and scholarly publications.*

HEBREW COLLEGE (1921). 43 Hawes St., Brookline, MA 02146. (617)232-8710. Pres. Samuel Schafler; Bd. Chmn. Leon Brock. Provides intensive programs of study in all areas of Jewish culture from high school through college and graduate school levels, also at branch in Hartford; maintains ongoing programs with most major local universities; offers the degrees of Master of Jewish Studies, Bachelor and Master of Hebrew Literature, and Bachelor and Master of Jewish Education, with teaching certification; trains men and women to teach, conduct, and supervise Jewish schools; operates Hebrew-speaking Camp Yavneh in Northwood, NH; offers extensive Ulpan program and courses for community. *Hebrew College Bulletin.*

HEBREW THEOLOGICAL COLLEGE (1922). 7135 N. Carpenter Rd., Skokie, IL 60077. (312)267-9800. Pres. Rabbi Don Well; Bd. Chmn. Colman Ginsparg. An institution of higher Jewish learning which includes a division of advanced Hebrew studies, a school of liberal arts and sciences, a rabbinical ordination program, a graduate school in Judaic studies and pastoral counseling; the Fasman Yeshiva High School; a high school summer program combining Torah studies and computer science courses; and a Jewish studies program. *Or Shmuel Torah Journal; quarterly newsletter.*

HEBREW UNION COLLEGE-JEWISH INSTITUTE OF RELIGION (1875). 3101 Clifton Ave., Cincinnati, OH 45220. (513)221-1875. Pres. Alfred Gottschalk; Exec. Dean Eugene Mihaly; Exec. V.-Pres. Uri D. Herscher; Chmn. Bd. of Govs. Richard J. Scheuer. Academic centers: 3101 Clifton Ave., Cincinnati, OH 45220 (1875), Samuel Greengus, Dean; 1 W. 4 St., NYC 10012 (1922), Paul M. Steinberg, Dean; 3077 University Ave., Los Angeles, CA 90007 (1954), Uri D. Herscher, Chief Admin. Off.; 13 King David St., Jerusalem, Israel 94101 (1963), Michael Klein, Dean. Prepares students for Reform rabbinate, cantorate, religious-school teaching and administration, community service, academic careers; promotes Jewish studies; maintains libraries and a museum; offers bachelor's, master's, and doctoral degrees; engages in archaeological excavations; publishes scholarly works through Hebrew Union College Press. *American Jewish Archives; Bibliographica Judaica; HUC-JIR Catalogue; Hebrew Union College Annual; Studies in Bibliography and Booklore; The Chronicle.*

———, AMERICAN JEWISH ARCHIVES (1947). 3101 Clifton Ave., Cincinnati, OH 45220. (513)221-1875. Dir. Jacob R. Marcus; Admin. Dir. Abraham Peck. Promotes the study and preservation of the Western Hemisphere Jewish experience through research, publications, collection of important source materials, and a vigorous public-outreach program. *American Jewish Archives; monographs, publications, and pamphlets.*

———, AMERICAN JEWISH PERIODICAL CENTER (1957). 3101 Clifton Ave., Cincinnati, OH 45220. (513)221-1875. Dir. Jacob R. Marcus; Codir. Herbert C. Zafren. Maintains microfilms of all American Jewish periodicals 1823–1925, selected periodicals since 1925. *Jewish Periodicals and Newspapers on Microfilm (1957); First Supplement (1960); Augmented Edition (1984).*

———, EDGAR F. MAGNIN SCHOOL OF GRADUATE STUDIES (1956). 3077 University Ave., Los Angeles, CA 90007. (213)-749-3424. Dir. Stanley Chyet. Supervises programs leading to PhD (Education), DHS, DHL, and MA degrees; participates in cooperative PhD programs with the University of Southern California.

———, JEROME H. LOUCHHEIM SCHOOL OF JUDAIC STUDIES (1969). 3077 University Ave. Los Angeles, CA 90007. (213)749-3424. Dir. David Ellenson. Offers programs leading to MA, BS, BA, and AA degrees; offers courses as part of the undergraduate program of the University of Southern California.

———, NELSON GLUECK SCHOOL OF BIBLICAL ARCHAEOLOGY (1963). 13 King David St., Jerusalem, Israel 94101. Dir. Avraham Biran. Offers graduate-level research programs in Bible and archaeology. Summer excavations are carried out by scholars and students. University credit may be earned by participants in excavations. Consortium of colleges, universities, and seminaries is affiliated with the school.

———, RHEA HIRSCH SCHOOL OF EDUCATION (1967). 3077 University Ave., Los Angeles, CA 90007. (213)749-3424. Dir. Sara S. Lee. Offers PhD and MA programs in Jewish and Hebrew education; conducts joint degree programs with University of Southern California; offers courses for Jewish teachers, librarians, and early educators on a nonmatriculating basis; conducts summer institutes for professional Jewish educators.

———, SCHOOL OF EDUCATION (1947). 1 W. 4 St., NYC 10012. (212)674-5300. V.-Pres. and Dean Paul M. Steinberg; Dir. Kerry Olitzky. Trains teachers and principals for Reform religious schools; offers MA degree with specialization in religious education; offers extension programs in various suburban centers.

———, SCHOOL OF GRADUATE STUDIES (1949). 3101 Clifton Ave., Cincinnati, OH 45220 (513)221-1875. Dean Samuel Greengus. Offers programs leading to MA and PhD degrees; offers program leading to DHL degree for rabbinic graduates of the college.

———, SCHOOL OF JEWISH COMMUNAL SERVICE (1968). 3077 University Ave., Los Angeles, CA 90007. (213)749-3424. Dir. Gerald B. Bubis. Offers certificate and master's degree to those employed in Jewish communal services, or preparing for such work; offers joint MA in Jewish education and communal service with Rhea Hirsch School; offers MA and MSW in conjunction with the University of Southern California School of Social Work, with the George Warren Brown School of Social Work of Washington University, and with the University of Pittsburgh School of Social Work; offers joint master's degrees in conjunction with USC in public administration or gerontology.

———, SCHOOL OF JEWISH STUDIES (1963). 13 King David St., Jerusalem, Israel, 94101. (02)20333. Dean Michael Klein. Offers first year of graduate rabbinic, cantorial, and Jewish education studies; program in biblical archaeology; program leading to ordination for Israeli students; undergraduate semester in Jerusalem and one-year work/study program on a kibbutz in cooperation with Union of American Hebrew Congregations.

———, SCHOOL OF SACRED MUSIC (1947). 1 W. 4 St., NYC 10012. (212)674-5300. V.-Pres. and Dean Paul M. Steinberg. Trains cantors and music personnel for congregations; offers MSM degree. *Sacred Music Press.*

———, SKIRBALL MUSEUM (1913; 1972 in Calif.). 3077 University Ave., Los Angeles, CA 90007. (213)749-3424. Dir. Nancy Berman; Curator Grace Grossman. Collects, preserves, researches, and exhibits art and artifacts made by or for Jews, or otherwise associated with Jews and Judaism. Provides opportunity to faculty and students to do research in the field of Jewish art. *Catalogues of exhibits and collections.*

HERZLIAH-JEWISH TEACHERS SEMINARY (1967). Division of Touro College. 30 W. 44 St., NYC 10036. (212)575-1819. Pres. Bernard Lander; Dir. Jacob Katzman.

———, GRADUATE SCHOOL OF JEWISH STUDIES (1981). 30 W. 44th St., NYC 10036. (212)575-0190. Pres. Bernard Lander; Dean Michael Shmidman. Offers programs leading to MA in Jewish studies, including Hebrew language and literature, Jewish education, history, philosophy, and sociology. Admits men and women who have bachelor's degrees and backgrounds in Hebrew, Yiddish, and Jewish studies.

———, JEWISH PEOPLE'S UNIVERSITY OF THE AIR. (212)575-1819. Dir. Jacob Katzman. The educational outreach arm of Touro College, it produces and disseminates Jewish educational and cultural programming for radio broadcast and on audio-cassettes.

INSTITUTE FOR COMPUTERS IN JEWISH LIFE (1978). 845 N. Michigan Ave., Suite 843, Chicago, IL 60611. (312)787-7856. Pres. Thomas Klutznick; Exec. V.-Pres. Irving J. Rosenbaum. Explores, develops, and disseminates applications of computer technology to appropriate areas of Jewish life, with special emphasis on Jewish education; provides access to the Bar-Ilan University Responsa Project; creates educational software for use in Jewish schools; provides consulting service and assistance for national Jewish organizations, seminaries, and synagogues. *Monitor.*

JEWISH CHAUTAUQUA SOCIETY, INC. (sponsored by NATIONAL FEDERATION OF TEMPLE BROTHERHOODS) (1893). 838 Fifth Ave., NYC 10021. (212)570-0707. Pres. Carl J. Burkons; Exec. Dir. Av Bondarin. Disseminates authoritative information on Jews and Judaism; assigns rabbis to lecture at colleges and secondary schools; endows courses in Judaism for college credit at universities; donates Jewish reference books to college libraries; sends rabbis to serve as counselor-teachers at Christian church summer camps and as chaplains at Boy Scout camps; sponsors institutes on Judaism for Christian clergy; produces motion pictures for public-service television and group showings. *Brotherhood.*

JEWISH EDUCATION IN MEDIA, INC. (1978). PO Box 180, Riverdale Sta., NYC 10471. (212)362-7633. Pres. Bernard Samers; Exec. Dir. Rabbi Mark S. Golub. Seeks to promote Jewish identity and commitment through the creation of innovative and entertaining media materials, including radio and television programming, film, and audio and video cassettes for synagogue and institutional use. Produces syndicated radio magazine, *L'Chayim.*

JEWISH EDUCATION SERVICE OF NORTH AMERICA, INC. (JESNA) (1981). 730 Broadway, NYC 10003. (212)529-2000. Pres. Bennett Yanowitz; Exec. V.-Pres. Jonathan Woocher. Coordinating, planning, and service agency for Jewish education in bureaus and federations; offers curricular advisement and maintains a National Educational Resource Center; runs regional pedagogic conferences; conducts evaluative surveys on Jewish education; engages in statistical and other educational research; provides community consultations; sponsors the National Board of License; administers Fellowships in Jewish Educational Leadership training program (FIJEL); provides placement of upper-level bureau and communal school personnel and educators. *Pedagogic Reporter; TRENDS; Information Research Bulletins; Jewish Education Directory; annual report; NISE Newsletter.*

JEWISH MINISTERS CANTORS ASSOCIATION OF AMERICA, INC. (1896). 3 W. 16 St., NYC 10011. (212)675-6601. Pres. Cantor Nathan H. Muchnick. Furthers and propagates traditional liturgy; places cantors in synagogues throughout the U.S. and Canada; develops the cantors of the future. *Kol Lakol.*

JEWISH RECONSTRUCTIONIST FOUNDATION (1940). 270 W. 89 St., NYC 10024. (212)-496-2960. Bd. Chmn. Jack Wolofsky; Exec. Dir. Rabbi Mordechai Liebling. Dedicated to the advancement of Judaism as the evolving religious civilization of the Jewish people. Coordinates the Federation of Reconstructionist Congregations and Havurot, Reconstructionist Rabbinical Association, and Reconstructionist Rabbinical College.

———, FEDERATION OF RECONSTRUCTIONIST CONGREGATIONS AND HAVUROT (1954). 270 W. 89 St., NYC 10024. (212)-496-2960. Pres. Lillian Kaplan; Exec. Dir. Rabbi Mordechai Liebling. Services affiliated congregations and havurot educationally and administratively; fosters the establishment of new Reconstructionist congregations and fellowship groups. Runs the Reconstructionist Press and provides programmatic materials. *Newsletter; Reconstructionist.*

———, RECONSTRUCTIONIST RABBINICAL ASSOCIATION (1975). Greenwood Ave. and Church Rd., Wyncote, PA 19095. (215)576-0800. Pres. Rabbi Joy Levitt; Exec. Dir. Rabbi David Klatzker. Professional organization for graduates of the Reconstructionist Rabbinical College and other rabbis who identify with Reconstructionist Judaism; cooperates with Federation of Reconstructionist Congregations and Havurot in furthering Reconstructionism in N. America. *Raayanot; newsletter.*

———, RECONSTRUCTIONIST RABBINICAL COLLEGE (*see* p. 451)

JEWISH TEACHERS ASSOCIATION—MORIM (1931). 45 E. 33 St., NYC 10016. (212)684-0556. Pres. Phyllis L. Pullman; V.-Pres. Eli Nieman. Protects teachers from abuse of seniority rights; fights the encroachment of anti-Semitism in education; provides legal counsel to protect teachers from discrimination; offers scholarships to qualified students; encourages teachers to assume active roles in Jewish communal and religious affairs. *Morim Jewish Teachers Association Newsletter.*

JEWISH THEOLOGICAL SEMINARY OF AMERICA (1886; reorg. 1902). 3080 Broadway, NYC 10027. (212)678-8000. Chancellor Ismar Schorsch; Chmn. Bd. of Directors and Exec. Com. Stephen M. Peck. Operates undergraduate and graduate programs in Judaica, professional schools for training Conservative rabbis and cantors, a pastoral psychiatry center, Melton Center for Jewish Education, the Jewish Museum, and such youth programs as the Ramah Camps, the OMETZ-Center for Conservative Judaism on Campus, and the Prozdor high-school division. Produces the "Eternal Light" radio and TV programs. *Academic Bulletin; JTS Bulletin; Seminary Progress.*

———, ALBERT A. LIST COLLEGE OF JEWISH STUDIES (formerly SEMINARY COLLEGE OF JEWISH STUDIES-TEACHERS INSTITUTE) (1909). 3080 Broadway, NYC 10027. (212)678-8826. Dean Anne Lapidus Lerner. Offers complete undergraduate program in Judaica leading to BA degree; conducts joint programs with Columbia University and Barnard enabling students to receive two BA degrees after four years.

———, AMERICAN STUDENT CENTER IN JERUSALEM (1962). PO Box 196, Neve Schechter, Jerusalem, Israel 91001. (02)-631121. Dean Reuven Hammer; Dir. Midreshet Yerushalayim, Baruch Feldstern. Offers year-in-Israel programs for students of college and postgraduate age in the field of Jewish studies. Rabbinical and cantorial students of the JTS spend a minimum of one year of their studies at Neve Schechter. Headquarters also for the Saul Lieberman Institute for Talmudic Studies, Shamma Friedman, Director.

———, CANTORS INSTITUTE AND SEMINARY COLLEGE OF JEWISH MUSIC (1952). 3080 Broadway, NYC 10027. (212)678-8038. Dean Rabbi Morton M. Leifman. Trains cantors, music teachers, and choral directors for congregations. Offers full-time programs in sacred music leading to degrees of BSM, MSM, and DSM, and diploma of *Hazzan.*

———, DEPARTMENT OF RADIO AND TELEVISION (1944). 3080 Broadway, NYC 10027. (212)678-8020. Exec. Prod. Marjorie Wyler. Produces radio and TV programs expressing the Jewish tradition in its broadest sense: The "Eternal Light" weekly radio program on NBC network; one hour-long documentary on NBC-TV; TV program on ABC. Distributes cassettes of programs at minimum charge.

———, GRADUATE SCHOOL (formerly INSTITUTE FOR ADVANCED STUDY IN THE HUMANITIES) (1968). 3080 Broadway, NYC 10027. (212)678-8024. Dean Shaye J. D. Cohen. Graduate programs leading to MA, DHL, and PhD degrees in Jewish studies, Bible, Jewish education, history, literature, philosophy, rabbinics, and medieval studies; dual degree with Columbia University School of Social Work.

———, JEWISH MUSEUM (*see* p. 437)

———, LOUIS FINKELSTEIN INSTITUTE FOR RELIGIOUS AND SOCIAL STUDIES (1938). 3080 Broadway, NYC 10027. (212)678-8815. Dir. Gordon Tucker. A scholarly and scientific fellowship of clergy and other religious teachers who desire authoritative information regarding some of the basic issues now confronting spiritually minded individuals.

———, MELTON RESEARCH CENTER FOR JEWISH EDUCATION (1960). 3080 Broadway, NYC 10027. (212)678-8031. Dirs. Eduardo Rauch, Barry W. Holtz. Develops new curricula and materials for Jewish education; recruits and prepares educators through seminars and in-service programs; maintains consultant and supervisory relationships with a limited number of pilot schools; sponsors "renewal" retreats for teachers and principals. *Melton Journal.*

———, NATIONAL RAMAH COMMISSION (1947). 3080 Broadway, NYC 10027. (212)678-8881. Pres. Irving Robbin; Dir. Burton I. Cohen. Sponsors 7 summer camps conducted in Hebrew in the U.S. and Canada; offers opportunities for qualified Seminary students and others to serve as counselors, administrators, specialists, etc. Offers special programs in U.S. and Israel, including Bert B. Weinstein National Ramah Staff Training Institute, Ramah Israel Seminars, the Ulpan Ramah Plus Program, and Tichon Ramah Yerushalayim.

———, PROZDOR (1951). 3080 Broadway, NYC 10027. (212)678-8824. Principal Beverly Gribetz. The high-school department of JTS, it provides a supplementary Jewish education for students who attend a secular (public or private) full-time high school. Classes in classical Jewish studies, with emphasis on Hebrew language, meet twice a week. *Prozdor Pages.*

———, RABBINICAL SCHOOL (1886). 3080 Broadway, NYC 10027. (212)678-8816. Dean Gordon Tucker. Offers a program of graduate and professional studies leading to the degree of Master of Arts and ordination; includes one year of study at the American Student Center in Jerusalem and pastoral psychiatry training.

———, SCHOCKEN INSTITUTE FOR JEWISH RESEARCH (1961). 6 Balfour St., Jerusalem, Israel, 92102. (02)631288. Dir. Shamma Friedman; Genl. Dir. Shmuel Glick. Incorporates Schocken library and its related research institutes in medieval Hebrew poetry and Jewish mysticism, as well as the Saul Lieberman Institute for Talmudic Research. *Schocken Institute Yearbook (P'raqim).*

———, UNIVERSITY OF JUDAISM (1947). 15600 Mulholland Dr., Los Angeles, CA 90077. (213)879-4114. Pres. David L. Lieber; Sr. V.-Pres. Max Vorspan. West Coast affiliate of JTS. Serves as center of undergraduate and graduate study of Judaica; offers preprofessional and professional programs in Jewish education, nonprofit management, and allied fields, including a prerabbinic program and joint program enabling students to receive BA from UCLA and BHL from U. of J. after four years of undergraduate study. Offers degree programs in Jewish and Western studies as well as a broad range of adult education and Jewish activities. *Direction Magazine; Bulletin of General Information.*

MACHNE ISRAEL, INC. (1940). 770 Eastern Pkwy., Brooklyn, NY 11213. (718)493-9250. Pres. Menachem M. Schneerson (Lubavitcher Rebbe); Dir., Treas. M.A. Hodakov; Sec. Nissan Mindel. The Lubavitcher movement's organ dedicated to the social, spiritual, and material welfare of Jews throughout the world.

MERKOS L'INYONEI CHINUCH, INC. (THE CENTRAL ORGANIZATION FOR JEWISH EDUCATION) (1940). 770 Eastern Pkwy., Brooklyn, NY 11213. (718)493-9250. Pres. Menachem M. Schneerson (Lubavitcher Rebbe); Dir., Treas. M.A. Hodakov; Sec. Nissan Mindel. The educational arm of the Lubavitcher movement. Seeks to promote Jewish education among Jews, regardless of their background, in the spirit of Torah-true Judaism; to establish contact with alienated Jewish youth; to stimulate concern and active interest in Jewish education on all levels; and to promote religious observance as a daily experience among all Jews; maintains worldwide network of regional offices, schools, summer camps, and Chabad-Lubavitch Houses; publishes Jewish educational literature in numerous languages and monthly journal in five languages: *Conversaciones con la juventud; Conversations avec les jeunes; Schmuessen mit Kinder un Yugent; Sihot la-No-ar; Talks and Tales.*

MESIVTA YESHIVA RABBI CHAIM BERLIN RABBINICAL ACADEMY (1905). 1593 Coney Island Ave., Brooklyn, NY 11230. (718)377-0777. Pres. Sol Eiger; Exec. Dir. Y. Mayer Lasker. Maintains fully accredited elementary and high schools; collegiate and postgraduate school for advanced Jewish studies, both in America and Israel; Camp Morris, a summer study retreat; Prof. Nathan Isaacs Memorial Library; Gur Aryeh Publications.

NATIONAL COMMITTEE FOR FURTHERANCE OF JEWISH EDUCATION (1941). 824 Eastern Pkwy., Brooklyn, NY 11213. (718)735-0200. Pres. J. James Plesser; Natl. Pres. Joseph Fisch; Exec. V.-Pres. Rabbi Jacob J. Hecht. Seeks to disseminate the ideals of Torah-true education among the youth of America; aids poor, sick, and needy in U.S. and Israel; provides aid to Iranian Jewish youth through the Iranian Children's Fund; maintains camp for underprivileged children; sponsors Hadar HaTorah, Machon Chana, and Ivy League Torah Study Program, seeking to win back college youth and others to Judaism; maintains schools and dormitory facilities, family and vocational counseling services. *Panorama; Passover Handbook; Seder Guide; Spiritual Suicide; Focus.*

NATIONAL COUNCIL OF YOUNG ISRAEL (1912). 3 W. 16 St., NYC 10011. (212)929-1525. Pres. Harold M. Jacobs; Exec. V.-Pres. Rabbi Ephraim H. Sturm. Maintains a program of spiritual, cultural, social, and communal activity aimed at the advancement and perpetuation of traditional, Torah-true Judaism; seeks to instill in American youth an understanding and appreciation of the ethical and spiritual values of Judaism. Sponsors kosher dining clubs and fraternity houses and an Israel program. *Viewpoint; Hashkafa series; Masorah newspaper.*

———, AMERICAN FRIENDS OF YOUNG ISRAEL SYNAGOGUES IN ISRAEL (1926). 3 W. 16 St., NYC 10011. (212)929-1525. Chmn. Jack Forgash; Dir. Israel Programs Isaac Hagler; Exec. V.-Pres. Rabbi Ephraim H. Sturm. Promotes Young Israel synagogues and youth work in synagogues in Israel.

———, ARMED FORCES BUREAU (1912). 3 W. 16 St., NYC 10011. (212)929-1525. Advises and guides the inductees into the armed forces with regard to Sabbath observance, *kashrut,* and Orthodox behavior. *Guide for the Orthodox Serviceman.*

———, EMPLOYMENT BUREAU (1912). 3 W. 16 St., NYC 10011. (212)929-1525. Exec. V.-Pres. Rabbi Ephraim H. Sturm; Employment Dir. Dorothy Stein. Operates an on-the-job training program under federal contract; helps secure employment, particularly for Sabbath observers and Russian immigrants; offers vocational guidance.

———, INSTITUTE FOR JEWISH STUDIES (1947). 3 W. 16 St., NYC 10011. (212)929-1525. Pres. Harold M. Jacobs; Exec. V.-Pres. Rabbi Ephraim H. Sturm. Introduces students to Jewish learning and knowledge; helps form adult branch schools; aids Young Israel synagogues in their adult education programs. *Bulletin.*

———, YOUNG ISRAEL COLLEGIATES AND YOUNG ADULTS (1951; reorg. 1982). 3 W. 16 St., NYC 10011. (212)929-1525. Chmn. Kenneth Block; Dir. Richard Stareshefsky. Organizes and operates kosher dining clubs on college and university campuses; provides information and counseling on *kashrut* observance at college; gives college-age youth understanding and appreciation of Judaism and information on issues important to Jewish community; arranges seminars and meetings, weekends and trips; operates Achva summer mission to Israel for ages 18–21 and 22–27.

———, YOUNG ISRAEL YOUTH (reorg. 1968). 3 W. 16 St., NYC 10011. (212)929-1525. Dir. Richard Stareshefsky. Fosters a program of spiritual, cultural, social, and communal activities for the advancement and perpetuation of traditional Torah-true Judaism; strives to instill an understanding and appreciation of the high ethical and spiritual values and to demonstrate compatibility of ancient faith of Israel with good Americanism. Operates Achva Summer Mission study program in Israel. *Monthly newsletter.*

NATIONAL JEWISH CENTER FOR LEARNING AND LEADERSHIP—CLAL (1974). 421 Seventh Ave., NYC 10001. (212)714-9500. Chmn. Robert E. Loup; Pres. Irving Greenberg; Exec. V.-Pres. Paul Jeser. Devoted to leadership education and policy guidance for the American Jewish community. Conducts weekend retreats and community gatherings as well as conferences on various topics. *Perspectives.*

NATIONAL JEWISH HOSPITALITY COMMITTEE (1973). 201 S. 18 St., Rm. 1519, Philadelphia, PA 19103. (215)546-8293. Pres. Rabbi Allen S. Maller; Exec. Dir. Steven S. Jacobs. Assists converts and prospective converts to Judaism, persons involved in intermarriages, and the parents of Jewish youth under the influence of cults and missionaries, as well as the youths themselves. *Special reports.*

NATIONAL JEWISH INFORMATION SERVICE FOR THE PROPAGATION OF JUDAISM, INC. (1960). 5174 W. 8 St., Los Angeles, CA 90036. (213)936-6033. Pres. Rabbi Moshe M. Maggal; V.-Pres. Lawrence J. Epstein; Sec. Rachel D. Maggal. Seeks to convert non-Jews to Judaism and return Jews to Judaism; maintains College for Jewish Ambassadors for the training of Jewish missionaries and the Correspondence Academy of Judaism for instruction on Judaismthroughthemail. *Voice of Judaism.*

NER ISRAEL RABBINICAL COLLEGE (1933). 400 Mt. Wilson Ln., Baltimore, MD 21208. (301)484-7200. Pres. Rabbi Jacob I. Ruderman; V.-Pres. Rabbi Herman N. Neuberger. Trains rabbis and educators for Jewish communities in America and worldwide. Offers bachelor's, master's, and doctoral degrees in talmudic law, as well as teacher's diploma. College has four divisions: Mechina High School, Rabbinical College, Teachers Training Institute, Graduate School. Maintains an active community-service division. Operates special program for Iranian Jewish students. *Ner Israel Bulletin; Alumni Bulletin; Ohr Hanair Talmudic Journal; Iranian B'nei Torah Bulletin.*

OZAR HATORAH, INC. (1946). 1 E. 33 St., NYC 10016. (212)686-7550. Pres. Joseph Shalom; Sec. Sam Sutton. Maintains schools for Jewish youth worldwide, providing religious and secular studies.

P'EYLIM—AMERICAN YESHIVA STUDENT UNION (1951). 3 W. 16 St., NYC 10011. (212)989-2500. Pres. Jacob Y. Weisberg; Dir. Avraham Hirsch. Aids and sponsors pioneer work by American graduate teachers and rabbis in new villages and towns in Israel; does religious, organizational, and educational work and counseling among new immigrant youth; maintains summer camps for poor immigrant youth in Israel; belongs to worldwide P'eylim movement which has groups in Argentina, Brazil, Canada, England, Belgium, the Netherlands, Switzerland, France, and Israel; engages in relief and educational work among North African immigrants in France and Canada, assisting them to relocate and reestablish a strong Jewish community life. *P'eylim Reporter; News from P'eylim; N'shei P'eylim News.*

RABBINICAL ALLIANCE OF AMERICA (IGUD HARABONIM) (1944). 3 W. 16 St., 4th fl., NYC 10011. (212)242-6420. Pres. Rabbi Abraham B. Hecht; Menahel Rabbinical Court Rabbi Herschel Kurzrock. Seeks to promulgate the cause of Torah-true Judaism through an organized rabbinate that is consistently Orthodox; seeks to elevate the position of Orthodox rabbis nationally, and to defend the welfare of Jews the world over. Also has Beth Din Rabbinical Court for Jewish divorces, litigation, marriage counseling and family problems. *Perspective; Nahalim; Torah Message of the Week.*

RABBINICAL ASSEMBLY (1900). 3080 Broadway, NYC 10027. (212)678-8060. Pres. Rabbi Kassel Abelson; Exec. V.-Pres. Rabbi Wolfe Kelman. Seeks to promote Conservative Judaism, and to foster the spirit of fellowship and cooperation among rabbis and other Jewish scholars; cooperates with the Jewish Theological Seminary of America and the United Synagogue of America. *Conservative Judaism; Proceedings of the Rabbinical Assembly.*

RABBINICAL COLLEGE OF TELSHE, INC. (1941). 28400 Euclid Ave., Wickliffe, OH 44092. (216)943-5300. Pres. Rabbi Mordecai Gifter; V.-Pres. Rabbi Abba Zalka Gewirtz. College for higher Jewish learning specializing in Talmudic studies and rabbinics; maintains a preparatory academy including a secular high school, postgraduate department, teacher-training school, and teachers seminary for women. *Pri Etz Chaim; Peer Mordechai; Alumni Bulletin.*

RABBINICAL COUNCIL OF AMERICA, INC. (1923; reorg. 1935). 275 Seventh Ave., NYC 10001. (212)807-7888. Pres. Rabbi Max N. Schreier; Exec. V.-Pres. Rabbi Binyamin Walfish. Promotes Orthodox Judaism in the community; supports institutions for study of Torah; stimulates creation of new traditional agencies. *Hadorom; Record; Sermon Manual; Tradition.*

RECONSTRUCTIONIST RABBINICAL COLLEGE (1968). Church Rd. and Greenwood Ave., Wyncote, PA 19095. (215)576-0800. Bd. Chmn. Samuel Blumenthal; Genl. Chmn. Aaron Ziegelman; Pres. Arthur Green. Coeducational. Trains rabbis for all areas of Jewish communal life: synagogues, academic and educational positions, Hillel centers, federation agencies; confers title of rabbi and grants degrees of Master and Doctor of Hebrew Letters. *RRC Report.*

RESEARCH INSTITUTE OF RELIGIOUS JEWRY, INC. (1941; reorg. 1954). 471 W. End Ave., NYC 10024. (212)874-7979. Chmn. Rabbi Oswald Besser; Sec. Marcus Levine. Engages in research and publishes studies concerning the situation of religious Jewry and its problems all over the world.

SHOLEM ALEICHEM FOLK INSTITUTE, INC. (1918). 3301 Bainbridge Ave., Bronx, NY 10467. (212)881-6555. Pres. Burt Levey; Sec. Noah Zingman. Aims to imbue children with Jewish values through teaching Yiddish language and literature, Hebrew and the Bible, Jewish history, the significance of Jewish holidays, folk and choral singing, and facts about Jewish life in America and Israel. *Kinder Journal* (Yiddish).

SOCIETY FOR HUMANISTIC JUDAISM (1969). 28611 W. Twelve Mile Rd., Farmington Hills, MI 48018. (313)478-7610. Pres. Lynne Master; Exec. Dir. Miriam Jerris. Serves as a voice for Jews who value their Jewish identity and who seek an alternative to conventional Judaism, who reject supernatural authority and affirm the right of individuals to be the masters of their own lives. Publishes educational and ceremonial materials; organizes congregations and groups. *Humanorah (quarterly newsletter).*

SOCIETY OF FRIENDS OF THE TOURO SYNAGOGUE, NATIONAL HISTORICAL SITE, INC. (1948). 85 Touro St., Newport, RI 02840. (401)847-4794. Pres. Burton Fischler; Exec. Sec. Rabbi Chaim Shapiro. Assists in the maintenance of the Touro Synagogue as a national historical site. *History of Touro Synagogue.*

SPERTUS COLLEGE OF JUDAICA (1925). 618 S. Michigan Ave., Chicago, IL 60605. (312)922-9012. Pres. Howard A. Sulkin; Bd. Chmn. Stuart Taussig; V.-Pres. for Academic Affairs Byron L. Sherwin. Provides Chicago-area colleges and universities with specialized undergraduate and graduate programs in Judaica and serves as a department of Judaic studies to these colleges and universities; serves as Midwest Jewish information center, through its Asher Library, Maurice Spertus Museum of Judaica, Katzin Memorial Rare Book Room, and Chicago Jewish Archives. Grants degrees of MA in Jewish education, Jewish studies, and Jewish communal service; BA and Bachelor of Judaic Studies. Has community outreach/extension studies program for adults.

SYNAGOGUE COUNCIL OF AMERICA (1926). 327 Lexington Ave., NYC 10016. (212)-686-8670. Pres. Rabbi Gilbert Klaperman; Exec. V.-Pres. Rabbi Henry D. Michelman. Serves as spokesman for, and coordinates policies of, national rabbinical and lay synagogal organizations of Conservative, Orthodox, and Reform branches of American Judaism.

TORAH SCHOOLS FOR ISRAEL—CHINUCH ATZMAI (1953). 167 Madison Ave., NYC 10016. (212)889-0606. Pres. Abraham Pam; Exec. Dir. Henach Cohen. Conducts information programs for the American Jewish community on activities of the independent Torah schools educational network in Israel; coordinates role of American members of international board of governors; funds special programs of Mercaz Hachinuch Ha-Atzmai B'Eretz Yisroel. *Israel Education Reporter.*

TORAH UMESORAH—NATIONAL SOCIETY FOR HEBREW DAY SCHOOLS (1944). 160 Broadway, NYC 10038. (212)227-1000. Pres. Sheldon Beren; Chmn. Exec. Com. David Singer; Exec. V.-Pres. Joshua Fishman. Establishes Hebrew day schools throughout U.S. and Canada and services them in all areas, including placement and curriculum guidance; conducts teacher-training institutes on campuses of major yeshivahs and seminars and workshops for in-service training of teachers; publishes textbooks and supplementary reading material. New Hemshech program offers Shabbatonim and Wisconsin summer camp for day-school students. *Olomeinu-Our World; Visions.*

———, INSTITUTE FOR PROFESSIONAL ENRICHMENT (1973). 22 E. 28 St., NYC 10016. (212)683-3216. Dir. Bernard Dov Milians. Provides enriched training and upgraded credentials for administrative, guidance, and classroom personnel of Hebrew day schools and for Torah-community leaders; offers graduate and undergraduate programs, in affiliation with accredited universities which award full degrees: MA in early childhood and elementary education; MS in family counseling; MBA in management; MS in special education, reading; BS in education; BA in human relations, social sciences, education, gerontology. *Professional Enrichment News (PEN).*

———, NATIONAL ASSOCIATION OF HEBREW DAY SCHOOL ADMINISTRATORS (1960). 1114 Ave. J, Brooklyn, NY 11230. Pres. David H. Schwartz. Coordinates the work of the fiscal directors of Hebrew day schools throughout the country. *NAHDSA Review.*

———, NATIONAL ASSOCIATION OF HEBREW DAY SCHOOL PARENT-TEACHER ASSOCIATIONS (1948). 160 Broadway, NYC 10038. (212)227-1000. Pres. Mrs. Henry C. Rhein; Exec. Sec. Mrs. Samuel Brand; Bd. Chmn. Mrs. Clarence Horwitz. Acts as a clearinghouse and service agency to PTAs of Hebrew day schools; organizes parent-education courses and sets up programs for individual PTAs. *Fundraising with a Flair; Monthly Sidrah Series Program; PTA with a Purpose for the Hebrew Day School.*

———, NATIONAL CONFERENCE OF YESHIVA PRINCIPALS (1956). 160 Broadway, NYC 10038. (212)227-1000. Pres. Rabbi Sholom Strajcher; Bd. Chmn. Rabbi Yitzchak Merkin; Exec. V.-Pres. Rabbi A. Moshe Possick. A professional organization of primary and secondary yeshivah day-school principals which seeks to make yeshivah day-school education more effective. *Newsletter; Directory of High Schools.*

———, NATIONAL YESHIVA TEACHERS BOARD OF LICENSE (1953). 160 Broadway, NYC 10038. (212)406-4190. Dir. Rabbi Zvi H. Shurin. Issues licenses to qualified instructors for all grades of the Hebrew day school and the general field of Torah education.

TOURO COLLEGE (1970). 30 W. 44 St., NYC 10036. (212)575-0190. Pres. Bernard Lander; Bd. Chmn. Max Karl. Chartered by NY State Board of Regents as a nonprofit four-year college with liberal arts programs leading to BA, BS, and MA degrees, emphasizing relevance of Jewish heritage to general culture of Western civilization. Offers JD degree and a biomedical program leading to the MD from Technion-Israel Institute of Technology, Haifa, and the University of Groningen, Holland.

———, COLLEGE OF LIBERAL ARTS AND SCIENCES. 30 W. 44 St., NYC 10036. (212)575-0196. Exec. Dean Stanley Boylan. Offers comprehensive Jewish studies along with studies in the arts, sciences, humanities, and preprofessional studies in health sciences, law, accounting, business, computer science, and finance. Coordinate and extension programs at Women's Division (17 W. 60 St., NYC) and Flatbush Center in Brooklyn.

———, DIVISION OF HEALTH SCIENCES. 30 W. 44 St., NYC 10036, and the Long Island campus in Huntington. Offers three programs: (1) Five-year program leading to MD degree from the Faculty of Medicine of Technion-Israel Institute of Technology, Haifa; includes one year of advanced clinical rotations in Israel; (2) Physician Assistant program; (3) Physical Therapist program.

———, FLATBUSH PROGRAM. 1277 E. 14 St., Brooklyn, NY 11230. Offers evening classes to students attending a yeshiva or seminary during the day; nine majors include accounting, business management, education, and computer science.

———, GRADUATE SCHOOL OF JEWISH STUDIES. 30 W. 44 St., NYC 10036. Offered in conjunction with Herzliah-Jewish Teachers Seminary Division (*see* p. 446).

———, INSTITUTE OF JEWISH LAW. Based at Fuchsberg Law Center, serves as a center and clearinghouse for study and teaching of Jewish law. Coedits *Dinei Israel* (Jewish Law Journal) with Tel Aviv University Law School.

———, JACOB D. FUCHSBERG LAW CENTER (1980). Long Island Campus, 300 Nassau Rd., Huntington, NY 11743. (516)421-2244. Dean Howard A. Glickstein. Offers studies leading to JD degree.

———, JEWISH PEOPLE'S UNIVERSITY OF THE AIR. Presents Sunday radio courses on New York stations WEVD and WNYC, carried by satellite to NPR's 320 affiliated stations nationwide; covers all aspects of Jewish culture and offers course outlines and cassettes.

———, SCHOOL OF GENERAL STUDIES. 240 E. 123 St., NYC 10021. Dean Alfredo Matthew. Offers educational opportunities to minority groups and older people; courses in the arts, sciences, humanities, and special programs of career studies.

UNION OF AMERICAN HEBREW CONGREGATIONS (1873). 838 Fifth Ave., NYC 10021. (212)249-0100. Pres. Rabbi Alexander M. Schindler; Bd. Chmn. Charles J. Rothschild, Jr. Serves as the central congregational body of Reform Judaism in the Western Hemisphere; serves its approximately 805 affiliated temples and membership with religious, educational, cultural, and administrative programs. *Keeping Posted; Reform Judaism.*

———, AMERICAN CONFERENCE OF CANTORS (1956). 1 Kalisa Way, Suite 104, Paramus, NJ 07652. (201)599-0910. Pres. Paul Silbersher; Exec. V.-Pres. Raymond Smolover. Members receive investiture and commissioning as cantors at ordination-investiture ceremonies at Hebrew Union College-Jewish Institute of Religion, Sacred School of Music. Through Joint Placement Commission, serves congregations seeking cantors and music directors. Dedicated to creative Judaism, preserving the best of the past, and encouraging new and vital approaches to religious ritual, music and ceremonies. *Koleinu.*

———, COMMISSION ON JEWISH EDUCATION (with CCAR and NATE) (1923). 838 Fifth Ave., NYC 10021. (212)249-0100. Chmn. Rabbi Murray Blackman; Dir. Rabbi Howard I. Bogot. Develops curricula and teachers' manuals; conducts pilot projects and offers educational guidance and consultation at all age levels to member congregations and affiliates and associate bodies. *Compass.*

———, COMMISSION ON SOCIAL ACTION OF REFORM JUDAISM (*see* p. 432)

———, COMMISSION ON SYNAGOGUE MANAGEMENT (with CCAR) (1962). 838 Fifth Ave., NYC 10021. (212)249-0100. Chmn. Dr. Paul Vanek; Dir. Joseph C. Bernstein. Assists congregations in management, finance, building maintenance, design, construction, and art aspects of synagogues; maintains the Synagogue Architectural Library.

———, NATIONAL ASSOCIATION OF TEMPLE ADMINISTRATORS (NATA) (1941). 1185 N. Sheridan Rd., Glencoe, IL 60022. (312)835-0724. Pres. Ilene H. Herst; Admin. Sec. Mark W. Weisstuch. Prepares and disseminates administrative information and procedures to member synagogues of UAHC; provides training of professional synagogue executives; formulates and establishes professional standards for the synagogue executive; provides placement services. *NATA Journal; Temple Management Manual.*

———, NATIONAL ASSOCIATION OF TEMPLE EDUCATORS (NATE) (1955). 707 Summerly Dr., Nashville, TN 37209-4218. (615)352-0322. Pres. Robert E. Tornberg; Exec. Sec. Richard M. Morin. Represents the temple educator within the general body of Reform Judaism; fosters the full-time profession of the temple educator; encourages the growth and development of Jewish religious education consistent with the aims of Reform Judaism; stimulates communal interest in and responsibility for Jewish religious education. *NATE News; Compass.*

———, NATIONAL FEDERATION OF TEMPLE BROTHERHOODS (1923). 838 Fifth Ave., NYC 10021. (212)570-0707. Pres. Carl J. Burkons; Exec. Dir. Av Bondarin. Promotes Jewish education among its members, along with participation in temple, brotherhood, and interfaith activities;

sponsors the Jewish Chautauqua Society. *Brotherhood.*

———, NATIONAL FEDERATION OF TEMPLE SISTERHOODS (1913). 838 Fifth Ave., NYC 10021. (212)249-0100. Pres. Dolores Wilkenfeld; Exec. Dir. Eleanor R. Schwartz. Serves more than 640 sisterhoods of Reform Judaism; promotes interreligious understanding and social justice; awards scholarships and grants to rabbinic students; provides braille and large-type Judaic materials for Jewish blind; supports projects for Israel, Soviet Jewry, and the aging; is an affiliate of UAHC and is the women's agency of Reform Judaism; works in behalf of the Hebrew Union College-Jewish Institute of Religion; cooperates with World Union for Progressive Judaism. *Leaders Line; Notes for Now.*

———, NORTH AMERICAN FEDERATION OF TEMPLE YOUTH (NFTY; formerly NATIONAL FEDERATION OF TEMPLE YOUTH) (1939). 838 Fifth Ave., NYC 10021. (212)249-0100. Dir. Ramie Arian; Pres. Leon Morris. Seeks to train Reform Jewish youth in the values of the synagogue and their application to daily life through service to the community and congregation; runs department of summer camps and national leadership training institute; arranges overseas academic tours, work programs, international student exchange programs, and college student programs in the U.S. and Israel, including accredited study programs in Israel. *Ani V'Atah; The Jewish Connection.*

UNION OF ORTHODOX JEWISH CONGREGATIONS OF AMERICA (1898). 45 W. 36 St., NYC 10018. (212)563-4000. Pres. Sidney Kwestel; Exec. V.-Pres. Rabbi Pinchas Stolper. Serves as the national central body of Orthodox synagogues; sponsors National Conference of Synagogue Youth, Our Way program for the Jewish deaf, Yachad program for developmentally disabled youth, Israel Center in Jerusalem, *aliyah* department, national OU *kashrut* supervision and certification service; provides educational, religious, and organizational guidance to synagogues and groups; represents the Orthodox Jewish community in relation to governmental and civic bodies and the general Jewish community. Publishes synagogue programming publications and books of Jewish interest. *Jewish Action magazine; OU Kosher Directory; OU Passover Directory; OU News Reporter; Synagogue Spotlight; Our Way magazine; Yachad magazine; Luach Limud Torah Diary Home Study Program.*

———, NATIONAL CONFERENCE OF SYNAGOGUE YOUTH (1954). 45 W. 36 St., NYC 10018. (212)563-4000. Pres. Howie Siegel; Dir. Rabbi Raphael Butler. Serves as central body for youth groups of Orthodox congregations; provides such national activities and services as educational guidance, Torah study groups, community service, programs consultation, Torah library, Torah fund scholarships, Ben Zakkai Honor Society, Friends of NCSY; conducts national and regional events including week-long seminars, summer Torah tours in over 200 communities, Israel summer seminar for teens and collegiates, cross-country tours, and Camp NCSY East. Divisions include Senior NCSY in 18 regions and 465 chapters, Junior NCSY for preteens, Our Way for the Jewish deaf, Yachad for the developmentally disabled, and NCSY in Israel. *Keeping Posted with NCSY; Face the Nation—President's Newsletter; Oreich Yomeinu—Education Newsletter.*

———, WOMEN'S BRANCH (1923). 156 Fifth Ave., NYC 10010. (212)929-8857. Pres. Gitti Needleman; UN-NGO Rep. Fanny Wald. Seeks to spread the understanding and practice of Orthodox Judaism and to unite all Orthodox women and their synagogal organizations; services affiliates with educational and programming materials, leadership, and organizational guidance, and has an NGO representative at the UN. *Hachodesh; Hakol.*

UNION OF ORTHODOX RABBIS OF THE UNITED STATES AND CANADA (1900). 235 E. Broadway, NYC 10002. (212)964-6337. Dir. Rabbi Hersh M. Ginsberg. Seeks to foster and promote Torah-true Judaism in the U.S. and Canada; assists in the establishment and maintenance of *yeshivot* in the U.S.; maintains committee on marriage and divorce and aids individuals with marital difficulties; disseminates knowledge of traditional Jewish rites and practices and publishes regulations on synagogal structure; maintains rabbinical court for resolving individual and communal conflicts. *HaPardes.*

UNION OF SEPHARDIC CONGREGATIONS, INC. (1929). 8 W. 70 St., NYC 10023. (212)873-0300. Pres. The Haham Solomon

Gaon; Bd. Chmn. Victor Tarry. Promotes the religious interests of Sephardic Jews; prepares and distributes Sephardic prayer books; provides religious leaders for Sephardic congregations.

UNITED LUBAVITCHER YESHIVOTH (1940). 841-853 Ocean Pkwy., Brooklyn, NY 11230. (718)859-7600. Pres. Eli N. Sklar; Chmn. Exec. Com. Rabbi S. Gourary. Supports and organizes Jewish day schools and rabbinical seminaries in the U.S. and abroad.

UNITED SYNAGOGUE OF AMERICA (1913). 155 Fifth Ave., NYC 10010. (212)533-7800. Pres. Franklin D. Kreutzer; Exec. V.-Pres. Benjamin Z. Kreitman; Sr. V.-Pres./Chief Exec. Off. Jerome M. Epstein. International organization of 850 Conservative congregations. Maintains 12 departments and 20 regional offices to assist its affiliates with religious, educational, youth, community, and administrative programming and guidance; aims to enhance the cause of Conservative Judaism, further religious observance, encourage establishment of Jewish religious schools, draw youth closer to Jewish tradition. Extensive Israel programs. *Program Suggestions; United Synagogue Review; Yearbook Directory and Buyers' Guide; Book Service Catalogue of Publications.*

———, COMMISSION ON JEWISH COMMUNITY AND PUBLIC POLICY (1958). 155 Fifth Ave., NYC 10010. Cochmn. Burton Citak, Rabbi Zachary Heller; Dir. Rabbi Benjamin Z. Kreitman. Consists of representatives of United Synagogue of America, Women's League for Conservative Judaism, Rabbinical Assembly, and Federation of Jewish Men's Clubs; reviews public issues and cooperates with civic and Jewish community organizations to achieve social-action goals. *Today: Hayom.*

———, COMMISSION ON JEWISH EDUCATION (1930). 155 Fifth Ave., NYC 10010. (212)260-8450. Cochmn. Rabbi Joel H. Zaiman, Harry S. Katz; Dir. Morton K. Siegel. Promotes higher educational standards in Conservative congregational schools and Solomon Schechter Day Schools and publishes material for the advancement of their educational programs. Provides guidance and resources for adult-education programs; publishes the *Jewish Tract* series; distributes El-Am edition of Talmud and black-and-white and color films of "Eternal Light" TV programs on Jewish subjects. *In Your Hands; Your Child; Kol Bana'yikh.*

———, JEWISH EDUCATORS ASSEMBLY (1951). 15 E. 26 St., NYC 10010. (212)532-4949. Pres. Rabbi Marim D. Charry; Exec. Dir. Benjamin Margolis. Advances the development of Jewish education on all levels in consonance with the philosophy of the Conservative movement. Promotes Jewish education as a basis for the creative continuity of the Jewish people. Serves as a forum for the exchange of ideas, programs, and educational media. *The Observer; bulletins; newsletters; Tamtzit.*

———, KADIMA (formerly PRE-USY; reorg. 1968). 155 Fifth Ave., NYC 10010. (212)-533-7800. Exec. Dir. Daniel B. Ripps. Involves Jewish preteens in a meaningful religious, educational, and social environment; fosters a sense of identity and commitment to the Jewish community and the Conservative movement; conducts synagogue-based chapter programs and regional Kadima days and weekends. *Mitzvah of the Month; Kadima Kesher; Chagim; Advisors Aid; Games; quarterly Kadima magazine.*

———, NATIONAL ASSOCIATION OF SYNAGOGUE ADMINISTRATORS (1948). 155 Fifth Ave., NYC 10010. (212)533-7800. Pres. Harvey L. Brown. Aids congregations affiliated with the United Synagogue of America to further aims of Conservative Judaism through more effective administration (PALS Program); advances professional standards and promotes new methods in administration; cooperates in United Synagogue placement services and administrative surveys. *NASA Newsletter; NASA Journal.*

———, UNITED SYNAGOGUE YOUTH OF (1951). 155 Fifth Ave., NYC 10010. (212)-533-7800. Pres. Charles Savenor; Exec. Dir. Rabbi Paul Freedman. Seeks to strengthen identification with Conservative Judaism, based on the personality development, needs, and interests of the adolescent, in a Mitzvah framework. *Achshav; Tikun Olam; A.J. Heschel Honor Society Newsletter; SATO Newsletter; USY Alumni Assn. Newsletter; USY Program Bank.*

VAAD MISHMERETH STAM (1976). 4902 16 Ave., Brooklyn, NY 11204. (718)438-4963. Exec. Dir. Rabbi Yakov Basch. A nonprofit consumer-protection agency dedicated to preserving and protecting the halakhic integrity of Torah scrolls, phylacteries, and *mezuzot.* Makes presentations and conducts examination campaigns in schools and synagogues. *The Jewish Quill.*

WEST COAST TALMUDICAL SEMINARY (Yeshiva Ohr Elchonon Chabad) (1953). 7215 Warring St., Los Angeles, CA 90046. (213)937-3763. Pres. Meilech DuBrow; Dean Rabbi Ezra Schochet. Provides facilities for intensive Torah education as well as Orthodox rabbinical training on the West Coast; conducts an accredited college preparatory high school combined with a full program of Torah-talmudic training and a graduate talmudical division on the college level. *Torah Quiz; Kobetz Migdal Ohr.*

WOMEN'S LEAGUE FOR CONSERVATIVE JUDAISM (1918). 48 E. 74 St., NYC 10021. (212)628-1600. Pres. Evelyn Auerbach; Exec. Bernice Balter. Constitutes parent body of Conservative (Masorti) women's groups in U.S., Canada, Puerto Rico, Mexico, and Israel; provides them with programs and resources in Jewish education, social action, Israel affairs, Canadian public affairs, leadership training, services to the disabled, community affairs, and publicity techniques; publishes books of Jewish interest; contributes to support of Jewish Theological Seminary and its residence halls. *Women's League Outlook; Ba'Olam.*

WORLD COUNCIL OF SYNAGOGUES (1957). 155 Fifth Ave., NYC 10010 (212)533-7693. Pres. Marshall Wolke; Exec. Dir. Barbara Kessel. International representative of Conservative organizations and congregations; promotes the growth and development of the Conservative movement in Israel and throughout the world; supports educational institutions overseas; holds biennial international conventions; represents the world Conservative movement on the Executive of the World Zionist Organization. *Jerusalem Newsletter; Spectrum.*

WORLD UNION FOR PROGRESSIVE JUDAISM, LTD. (1926). 838 Fifth Ave., NYC 10021. (212)249-0100. Pres. Gerard Daniel; Exec. Dir. Richard G. Hirsch; N. Amer. Dir. Martin Strelzer. International umbrella organization of Liberal Judaism; promotes and coordinates efforts of Liberal congregations throughout the world; starts new congregations, recruits rabbis and rabbinical students for all countries; organizes international conferences of Liberal Jews. *International Conference Reports; News and Views; Shalhevet* (Israel); *Teshuva* (Argentina); *Ammi.*

YAVNE HEBREW THEOLOGICAL SEMINARY (1924). PO Box 185, Brooklyn, NY 11218. (718)436-5610. Pres. Nathan Shapiro; Exec. Dir. Rabbi Solomon K. Shapiro. School for higher Jewish learning; maintains Machon Maharshal branch in Jerusalem for higher Jewish education and for an exchange student program. *Otzar Hashe'elot Vehateshuvot; Yavne Newsletter.*

YESHIVA UNIVERSITY (1886). 500 W. 185 St., NYC 10033. (212)960-5400. Pres. Norman Lamm; Chmn. Bd. of Trustees, Herbert Tenzer. The nation's oldest and largest independent university founded under Jewish auspices, with a broad range of undergraduate, graduate, and professional schools, a network of affiliates, publications, a widespread program of research and community outreach, and a museum. Curricula lead to bachelor's, master's, doctoral, and professional degrees. Undergraduate schools provide general studies curricula supplemented by courses in Jewish learning; graduate schools prepare for careers in medicine, law, social work, Jewish education, psychology, Semitic languages, literatures, and cultures, and other fields. It has six undergraduate schools, seven graduate and professional schools, and three affiliates, with its four main centers located in Manhattan and the Bronx. *Alumni Review/Inside YU.*

Undergraduate schools for men at Main Center: Yeshiva College (Dean Norman Rosenfeld) provides liberal arts and sciences curricula; grants BA and BS degrees. Isaac Breuer College of Hebraic Studies (Dean Rabbi Jacob M. Rabinowitz) awards Hebraic Studies and Hebrew teacher's diploma, AA, BA, and BS. James Striar School of General Jewish Studies (Dir. Rabbi Benjamin Yudin) grants AA degree. Yeshiva Program/Mazer School of Talmudic Studies (Dean Rabbi Zevulun Charlop) offers advanced course of study in talmudic texts and commentaries.

Undergraduate school for women at Midtown Center, 245 Lexington Ave., NYC 10016: Stern College for Women (Dean Karen Bacon) offers liberal arts and sciences curricula supplemented by Jewish studies courses; awards BA, BS, BS in education, AA, Jewish Studies certificate, Hebrew teacher's diploma.

Sy Syms School of Business at Main Center (Dean Michael Schiff) offers undergraduate business study in conjunction with study at Yeshiva College or Stern College; grants BS in business.

Sponsors one high school for boys (Manhattan) and one for girls (Queens).

Universitywide services include the Irving and Hanni Rosenbaum Aliyah Incentive Fund; Jacob E. Safra Institute of Sephardic Studies; Ivan L. Tillem Program for Special Services for the Jewish Elderly; Holocaust Studies Program; Interdisciplinary Conference on Bereavement and Grief; Yeshiva University Gerontological Institute; Yeshiva University Museum; Yeshiva University Press.

———, ALBERT EINSTEIN COLLEGE OF MEDICINE (1955). 1300 Morris Pk. Ave., Bronx, NY 10461. (212)430-2000. Pres. Norman Lamm; Chmn. Bd. of Overseers Burton P. Resnick; Dean Dr. Dominick P. Purpura. Prepares physicians, conducts research in the health sciences, and provides patient care; awards MD degree; includes Sue Golding Graduate Division of Medical Sciences (Dir. Dr. Leslie Leinwand), which grants PhD degree. Einstein College's clinical facilities and affiliates encompass Jack D. Weiler Hospital of Albert Einstein College of Medicine, Bronx Municipal Hospital Center, Montefiore Hospital and Medical Center, and the Rose F. Kennedy Center for Research in Mental Retardation and Human Development. *Einstein; AECOM Today; Einstein Quarterly Journal of Biology and Medicine.*

———, ALUMNI OFFICE, 500 W. 185 Street, NYC 10033. (212)960-5373. Dir. E. Yechiel Simon. Seeks to foster a close allegiance of alumni to their alma mater by maintaining ties with all alumni and servicing the following associations: Yeshiva College Alumni (Pres. Henry Rothman); Stern College Alumnae (Pres. Rachel E. Oppenheim); Albert Einstein College of Medicine Alumni (Pres. Dr. Marvin Kirschner); Ferkauf Graduate School Alumni (Pres. Alvin I. Schiff); Wurzweiler School of Social Work Alumni (Pres. Eileen Stein Himber); Bernard Revel Graduate School—Harry Fischel School Alumni (Pres. Bernard Rosensweig); Rabbinic Alumni (Pres. Rabbi Steven Dworken); Benjamin N. Cardozo School of Law Alumni (Pres. Noel Ferris). Alumni Council (Chmn. Abraham S. Guterman) offers guidance to Pres. and Bd. of Trustees on university's academic development and service activities. *Alumni Review/Inside; AECOM Alumni News; Jewish Social Work Forum.*

———, BELFER INSTITUTE FOR ADVANCED BIOMEDICAL STUDIES (1978). 1300 Morris Pk. Ave., Bronx, NY 10461. (212)430-2801. Dir. Dr. Ernest R. Jaffé. Integrates and coordinates the Medical College's postdoctoral research and training-grant programs in the basic and clinical biomedical sciences in the College of Medicine. Awards certificate as Research Fellow or Research Associate on completion of training.

———, BENJAMIN N. CARDOZO SCHOOL OF LAW (1976). 55 Fifth Ave., NYC 10003. (212)790-0310. Pres. Norman Lamm; Bd. Chmn. Jacob Burns; Dean Monroe E. Price. Provides innovative courses of study within a traditional legal framework; program includes judicial internships; grants Doctor of Law (JD) degree. Center for Professional Development assists students in obtaining employment. Leonard and Bea Diener Institute of Jewish Law explores American and Jewish jurisprudence. Bet Tzedek Legal Services Clinic provides services to low-income individuals; Samuel & Ronnie Heyman Center on Corporate Governance supports programs such as Tax Court Clinic. *Cardozo Law Review; Arts and Entertainment Law Journal; Women's Annotated Legal Bibliography; Assoc. of Student Internatl. Law Societies Internatl. Law Journal; Cardozo Law Forum.*

———, BERNARD REVEL GRADUATE SCHOOL (1937). 500 W. 185 St., NYC 10033. (212)960-5253. Dean Leo Landman. Offers graduate work in Judaic studies and Semitic languages, literatures, and cultures; confers MS, MA, and PhD degrees.

———, BROOKDALE INSTITUTE FOR THE STUDY OF GERONTOLOGY (WURZWEILER SCHOOL OF SOCIAL WORK) (1978). 2495 Amsterdam Ave., NYC 10033. (212)960-0808. Dir. Celia B. Weisman. Aims to further advanced education in the field of gerontology and to introduce gerontology into the curriculum in the undergraduate and graduate schools.

———, DAVID J. AZRIELI GRADUATE INSTITUTE OF JEWISH EDUCATION AND ADMINISTRATION (1945). 245 Lexington Ave., NYC 10016. (212)340-7705. Dir. Yitzchak Handel. Offers MS degree in Jewish elementary and secondary education; specialist's certificate and EdD programs in administration and supervision of Jewish education. Block Summer Education Program in administration and supervision of Jewish education. Prepares teachers and administrators in Jewish education for positions throughout the world.

———, FERKAUF GRADUATE SCHOOL OF PSYCHOLOGY (1957). 1300 Morris Pk. Ave., 5th fl., NYC 10461. (212)430-4201. Dean Morton Berger. Offers MA in general psychology; PsyD in clinical and school psychology; and PhD in clinical, developmental-experimental (concentration in health) and school psychology. Center for Psychological and Psychoeducation Services offers counseling, diagnostic evaluation, and psychotherapy.

———, HARRY FISCHEL SCHOOL FOR HIGHER JEWISH STUDIES (1945). 500 W. 185 St., NYC 10033. Dean Leo Landman. Offers summer graduate programs in Judaic studies and Semitic languages, literatures, and cultures; confers MS, MA, and PhD degrees.

———, (affiliate) RABBI ISAAC ELCHANAN THEOLOGICAL SEMINARY (1896). 2540 Amsterdam Ave., NYC 10033. (212)960-5344. Chmn. Bd. of Trustees Judah Feinerman; Dean Rabbi Zevulun Charlop. Offers comprehensive program for preparing Orthodox rabbis; grants *semikhah* (ordination) and the degrees of Master of Religious Education, Master of Hebrew Literature, Doctor of Religious Education, and Doctor of Hebrew Literature. Includes Rabbi Joseph B. Soloveitchik Center of Rabbinic Studies, Marcos and Adina Katz Kollel (Institute for Advanced Research in Rabbinics, Dir. Rabbi Hershel Schachter), Kollel L'Horaah (Yadin Yadin; Dir. Rabbi J. David Bleich), Caroline and Joseph S. Gruss Kollel Elyon (Dir. Rabbi Aharon Kahn), Chaver Program (Dir. Rabbi J. David Bleich), Caroline and Joseph S. Gruss Institute in Jerusalem (Dir. Rabbi Aharon Lichtenstein). Brookdale Chaplaincy Internship Program trains prospective rabbis to work effectively with the elderly. Maybaum Sephardic Fellowship Program trains rabbis for service in Sephardic communities here and abroad. Morris and Nellie L. Kawaler Rabbinic Training Program emphasizes professional aspects of the rabbinate. Philip and Sarah Belz School of Jewish Music (Dir. Cantor Bernard Beer) provides professional training of cantors and other musical personnel; awards Associate Cantor's certificate and cantorial diploma. Max Stern Division of Communal Services (Assoc. Dir. Rabbi Kenneth Hain) provides personal and professional service to the rabbinate and related fields, as well as educational, consultative, organizational, and placement services to congregations, schools, and communal organizations throughout North America and abroad. Dr. Joseph and Rachel Ades Sephardic Community Outreach Program provides educational, religious, and cultural programs and personnel to Sephardic communities. Stone-Sapirstein Center for Jewish Education identifies and trains future educators through programs of learning, service, and internship; works with schools in the community and across the country; sponsors academic programs, lectures, and special projects throughout the university. National Commission on Torah Education and Educators Council of America formulate uniform educational standards, provide guidance to professional staffs, rabbis, and lay leaders with regard to curriculum, and promote Jewish education. Camp Morasha (Dir. Zvi Reich) offers Jewish studies program.

———, WOMEN'S ORGANIZATION (1928). 500 W. 185 St., NYC 10033. Pres. Ann Arbesfeld; Dir. Deborah Steinhorn. Supports Yeshiva University's national scholarship program for students training in education, community service, law, medicine, and other professions, and its development program. *YUWO News Briefs.*

———, WURZWEILER SCHOOL OF SOCIAL WORK (1957). 500 W. 185 St., NYC 10033. Chmn. Bd. of Governors Herbert H. Schiff; Dean Samuel Goldstein. Offers graduate programs in social casework, social group work, community social work; grants MSW and DSW degrees; two-year, full-time Concurrent Plan (Dir. Naomi

Lazarus) combines classroom study and supervised field instruction; the Extended Plan permits a period of up to five years to complete requirements for some master's degree candidates. Block Education Plan (Dir. Frances A. Sosnoff) provides field instruction in Jewish communities in the U.S., Canada, Europe, and Israel. Clergy Plan (Dir. Naomi Lazarus) provides training in counseling for clergymen of all denominations. Plan for Employed Persons (Dir. Naomi Lazarus) is specifically designed for people working in social agencies.

———, (affiliate) YESHIVA UNIVERSITY OF LOS ANGELES (1977). 9760 W. Pico Blvd., Los Angeles, CA 90035. (213)553-4478. Dean Rabbi Marvin Hier; Bd. Chmn. Samuel Belzberg; Dir. Academic Programs Rabbi Sholom Tendler. Grants BA degree in Jewish studies. Has university program and graduate studies department. Also provides Jewish studies program for beginners. Affiliates are Yeshiva University of Los Angeles High School and the Jewish Studies Institute.

———, SIMON WIESENTHAL CENTER (1977). 9760 W. Pico Blvd., Los Angeles, CA 90035. (213)553-9036. Dean Rabbi Marvin Hier; Assoc. Dean Rabbi Abraham Cooper; Dir. Dr. Gerald Margolis. Branch Offices: 5715 N. Lincoln Ave., Suite #16, Chicago, IL 60659, (312)989-0022; 342 Madison Ave., Suite #320, NYC, 10017, (212)370-0320. Dedicated to preserving memory of the Holocaust through education and awareness. Programs: museum; library; archives; "Testimony to Truth" Oral History Program; educational outreach; Scholars' Forum; International Social Action Agenda. *Simon Wiesenthal Center Annual; Response Magazine; Page One* (syndicated weekly radio news magazine presenting contemporary Jewish issues).

YESHIVATH TORAH VODAATH AND MESIVTA RABBINICAL SEMINARY (1918). 425 E. 9 St., Brooklyn, NY 11218. (718)-941-8000. Pres. Henry Hirsch; Bd. Chmn. Fred F. Weiss; Sec. Earl H. Spero. Offers Hebrew and secular education from elementary level through rabbinical ordination and postgraduate work; maintains a teachers institute and community-service bureau; maintains a dormitory and a nonprofit camp program for boys. *Chronicle; Mesivta Vanguard; Thought of the Week; Torah Vodaath News.*

———, ALUMNI ASSOCIATION (1941). 425 E. 9 St., Brooklyn, NY 11218. (718)941-8000. Pres. Marcus Saffer; Bd. Chmn. Seymour Pluchenik. Promotes social and cultural ties between the alumni and the schools through fund raising; offers vocational guidance to students; operates Camp Torah Vodaath; sponsors research fellowship program for boys. *Annual Journal; Hamesivta Torah periodical.*

SOCIAL, MUTUAL BENEFIT

AMERICAN FEDERATION OF JEWS FROM CENTRAL EUROPE, INC. (1942). 570 Seventh Ave., NYC 10018. (212)921-3871. Pres. K. Peter Lekisch; Bd. Chmn. Curt C. Silberman; Exec. Asst. Katherine Rosenthal. Seeks to safeguard the rights and interests of American Jews of Central European descent, especially in reference to restitution and indemnification; through its Research Foundation for Jewish Immigration, sponsors research and publications on the history of Central European Jewry and the history of its immigration and acculturation in the U.S.; sponsors a social program for needy Nazi victims in the U.S. in cooperation with United Help, Inc. and other specialized social agencies; undertakes cultural activities, annual conferences, publications, and lecture programs; member, Council of Jews from Germany.

AMERICAN SEPHARDI FEDERATION (1973). 8 W. 40 St., Suite 1607, NYC 10018. (212)-730-1210. Pres. Leon Levy; Exec. V.-Pres. Joshua Toledano. Seeks to preserve the Sephardi heritage in the U.S., Israel, and throughout the world by fostering and supporting religious and cultural activities of Sephardi congregations, organizations, and communities, and uniting them in one overall organization; supports Jewish institutions of higher learning and those that train Sephardi lay and religious leaders; assists Sephardi charitable, cultural, religious, and educational institutions everywhere; publishes and/or disseminates books and other literature dealing with Sephardi culture and tradition in the U.S.; organizes youth and young-adult activities throughout the U.S.; supports efforts of the World Sephardi Federation to alleviate social disparities in Israel. *Sephardic Connection; Sephardic Highlights.*

AMERICAN VETERANS OF ISRAEL (1949). c/o Samuel E. Alexander, 548 E. Walnut St., Long Beach, NY 11561. (516)431-8316. Pres. Murray Aronoff; Sec. Samuel E. Alexander. Maintains contact with American and Canadian volunteers who served in Aliyah Bet and/or Israel's War of Independence; promotes Israel's welfare; holds memorial services at grave of Col. David Marcus; is affiliated with World Mahal. *Newsletter.*

ASSOCIATION OF YUGOSLAV JEWS IN THE UNITED STATES, INC. (1941). 247 W. 99 St., NYC 10025. (212)865-2211. Pres. Sal Musafia; Sec.-Treas. Mile Weiss. Assists all Jews originally from Yugoslavia; raises funds for Israeli agencies and institutions. *Bulletin.*

BNAI ZION—THE AMERICAN FRATERNAL ZIONIST ORGANIZATION (1908). 136 E. 39 St., NYC 10016. (212)725-1211. Pres. Ernest Zelig; Exec. V.-Pres. Mel Parness. Fosters principles of Americanism, fraternalism, and Zionism; offers life insurance, Blue Cross and Blue Shield and other benefits to its members. Sponsors various projects in Israel: settlements, youth centers, medical clinics, Bnai Zion Home for Retarded Children (in Rosh Ha'ayin), the Haifa Medical Center, and the Herman Z. Quittman Center in Hakfar Hashwedi in Jerusalem. Has Young Leadership Division. *Bnai Zion Voice; Bnai Zion Foundation Newsletter; The Challenge; Haifa Happenings.*

BRITH ABRAHAM (1887). 136 E. 39 St., NYC 10016. (212)725-1211. Grand Master Robert Freeman. Protects Jewish rights and combats anti-Semitism; supports Soviet and Ethiopian emigration and the safety and dignity of Jews worldwide; furnishes regular financial assistance to Beit Halochem for the Israeli war disabled, Haifa Medical Center, Rosh Ha'ayin Home for Retarded Children, Kupat Cholim diagnostic centers, libraries, educational facilities, and other institutions to relieve the social burdens on the Israeli economy; aids and supports various programs and projects in the U.S.: Hebrew Excellence Program—Gold Medal presentation in high schools and colleges; Camp Loyaltown; Brith Abraham and Bnai Zion Foundations. *Voice.*

BRITH SHOLOM (1905). 3939 Conshohocken Ave., Philadelphia, PA 19131. (215)878-5696. Pres. Albert Bernbaum; Exec. Dir. Mervin L. Krimins. Fraternal organization devoted to community welfare, protection of rights of Jewish people, and activities which foster Jewish identity and provide support for Israel; sponsors Brith Sholom House for senior citizens in Philadelphia and Brith Sholom Beit Halochem in Haifa, a rehabilitation center for Israel's permanently war-wounded. *Brith Sholom Presents; monthly news bulletin.*

CENTRAL SEPHARDIC JEWISH COMMUNITY OF AMERICA (1940). 8 W. 70 St., NYC 10023. (212)787-2850. Pres. Morris Halfon; Sec. Isaac Molho. Seeks to foster Sephardic culture, education, and communal institutions. Sponsors wide range of activities; raises funds for Sephardic causes in U.S. and Israel.

FREE SONS OF ISRAEL (1849). 180 Varick St., 14th fl., NYC 10014. (212)924-6566. Grand Master Robert Grant; Grand Sec. Stanley Siflinger. Promotes fraternalism; supports State of Israel, UJA, Soviet Jewry, Israel Bonds, and other Jewish charities; fights anti-Semitism; awards scholarships. *National Reporter; Digest.*

JEWISH LABOR BUND (Directed by WORLD COORDINATING COMMITTEE OF THE BUND) (1897; reorg. 1947). 25 E. 21 St., NYC 10010. (212)475-0059. Exec. Sec. Joel Litewka. Coordinates activities of Bund organizations throughout the world and represents them in the Socialist International; spreads the ideas of socialism as formulated by the Jewish Labor Bund; publishes books and periodicals on world problems, Jewish life, socialist theory and policy, and on the history, activities, and ideology of the Jewish Labor Bund. *Unser Tsait* (U.S.); *Lebns-Fragn* (Israel); *Unser Gedank* (Australia); *Unser Shtimme* (France).

ROUMANIAN JEWISH FEDERATION OF AMERICA, INC. (1956). 135 W. 106 St., #2M, NYC 10025. (212)866-0692. Pres. Charles H. Kremer; Sec. Treas. Marian Marcu. Interested in protecting the welfare, preserving the culture, and easing the plight of Jews of Rumanian descent throughout the world. Works to influence the Rumanian government to grant freedom of worship to Jews and permission for their emigration to Israel.

SEPHARDIC JEWISH BROTHERHOOD OF AMERICA, INC. (1915). 97-29 64 Rd., Rego

Park, NY 11374. (718)459-1600. Pres. Bernard Ouziel; Sec. Michael Cohen. Promotes the industrial, social, educational, and religious welfare of its members; offers funeral and burial benefits, scholarships, and aid to the needy. *Sephardic Brother.*

UOTS, INC. (1846). 212 Fifth Ave., NYC 10010. (212)679-6790. Pres. Sylvia Fishgall; Exec. Off. Dorothy B. Giuriceo. Philanthropic, community service, especially for cancer victims; supports camps for children with cancer.

WORKMEN'S CIRCLE (1900). 45 E. 33 St., NYC 10016. (212)889-6800. Pres. Barnett Zumoff; Exec. Dir. Jack Noskowitz. Provides fraternal benefits and activities, Jewish educational programs, secularist Yiddish schools for children, and community activities; supports institutions in Israel and promotes public-affairs activities in the U.S. on international and national issues. Underwrites "Folksbiene," worldwide Yiddish cultural, music, and theatrical festivals. Allied to *Jewish Forward* and WEVD. *Workmen's Circle Call; Kultur un Leben.*

———, DIVISION OF JEWISH LABOR COMMITTEE (*see* p. 433)

SOCIAL WELFARE

AMC CANCER RESEARCH CENTER (formerly JEWISH CONSUMPTIVES' RELIEF SOCIETY, 1904; incorporated as AMERICAN MEDICAL CENTER AT DENVER, 1954). 1600 Pierce, Denver, CO 80214. (303)233-6501. Pres. Dr. Marvin A. Rich. Dedicated to advancing knowledge of cancer prevention, detection, diagnosis, and treatment through programs of laboratory, clinical, and community cancer control research. *Quarterly bulletin; annual report.*

AMERICAN JEWISH CORRECTIONAL CHAPLAINS ASSOCIATION, INC. (formerly NATIONAL COUNCIL OF JEWISH PRISON CHAPLAINS) (1937). 10 E. 73 St., NYC 10021-4194. (212)879-8415. (Cooperates with the New York Board of Rabbis and Jewish Family Service.) Pres. Rabbi Irving Koslowe; Exec. Dir. Rabbi Paul L. Hait; Assoc. Dir. Rabbi Moses A. Birnbaum. Provides religious services and guidance to Jewish men and women in penal and correctional institutions; serves as a liaison between inmates and their families; upgrades the quality of correctional ministrations through conferences, professional workshops, and conventions. *Bulletin.*

AMERICAN JEWISH SOCIETY FOR SERVICE, INC. (1949). 15 E. 26 St., Rm. 1302, NYC 10010. (212)683-6178. Pres. E. Kenneth Marx; Exec. Dir. Elly Saltzman. Conducts voluntary work-service camps each summer to enable high school juniors and seniors to perform humanitarian service.

ASSOCIATION OF JEWISH COMMUNITY ORGANIZATION PERSONNEL (1969). 1175 College Ave., Columbus, OH 43209. (614)-237-7686. Pres. Herman Markowitz; Exec. Dir. Ben Mandelkorn. An organization of professionals engaged in areas of fund raising, endowments, budgeting, social planning, financing, administration and coordination of services. Objectives are to develop and enhance professional practices in Jewish communal work; to maintain and improve standards, practices, scope and public understanding of the field of community organization, as practiced through local federations, national agencies, other organizations, settings, and private practitioners.

ASSOCIATION OF JEWISH FAMILY AND CHILDREN'S AGENCIES (1972). 3084 State Hwy. 27, Suite 1—PO Box 248, Kendall Park, NJ 08824-0248. (201)821-0909. Pres. Bernard B. Nebenzahl; Exec. Dir. Bert J. Goldberg. The national service organization for Jewish family and children's agencies in Canada and the U.S. Reinforces member agencies in their efforts to sustain and enhance the quality of Jewish family and communal life. Operates the Elder Support Network for the National Jewish Community. *Bimonthly Bulletin; Directory; Job Openings Memo.*

ASSOCIATION OF JEWISH FAMILY AND CHILDREN'S AGENCY PROFESSIONALS (1965). c/o NYANA, 225 Park Ave. S., NYC 10003. (212)674-7400. Pres. Arnold Marks; Exec. Dir. Solomon H. Green. Brings together Jewish caseworkers and related professionals in Jewish family, children's, and health services. Seeks to improve personnel standards, further Jewish continuity and identity, and strengthen Jewish family life; provides forums for professional discussion at national conference of Jewish communal service and regional meetings; takes action on social-policy issues. *Newsletter.*

BARON DE HIRSCH FUND (1891). 130 E. 59 St., NYC 10022. (212)836-1798. Pres. Ezra Pascal Mager; Mng. Dir. Lauren Katzowitz. Aids Jewish immigrants and their children in the U.S. and Israel by giving grants to agencies active in educational and vocational fields; has limited program for study tours in U.S. by Israeli agriculturists.

B'NAI B'RITH INTERNATIONAL (1843). 1640 Rhode Island Ave., NW, Washington, DC 20036. (202)857-6600. Pres. Seymour D. Reich; Exec. V.-Pres. Daniel Thursz. International Jewish organization with affiliates in 43 countries. Offers programs designed to insure the preservation of Jewry and Judaism: Jewish education, community volunteer service to aid the needy, expansion of human rights, assistance to Israel, housing for the elderly, leadership training for youths and adults, rights of Soviet Jews and Jews of other countries to emigrate. *The International Jewish Monthly; Shofar; Insider.*

———, ANTI-DEFAMATION LEAGUE OF (*see* p. 432)

———, CAREER AND COUNSELING SERVICES (1938). 1640 Rhode Island Ave. NW, Washington, DC 20036. (202)857-6532. Chmn. Burton M. Wanetik; Natl. Dir. Max F. Baer. Offers educational and career counseling to Jewish youth and adults on a group and individual basis through professionally staffed centers in New York, North Jersey, and Philadelphia.

———, HILLEL FOUNDATIONS, INC. (*see* p. 443)

———, KLUTZNICK MUSEUM (*see* p. 436)

———, YOUTH ORGANIZATION (*see* p. 443)

B'NAI B'RITH WOMEN (1897). 1640 Rhode Island Ave., NW, Washington, DC 20036. (202)857-6689. Pres. Irma Gertler; Exec. Dir. Elaine Binder. Promotes the principles of social advancement through education, action, and service. Offers programs that contribute to preservation of Jewish life and values; supports treatment of emotionally disturbed boys in BBW Children's Home, Group House in Israel; advocacy for women's rights. *Jewish Woman.*

CITY OF HOPE NATIONAL MEDICAL CENTER AND BECKMAN RESEARCH INSTITUTE (1913). 1500 E. Duarte Rd., Duarte, CA 91010. (818)359-8111. Pres. and Chief Exec. Off. Dr. Sanford M. Shapero; Bd. Chmn. Abraham S. Bolsky. Offers care to those with cancer and major diseases, medical consultation service for second opinions, and pilot research programs in genetics, immunology, and the basic life process. *Pilot; President's Newsletter; City of Hope Quarterly.*

CONFERENCE OF JEWISH COMMUNAL SERVICE (1899). 3084 State Hwy., Suite 1, Kendall Park, NJ 08824-1657. (201)821-1871. Pres. Ethel Taft; Exec. Dir. Joel Ollander. Serves as forum for all professional philosophies in community service, for testing new experiences, proposing new ideas, and questioning or reaffirming old concepts; umbrella organization for eight major Jewish communal service groups. Concerned with advancement of professional personnel practices and standards. *Concurrents; Journal of Jewish Communal Service.*

COUNCIL OF JEWISH FEDERATIONS, INC. (1932). 730 Broadway, NYC 10003. (212)-475-5000. Pres. Mandell Berman; Exec. V.-Pres. Carmi Schwartz. Provides national and regional services to 200 associated federations embracing 800 communities in the U.S. and Canada, aiding in fund raising, community organization, health and welfare planning, personnel recruitment, and public relations. *Directory of Jewish Federations, Welfare Funds and Community Councils; Directory of Jewish Health and Welfare Agencies* (biennial); *annual report.*

HOPE CENTER FOR THE RETARDED (1965). 3601 Martin L. King Blvd., Denver, CO 80205. (303)388-4801. Pres. Lester Goldstein; Exec. Dir. George E. Brantley; Sec. Helen Fonda. Provides services to developmentally disabled of community: preschool training, day training and work activities center, speech and language pathology, occupational arts and crafts, recreational therapy, and social services.

INTERNATIONAL COUNCIL ON JEWISH SOCIAL AND WELFARE SERVICES (1961). c/o American Jewish Joint Distribution Committee, 711 Third Ave., NYC 10017. (NY liaison office with UN headquarters.) (212)687-6200. Chmn. Hon. L.H.L. Cohen; Exec. Sec. Leon Leiberg. Provides for exchange of views and information among member agencies on problems of

Jewish social and welfare services, including medical care, old age, welfare, child care, rehabilitation, technical assistance, vocational training, agricultural and other resettlement, economic assistance, refugees, migration, integration and related problems, representation of views to governments and international organizations. Members: six national and international organizations.

JEWISH BRAILLE INSTITUTE OF AMERICA, INC. (1931). 110 E. 30 St., NYC 10016. (212)889-2525. Pres. Jane Evans; Exec. V.-Pres. Gerald M. Kass. Serves the religious, cultural, and educational needs of the Jewish blind, visually impaired, and reading-disabled by producing books of Judaica, including prayer books in Hebrew and English braille, large print, and on audio cassettes. Maintains free lending library of Hebrew, English, Yiddish, and other-language cassettes for the Jewish blind, visually impaired, and reading-disabled in 40 countries. *Jewish Braille Review; JBI Voice; Or Chadash.*

JEWISH CONCILIATION BOARD OF AMERICA, INC. (1930). 235 Park Ave. S., NYC 10003. (212)777-9034. Pres. Milton J. Schubin; Exec. Dir. Beatrice Lampert. Offers dispute-resolution services to families, individuals, and organizations. Social-work, rabbinic, and legal expertise are available for family and divorce mediation and arbitration. Fee—sliding scale.

JEWISH FUND FOR JUSTICE (1984). 1334 G St., NW, Suite 601, Washington, DC 20005. (202)638-0550. Pres. Si Kahn; Exec. Dir. Lois Roisman. A national grant-making institution supporting efforts to combat poverty in the U.S. Acts as a catalyst to increase Jewish communal and individual involvement in social-justice issues; participates in grant-making coalitions with other religious and ethnic groups. *Newsletter.*

JWB (1917). 15 E. 26 St., NYC 10010. (212)-532-4949. Pres. Donald R. Mintz; Exec. V.-Pres. Arthur Rotman. Leadership agency for North American network of Jewish community centers, YM-YWHAs, and camps, serving one million Jews. Provides Jewish educational and cultural programming through JWB Jewish Book and Music Councils, Lecture Bureau. U.S. government-accredited agency serving Jewish military families and hospitalized VA patients through JWB Jewish Chaplains Council. *JWB Circle; JWBriefing; Zarkor; JWB Personnel Reporter.*

———, JEWISH BOOK COUNCIL (*see* p. 438)

———, JEWISH CHAPLAINS COUNCIL (formerly COMMISSION ON JEWISH CHAPLAINCY) (1940). 15 E. 26 St., NYC 10010. Chmn. Rabbi Aaron Landes; Dir. Rabbi David Lapp. Recruits, endorses, and serves Jewish military and Veterans Administration chaplains on behalf of the American Jewish community and the three major rabbinic bodies; trains and assists Jewish lay leaders where there are no chaplains, for service to Jewish military personnel, their families, and hospitalized veterans. *Chaplines newsletter.*

———, JEWISH MUSIC COUNCIL (*see* p. 438)

———, LECTURE BUREAU (*see* p. 438)

LEVI ARTHRITIS HOSPITAL (sponsored by B'nai B'rith) (1914). 300 Prospect Ave., Hot Springs, AR 71901. (501)624-1281. Pres. Harry Levitch; Chief Exec. Off. Patrick G. McCabe, Jr. Maintains a nonprofit, nonsectarian hospital for treatment of sufferers from arthritis; offers postoperative bone and joint surgery rehabilitation; stroke rehabilitation; and posttrauma rehabilitation. *Levi Voice.*

NATIONAL ASSOCIATION OF JEWISH FAMILY, CHILDREN'S AND HEALTH PROFESSIONALS (*see* Association of Jewish Family and Children's Agency Professionals)

NATIONAL ASSOCIATION OF JEWISH VOCATIONAL SERVICES (formerly JEWISH OCCUPATIONAL COUNCIL) (1940). 225 Park Ave. S., 17th fl., NYC 10003. (212)529-7474. Pres. Harold E. Friedman; Exec. Dir. Harvey P. Goldman. Acts as coordinating body for all Jewish agencies in U.S., Canada, and Israel, having programs in educational-vocational guidance, job placement, vocational rehabilitation, skills-training, sheltered workshops, and occupational research. *Newsletter; NAJVS Reports.*

NATIONAL CONGRESS OF JEWISH DEAF (1956; inc. 1961). 4960 Sabal Palm Blvd., Bldg. 7, Tamarac, FL 33319. TTY (301)-345-8612. Pres. Dr. Martin Florsheim; Exec. Dir. Alexander Fleischman. Congress of Jewish congregations, service organizations, and associations located throughout the U.S. and Canada, advocating religious and cultural ideals and fellowship for the Jewish deaf. Publishes *Signs of Judaism,* a guide to American Sign Language. Affiliated with World Organization of Jewish Deaf.

NATIONAL COUNCIL OF JEWISH PRISON CHAPLAINS, INC. (*see* American Jewish Correctional Chaplains Association, Inc.)

NATIONAL COUNCIL OF JEWISH WOMEN (1893). 15 E. 26 St., NYC 10010. (212)532-1740. Pres. Lenore Feldman; Exec. Dir. Dadie Perlov. Furthers human welfare through program of community service, education, advocacy for children and youth, aging, women's issues, constitutional rights, Jewish life and Israel. Promotes education for the disadvantaged in Israel through the NCJW Research Institute for Innovation in Education at Hebrew University, Jerusalem. Promotes welfare of children in U.S. through Center for the Child. *NCJW Journal; Washington Newsletter.*

NATIONAL INSTITUTE FOR JEWISH HOSPICE (1985). 6363 Wilshire Blvd., Suite 126, Los Angeles, CA 90048. (213) HOSPICE. Pres. Rabbi Maurice Lamm. Serves as a national Jewish hospice resource center. Through conferences, research, publications, video training courses, referral, and counseling services offers guidance, training, and information to patients, family members, clergy of all faiths, professional caregivers, and volunteers who work with seriously ill Jews.

NATIONAL JEWISH CENTER FOR IMMUNOLOGY AND RESPIRATORY MEDICINE (formerly NATIONAL JEWISH HOSPITAL/NATIONAL ASTHMA CENTER) (1899). 1400 Jackson St., Denver, CO 80206. (303)388-4461; 1-800-222-5864; Pres. Michael K. Schonbrun; V.-Pres. Public Affairs, Jerry L. Colness. Leading medical center for study and treatment of respiratory diseases, allergies, and immune system disorders. Clinical emphasis on asthma, emphysema, tuberculosis, chronic bronchitis, and interstitial lung diseases; immune system disorders such as juvenile rheumatoid arthritis and immune deficiency disorders. *New Directions; Update; annual report; Lung Line Letter.*

NATIONAL JEWISH COMMITTEE ON SCOUTING (Boy Scouts of America) (1926). 1325 Walnut Hill La., Irving, TX 75038-3096. (214)580-2059. Chmn. Murray L. Cole; Dir. Fred Tichauer. Seeks to bring Jewish youth and adults closer to Judaism through Scouting programs. Works through local Jewish committees on Scouting to establish Tiger Cub groups (1st grade), Cub Scout packs, Boy Scout troops, and coed Explorer posts in synagogues, Jewish community centers, day schools, and other Jewish organizations wishing to draw Jewish youth. Support materials and resources on request. *Hatsofe.*

NATIONAL JEWISH GIRL SCOUT COMMITTEE (1972). Synagogue Council of America, 327 Lexington Ave., NYC 10016. (212)686-8670. Chmn. Rabbi Herbert W. Bomzer; Field Chmn. Adele Wasko. Under the auspices of the Synagogue Council of America, serves to further Jewish education by promoting Jewish award programs, encouraging religious services, promoting cultural exchanges with Israeli Boy & Girl Scouts Federation, and extending membership in the Jewish community by assisting councils in organizing Girl Scout troops and local Jewish Girl Scout committees. *Newsletter.*

NORTH AMERICAN ASSOCIATION OF JEWISH HOMES AND HOUSING FOR THE AGING (1960). 2525 Centerville Rd., Dallas, TX 75228. (214)327-4503. Pres. Richard S. Lamden; Exec. V.-Pres. Herbert Shore. Represents a community of not-for-profit charitable homes and housing for the Jewish aging; promotes excellence in performance and quality of service through fostering communication and education and encouraging advocacy for the aging.

WORLD CONFEDERATION OF JEWISH COMMUNITY CENTERS (1947). 15 E. 26 St., NYC 10010. (212)532-4949. Pres. Ralph Goldman; Exec. Dir. Don Scher. Serves as a council of national and continental federations of Jewish community centers; fosters development of the JCC movement worldwide; provides a forum for exchange of information among centers. *Newsletter.*

ZIONIST AND PRO-ISRAEL

ALYN—AMERICAN SOCIETY FOR HANDICAPPED CHILDREN IN ISRAEL (1954). 19 W. 44 St., NYC 10036. (212)869-8085. Chmn. Simone P. Blum; Exec. Dir. Nathan N. Schorr. Supports the work of

ALYN Orthopaedic Hospital and Rehabilitation Center for Physically Handicapped Children, located in Jerusalem, which encompasses a 100-bed hospital and outpatient clinics, and houses the Helena Rubinstein Foundation Research Institute for research in neuromuscular diseases. *ALYN News.*

AMERICA-ISRAEL CULTURAL FOUNDATION, INC. (1939). 485 Madison Ave., NYC 10022. (212)751-2700. Bd. Chmn. Isaac Stern; Pres. Carl Glick. Membership organization supporting Israeli cultural institutions, such as Israel Philharmonic and Israel Chamber Orchestra, Tel Aviv Museum, Rubin Academies, Bat Sheva Dance Co., Omanut La'am, and Tzlil Am; sponsors cultural exchange between U.S. and Israel; awards scholarships in all arts to young Israelis for study in Israel. *Hadashot.*

AMERICA-ISRAEL FRIENDSHIP LEAGUE, INC. (1971). 134 E. 39 St., NYC 10016. (212)213-8630. Pres. Herbert Tenzer; Exec. V.-Pres. Ilana Artman. A nonsectarian, nonpartisan organization which seeks to broaden the base of support for Israel among Americans of all faiths and backgrounds. Activities include educational exchanges, tours of Israel for American leadership groups, symposia and public education activities, and the dissemination of printed information. *Newsletter.*

AMERICAN ASSOCIATES, BEN-GURION UNIVERSITY OF THE NEGEV (1973). 342 Madison Ave., Suite 1924, NYC 10173. (212)-687-7721. Pres. Arnold Forster; Bd. Chmn. Irwin H. Goldenberg; Exec. V.-Pres. Donald L. Gartner. Serves as the university's publicity and fund-raising link to the U.S. The Associates are committed to publicizing university activities and curricula, securing student scholarships, transferring contributions, and encouraging American interest in the university. *AABGU Reporter; BGU Bulletin; Negev.*

AMERICAN COMMITTEE FOR SHAARE ZEDEK HOSPITAL IN JERUSALEM, INC. (1949). 49 W. 45 St., NYC 10036. (212)-354-8801. Pres. Charles Bendheim; Bd. Chmn. Ludwig Jesselson; Sr. Exec. V.-Pres. Morris Talansky. Raises funds for the various needs of the Shaare Zedek Medical Center, Jerusalem, such as equipment and medical supplies, nurse training, and research; supports exchange program between Shaare Zedek Medical Center and Albert Einstein College of Medicine, NY. *Heartbeat magazine.*

AMERICAN COMMITTEE FOR SHENKAR COLLEGE IN ISRAEL, INC. (1971). 855 Ave. of the Americas, NYC 10001. (212)-947-1597. Pres. David Pernick; Exec. Dir. Charlotte Fainblatt. Raises funds for capital improvement, research and development projects, laboratory equipment, scholarships, lectureships, fellowships, and library/archive collections at Shenkar College in Israel, Israel's only fashion and textile technology college. Accredited by the Council of Higher Education, the college is the chief source of personnel for Israel's fashion and apparel industry. *Shenkar Bulletin.*

AMERICAN COMMITTEE FOR THE WEIZMANN INSTITUTE OF SCIENCE (1944). 515 Park Ave., NYC 10022. (212)752-1300. Pres. Maurice M. Weiss; Bd. Chmn. Norman D. Cohen; Exec. V.-Pres. Bernard N. Samers. Through 13 regional offices in the U.S. raises funds for the Weizmann Institute in Rehovot, Israel, and disseminates information about the scientific research under way there. *Interface; Rehovot; Research.*

AMERICAN FRIENDS OF HAIFA UNIVERSITY (1972). 41 E. 42 St., #828, NYC 10017. (212)818-9050. Pres. Sigmund Strochlitz; Exec. V.-Pres. Michael Weisser. Promotes, encourages, and aids higher and secondary education, research, and training in all branches of knowledge in Israel and elsewhere; aids in the maintenance and development of Haifa University; raises and allocates funds for the above purposes; provides scholarships; promotes exchanges of teachers and students. *Newsletter.*

AMERICAN FRIENDS OF RAMAT HANEGEV COLLEGE INC. (1983). 118 E. 25 St., NYC 10010. (212)460-8700. Pres. Meir Levin; Sec.-Treas. Jehuda J. Levin. Represents Ramat HaNegev College in fund raising and public relations in the U.S. Through various activities aids the college's efforts to improve the well-being of the Negev towns of Yeruham, Dimona, and Mitzpeh Ramon, and the development of the Negev south of Beersheva. *Newsletter.*

AMERICAN FRIENDS OF THE HAIFA MARITIME MUSEUM, INC. (1977). 236 Fifth Ave., NYC 10001. (212)696-8084. Chmn.

and Treas. Bernard Weissman; Pres. Stephen K. Haber. Supports National Maritime Museum in Haifa. Promotes interest in maritime life among American Jews.

AMERICAN FRIENDS OF THE HEBREW UNIVERSITY (1925; inc. 1931). 11 E. 69 St., NYC 10021. (212)472-9800. Pres. Fred S. Lafer; Exec. V.-Pres. Robert A. Pearlman; Bd. Chmn. Harvey L. Silbert. Fosters the growth, development, and maintenance of the Hebrew University of Jerusalem; collects funds and conducts programs of information throughout the U.S., interpreting the work of the university and its significance; administers American student programs and arranges exchange professorships in the U.S. and Israel. *News from the Hebrew University of Jerusalem; Scopus magazine.*

AMERICAN FRIENDS OF THE ISRAEL MUSEUM (1968). 10 E. 40 St., Suite 1208, NYC 10016. (212)683-5190. Pres. Maureen Cogan; Exec. Dir. Michele Cohn Tocci. Raises funds for special projects of the Israel Museum in Jerusalem; solicits works of art for exhibition and educational purposes. *Newsletter.*

AMERICAN FRIENDS OF THE JERUSALEM MENTAL HEALTH CENTER—EZRATH NASHIM, INC. (1895). 10 E. 40 St., Suite 2701, NYC 10016. (212)725-8175. Pres. Burton G. Greenblatt; Exec. Dir. Mira Berman. Supports research, education, and patient care at the Jerusalem Mental Health Center, which includes a 250-bed hospital, comprehensive outpatient clinic, drug abuse clinic, geriatric center, and the Jacob Herzog Psychiatric Research Center; Israel's only nonprofit, voluntary psychiatric hospital; used as a teaching facility by Israel's major medical schools. *Friend to Friend; To Open the Gates of Healing.*

AMERICAN FRIENDS OF THE SHALOM HARTMAN INSTITUTE (1976). 1735 Jefferson Davis Hwy., Crystal City, Arlington, VA 22202. (703)769-1240. Chmn. Robert P. Kogod; Dir. Ruth S. Frank. Supports the Shalom Hartman Institute, Jerusalem, an institute of higher education and research center, devoted to applying the teachings of classical Judaism to the issues of modern life. Founded in 1976 by David Hartman, the institute includes Beit Midrash and centers for philosophy, theology, *halakhah,* political thought, and medical science, an experimental school, and programs for lay leadership. *A Word from Jerusalem.*

AMERICAN FRIENDS OF THE TEL AVIV MUSEUM (1974). 133 E. 58 St., Suite 704, NYC 10022. (212)319-0555. Pres. Roy V. Titus; Chmn. Milton J. Schubin; Exec. Dir. Jane M. Rogul. Solicits contributions of works of art to enrich the Tel Aviv Museum collection; raises funds to support development, maintenance, and expansion of the museum and its educational and cultural programs. *Exhibition catalogues.*

AMERICAN FRIENDS OF THE TEL AVIV UNIVERSITY, INC. (1955). 360 Lexington Ave., NYC 10017. (212)687-5651. Bd. Chmn. Lally Weymouth; Exec. V.-Pres. Jules Love. Promotes, encourages, aids, and advances higher education at Tel Aviv University and elsewhere. Among the many projects in the university's more than 50 research institutes are the Moshe Dayan Center for Middle Eastern & African Studies, the Jaffe Center for Strategic Studies; 25 institutes in different fields of medicine; and the Institute for Cereal Crops Improvement. *Tel Aviv University Report; AFTAU Newsletter.*

AMERICAN ISRAEL PUBLIC AFFAIRS COMMITTEE (AIPAC) (1954). 500 N. Capitol St., NW, Washington, DC 20001. (202)-638-2256. Pres. Robert Asher; Exec. Dir. Thomas A. Dine. Registered to lobby on behalf of legislation affecting U.S.-Israel relations; represents Americans who believe support for a secure Israel is in U.S. interest. Works for a strong U.S.-Israel relationship. *Near East Report; AIPAC Papers on U.S.-Israel Relations.*

AMERICAN-ISRAELI LIGHTHOUSE, INC. (1928; reorg. 1955). 30 E. 60 St., NYC 10022. (212)838-5322. Pres. Mrs. Leonard F. Dank; Sec. Frances Lentz. Provides education and rehabilitation for the blind and physically handicapped in Israel to effect their social and vocational integration into the seeing community; built and maintains Rehabilitation Center for the Blind (Migdal Or) in Haifa. *Tower.*

AMERICAN JEWISH LEAGUE FOR ISRAEL (1957). 30 E. 60 St., NYC 10022. (212)371-1583. Pres. Rabbi Reuben M. Katz; Bd. Chmn. Rabbi Aaron Decter. Seeks to unite all those who, notwithstanding differing philosophies of Jewish life, are committed to the historical ideals of Zionism; works, independently of class or party, for the welfare of Israel as a whole. Not identified with any political parties in Israel. *Bulletin of the American Jewish League for Israel.*

AMERICAN PHYSICIANS FELLOWSHIP, INC. FOR MEDICINE IN ISRAEL (1950). 2001 Beacon St., Brookline, MA 02146. (617)-232-5382. Pres. Dr. Edward H. Kass; Sec. Dr. Manuel M. Glazier. Helps Israel become a major world medical center; secures fellowships for selected Israeli physicians and arranges lectureships in Israel by prominent American physicians; supports Jerusalem Academy of Medicine; coordinates U.S. and Canadian medical and paramedical emergency volunteers to Israel; maintains Israel Institute of the History of Medicine; contributes medical books, periodicals, instruments, and drugs. *APF News.*

AMERICAN RED MAGEN DAVID FOR ISRAEL, INC. (1940). 888 Seventh Ave., NYC 10106. (212)757-1627. Natl. Chmn. Joseph Handleman; Pres. Louis Rosenberg; Exec. V.-Pres. Benjamin Saxe. An authorized tax-exempt organization; the sole support arm in the U.S. of Magen David Adom, Israel's Red Cross Service; raises funds for MDA's emergency medical services for Israel's military and civilian population, supplies ambulances, bloodmobiles, and mobile cardiac rescue units serving all hospitals and communities throughout Israel; supports MDA's 73 emergency medical clinics and helps provide training and equipment for volunteer emergency paramedical corps. *Lifeline.*

AMERICAN SOCIETY FOR TECHNION-ISRAEL INSTITUTE OF TECHNOLOGY (1940). 810 Seventh Ave., NYC 10019. (212)262-6200. Pres. Edward R. Goldberg; Exec. V.-Pres. Melvyn H. Bloom. Supports the work of the Technion-Israel Institute of Technology, Haifa, Israel's oldest university and premier technological institute, which educates 8,000 students in 20 engineering departments, in science and in medical school, and conducts research across a broad spectrum of science and technology. *Technion magazine; Technion-USA; UPDATE: News for ATS Insiders.*

AMERICAN SOCIETY FOR THE PROTECTION OF NATURE IN ISRAEL (1986). 475 Fifth Ave., 23rd fl., NYC 10017. (212)685-3380. Hon. Chmn. Samuel W. Lewis; Pres. Daniel M. Singer; Exec. Dir. Lynn Holstein. Seeks to increase the American public's awareness of, and support for, the critical conservation efforts conducted in Israel by the Society for the Protection of Nature in Israel (SPNI). Conducts educational programs and outdoor activities in the U.S. *Israel-Land and Nature (published in Israel).*

AMERICAN ZIONIST FEDERATION (1939; reorg. 1949 and 1970). 515 Park Ave., NYC 10022. (212)371-7750. Pres. Benjamin Cohen; Exec. Dir. Karen Rubinstein. Coordinates the work of the Zionist constituency in the areas of education, *aliyah,* youth and young leadership and public and communal affairs. Seeks to involve the Zionist and broader Jewish community in programs and events focused on Israel and Zionism (e.g., Zionist Shabbat, Scholars-in-Residence, Yom Yerushalayim) and through these programs to develop a greater appreciation for the Zionist idea among American Jewry. Composed of 16 national Zionist organizations, 10 Zionist youth movements, and affiliated organizations. Offices in Boston, Chicago, Los Angeles, New York. Groups in Baltimore, Detroit, Philadelphia, Pittsburgh, Rochester, Washington, DC. *Issue Analysis, Spectrum.*

AMERICAN ZIONIST YOUTH FOUNDATION, INC. (1963). 515 Park Ave., NYC 10022. (212)751-6070. Bd. Chmn. Leon Levy; Exec. Dir. Ruth Kastner. Heightens Zionist awareness among Jewish youth through programs and services geared to high-school and college-age youngsters. Sponsors educational tours to Israel, study in leading institutions of science, scholarship, and the arts; sponsors field workers on campus and in summer camps; prepares and provides specialists who present and interpret the Israel experience for community centers and federations throughout the country. *Activist Newsletter; Guide to Education and Programming Material; Programs in Israel.*

———, AMERICAN ZIONIST YOUTH COUNCIL (1951). 515 Park Ave., NYC 10022. (212)751-6070. Chmn. Marc Sussman. Acts as spokesman and representative of Zionist youth in interpreting Israel to the youth of America; represents, coordinates, and implements activities of the Zionist youth movements in the U.S.

AMERICANS FOR A SAFE ISRAEL (1971). 114 E. 28 St., NYC 10016. (212)696-2611. Chmn. Herbert Zweibon; Dir. Joseph Puder. Seeks to educate the public to the necessity of a militarily strong Israel within defensible borders, viz., those which include Judea, Samaria, Gaza, and the Golan. Holds that a strong Israel is essential for the security of the free world. Produces pamphlets, magazines, videotapes, and radio shows and provides speakers; promotes college-campus activity and provides a congressional resource center. *Outpost.*

AMERICANS FOR PROGRESSIVE ISRAEL (1949). 150 Fifth Ave., Suite 911, NYC 10011. (212)255-8760. Pres. Harry Movchine. A socialist Zionist movement that calls for a just and durable peace between Israel and its Arab neighbors; works for the liberation of all Jews; seeks the democratization of Jewish communal and organizational life; promotes dignity of labor, social justice, and a deeper understanding of Jewish heritage. Affiliate of American Zionist Federation, World Union of Mapam, Hashomer Hatzair, and Kibbutz Artzi Fed. of Israel. *Israel Horizons; Progressive Israel; API Newsletter.*

AMIT WOMEN (formerly AMERICAN MIZRACHI WOMEN) (1925). 817 Broadway, NYC 10003. (212)477-4720. Pres. Daisy Berman; Exec. Dir. Marvin Leff. The State of Israel's official *reshet* (network) for religious secondary technological education; conducts social service, child care, Youth Aliyah villages, and vocational-educational programs in Israel in an environment of traditional Judaism; promotes cultural activities for the purpose of disseminating Zionist ideals and strengthening traditional Judaism in America. *AMIT Woman.*

AMPAL—AMERICAN ISRAEL CORPORATION (1942). 10 Rockefeller Plaza, NYC 10020. (212)586-3232. Pres. Michael Arnon. Finances and invests in Israeli economic enterprises; mobilizes finance and investment capital in the U.S. through sale of own debenture issues and utilization of bank credit lines. *Annual report; prospectuses.*

ARZA—ASSOCIATION OF REFORM ZIONISTS OF AMERICA (1977). 838 Fifth Ave., NYC 10021. (212)249-0100. Pres. Rabbi Charles Kroloff; Exec. Dir. Rabbi Eric Yoffie. Individual Zionist membership organization devoted to achieving Jewish pluralism in Israel and strengthening the Israeli Reform movement. Chapter activities in the U.S. concentrate on these issues, and on strengthening American public support for Israel. *ARZA Newsletter.*

BAR-ILAN UNIVERSITY IN ISRAEL (1955). 853 Seventh Ave., NYC 10019. (212)315-1990. Chancellor Emanuel Rackman; Pres. Michael Albeck; Chmn. Global Bd. of Trustees Ludwig Jesselson; Acting Pres. Amer. Bd. of Overseers Belda Lindenbaum. Supports Bar-Ilan University, a liberal arts and sciences institution, located in Ramat-Gan, Israel, and chartered by Board of Regents of State of NY. *Update; Bar-Ilan News.*

BETAR ZIONIST YOUTH MOVEMENT, INC. (1935). 9 E. 38 St., NYC 10016. (212)696-0080. Pres. Mitch Chupak. Teaches Jewish youth love of the Jewish people and prepares them for *aliyah;* emphasizes learning Hebrew; keeps its members ready for mobilization in times of crisis; stresses Jewish pride and self-respect; seeks to aid and protect Jewish communities everywhere. *Herut; Etgar.*

BOYS TOWN JERUSALEM FOUNDATION OF AMERICA INC. (1948). 91 Fifth Ave., Suite 601, NYC 10003. (212)242-1118. Pres. Michael J. Scharf; Exec. V.-Pres. Rabbi Ronald L. Gray. Raises funds for Boys Town Jerusalem, which was established in 1948 to offer a comprehensive academic, religious, and technical education to disadvantaged Israeli and immigrant boys from 39 different countries, including Ethiopia and Iran. Enrollment: over 1,500 students in jr. high school, academic and technical high school, and a college of applied engineering. *BTJ Newsbriefs; Your Town Magazine.*

COUNCIL FOR A BEAUTIFUL ISRAEL ENVIRONMENTAL EDUCATION FOUNDATION (1973). 350 Fifth Ave., 19th fl., NYC 10118. (212)947-5709. Pres. Ruth Baum; Admin. Dir. Donna Lindemann. A support group for the Israeli body, whose activities include education, town planning, lobbying for legislation to protect and enhance the environment, preservation of historical sites, the improvement and beautification of industrial and commercial areas, and renovating bomb shelters into parks and playgrounds. *Quarterly newsletter.*

DROR—YOUNG KIBBUTZ MOVEMENT—HABONIM (1948). 27 W. 20 St., NYC 10011. (212)675-1168. Exec. Dir. Yoel Skolnick. Provides an opportunity for individuals who have spent time in Israel, on a kibbutz program, to continue their contact with the kibbutz movement through regional and national activities and seminars; sponsors two *garinim* to kibbutz each year and a teenage summer program. *New Horizons.*

———, CHAVURAT HAGALIL (1978). Exec. Dir. Shlomo Ravid. Aids those aged 27–35 in making *aliyah* to a kibbutz. Affiliated with TAKAM kibbutz association.

———, GARIN YARDEN, THE YOUNG KIBBUTZ MOVEMENT (1976). Exec. Dir. Shlomo Ravid. Aids those aged 19–26 interested in making *aliyah* to a kibbutz; affiliated with TAKAM kibbutz association.

EMUNAH WOMEN OF AMERICA (formerly HAPOEL HAMIZRACHI WOMEN'S ORGANIZATION) (1948). 370 Seventh Ave., NYC 10001. (212)564-9045. Pres. Beverly Segal; Exec. Dir. Shirley Singer. Maintains and supports 200 educational and social-welfare institutions in Israel within a religious framework, including nurseries, day-care centers, vocational and teacher-training schools for the underprivileged. Also involved in absorption of Ethiopian immigrants. *The Emunah Woman; Lest We Forget; Emunah Connection.*

FEDERATED COUNCIL OF ISRAEL INSTITUTIONS—FCII (1940). 4702 15 Ave., Brooklyn, NY 11219. (718)972-5530. Bd. Chmn. Z. Shapiro; Exec. V.-Pres. Rabbi Julius Novack. Central fund-raising organization for over 100 affiliated institutions; handles and executes estates, wills, and bequests for the traditional institutions in Israel; clearinghouse for information on budget, size, functions, etc. of traditional educational, welfare, and philanthropic institutions in Israel, working cooperatively with the Israeli government and the overseas department of the Council of Jewish Federations. *Annual financial reports and statistics on affiliates.*

FRIENDS OF LABOR ISRAEL (1986). 27 W. 20 St. (9), NYC 10011. (212)255-1796. Exec. Dir. Simmy Ziv-El; Asst. Dir. Ronny Brawer. The Israel Labor movement's newest support organization in the U.S. was established to bolster Labor representation in the World Zionist Congress and to promote a dialogue between labor leaders and American Jewry. *Folio.*

FRIENDS OF THE ISRAEL DEFENSE FORCES (1981). 15 E. 26 St., NYC 10010. (212)684-0669. Bd. Chmn. Henry Plitt; Natl. Dir. Martin Gallanter. Supports the *Agudah Lema'an Hahayal,* Israel's Assoc. for the Well-Being of Soldiers, founded in the early 1940s, which provides social, recreational, and educational programs for soldiers, special services for the sick and wounded, and much more. *Newsletter.*

FUND FOR HIGHER EDUCATION (1970). 1500 Broadway, Suite 800, NYC 10036. (212)354-4660. V.-Pres. Sondra G. Kolker. Supports, on a project-by-project basis, institutions of higher learning in the U.S. and Israel. *In Response II; annual report; FHE brochure.*

GIVAT HAVIVA EDUCATIONAL FOUNDATION, INC. (1966). 150 Fifth Ave., Suite 911, NYC 10011. (212)255-2992. Chmn. Lucille R. Perlman. Supports programs in Israel to further Jewish-Arab rapprochement, narrow economic and educational gaps within Israeli society, and improve educational opportunities for various disadvantaged youth. Affiliated with the Givat Haviva Center of the Kibbutz Artzi Federation, the Menachem Bader Fund, and other projects. In the U.S., GHEF, Inc. sponsors educational seminars, public lectures and parlor meetings with Israeli speakers, as well as individual and group trips to Israel. *News from Givat Haviva; special reports.*

GOLDA MEIR ASSOCIATION (1984). 33 E. 67 St., NYC 10021. (212)570-1443. Pres. Alfred H. Moses; Exec. Dir. Avner Tavori. North American support group for the Israeli association, whose large-scale educational programs address the issues of democracy in Israel, Sephardi-Ashkenazi integration, religious pluralism, the peace process, and relations between Israeli Jews and Arabs. Its "Project Democracy" is the largest program dealing with the tide of extremism sweeping Israel's youth. *Newsletter.*

HABONIM-DROR NORTH AMERICA (1934). 27 W. 20 St., 9th fl., NYC 10011. (212)255-1796. Sec.-Gen. Chuck Buxbaum; Exec. Off. Jeff Dolgin. Fosters identification with pioneering in Israel; stimulates study of Jewish life, history, and culture; sponsors community-action projects, seven summer camps in North America, programs in Israel, and *garinei aliyah* to Kibbutz Ravid. *Batnua; Progressive Zionist Journal; Bimat Hamaapilim.*

HADASSAH, THE WOMEN'S ZIONIST ORGANIZATION OF AMERICA, INC. (1912). 50 W. 58 St., NYC 10019. (212)355-7900. Pres. Ruth Popkin; Exec. Dir. Zmira Goodman. In America helps interpret Israel to the American people; provides basic Jewish education as a background for intelligent and creative Jewish living; sponsors Hashachar, largest Zionist youth movement in U.S., which has four divisions: Young Judaea, Intermediate Judaea, Senior Judaea, and Hamagshimim; operates six Zionist youth camps in this country; supports summer and all-year courses in Israel. Maintains in Israel Hadassah-Hebrew University Medical Center for healing, teaching, and research; Hadassah Community College; Seligsberg/Brandeis Comprehensive High School; and Hadassah Vocational Guidance Institute. Is largest organizational contributor to Youth Aliyah and to Jewish National Fund for land purchase and reclamation. *Update; Headlines; Hadassah Magazine.*

———, HASHACHAR (formerly YOUNG JUDAEA and JUNIOR HADASSAH) (1909; reorg. 1967). 50 W. 58 St., NYC 10019. (212)355-7900. Pres. of Senior Judaea (high-school level) James Licht; Coordinator of Hamagshimim (college level) Gil Preuss; Natl. Dir. Paul Goldberg. Seeks to educate Jewish youth from the ages of 9–27 toward Jewish and Zionist values, active commitment to and participation in the American and Israeli Jewish communities; maintains summer camps and year programs in Israel. *Hamagshimim Journal; Kol Hat'nua; The Young Judaean.*

HASHOMER HATZAIR, SOCIALIST ZIONIST YOUTH MOVEMENT (1923). 150 Fifth Ave., Suite 911, NYC 10011. (212)929-4955. Sec. Tzvi Fleisher; Central Shaliach Ariel Hurvitz. Seeks to educate Jewish youth to an understanding of Zionism as the national liberation movement of the Jewish people. Promotes *aliyah* to *kibbutzim.* Affiliated with AZYC and Kibbutz Artzi Federation. Espouses socialist ideals of peace, justice, democracy, and brotherhood. *Young Guard.*

HERUT ZIONISTS OF AMERICA, INC. (1925). 9 E. 38 St., Suite 1000, NYC 10016. (212)-696-0900. Pres. Hart N. Hasten; Exec. Dir. Glenn Mones. American branch of worldwide movement founded by Ze'ev Jabotinsky. Affiliated with Herut political party in Israel. Supports Israeli peace with security, free enterprise economy, and rights to settlement in the territories. Subsidiaries: Betar Zionist Youth; Tagar Zionist Student Activist Movement; Tel-Hai Fund, Inc. *The Herut Letter.*

JEWISH NATIONAL FUND OF AMERICA (1901). 42 E. 69 St., NYC 10021. (212)879-9300. Pres. Joseph P. Sternstein; Exec. V.-Pres. Samuel I. Cohen. Exclusive fund-raising agency of the world Zionist movement for the afforestation, reclamation, and development of the land of Israel, including construction of roads, parks, and recreational areas, preparation of land for new communities and industrial facilities; helps emphasize the importance of Israel in schools and synagogues throughout the U.S. *JNF Almanac; Land and Life.*

KEREN OR, INC. (1956). 1133 Broadway, NYC 10010. (212)255-1180. Bd. Chmn. Dr. Edward L. Steinberg; Pres. Dr. Albert Hornblass; Exec. Dir. Paul H. Goldenberg. Funds the Keren Or Center for Multihandicapped Blind Children, in Jerusalem, providing long-term basic training, therapy, rehabilitative, and early childhood education to the optimum level of the individual; with major hospitals, conducts outpatient clinics in Haifa and Be'er Sheva; involved in research into causes of multihandicapped blind birth; campaign under way for new multipurpose building on government land-grant in Ramot.

LABOR ZIONIST ALLIANCE (formerly FARBAND LABOR ZIONIST ORDER; now uniting membership and branches of POALE ZION—UNITED LABOR ZIONIST ORGANIZATION OF AMERICA and AMERICAN HABONIM ASSOCIATION) (1913). 275 Seventh Ave., NYC 10001. (212)989-0300. Pres. Ezra Spicehandler; Exec. Dir. Rabbi Arthur Seltzer. Seeks to enhance Jewish life, culture, and education in U.S. and Canada; aids in building State of Israel as a cooperative commonwealth, and its Labor movement organized in the Histadrut; supports efforts toward a more democratic society throughout the world; furthers the democratization of the Jewish community in America and the welfare of Jews everywhere; works with labor and liberal forces in America. *Jewish Frontier; Yiddisher Kempfer.*

LEAGUE FOR LABOR ISRAEL (1938; reorg. 1961). 275 Seventh Ave., NYC 10001. (212)989-0300. Pres. Ezra Spicehandler; Exec. Dir. Rabbi Arthur Seltzer. Conducts Labor Zionist educational and cultural activities, for youth and adults, in the American Jewish community. Promotes educational travel to Israel.

MERCAZ (1979). 155 Fifth Ave., NYC 10010. (212)533-7800. Pres. Simon Schwartz; Exec. Dir. Hindy Kisch. The U.S. Zionist action organization for Conservative/Masorti Judaism, Mercaz works to attain religious rights for the Masorti movement in Israel. It fosters Zionist education and develops young leadership, sponsoring an annual mission to Israel. *Hatzioni Newsletter.*

NA'AMAT USA, THE WOMEN'S LABOR ZIONIST ORGANIZATION OF AMERICA, INC. (formerly PIONEER WOMEN/NA'AMAT) (1925; reorg. 1985). 200 Madison Ave., Suite 1808, NYC 10016. (212)725-8010. Pres. Gloria Elbling; Exec. Dir. Tehila Elpern. Part of a world movement of working women and volunteers, Na'amat USA helps provide social, educational, and legal services for women, teenagers, and children in Israel. It also advocates legislation for women's rights and child welfare in the U.S., furthers Jewish education, and supports Habonim-Dror, the Labor Zionist youth movement. *Na'amat Woman magazine.*

NATIONAL COMMITTEE FOR LABOR ISRAEL—HISTADRUT (1923). 33 E. 67 St., NYC 10021. (212)628-1000. Pres. Aaron L. Solomon; Exec. V.-Pres. Eliezer Rafaeli. Represents the Histadrut—Israel's General Federation of Labor; raises funds for Histadrut's network of social and welfare services in Israel, including Kupat Holim—the comprehensive health care organization which takes care of 80% of Israel's population—a vocational-school network, senior-citizen homes, and others. *Backdrop Histadrut; Amal Newsletter.*

NEW ISRAEL FUND (1979). 111 W. 40 St., Suite 2600, NYC 10018. (212)302-0066. Pres. David Arnow; Exec. Dir. Jonathan Jacoby. Supports the citizens'-action efforts of Israelis working to achieve social justice and to protect and strengthen the democratic process in Israel. Also seeks to enrich the quality of the relationships between Israelis and North American Jews through deepened mutual understanding. *A Guide to Arab-Jewish Peacemaking in Israel; quarterly bulletin; annual report.*

PEC ISRAEL ECONOMIC CORPORATION (formerly PALESTINE ECONOMIC CORPORATION) (1926). 511 Fifth Ave., NYC 10017. (212)687-2400. Pres. Joseph Ciechanover; Exec. V.-Pres. Frank J. Klein; Sec.-Asst. Treas. William Gold. Primarily engaged in the business of organizing, financing, and administering business enterprises located in or affiliated with enterprises in the State of Israel, through holdings of equity securities and loans. *Annual report.*

PEF ISRAEL ENDOWMENT FUNDS, INC. (1922). 41 E. 42 St., Suite 607, NYC 10017. (212)599-1260. Chmn. Sidney Musher; Sec. Harvey Brecher. Uses funds for Israeli educational and philanthropic institutions and for constructive relief, modern education, and scientific research in Israel. *Annual report.*

PIONEER WOMEN/NA'AMAT (*see* Na'amat USA)

POALE AGUDATH ISRAEL OF AMERICA, INC. (1948). 3190 Bedford Ave., Brooklyn, NY 11210. (718)377-4111. Pres. Rabbi Fabian Schonfeld; Exec. V.-Pres. Rabbi Moshe Malinowitz. Aims to educate American Jews to the values of Orthodoxy and *aliyah;* supports *kibbutzim,* trade schools, *yeshivot, moshavim, kollelim,* research centers, and children's homes in Israel. *PAI News; She'arim; Hamayan.*

———, WOMEN'S DIVISION OF (1948). Pres. Aliza Widawsky; Presidium: Sarah Ivanisky, Miriam Lubling, Bertl Rittenberg. Assists Poale Agudath Israel to build and support children's homes, kindergartens, and trade schools in Israel. *Yediot PAI.*

PROGRESSIVE ZIONIST CAUCUS (1982). 27 W. 20 St., NYC 10011. (212)675-1168. Pres. Shlomo Ravid; Dir. Rebecca Rowe. A campus-based grassroots organization committed to a progressive Zionist agenda. Students organize local and regional educational, cultural, and political activities, such as speakers, films, *Kabbalot Shabbat,* and Arab-Jewish dialogue groups. The PZC Kvutzat Aliyah is a support framework for individuals interested in *aliyah* to a city or town. *La'Inyan.*

RELIGIOUS ZIONISTS OF AMERICA 25 W. 26 St., NYC 10010. (212)689-1414.

———, BNEI AKIVA OF NORTH AMERICA (1934). 25 W. 26 St., NYC 10010. (212)-889-5260. Pres. Yitz Feigenbaum; V.-Pres. Admin. Jerry Yudkowsky. Seeks to interest youth in *aliyah* to Israel and social justice through pioneering *(halutziut)* as an integral part of their religious observance; sponsors five summer camps, a leadership training camp for eleventh graders, a work-study program on a religious kibbutz for high school graduates, summer tours to Israel; establishes nuclei of college students for kibbutz or other settlement. *Akivon; Hamvaser; Pinkas Lamadrich; Daf Rayonot; Ma'Ohalai Torah; Zraim.*

———, MIZRACHI-HAPOEL HAMIZRACHI (1909; merged 1957). 25 W. 26 St., NYC 10010. (212)689-1414. Pres. Hermann Merkin; Exec. V.-Pres. Israel Friedman. Disseminates ideals of religious Zionism; conducts cultural work, educational program, public relations; raises funds for religious educational institutions in Israel, including *yeshivot hesder* and Bnei Akiva. *Newsletters; Kolenu.*

———, MIZRACHI PALESTINE FUND (1928). 25 W. 26 St., NYC 10010. Chmn. Joseph Wilon; Sec. Israel Friedman. Fund-raising arm of Mizrachi movement.

———, NATIONAL COUNCIL FOR TORAH EDUCATION OF MIZRACHI-HAPOEL HAMIZRACHI (1939). 25 W. 26 St., NYC 10010. Pres. Israel Shorr; Dir. Meyer Golombek. Organizes and supervises *yeshivot* and Talmud Torahs; prepares and trains teachers; publishes textbooks and educational materials; conducts a placement agency for Hebrew schools; organizes summer seminars for Hebrew educators in cooperation with Torah Department of Jewish Agency; conducts *ulpan.*

———, NOAM-MIZRACHI NEW LEADERSHIP COUNCIL (formerly NOAM-HAMISHMERET HATZEIRA) (1970). 25 W. 26 St., NYC 10010. (212)684-6091. Pres. Rabbi Marc Schneier. Develops new religious Zionist leadership in the U.S. and Canada; presents young religious people with various alternatives for settling in Israel through *garinei aliyah* (core groups); meets the religious, educational, and social needs of Jewish young adults and young couples. *Forum.*

SOCIETY OF ISRAEL PHILATELISTS (1948). 27436 Aberdeen, Southfield, MI 48076. (313)557-0887. Pres. Stanley H. Raffel; Exec. Sec. Irvin Girer. Promotes interest in, and knowledge of, all phases of Israel philately through sponsorship of chapters and research groups, maintenance of a philatelic library, and support of public and private exhibitions. *Israel Philatelist; monographs; books.*

STATE OF ISRAEL BONDS (1951). 730 Broadway, NYC 10003. (212)677-9650. Intnl. Chmn. David B. Hermelin; Pres. Yehudah Halevy; Exec. V.-Pres. Morris Sipser. Seeks to provide large-scale investment funds for the economic development of the State of Israel through the sale of State of Israel bonds in the U.S., Canada, Western Europe, and other parts of the free world.

THEODOR HERZL FOUNDATION (1954). 515 Park Ave., NYC 10022. (212)752-0600. Chmn. Kalman Sultanik; Sec. Isadore Hamlin. Cultural activities, lectures, conferences, courses in modern Hebrew and Jewish subjects, Israel, Zionism, and Jewish history. *Midstream.*

———, HERZL PRESS. Chmn. Kalman Sultanik; Editor Mordecai S. Chertoff. Publishes books and pamphlets on Israel, Zionism, and general Jewish subjects.

———, THEODOR HERZL INSTITUTE. Chmn. Jacques Torczyner; Dir. Sidney Rosenfeld. Program geared to review of contemporary problems on Jewish scene here and abroad, presentation of Jewish heritage values in light of Zionist experience of the ages, study of modern Israel, and Jewish social research with particular consideration of history and impact of Zionism. Lectures, forums, Encounter with Creativity; musicales, recitals, concerts; holiday celebrations; visual art programs, Nouveau Artist Introductions. *Annual Program Preview; Herzl Institute Bulletin.*

UNITED CHARITY INSTITUTIONS OF JERUSALEM, INC. (1903). 1141 Broadway, NYC 10001. (212)683-3221. Pres. Rabbi Zevulun Charlop; Sec. Sam Gabel. Raises funds for the maintenance of schools, kitchens, clinics, and dispensaries in Israel; free loan foundations in Israel.

UNITED ISRAEL APPEAL, INC. (1925). 515 Park Ave., NYC 10022. (212)688-0800. Chmn. Henry Taub; Exec. V.-Chmn. Irving Kessler. As principal beneficiary of the United Jewish Appeal, serves as link between American Jewish community and Jewish Agency for Israel, its operating agent; assists in resettlement and absorption of refugees in Israel, and supervises flow of funds and expenditures for this purpose.

UNITED STATES COMMITTEE SPORTS FOR ISRAEL, INC. (1948). 275 S. 19 St., Suite 1203, Philadelphia, PA 19103. (215)546-4700. Pres. Robert E. Spivak; Exec. Dir. Barbara G. Lissy. Sponsors U.S. participation in, and fields and selects U.S. team for, World Maccabiah Games in Israel every four years; promotes education and sports programs in Israel; provides funds and technical and material assistance to Wingate Institute for Physical Education and Sport in Israel; sponsors coaching programs in Israel. *USCSFI Newsletter; commemorative Maccabiah Games journal.*

WOMEN'S LEAGUE FOR ISRAEL, INC. (1928). 515 Park Ave., NYC 10022. (212)838-1997. Pres. Muriel Lunden; Sr. V.-Pres. Linda Anopolsky; Exec. Dir. Bernice Backon. Promotes the welfare of young people in Israel; built and maintains homes in Jerusalem, Haifa, Tel Aviv, and Natanya; in cooperation with Ministry of Labor and Social Affairs, operates live-in vocational training center for girls, including handicapped, in Natanya, and weaving workshop for the blind. *WLI Bulletin.*

WORLD CONFEDERATION OF UNITED ZIONISTS (1946; reorg. 1958). 30 E. 60 St., NYC 10022. (212)371-1452. Copres. Bernice S. Tannenbaum, Kalman Sultanik, Melech Topiol. Promotes Zionist education, sponsors nonparty youth movements in the Diaspora, and strives for an Israel-oriented creative Jewish survival in the Diaspora. *Zionist Information Views.*

WORLD ZIONIST ORGANIZATION—AMERICAN SECTION (1971). 515 Park Ave., NYC 10022. (212)752-0600. Chmn. Bernice S. Tannenbaum; Exec. V.-Chmn. Isadore Hamlin. As the American section of the overall Zionist body throughout the world, it operates primarily in the field of *aliyah* from the free countries, education in the Diaspora, youth and *hechalutz,* organization and information, cultural institutions, publications; conducts a worldwide Hebrew cultural program including special seminars and pedagogic manuals; disperses information and assists in research projects concerning Israel; promotes, publishes, and distributes books, periodicals, and pamphlets concerning developments in Israel, Zionism, and Jewish history. *Israel Scene; Five Fifteen.*

———, DEPARTMENT OF EDUCATION AND CULTURE (1948). 515 Park Ave., NYC 10022. (212)752-0600. Exec. Counselor Arthur Levine; Exec. Dir. Mordecai Peled. Seeks to foster a wider and deeper knowledge of the Hebrew language and literature and a better understanding and fuller appreciation of the role of Israel in the destiny of Jewry and Judaism, to introduce the study of Israel as an integral part of the Jewish school curriculum, and to initiate and sponsor educational projects designed to implement these objectives.

———, NORTH AMERICAN ALIYAH MOVEMENT (1968). 515 Park Ave., NYC 10022. (212)752-0600. Exec. Dir. Robert Berl. Promotes and facilitates *aliyah* and *klitah* from the U.S. and Canada to Israel; serves as a social framework for North American immigrants to Israel. *Aliyon; NAAM Newsletter; Coming Home.*

———, ZIONIST ARCHIVES AND LIBRARY OF THE (1939). 515 Park Ave., NYC 10022. (212)753-2167. Dir. and Librarian Esther Togman. A depository for books, pamphlets, newspapers, periodicals, ephemera, and archival material; a primary center in the U.S. for research and authentic information on Israel, Zionism, the Middle East, and Jewish life in the Diaspora.

ZIONIST ORGANIZATION OF AMERICA (1897). ZOA House, 4 E. 34 St., NYC 10016. (212)481-1500. Pres. Alleck A. Resnick; Exec. V.-Pres. Paul Flacks. Public affairs programming to foster the unity of the Jewish people through General Zionism; parent organization of four institutes which promote the understanding of Zionism within the Jewish and non-Jewish world; sponsors of Masada Youth summer programs in Israel, ZOA House in Tel Aviv, and international high school programs at Kfar Silver, Ashkelon. *American Zionist.*

PROFESSIONAL ASSOCIATIONS*

AMERICAN CONFERENCE OF CANTORS, UNION OF AMERICAN HEBREW CONGREGATIONS (Religious, Educational)

AMERICAN JEWISH CORRECTIONAL CHAPLAINS ASSOCIATION, INC. (Social Welfare)

AMERICAN JEWISH PRESS. ASSOCIATION (Cultural)

AMERICAN JEWISH PUBLIC RELATIONS SOCIETY (1957). 234 Fifth Ave., NYC 10001. (212)697-5895. Pres. Robert L. Kern; Treas. Hyman Brickman. Advances professional status of workers in the public-relations field in Jewish communal service; upholds a professional code of ethics and standards; serves as a clearinghouse for employment opportunities; exchanges professional information and ideas; presents awards for excellence in professional attainments, including the "Maggid Award" for outstanding literary or artistic achievement which enhances Jewish life. *AJPRS Newsletter; AJPRS Directory.*

ASSOCIATION OF HILLEL/JEWISH CAMPUS PROFESSIONALS (Religious, Educational)

ASSOCIATION OF JEWISH CENTER WORKERS (Community Relations)

ASSOCIATION OF JEWISH CHAPLAINS OF THE ARMED FORCES (Religious, Educational)

ASSOCIATION OF JEWISH COMMUNITY ORGANIZATION PERSONNEL (Social Welfare)

ASSOCIATION OF JEWISH COMMUNITY RELATIONS WORKERS (Community Relations)

CANTORS ASSEMBLY (Religious, Educational)

CENTRAL CONFERENCE OF AMERICAN RABBIS (Religious, Educational)

CONFERENCE OF JEWISH COMMUNAL SERVICE (Social Welfare)

COUNCIL OF JEWISH ORGANIZATIONS IN CIVIL SERVICE (Community Relations)

JEWISH CHAPLAINS COUNCIL, JWB (Social Welfare)

JEWISH EDUCATORS ASSEMBLY, UNITED SYNAGOGUE OF AMERICA (Religious, Educational)

JEWISH MINISTERS CANTORS ASSOCIATION OF AMERICA, INC. (Religious, Educational)

JEWISH TEACHERS ASSOCIATION—MORIM (Religious, Educational)

NATIONAL ASSOCIATION OF HEBREW DAY SCHOOL ADMINISTRATORS, TORAH UMESORAH (Religious, Educational)

NATIONAL ASSOCIATION OF SYNAGOGUE ADMINISTRATORS, UNITED SYNAGOGUE OF AMERICA (Religious, Educational)

NATIONAL ASSOCIATION OF TEMPLE ADMINISTRATORS, UNION OF AMERICAN HEBREW CONGREGATIONS (Religious, Educational)

NATIONAL ASSOCIATION OF TEMPLE EDUCATORS, UNION OF AMERICAN HEBREW CONGREGATIONS (Religious, Educational)

NATIONAL CONFERENCE OF YESHIVA PRINCIPALS, TORAH UMESORAH (Religious, Educational)

RABBINICAL ASSEMBLY (Religious, Educational)

RABBINICAL COUNCIL OF AMERICA (Religious, Educational)

RECONSTRUCTIONIST RABBINICAL ASSOCIATION, JEWISH ◦ RECONSTRUCTIONIST FOUNDATION (Religious, Educational)

UNION OF ORTHODOX RABBIS OF THE U.S. AND CANADA (Religious, Educational)

WORLD CONFERENCE OF JEWISH COMMUNAL SERVICE (Community Relations)

WOMEN'S ORGANIZATIONS*

AMIT WOMEN (Zionist and Pro-Israel)

B'NAI B'RITH WOMEN (Social Welfare)

BRANDEIS UNIVERSITY NATIONAL WOMEN'S COMMITTEE (1948). 415 South St., Waltham, MA 02254. (617)647-2194. Pres. Barbara J. Ehrlich; Exec. Dir. Carol S. Rabinovitz. Responsible for support and maintenance of Brandeis University libraries; sponsors University on Wheels and,

*For fuller listing see under categories in parentheses.

through its chapters, study-group programs based on faculty-prepared syllabi, volunteer work in educational services, and a program of New Books for Old sales; constitutes largest "Friends of a Library" group in U.S. *Imprint.*

HADASSAH, THE WOMEN'S ZIONIST ORGANIZATION OF AMERICA (Zionist and Pro-Israel)

NA'AMAT USA, THE WOMEN'S LABOR ZIONIST ORGANIZATION OF AMERICA (Zionist and Pro-Israel)

NATIONAL COUNCIL OF JEWISH WOMEN (Social Welfare)

NATIONAL FEDERATION OF TEMPLE SISTERHOODS, UNION OF AMERICAN HEBREW CONGREGATIONS (Religious, Educational)

UOTS (Social, Mutual Benefit)

WOMEN'S AMERICAN ORT, AMERICAN ORT FEDERATION (Overseas Aid)

WOMEN'S BRANCH OF THE UNION OF ORTHODOX JEWISH CONGREGATIONS OF AMERICA (Religious, Educational)

WOMEN'S DIVISION OF POALE AGUDATH ISRAEL OF AMERICA (Zionist and Pro-Israel)

WOMEN'S DIVISION OF THE JEWISH LABOR COMMITTEE (Community Relations)

WOMEN'S DIVISION OF THE UNITED JEWISH APPEAL (Overseas Aid)

WOMEN'S LEAGUE FOR CONSERVATIVE JUDAISM (Religious, Educational)

WOMEN'S LEAGUE FOR ISRAEL, INC. (Zionist and Pro-Israel)

WOMEN'S ORGANIZATION, YESHIVA UNIVERSITY (Religious, Educational)

YOUTH AND STUDENT ORGANIZATIONS*

AMERICAN ZIONIST YOUTH FOUNDATION (Zionist and Pro-Israel)

———, AMERICAN ZIONIST YOUTH COUNCIL

B'NAI B'RITH HILLEL FOUNDATIONS (Religious, Educational)

B'NAI B'RITH YOUTH ORGANIZATION (Religious, Educational)

BNEI AKIVA OF NORTH AMERICA, RELIGIOUS ZIONISTS OF AMERICA (Zionist and Pro-Israel)

BNOS AGUDATH ISRAEL, AGUDATH ISRAEL OF AMERICA, GIRLS' DIVISION (Religious, Educational)

DROR—YOUNG KIBBUTZ MOVEMENT—HABONIM (Zionist and Pro-Israel)

HABONIM-DROR NORTH AMERICA (Zionist and Pro-Israel)

HASHACHAR, HADASSAH (Zionist and Pro-Israel)

HASHOMER HATZAIR, SOCIALIST ZIONIST YOUTH MOVEMENT (Zionist and Pro-Israel)

JEWISH STUDENT PRESS SERVICE (1970)—JEWISH STUDENT EDITORIAL PROJECTS, JEWISH PRESS FEATURES. 15 E. 26 St., Suite 1350, NYC 10010. (212)679-1411. Dir. Suzanne Dashman; Editor Larry Yudelson. Serves all Jewish student and young adult publications, as well as many Anglo-Jewish newspapers, in North America, through monthly feature packets of articles and graphics. Holds annual national and local editors' conference for member publications. Provides technical and editorial assistance; maintains Israel Bureau. *Jewish Press Features.*

KADIMA, UNITED SYNAGOGUE OF AMERICA (Religious, Educational)

NATIONAL CONFERENCE OF SYNAGOGUE YOUTH, UNION OF ORTHODOX JEWISH CONGREGATIONS OF AMERICA (Religious, Educational)

NOAM-MIZRACHI NEW LEADERSHIP COUNCIL, RELIGIOUS ZIONISTS OF AMERICA (Zionist and Pro-Israel)

NORTH AMERICAN FEDERATION OF TEMPLE YOUTH, UNION OF AMERICAN HEBREW CONGREGATIONS (Religious, Educational)

NORTH AMERICAN JEWISH STUDENTS APPEAL (1971). 165 Pidgeon Hill Rd., Huntington Station, NY 11746. (516)385-8771. Pres. Cindy Rubin; Chmn. Gerald A.

*For fuller listing see under categories in parentheses.

Flanzbaum; Exec. Dir. Brenda Gevertz. Serves as central fund-raising mechanism for five national, independent Jewish student organizations; insures accountability of public Jewish communal funds used by these agencies; assists Jewish students undertaking projects of concern to Jewish communities; advises and assists Jewish organizations in determining student project feasibility and impact; fosters development of Jewish student leadership in the Jewish community. Beneficiaries include local and regional Jewish student projects; current constituents include Jewish Student Press Service, Student Struggle for Soviet Jewry, *Response,* Yugntruf Youth for Yiddish, and the newest constituent, Progressive Zionist Caucus.

NORTH AMERICAN JEWISH STUDENTS' NETWORK (1969). 501 Madison Ave., 17th fl., NYC 10022. (212)755-5770. Pres. Moshe Ronen; Natl. Chmn. Ayall Schanzer; Exec. Dir. Alan Oirich. Coordinates information and programs among all Jewish student organizations in North America; promotes development of student-controlled Jewish student organizations; maintains contacts and coordinates programs with Jewish students throughout the world through the World Union of Jewish Students; runs the Jewish Student Speakers Bureau; sponsors regional, national, and North American conferences. *Network Spectrum; Jewish Students of America.*

STUDENT STRUGGLE FOR SOVIET JEWRY (Community Relations)

UNITED SYNAGOGUE YOUTH, UNITED SYNAGOGUE OF AMERICA (Religious, Educational)

YOUNG ISRAEL COLLEGIATES AND YOUNG ADULTS, NATIONAL COUNCIL OF YOUNG ISRAEL (Religious, Educational)

YUGNTRUF YOUTH FOR YIDDISH (1964). 3328 Bainbridge Ave., Bronx, NY 10467. (212)654-8540. Chmn. Itzek Gottesman; Editor Paul Glasser. A worldwide, nonpolitical organization for high school and college students with a knowledge of, or interest in, Yiddish. Spreads the love and use of the Yiddish language; organizes artistic and social activities, including annual conference for young adults; sponsors Yiddish-speaking preschool for non-Orthodox children; disseminates new Yiddish teaching materials. *Yugntruf.*

ZEIREI AGUDATH ISRAEL, AGUDATH ISRAEL OF AMERICA, YOUNG MEN'S DIVISION (Religious, Educational)

CANADA

CANADA-ISRAEL SECURITIES, LTD., STATE OF ISRAEL BONDS (1953). 1255 University St., #200, Montreal, PQ H3B 3B2. (514)-878-1871. Pres. Melvyn A. Dobrin; Exec. V.-Pres. Julius Briskin. Sells Israel bonds and notes.

CANADIAN ASSOCIATION FOR LABOR ISRAEL (HISTADRUT) (1944). 4770 Kent Ave., Suite 301, Montreal, PQ H3W 1H2. Pres. Harry J. F. Bloomfield; Exec. Dir. Michael E. Meyer. Raises funds for Histadrut medical, cultural, and educational programs for the workers and families of Israel. Public relations work with trade unions to inform and educate them about the State of Israel.

CANADIAN B'NAI BRITH (1964). 15 Hove St., Suite 200, Downsview, ONT M3H 4Y8. (416)633-6224. Pres. Ralph Snow; Exec. V.-Pres. Frank Dimant. Canadian Jewry's senior organization; makes representations to all levels of government on matters of Jewish concern; promotes humanitarian causes and educational programs, community volunteer projects, adult Jewish education, and leadership development; dedicated to human rights; sponsors youth programs of B'nai Brith Youth Org. and Hillel. *Covenant; Communiqué; Hillel Voice.*

———, INSTITUTE FOR INTERNATIONAL AND GOVERNMENTAL AFFAIRS (1987). Identifies and protests the abuse of human rights throughout the world. Monitors the condition of Jewish communities worldwide and advocates on their behalf when they experience serious violations of their human rights. *Comment.*

———, LEAGUE FOR HUMAN RIGHTS (1970). (416)633-6227. Chmn. Harry Bick. Dedicated to monitoring human rights, combating racism and racial discrimination, and preventing bigotry and anti-Semitism, through education and community relations. Sponsors Holocaust Education Programs, the R. Lou Ronson Research Institute on Anti-Semitism; distributor of Anti-Defamation League materials in Canada. *Review of Anti-Semitism.*

CANADIAN FOUNDATION FOR JEWISH CULTURE (1965). 4600 Bathurst St., Willowdale, ONT M2R 3V2. (416)635-2883. Pres. Mira Koschitzky; Exec. Sec. Edmond Y. Lipsitz. Promotes Jewish studies at university level and encourages original research and scholarship in Jewish subjects; awards annual scholarships and grants-in-aid to scholars in Canada.

CANADIAN FRIENDS OF THE ALLIANCE ISRAÉLITE UNIVERSELLE (1958). PO Box 578 Victoria Station, Montreal, PQ H3Z 2Y6. (514)481-3552. Pres. Joseph Nuss. Supports the educational work of the Alliance.

CANADIAN FRIENDS OF THE HEBREW UNIVERSITY (1944). 208-1 Yorkdale Rd., Toronto, ONT M6A 3A1. (416)789-2633. Pres. Gerald Halbert; Exec. V.-Pres. Shimon Arbel. Represents and publicizes the Hebrew University in Canada; serves as fund-raising arm for the university in Canada; processes Canadians for study at the university. *Scopus; Ha-Universita.*

CANADIAN JEWISH CONGRESS (1919; reorg. 1934). 1590 Dr. Penfield Ave., Montreal, PQ H3G 1C5. (514)931-7531. Pres. Dorothy Reitman; Exec. V.-Pres. Alan Rose. The official voice of Canadian Jewish communities at home and abroad; acts on all matters affecting the status, rights, concerns and welfare of Canadian Jewry; internationally active on behalf of Soviet Jewry, Jews in Arab lands, Holocaust remembrance and restitution; largest Jewish archives in Canada. *National Small Communities Newsletter; Community Relations Newsletter; Intercom; National Archives Newsletter; Bulletin du Congrès Juif Canadien; Ottawa Digest.*

CANADIAN ORT ORGANIZATION (Organization of Rehabilitation Through Training) (1942). 5165 Sherbrooke St. W., Suite 208, Montreal, PQ H4A 1T6. (514)481-2787. Pres. Dr. Victor C. Goldbloom; Exec. Dir. Mac Silver. Carries on fund-raising projects in support of the worldwide vocational-training-school network of ORT. *ORT Reporter.*

———, WOMEN'S CANADIAN ORT (1948). 3101 Bathurst St., Suite 604, Toronto, ONT M6A 2A6. (416)787-0339. Pres. Harriet Morton; Exec. Dir. Diane Uslaner. *Focus.*

CANADIAN SEPHARDI FEDERATION (1973). c/o Or Haemet School, 210 Wilson Ave., Toronto, ONT M5M 3B1. (416)483-8968. Acting Pres. Maurice Benzacar; Sec. Laeticia Benabou. Preserves and promotes Sephardic identity, particularly among youth; works for the unity of the Jewish people; emphasizes relations between Sephardi communities all over the world; seeks better situation for Sephardim in Israel; supports Israel by all means. Participates in *La Voix Sépharade, Le Monde Sépharade,* and *Sephardi World.*

CANADIAN YOUNG JUDAEA (1917). 788 Marlee Ave., Toronto, ONT M6B 3K1. (416)787-5350. Exec. Dir. Alon Szpindel; Natl. Shaliach Roy Tamir. Strives to attract Jewish youth to Zionism, with goal of *aliyah;* operates six summer camps in Canada and one in Israel; is sponsored by Canadian Hadassah-WIZO and Zionist Federation of Canada, and affiliated with Hanoar Hatzioni in Israel. *Judaean; The Young Judaean.*

CANADIAN ZIONIST FEDERATION (1967). 5250 Decarie Blvd., Suite 550, Montreal, PQ H3X 2H9. (514)486-9526. Pres. David J. Azrieli; Exec. Dir. Rabbi Meyer Krentzman. Umbrella organization of all Zionist and Israel-related groups in Canada; carries on major activities in all areas of Jewish life through its departments of education and culture, *aliyah,* youth and students, public affairs, and fund raising for the purpose of strengthening the State of Israel and the Canadian Jewish community. *Canadian Zionist.*

———, BUREAU OF EDUCATION AND CULTURE (1972). Pres. David J. Azrieli; Exec. Dir. Rabbi Meyer Krentzman. Provides counseling by pedagogic experts, in-service teacher-training courses and seminars in Canada and Israel; national pedagogic council and research center; distributes educational material and teaching aids; conducts annual Bible contest and Hebrew-language courses for adults. *Al Mitzpe Hachinuch.*

FRIENDS OF PIONEERING ISRAEL (1950s). 1111 Finch Ave. W., Suite 154, Downsview, ONT M35 2E5 (416)736-0977. Exec. Dir. Yigal Gilboa. Acts as a progressive voice within the Jewish community on Israeli and Canadian issues; expresses socialist and Zionist viewpoints; serves as a focal point for work of the progressive Zionist elements in Canada; acts as Canadian representative of Mapam and as the Canadian distributor of *New Outlook—Mideast Monthly.* Activities include lectures on political and Jewish topics open to the public; Jewish holiday celebrations.

HADASSAH—WIZO ORGANIZATION OF CANADA (1917). 1310 Greene Ave., Suite 900, Montreal, PQ H3Z 2B8. (514)937-9431. Pres. Cecily Peters; Exec. V.-Pres. Lily Frank. Extends material and moral support to the people of Israel requiring such assistance; strengthens and fosters Jewish ideals; encourages Hebrew culture in Canada and promotes Canadian ideals of democracy. *Orah magazine.*

JEWISH IMMIGRANT AID SERVICES OF CANADA (JIAS) (1919). 5151 Cote Ste. Catherine Rd., Montreal, PQ H3W 1M6. (514)-342-9351. Pres. Dr. Harold Ashley; Exec. Dir. Herb Abrams. Serves as a national agency for immigration and immigrant welfare. *JIAS Bulletin.*

JEWISH NATIONAL FUND OF CANADA (KEREN KAYEMETH LE'ISRAEL, INC.) (1902). 1980 Sherbrooke St. W., Suite 500, Montreal, PQ H3H 2M7. (514)934-0313. Pres. Saul B. Zitzerman; Exec. V.-Pres. Michael Goldstein. Fund-raising organization affiliated with the World Zionist Organization; involved in afforestation, soil reclamation, and development of the land of Israel, including the construction of roads and preparation of sites for new settlements; provides educational materials and programs to Jewish schools across Canada.

LABOR ZIONIST MOVEMENT OF CANADA (1939). 4770 Kent Ave., Montreal, PQ H3W 1H2. (514)342-9710. Admin. V.-Pres. Abraham Shurem. Disseminates information and publications on Israel and Jewish life; arranges special events, lectures, and seminars; coordinates communal and political activities of its constituent bodies (Pioneer Women/Na'amat, Labor Zionist Alliance, Poale Zion party, Habonim-Dror Youth, Israel Histadrut, affiliated Hebrew elementary and high schools in Montreal and Toronto). *Bulletin.*

MIZRACHI-HAPOEL HAMIZRACHI ORGANIZATION OF CANADA (1941). 159 Almore Ave., Downsview, ONT M3H 2H9. (416)-630-7575. Pres. Kurt Rothschild; Exec. Dir. Rabbi Menachem Gopin. Promotes religious Zionism, aimed at making Israel a state based on Torah; maintains Bnei Akiva, a summer camp, adult education program, and touring department; supports Mizrachi-Hapoel Hamizrachi and other religious Zionist institutions in Israel which strengthen traditional Judaism. *Mizrachi Newsletter; Or Hamizrach Torah Quarterly.*

NATIONAL COUNCIL OF JEWISH WOMEN OF CANADA (1947). 1110 Finch Ave. W., #518, Downsview, ONT M3J 2T2. (416)-665-8251. Pres. Penny Yellen; Exec. Dir. Eleanor Appleby. Dedicated to furthering human welfare in Jewish and non-Jewish communities, locally, nationally, and internationally; provides essential services, and stimulates and educates the individual and the community through an integrated program of education, service, and social action. *New Edition.*

NATIONAL JOINT COMMUNITY RELATIONS COMMITTEE OF CANADIAN JEWISH CONGRESS (1936). 4600 Bathurst St., Willowdale, ONT M2R 3V2 (416)635-2883. Cochmn. Victor Goldbloom, Joseph J. Wilder; Exec. Dir. Manuel Prutschi. Seeks to safeguard the status, rights, and welfare of Jews in Canada; to combat anti-Semitism and promote understanding and goodwill among all ethnic and religious groups. *Community Relations Report.*

UNITED JEWISH TEACHERS' SEMINARY (1946). 5237 Clanranald Ave., Montreal, PQ H3X 2S5. (514)489-4401. Dir. A. Aisenbach. Trains teachers for Yiddish and Hebrew schools under auspices of Canadian Jewish Congress. *Yitonenu.*

ZIONIST ORGANIZATION OF CANADA (1892; reorg. 1919). 788 Marlee Ave., Toronto, ONT M6B 3K1. (416)781-3571. Pres. Max Goody; Exec. V.-Pres. George Liban. Furthers general Zionist aims by operating six youth camps in Canada and one in Israel; maintains Zionist book club; arranges programs, lectures; sponsors Young Judaea, Youth Centre Project in Jerusalem Forest, Israel.

Jewish Federations, Welfare Funds, Community Councils

UNITED STATES

ALABAMA

BIRMINGHAM

BIRMINGHAM JEWISH FEDERATION (1936; reorg. 1971); PO Box 130219 (35213); (205)-879-0416. Pres. Suzanne Bearman; Exec. Dir. Richard Friedman.

MOBILE

MOBILE JEWISH WELFARE FUND, INC. (inc. 1966); 1 Office Park, Suite 219 (36609); (205)-343-7197. Pres. Gerald A. Friedlander; Admin. Barbara V. Paper.

MONTGOMERY

JEWISH FEDERATION OF MONTGOMERY, INC. (1930); PO Box 20058 (36120); (205)-277-5820. Pres. Jake Aronov; Sec. Ellen Loeb.

ARIZONA

PHOENIX

JEWISH FEDERATION OF GREATER PHOENIX (incl. surrounding communities) (1940); 32 West Coolidge (85015); (602)274-1800. Pres. Seymour Sacks; Exec. Dir. Harold Morgan.

TUCSON

JEWISH FEDERATION OF SOUTHERN ARIZONA (1942); 635 N. Craycroft (85711); (602)327-7957. Pres. Jerry Sonenblick; Exec. V. Pres. Charles Plotkin.

ARKANSAS

LITTLE ROCK

JEWISH FEDERATION OF LITTLE ROCK (1911); 4942 West Markham, Suite 5 (72205); (501)663-3571. Pres. Jane B. Mendel; Exec. Dir. Nanci Goldman.

CALIFORNIA

FRESNO

JEWISH FEDERATION OF FRESNO (inc. 1978); 5094 N. West Ave. (93711); (209)432-2162. Pres. Lee Horwitz; Exec. Dir. Carol Reba.

LONG BEACH

JEWISH FEDERATION OF GREATER LONG BEACH AND WEST ORANGE COUNTY (1937); (sponsors UNITED JEWISH WELFARE FUND); 3801 E. Willow St. (90815); (213)-426-7601. Pres. Gordon Lentzner; Exec. Dir. Sandi Goldstein.

LOS ANGELES

JEWISH FEDERATION COUNCIL OF GREATER LOS ANGELES (1912; reorg. 1959); (sponsors UNITED JEWISH FUND); 6505 Wilshire Blvd. (90048); (213)852-1234. Pres. Stanley Hirsh; Exec. V. Pres. Wayne Feinstein.

OAKLAND

JEWISH FEDERATION OF THE GREATER EAST BAY (1918); 3245 Sheffield Ave.

This directory is based on information supplied by the Council of Jewish Federations.

(94602); (415)533-7462. Pres. Amy R. Sternberg; Exec. V. Pres. Ami Nahshon.

ORANGE COUNTY

JEWISH FEDERATION OF ORANGE COUNTY (1964; inc. 1965); (sponsors UNITED JEWISH WELFARE FUND); 1385 Warner Ave., Suite. A, Tustin (92680-6442); (714)259-0655. Pres. Jeff Schulein; Exec. Dir. Merv Lemmerman.

PALM SPRINGS

JEWISH FEDERATION OF PALM SPRINGS-DESERT AREA (1971); 611 S. Palm Canyon Dr. Suite. 215 (92264); (619)325-7281. Pres. Sondra Landau; Exec. Dir. Nat Bent.

SACRAMENTO

JEWISH FEDERATION OF SACRAMENTO (1948); PO Box 254589 (95865); (916)486-0906. Pres. Kenneth Goore; Exec. Dir. Arnold Feder.

SAN DIEGO

UNITED JEWISH FEDERATION OF SAN DIEGO COUNTY (1936); 4797 Mercury St. (92111); (619)571-3444. Pres. Howard Brotman; Exec. V. Pres. Stephen M. Abramson.

SAN FRANCISCO

JEWISH COMMUNITY FEDERATION OF SAN FRANCISCO, THE PENINSULA, MARIN, AND SONOMA COUNTIES (1910; reorg. 1955); 121 Steuart St. (94105); (415)777-0411. Pres. Laurence E. Myers; Exec. Dir. Rabbi Brian Lurie.

SAN JOSE

JEWISH FEDERATION OF GREATER SAN JOSE (incl. Santa Clara County except Palo Alto and Los Altos) (1930; reorg. 1950); 14855 Oka Rd., Los Gatos (95030); (408)358-3033. Pres. Sherman Naymark; Exec. Dir. Michael Papo.

COLORADO

DENVER

ALLIED JEWISH FEDERATION OF DENVER (1936); (sponsors ALLIED JEWISH CAMPAIGN); 300 S. Dahlia St. (80222); (303)321-3399. Pres. Warren Toltz; Exec. Dir. Sheldon Steinhauser.

CONNECTICUT

BRIDGEPORT

JEWISH FEDERATION OF GREATER BRIDGEPORT, INC. (1936; reorg. 1981); (sponsors UNITED JEWISH CAMPAIGN); 4200 Park Ave. (06604); (203)372-6504. Pres. Irving Kern; Exec. Dir. Gerald A. Kleinman.

DANBURY

JEWISH FEDERATION OF GREATER DANBURY (1945); 54 Main St., Suite E (06810); (203)792-6353. Pres. Melvin Pollack; Exec. Dir. Sharon Garelick.

EASTERN CONNECTICUT

JEWISH FEDERATION OF EASTERN CONNECTICUT, INC. (1950; inc. 1970); 28 Channing St., New London (06320); (203)442-8062. Pres. Reuben Levin; Exec. Dir. Jerome E. Fischer.

GREENWICH

GREENWICH JEWISH FEDERATION (1956); 22 W. Putnam Ave., Suite 18 (06830); (203)-622-1434. Pres. Joan Mann; Exec. Dir. Mona Abramson.

HARTFORD

GREATER HARTFORD JEWISH FEDERATION (1945); 333 Bloomfield Ave., W. Hartford (06117); (203)232-4483. Pres. Richard Suisman; Exec. Dir. Don Cooper.

NEW HAVEN

NEW HAVEN JEWISH FEDERATION (1928); 419 Whalley Ave. (06511); (203)562-2137. Pres. Dr. Milton Wallack; Exec. Dir. Susan Shimelman.

NORWALK

JEWISH FEDERATION OF GREATER NORWALK, INC. (1946; reorg. 1964); Shorehaven Rd., E. Norwalk (06855); (203)853-3440. Pres. Andrew Glickson; Interim Exec. Dir. Robert Kessler.

STAMFORD

UNITED JEWISH FEDERATION (inc. 1973); 1035 Newfield Ave., PO Box 3038 (06905); (203)322-6935. Pres. Melvin Goldstein; Exec. Dir. Debra Stein.

WATERBURY

JEWISH FEDERATION OF WATERBURY, INC. (1938); 359 Cooke St. (06710); (203)756-7234. Pres. Gary Broder; Exec. Dir. Eli J. Skora.

WESTPORT, WESTON, WILTON

UNITED JEWISH APPEAL OF WESTPORT, WESTON & WILTON (inc. 1980); 49 Richmondville Ave., (06880); (203)266-1908. Pres. Dorothy Thau; Exec. Dir. Robert Kessler.

DELAWARE

WILMINGTON

Jewish Federation of Delaware, Inc. (1934); 101 Garden of Eden Rd. (19803); (302)478-6200. Pres. Stephen E. Herrmann; Exec. V. Pres. Robert N. Kerbel.

DISTRICT OF COLUMBIA

WASHINGTON

United Jewish Appeal-Federation of Greater Washington, Inc. (1935); 7900 Wisconsin Ave., Bethesda, MD (20814-3698); (301)652-6480. Pres. Joseph B. Gildenhorn; Exec. V. Pres. Ted B. Farber.

FLORIDA

DAYTONA BEACH

Jewish Federation of Volusia & Flagler Counties, Inc.; 533 Seabreeze Blvd., Suite 300 (32018-3996); (904)255-6260. Pres. Dr. Michael D. Kohen; Exec. Dir. Iris Gardener.

FT. LAUDERDALE

Jewish Federation of Greater Ft. Lauderdale (1968); 8358 W. Oakland Pk. Blvd. (33351); (305)748-8400. Pres. Sheldon Polish; Exec. Dir. Kenneth B. Bierman.

JACKSONVILLE

Jacksonville Jewish Federation (1935); 10829 Old St. Augustine Rd. (32223); (904)262-2800. Pres. Elliot Zisser; Exec. V. Pres. Isaac Lakritz.

LEE COUNTY

Jewish Federation of Lee County (1974); 3628 Evans Ave., Ft. Myers (33901); (813)275-3554. Pres. Dr. Ingeborg Mauksch.

MIAMI

Greater Miami Jewish Federation, Inc. (1938); 4200 Biscayne Blvd. (33137); (305)576-4000. Pres. Aaron Podhurst; Exec. V. Pres. Myron J. Brodie.

ORLANDO

Jewish Federation of Greater Orlando (1949); 851 N. Maitland Ave., PO Box 1508, Maitland (32751); (407)645-5933. Pres. Susan Bierman; Exec. Dir. Jordan Harburger.

PALM BEACH COUNTY

Jewish Federation of Palm Beach County, Inc. (1938); 501 S. Flagler Dr., Suite 305, W. Palm Beach (33401); (407)832-2120. Pres. Erwin Blonder; Exec. Dir. Jeffrey L. Klein.

PINELLAS COUNTY (incl. Clearwater and St. Petersburg)

Jewish Federation of Pinellas County, Inc. (1950; reincorp. 1974); 301 S. Jupiter Ave., Clearwater (34615); (813)446-1033. Pres. Rabbi Ira Youdovin; Exec. Dir. Robert F. Tropp.

SARASOTA

Sarasota-Manatee Jewish Federation (1959); 580 S. McIntosh Rd. (34232); (813)-371-4546. Pres. Max Bussel; Exec. Dir. Jack Weintraub.

SOUTH BROWARD

Jewish Federation of South Broward, Inc. (1943); 2719 Hollywood Blvd., Hollywood (33020); (305)921-8810. Pres. Ron Rothchild; Exec. Dir. Sumner G. Kaye.

SOUTH COUNTY

South County Jewish Federation (inc. 1979); 336 NW Spanish River Blvd., Boca Raton (33431); (305)368-2737. Pres. James Nobil; Exec. Dir. Rabbi Bruce S. Warshal.

TAMPA

Tampa Jewish Federation (1941); 2808 Horatio (33609); (813)875-1618. Pres. Douglas B. Cohn; Exec. V. Pres. Gary S. Alter.

GEORGIA

ATLANTA

Atlanta Jewish Federation, Inc. (1905; reorg. 1967); 1753 Peachtree Rd. NE (30309); (404)873-1661. Pres. Betty R. Jacobson; Exec. Dir. David I. Sarnat.

AUGUSTA

Augusta Jewish Federation (1937); PO Box 3251, Sibley Rd. (30904); (404)736-1818. Pres. David Alalof; Exec. Dir. Louis Goldman.

COLUMBUS

Jewish Welfare Federation of Columbus, Inc. (1941); PO Box 6313 (31907); (404)568-6668. Pres. Warren Pomerance; Sec. Irene Rainbow.

SAVANNAH

Savannah Jewish Council (1943); (sponsors UJA-Federation Campaign); PO Box 23527 (31403); (912)355-8111. Pres. Sheldon Tanenbaum; Exec. Dir. Stan Ramati.

HAWAII

HONOLULU

JEWISH FEDERATION OF HAWAII (1956); 677 Ala Moana, Suite 813 (96813); (808)531-4634. Pres. Gerald Clay; Exec. Dir. Nathan Stein.

ILLINOIS

CHAMPAIGN-URBANA

CHAMPAIGN-URBANA JEWISH FEDERATION (member Central Illinois Jewish Federation) (1929); 503 E. John St., Champaign (61820); (217)367-9872. Pres. Daniel Bloomfield; Exec. Dir. Jane Yairi.

CHICAGO

JEWISH FEDERATION OF METROPOLITAN CHICAGO (1900); 1 S. Franklin St. (60606); (312)346-6700. Pres. Maynard I. Wishner; Exec. V. Pres. Steven B. Nasatir.

JEWISH UNITED FUND OF METROPOLITAN CHICAGO (1968); 1 S. Franklin St. (60606); (312)346-6700. Pres. Richard L. Wexler; Exec. Dir. Steven B. Nasatir.

DECATUR

DECATUR JEWISH FEDERATION (member Central Illinois Jewish Federation) (1942); c/o Temple B'nai Abraham, 1326 W. Eldorado (62522); (217)429-5740. Pres. Cheri Kalvort; Treas. Marvin Tick.

ELGIN

ELGIN AREA JEWISH WELFARE CHEST (1938); 330 Division St. (60120); (312)741-5656. Pres. Charles Zimmerman; Treas. Stuart Hanfling.

PEORIA

JEWISH FEDERATION OF PEORIA (1933; inc. 1947); 3100 N. Knoxville, Suite 19 (61603); (309)686-0611. Pres. Dr. Thomas Halperin; Exec. Dir. Barry Nove.

QUAD CITIES

JEWISH FEDERATION OF THE QUAD CITIES (incl. Rock Island, Moline, Davenport, Bettendorf) (1938; comb. 1973); 224 18 St., Suite 511, Rock Island (61201); (309)793-1300. Pres. Martin Rich; Exec. Dir. Ida Kramer.

ROCKFORD

ROCKFORD JEWISH COMMUNITY COUNCIL (1937); 1500 Parkview Ave. (61107); (815)-399-5497. Pres. Murray Monosoff; Exec. Dir. Tony Toback.

SOUTHERN ILLINOIS

JEWISH FEDERATION SERVING SOUTHERN ILLINOIS, SOUTHEASTERN MISSOURI AND WESTERN KENTUCKY (1941); 6464 W. Main, Suite 7A, Belleville (62223); (618)398-6100. Pres. Carol Korein; Exec. Dir. Rabbi Zalman Stein.

SPRINGFIELD

SPRINGFIELD JEWISH FEDERATION (1941); 730 E. Vine St. (62703); (217)528-3446. Pres. Gloria Schwartz; Exec. Dir. Lenore Loeb.

INDIANA

EVANSVILLE

EVANSVILLE JEWISH COMMUNITY COUNCIL, INC. (1936; inc. 1964); PO Box 5026 (47715); (812)477-7050. Pres. Alan Shovers; Exec. Sec. Maxine P. Fink.

FORT WAYNE

FORT WAYNE JEWISH FEDERATION (1921); 227 E. Washington Blvd. (46802); (219)422-8566. Pres. Lawrence Adelman; Exec. Dir. Vivian Lansky.

INDIANAPOLIS

JEWISH WELFARE FEDERATION, INC. (1905); 615 N. Alabama St., Suite 412 (46204); (317)637-2473. Pres. Jerry Litwack; Exec. V. Pres. Harry Nadler.

LAFAYETTE

FEDERATED JEWISH CHARITIES (1924); PO Box 708 (47902); (317)742-9081. Pres. Arnold Cohen; Finan. Sec. Louis Pearlman, Jr.

MICHIGAN CITY

MICHIGAN CITY UNITED JEWISH WELFARE FUND; 2800 Franklin St. (46360); (219)874-4477. Pres. Nate Winski; Treas. Harold Leinwand.

NORTHWEST INDIANA

THE JEWISH FEDERATION, INC. (1941; reorg. 1959); 2939 Jewett St., Highland (46322); (219)972-2251. Pres. Alan Hurst.

SOUTH BEND

JEWISH FEDERATION OF ST. JOSEPH VALLEY (1946); 105 Jefferson Centre, Suite 804 (46601); (219)233-1164. Pres. Dr. Joseph Wind; Exec. V. Pres. Michael A. Bierman.

IOWA

DES MOINES

JEWISH FEDERATION OF GREATER DES MOINES (1914); 910 Polk Blvd. (50312);

(515)277-6321. Pres. Martin Brody; Acting Exec. Dir. Elaine Steinger.

SIOUX CITY

JEWISH FEDERATION (1921); 525 14 St. (51105); (712)258-0618. Pres. Sandra Baron; Exec. Dir. Doris Rosenthal.

KANSAS

WICHITA

MID-KANSAS JEWISH FEDERATION, INC. (1935); 400 N. Woodlawn, Suite 8 (67208); (316)686-4741. Pres. Hilary Zarnow; Exec. Dir. Beverly Jacobs.

KENTUCKY

LEXINGTON

CENTRAL KENTUCKY JEWISH FEDERATION (1976); 333 Waller, Suite 5 (40504); (606)-252-7622. Pres. Gail Cohen; Admin. Linda Ravvin.

LOUISVILLE

JEWISH COMMUNITY FEDERATION OF LOUISVILLE, INC. (1934); (sponsors UNITED JEWISH CAMPAIGN); PO Box 33035 (40232), 3630 Dutchman's Lane (40205); (502)451-8840. Pres. Michael Shaikun; Exec. Dir. Dr. Franklin B. Fogelson.

LOUISIANA

ALEXANDRIA

THE JEWISH WELFARE FEDERATION AND COMMUNITY COUNCIL OF CENTRAL LOUISIANA (1938); 1227 Southhampton (71303); (318)445-4785. Pres. Alvin Mykoff; Sec.-Treas. Roeve Weill.

BATON ROUGE

JEWISH FEDERATION OF GREATER BATON ROUGE (1971); 11744 Haymarket Ave., Suite B; P.O. Box 80827 (70898); (504)291-5895. Pres. Eleanor Fraenkel; Exec. Dir. Yigal Bander.

NEW ORLEANS

JEWISH FEDERATION OF GREATER NEW ORLEANS (1913; reorg. 1977); 1539 Jackson Ave. (70130); (504)525-0673. Pres. Dr. Marshall Gottsegen; Exec. Dir. Jane Buchsbaum.

SHREVEPORT

SHREVEPORT JEWISH FEDERATION (1941; inc. 1967); 2032 Line Ave. (71104); (318)221-4129. Pres. Melvin Goldberg; Exec. Dir. Monty Pomm.

MAINE

LEWISTON-AUBURN

LEWISTON-AUBURN JEWISH FEDERATION (1947); (sponsors UNITED JEWISH APPEAL); 74 Bradman St., Auburn (04210); (207)786-4201. Pres. Joel Goodman.

PORTLAND

JEWISH FEDERATION COMMUNITY COUNCIL OF SOUTHERN MAINE (1942); (sponsors UNITED JEWISH APPEAL); 57 Ashmont St. (04103); (207)773-7254. Pres. Larry Plotkin; Admin. Cecelia E. Levine.

MARYLAND

BALTIMORE

ASSOCIATED JEWISH CHARITIES & WELFARE FUND, INC. (a merger of the Associated Jewish Charities & Jewish Welfare Fund) (1920; reorg. 1969); 101 W. Mt. Royal Ave. (21201); (301)727-4828. Chmn. Samuel Himmelrich; Pres. Darrell D. Friedman.

MASSACHUSETTS

BERKSHIRE COUNTY

JEWISH FEDERATION OF THE BERKSHIRES (1940); 235 East St., Pittsfield (01201); (413)-442-4360. Pres. Alexandra Warshaw; Exec. Dir. Rhoda Kaminstein.

BOSTON

COMBINED JEWISH PHILANTHROPIES OF GREATER BOSTON, INC. (1895; reorg. 1961); One Lincoln Plaza (02110); (617)330-9500. Pres. Joel B. Sherman; Exec. V. Pres. Barry Shrage.

FRAMINGHAM

GREATER FRAMINGHAM JEWISH FEDERATION (1968; inc. 1969); 76 Salem End Rd., Framingham Centre (01701); (617)879-3301. Pres. Carl Chudnofsky; Exec. Dir. Lawrence Lowenthal.

LEOMINSTER

LEOMINSTER JEWISH COMMUNITY COUNCIL, INC. (1939); 268 Washington St. (01453); (617)534-6121. Pres. Milton Kline; Sec. Treas. Howard J. Rome.

MERRIMACK VALLEY

MERRIMACK VALLEY UNITED JEWISH COMMUNITIES (Serves Lowell, Lawrence, Andover, Haverhill, and Newburyport) 805 Turnpike St., N. Andover (01845). Pres. Larry Ansin; Exec. Dir. Leonard Gravitz.

NEW BEDFORD

Jewish Federation of Greater New Bedford, Inc. (1938; inc. 1954); 467 Hawthorn St., N. Dartmouth (02747); (617)997-7471. Pres. Barry Russell; Exec. Dir. Larry A. Katz.

NORTH SHORE

Jewish Federation of the North Shore, Inc. (1938); 4 Community Rd., Marblehead (01945); (617)598-1810. Pres. Dr. Bertil F. Wolf; Exec. Dir. Bruce Yudewitz.

SPRINGFIELD

Jewish Federation of Greater Springfield, Inc. (1925); (sponsors SJF/UJA Campaign); 1160 Dickinson (01108); (413)-737-4313. Pres. Betsy Gaberman; Exec. Dir. Joel Weiss.

WORCESTER

Worcester Jewish Federation, Inc. (1947; inc. 1957); (sponsors Jewish Welfare Fund); 633 Salisbury St. (01609); (617)756-1543. Pres. Gilbert Slovin; Exec. Dir. Joseph Huber.

MICHIGAN

DETROIT

Jewish Welfare Federation of Detroit (1899); (sponsors Allied Jewish Campaign); Fred M. Butzel Memorial Bldg., 163 Madison (48226); (313)965-3939. Pres. Dr. Conrad L. Giles; Exec. V. Pres. Martin Kraar.

FLINT

Flint Jewish Federation (1936); 619 Clifford St. (48502); (313)767-5922; Pres. Peter Goodstein; Exec. Dir. David Nussbaum.

GRAND RAPIDS

Jewish Community Fund of Grand Rapids (1930); 1410 Pontiac SE (49506); (616)452-6619. Pres. Joseph N. Schwartz; Admin. Dir. Barbara Kravitz.

MINNESOTA

DULUTH-SUPERIOR

Jewish Federation & Community Council (1937); 1602 E. 2 St. (55812); (218)724-8857. Pres. Aaron Glazman; Sec. Admin. Gloria Vitullo.

MINNEAPOLIS

Minneapolis Federation for Jewish Service (1929; inc. 1930); 7600 Wayzata Blvd. (55426); (612)593-2600. Pres. Sheldon Levin; Exec. Dir. Herman Markowitz.

ST. PAUL

United Jewish Fund and Council (1935); 790 S. Cleveland, Suite 201 (55116); (612)690-1707. Pres. Rhoda Mains; Exec. Dir. Robert M. Hyfler.

MISSISSIPPI

JACKSON

Jackson Jewish Welfare Fund, Inc. (1945); PO Box 12329 (39211); (601)944-0607. Pres. Jonathan Larkin; V. Pres. Ruth Friedman.

MISSOURI

KANSAS CITY

Jewish Federation of Greater Kansas City (1933); 25 E. 12 St., 10th fl. (64106); (816)421-5808. Pres. Suzanne Parelman; Exec. Dir. Sol Koenigsberg.

ST. JOSEPH

United Jewish Fund of St. Joseph (1915); 509 Woodcrest Dr. (64506); (816)-279-7154. Pres. Lou Silverglat; Exec. Sec. Martha Rothstein.

ST. LOUIS

Jewish Federation of St. Louis (incl. St. Louis County) (1901); 12 Millstone Campus Dr. (63146); (314)432-0020. Pres. Thomas R. Green; Exec. V. Pres. William Kahn.

NEBRASKA

LINCOLN

Lincoln Jewish Welfare Federation, Inc. (1931; inc. 1961); PO Box 80014 (68501); (402)423-5695. Pres. Betty Polsky; Exec. Dir. Robert Pitlor.

OMAHA

Jewish Federation of Omaha (1903); 333 S. 132 St. (68154-2198); (402)334-8200. Pres. Mort Trachtenbarg.

NEVADA

LAS VEGAS

Jewish Federation of Las Vegas (1973); 1030 E. Twain Ave. (89109); (702)732-0556. Pres. Arnold Rosencrantz; Exec. Dir. Norman Kaufman.

NEW HAMPSHIRE

MANCHESTER

JEWISH FEDERATION OF GREATER MANCHESTER (1974); 698 Beech St. (03104); (603)627-7679. Pres. Gary Wallin; Exec. Dir. Earnest Siegel.

NEW JERSEY

ATLANTIC COUNTY

FEDERATION OF JEWISH AGENCIES OF ATLANTIC COUNTY (1924); 5321 Atlantic Ave., Ventnor City (08406); (609)822-7122. Pres. James Cooper; Exec. Dir. Bernard Cohen.

BERGEN COUNTY

UNITED JEWISH COMMUNITY OF BERGEN COUNTY (inc. 1978); 111 Kinderkamack Rd., PO Box 4176, N. Hackensack Station, River Edge (07661); (201)488-6800. Pres. Eli Warach; Exec. V. Pres. Dr. James Young.

CENTRAL NEW JERSEY

JEWISH FEDERATION OF CENTRAL NEW JERSEY (1940; merged 1973); (sponsors UNITED JEWISH CAMPAIGN); Green Lane, Union (07083); (201)351-5060. Pres. Jim Shrager; Exec. V. Pres. Burton Lazarow.

CLIFTON-PASSAIC

JEWISH FEDERATION OF GREATER CLIFTON-PASSAIC (1933); (sponsors UNITED JEWISH CAMPAIGN); 199 Scoles Ave., Clifton (07012). (201)777-7031. Pres. Seymour Bitterman; Exec. Dir. Yosef Muskin.

CUMBERLAND COUNTY

JEWISH FEDERATION OF CUMBERLAND COUNTY (inc. 1971); (incl. JEWISH COMMUNITY COUNCIL and ALLIED JEWISH APPEAL); 629 Wood St., Suite 204, Vineland (08360); (609)696-4445. Pres. Ronald Macon; Exec. Dir. Daniel Lepow.

ENGLEWOOD

(Merged with Bergen County)

JERSEY CITY

UNITED JEWISH APPEAL (1939); 71 Bentley Ave. (07304); (201)332-6644. Chmn. Mel Blum; Exec. Sec. Madeline Mazer.

MERCER COUNTY

JEWISH FEDERATION OF MERCER AND BUCKS COUNTIES NJ/PA (formerly Delaware Valley); (1929; reorg. 1982); 999 Lower Ferry Rd., Trenton (08628); (609)883-5000. Pres. Lionel A. Kaplan; Exec. Dir. Haim Morag. (Also see listing under Pennsylvania.)

METROWEST NEW JERSEY

UNITED JEWISH FEDERATION OF METROWEST (1923); (sponsors UNITED JEWISH APPEAL); 60 Glenwood Ave., E. Orange (07017); (201)673-6800; (212)943-0570. Pres. Sam Oolie; Exec. V. Pres. Howard E. Charish.

MIDDLESEX COUNTY

JEWISH FEDERATION OF GREATER MIDDLESEX COUNTY (formerly Northern Middlesex County and Raritan Valley) (org. 1948; reorg. 1985), (sponsors UNITED JEWISH APPEAL); 100 Metroplex Dr., Suite 101, Edison (08817); (201)985-1234. Pres. Larry Zicklin; Exec. Dir. Michael Shapiro.

MONMOUTH COUNTY

JEWISH FEDERATION OF GREATER MONMOUTH COUNTY (formerly Shore Area) (1971); 100 Grant Ave., PO Box 210, Deal (07723-0210); (201)531-6200-1. Pres. Dr. Lawrence Karasic; Exec. Dir. Marvin Relkin.

MORRIS-SUSSEX COUNTY

(Merged with MetroWest NJ)

NORTH JERSEY

JEWISH FEDERATION OF NORTH JERSEY (formerly Jewish Community Council) (1933); (sponsors UNITED JEWISH APPEAL DRIVE); 1 Pike Dr., Wayne (07470); (201)-595-0555. Pres. Alvin Reisbaum; Exec. Dir. Barry Rosenberg.

NORTHERN MIDDLESEX COUNTY

(See Middlesex County)

OCEAN COUNTY

OCEAN COUNTY JEWISH FEDERATION (1977); 301 Madison Ave., Lakewood (08701); (201)363-0530. Pres. Robert Singer; Exec. Dir. Michael Ruvel.

RARITAN VALLEY

(See Middlesex County)

SOMERSET COUNTY

JEWISH FEDERATION OF SOMERSET COUNTY (1960); 120 Finderne Ave., Bridgewater (08807); (201)725-6994. Pres. Ted Gast; Exec. Dir. Elaine Auerbach.

SOUTHERN NEW JERSEY

JEWISH FEDERATION OF SOUTHERN NEW JERSEY (incl. Camden, Burlington, and Gloucester Counties) (1922); (sponsors ALLIED JEWISH APPEAL); 2393 W. Marlton

Pike, Cherry Hill (08002); (609)665-6100. Pres. Dr. Eugene Bass; Exec. V. Pres. Stuart Alperin.

NEW MEXICO

ALBUQUERQUE

JEWISH FEDERATION OF GREATER ALBUQUERQUE, INC. (1938); 12800 Lomas NE, Suite F (87112); (505)292-1061. Pres. Arthur Gardenswartz; Exec. Dir. Elisa M. Simon.

NEW YORK

ALBANY

(Merged with Schenectady; see Northeastern New York)

BROOME COUNTY

JEWISH FEDERATION OF BROOME COUNTY (1937; inc. 1958); 500 Clubhouse Rd., Binghamton (13903); (607)724-2332. Pres. Victoria Rouff; Exec. Dir. Mark Steiner.

BUFFALO

JEWISH FEDERATION OF GREATER BUFFALO, INC. (1903); (sponsors UNITED JEWISH FUND CAMPAIGN); 787 Delaware Ave. (14209); (716)886-7750. Pres. Joel Lippman; Exec. Dir. Harry Kosansky.

ELMIRA

ELMIRA JEWISH WELFARE FUND, INC. (1942); PO Box 3087 (14905); (607)734-8122. Pres. Kurt Wohl; Exec. Dir. Cy Leveen.

KINGSTON

JEWISH FEDERATION OF GREATER KINGSTON, INC. (inc. 1951); 159 Green St. (12401); (914)338-8131. Pres. Dr. Howard Rothstein; Exec. Dir. Ira H. Minot.

NEW YORK

UJA-FEDERATION OF JEWISH PHILANTHROPIES OF NEW YORK, INC. (incl. Greater NY; Westchester, Nassau, and Suffolk Counties) (Fed. org. 1917; UJA 1939; merged 1986); 130 E. 59 St. (10022); (212)980-1000. Pres. Peggy Tishman; Bd. Chmn. Joseph Gurwin; Exec. V. Pres.'s Ernest W. Michel, Stephen D. Solender.

NIAGARA FALLS

JEWISH FEDERATION OF NIAGARA FALLS, NY, INC. (1935); Temple Beth Israel, Rm. #5, College & Madison Ave. (14305); (716)-284-4575. Pres. Howard Kushner; Exec. Dir. Linda Boxer.

NORTHEASTERN NEW YORK

UNITED JEWISH FEDERATION OF NORTHEASTERN NEW YORK (formerly Albany and Schenectady) (1986); Latham Circle Mall, 800 New Loudon Rd., Latham (12110); (518)783-7800. Pres. Malka Evans; Exec. Dir. Norman J. Schimelman.

ORANGE COUNTY

JEWISH FEDERATION OF GREATER ORANGE COUNTY (1977); 360 Powell Ave., Newburgh (12550); (914)562-7860. Pres. Harold Levine.

ROCHESTER

JEWISH COMMUNITY FEDERATION OF ROCHESTER, NY, INC. (1939); 441 East Ave. (14607); (716)461-0490. Pres. Paul Goldberg; Exec. Dir. Avrom Fox.

ROCKLAND COUNTY

UNITED JEWISH COMMUNITY OF ROCKLAND COUNTY (1985); 300 N. Main St., Suite 311, Spring Valley (10977); (914)352-7100. Pres. Barbara Grau; Exec. Dir. Robert Posner.

SCHENECTADY

(Merged with Albany; see Northeastern New York)

SYRACUSE

SYRACUSE JEWISH FEDERATION, INC. (1918); 2223 E. Genesee St., PO Box 510, DeWitt (13214); (315)422-4104. Pres. Helen Marcum; Exec. V. Pres. Barry Silverberg.

TROY

TROY JEWISH COMMUNITY COUNCIL, INC. (1936); 2430 21 St. (12180); (518)274-0700. Pres. Steven Ginsberg.

UTICA

JEWISH FEDERATION OF UTICA, NY, INC. (1933; inc. 1950); (sponsors UNITED JEWISH APPEAL OF UTICA); 2310 Oneida St. (13501); (315)733-2343. Pres. Ann Siegel; Exec. Dir. Meyer L. Bodoff.

NORTH CAROLINA

ASHEVILLE

WESTERN NORTH CAROLINA JEWISH FEDERATION (1935); 236 Charlotte St. (28801); (704)253-0701. Pres. Robert J. Deutsch; Exec. Dir. Ellen Sandweiss-Hodges.

CHARLOTTE

CHARLOTTE JEWISH FEDERATION (1938); PO Box 13369 (28211); (704)366-5007. Pres.

Mrs. Bobbi Bernstein; Exec. Dir. Michael Minkin.

DURHAM-CHAPEL HILL

Durham-Chapel Hill Jewish Federation & Community Council (1979); 205 Mt. Bolus Rd., Chapel Hill (27514); (919)-967-6916. Pres. Lee M. Marcus.

GREENSBORO

Greensboro Jewish Federation (1940); 713A N. Greene St. (27401); (919)272-3189. Pres. Joel Liebling; Exec. Dir. Marilyn Chandler.

OHIO

AKRON

Akron Jewish Community Federation (1935); 750 White Pond Dr. (44320); (216)-867-7850. Pres. Martin Spector; Exec. Dir. Stanley H. Bard.

CANTON

Canton Jewish Community Federation (1935; reorg. 1955); 2631 Harvard Ave., NW (44709); (216)452-6444. Pres. Neil Genshaft; Exec. Dir. Jay Rubin.

CINCINNATI

Jewish Federation of Cincinnati (merger of the Associated Jewish Agencies and Jewish Welfare Fund) (1896; reorg. 1967); 1811 Losantiville, Suite 320 (45237); (513)351-3800. Pres. David Lazarus; Exec. V. Pres. Aubrey Herman.

CLEVELAND

Jewish Community Federation of Cleveland (1903); 1750 Euclid Ave. (44115); (216)566-9200. Pres. Amb. Milton A. Wolf; Exec. Dir. Stephen H. Hoffman.

COLUMBUS

Columbus Jewish Federation (1926); 1175 College Ave. (43209); (614)237-7686. Pres. B. Lee Skilken; Exec. Dir. Alan Gill.

DAYTON

Jewish Federation of Greater Dayton (1910); 4501 Denlinger Rd. (45426); (513)854-4150. Pres. Bernard Rabinowitz; Exec. V. Pres. Peter H. Wells.

STEUBENVILLE

Jewish Community Council (1938); PO Box 472 (43952); (614)282-9031. Pres. Morris Denmark; Exec. Sec. Mrs. Joseph Freedman.

TOLEDO

Jewish Federation of Greater Toledo (1907; reorg. 1960); 6505 Sylvania Ave., PO Box 587, Sylvania (43560); (419)885-4461. Pres. Marla Levine; Exec. Dir. Steven J. Edelstein.

YOUNGSTOWN

Youngstown Area Jewish Federation (1935); PO Box 449, 505 Gypsy Lane (44501); (216)746-3251. Pres. Lawrence J. Heselov; Exec. V. Pres. Sam Kooperman.

OKLAHOMA

OKLAHOMA CITY

Jewish Federation of Greater Oklahoma City (1941); 3022 NW Expressway #116 (73112); (405)949-0111. Pres. Charles Fagin; Exec. Dir. Garth Potts.

TULSA

Jewish Federation of Tulsa (1938); (sponsors United Jewish Campaign); 2021 E. 71 St. (74136); (918)495-1100. Pres. Edward I. Cohen; Exec. Dir. David Bernstein.

OREGON

PORTLAND

Jewish Federation of Portland (incl. state of Oregon and adjacent Washington communities) (1920; reorg. 1956); 6651 SW Capitol Highway (97219); (503)245-6219. Pres. Dr. Leonard Goldberg; Exec. Dir. Charles Schiffman.

PENNSYLVANIA

ALLENTOWN

Jewish Federation of Allentown; 702 N. 22 St. (18104); (215)821-5500. Pres. Daniel Pomerantz; Exec. Dir. Ivan C. Schonfeld.

ALTOONA

Federation of Jewish Philanthropies (1920; reorg. 1940; inc. 1944); 1308 17 St. (16601); (814)944-4072. Pres. Morley Cohn.

BUCKS COUNTY

Jewish Federation of Mercer and Bucks Counties NJ/PA (formerly Delaware Valley); (1929; reorg. 1982); 999 Lower Ferry Rd., Trenton, NJ (08628); (609)883-5000. Pres. Lionel A. Kaplan; Exec. Dir. Haim Morag. (Also see listing under New Jersey.)

ERIE

JEWISH COMMUNITY COUNCIL OF ERIE (1946); 701 G. Daniel Baldwin Bldg., 1001 State St. (16501); (814)455-4474. Pres. Leonard Lechtner.

HARRISBURG

UNITED JEWISH FEDERATION OF GREATER HARRISBURG (1941); 100 Vaughn St. (17110); (717)236-9555. Pres. Morton Spector; Exec. Dir. Elliot Gershenson.

JOHNSTOWN

UNITED JEWISH FEDERATION OF JOHNSTOWN (1938); 922 Windan Lane (15905); (814)535-6756. Pres. Isadore Suchman.

PHILADELPHIA

FEDERATION OF JEWISH AGENCIES OF GREATER PHILADELPHIA (1901; reorg. 1956); 226 S. 16 St. (19102); (215)893-5600. Pres. Miriam A. Schneirov; Exec. V. Pres. Robert P. Forman.

PITTSBURGH

UNITED JEWISH FEDERATION OF GREATER PITTSBURGH (1912; reorg. 1955); 234 McKee Pl. (15213); (412)681-8000. Pres. Leon L. Netzer; Exec. V. Pres. Howard M. Rieger.

READING

JEWISH FEDERATION OF READING, PA., INC. (1935; reorg. 1972); (sponsors UNITED JEWISH CAMPAIGN); 1700 City Line St. (19604); (215)921-2766. Pres. Victor Hammel; Exec. Dir. Daniel Tannenbaum.

SCRANTON

SCRANTON-LACKAWANNA JEWISH FEDERATION (incl. Lackawanna County) (1945); 601 Jefferson Ave. (18510); (717)961-2300. Pres. Dr. Alvin Greenwald; Exec. Dir. Seymour Brotman.

WILKES-BARRE

JEWISH FEDERATION OF GREATER WILKES-BARRE (1935); (sponsors UNITED JEWISH CAMPAIGN); 60 S. River St. (18702); (717)-822-4146. Pres. Dr. David Greenwald; Exec. Dir. Marty Erann.

RHODE ISLAND

PROVIDENCE

JEWISH FEDERATION OF RHODE ISLAND (1945); 130 Sessions St. (02906); (401)421-4111. Pres. Norman Tilles; Exec. V. Pres. Elliot Cohan.

SOUTH CAROLINA

CHARLESTON

CHARLESTON JEWISH FEDERATION (1949); 1645 Raoul Wallenberg Blvd., PO Box 31298 (29407); (803)571-6565. Pres. Ellis I. Kahn Exec. Dir. Michael Wise.

COLUMBIA

COLUMBIA UNITED JEWISH WELFARE FEDERATION (1960); 4540 Trenholm Rd., PO Box 6968 (29206); (803)787-0580. Pres. Howard Weiss; Exec. Dir. Alex Grossberg.

SOUTH DAKOTA

SIOUX FALLS

JEWISH WELFARE FUND (1938); National Reserve Bldg., 513 S. Main Ave. (57102); (605)336-2880. Pres. Laurence Bierman; Exec. Sec. Louis R. Hurwitz.

TENNESSEE

CHATTANOOGA

CHATTANOOGA JEWISH FEDERATION (1931); 5326 Lynnland Terrace, PO Box 8947 (37411); (615)894-1317. Pres. Robert H. Siskin; Exec. Dir. Morris Rombro.

KNOXVILLE

KNOXVILLE JEWISH FEDERATION (1939); 6800 Deane Hill Dr., PO Box 10882 (37919); (615)693-5837. Pres. Arnold Schwarzbart; Exec. Dir. Conrad J. Koller.

MEMPHIS

MEMPHIS JEWISH FEDERATION (incl. Shelby County) (1935); 6560 Poplar Ave., PO Box 38268 (38138); (901)767-7100. Pres. Edward R. Young; Exec. Dir. Leslie S. Gottlieb.

NASHVILLE

JEWISH FEDERATION OF NASHVILLE & MIDDLE TENNESSEE (1936); 801 Perry Warner Blvd. (37205); (615)356-3242. Pres. David Steine, Jr.; Exec. Dir. Dr. Jay M. Pilzer.

TEXAS

AUSTIN

JEWISH COMMUNITY COUNCIL OF AUSTIN (1939); reorg. 1956); 11713 Jollyville Rd. (78759); (512)331-1144. Pres. David Kruger; Exec. Dir. Marilyn Stahl.

CORPUS CHRISTI

COMBINED JEWISH APPEAL OF CORPUS CHRISTI (1962); 750 Everhart Rd. (78411);

(512)855-6239. Pres. Charles Doraine; Acting Exec. Dir. Rosalind Lieberman.

CORPUS CHRISTI JEWISH COMMUNITY COUNCIL (1953); 750 Everhart Rd. (78411); (512)855-6239. Pres. Howard Bazarsky; Acting Exec. Dir. Rosalind Lieberman.

DALLAS

JEWISH FEDERATION OF GREATER DALLAS (1911); 7800 Northaven Rd., Suite A (75230); (214)369-3313. Pres. Howard Schultz; Exec. Dir. Morris A. Stein.

EL PASO

JEWISH FEDERATION OF EL PASO, INC. (incl. surrounding communities) (1937); 405 Wallenberg Dr., PO Box 12097 (79913-0097); (915)584-4437. Pres. Beth Lipson; Exec. Dir. David Brown.

FORT WORTH

JEWISH FEDERATION OF FORT WORTH AND TARRANT COUNTY (1936); 6801 Dan Danciger Rd. (76133); (817)292-3081. Pres. Sandra Freed; Exec. Dir. Rabbi Howard J. Hirsch.

GALVESTON

GALVESTON COUNTY JEWISH WELFARE ASSOCIATION (1936); PO Box 146 (77553); (409)763-5241. Pres. Dr. Mark Sanders; Treas. Harold Levine.

HOUSTON

JEWISH FEDERATION OF GREATER HOUSTON (1936); 5603 S. Braeswood Blvd. (77096); (713)729-7000. Pres. Harold Raizes; Exec. Dir. Hans Mayer.

SAN ANTONIO

JEWISH FEDERATION OF SAN ANTONIO (incl. Bexar County) (1922); 8434 Ahern Dr. (78216); (512)341-8234. Pres. Russell Davis; Exec. Dir. Alan Bayer.

WACO

JEWISH FEDERATION OF WACO AND CENTRAL TEXAS (1949); PO Box 8031 (76714-8031); (817)776-3740. Pres. Simone Bauer; Exec. Sec. Martha Bauer.

UTAH

SALT LAKE CITY

UNITED JEWISH COUNCIL AND SALT LAKE JEWISH WELFARE FUND (1936); 2416 E. 1700 S. (84108); (801)581-0098. Pres. Richard McGillis; Exec. Dir. Bernard Solomon.

VIRGINIA

NEWPORT NEWS—HAMPTON—WILLIAMSBURG

UNITED JEWISH COMMUNITY OF THE VIRGINIA PENINSULA, INC. (1942); 2700 Spring Rd., Newport News (23606); (804)930-1422. Pres. Rhoda H. Mazur; Exec. Dir. Norman Olshansky.

RICHMOND

JEWISH COMMUNITY FEDERATION OF RICHMOND (1935); 5403 Monument Ave., PO Box 8237 (23226); (804)288-0045. Pres. Dr. Walter N. Rashan; Exec. Dir. Robert S. Hyman.

ROANOKE

JEWISH COMMUNITY COUNCIL (1974); PO Box 1074 (24005). Chmn. Albert Lippmann.

TIDEWATER

UNITED JEWISH FEDERATION OF TIDEWATER (incl. Norfolk, Portsmouth, and Virginia Beach) (1937); 7300 Newport Ave., PO Box 9776, Norfolk (23505); (804)489-8040. Pres. Bootsie Goldmeier; Exec. V. Pres. A. Robert Gast.

WASHINGTON

SEATTLE

JEWISH FEDERATION OF GREATER SEATTLE (incl. King County, Everett, and Bremerton) (1926); 510 Securities Bldg., 1904 Third Ave. (98101); (206)622-8211. Pres. Eileen Gilman; Exec. Dir. Rabbi Melvin L. Libman.

WEST VIRGINIA

CHARLESTON

FEDERATED JEWISH CHARITIES OF CHARLESTON, INC. (1937); PO Box 1613 (25326); (304)346-7500. Pres. Carl Lehman; Exec. Sec. William H. Thalheimer.

WISCONSIN

KENOSHA

KENOSHA JEWISH WELFARE FUND (1938); 6537 Seventh Ave. (53140); (414)658-8635. Pres. Nathaniel S. Lepp; Sec.-Treas. Mrs. S. M. Lapp.

MADISON

MADISON JEWISH COMMUNITY COUNCIL, INC. (1940); 310 N. Midvale Blvd., Suite 325 (53705); (608)231-3426. Pres. Louis Swedarsky; Exec. Dir. Steven H. Morrison.

MILWAUKEE

MILWAUKEE JEWISH FEDERATION, INC. (1902); 1360 N. Prospect Ave. (53202); (414)-271-8338. Pres. R. Todd Lappin; Exec. V. Pres. Robert Aronson.

RACINE

RACINE JEWISH WELFARE COUNCIL (1946); 944 S. Main St. (53403); (414)633-7093. Chmn. Arthur Schaefer.

CANADA

ALBERTA

CALGARY

CALGARY JEWISH COMMUNITY COUNCIL (1962); 1607 90th Ave. SW (T2V 4V7); (403)-253-8600. Pres. Hal Joffe; Exec. Dir. Drew J. Staffenberg.

EDMONTON

JEWISH FEDERATION OF EDMONTON (1954; reorg. 1982); 7200 156 St. (T5R 1X3); (403)-487-5120. Pres. Shelly Maerov; Exec. Dir. Howard Bloom.

BRITISH COLUMBIA

VANCOUVER

JEWISH FEDERATION OF GREATER VANCOUVER (1932); 950 W. 41 Ave. (V5Z 2N7); (604)266-8371. Pres. Ronald Coleman; Exec. Dir. Steve Drysdale.

MANITOBA

WINNIPEG

WINNIPEG JEWISH COMMUNITY COUNCIL (1938; reorg. 1973); (sponsors COMBINED JEWISH APPEAL OF WINNIPEG); 370 Hargrave St. (R3B 2K1); (204)943-0406. Pres. Evelyn Katz; Exec. Dir. Robert Freedman.

ONTARIO

HAMILTON

HAMILTON JEWISH FEDERATION (1932; merged 1971); (sponsors UNITED JEWISH WELFARE FUND); PO Box 7258, 1030 Lower Lion Club Rd., Ancaster (L9G3N6); (416)-648-0605. Pres. Phillip Leon; Exec. Dir. Sid Brail.

LONDON

LONDON JEWISH COMMUNITY COUNCIL (1932); 536 Huron St. (N5Y 4J5); (519)673-3310. Pres. Gloria Gilbert; Exec. Dir. Gerald Enchin.

OTTAWA

JEWISH COMMUNITY COUNCIL OF OTTAWA (1934); 151 Chapel St. (K1N 7Y2); (613)232-7306. Pres. Steven Victor.

TORONTO

TORONTO JEWISH CONGRESS (1937); 4600 Bathurst St.; Willowdale (M2R 3V2); (416)-635-2883. Pres. Herb Rosenfeld; Exec. Dir. Steven Ain.

WINDSOR

JEWISH COMMUNITY COUNCIL (1938); 1641 Ouellette Ave. (N8X 1K9); (519)973-1772. Pres. Richard Rosenthal; Exec. Dir. Joseph Eisenberg.

QUEBEC

MONTREAL

ALLIED JEWISH COMMUNITY SERVICES (1965); 5151 Cote St. Catherine Rd. (H3W 1M6); (514)735-3541. Pres. Peter Wolkove; Exec. Dir. John Fishel.

Jewish Periodicals[1]

UNITED STATES

ARIZONA

ARIZONA POST (1946). 635 N. Craycroft, #202, Tucson, 85711. (602)325-5864. Sandra R. Heiman. Semiweekly. Jewish Federation of S. Arizona.

GREATER PHOENIX JEWISH NEWS (1947). PO Box 26590, Phoenix, 85068. (602)870-9470. Flo Eckstein. Weekly.

CALIFORNIA

B'NAI B'RITH MESSENGER (1897). 2510 W. 7 St., Los Angeles, 90057. (213)380-5000. Rabbi Yale Butler. Weekly.

B'NAI B'RITH MESSENGER-Bay Area Edition (1986). 904 Irving St., Suite 236, San Francisco, 94122. (415)387-1744. Janet Gallin. Monthly.

HERITAGE-SOUTHWEST JEWISH PRESS (1914). 2130 S. Vermont Ave., Los Angeles, 90007. Dan Brin. Weekly. (Also SAN DIEGO JEWISH PRESS-HERITAGE, San Diego [weekly]; CENTRALCALIFORNIA JEWISH HERITAGE, Sacramento and Fresno area [monthly]; ORANGE COUNTY JEWISH HERITAGE, Orange County area [weekly].)

JEWISH JOURNAL (1986). 3660 Wilshire Blvd., Suite 204, Los Angeles, 90010. (213)738-7778. Gene Lichtenstein. Weekly.

JEWISH SPECTATOR (1935). PO Box 2016, Santa Monica, 90406. (213)393-9063. Trude Weiss-Rosmarin. Quarterly.

JEWISH STAR (1956). 109 Minna St., Suite 323, San Francisco, 94105. (415)421-4874. Nevon Stuckey. Bimonthly.

NATIONAL JEWISH DAILY AND ISRAEL TODAY (1973). 6742 Van Nuys Blvd., Van Nuys, 91405. (818)786-4000. Phil Blazer. Daily.

NORTHERN CALIFORNIA JEWISH BULLETIN (1946). 121 Steuart St., Suite 302, San Francisco, 94105. (415)957-9340. Marc Klein. Weekly. San Francisco Jewish Community Publications Inc.

SAN DIEGO JEWISH TIMES (1979). 2592 Fletcher Pkwy., El Cajon, 92020. (619)-463-5515. Carol Rosenberg. Biweekly.

TIKKUN (1986). 5100 Leona St., Oakland, 94619. (415)482-0805. Michael Lerner. Bimonthly. Institute for Labor & Mental Health.

WESTERN STATES JEWISH HISTORY (1968). 2429 23 St., Santa Monica, 90405. (213)-450-2946. Norton B. Stern. Quarterly. Western States Jewish History Association.

COLORADO

INTERMOUNTAIN JEWISH NEWS (1913). 1275 Sherman St., Suite 214, Denver, 80203. (303)861-2234. Miriam H. Goldberg. Weekly.

CONNECTICUT

CONNECTICUT JEWISH LEDGER (1929). PO Box 1688, Hartford, 06101. (203)233-2148. Berthold Gaster. Weekly.

DISTRICT OF COLUMBIA

B'NAI B'RITH INTERNATIONAL JEWISH MONTHLY (1886 under the name MENORAH). 1640 Rhode Island Ave., NW,

[1]The information in this directory is based on replies to questionnaires circulated by the editors. For organization bulletins, see the directory of Jewish organizations.

Washington, 20036. (202)857-6645. Marc Silver. Ten times a year. B'nai B'rith.

JEWISH VETERAN (1896). 1811 R St., NW, Washington, 20009. (202)265-6280. Pearl Laufer. Bimonthly. Jewish War Veterans of the U.S.A.

MOMENT (1975). 3000 Connecticut Ave., NW, Washington, 20008. (202)387-8888. Hershel Shanks. Monthly (except Jan./ Feb. and July/Aug.) Jewish Education Ventures.

NEAR EAST REPORT (1957). 500 N. Capitol St., NW, Washington, 20001. (202)638-1225. Eric Rozenman. Weekly. Near East Research, Inc.

QUARTERLY REPORT. 1819 H Street, NW, Suite 410, Washington, 20006. (202)775-9770. Micah H. Naftalin. Quarterly. Union of Councils for Soviet Jews.

WASHINGTON JEWISH WEEK (1965). 1910 K St., NW, #601, Washington, 20006. (202)872-1100. Lisa S. Lenkiewicz. Weekly.

FLORIDA

JEWISH FLORIDIAN GROUP (1927). 120 NE 6 St., Miami, 33101. (305)373-4605. Leo Mindlin. Weekly.

JEWISH JOURNAL (1977). PO Box 189006, Ft. Plantation, 33313. (305)581-2244. Dorothy P. Rubin. Weekly.

JEWISH WORLD (1982). 2405 Mercer Ave., W. Palm Beach, 33401. (305)833-8331. Martin Pomerance. Weekly.

MIAMI JEWISH TRIBUNE (1986). 3550 Biscayne Blvd., Suite 600, Miami, 33137. (305)576-9500. David Frank. Weekly.

SOUTHERN JEWISH WEEKLY (1924). PO Box 3297, Jacksonville, 32206. (904)634-1469. Isadore Moscovitz. Weekly.

GEORGIA

ATLANTA JEWISH TIMES (formerly SOUTHERN ISRAELITE). PO Box 250287, Atlanta, 30325. (404)355-6139. Vida Goldgar. Weekly.

JEWISH CIVIC PRESS (1965). 3330 Peachtree Rd. NE, Atlanta, 30326. (404)262-6786. Abner Tritt. Monthly.

ILLINOIS

CHICAGO JUF NEWS (1972). 1 S. Franklin St., Chicago, 60606. (312)444-2853. Joseph Aaron. Monthly. Jewish Federation of Metropolitan Chicago.

JEWISH COMMUNITY NEWS (1941). 6464 W. Main, Suite 7A, Belleville, 62223. (618)-398-6100. Zalman Stein. Bimonthly. Jewish Federation of Southern Illinois.

SENTINEL (1911). 323 S. Franklin St., Chicago, 60606. (312)663-1101. J. I. Fishbein. Weekly.

INDIANA

ILLIANA NEWS (1975). 2939 Jewett St., Highland, 46322. (219)972-2250. Barnett Labowitz. Ten times a year. Jewish Federation, Inc./Northwest Indiana.

INDIANA JEWISH POST AND OPINION (1935). PO Box 449097, Indianapolis, 46202. (317)927-7800. Gabriel Cohen. Weekly.

NATIONAL JEWISH POST AND OPINION. PO Box 449097, Indianapolis, 46202. (317)-927-7800. Gabriel Cohen. Weekly.

KENTUCKY

KENTUCKY JEWISH POST AND OPINION (1931). 1551 Bardstown Rd., Louisville, 40205. (502)459-1914. Gabriel Cohen. Weekly.

LOUISIANA

JEWISH CIVIC PRESS (1965). PO Box 15500, 924 Valmont St., New Orleans, 70115. (504)895-8784. Abner Tritt. Monthly.

JEWISH TIMES (1974). 1539 Jackson Ave., Suite 323, New Orleans, 70130. (504)524-3147. Fred Shochet, Leah Paller. Biweekly.

MARYLAND

BALTIMORE JEWISH TIMES (1919). 2104 N. Charles St., Baltimore, 21218. (301)752-3504. Gary Rosenblatt. Weekly.

MASSACHUSETTS

AMERICAN JEWISH HISTORY (1893). 2 Thornton Rd., Waltham, 02154. (617)891-8110. Marc Lee Raphael. Quarterly. American Jewish Historical Society.

BOSTON JEWISH TIMES (1945). Box 18427, Boston, 02118. (617)357-8635. Sten Lukin. Weekly.

JEWISH ADVOCATE (1902). 1168-70 Commonwealth Ave., Boston, 02134. (617)277-8988. Bernard M. Hyatt. Weekly.

JEWISH REPORTER (1970). 76 Salem End Rd., Framingham, 01701. (617)879-3300. Sheila Abrahams, Jodie Holzwasser. Monthly. Metro West Jewish Federation.

JEWISH WEEKLY NEWS (1945). PO Box 1569, Springfield, 01101. (413)739-4771. Leslie B. Kahn. Weekly.

JOURNAL OF THE NORTH SHORE JEWISH COMMUNITY. 564 Loring Ave., Salem, 01970. (617)741-1558. Barbara Wolf. Fortnightly. Jewish Federation of the North Shore.

MICHIGAN

DETROIT JEWISH NEWS (1942). 20300 Civic Center Dr., Suite 240, Southfield, 48076. (313)354-6060. Gary Rosenblatt. Weekly.

HUMANISTIC JUDAISM (1968). 28611 W. Twelve Mile Rd., Farmington Hills, 48018. (313)478-7610. M. Bonnie Cousens, Ruth D. Feldman. Quarterly. Society for Humanistic Judaism.

MICHIGAN JEWISH HISTORY (1960). 6600 W. Maple Rd., W. Bloomfield, 48033. (313)661-1000. Phillip Applebaum. Semiannually. Jewish Historical Society of Michigan.

MINNESOTA

AMERICAN JEWISH WORLD (1912). 4509 Minnetonka Blvd., Minneapolis, 55416. (612)920-7000. Stacey R. Bush. Weekly.

MISSOURI

KANSAS CITY JEWISH CHRONICLE (1920). 7373 W. 107 St., Overland Park, 66212. (913)648-4620. Ruth Baum Bigus. Weekly.

MISSOURI JEWISH POST (1948). 9531 Lackland, Suite 207, St. Louis, 63114. (314)423-3088. Kathie Sutin. Weekly.

ST. LOUIS JEWISH LIGHT (1947). 12 Millstone Campus Dr., St. Louis, 63146. (314)-432-3353. Robert A. Cohn. Weekly. Jewish Federation of St. Louis.

NEBRASKA

JEWISH PRESS (1921). 333 S. 132 St., Omaha, 68154. (402)334-8200. Morris Maline. Weekly. Jewish Federation of Omaha.

NEVADA

JEWISH REPORTER (1976). 1030 E. Twain Ave., Las Vegas, 89109. (702)732-0556. Marla Gerecht. Monthly. Jewish Federation of Las Vegas.

LAS VEGAS ISRAELITE (1965). PO Box 14096, Las Vegas, 89114. (702)876-1255. Michael Tell. Biweekly.

NEW JERSEY

JEWISH COMMUNITY VOICE (1941). 2393 W. Marlton Pike, Cherry Hill, 08002. (609)-665-6100. Harriet Kessler. Biweekly. Jewish Federation of Southern NJ.

JEWISH HORIZON (1981). 1391 Martine Ave., Scotch Plains, 07076. (201)889-9200. Fran Gold. Weekly. Jewish Federation of Central NJ.

JEWISH NEWS (1947). 60 Glenwood Ave., E. Orange, 07017. (201)678-3900. Charles Baumohl. Weekly. United Jewish Federation of MetroWest.

JEWISH RECORD (1939). 1537 Atlantic Ave., Atlantic City, 08401. (609)344-5119. Martin Korik. Weekly.

JEWISH STANDARD (1931). 385 Prospect Ave. Hackensack, 07601. (201)342-1115. Lois Goldrich. Weekly.

JEWISH STAR (1985). 100 Metroplex Dr., Edison, 08817. (201)985-1234. Mindy Belfer. Bimonthly. Jewish Federation of Greater Middlesex County.

JOURNAL OF JEWISH COMMUNAL SERVICE (1899). 3084 State Hwy. 27, Suite 1, Kendall Pk, NJ 08824-1657. (201)821-1871. Sanford N. Sherman. Quarterly. Conference of Jewish Communal Service.

NEW YORK

AFN SHVEL (1941). 200 W. 72 St., Suite 40, NYC, 10023. (212)787-6675. Mordkhe Schaechter. Quarterly. Yiddish. League for Yiddish, Inc.

ALBANY JEWISH WORLD (1965). 1104 Central Ave., Albany, 12205. (518)459-8455. Laurie J. Clevenson. Weekly.

ALGEMEINER JOURNAL (1972). 404 Park Ave. S., NYC, 10016. (212)689-3390. Gershon Jacobson. Weekly. Yiddish.

AMERICAN JEWISH YEAR BOOK (1899). 165 E. 56 St., NYC, 10022. (212)751-4000. David Singer. Annually. American Jewish Committee and Jewish Publication Society.

AMERICAN ZIONIST (1910). 4 E. 34 St., NYC, 10016. (212)481-1500. Carol Binen. Quarterly. Zionist Organization of America.

AMIT WOMAN (1925). 817 Broadway, NYC, 10003. (212)477-4720. Micheline Ratzersdorfer. Five times a year. AMIT Women (formerly American Mizrachi Women).

AUFBAU (1934). 2121 Broadway, NYC, 10023. (212)873-7400. Gert Niers, Henry Marx. Fortnightly. German. New World Club, Inc.

BITZARON (1939). PO Box 623, Cooper Station, NYC, 10003. (212)598-3958. Hayim Leaf. Bimonthly. Hebrew. Hebrew Literary Foundation.

BUFFALO JEWISH REVIEW (1918). 15 E. Mohawk St., Buffalo, 14203. (716)854-2192. Harlan C. Abbey. Weekly. Kahaal Nahalot Israel.

COMMENTARY (1945). 165 E. 56 St., NYC, 10022. (212)751-4000. Norman Podhoretz. Monthly. American Jewish Committee.

CONGRESS MONTHLY (1933). 15 E. 84 St., NYC, 10028. (212)879-4500. Maier Deshell. Seven times a year. American Jewish Congress.

CONSERVATIVE JUDAISM (1945). 3080 Broadway, NYC, 10027. (212)678-8863. Rabbi David Silverman. Quarterly. Rabbinical Assembly.

CONTEMPORARY JEWRY (1974 under the name JEWISH SOCIOLOGY AND SOCIAL RESEARCH). Center for Jewish Studies, CUNY Graduate School and University Center, 33 W. 42 St., NYC, 10036. (212)-790-4404. Paul Ritterband. Semiannually. Association for the Social Scientific Study of Jewry.

ECONOMIC HORIZONS (1953). 500 Fifth Ave., NYC, 10110. (212)354-6510. Ronnie Bassan. Quarterly. American-Israel Chamber of Commerce and Industry, Inc.

HADAROM (1957). 275 Seventh Ave. NYC, 10001. (212)807-7888. Rabbi Gedalia Schwartz. Annually. Hebrew. Rabbinical Council of America.

HADASSAH MAGAZINE (1921). 50 W. 58 St., NYC, 10019. (212)355-7900. Alan M. Tigay. Monthly (except for combined issues of June–July and Aug.–Sept.). Hadassah, Women's Zionist Organization of America.

HADOAR (1921). 1841 Broadway, Rm. 510, NYC, 10023. (212)581-5151. Shlomo Shamir. Weekly. Hebrew. Histadruth Ivrith of America.

ISRAEL HORIZONS (1952). 150 Fifth Ave., Suite 911, NYC, 10011. (212)255-8760. Arieh Lebowitz. Bimonthly. Americans for Progressive Israel.

ISRAEL QUALITY (1976). 500 Fifth Ave., Suite 5416, NYC, 10110. (212)354-6510. Beth Belkin. Quarterly. American-Israel Chamber of Commerce and Industry, Inc. and Government of Israel Trade Center.

JEWISH ACTION (1950). 45 W. 36 St., NYC, 10018. (212)563-4000. Heidi Tenzer. Quarterly. Union of Orthodox Jewish Congregations of America.

JEWISH BOOK ANNUAL (1942). 15 E. 26 St., NYC, 10010. (212)532-4949. Jacob Kabakoff. Annually. English-Hebrew-Yiddish. JWB Jewish Book Council.

JEWISH BOOK WORLD (1945). 15 E. 26 St., NYC, 10010. (212)532-4949. William Wollheim. Quarterly. JWB Jewish Book Council.

JEWISH BRAILLE INSTITUTE VOICE (1978). 110 E. 30 St., NYC, 10016. (212)889-2525. Jacob Freid. Ten times a year (audio cassettes). Jewish Braille Institute of America, Inc.

JEWISH BRAILLE REVIEW (1931). 110 E. 30 St., NYC, 10016. (212)889-2525. Jacob Freid. Ten times a year. English braille. Jewish Braille Institute of America, Inc.

JEWISH CURRENT EVENTS (1959). 430 Keller Ave., Elmont, 11003. Samuel Deutsch. Biweekly.

JEWISH CURRENTS (1946). 22 E. 17 St., Suite 601, NYC, 10003. (212)924-5740. Morris U. Schappes. Monthly. Association for Promotion of Jewish Secularism, Inc.

JEWISH EDUCATION (1929). 426 W. 58 St., NYC, 10019. (212)245-8200. Alvin I. Schiff. Quarterly. Council for Jewish Education.

JEWISH FORWARD (1897). 45 E. 33 St., NYC, 10016. (212)889-8200. Mordecai Shtrigler. Weekly. Yiddish and English. Forward Association, Inc.

JEWISH FRONTIER (1934). 275 Seventh Ave., 17th fl., NYC, 10001. (212)645-8121. Nahum Guttman. Monthly. Labor Zionist Letters, Inc.

JEWISH GUARDIAN (1974). GPO Box 2143, Brooklyn, 11202. (718)384-4661. Pinchus David. Irregularly. English-Hebrew. Neturei Karta of U.S.A.

JEWISH JOURNAL (1969). 8723 Third Ave., Brooklyn, 11209. (718)238-6600. Amos Neufeld. Weekly.

JEWISH LEDGER (1924). 3385 Brighton-Henrietta T.L. Rd., Rochester, 14623. (716)-427-2434. Barbara Morgenstern. Weekly.

JEWISH MUSIC NOTES (1945). 15 E. 26 St., NYC, 10010. (212)532-4949. Laura Leon-Cohen. Quarterly. JWB Jewish Music Council.

JEWISH OBSERVER (1963). 84 William St., NYC, 10038. (212)797-9000. Rabbi Nisson Wolpin. Monthly (except July and Aug.). Agudath Israel of America.

JEWISH OBSERVER (1978). PO Box 510, DeWitt, 13214. (315)422-4104. Judith Rubenstein. Fortnightly. Syracuse Jewish Federation, Inc.

JEWISH POST AND RENAISSANCE (1977). 57 E. 11 St., NYC, 10003. (212)420-0042. Charles Roth. Monthly.

JEWISH PRESS (1950). 338 Third Ave., Brooklyn, 11215. (718)330-1100. Sholom Klass. Weekly.

JEWISH SOCIAL STUDIES (1939). 2112 Broadway, Rm. 206, NYC, 10023. (212)-724-5336. Tobey B. Gitelle. Quarterly. Conference on Jewish Social Studies, Inc.

JEWISH TELEGRAPHIC AGENCY COMMUNITY NEWS REPORTER (1962). 165 W. 46 St., Suite 511, NYC, 10036. (212)575-9370. Mark Joffe. Weekly.

JEWISH TELEGRAPHIC AGENCY DAILY NEWS BULLETIN (1917). 165 W. 46 St., Suite 511, NYC, 10036. (212)575-9370. Mark Joffe. Daily.

JEWISH TELEGRAPHIC AGENCY WEEKLY NEWS DIGEST (1933). 165 W. 46 St., Suite 511, NYC, 10036. (212)575-9370. Mark Joffe. Weekly.

JEWISH WEEK (1876; reorg. 1970). 1 Park Ave., NYC, 10016. (212)686-2320. Phillip Ritzenberg. Weekly.

JOURNAL OF REFORM JUDAISM (1953). 192 Lexington Ave., NYC, 10016. (212)684-4990. Samuel Stahl. Quarterly. Central Conference of American Rabbis.

JUDAISM (1952). 15 E. 84 St., NYC, 10028. (212)879-4500. Robert Gordis. Quarterly. American Jewish Congress.

JWB CIRCLE (1946). 15 E. 26 St., NYC, 10010. (212)532-4949. Shirley Frank. Bimonthly. JWB.

KIBBUTZ JOURNAL (1984). 27 W. 20 St., 9th fl., NYC, 10011. (212)255-1338. Becky Rowe. Irregularly. Kibbutz Aliya Desk.

KOL HAT'NUA (1943). 50 W. 58 St., NYC, 10019. (212)355-7900. Heather Paskoff. Irregularly. Young Judaea.

KOSHER DIRECTORY (1925). 45 W. 36 St., NYC, 10018. (212)563-4000. Tziporah Spear. Annually. Union of Orthodox Jewish Congregations of America.

KOSHER DIRECTORY, PASSOVER EDITION (1923). 45 W. 36 St., NYC, 10018. (212)-563-4000. Tziporah Spear. Annually. Union of Orthodox Jewish Congregations of America.

KULTUR UN LEBN—CULTURE AND LIFE (1967). 45 E. 33 St., NYC, 10016. (212)-889-6800. Joseph Mlotek. Quarterly. Yiddish. Workmen's Circle.

LAMISHPAHA. (1963). 1841 Broadway, Rm. 510, NYC, 10023. (212)581-5151. Hanita Brand. Monthly (except July and Aug.). Hebrew. Histadruth Ivrith of America.

LILITH—THE JEWISH WOMEN'S MAGAZINE (1976). 250 W. 57 St., NYC, 10019. (212)-757-0818. Susan Weidman Schneider. Quarterly.

LONG ISLAND JEWISH WORLD (1971). 115 Middle Neck Rd., Great Neck, 11021. (516)829-4000. Jerome W. Lippman. Weekly.

MARTYRDOM AND RESISTANCE (1974). 48 W. 37 St., 9th fl., NYC 10018. (212)564-1865. Eli Zborowski. Bimonthly.

MELTON JOURNAL (1982). 3080 Broadway, NYC, 10027. (212)678-8032. Eduardo Rauch, Barry W. Holtz. Biannually. Melton Research Center for Jewish Education.

MIDSTREAM (1954). 515 Park Ave., NYC, 10022. (212)752-0600. Joel Carmichael. Monthly (bimonthly June–Sept.). Theodor Herzl Foundation, Inc.

MODERN JEWISH STUDIES ANNUAL (1977). Queens College, Kiely 802, 65-30 Kissena

Blvd., Flushing, 11367. (718)520-7067. Joseph C. Landis. Annually. American Association of Professors of Yiddish.

MORNING FREIHEIT (1922). 43 W. 24 St., NYC, 10010. (212)255-7661. Paul Novick. Weekly. Yiddish.

NA'AMAT WOMAN (1926). 200 Madison Ave., Suite 1808, NYC, 10016. (212)725-8010. Judith A. Sokoloff. Five times a year. English-Yiddish-Hebrew. NA'AMAT USA, the Women's Labor Zionist Organization of America

OLOMEINU—OUR WORLD (1945). 160 Broadway, NYC, 10038. (212)227-1000. Rabbi Yaakov Fruchter, Rabbi Nosson Scherman. Monthly. English-Hebrew. Torah Umesorah-National Society for Hebrew Day Schools.

OR CHADASH (1981). 110 E. 30 St., NYC, 10016. (212)889-2525. Joanne Jahr. Two to four times a year (audio cassettes). Hebrew. Jewish Braille Institute of America, Inc.

PEDAGOGIC REPORTER (1949). 730 Broadway, NYC, 10003. (212)529-2000. Mordecai H. Lewittes. Quarterly. Jewish Education Service of North America, Inc.

PRESENT TENSE (1973). 165 E. 56 St., NYC, 10022. (212)751-4000. Murray Polner. Bimonthly. American Jewish Committee.

PROCEEDINGS OF THE AMERICAN ACADEMY FOR JEWISH RESEARCH (1920). 3080 Broadway, NYC, 10027. (212)678-8864. Isaac E. Barzilay. Annually. Hebrew-Arabic-English. American Academy for Jewish Research.

RABBINICAL COUNCIL RECORD (1953). 275 Seventh Ave. NYC, 10001. (212)807-7888. Rabbi Louis Bernstein. Quarterly. Rabbinical Council of America.

RECONSTRUCTIONIST (1935). 270 W. 89 St., NYC, 10024. (212)496-2960. Jacob J. Staub. Eight times a year. Federation of Reconstructionist Congregations and Havurot.

REFORM JUDAISM (1972; formerly DIMENSIONS IN AMERICAN JUDAISM). 838 Fifth Ave., NYC, 10021. (212)249-0100. Aron Hirt-Manheimer. Quarterly. Union of American Hebrew Congregations.

REPORTER. 500 Clubhouse Rd., Binghamton, 13903. (607)724-2360. Marc Goldberg. Weekly. Jewish Federation of Broome County.

RESPONSE (1967). 27 W. 20 St., 9th fl., NYC, 10011. (212)675-1168. Cindy Rubin. Quarterly. Jewish Educational Ventures, Inc.

SHEVILEY HA-HINNUKH (1939). 426 W. 58 St., NYC, 10019. (212)713-0290. Zvulun Ravid. Quarterly. Hebrew. Council for Jewish Education.

SH'MA (1970). Box 567, 23 Murray Ave., Port Washington, 11050. (516)944-9791. Eugene B. Borowitz. Biweekly (except June, July, Aug.).

SHMUESSEN MIT KINDER UN YUGENT (1942). 770 Eastern Pkwy., Brooklyn, 11213. (718)493-9250. Nissan Mindel. Monthly. Yiddish. Merkos L'Inyonei Chinuch, Inc.

SPECTRUM (1982). 515 Park Ave., NYC, 10022. (212)371-7750. Karen Rubinstein. Quarterly. American Zionist Federation.

SYNAGOGUE LIGHT (1933). 47 Beekman St., NYC, 10038. (212)227-7800. Rabbi Meyer Hager. Semiannually. Union of Chasidic Rabbis.

TALKS AND TALES (1942). 770 Eastern Pkwy., Brooklyn, 11213. (718)493-9250. Nissan Mindel. Monthly (also Hebrew, French, and Spanish editions). Merkos L'Inyonei Chinuch, Inc.

TRADITION (1958). 275 Seventh Ave., NYC, 10001. (212)807-7888. Walter Wurzburger. Quarterly. Rabbinical Council of America.

TRENDS (1982). 730 Broadway, NYC, 10003. (212)529-2000. Leora W. Isaacs. Semiannually. Jewish Education Service of North America, Inc.

UNITED SYNAGOGUE REVIEW (1943). 155 Fifth Ave., NYC, 10010. (212)533-7800. Ruth M. Perry. United Synagogue of America.

UNSER TSAIT (1941). 25 E. 21 St., NYC, 10010. (212)475-0059. Editorial committee. Monthly. Yiddish. Jewish Labor Bund.

WOMEN'S AMERICAN ORT REPORTER (1966). 315 Park Ave. S., NYC, 10010. (212)505-7700. Elie Faust-Levy. Quarterly. Women's American ORT, Inc.

WOMEN'S LEAGUE OUTLOOK (1930). 48 E. 74 St., NYC, 10021. (212)628-1600. Lynne Heller. Quarterly. Women's League for Conservative Judaism.

WORKMEN'S CIRCLE CALL (1934). 45 E. 33 St., NYC, 10016. (212)889-6800. Walter L. Kirschenbaum. Bimonthly. Workmen's Circle.

YEARBOOK OF THE CENTRAL CONFERENCE OF AMERICAN RABBIS (1890). 192 Lexington Ave., NYC, 10016. (212)684-4990. Elliot L. Stevens. Annually. Central Conference of American Rabbis.

YIDDISH (1973). Queens College, Kiely 802, 65-30 Kissena Blvd., Flushing, 11367. (718)520-7067. Joseph C. Landis. Quarterly. Queens College Press.

YIDDISHE HEIM (1958). 770 Eastern Pkwy., Brooklyn, 11213. (718)493-9250. Rachel Altein. Quarterly. English-Yiddish. Neshei Ub'nos Chabad.

YIDDISHE KULTUR (1938). 1123 Broadway, Rm. 305, NYC, 10010. (212)243-1304. Itche Goldberg. Monthly (except June–July, Aug.–Sept.). Yiddish. Yiddishe Kultur Farband, Inc.—YKUF.

YIDDISHE VORT (1953). 5 Beekman St., NYC, 10038. (212)797-9000. Joseph Friedenson. Monthly. Yiddish. Agudath Israel of America.

YIDDISHER KEMFER (1906). 275 Seventh Ave., NYC, 10001. (212)675-7808. Mordechai Strigler. Weekly. Yiddish. Labor Zionist Letters, Inc.

YIDISHE SHPRAKH (1941). 1048 Fifth Ave., NYC, 10028. (212)231-7905. Mordkhe Schaechter. Irregularly. Yiddish. Yivo Institute for Jewish Research, Inc.

YIVO ANNUAL OF JEWISH SOCIAL SCIENCE (1946). 1048 Fifth Ave., NYC, 10028. (212)535-6700. Irregularly. Yivo Institute for Jewish Research, Inc.

YIVO BLETER (1931). 1048 Fifth Ave., NYC, 10028. (212)535-6700. Editorial board. Irregularly. Yiddish. Yivo Institute for Jewish Research, Inc.

YOUNG ISRAEL VIEWPOINT (1952). 3 W. 16 St., NYC, 10011. (212)929-1525. Steve K. Walz. Bimonthly. National Council of Young Israel.

YOUNG JUDAEAN (1912). 50 W. 58 St., NYC, 10019. (212)303-8268. Mordecai Newman. Six times a year. Hadassah Zionist Youth Commission.

YUGNTRUF (1964). 3328 Bainbridge Ave., Bronx, 10467. (212)654-8540. Hershl Glasser. Quarterly. Yiddish. Yugntruf Youth for Yiddish.

NORTH CAROLINA

AMERICAN JEWISH TIMES—OUTLOOK (1934; reorg. 1950). PO Box 33218, Charlotte, 28233. (704)372-3296. Ruth Goldberg. Monthly. The Blumenthal Foundation.

OHIO

THE AMERICAN ISRAELITE (1854). 906 Main St., Rm. 505, Cincinnati, 45237. (513)621-3145. Phyllis R. Singer. Weekly.

AMERICAN JEWISH ARCHIVES (1947). 3101 Clifton Ave., Cincinnati, 45220. (513)221-1875. Jacob R. Marcus, Abraham J. Peck. Semiannually. American Jewish Archives of Hebrew Union College—Jewish Institute of Religion.

CLEVELAND JEWISH NEWS (1964). 13910 Cedar Rd., University Hts., 44118. (216)-371-0800. Cynthia Dettelbach. Weekly. Cleveland Jewish Publication Co.

DAYTON JEWISH CHRONICLE (1961). 118 Salem Ave., Dayton, 45406. (513)222-0783. Leslie Cohen Zukowsky. Weekly.

INDEX TO JEWISH PERIODICALS (1963). PO Box 18570, Cleveland Hts., 44118. (216)-321-7296. Miriam Leikind, Bess Rosenfeld, Jean H. Foxman. Semiannually.

OHIO JEWISH CHRONICLE (1921). 2831 E. Main St., Columbus, 43209. (614)237-4296. Judith Franklin, Steve Pinsky, Diane Levi. Weekly.

STARK JEWISH NEWS (1920). 2631 Harvard Ave. NW, Canton, 44709. (216)452-6444. Adele Gelb. Monthly. Canton Jewish Community Federation.

STUDIES IN BIBLIOGRAPHY AND BOOKLORE (1953). 3101 Clifton Ave., Cincinnati, 45220. (513)221-1875. Herbert C. Zafren. Irregularly. English-Hebrew-German. Library of Hebrew Union College—Jewish Institute of Religion.

YOUNGSTOWN JEWISH TIMES (1935). PO Box 777, Youngstown, 44501. (216)746-6192. Harry Alter. Fortnightly.

OKLAHOMA

SOUTHWEST JEWISH CHRONICLE (1929). 314-B N. Robinson St., Oklahoma City, 73102. (405)236-4226. E. F. Friedman. Quarterly.

TULSA JEWISH REVIEW (1930). 2021 E. 71 St., Tulsa, 74136. (918)495-1100. Dianna Aaronson. Monthly. Tulsa Section, National Council of Jewish Women.

PENNSYLVANIA

JEWISH CHRONICLE (1962). 5600 Baum Blvd., Pittsburgh, 15206. (412)687-1000. Joel Roteman. Weekly. Pittsburgh Jewish Publication and Education Foundation.

JEWISH EXPONENT (1887). 226 S. 16 St., Philadelphia, 19102. (215)893-5740. Albert Erlick. Weekly. Federation of Jewish Agencies of Greater Philadelphia.

JEWISH QUARTERLY REVIEW (1910). 250 N. Highland Ave., Merion, 19149. (215)-667-1830. Leon Nemoy, Bernard Lewis, David M. Goldenberg. Quarterly.

JEWISH TIMES OF THE GREATER NORTHEAST (1925). 2417 Welsh Rd., Philadelphia, 19114. (215)464-3900. Leon E. Brown. Weekly. Federation of Jewish Agencies of Greater Philadelphia.

NEW MENORAH (1979). 6723 Emlen St., Philadelphia, 19119. (215)849-5385. Arthur Waskow, Shana Margolin. Quarterly. P'nai Or Religious Fellowship.

RHODE ISLAND

RHODE ISLAND JEWISH HISTORICAL NOTES (1954). 130 Sessions St., Providence, 02906. (401)331-1360. Michael Fink. Annually. Rhode Island Jewish Historical Association.

TENNESSEE

HEBREW WATCHMAN (1925) 4646 Poplar Ave., Suite 232, Memphis, 38117. (901)-763-2215. Herman I. Goldberger. Weekly.

TEXAS

JEWISH CIVIC PRESS (1965). PO Box 35656, Houston, 77235. (713)491-1512. Abner Tritt. Monthly.

JEWISH HERALD-VOICE (1908). PO Box 153, Houston, 77001. (713)630-0391. Joseph W. and Jeanne F. Samuels. Weekly.

JEWISH JOURNAL OF SAN ANTONIO (1973). 8434 Ahern, San Antonio, 78216. (512)-341-8234. Gaylon Young. Monthly. Jewish Federation of San Antonio.

TEXAS JEWISH POST (1947). PO Box 742, Fort Worth, 76101. (817)927-2831. 11333 N. Central Expressway, Dallas, 75243. (214)692-7283. Jimmy Wisch. Weekly.

VIRGINIA

UJF NEWS (1959). 7300 Newport Ave., Norfolk, 23505. (804)489-8040. Reba Karp. Weekly. United Jewish Federation of Tidewater.

WASHINGTON

JEWISH TRANSCRIPT (1924). 1904 3rd St., Suite 510, Seattle, 98101. (206)624-0136. Craig Degginger. Bimonthly. Jewish Federation of Greater Seattle.

M'GODOLIM: THE JEWISH QUARTERLY (1979). 2921 E. Madison St., #7, Seattle, 98112-4237. (206)322-1431. Keith S. Gormezano. Quarterly. Hebrew-English.

WISCONSIN

WISCONSIN JEWISH CHRONICLE (1921). 1360 N. Prospect Ave., Milwaukee, 53202. (414)271-2992. Arthur J. Stegeman. Weekly. Milwaukee Jewish Federation.

NEWS SYNDICATES

JEWISH STUDENT PRESS SERVICE (1970). 15 E. 26 St., Suite 1350, NYC, 10010. (212)-679-1411. Larry Yudelson.

JEWISH TELEGRAPHIC AGENCY, INC. (1917). 165 W. 46 St., NYC., 10036. (212)-575-9370. Mark Joffe.

CANADA

BULLETIN DU CONGRES JUIF CANADIEN (Région du Québec) (1952). 1590 Dr. Penfield Ave., Montreal, QUE H3G 1C5. (514)931-7531. Irregularly. French. Canadian Jewish Congress.

CANADIAN JEWISH HERALD (1977). 17 Anselme Lavigne Blvd., Dollard des Ormeaux, QUE H9A 1N3. (514)684-7667. Dan Nimrod. Irregularly.

CANADIAN JEWISH NEWS (1960). 10 Gateway Blvd., Toronto, ONT M4P 1P1. (416)422-2331. Maurice Lucow. Weekly.

CANADIAN JEWISH OUTLOOK (1963). 6184 Ash St., #3, Vancouver, BC V5Z 3G9. (604)324-5101. Ben Chud, Henry Rosenthal. Monthly.

CANADIAN ZIONIST (1934). 5250 Decarie Blvd., Suite 550, Montreal, QUE H3X 2H9. (514)486-9526. Glenna Uline. Five times a year. Canadian Zionist Federation.

JEWISH EAGLE (1907). 4180 De Courtrai, Rm. 218, Montreal, QUE H3S 1C3. (514)-735-6577. B. Hirshtal. Weekly. Yiddish-Hebrew-French.

JEWISH POST (1925). 117 Hutchings St., Winnipeg, MAN R2X 2V4. (204)694-3332. Matt Bellan. Weekly.

JEWISH STANDARD (1929). 77 Mowat Ave., Toronto, ONT M6K 3E3. (416)537-2696. Julius Hayman. Semimonthly.

JEWISH WESTERN BULLETIN (1930). 3268 Heather St., Vancouver, BC V5Z 3K5. (604)879-6575. Samuel Kaplan. Weekly.

JOURNAL OF PSYCHOLOGY AND JUDAISM (1976). 1747 Featherston Dr., Ottawa, ONT K1H 6P4. (613)731-9119. Reuven P. Bulka. Quarterly. Center for the Study of Psychology and Judaism.

OTTAWA JEWISH BULLETIN & REVIEW (1954). 151 Chapel St., Ottawa, ONT K1N 7Y2. (613)232-7306. Cynthia Engel. Biweekly. Jewish Community Council of Ottawa.

UNDZER VEG (1932). 272 Codsell Ave., Downsview, ONT M3H 3X2. (416)636-4024. Joseph Kage. Irregularly. Yiddish-English. Achdut HaAvoda-Poale Zion of Canada.

WESTERN JEWISH NEWS (1926). 400-259 Portage Ave., Winnipeg, MAN R3C 2G6. (204)942-6361. Cheryl Fogel. Weekly. English-Hebrew.

WINDSOR JEWISH COMMUNITY BULLETIN (1938). 1641 Ouellette Ave., Windsor, ONT N8X 1K9. (519)973-1772. Joseph Eisenberg. Irregularly. Windsor Jewish Community Council.

Obituaries: United States[1]

AGUS, JACOB BERNARD, rabbi, scholar; b. Swislocz, Poland, Nov. 8, 1911; d. Baltimore, Md., Sept. 26, 1986; in U.S. since 1927. Educ.: Yeshiva U.(ordination, Rabbi Isaac Elchanan Theol. Sem.); Harvard U. (PhD). Rabbi: Orthodox congregations in Norfolk, Va., Cambridge, Mass., and Chicago, Ill., 1936–42; Beth Abraham United Cong. (Conservative), Dayton, Ohio, 1942–50; Beth El Cong., Baltimore, Md., 1950–80; rabbi emer. since 1980. Prof.: Mt. St. Mary's Seminary, Dropsie Coll., Temple U., Reconstructionist Rabbinical Coll.; lect. on the Gospels and the Ethics of the Fathers, Baltimore Roman Catholic Archdiocese Inst. An early architect of interfaith programs, he was an adviser to Vatican II and to Cardinal Bea, and a member of the Jewish-Christian-Moslem Trialogue, Georgetown U.'s Kennedy Inst. on Ethics. Pres., Baltimore Bd. of Rabbis, 1976–78. Mem. exec. com. Amer. Jewish Philosophical Conf. A leader of the liberal wing of the Conservative movement, he held important positions in its Rabbinical Assembly: founder and 40-year mem. Com. on Law and Standards; chmn. Ideological Conf.; natl. chmn. and treas. Prayer Book Comm. Consulting ed. *Encyclopaedia Britannica,* 1957–69; assoc. ed. *Journal of Ecumenical Studies,* 1978–85; ed. bd. *Judaism.* Author: nine books, including *Modern Philosophies of Judaism* (1941), *Guideposts in Modern Judaism* (1954), *The Evolution of Jewish Thought* (1959), *The Meaning of Jewish History* (1964), *Jewish Identity in an Age of Ideologies* (1978), *The Jewish Quest* (1984), and many scholarly articles.

ALPERT, NISSON, rabbi, scholar; b. Polonka, Lithuania, Dec. 15, 1927; d. NYC, May 26, 1986; in U.S. since 1940. Educ.: Yeshiva Mesivta Tiferet Jerusalem, NYC, where he was ordained by Rabbi Moshe Feinstein and where he later served as a *rosh yeshivah* (professor of Talmud). Rabbi: Cong. Chevra Bechurim B'nai Menashe Ahavas Achim, NYC, for 27 years; Cong. Agudath Israel of Long Island, for 5 years. *Rosh yeshivah,* Rabbi Isaac Elchanan Theol. Sem., Yeshiva U., since 1967; *rosh kollel l'horaah* at RIETS (mentor of a training group for experts in rabbinic law). Founder and pres. P'eylim (organization to help immigrant children); pres. United Jewish Council of the (Lower) East Side. Mem.: Ezras Torah, Chinuch Atzmai, Union of Orthodox Rabbis of the U.S., Agudath Israel. Author: *M'eri: Baba Metzia;* ed., English transl. of Alexander Friedman's *Maayanei Torah* (Wellsprings of Torah).

ALTMAN, SHALOM, musician, educator; b. NYC, Mar. 6, 1911; d. Philadelphia, Pa., July 19, 1986. Educ.: Juilliard School of Music; NYU. Prof. of music and dir. Bertha and Monte H. Tyson Music Dept., Gratz Coll. Founder and pres. Natl. Jewish Music Council; pres. Educators' Council, Jewish Natl. Fund; mem. Jewish Welfare Bd. Cultural Comm. Conductor of Jewish music groups, composer, author of columns on music, and editor of Jewish song books. Recipient: Kavod Award, Cantors

[1]Including Jewish residents of the United States who died between January 1 and December 31, 1986.

Assembly, and other honors. Composer of popular melody to "*Lo Yisa Goy,*" found in several sources, not always attributed.

AUSUBEL, NATHAN, author; b. Lezajsk, Galicia, Poland, June 15, 1899; d. Callicoon, N.Y., Nov. 23, 1986; in U.S. since 1906. Served with Jewish Legion in Palestine under Field Marshal Edmund Allenby, 1918. Largely self-educated. Editor, Crown Publishers, in 1940s; mostly self-employed thereafter. Author: *Superman, The Life of Frederick the Great* (1931), *A Treasury of Jewish Folklore* (1948), *A Treasury of Jewish Humor* (1951), *A Pictorical History of the Jewish People* (1953), *A Treasury of Jewish Poetry* (1957), *The Book of Jewish Knowledge* (1964), and other works; ed., *Voices of History,* annual volumes including speeches and state papers of world leaders.

BLAU, JOSEPH L., professor; b. Brooklyn, N.Y., May 6, 1909; d. NYC, Dec. 28, 1986. Educ.: Columbia U. (BA, MA, PhD). Teacher, NYC high schools, 1933–46; joined Columbia faculty in 1944; helped form religion dept. in 1961; prof. of religion, 1963, chmn. of dept., 1966–77; prof. emer. since 1977. Visiting prof.: California Inst. of Technology, Vassar Coll., and elsewhere. V.-pres., Conf. on Jewish Social Studies; mem.: Com. on the History of Religions, Amer. Council of Learned Societies; Amer. Philosophical Assn.; Amer. Acad. for Jewish Research; Amer. Humanist Assn.; Conf. on Jewish Relations, and other groups; ed. bds. of the *Review of Religion, Jewish Social Studies,* other publications. Author: more than 15 books, including *Men and Movements in American Philosophy* (1952; transl. into six languages), *Modern Varieties of Judaism* (1966), *Judaism in America: From Curiosity to Third Faith* (1976). Ed.: *Cornerstones of Religious Freedom in America* (1944). Recipient: Festschrift: *History, Religion and Spiritual Democracy: Essays in Honor of Joseph L. Blau* (1980); Leadership Award, North Amer. Com. for Humanism, for his leadership in the N.Y. Society for Ethical Culture; named Distinguished Scholar in the Philosophy of Religion by the Com. for Scientific Examination of Religion.

BRICKMAN, WILLIAM W., professor, author; b. NYC, June 30, 1913; d. Philadelphia, Pa., June 22, 1986. Educ.: CCNY; NYU (PhD). Historian, German instr., and counterintelligence agent, U.S. armed forces, WWII. Instr., asst. prof., assoc. prof., prof., School of Educ., NYU, 1948–62; chmn. dept. of history of educ., 1952–57; prof., Grad. School of Educ., U. of Pa., 1962–81; prof. emer since 1981; also at U. of Pa.: mem. faculty, Grad. School of Arts and Sciences, Dept. of International Relations, Slavic Center, Middle East Center, and chmn., Dept. of English as a Second Language. Dean, Touro Coll. (NYC), 1977–79. Numerous visiting professorships and lectureships. Founder and first pres., Comparative Educ. Soc.; mem.: Natl. Fulbright Selection Com., Coll. Entrance Examination Bd., and many professional and educational associations. Fluent in 20 languages and an expert on education in the USSR. Chmn. Educ. Comm., Union of Orthodox Congs. of Amer.; mem. Acad. Adv. Council, Yeshiva U.; consultant, Torah Umesorah. Author: numerous books, pamphlets, articles in journals, and encyclopedia entries.

BURSTEIN, PESACH, actor, singer; b. Warsaw, Poland, Apr. 15, 1896; d. NYC, Apr. 6, 1986. Educ. in Berdiansk, Russia. Began stage career at age 15, running away from home to join a theater troupe. Brought to the U.S. by Boris Thomashevsky in 1923; his immediate success on Broadway in *The Jolly Tailor* (with Rudolph Schildkraut and Ludwig Satz) was soon followed by a 20-year contract with Columbia Records. He toured with his own theatrical companies throughout the world—becoming known as the Yiddish Maurice Chevalier—playing in melodramas, comedies, and musicals, often with his actress wife, Lillian Lux. Dividing his later years between New York and Tel Aviv, in 1968 he returned to Broadway with his wife and actor son, Mike Burstein, in a production of *The Megilla of Itzik Manger.* Mem.: Hebrew Actors' Union since 1927; theater unions in Israel and Argentina. Author: *Geshpielt a Leben* (A Life at Play), a memoir published in Israel. Recipient: Goldfaden Award for lifetime achievement, Congress of Jewish Culture, 1985; Itzik Manger Award (Israel), 1986.

COHEN, ARTHUR A., writer, publisher; b. NYC, June 25, 1928; d. NYC, Oct. 31, 1986. Educ.: U. of Chicago; Jewish Theol. Sem. of Amer. Cofounder and pres. Noonday Press, 1951–54; founder, pres. Meridian Books, 1954–60; dir. religion dept., Holt, Rinehart, and Winston, 1962–64, ed.-in-chief and v.-pres., 1964–68;

managing ed. Documents of 20th Century Art, Viking Press, 1968–75; founder and pres. Ex Libris bookstore, specializing in rare works on 20th-century art, since 1974. Visiting lect. in religion at Brown U. and in theol. at Jewish Inst. of Religion. Bd. mem.: PEN Amer. Center, 1977–86; YIVO Inst. for Jewish Research, 1983–85; chmn. of YIVO, 1985–86. Author: five novels, including *In the Days of Simon Stern* (1973); *An Admirable Woman* (1983); numerous nonfiction books and articles, including *Martin Buber* (1957), *The Natural and Supernatural Jew: An Historical and Theological Introduction* (1962), *The Tremendum: A Theological Interpretation of the Holocaust* (1981), *Herbert Bayer: The Complete Works* (1984); two posthumous works: *Artists and Enemies: Three Novellas* and *A Handbook of Jewish Religious Thought,* ed. with Paul Mendes-Flohr. Recipient: many honors, including Edward Lewis Wallant Award (1973), Natl. Jewish Book Award (1984), George Wittenborn Memorial Award (1986), hon. doctorate, Spertus Coll., Chicago (1985).

COLODNER, SOLOMON, educator; b. Prusneh, Russia, May 26, 1908; d. NYC, Oct. 24, 1986; in U.S. since 1914. Educ.: Dropsie Coll. (PhD). Principal: Temple B'nai Abraham, Newark, N.J.; Forest Hills Jewish Center, Forest Hills, N.Y.; teacher of Hebrew, Hunter Coll., NYC; instr., Hebrew Union Coll.; educ. consultant, Westchester (N.Y.) Assn. of Hebrew Schools; developer of Talking Books for the Blind in Hebrew, Yiddish, and other languages. A founder, Jewish Educators Assembly. Recipient: Jewish Braille Inst. Award; Scrolls of Honor from Jewish Educators Assembly and Council of Jewish Education.

DRACHSLER, LEO M., lawyer; b. Sucany, Czechoslovakia (Austria-Hungary), Sept. 6, 1899; d. Alexandria, Va., Jan. 3, 1986; in U.S. since 1903. Educ.: CCNY; Columbia U. School of Law. From 1924 to 1933 practiced in law offices of Judge Samuel Seabury and Samuel Untermeyer; held various U.S. govt. positions 1933–46; member, prosecution staff, internatl. military tribunal, Nuremberg, Germany, 1946–47; special adviser U.S. Displaced Persons Comm., Munich, 1948–49; judge U.S. military govt. courts in Germany, 1949–50; resumed general law practice in NYC in 1951; retired 1965. Special adviser: NYC Human Resources Admin., UN Dept. of Econ. and Social Affairs; NYC Bar Assoc. com. on civil rights; dir., NYC Service Corps of Volunteer Lawyers; numerous other professional and civic affiliations.

EDELSBERG, HERMAN, lawyer, communal worker; b. NYC, Apr. 14, 1909; d. Washington, D.C., Oct. 30, 1986. Educ.: CCNY; Brooklyn Law School of St. Lawrence U. Served with U.S. Foreign Economic Admin., Bd. of Economic Warfare, and Office of Price Admin., 1941–45; counsel and staff dir. Senate Subcommittee on Foreign Trade, 1945–46; Washington rep. B'nai B'rith Anti-Defamation League, 1948–1967; exec. dir. U.S. Equal Employment Opportunity Comm., 1965–67; dir. Internatl. Council, B'nai B'rith, 1967–77. Mem. Civil Liberties Clearing House; chmn. Washington Hebrew Cong. Author: *Not for Myself Alone.* Recipient: Americans for Democratic Action (D.C.) Award for Civil Rights Achievement.

EICHHORN, DAVID M., rabbi, communal worker; b. Columbia, Pa., Jan. 6, 1906; d. Melbourne, Fla., July 16, 1986. Educ.: U. of Cincinnati; Hebrew Union Coll. Chaplain U.S. army, 1942–45, serving in France and Germany; thereafter lt. col. U.S. army reserves. Conducted the first religious service in Dachau concentration camp after liberation. Rabbi: Springfield, Mass., 1932–34; Texarkana, Ark., 1935–38; Fla. Hillel Founds., 1939–42. Dir., field activities, Comm. on Jewish Chaplaincy, Natl. Jewish Welfare Bd., 1945–70; founder, Temple Israel, Merritt Island, Fla., 1970. Author: seven books, including *Jewish Intermarriage: Fact and Fiction, Conversion to Judaism, Joys of Jewish Folklore.* Recipient: hon. doctorates, Hebrew Union Coll.

FEINBERG, ABRAHAM L., rabbi, author; b. Bellaire, Ohio, Sept. 14, 1899; d. Reno, Nev., Oct. 5, 1986. Educ.: U. of Cincinnati; Heb. Union Coll.; U. of Toronto (LLD). Rabbi: Temple Israel, NYC, 1927–30; Mt. Neboh Temple, NYC, 1935–38; Holy Blossom Temple, Toronto, Canada, 1943–61; rabbi-in-residence, Glide Memorial United Methodist Church, San Francisco, which served vagrants and other outcasts, 1960s. In the 1930s was a popular singer on radio; in the 1960s and thereafter was an outspoken civil rights and peace activist. Author: *Hanoi Diary, Storm the Gates of Jericho, Sex and the Pulpit,* and shorter pieces. Recipient: Civil Libertarian of the Year designation in 1986 by the ACLU of Nev.

FEINSTEIN, MOSHE, rabbi, talmudic scholar; b. Uzda, Russia, Mar. 5, 1895; d. NYC, Mar. 23, 1986. Educ.: Yeshivas of Slutzk and Schklov, Russia. Rabbi of Usda, 1916–18; of Luban, USSR, 1921–37, when he was placed under house arrest for religious activities. Came to U.S. through international intervention in 1937. Regarded as the rabbinic "giant of his generation," he was an internationally recognized *posek,* an authority on the application of *halakhah* (Jewish law) to modern issues. Chmn., at his death, Council of Sages, Agudath Israel of Amer.; pres. Union of Orthodox Rabbis in Amer. and Canada, 1966–76. Author: *Dibrot Moshe,* seven vols. of Talmud commentary (starting 1946) and *Igrot Moshe,* seven vols. of responsa to questions on Jewish law (starting 1959).

GLASER, JULIUS S., businessman; b. Boston, Mass., June 13, 1916; d. White Plains, N.Y., Sept. 10, 1986. Educ.: Williams Coll. Pres. Glaser-Steers Corp., 1950–60; v.pres., AMETEK, Inc., 1960–68; bd. chmn. Schocken Books, 1975–81, pres., 1981–84. Chmn., Labor Zionist Letters; exec. bd. mem., Labor Zionist Alliance.

GOLDSTEIN, ISRAEL, rabbi, communal leader; b. Philadelphia, Pa., June 18, 1896; d. Jerusalem, Israel, Apr. 11, 1986. Educ.: U. of Pa.; Jewish Theol. Sem. of Amer. (ordination and DHL). Rabbi, Cong. B'nai Jeshurun, NYC, 1918–60. Cofounder, Natl. Conf. of Christians and Jews, 1928, and cochmn. of its Commission on Religious Orgs., 1930–32; pres. Young Judea, 1926–28; pres. N.Y. Bd. of Rabbis, 1928–30; pres. Jewish Natl. Fund, 1934–43; chmn. United Palestine Appeal, 1935–39; cochmn. UJA, 1939–45; pres. Zionist Org. of Amer., 1943–46; pres. Synagogue Council of Amer., 1943–45; consultant, U.S. delegation, UN Founding Conf., San Francisco, 1945; cofounder Brandeis U., 1946–48; mem. Jewish Agency Exec., 1948–71; treas. Jewish Agency, 1949; pres. and later chmn. Jewish Restitution Successor Org., 1952–60; v.-chmn. Conf. on Jewish Material Claims Against Germany, 1953–70; pres. Amer. Jewish Cong., 1952–59. Continued his activities after moving to Israel in 1960; chmn. Keren Hayesod-United Israel Appeal, 1961–71; deputy chmn. bd. of govs., Hebrew U. and Weizmann Inst. of Science; bd. mem. Haifa U. Author: many articles and 14 books, including *A Century of Judaism in New York, Shanah b'Yisrael, American Jewry Comes of Age, Israel at Home and Abroad.* Recipient: Distinguished Citizen of Jerusalem award (1976); academic chairs in his name at Jewish Theol. Sem. and Hebrew U.; syn. in his name at Hebrew U. and a youth village in Jerusalem.

GOLDSTEIN, NOAH, rabbi; b. U.S., Nov. 24, 1927; d. Flushing, N.Y., Jan. 14, 1986. Educ.: Yeshiva Coll.; Rabbi Isaac Elchanan Theol. Sem.(ordination); Harvard U., Yeshiva U. (DHL). Rabbi, Cong. Sons of Israel and Anshe Sfard and exec. dir. Hebrew Community Center, Peabody, Mass., 1952–62; teacher, Marsha Stern Talmudic Acad. and Yeshiva U. High School for Boys, and professor of Talmud, RIETS, 1962–86; rabbi, Cong. Ohab Zedek, Yonkers, N.Y., 1973–79; asst. to registrar Yeshiva U., 1979–81; ed. since 1982 of *Chavrusa,* publication of RIETS alumni assn., and of the newsletter of the Educators Council of Amer. Mem.: Rabbinical Council of Amer., United Rabbinic Chaplaincy Council of Mass., Natl. Council of Prison Chaplains.

GREENBERG, HENRY BENJAMIN (HANK), baseball star; b. NYC, Jan. 1, 1911; d. Beverly Hills, Cal., Sept. 4, 1986. Played in minor leagues, 1930–33; Detroit Tigers, 1933–41, 1945–46, playing in four World Series; joined Pittsburgh Pirates, 1947, as highest-paid player in baseball; served U.S. Air Force 1941–45, first baseball star in uniform. Lifetime batting average of .313, with 331 home runs. Co-owner and gen. mgr. Cleveland Indians, 1947–57; v.-pres. and gen. mgr. Chicago White Sox, from 1959 on. Recipient: American League Most Valuable Player Award 1935, 1940; Baseball Hall of Fame, 1956—first Jew chosen.

HELLMAN, YEHUDA, journalist, communal worker; b. Riga, Latvia, Feb. 10, 1920; d. St. Louis, Mo., May 17, 1986; in U.S. since 1946. Educ.: Hebrew U. of Jerusalem; Amer. U. of Beirut, Lebanon. European and Middle East correspondent for the *Jerusalem Post,* Overseas News Agency, JTA; exec. v.-chmn., Conf. of Presidents of Major Amer. Jewish Orgs., since 1959. Mem.: internatl. steering com., World Conf. on Soviet Jewry; former secy. gen. World Council of Jewish Orgs.

HOBSON, LAURA Z., writer; b. NYC, June 19, 1900; d. NYC, Feb. 28, 1986. Educ.:

Cornell U. Acclaimed author of nine novels, an autobiography, hundreds of short stories and magazine pieces, news features, and advertising copy. *Gentleman's Agreement,* her 1947 novel about anti-Semitism in the U.S., topped best-seller lists for months, was translated into 13 languages, sold 1.6 million copies, and was made into a hit movie that won 50 awards, including the Academy Award and best-film citation of the New York Film Critics. Other novels include *The Trespassers, First Papers,* and *Consenting Adults.*

JAVITS, JACOB K., politician, statesman; b. NYC, May 18, 1904; d. Palm Beach, Fla., Mar. 7, 1986. Educ.: Columbia U.; NYU Law School (working his way through with jobs in a printshop and pipe factory). Partner, with his brother, Javits & Javits, 1927–42; U.S. army 1942–46; served four terms U.S. House of Reps., 1946–54, representing an upper Manhattan district with many German Jewish residents; NY State Atty. Gen., 1954–56; four terms in U.S. Senate, 1956–80. One of the longest-serving members of Congress, he was a political maverick, a Republican liberal who frequently defeated well-known Democrats in largely Democratic bastions. Regarded by admirers and detractors alike as one of the most intelligent, industrious, and effective members of the Senate. A leading advocate of three major pieces of legislation: the War Powers Act, Erisa Act (for guarantees of private-sector pensions), and the Natl. Endowment for the Arts & Humanities; supported major legislation on banking and currency, foreign affairs, social welfare; a staunch supporter of Israel. Mem.: numerous affiliations, including Central Syn. (NYC); B'nai B'rith and the Anti-Defamation League (ADL hon. v.-chmn. for 25 years); Zionist Org. of Amer., Amer. J. Com., UJA-Federation, and the Amer.-Israel Cultural Found.; bd. mem. Amer. ORT; science fellow and founder Albert Einstein Coll. of Med.; trustee Amer. Friends of Hebrew U.; bd. chmn. Bellevue Hosp. Assn. Author: Several books, including *Order of Battle: A Republican's Call to Reason,* and *Javits: The Autobiography of a Public Man,* and many articles. Recipient: Presidential Medal of Freedom, 1983; Charles Evans Hughes Gold Medal;, UJA-Federation Lifetime Achievement Award for Public Service; Agudath Israel Humanitarian Award; ADL Haym Salomon Award;, ORT Community Achievement Award; convention center in NYC named in his honor, and also a federal office building.

KAMENETZKY, JACOB, rabbi, authority on talmudic law; b. near Minsk, Russia, Jan. 1890; d. Baltimore, Md., Mar.10, 1986. In U.S. since 1945. Educ.: Slobodka Yeshiva; Kovno *kollel* (advanced talmudic inst.). Rabbi: Tzitovyan, Poland, 1926–37; Seattle, Wash., 1937–39(?); Toronto, Canada, 1939(?)-45; Talmud professor, Mesivta Torah Vodaath Sem. (NYC), beginning 1945, and dean, 1948–68. Sr. mem. Moetzes Gedolei HaTorah (Council of Torah Sages) of Agudath Israel.

KNOX, ISRAEL, professor, author; b. Rogachev, Russia, May 3, 1904; d. NYC, June 9, 1986. In U.S. since 1911. Educ.: CCNY; Columbia U. (PhD). Dir. Workmen's Circle English-speaking div., 1937–47; asst. prof. of philosophy, U. of Ohio 1947–51; prof. NYU 1951–72, prof. emer. 1972–86; prof. and dean, Herzliah Jewish Teachers' Sem., late 1970s. Pres. World Congress for Jewish Culture. Author: *Rabbi in America: The Story of Isaac Mayer Wise; Anthology of Holocaust Literature* (ed.); articles in many periodicals, including *Journal of Philosophy, Ethics, Menorah Journal, Commentary, Jewish Social Studies, Zukunft.*

LANDAU, IDA BIENSTOCK, journalist; b. Hartford, Conn., Nov. 18, 1899; d. Los Angeles, Cal., May 4, 1986. Educ.: NYU Law School. Marriage to a noncitizen—Jacob Landau, founder and managing dir. of the Jewish Telegraphic Agency, in 1921—cost her her citizenship and the right to practice law. (After the case attracted national attention, Congress enacted the Case Act, which restored citizenship rights of women married to foreigners.) Asst. mgr. JTA, 1928–51; mgr. Overseas News Agency, 1942–51; organized and served as pres. and gen. mgr. Transworld Features Syndicate, 1951–65; dir. Agencia Periodistica Latino-Americana (APLA), 1951–65; as a war correspondent, covered Bermuda Refugee Conf. 1943, and refugee situation in Europe, 1945–46. Founder-mem. Delta Phi Epsilon sorority.

LIPMANN, FRITZ A., biochemist, physician; b. Koenigsberg, Germany, June 12, 1899; d. Poughkeepsie, N.Y., July 24, 1986; in U.S. since 1939. Educ.: Univs. of Munich, Berlin (MD, PhD), Marseilles,

Copenhagen. Faculty, Cornell Med. School, 1939–41; Mass. Gen. Hosp. 1941–57; prof. Harvard Med. School, 1949–57; prof. Rockefeller U., 1957–70, emer. since 1970. Author: *Wanderings of a Biochemist;* many articles and papers. Recipient: Nobel Prize in Physiology or Medicine (1953), Natl. Medal of Science (1966), hon. doctorates from U. of Marseilles, Copenhagen, Harvard, Chicago, Rockefeller.

MALAMUD, BERNARD, writer; b. NYC, Apr. 26, 1914; d. NYC, Mar. 18, 1986. Educ.: CCNY; Columbia U. Taught in NYC high schools, 1940–49; faculty mem.: Oregon State U. 1949–61; Bennington Coll. (Vt.), 1961–86; visiting lect. Harvard U., 1966–68. Mem. Amer. Acad. of Arts & Letters; Amer. PEN (pres., 1979–81). Author: *The Natural* (1952), *The Magic Barrel* (1958), *The Assistant* (1957), *The Fixer* (1967), *Rembrandt's Hat* (1973), *Dubin's Lives* (1979), *God's Grace* (1982), and other works. Recipient: many honors, including Natl. Book Award for *The Magic Barrel;* a second NBA and a Pulitzer Prize for *The Fixer,* based on the Mendel Beiliss ritual murder case in Russia; Rosenthal Award, Natl. Inst. of Arts & Letters; Gold Medal, Amer. Acad. and Inst. for Arts & Letters; Vt. Governor's Award for Excellence in the Arts; Brandeis Creative Arts Award.

MARSHALL, JAMES, lawyer, communal worker; b. NYC, May 12, 1896; d. NYC, Aug. 11, 1986. Educ.: Columbia U. School of Journalism, Law School. Served in U.S. Army Sanitation Corps., WW I. Assoc. Guggenheimer, Untermeyer & Marshall (the law firm of his father, Louis Marshall), 1921–34; founder counsel, Marshall, Bratter, Greene, Allison & Tucker, 1934–82; counsel, Burns Summit Rovins & Feldesman, 1982–86. Adj. lect. and prof., NYU Grad. School of Public Admin., 1953–65. Manhattan mgr., Fiorello H. LaGuardia's first mayoral campaign, 1933; mem. NYC Bd. of Educ., 1933–52, pres. 1938–42. Helped to create UNESCO, served on U.S. Natl. Comm. for UNESCO for several years, and was a mem. of U.S. delegations to UNESCO in 1946, 1947, and 1950. Active in behalf of the NYC Citizens Com. for Children; PEN Amer. Center; Natl. Resources Defense Council; Adirondack Council; Council of the Wilderness Soc.; Martha Graham Found.; NAACP. Joined exec. com. Amer. Jewish Com., 1930, and thereafter served in various capacities; at the time of his death was hon. v.-pres. and mem. bd. of govs. A founder, v.-pres., and bd. chmn. Amer. Friends of Hebrew U.; mem. exec. com. Amer. Jewish Joint Distribution Com. Author: books on political science, legal psychology, a novel, children's stories, and numerous articles. Last book: *The Devil in the Classroom: Hostility in American Education* (1985). Recipient: Butler Silver Medal, Columbia U.; Public Educ. Assn. Gold Medal; Public Service Award, Amer. Veterans, and many other honors.

NADELMANN, LUDWIG, rabbi; b. Berlin, Germany, Apr. 29, 1928; d. White Plains, N.Y., Dec. 6, 1986; in U.S. since 1946. Educ.: Yeshiva U.; Jewish Theol. Sem. of Amer.; Columbia U.; Dropsie Coll. Rabbi: Beth Shalom Syn., White Plains, N.Y., 1959–62; Genesis Hebrew Center, Tuckahoe, N.Y., 1963–73; exec. v.-pres. Jewish Reconstructionist Found., 1973–82; founder-rabbi Cong. M'vakshe Derekh, Scarsdale, N.Y., 1982–86. Assoc. ed. *The Reconstructionist;* pres. Westchester Bd. of Rabbis, 1967–70; mem.: Rabbinical Assembly, Amer. Jewish Com., Leo Baeck Inst., Reconstructionist Rabbinical Assn. Author: *The Role of Jewish Tradition in the Thought of Martin Buber, Jewish Peoplehood: An Analysis;* obituary essay on Mordecai Kaplan in 1985 AJYB.

PERLSTEIN, HARRIS, businessman, communal worker; b. NYC, Aug. 18, 1892; d. Chicago, Ill., Aug. (?), 1986. Educ.: Armour Inst. of Technology; Ill. Inst. of Technology. In the brewing industry since 1914, he was chmn. emer. of the Pabst Brewing Co. at the time of his death. In the 1930s, as a bd. member, later pres., of the Jewish Fed. of Metro. Chicago, he helped organize and headed the Jewish Welfare Fund, raising over $2 million for ship passage of Jews escaping Europe. Bd. mem.: State Bd. of Public Welfare, Ill.; Ill. Inst. of Technology; U.S. Brewers Assn.; Public Welfare Comms., Ill. Gen. chmn. Combined Jewish Appeal, 1938, 1946; bd. mem. Amer. Jewish Joint Distribution Com. Recipient: hon. doctorate, ITT; Jewish Fed. Julius Rosenwald Memorial Award; Amer. Jewish Com. Human Rights Award; Man of the Year, Israel Bonds.

PILCH, JUDAH, educator, author; b. Vachnikov, Russia, Sept. 7, 1902; d. Los Angeles, Cal., Jan. 29, 1986; in U.S. since 1923. Educ.: Yeshiva of Constantinople,

Turkey; Lewis Inst. of Chicago; Columbia U.; Dropsie Coll. (PhD). Lect. Coll. of Jewish Studies, Chicago, 1929–39; dir.: Jewish Educ. Assn., Rochester, N.Y., 1939–44; Jewish Educ. Com., NYC, 1944–49; Amer. Assn. for Jewish Educ. 1949–52, exec. dir. 1952–60; dir. AAJE Natl. Curriculum Research Inst., 1960–68; prof. of educ., Hebrew Union Coll., L.A., 1972–73; prof. U. of Judaism, L.A., 1972–78. Pres.: Natl. Council for Jewish Educ., 1948–50; Natl. Conf. of Jewish Communal Services, 1954–55; v.-pres. Religious Educ. Assn. of U.S. and Canada 1952–59, chmn. exec. com. 1959–70; pres. Histadrut Ivrit of Amer. 1959–71; chmn. Amer. Bible Contest, 1959–70. Author: numerous works, including: *The History of Modern Jewish Education in the U.S.* and *The Jewish Catastrophe in Europe* (ed.). Recipient: Distinguished Public Service Award, Jewish Tercentenary Comm.; hon. doctorate, Jewish Teachers Sem. and Jewish People's U., and other honors.

PRITZKER, ABRAM N., businessman, civic leader; b. Chicago, Ill., Jan. 6, 1896; d. Chicago, Feb. 8, 1986. Educ.: Harvard Law School. Partner, Pritzker, Pritzker & Clinton. Founder of the family-owned Marmon Group that owned some 266 companies and subsidiaries, including 140 Hyatt Hotels, Braniff Airlines, and *McCall's* magazine. Benefactor, U. of Chicago School of Medicine, Yeshiva U., Boys Town Jerusalem, Israel Bonds, other institutions. Dir. Jewish Fed. of Chicago. Recipient: many honors, including a chair in his name at Yeshiva U. and med. school named for him at U. of Chicago.

RESNIKOFF, NATHALIE, communal worker; b. NYC, Oct. 4, 1910; d. NYC, Nov. 8, 1986. Natl. pres. AMIT Women (formerly Amer. Mizrachi Women), 1962–65; hon. natl. pres., 1965–86; cochairwoman of its Israeli Comm.; delegate to the World Zionist Congress and a mem. of its Actions Com.

RICH, JACOB C., journalist; b. Minsk, Russia, Oct. 31, 1894; d. NYC, Nov. 26, 1986; in U.S. since 1906. Educ.: Boston Latin School; studied at Harvard. Editorial writer, city ed., columnist *Jewish Daily Forward* 1920–83; ed. Hatters' Union newspaper; articles in: *Saturday Evening Post, American Mercury,* N.Y. *World-Telegram,* the *New Leader,* and various union periodicals. Pres. Atlantic Labor Press Conf.; v.-pres. Tamiment Inst. Recipient: several honors, including a fete at Harvard library and awards for Hatters' Union paper.

RICKOVER, HYMAN G., engineer; naval officer; b. (?), Poland, Jan. 27, 1900; d. Arlington, Va., July 8, 1986; in U.S. since 1904. Educ.: U.S. Naval Acad.; Columbia U. The longest-serving officer in U.S. Navy history (63 years) and the first Jewish admiral, he was the father of the nuclear submarine, creator of the nuclear defense fleet, and a leader in the establishment of the first all-civilian nuclear power plant. He was a controversial figure throughout his career, a crusty and outspoken personality who opposed navy bureaucracy and insisted on innovation and quality control. Served aboard submarines, 1929–33; skipper of minesweeper, 1937–39; various engineering and admin. posts, 1933–37; head elect. section, Bureau of Ships, 1939–45; assigned to atomic submarine project, Oak Ridge, 1946; from 1949 on, headed newly created Nuclear Power Div., Bureau of Ships, and the Naval Reactors Branch, Atomic Energy Comm. Appointed admiral 1952, after being twice passed over, and following a public outcry. Presided over development of the *Nautilus,* the first nuclear submarine, launched in 1954. On retirement in 1982, urged outlawing of both nuclear weapons and power. Established: Center for Excellence in Educ., 1982; Rickover Science Inst. in Israel, 1981, enabling top Israeli science students to study in U.S. Recipient: two congressional Gold Medals for distinguished service; Presidential Medal of Freedom, 1980; honored by commissioning of submarine *Hyman G. Rickover,* 1984.

ROSE, DAVID, builder, communal worker; b. Jerusalem, Palestine, Dec. 24, 1891; d. NYC, July 16, 1986; in U.S. since 1892. Educ.: CCNY. Cofounder (1927), chmn., chmn. emer., Rose Associates, N.Y. real-estate development firm. Acquiring an interest in medical technology in his later years, he helped to design and build the hyperbaric chamber at Mt. Sinai Hosp., NYC, and an artificial kidney machine at U. of Utah. Construction consultant for Salk Inst., Cal., and Hadassah Hosp., Jerusalem. Cofounder Found. for Medical Technology; trustee New School for Social Research; board mem. Bronx-Riverdale YM-YWHA; pres., hon. pres., bd. chmn., lifetime trustee, Amer. Soc. for Technion, and v.-pres. Technion's internatl. bd. of govs.; cofounder Inst. on Amer. Jewish-Israeli Relations, Amer. Jewish Com. Recipient: Fiorello LaGuardia Award, New School for Social Research; Scopus Award, Amer. Friends of Hebrew U.; hon. doctorates: Technion, Israel; Bard Coll.

ROTHSCHILD, RICHARD C., author, organization exec.; b. Chicago, Ill., Mar. 24, 1895; d. NYC, Jan. 13, 1986. Educ.: Yale U. Ensign, U.S. Navy Aviation, WWI. Acct. exec. J. Walter Thompson and the Rothschild Co., 1920s and early 1930s; dir. *Parents Magazine,* 1928–46; lect. in philosophy, New School for Social Research, 1935–38; dir. of public information, Amer. Jewish Com., 1940–50, where he planned and directed a campaign against anti-Semitism; consultant to U.S. Coord. of Inter-Amer. Affairs, 1941–45. Mem.: Manhattan Council, N.Y. State Comm. Against Discrimination, 1953–64. Author: *Paradoxy: The Destiny of Modern Thought, Reality and Illusion,* and *Three Gods Give an Evening to Politics.*

ROTHSTEIN, JOSEPH, rabbi, communal worker; b. Yonkers, N.Y., Nov. 18, 1916; d. Philadelphia, Pa., Feb. 14, 1986. Educ.: Yeshiva U.; NYU; Wurzweiler School of Social Work (gerontology). Congregations in N.Y., Ont., Mass., S.C., 1942–45; admin. and sr. chaplain, Jewish Community Chaplaincy Service of Greater Phila., 1955–82; rabbi, Ahavath Israel Cong., 1962–77; Temple Beth Ami, 1982–85, both in Phila. Natl. pres. Amer. Correctional Chaplains Assn.; pres. Rabbinical Council of America, Phila. region; v.-pres.: Y.U. Rabbinical Alumni; Talmudical Yeshiva of Phila.; Religious Zionist Council of Phila.; bd. mem.: Assn. of Mental Health Chaplains of Amer.; Advisory Comm. to City Prisons; Interfaith Comm. on Chaplaincy for Commonwealth of Pa. Author: *Sense and Essence, Meeting Life's Challenges Through Pastoral Care.* Recipient: citations for meritorious humanitarian service from many orgs., including Amer. Correctional Chaplains Assn., Einstein Medical Center, Yeshiva U., UJA.

ROTHSTEIN, SAMUEL, lawyer, communal worker; b. (?), Poland, (?), 1904; d. Belvedere, Cal., Apr. 7, 1986; in U.S. since 1906. Educ.: NYU Law School. Pres. United Synagogue of Amer.,1944–50, then hon. pres. for life. Helped organize World Council of Synagogues, 1957. Hon. v.-pres. East Midwood Jewish Center, Brooklyn, N.Y.; founding mem., hon. v.-pres. Amer. Jewish League for Israel.

RUBLOFF, ARTHUR, businessman, philanthropist; b. Duluth, Minn., June 25, 1902; d. Chicago, Ill., May 24, 1986. Entered real estate business in 1919; founded Arthur Rubloff & Co. 1930; partner, pres., and chmn. until 1969; founder and chmn. Rubloff Development, 1971–86. V. chmn., chmn., chmn. emer., Northwestern U. Advisory Council; life trustee Art Inst. of Chicago and largest single contributor in its history; bd. mem. Horatio Alger Assn.; trustee Roosevelt U.; fellow Brandeis U.; trustee Hull House Assn.; dir. Lincoln Park Zoological Soc. Recipient: numerous honors including Horatio Alger Award, Amer. School & Colls. Assn.; Award of Merit, Veterans of Foreign Wars; B'nai B'rith Humanitarian Award; Harvard Club Man of the Year; hon. doctorates from Lewis U., Northwestern U., St. Xavier Coll.

SCHRAYER, MAX R., insurance executive, communal worker; b. Chicago, Ill., Nov. 17, 1902; d. Chicago, Ill., Sept. 17, 1986. Educ.: U. of Michigan Coll. of Engineering. Bd. chmn., Associated Agencies, Inc., insurance co. Numerous community activities, including: pres. Better Govt. Assn. 1967–70, v.-chmn. bd. of trustees, Roosevelt U. Bd. mem.: Jewish Fed. of Metro. Chicago, Amer. Jewish Joint Distribution Com., Jewish Telegraphic Agency, Jewish Publication Soc., Amer. Soc. for Technion, Temple Sholom; pres.: K.A.M. Cong., 1941–48; Beth Am Cong. 1952–54; Chicago Fed., Union of Amer. Hebrew Congs., 1948–50; chmn. Combined Jewish Appeal of Metro. Chicago, 1964, 1965; genl. chmn. Jewish United Fund of Metro. Chicago, 1979. Recipient: Jewish Community Centers Senior Adult Award; Julius Rosenwald Award, Jewish Fed. of Metro. Chicago; Freedom Award, Roosevelt U.

SCHWARTZ, DAVID, businessman, philanthropist; b. NYC, July 27, 1902; d. NYC, Dec. 28, 1985. Educ.: NYC public schools. From small beginnings in 1924, built Jonathan Logan, the largest independent dress manufacturing co. in the U.S. Major benefactor, NYU Hosp.; Tufts Coll.; supporter of Brandeis U., Yeshiva U., Albert Einstein Coll. of Med., Benjamin N. Cardozo Law School, Hebrew U. and its Harry S.

Truman Research Inst.; assoc. chmn. Amer. Jewish Com. Appeal for Human Relations.

SHANKMAN, JACOB KESTIN, rabbi; b. Chelsea, Mass., Oct. 22, 1904; d. New Rochelle, N.Y., Feb. 4, 1986. Educ.: Harvard U.; Hebrew Union Coll. Rabbi: Cong. B'rith Sholom, Troy, N.Y., 1930–37; Temple Israel, New Rochelle, N.Y., 1937–73, emer. thereafter; chaplain (lt. com.) U.S. Navy, WW II. Bd. mem.: Amer. Red Cross, Council of Social Agencies, Salvation Army, Community Chest/United Way; lect. and mem. president's adv. council, Coll. of New Rochelle. Pres.: Assn. of Reform Rabbis of N.Y.; Westchester Bd. of Rabbis; exec. bd. mem. Central Conf. of American Rabbis and chmn. of its coms. on church & state, ethics, others; chmn., pres., N. Amer. bd., World Union for Progressive Judaism; helped found Cong. Har-El, Jerusalem, and dedicated Yahel, first Reform kibbutz in Israel. Recipient: hon. doctorate, Heb. Union Coll., and many awards from civic groups.

SHUSTER, ZACHARIAH, communal worker; b. Kovno, Lithuania, (?), 1902; d. NYC, Feb. 15, 1986; in U.S. since 1927. Fluent in seven languages and possessing extensive knowledge of Judaism and Christianity as well as international affairs, he was foreign affairs expert for the Amer. Jewish Com., 1938–86: mem. of its delegation to the UN founding conf., San Francisco, 1945; dir. of its European office, Paris, 1948–74, where he led programs to rebuild postwar Jewish communities in Europe and N. Africa; adviser on relations with the Vatican and the World Council of Churches and representative to the Second Vatican Council, 1962; consultant, natl. office, 1974–86. Author: frequent articles in *The Nation, Commentary, Menorah Journal, Contemporary Jewish Record, Hadoar, Zukunft.*

SMOLAR, BORIS, journalist; b. Rovno, Ukraine, (?), 1897; d. NYC, Jan. 31, 1986; in U.S. since 1919. Educ.: Medill School of Journalism, Northwestern U. Ed. staff *Chicago Jewish Daily Forward* until 1924; roving reporter *New York World* and European corresp. Jewish Telegraphic Agency, 1924–28; JTA ed.-in-chief, 1928–67; established JTA office in Moscow, 1928; corresp. in Berlin, 1932, until expelled; coverage of Palestine in pre-Israel years. Author: numerous books in Yiddish and Hebrew and *In the Service of My People* and *Soviet Jewry Today and Tomorrow* in English. Recipient: numerous citations and awards, including Bronze Peace Medal and Silver Shekel Medal from the Israeli govt.; Amoris Alumna Pax Medal from Pope Paul VI. In his honor, the Council of Jewish Feds. and Welfare Funds established the Smolar Award for Excellence in Jewish Journalism.

SONNEBORN, RUDOLF G., businessman, communal worker; b. Baltimore, Md., June 22, 1898; d. Danbury, Conn., June 1, 1986. Educ.: Johns Hopkins U. Associated with L. Sonneborn Sons, family company producing petrochemicals and specialty petroleum products, beginning in 1919 and serving as pres. early 1940s to 1960; dir. Witco Corp., which absorbed Sonneborn, until 1968. In 1919, on a mission to Palestine for World Zionist Org., began friendships with David Ben-Gurion and Chaim Weizmann; during World War II raised funds for Jewish refugees in Europe; in 1947, at Ben-Gurion's request, founded Materials for Israel, also known as the Sonneborn Inst., a secret supply source of arms for the Haganah; after 1948 was a leading fund-raiser for UJA and United Palestine Appeal, Israel Bonds, and the ZOA. Chmn. Ampal-Amer. Israel Corp., 1952–70; active in Amer. Financial and Development Corp. and Israel Investors. Recipient: many honors and awards from Jewish orgs. in the U.S. and Israel.

SPERTUS, MAURICE, businessman, philanthropist; b. Lubech, Chernigov, Russia, Sept. 16, 1902; d. Chicago, Ill., June 19, 1986; in U.S. since 1923. Educ.: U. of Kiev. Cofounder Intercraft Industries Corp., internatl. manufacturer of picture frames, 1933. Cofounder and trustee Spertus Coll. of Judaica (formerly Coll. of Jewish Studies), 1961–86; founder Spertus Museum, which houses one of the nation's largest permanent collections of Judaica; natl. v.-pres. Amer. Technion Soc., 1950–86; v.-pres. and dir. Jewish Fed. of Metro. Chicago 1970–80. Recipient: hon. doctorate, Spertus Coll.

SUHL, YURI, writer; b. Podayetz, Galicia, July 30, 1908; d. Martha's Vineyard, Mass., Nov. 8, 1986; in U.S. since 1923. Educ.: CCNY; NYU; Jewish Workers U. Author: four vols. of poetry in Yiddish; children's books, including *Uncle Misha's Partisans* (winner of Jewish Book Council Award), *Simon Boom Goes to a Wedding,* (winner of Lewis Carroll Shelf Award) and *The Purim Goat;* two autobiographical novels, *One Foot in America* and *Cowboy on a Wooden Horse;* the biography *Ernestine L. Rose and the Battle for Human Rights;* and *They Fought Back: The Story of Jewish Resistance in Europe* (ed., transl.). Identified politically as a socialist, he was active in efforts to prevent the execution of Julius and Ethel Rosenberg. Was also an outspoken critic of persecution of Jews in Poland and the USSR.

TOUBIN, ISAAC, rabbi, communal worker; b. NYC, May 22, 1915; d. NYC, Mar. 23, 1986. Educ.: Yeshiva U., Jewish Theol. Sem. of Amer. (ordination; DHL). During WW II, dir. European office, Jewish Welfare Bd. and dir. of its Greater N.Y. Army and Navy Com.; asst. dir., natl. exec. dir. Amer. Jewish Cong. 1946–60; exec. v. pres. Amer. Assn. for Jewish Educ. (now Jewish Educ. Service of N. Amer., JESNA) 1960–78; mem. and High Holy Days rabbi, Park Ave. Synagogue, NYC; hon. trustee, the Jewish Museum, NYC.

WALDMAN, JONAH H., rabbi; b. (?), Lithuania, (?), 1910; d. Rockville, Md., Aug. 19, 1986; in U.S. since 1921. Educ.: Boston U.; Boston Hebrew Teachers Coll.; Boston Yeshiva; Ohel Torah Yeshiva. Rabbi, Agudath Achim Cong., Washington, D.C. 1941–78; rabbi emer. Har Tzeon-Agudath Achim, a merged cong., in Silver Spring, Md., since 1978. Pres.: Washington Bd. of Rabbis; Hebrew Cultural Assn.; principal, Hebrew Acad. of Greater Washington; exec. com. mem.: Jewish Comm. Council; Histadrut Ivrit of Amer.

WIRNIK, RACHMIEL, journalist; b. Kovel, Volyn, Poland, Dec. 15, 1913; d. NYC, Dec. 26, 1986; in U.S. since ca. 1965. Educ.: yeshivah and Tarbut Gymnasia, Kovel; Warsaw Hochschule for Journalism. Began to write for *Unser Leben* in 1932; head of Betar Youth Org. in the 1930s and ed. of the Yiddish Revisionist Zionist publication *Medinat Yisrael;* worked closely with Zeev Jabotinsky and Menachem Begin; emigrated to Palestine in 1941 and was active in Herut party; after establishment of Israel edited Zionist publications in Israel and later in Paris; in U.S. edited ZINS, the weekly news bulletin of the World Union of Genl. Zionists, which he also served as exec. dir. Frequent contrib. to publications worldwide.

WUNDOHL, FRANK F., journalist; b. Philadelphia, Pa., Oct. 7, 1929; d. Elizabeth, N.J., May 17, 1986. Educ.: Temple U. News posts at WCAU-TV Phila.; *Philadelphia Daily News; Courier-Post,* S. Jersey; *Daily Intelligencer,* Doylestown, Pa.; information dir. Albert Einstein Medical Center, Phila., 1967–73; ed. *Jewish Exponent,* Phila., 1973–81; dir. of communications Jewish Welfare Bd., since 1981. Bd. mem. Jewish Telegraphic Agency; pres. Amer. Jewish Press Assn., 1978–81; v.-pres. Amer. Jewish Public Relations Soc. Recipient: Council of Federations Boris Smolar Award for Excellence in N. Amer. Jewish Journalism; AJPA Simon Rockower and Joseph Poliakoff Awards.

WYZANSKI, CHARLES E., Jr., federal judge; b. Boston, Mass., May 27, 1906; d. Cambridge, Mass., Sept. 3, 1986. Educ.: Harvard Coll., Harvard Law School. After private practice with Ropes, Gray became law secy. to Justice Augustus Hand, 1930–31, and to Justice Learned Hand, 1932–33; solicitor, U.S. Labor Dept. 1933–35, where he devised plans to facilitate immigration of refugees; in the Solicitor General's Office, 1935–37, he argued cases before the Supreme Court supporting the Social Security Act and Natl. Labor Relations Act; assoc. Ropes, Gray, 1938–41; appointed by Franklin D. Roosevelt to Mass. fed. dist. court, 1941; chief judge 1965–71; sr. judge, 1971–86, sitting on federal district courts in San Francisco and Boston, and appeals courts in Chicago, NYC, Richmond, and Washington; Internatl. Administrative Court, Geneva, Switzerland, 1950–55. Regarded as an activist judge, he overturned corporal punishment in Boston schools, invalidated the Selective Service Act, and ruled the Vietnam War unconstitutional. Lect. Harvard Coll., 1942–43, 1949–50. Mem. Harvard Bd. of Overseers, 1943–49 and 1951–57; pres. 1953–57. Author: *Whereas: A Judge's Premises* (paperback title, *The New Meaning of Justice);* many learned and more popular articles and published opinions.

YAFFE, RICHARD, journalist, communal worker; b. Reading, Pa., June 10, 1903; d. NYC, Oct. 30, 1986. Educ.: Boston U., Harvard U. Reporter: beginning 1926, *Atlantic City Times; Philadelphia Inquirer; NY Post,* 1935–38; foreign ed. PM (NYC), 1940–49; Eastern Europe corresp. CBS 1949–51; UN corresp. *Al Hamishmar*

(Israel); assoc. ed. NY *Jewish Week;* ed.-in-chief *Israel Horizons* (voice of Mapam in the U.S.); Amer. bureau chief *London Jewish Chronicle;* contrib. to *Aufbau, National Jewish Monthly, Congress Weekly.* With Heywood Broun, helped organize American Newspaper Guild. A vocal opponent of McCarthyism in the 50s; a lifelong fighter for progressive political causes. Mem.: Foreign Press Assn.; Overseas Press Club; UN Press Assn. Cofounder Americans for a Progressive Israel; Givat Haviva Educ. Found.; active in behalf of the Jewish Natl. Fund, World Zionist Org.-Amer. Section, Amer. Zionist Youth Fed. Author: *Yugoslavia's Way, Nathan Rapaport: Sculptures and Monument, A Short History of American Jews,* numerous articles. Recipient: Council of Jewish Feds. first Special Citation for Lifetime Achievement in Jewish Journalism (1986).

ZUCKERMAN, PAUL, businessman, philanthropist; b. Constantinople, Turkey, May 31, 1912; d. Detroit, Mich., Jan. 8, 1986; in U.S. since 1914. From first job as a truck driver, rose to become "the peanut butter king," its largest producer and distributor in the world; chmn. Velvet-O'Donnell Corp.; dir. Super Sol Markets, Israel. Known as a generous contributor and "fund-raising genius" in behalf of numerous causes, including: United Found. of Detroit; Detroit Round Table; Natl. Conf. of Christians and Jews; Michigan Soc. for the Mentally Diseased; Sinai Hosp. of Detroit; lifetime trustee, Detroit Inst. of Arts; founder, the Angels (cancer research); chmn. U.S. Food for Peace, Detroit. Pres. natl. UJA, 1975–76; gen. chmn., 1972–74; chmn. Israel Emergency Fund, 1967; treas. United Israel Appeal; chmn. World Fund Raising Com., Jewish Agency; exec. com. mem., AIPAC; v.-pres. Amer. ORT; dir. Boys Town, Jerusalem; pres. AKIM, U.S.A.; bd. mem.: Ben-Gurion U., Amer. Friends of Hebrew U., ZOA, Israel Bonds, Amer. Jewish Joint Distribution Com., Magen David Adom. Recipient: hon. doctorates from Siena Heights Coll., Bar Ilan U.; hon. fellowship, Hebrew U.; Amer. Jewish Com. Human Rights Medallion; Brandeis Award, ZOA; Jewish War Veterans citation, and many other honors.

Calendars

SUMMARY JEWISH CALENDAR, 5748–5752 (Sept. 1987-Aug. 1992)

HOLIDAY	5748			5749			5750			5751			5752		
		1987			1988			1989			1990			1991	
Rosh Ha-shanah, 1st day	Th	Sept.	24	M	Sept.	12	Sa	Sept.	30	Th	Sept.	20	M	Sept.	9
Rosh Ha-shanah, 2nd day . . .	F	Sept.	25	T	Sept.	13	S	Oct.	1	F	Sept.	21	T	Sept.	10
Fast of Gedaliah	S	Sept.	27	W	Sept.	14	M	Oct.	2	S	Sept.	23	W	Sept.	11
Yom Kippur	Sa	Oct.	3	W	Sept.	21	M	Oct.	9	Sa	Sept.	29	W	Sept.	18
Sukkot, 1st day	Th	Oct.	8	M	Sept.	26	Sa	Oct.	14	Th	Oct.	4	M	Sept.	23
Sukkot, 2nd day	F	Oct.	9	T	Sept.	27	S	Oct.	15	F	Oct.	5	T	Sept.	24
Hosha'na' Rabbah	W	Oct.	14	S	Oct.	2	F	Oct.	20	W	Oct.	10	S	Sept.	29
Shemini 'Aẓeret	Th	Oct.	15	M	Oct.	3	Sa	Oct.	21	Th	Oct.	11	M	Sept.	30
Simḥat Torah	F	Oct.	16	T	Oct.	4	S	Oct.	22	F	Oct.	12	T	Oct.	1
New Moon, Ḥeshwan, 1st day .	F	Oct.	23	T	Oct.	11	S	Oct.	29	F	Oct.	19	T	Oct.	8
New Moon, Ḥeshwan, 2nd day .	Sa	Oct.	24	W	Oct.	12	M	Oct.	30	Sa	Oct.	20	W	Oct.	9
New Moon, Kislew, 1st day . .	S	Nov.	22	Th	Nov.	10	T	Nov.	28	S	Nov.	18	Th	Nov.	7
New Moon, Kislew, 2nd day . .							W	Nov.	29				F	Nov.	8
Ḥanukkah, 1st day	W	Dec.	16	S	Dec.	4	Sa	Dec.	23	W	Dec.	12	M	Dec.	2
New Moon, Ṭevet, 1st day . .	M	Dec.	21	F	Dec.	9	Th	Dec.	28	M	Dec.	17	Sa	Dec.	7
New Moon, Ṭevet, 2nd day . .	T	Dec.	22				F	Dec.	29	T	Dec.	18	S	Dec.	8
								1990							
Fast of 10th of Ṭevet	Th	Dec.	31	S	Dec.	18	S	Jan.	7	Th	Dec.	27	T	Dec.	17

	1988			1989			1990			1991			1992		
New Moon, Shevat	W	Jan.	20	Sa	Jan.	7	Sa	Jan.	27	W	Jan.	16	M	Jan.	6
Hamishshah-'asar bi-Shevat	W	Feb.	3	Sa	Jan.	21	Sa	Feb.	10	W	Jan.	30	M	Jan.	20
New Moon, Adar I, 1st day	Th	Feb.	18	S	Feb.	5	S	Feb.	25	Th	Feb.	14	T	Feb.	4
New Moon, Adar I, 2nd day	F	Feb.	19	M	Feb.	6	M	Feb.	26	F	Feb.	15	W	Feb.	5
New Moon, Adar II, 1st day				T	Mar.	7							Th	Mar.	5
New Moon, Adar II, 2nd day				W	Mar.	8							F	Mar.	6
Fast of Esther	W	Mar.	2	M	Mar.	20	Th	Mar.	8	W	Feb.	27	W	Mar.	18
Purim	Th	Mar.	3	T	Mar.	21	S	Mar.	11	Th	Feb.	28	Th	Mar.	19
Shushan Purim	F	Mar.	4	W	Mar.	22	M	Mar.	12	F	Mar.	1	F	Mar.	20
New Moon, Nisan	Sa	Mar.	19	Th	Apr.	6	T	Mar.	27	Sa	Mar.	16	Sa	Apr.	4
Passover, 1st day	Sa	Apr.	2	Th	Apr.	20	T	Apr.	10	Sa	Mar.	30	Sa	Apr.	18
Passover, 2nd day	S	Apr.	3	F	Apr.	21	W	Apr.	11	S	Mar.	31	S	Apr.	19
Passover, 7th day	F	Apr.	8	W	Apr.	26	M	Apr.	16	F	Apr.	5	F	Apr	24
Passover, 8th day	Sa	Apr.	9	Th	Apr.	27	T	Apr.	17	Sa	Apr.	6	Sa	Apr.	25
Holocaust Memorial Day	Th	Apr.	14	T	May	2	S	Apr.	22	Th	Apr.	11	Th	Apr.	30
New Moon, Iyar, 1st day	S	Apr.	17	F	May	5	W	Apr.	25	S	Apr.	14	S	May	3
New Moon, Iyar, 2nd day	M	Apr.	18	Sa	May	6	Th	Apr.	26	M	Apr.	15	M	May	4
Israel Independence Day	F	Apr.	22*	W	May	10	M	Apr.	30	F	Apr.	19*	F	May	8*
Lag Ba-'omer	Th	May	5	T	May	23	S	May	13	Th	May	2	Th	May	21
Jerusalem Day	S	May	15	F	June	2*	W	May	23	S	May	12	S	May	31
New Moon, Siwan	T	May	17	S	June	4	F	May	25	T	May	14	T	Jun	2
Shavu'ot, 1st day	S	May	22	F	June	9	W	May	30	S	May	19	S	Jun	7
Shavu'ot, 2nd day	M	May	23	Sa	June	10	Th	May	31	M	May	20	M	Jun	8
New Moon, Tammuz, 1st day	W	June	15	M	July	3	Sa	June	23	W	June	12	W	July	1
New Moon, Tammuz, 2nd day	Th	June	16	T	July	4	S	June	24	Th	June	13	Th	July	2
Fast of 17th of Tammuz	S	July	3	Th	July	20	T	July	10	S	June	30	S	July	19
New Moon, Av	F	July	15	W	Aug.	2	M	July	23	F	July	12	F	July	31
Fast of 9th of Av	S	July	24	Th	Aug.	10	T	July	31	S	July	21	S	Aug.	9
New Moon, Elul, 1st day	Sa	Aug.	13	Th	Aug.	31	T	Aug.	21	Sa	Aug.	10	Sa	Aug.	29
New Moon, Elul, 2nd day	S	Aug.	14	F	Sept.	1	W	Aug.	22	S	Aug.	11	S	Aug.	30

*Observed Thursday, a day earlier, to avoid conflict with the Sabbath.

CONDENSED MONTHLY CALENDAR (1987–1989)

1987, Jan. 2–Jan. 30] ṬEVET (29 DAYS) [5747

Civil Date	Day of the Week	Jewish Date	SABBATHS, FESTIVALS, FASTS	PENTATEUCHAL READING	PROPHETICAL READING
Jan. 2	F	Ṭevet 1	New Moon, second day; Ḥanukkah, seventh day	Num. 28:1–15 Num. 7:48–53	
3	Sa	2	Mi-ḳez; Ḥanukkah, eighth day	Gen. 41:1–44:17 Num. 7:54–8:4	Zechariah 2:14–4:7
10	Sa	9	Wa-yiggash	Gen. 44:18–47:27	Ezekiel 37:15–28
11	S	10	Fast of 10th of Ṭevet	Exod. 32:11–14 34:1–10	Isaiah 55:6–56:8 (afternoon only)
17	Sa	16	Wa-yeḥi	Gen. 47:28–50:26	I Kings 2:1–12
24	Sa	23	Shemot	Exod. 1:1–6:1	Isaiah 27:6–28:13 29:22–23 *Jeremiah 1:1–2:3*

Italics are for Sephardi Minhag.

1987, Jan. 31–Mar. 1] SHEVAṬ (30 DAYS) [5747

Civil Date	Day of the Week	Jewish Date	SABBATHS, FESTIVALS, FASTS	PENTATEUCHAL READING	PROPHETICAL READING
Jan. 31	Sa	Shevaṭ 1	Wa-'era'; New Moon	Exod. 6:2–9:35 Num. 28:9–15	Isaiah 66:1–24
Feb. 7	Sa	8	Bo'	Exod. 10:1–13:16	Jeremiah 46:13–28
14	Sa	15	Be-shallaḥ (Shabbat Shirah); Ḥamishshah-'asar bi-Shevaṭ	Exod. 13:17–17:16	Judges 4:4–5:31 *Judges 5:1–31*
21	Sa	22	Yitro	Exod. 18:1–20:23	Isaiah 6:1–7:6 9:5–6 *Isaiah 6:1–13*
28	Sa	29	Mishpaṭim (Shabbat Sheḳalim)	Exod. 21:1–24:18 Exod. 30:11–16	II Kings 12:1–17 *II Kings 11:17–12:17* *I Samuel 20:18, 42*
Mar. 1	S	30	New Moon, first day	Num. 28:1–15	

Italics are for Sephardi Minhag.

1987, Mar. 2–Mar. 30] ADAR (29 DAYS) [5747

Civil Date	Day of the Week	Jewish Date	SABBATHS, FESTIVALS, FASTS	PENTATEUCHAL READING	PROPHETICAL READING
Mar. 2	M	Adar 1	New Moon, second day	Num. 28:1–15	
7	Sa	6	Terumah	Exod. 25:1–27:19	I Kings 5:26–6:13
12	Th	11	Fast of Esther	Exod. 32:11–14 34:1–10	Isaiah 55:6–56:8 (afternoon only)
14	Sa	13	Teẓawweh (Shabbat Zakhor)	Exod. 27:20–30:10 Deut. 25:17–19	I Samuel 15:2–34 *I Samuel 15:1–34*
15	S	14	Purim	Exod. 17:8–16	Book of Esther (night before and in the morning)
16	M	15	Shushan Purim		
21	Sa	20	Ki tissa' (Shabbat Parah)	Exod. 30:11–34:35 Num. 19:1–22	Ezekiel 36:16–38 *Ezekiel 36:16–36*
28	Sa	27	Wa-yaḳhel, Peḳude (Shabbat Ha-ḥodesh)	Exod. 35:1–40:38 Exod. 12:1–20	Ezekiel 45:16–46:18 *Ezekiel 45:18–46:15*

Italics are for Sephardi Minhag.

1987, Mar. 31–Apr. 29] NISAN (30 DAYS) [5747

Civil Date	Day of the Week	Jewish Date	SABBATHS, FESTIVALS, FASTS	PENTATEUCHAL READING	PROPHETICAL READING
Mar. 31	T	Nisan 1	New Moon	Num. 28:1–15	
Apr. 4	Sa	5	Wa-yikra'	Levit. 1:1–5:26	Isaiah 43:21–44:24
11	Sa	12	Ẓaw (Shabbat Ha-gadol)	Levit. 6:1–8:36	Malachi 3:4–24
13	M	14	Fast of Firstborn		
14	T	15	Passover, first day	Exod. 12:21–51 Num. 28:16–25	Joshua 5:2–6:1, 27
15	W	16	Passover, second day	Levit. 22:26–23:44 Num. 28:16–25	II Kings 23:1–9, 21–25
16	Th	17	Ḥol Ha-mo'ed, first day	Exod. 13:1–16 Num. 28:19–25	
17	F	18	Ḥol Ha-mo'ed, second day	Exod. 22:24–23:19 Num. 28:19–25	
18	Sa	19	Ḥol Ha-mo'ed, third day	Exod. 33:12–34:26 Num. 28:19–25	Ezekiel 37:1–14
19	S	20	Ḥol Ha-mo'ed, fourth day	Num. 9:1–14 Num. 28:19–25	
20	M	21	Passover, seventh day	Exod. 13:17–15:26 Num. 28:19–25	II Samuel 22:1–51
21	T	22	Passover, eighth day	Deut. 15:19–16:17 Num. 28:19–25	Isaiah 10:32–12:6
25	Sa	26	Shemini	Levit. 9:1–11:47	II Samuel 6:1–7:17
26	S	27	Holocaust Memorial Day		
29	W	30	New Moon, first day	Num. 28:1–15	

1987, Apr. 30–May 28] IYAR (29 DAYS) [5747

Civil Date	Day of the Week	Jewish Date	SABBATHS, FESTIVALS, FASTS	PENTATEUCHAL READING	PROPHETICAL READING
Apr. 30	Th	Iyar 1	New Moon, second day	Num. 28:1–15	
May 2	Sa	3	Tazria', Meẓora'	Levit. 12:1–15:33	II Kings 7:3–20
4	M	5	Israel Independence Day		
9	Sa	10	Aḥare mot, Ḳedoshim	Levit. 16:1–20:27	Amos 9:7–15 *Ezekiel 20:2–20*
16	Sa	17	Emor	Levit. 21:1–24:23	Ezekiel 44:15–31
17	S	18	Lag Ba-'omer		
23	Sa	24	Be-har, Be-ḥuḳḳotai	Levit. 25:1–27:34	Jeremiah 16:19–17:14
27	W	28	Jerusalem Day		

1987, May 29–June 27] SIWAN (30 DAYS) [5747

Civil Date	Day of the Week	Jewish Date	SABBATHS, FESTIVALS, FASTS	PENTATEUCHAL READING	PROPHETICAL READING
May 29	F	Siwan 1	New Moon	Num. 28:1–15	
30	Sa	2	Be-midbar	Num. 1:1–4:20	Hosea 2:1–22
June 3	W	6	Shavu'ot, first day	Exod. 19:1–20:23 Num. 28:26–31	Ezekiel 1:1–28 3:12
4	Th	7	Shavu'ot, second day	Deut. 15:19–16:17 Num. 28:26–31	Habbakuk 3:1–19 *Habbakuk 2:20–3:19*
6	Sa	9	Naso'	Num. 4:21–7:89	Judges 13:2–25
13	Sa	16	Be-ha'alotekha	Num. 8:1–12:16	Zechariah 2:14–4:7
20	Sa	23	Shelaḥ lekha	Num. 13:1–15:41	Joshua 2:1–24
27	Sa	30	Ḳoraḥ; New Moon, first day	Num. 16:1–18:32 Num. 28:9–15	Isaiah 66:1–24 *Isaiah 66:1–24* *I Samuel 20:18, 42*

Italics are for Sephardi Minhag.

1987, June 28–July 26] TAMMUZ (29 DAYS) [5747

Civil Date	Day of the Week	Jewish Date	SABBATHS, FESTIVALS, FASTS	PENTATEUCHAL READING	PROPHETICAL READING
June 28	S	Tammuz 1	New Moon, second day	Num. 28:1–15	
July 4	Sa	7	Ḥuḳḳat	Num. 19:1–22:1	Judges 11:1–33
11	Sa	14	Balaḳ	Num. 22:2–25:9	Micah 5:6–6:8
14	T	17	Fast of 17th of Tammuz	Exod. 32:11–14 34:1–10	Isaiah 55:6–56:8 (afternoon only)
18	Sa	21	Pineḥas	Num. 25:10–30:1	Jeremiah 1:1–2:3
25	Sa	28	Maṭṭot, Masʿe	Num. 30:2–36:13	Jeremiah 2:4–28 3:4 *Jeremiah 2:4–28* *4:1–2*

Italics are for Sephardi Minhag.

1987, July 27–Aug. 25] AV (30 DAYS) [5747

Civil Date	Day of the Week	Jewish Date	SABBATHS, FESTIVALS, FASTS	PENTATEUCHAL READING	PROPHETICAL READING
July 27	M	Av 1	New Moon	Num. 28:1–15	
Aug. 1	Sa	6	Devarim (Shabbat Ḥazon)	Deut. 1:1–3:22	Isaiah 1:1–27
4	T	9	Fast of 9th of Av	Morning: Deut. 4:25–40 Afternoon: Exod. 32:11–14 34:1–10	(Lamentations is read the night before.) Jeremiah 8:13–9:23 (morning) Isaiah 55:6–56:8 (afternoon)
8	Sa	13	Wa-etḥannan (Shabbat Naḥamu)	Deut. 3:23–7:11	Isaiah 40:1–26
15	Sa	20	‘Ekev	Deut. 7:12–11:25	Isaiah 49:14–51:3
22	Sa	27	Re’eh	Deut. 11:26–16:17	Isaiah 54:11–55:5
25	T	30	New Moon, first day	Num. 28:1–15	

1987, Aug. 26–Sept. 23] ELUL (29 DAYS) [5747

Civil Date	Day of the Week	Jewish Date	SABBATHS, FESTIVALS, FASTS	PENTATEUCHAL READING	PROPHETICAL READING
Aug. 26	W	Elul 1	New Moon, second day	Num. 28:1–15	
29	Sa	4	Shofeṭim	Deut. 16:18–21:9	Isaiah 51:12–52:12
Sept. 5	Sa	11	Ki teẓe’	Deut. 21:10–25:19	Isaiah 54:1–10
12	Sa	18	Ki tavo’	Deut. 26:1–29:8	Isaiah 60:1–22
19	Sa	25	Niẓẓavim, Wa-yelekh	Deut. 29:9–31:30	Isaiah 61:10–63:9

Civil Date	Day of the Week	Jewish Date	SABBATHS, FESTIVALS, FASTS	PENTATEUCHAL READING	PROPHETICAL READING
Sept. 24	Th	Tishri 1	Rosh Ha-shanah, first day	Gen. 21:1–34 Num. 29:1–6	I Samuel 1:1–2:10
25	F	2	Rosh Ha-shanah, second day	Gen. 22:1–24 Num. 29:1–6	Jeremiah 31:2–20
26	Sa	3	Ha'azinu (Shabbat Shuvah)	Deut. 32:1–52	Hosea 14:2–10 Micah 7:18–20 Joel 2:15–27 *Hosea 14:2–10* *Micah 7:18–20*
27	S	4	Fast of Gedaliah	Exod. 32:11–14 34:1–10	Isaiah 55:6–56:8 (afternoon only)
Oct. 3	Sa	10	Yom Kippur	Morning: Levit. 16:1–34 Num. 29:7–11 Afternoon: Levit. 18:1–30	Isaiah 57:14–58:14 Jonah 1:1–4:11 Micah 7:18–20
8	Th	15	Sukkot, first day	Levit. 22:26–23:44 Num. 29:12–16	Zechariah 14:1–21
9	F	16	Sukkot, second day	Levit. 22:26–23:44 Num. 29:12–16	I Kings 8:2–21
10	Sa	17	Ḥol Ha-mo'ed, first day	Exod. 33:12–34:26 Num. 29:17–22	Ezekiel 38:18–39:16
11-13	S-T	18-20	Ḥol Ha-mo'ed, second to fourth days	S Num. 29:20–28 M Num. 29:23–31 T Num. 29:26–34	
14	W	21	Hosha'na' Rabbah	Num. 29:26–34	
15	Th	22	Shemini 'Aẓeret	Deut. 14:22–16:17 Num. 29:35–30:1	I Kings 8:54–66
16	F	23	Simḥat Torah	Deut. 33:1–34:12 Gen. 1:1–2:3 Num. 29:35–30:1	Joshua 1:1–18 *Joshua 1:1–9*
17	Sa	24	Be-re'shit	Gen. 1:1–6:8	Isaiah 42:5–43:10 *Isaiah 42:5–21*
23	F	30	New Moon, first day	Num. 28:1–15	

Italics are for Sephardi Minhag.

Civil Date	Day of the Week	Jewish Date	SABBATHS, FESTIVALS, FASTS	PENTATEUCHAL READING	PROPHETICAL READING
Oct. 24	Sa	Ḥeshwan 1	Noaḥ; New Moon, second day	Gen. 6:9–11:32 Num. 28:9–15	Isaiah 66:1–24
31	Sa	8	Lekh lekha	Gen. 12:1–17:27	Isaiah 40:27–41:16
Nov. 7	Sa	15	Wa-yera'	Gen. 18:1–22:24	II Kings 4:1–37 *II Kings 4:1–23*
14	Sa	22	Ḥayye Sarah	Gen. 23:1–25:18	I Kings 1:1–31
21	Sa	29	Toledot	Gen. 25:19–28:9	I Samuel 20:18–42

Civil Date	Day of the Week	Jewish Date	SABBATHS, FESTIVALS, FASTS	PENTATEUCHAL READING	PROPHETICAL READING
Nov. 22	S	Kislew 1	New Moon	Num. 28:1–15	
28	Sa	7	Wa-yeẓe'	Gen. 28:10–32:3	Hosea 12:13–14:10 *Hosea 11:7–12:12*
Dec. 5	Sa	14	Wa-yishlaḥ	Gen. 32:4–36:43	Hosea 11:7–12:12 *Obadiah 1:1–21*
12	Sa	21	Wa-yeshev	Gen. 37:1–40:23	Amos 2:6–3:8
16-18	W-F	25-27	Ḥanukkah, first to third days	W Num. 7:1–17 Th Num. 7:18–29 F Num. 7:24–35	
19	Sa	28	Mi-ḳeẓ; Ḥanukkah, fourth day	Gen. 41:1–44:17 Num. 7:30–35	Zechariah 2:14–4:7
20	S	29	Ḥanukkah, fifth day	Num. 7:36–47	
21	M	30	New Moon, first day; Ḥanukkah, sixth day	Num. 28:1–15 Num. 7:42–47	

Italics are for Sephardi Minhag.

Civil Date	Day of the Week	Jewish Date	SABBATHS, FESTIVALS, FASTS	PENTATEUCHAL READING	PROPHETICAL READING
Dec. 22	T	Ṭevet 1	New Moon, second day; Ḥanukkah, seventh day	Num. 28:1–15 Num. 7:48–53	
23	W	2	Ḥanukkah, eighth day	Num. 7:54–8:4	
26	Sa	5	Wa-yiggash	Gen. 44:18–47:27	Ezekiel 37:15–28
31	Th	10	Fast of 10th of Ṭevet	Exod. 32:11–14 34:1–10	Isaiah 55:6–56:8 (afternoon only)
Jan. 2	Sa	12	Wa-yeḥi	Gen. 47:28–50:26	I Kings 2:1–12
9	Sa	19	Shemot	Exod. 1:1–6:1	Isaiah 27:6–28:13 29:22–23 *Jeremiah 1:1–2:3*
16	Sa	26	Wa-'era'	Exod. 6:2–9:35	Ezekiel 28:25–29:21

1988, Jan. 20–Feb. 18] SHEVAṬ (30 DAYS) [5748

Civil Date	Day of the Week	Jewish Date	SABBATHS, FESTIVALS, FASTS	PENTATEUCHAL READING	PROPHETICAL READING
Jan. 20	W	Shevaṭ 1	New Moon	Num. 28:1–15	
23	Sa	4	Bo'	Exod. 10:1–13:16	Jeremiah 46:13–28
30	Sa	11	Be-shallaḥ (Shabbat Shirah)	Exod. 13:17–17:16	Judges 4:4–5:31 *Judges 5:1–31*
Feb. 3	W	15	Ḥamishshah–'asar bi-Shevaṭ		
6	Sa	18	Yitro	Exod. 18:1–20:23	Isaiah 6:1–7:6 9:5–6 *Isaiah 6:1–13*
13	Sa	25	Mishpaṭim (Shabbat Sheḳalim)	Exod. 21:1–24:18 Exod. 30:11–16	II Kings 12:1–17 *II Kings 11:17–12:17*
18	Th	30	New Moon, first day	Num. 28:1–15	

Italics are for Sephardi Minhag.

1988, Feb. 19–Mar. 18] ADAR (29 DAYS) [5748

Civil Date	Day of the Week	Jewish Date	SABBATHS, FESTIVALS, FASTS	PENTATEUCHAL READING	PROPHETICAL READING
Feb. 19	F	Adar 1	New Moon	Num. 28:1–15	
20	Sa	2	Terumah	Exod. 25:1–27:19	I Kings 5:26–6:13
27	Sa	9	Teẓawweh (Shabbat Zakhor)	Exod. 27:20–30:10 Deut. 25:17–19	I Samuel 15:2–34 *I Samuel 15:1–34*
Mar. 2	W	13	Fast of Esther	Exod. 32:11–14 34:1–10	Isaiah 55:6–56:8 (afternoon only)
3	Th	14	Purim	Exod. 17:8–16	Book of Esther (night before and in the morning)
4	F	15	Shushan Purim		
5	Sa	16	Ki tissa'	Exod. 30:11–34:35	I Kings 18:1–39 *I Kings 18:20–39*
12	Sa	23	Wa-yakhel, Pekude (Shabbat Parah)	Exod. 35:1–40:38 Num. 19:1–22	Ezekiel 36:16–38 *Ezekiel 36:16–36*

Italics are for Sephardi Minhag.

1988, Mar. 19–Apr. 17] NISAN (30 DAYS) [5748

Civil Date	Day of the Week	Jewish Date	SABBATHS, FESTIVALS, FASTS	PENTATEUCHAL READING	PROPHETICAL READING
Mar. 19	Sa	Nisan 1	Wa-yiḳra' (Shabbat Ha-ḥodesh); New Moon	Levit. 1:1–5:26 Exod. 12:1–20 Num. 28:9–15	Ezekiel 45:16–46:18 *Ezekiel 45:18–46:15* *Isaiah 66:1, 23*
26	Sa	8	Ẓaw (Shabbat Ha-gadol)	Levit. 6:1–8:36	Malachi 3:4–24
Apr. 1	F	14	Fast of Firstborn		
2	Sa	15	Passover, first day	Exod. 12:21–51 Num. 28:16–25	Joshua 5:2–6:1, 27
3	S	16	Passover, second day	Levit. 22:26–23:44 Num. 28:16–25	II Kings 23: 1–9, 21–25
4	M	17	Ḥol Ha-mo'ed, first day	Exod. 13:1–16 Num. 28:19–25	
5	T	18	Ḥol Ha-mo'ed, second day	Exod. 22:24–23:19 Num. 28:19–25	
6	W	19	Ḥol Ha-mo'ed, third day	Exod. 34:1–26 Num. 28:19–25	
7	Th	20	Ḥol Ha-mo'ed, fourth day	Num. 9:1–14 Num. 28:19–25	
8	F	21	Passover, seventh day	Exod. 13:17–15:26 Num. 28:19–25	II Samuel 22:1–51
9	Sa	22	Passover, eighth day	Deut. 15:19–16:17 Num. 28:19–25	Isaiah 10:32–12:6
14	Th	27	Holocaust Memorial Day		
16	Sa	29	Shemini	Levit. 9:1–11:47	I Samuel 20:18–42
17	S	30	New Moon, first day	Num. 28:1–15	

Italics are for Sephardi Minhag.

Civil Date	Day of the Week	Jewish Date	SABBATHS, FESTIVALS, FASTS	PENTATEUCHAL READING	PROPHETICAL READING
Apr. 18	M	Iyar 1	New Moon, second day	Num. 28:1–15	
22	F*	5	Israel Independence Day		
23	Sa	6	Tazria‘, Meẓora‘	Levit. 12:1–15:33	II Kings 7:3–20
30	Sa	13	Aḥare mot, Ḳedoshim	Levit. 16:1–20:27	Amos 9:7–15 *Ezekiel 20:2–20*
May 5	Th	18	Lag Ba-‘omer		
7	Sa	20	Emor	Levit. 21:1–24:23	Ezekiel 44:15–31
14	Sa	27	Be-har, Be-ḥuḳḳotai	Levit. 25:1–27:34	Jeremiah 16:19–17:14
15	S	28	Jerusalem Day		

*Observed Thursday, a day earlier, to avoid conflict with the Sabbath.

Civil Date	Day of the Week	Jewish Date	SABBATHS, FESTIVALS, FASTS	PENTATEUCHAL READING	PROPHETICAL READING
May 17	T	Siwan 1	New Moon	Num. 28:1–15	
21	Sa	5	Be-midbar	Num. 1:1–4:20	Hosea 2:1–22
22	S	6	Shavu‘ot, first day	Exod. 19:1–20:23 Num. 28:26–31	Ezekiel 1:1–28 3:12
23	M	7	Shavu‘ot, second day	Deut. 15:19–16:17 Num. 28:26–31	Habbakuk 3:1–19 *Habbakuk 2:20–3:19*
28	Sa	12	Naso’	Num. 4:21–7:89	Judges 13:2–25
June 4	Sa	19	Be-ha‘alotekha	Num. 8:1–12:16	Zechariah 2:14–4:7
11	Sa	26	Shelaḥ lekha	Num. 13:1–15:41	Joshua 2:1–24
15	W	30	New Moon, first day	Num. 28:1–15	

Italics are for Sephardi Minhag.

1988, June 16–July 14] TAMMUZ (29 DAYS) [5748

Civil Date	Day of the Week	Jewish Date	SABBATHS, FESTIVALS, FASTS	PENTATEUCHAL READING	PROPHETICAL READING
June 16	Th	Tammuz 1	New Moon, second day	Num. 28:1–15	
18	Sa	3	Ḳoraḥ	Num. 16:1–18:32	I Samuel 11:14–12:22
25	Sa	10	Ḥuḳḳat	Num. 19:1–22:1	Judges 11:1–33
July 2	Sa	17	Balaḳ	Num. 22:2–25:9	Micah 5:6–6:8
3	S	18	Fast of 17th of Tammuz	Exod. 32:11–14 34:1–10	Isaiah 55:6–56:8 (afternoon only)
9	Sa	24	Pineḥas	Num. 25:10–30:1	Jeremiah 1:1–2:3

1988, July 15–Aug. 13] AV (30 DAYS) [5748

Civil Date	Day of the Week	Jewish Date	SABBATHS, FESTIVALS, FASTS	PENTATEUCHAL READING	PROPHETICAL READING
July 15	F	Av 1	New Moon	Num. 28:1–15	
16	Sa	2	Maṭṭot, Mas'e	Num. 30:2–36:13	Jeremiah 2:4–28 3:4 *Jeremiah 2:4–28 4:1–2*
23	Sa	9	Devarim (Shabbat Ḥazon)	Deut. 1:1–3:22	Isaiah 1:1–27
24	S	10	Fast of 9th of Av	Morning: Deut. 4:25–40 Afternoon: Exod. 32:11–14 34:1–10	(Lamentations is read the night before.) Jeremiah 8:13–9:23 (morning) Isaiah 55:6–56:8 (afternoon)
30	Sa	16	Wa-ethḥannan (Shabbat Naḥamu)	Deut. 3:23–7:11	Isaiah 40:1–26
Aug. 6	Sa	23	'Eḳev	Deut. 7:12–11:25	Isaiah 49:14–51:3
13	Sa	30	Re'eh; New Moon, first day	Deut. 11:26–16:17 Num. 28:9–15	Isaiah 66:1–24 *Isaiah 66:1–24 I Samuel 20:18, 42*

1988, Aug. 14–Sept. 11] ELUL (29 DAYS) [5748

Civil Date	Day of the Week	Jewish Date	SABBATHS, FESTIVALS, FASTS	PENTATEUCHAL READING	PROPHETICAL READING
Aug. 14	S	Elul 1	New Moon, second day	Num. 28:1–15	
20	Sa	7	Shofeṭim	Deut. 16:18–21:9	Isaiah 51:12–52:12
27	Sa	14	Ki teẓe'	Deut. 21:10–25:19	Isaiah 54:1–55:5
Sept. 3	Sa	21	Ki tavo'	Deut. 26:1–29:8	Isaiah 60:1–22
10	Sa	28	Niẓẓavim	Deut. 29:9–30:20	Isaiah 61:10–63:9

Italics are for Sephardi Minhag.

Civil Date	Day of the Week	Jewish Date	SABBATHS, FESTIVALS, FASTS	PENTATEUCHAL READING	PROPHETICAL READING
Sept. 12	M	Tishri 1	Rosh Ha-shanah, first day	Gen. 21:1–34 Num. 29:1–6	I Samuel 1:1–2:10
13	T	2	Rosh Ha-shanah, second day	Gen. 22:1–24 Num. 29:1–6	Jeremiah 31:2–20
14	W	3	Fast of Gedaliah	Exod. 32:11–14 34:1–10	Isaiah 55:6–56:8 (afternoon only)
17	Sa	6	Wa-yelekh (Shabbat Shuvah)	Deut. 31:1–30	Hosea 14:2–10 Micah 7:18–20 Joel 2:15–27 *Hosea 14:2–10* *Micah 7:18–20*
21	W	10	Yom Kippur	Morning: Levit. 16:1–34 Num. 29:7–11 Afternoon: Levit. 18:1–30	Isaiah 57:14–58:14 Jonah 1:1–4:11 Micah 7:18–20
24	Sa	13	Ha'azinu	Deut. 32:1–52	II Samuel 22:1–51
26	M	15	Sukkot, first day	Levit. 22:26–23:44 Num. 29:12–16	Zechariah 14:1–21
27	T	16	Sukkot, second day	Levit. 22:26–23:44 Num. 29:12–16	I Kings 8:2–21
28–30	W-F	17–19	Ḥol Ha-mo'ed, first to third days	W Num. 29:17–25 Th Num. 29:20–28 F Num. 29:23–31	
Oct. 1	Sa	20	Ḥol Ha-mo'ed, fourth day	Exod. 33:12–34:26 Num. 29:26–31	Ezekiel 38:18–39:16
2	S	21	Hosha'na' Rabbah	Num. 29:26–34	
3	M	22	Shemini 'Aẓeret	Deut. 14:22–16:17 Num. 29:35–30:1	I Kings 8:54–66
4	T	23	Simḥat Torah	Deut. 33:1–34:12 Gen. 1:1–2:3 Num. 29:35–30:1	Joshua 1:1–18 *Joshua 1:1–9*
8	Sa	27	Be-re'shit	Gen. 1:1–6:8	Isaiah 42:5–43:10 *Isaiah 42:5–21*
11	T	30	New Moon, first day	Num. 28:1–15	

Italics are for Sephardi Minhag.

1988, Oct. 12–Nov. 9] ḤESHWAN (30 DAYS) [5749

Civil Date	Day of the Week	Jewish Date	SABBATHS, FESTIVALS, FASTS	PENTATEUCHAL READING	PROPHETICAL READING
Oct. 12	W	Ḥeshwan 1	New Moon, second day	Num. 28:1–15	
15	Sa	4	Noaḥ	Gen. 6:9–11:32	Isaiah 54:1–55:5 *Isaiah 54:1–10*
22	Sa	11	Lekh lekha	Gen. 12:1–17:27	Isaiah 40:27–41:16
29	Sa	18	Wa-yera'	Gen. 18:1–22:24	II Kings 4:1–37 *II Kings 4:1–23*
Nov. 5	Sa	25	Ḥayye Sarah	Gen. 23:1–25:18	I Kings 1:1–31

1988, Nov. 10–Dec. 8] KISLEW (29 DAYS) [5749

Civil Date	Day of the Week	Jewish Date	SABBATHS, FESTIVALS, FASTS	PENTATEUCHAL READING	PROPHETICAL READING
Nov. 10	Th	Kislew 1	New Moon	Num. 28:1–15	
12	Sa	3	Toledot	Gen. 25:19–28:9	Malachi 1:1–2:7
19	Sa	10	Wa-yeẓe'	Gen. 28:10–32:3	Hosea 12:13–14:10 *Hosea 11:7–12:12*
26	Sa	17	Wa-yishlaḥ	Gen. 32:4–36:43	Hosea 11:7–12:12 *Obadiah 1:1–21*
Dec. 3	Sa	24	Wa-yeshev	Gen. 37:1–40:23	Amos 2:6–3:8
4–8	S-Th	25–29	Ḥanukkah, first to fifth days	S Num. 7:1–17 M Num. 7:18–29 T Num. 7:24–35 W Num. 7:30–41 Th Num. 7:36–47	

Italics are for Sephardi Minhag.

1988, Dec. 9–Jan. 6, 1989] ṬEVET (29 DAYS) [5749

Civil Date	Day of the Week	Jewish Date	SABBATHS, FESTIVALS, FASTS	PENTATEUCHAL READING	PROPHETICAL READING
Dec. 9	F	Ṭevet 1	New Moon; Ḥanukkah, sixth day	Num. 28:1–15 Num. 7:42–47	
10	Sa	2	Mi-ḳeẓ; Ḥanukkah, seventh day	Gen. 41:1–44:17 Num. 7:48–53	Zechariah 2:14–4:7
11	S	3	Ḥanukkah, eighth day	Num. 7:54–8:4	
17	Sa	9	Wa-yiggash	Gen. 44:18–47:27	Ezekiel 37:15–28
18	S	10	Fast of 10th of Ṭevet	Exod. 32:11–14 34:1–10	Isaiah 55:6–56:8 (afternoon only)
24	Sa	16	Wa-yeḥi	Gen. 47:28–50:26	I Kings 2:1–12
31	Sa	23	Shemot	Exod. 1:1–6:1	Isaiah 27:6–28:13 29:22–23 *Jeremiah 1:1–2:3*

Italics are for Sephardi Minhag.

1989, Jan. 7–Feb. 5] SHEVAṬ (30 DAYS) [5749

Civil Date	Day of the Week	Jewish Date	SABBATHS, FESTIVALS, FASTS	PENTATEUCHAL READING	PROPHETICAL READING
Jan. 7	Sa	Shevat 1	Wa-'era'; New Moon	Exod. 6:2–9:35 Num. 28:9–15	Isaiah 66:1–24
14	Sa	8	Bo'	Exod. 10:1–13:16	Jeremiah 46:13–28
21	Sa	15	Be-shallaḥ (Shabbat Shirah); Ḥamishshah-'asar bi-Shevaṭ	Exod. 13:17–17:16	Judges 4:4–5:31 *Judges 5:1–31*
28	Sa	22	Yitro	Exod. 18:1–20:23	Isaiah 6:1–7:6 9:5–6 *Isaiah 6:1–13*
Feb. 4	Sa	29	Mishpaṭim	Exod. 21:1–24:18	I Samuel 20:18–42
5	S	30	New Moon, first day	Num. 28:1–15	

1989, Feb. 6–Mar. 7] ADAR I (30 DAYS) [5749

Civil Date	Day of the Week	Jewish Date	SABBATHS, FESTIVALS, FASTS	PENTATEUCHAL READING	PROPHETICAL READING
Feb. 6	M	I Adar 1	New Moon, second day	Num. 28:1–15	
11	Sa	6	Terumah	Exod. 25:1–27:19	I Kings 5:26–6:13
18	Sa	13	Teẓawweh	Exod. 27:20–30:10	Ezekiel 43:10–27
25	Sa	20	Ki tissa'	Exod. 30:11–34:35	I Kings 18:1–39 *I Kings 18:20–39*
Mar. 4	Sa	27	Wa-yakhel (Shabbat Sheḳalim)	Exod. 35:1–38:20 Exod. 30:11–16	II Kings 12:1–17 *II Kings 11:17–12:17*
7	T	30	New Moon, first day	Num. 28:1–15	

Italics are for Sephardi Minhag.

1989, Mar. 8–Apr. 5] ADAR II (29 DAYS) [5749

Civil Date	Day of the Week	Jewish Date	SABBATHS, FESTIVALS, FASTS	PENTATEUCHAL READING	PROPHETICAL READING
Mar. 8	W	II Adar 1	New Moon, second day	Num. 28:1–15	
11	Sa	4	Pekude	Exod. 38:21–40:38	I Kings 7:51–8:21 *I Kings 7:40–50*
18	Sa	11	Wa-yikra' (Shabbat Zakhor)	Levit. 1:1–5:26 Deut. 25:17–19	I Samuel 15:2–34 *I Samuel 15:1–34*
20	M	13	Fast of Esther	Exod. 32:11–14 34:1–10	Isaiah 55:6–56:8 (afternoon only)
21	T	14	Purim	Exod. 17:8–16	Book of Esther (night before and in the morning)
22	W	15	Shushan Purim		
25	Sa	18	Zaw (Shabbat Parah)	Levit. 6:1–8:36 Num. 19:1–22	Ezekiel 36:16–38 *Ezekiel 36:16–36*
Apr. 1	Sa	25	Shemini (Shabbat Ha-hodesh)	Levit. 9:1–11:47 Exod. 12:1–20	Ezekiel 45:16–46:18 *Ezekiel 45:18–46:15*

Italics are for Sephardi Minhag.

1989, Apr. 6–May 5] NISAN (30 DAYS) [5749

Civil Date	Day of the Week	Jewish Date	SABBATHS, FESTIVALS, FASTS	PENTATEUCHAL READING	PROPHETICAL READING
Apr. 6	Th	Nisan 1	New Moon	Num. 28:1–15	
8	Sa	3	Tazria'	Levit. 12:1–13:59	II Kings 4:42–5:19
15	Sa	10	Meẓora' (Shabbat Ha-gadol)	Levit. 14:1–15:33	Malachi 3:4–24
19	W	14	Fast of Firstborn		
20	Th	15	Passover, first day	Exod. 12:21–51 Num. 28:16–25	Joshua 5:2–6:1, 27
21	F	16	Passover, second day	Levit. 22:26–23:44 Num. 28:16–25	II Kings 23:1–9, 21–25
22	Sa	17	Ḥol Ha-mo'ed, first day	Exod. 33:12–34:26 Num. 28:19–25	Ezekiel 37:1–14
23	S	18	Ḥol Ha-mo'ed, second day	Exod. 13:1–16 Num. 28:19–25	
24	M	19	Ḥol Ha-mo'ed, third day	Exod. 22:24–23:19 Num. 28:19–25	
25	T	20	Ḥol Ha-mo'ed, fourth day	Num. 9:1–14 Num. 28:19–25	
26	W	21	Passover, seventh day	Exod. 13:17–15:26 Num. 28:19–25	II Samuel 22:1–51
27	Th	22	Passover, eighth day	Deut. 15:19–16:17 Num. 28:19–25	Isaiah 10:32–12:6
29	Sa	24	Aḥare mot	Levit. 16:1–18:30	Amos 9:7–15
May 2	T	27	Holocaust Memorial Day		
5	F	30	New Moon, first day	Num. 28:1–15	

1989, May 6–June 3] IYAR (29 DAYS) [5749

Civil Date	Day of the Week	Jewish Date	SABBATHS, FESTIVALS, FASTS	PENTATEUCHAL READING	PROPHETICAL READING
May 6	Sa	Iyar 1	Ḳedoshim; New Moon, second day	Levit. 19:1–20:27 Num. 28:9–15	Isaiah 66:1–24
10	W	5	Israel Independence Day		
13	Sa	8	Emor	Levit. 21:1–24:23	Ezekiel 44:15–31
20	Sa	15	Be-har	Levit. 25:1–26:2	Jeremiah 32:6–27
23	T	18	Lag Ba-'omer		
27	Sa	22	Be-ḥuḳḳotai	Levit. 26:3–27:34	Jeremiah 16:19–17:14
June 2	F*	28	Jerusalem Day		
3	Sa	29	Be-midbar	Num. 1:1–4:20	I Samuel 20:18–42

*Observed Thursday, a day earlier, to avoid conflict with the Sabbath.

1989, June 4–July 3] SIWAN (30 DAYS) [5749

Civil Date	Day of the Week	Jewish Date	SABBATHS, FESTIVALS, FASTS	PENTATEUCHAL READING	PROPHETICAL READING
June 4	S	Siwan 1	New Moon	Num. 28:1–15	
9	F	6	Shavu'ot, first day	Exod. 19:1–20:23 Num. 28:26–31	Ezekiel 1:1–28 3:12
10	Sa	7	Shavu'ot, second day	Deut. 15:19–16:17 Num. 28:26–31	Habbakuk 3:1–19 *Habbakuk 2:20–3:19*
17	Sa	14	Naso'	Num. 4:21–7:89	Judges 13:2–25
24	Sa	21	Be-ha'alotekha	Num. 8:1–12:16	Zechariah 2:14–4:7
July 1	Sa	28	Shelaḥ lekha	Num. 13:1–15:41	Joshua 2:1–24
3	M	30	New Moon, first day	Num. 28:1–15	

Italics are for Sephardi Minhag.

1989, July 4–Aug. 1] TAMMUZ (29 DAYS) [5749

Civil Date	Day of the Week	Jewish Date	SABBATHS, FESTIVALS, FASTS	PENTATEUCHAL READING	PROPHETICAL READING
July 4	T	Tammuz 1	New Moon, second day	Num. 28:1–15	
8	Sa	5	Ḳoraḥ	Num. 16:1–18:32	I Samuel 11:14–12:22
15	Sa	12	Ḥuḳḳat, Balaḳ	Num. 19:1–25:9	Micah 5:6–6:8
20	Th	17	Fast of 17th of Tammuz	Exod. 32:11–14 34:1–10	Isaiah 55:6–56:8 (afternoon only)
22	Sa	19	Pineḥas	Num. 25:10–30:1	Jeremiah 1:1–2:3
29	Sa	26	Maṭṭot, Mas'e	Num. 30:2–36:13	Jeremiah 2:4–28 3:4 *Jeremiah 2:4–28* *4:1–2*

Italics are for Sephardi Minhag.

1989, Aug. 2–Aug. 31] AV (30 DAYS) [5749

Civil Date	Day of the Week	Jewish Date	SABBATHS, FESTIVALS, FASTS	PENTATEUCHAL READING	PROPHETICAL READING
Aug. 2	W	Av 1	New Moon	Num. 28:1–15	
5	Sa	4	Devarim (Shabbat Ḥazon)	Deut. 1:1–3:22	Isaiah 1:1–27
10	Th	9	Fast of 9th of Av	Morning: Deut. 4:25–40 Afternoon: Exod. 32:11–14 34:1–10	(Lamentations is read the night before.) Jeremiah 8:13–9:23 (morning) Isaiah 55:6–56:8 (afternoon)
12	Sa	11	Wa-etḥannan (Shabbat Naḥamu)	Deut. 3:23–7:11	Isaiah 40:1–26
19	Sa	18	'Eḳev	Deut. 7:12–11:25	Isaiah 49:14–51:3
26	Sa	25	Re'eh	Deut. 11:26–16:17	Isaiah 54:11–55:5
31	Th	30	New Moon, first day	Num. 28:1–15	

1989, Sept. 1–Sept. 29] ELUL (29 DAYS) [5749

Civil Date	Day of the Week	Jewish Date	SABBATHS, FESTIVALS, FASTS	PENTATEUCHAL READING	PROPHETICAL READING
Sept. 1	F	Elul 1	New Moon, second day	Num. 28:1–15	
2	Sa	2	Shofeṭim	Deut. 16:18–21:9	Isaiah 51:12–52:12
9	Sa	9	Ki teẓe'	Deut. 21:10–25:19	Isaiah 54:1–10
16	Sa	16	Ki tavo'	Deut. 26:1–29:8	Isaiah 60:1–22
23	Sa	23	Niẓẓavim, Wa-yelekh	Deut. 29:9–31:30	Isaiah 61:10–63:9

Civil Date	Day of the Week	Jewish Date	SABBATHS, FESTIVALS, FASTS	PENTATEUCHAL READING	PROPHETICAL READING
Sept. 30	Sa	Tishri 1	Rosh Ha-shanah, first day	Gen. 21:1–34 Num. 29:1–6	I Samuel 1:1–2:10
Oct. 1	S	2	Rosh Ha-shanah, second day	Gen. 22:1–24 Num. 29:1–6	Jeremiah 31:2–20
2	M	3	Fast of Gedaliah	Exod. 32:11–14 34:1–10	Isaiah 55:6–56:8 (afternoon only)
7	Sa	8	Ha'azinu (Shabbat Shuvah)	Deut. 32:1–52	Hosea 14:2–10 Micah 7:18–20 Joel 2:15–27 *Hosea 14:2–10* *Micah 7:18–20*
9	M	10	Yom Kippur	Morning: Levit. 16:1–34 Num. 29:7–11 Afternoon: Levit. 18:1–30	Isaiah 57:14–58:14 Jonah 1:1–4:11 Micah 7:18–20
14	Sa	15	Sukkot, first day	Levit. 22:26–23:44 Num. 29:12–16	Zechariah 14:1–21
15	S	16	Sukkot, second day	Levit. 22:26–23:44 Num. 29:12–16	I Kings 8:2–21
16–19	M–Th	17–20	Hol Ha-mo'ed, first to fourth days	M Num. 29:17–25 T Num. 29:20–28 W Num. 29:23–31 Th Num. 29:26–34	
20	F	21	Hosha'na' Rabbah	Num. 29:26–34	
21	Sa	22	Shemini 'Aẓeret	Deut. 14:22–16:17 Num. 29:35–30:1	I Kings 8:54–66
22	S	23	Simḥat Torah	Deut. 33:1–34:12 Gen. 1:1–2:3 Num. 29:35–30:1	Joshua 1:1–18 *Joshua 1:1–9*
28	Sa	29	Be-re'shit	Gen. 1:1–6:8	I Samuel 20:18–42
29	S	30	New Moon, first day	Num. 28:1–15	

Italics are for Sephardi Minhag.

Civil Date	Day of the Week	Jewish Date	SABBATHS, FESTIVALS, FASTS	PENTATEUCHAL READING	PROPHETICAL READING
Oct. 30	M	Ḥeshwan 1	New Moon, second day	Num. 28:1–15	
Nov. 4	Sa	6	Noaḥ	Gen. 6:9–11:32	Isaiah 54:1–55:5 *Isaiah 54:1–10*
11	Sa	13	Lekh lekha	Gen. 12:1–17:27	Isaiah 40:27–41:16
18	Sa	20	Wa-yera'	Gen. 18:1–22:24	II Kings 4:1–37 *II Kings 4:1–23*
25	Sa	27	Ḥayye Sarah	Gen. 23:1–25:18	I Kings 1:1–31
28	T	30	New Moon, first day	Num. 28:1–15	

1989, Nov. 29–Dec. 28] KISLEW (30 DAYS) [5750

Civil Date	Day of the Week	Jewish Date	SABBATHS, FESTIVALS, FASTS	PENTATEUCHAL READING	PROPHETICAL READING
Nov. 29	W	Kislew 1	New Moon, second day	Num. 28:1–15	
Dec. 2	Sa	4	Toledot	Gen. 25:19–28:9	Malachi 1:1–2:7
9	Sa	11	Wa-yeẓe'	Gen. 28:10–32:3	Hosea 12:13–14:10 *Hosea 11:7–12:12*
16	Sa	18	Wa-yishlaḥ	Gen. 32:4–36:43	Hosea 11:7–12:12 *Obadiah 1:1–21*
23	Sa	25	Wa-yeshev; Ḥanukkah, first day	Gen. 37:1–40:23 Num. 7:1–17	Zechariah 2:14–4:7
24–27	S–W	26–29	Ḥanukkah, second to fifth days	S Num. 7:18–29 M Num. 7:24–35 T Num. 7:30–41 W Num. 7:36–47	
28	Th	30	New Moon, first day; Ḥanukkah, sixth day	Num. 28:1–15 Num. 7:42–47	

Italics are for Sephardi Minhag.

1989, Dec. 29–Jan. 26, 1990] ṬEVET (29 DAYS) [5750

Civil Date	Day of the Week	Jewish Date	SABBATHS, FESTIVALS, FASTS	PENTATEUCHAL READING	PROPHETICAL READING
Dec. 29	F	Ṭevet 1	New Moon, second day; Ḥanukkah, seventh day	Num. 28:1–15 Num. 7:48–53	
30	Sa	2	Mi-ḳez; Ḥanukkah, eighth day	Gen. 41:1–44:17 Num. 7:54–8:4	I Kings 7:40–50
Jan. 6	Sa	9	Wa-yiggash	Gen. 44:18–47:27	Ezekiel 37:15–28
7	S	10	Fast of 10th of Ṭevet	Exod. 32:11–14 34:1–10	Isaiah 55:6–56:8 (afternoon only)
13	Sa	16	Wa-yeḥi	Gen. 47:28–50:26	I Kings 2:1–12
20	Sa	23	Shemot	Exod. 1:1–6:1	Isaiah 27:6–28:13 29:22–23 *Jeremiah 1:1–2:3*

Italics are for Sephardi Minhag.

SELECTED ARTICLES OF INTEREST IN RECENT VOLUMES OF THE AMERICAN JEWISH YEAR BOOK

Article	Author and Reference
The American Jewish Family Today	Steven Martin Cohen 82:136–154
Attitudes of American Jews Toward Israel: Trends Over Time	Eytan Gilboa 86:110–125
The Bitburg Controversy	Deborah E. Lipstadt 87:21–37
California Jews: Data from the Field Polls	Alan M. Fisher and Curtis K. Tanaka 86:196–218
A Century of Conservative Judaism in the United States	Abraham J. Karp 86:3–61
A Century of Jewish History, 1881–1981: The View from America	Lucy S. Dawidowicz 82:3–98
The "Civil Judaism" of Communal Leaders	Jonathan S. Woocher 81:149–169
The Demographic Consequences of U.S. Jewish Population Trends	U.O. Schmelz and Sergio DellaPergola 83:141–187
The Demography of Latin American Jewry	U.O. Schmelz and Sergio DellaPergola 85:51–102
Israelis in the United States: Motives, Attitudes, and Intentions	Dov Elizur 80:53–67
Jewish Education Today	Walter I. Ackerman 80:130–148
Jewish Survival: The Demographic Factors	U.O. Schmelz 81:61–117
Jews in the United States: Perspectives from Demography	Sidney Goldstein 81:3–59
The Labor Market Status of American Jews: Patterns and Determinants	Barry R. Chiswick 85:131–153
Latin American Jewry Today	Judith Laikin Elkin 85:3–49

OBITUARIES

Leo Baeck	By Max Gruenewald 59:478–82
Jacob Blaustein	By John Slawson 72:547–57
Martin Buber	By Seymour Siegel 67:37–43
Abraham Cahan	By Mendel Osherowitch 53:527–29
Albert Einstein	By Jacob Bronowski 58:480–85
Felix Frankfurter	By Paul A. Freund 67:31–36
Louis Ginzberg	By Louis Finkelstein 56:573–79
Jacob Glatstein	By Shmuel Lapin 73:611–17
Sidney Goldmann	By Milton R. Konvitz 85:401–03
Hayim Greenberg	By Marie Syrkin 56:589–94
Abraham Joshua Heschel	By Fritz A. Rothschild 74:533–44
Horace Meyer Kallen	By Milton R. Konvitz 75:55–80
Mordecai Kaplan	By Ludwig Nadelmann 85:404–11
Herbert H. Lehman	By Louis Finkelstein 66:3–20
Judah L. Magnes	By James Marshall 51:512–15
Alexander Marx	By Abraham S. Halkin 56:580–88
Reinhold Niebuhr	By Seymour Siegel 73:605–10
Joseph Proskauer	By David Sher 73:618–28
Maurice Samuel	By Milton H. Hindus 74:545–53
Leo Strauss	By Ralph Lerner 76:91–97
Max Weinreich	By Lucy S. Dawidowicz 70:59–68
Chaim Weizmann	By Harry Sacher 55:462–69
Stephen S. Wise	By Philip S. Bernstein 51:515–18
Harry Austryn Wolfson	By Isadore Twersky 76:99–111

Index